LEGAL STUDIES OF THE
WILLIAM NELSON CROMWELL FOUNDATION

LEGAL ETHICS

LEGAL ETHICS

By HENRY S. DRINKER

MEMBER OF THE PHILADELPHIA BAR
CHAIRMAN OF THE STANDING COMMITTEE
ON PROFESSIONAL ETHICS AND GRIEVANCES
OF THE AMERICAN BAR ASSOCIATION

Published under the auspices of
THE
WILLIAM NELSON CROMWELL
FOUNDATION

Trustees

Columbia University Press, New York

COPYRIGHT 1953, COLUMBIA UNIVERSITY PRESS, NEW YORK
MANUFACTURED IN THE UNITED STATES OF AMERICA

First printing 1953
Second printing 1954

PUBLISHED IN GREAT BRITAIN, CANADA, INDIA, AND PAKISTAN
BY GEOFFREY CUMBERLEGE, OXFORD UNIVERSITY PRESS
LONDON, TORONTO, BOMBAY, AND KARACHI

This book is gratefully dedicated to

DAVID A. SIMMONS

WILLIS SMITH

CARL B. RIX

TAPPAN GREGORY

FRANK E. HOLMAN

HAROLD J. GALLAGHER

CODY FOWLER

HOWARD L. BARKDULL

ROBERT G. STOREY

the nine Presidents of the American Bar Association under whom it has been my great pleasure to serve as Chairman of its Ethics Committee.

FOREWORD

THE WILLIAM NELSON CROMWELL FOUNDATION was created by Mr. Cromwell on May 26, 1930, by a deed of trust naming various prominent members of the New York Bar as Trustees. Among its stated purposes were:

(5) Cultivation of the highest standards of ethics, honor and conduct in the practice of Law and the preparation and dissemination of rules, codes, treatises and literature upon said subjects.

Mr. Cromwell had had a lifelong interest in legal ethics and in elevating the standards of the bar.

Before Mr. Cromwell's death on July 19, 1948, the Foundation had insufficient funds to engage in many activities. However, by his will he left a substantial amount to the Foundation, so that by 1950 it was in a position to look for worthwhile projects.

Prior to the meeting of the Trustees held on June 5, 1950, the individual members were called on for suggestions for future projects. One suggestion was that the Foundation arrange for and finance a new book on legal ethics. This was made in view of the purpose quoted above, and the fact that Judge Sharswood's lectures on legal ethics delivered at the University of Pennsylvania Law School in 1854 and subsequently published was almost the only work obtainable.

A Committee of the Trustees was appointed, and the members made an extensive investigation of the project. A primary question was what type of person could best write the book. It seemed clear to the Committee and to the Board of Trustees that the ideal author would be a leading member of the bar who had for many years practiced law and thus had encountered in private practice the problems about which he was to write.

When the Committee was instructed to proceed, it found that, by a happy coincidence, Mr. Henry S. Drinker, of the Philadelphia Bar, had already commenced the preparation of a book on legal ethics. The Committee immediately made arrangements to finance the preparation and publication of his book.

When the question arose as to the method of distribution and sale of the book, both Mr. Drinker and the Foundation were in complete accord that the desirable approach was to obtain a wide distribution among practicing lawyers and to make the book available at a low price to lawyers, law schools, and law students. In support of this policy, the Foundation has agreed to supply all of the funds necessary for the publication of the book. It is not seeking to be reimbursed, nor will it be, for its large outlay in the matter by the subsequent sales of the volume.

Another coincidence which may be noted is that Judge Sharswood, when he delivered his lectures almost one hundred years ago, was a leading member of the Philadelphia Bar and his lectures were delivered at the University of Pennsylvania Law School. Mr. Drinker is also a leading member of the Philadelphia Bar and has delivered lectures on legal ethics at the University of Pennsylvania Law School. He has been for many years Chairman of the American Bar Association's Standing Committee on Professional Ethics and Grievances. The Foundation was fortunate indeed to find an author so well-equipped for the task.

JOHN W. DAVIS

New York, N.Y.
April 14, 1953.

PREFACE

Most lawyers know of Judge George Sharswood's *Professional Ethics;* many have read it. Very few, however, have read or even know of any other book on the subject.

While the principles stated by Judge Sharswood are still sound, the lectures which formed the basis for his little book were delivered at the new Law School of the University of Pennsylvania more than a hundred years ago—first published in 1854—when law was practiced in a very different world from that in which we now live, and long before the adoption of the Canons of Ethics by the bar associations and the construction thereof by their ethics committees. The two principal treatises on the subject—George W. Warvelle, *Legal Ethics,* and Edward M. Thornton, *Attorneys at Law*—were published the first in 1902 and the second in 1914. The four excellent case books on Legal Ethics [1] were intended for and primarily adapted to teaching in the law schools, and do not cover the important amendments to the Canons in 1937, and their construction by the various ethics committees.

To many lawyers it has therefore seemed essential that our lawyers and law students should have a modern book on the subject which would apply the eternal principles to present conditions, embody those dealing with the new developments, such as advertising, matrimonial litigation, fee splitting, etc., and also make available a summary of the principles established by the many written decisions which have been rendered during the past thirty years by the ethics committees of the different bar associations construing the Canons.

[1] George P. Costigan, *Cases on the Legal Profession and Its Ethics* (1917; revised 1933); Elliott E. Cheatham, *Cases and Materials on the Legal Profession* (1938); Frederic C. Hicks, *Organization and Ethics of the Bench and Bar* (1932); Herschel Whitfield Arant, *Cases and Other Materials on the American Bar and Its Ethics* (1933). See also Weeks, *Attorneys* (1878, 1892).

In the course of my duties as Chairman of the Ethics Committee of the American Bar Association, I have accumulated and studied all the obtainable opinions of the various committees,[2] which, I believe, constitute the only available collection. Encouraged and very materially assisted by The William Nelson Cromwell Foundation, it therefore seemed fitting that I should write this book.[3]

My primary aim has been to make readily available to the chairmen and members of the various ethics committees throughout the country, as well as to lawyers confronted with ethical problems, a summary of the decisions by such committees. I have not considered it necessary to cover all the many statutory provisions and reported court decisions on many of the points covered, restricting my references to a few of the leading ones, with citations of some of the articles in the law journals. In citing or referring to a Committee decision whose soundness seems to me seriously questionable, I have so indicated, either in the text or in a footnote. On debatable questions I have endeavored to cite representative decisions on both sides. Where I say that a lawyer "may properly" do thus and so, I mean without violating the Canons as construed by the committees.[4]

Finally, there is in this work some deliberate duplication of citations and discussions of principles; I believe that readers, who will in the main be using this work to ascertain the proprieties of specific

[2] The volume published in 1947 by the American Bar Association Committee contains 274 opinions. Thirteen subsequent opinions have been printed and issued in the American Bar Association Journal. The Committee of the Association of the Bar of the City of New York has issued 1,183 opinions, which, with the 423 opinions of the Committee of the New York County Lawyer's Association, are on file in the library of the Bar Association, 42 West 44th Street, New York City. They are referred to herein in this style: N.Y. City 624; N.Y. County 219.

Some 300 hitherto unpublished opinions rendered by the American Bar Association Committee are here published for the first time, with the approval of the present Committee, as Appendix A. They are referred to herein in this style: App. A, *198*.

The Michigan Committee has published 154 opinions, the Chicago Bar Association Committee 36, the Cleveland Committee 30, the Ohio State Bar Committee 10, the California Committee 53, the Texas Committee 43, the Missouri Committee 86, and other committees varying numbers. There are, I understand, about 200 opinions by the North Carolina Committee, which are in the course of preparation for publication, but they are not yet available so could not be referred to herein.

The opinions of the committees which have not numbered their opinions consecutively are referred to by what seems the most feasible method.

Copies of these opinions are available for inspection at the headquarters of the different associations.

[3] Neither the American Bar Association Ethics Committee, nor The Cromwell Foundation, nor the individual members of either are, however, responsible for it.

[4] This applies particularly to the insurance cases discussed in Chapter VI.

aspects of conduct, will prefer to have the statements and authorities for a given proposition gathered under its heading.

The present book does not purport to cover, except incidentally, questions of substantive law, such as the inherent authority and powers of lawyers, lawyers' liens,[5] and similar problems. Nor does it enumerate the instances in which the Codes or Canons adopted in the different states differ, in various particulars, from the American Bar Association Canons; or cover questions of conflict of laws.[6]

What, it may be asked, is meant by Ethics, as applied to the legal profession?

An exact definition is, of course, impossible. Bouvier's is as follows: Legal Ethics is "that branch of moral science which treats of the duties which a member of the legal profession owes to the public, the court, to his professional brethren and to his client." [7]

Many of the principles governing the propriety of the lawyer's conduct are embodied in statutes and court decisions, as well as in the Canons. Many are found in the "customs of the bar," referred to in Canon 25, the observance of which might be considered Legal Etiquette rather than Ethics.

The Canons, particularly those adopted from time to time after the original 32 of 1908, are not in any logical order corresponding to their numbers. For example, advertising and solicitation is covered by Canons 27, 40, 43, 45, and 46; the duty to clients by at least twenty of them; that to the Court by Canons 1, 2, 21, 22, 41, and others; that to other lawyers by Canons 7, 17, 25, 33, 34, etc. Accordingly, in discussing the duties of lawyers I have not followed the numerical order of the Canons.

Prior to discussing these obligations I have given a very brief account of the origin and history of the bar in England and in this country, and of the bar associations, the adoptions of the Canons of Ethics, and the constitutions and functions of their Ethics and

5 See Cheatham, Case Book, pp. 349–50, 376–78; Arant, Case Book, pp. 317–33, 409–14.

6 See 52 Col. L. Rev. 1039, 1050–53 (1952).

7 See also Felix S. Cohen, *Ethical Systems and Legal Ideals* (1933), p. 7: Ethics "is the study of the meaning and application of judgments of *good, bad, right, wrong, etc.* and every valuation of law involves an ethical judgment."

Charles A. Boston, *The Source and Formulation of Ethical Precepts,* 78 Cent. L. Jour. 400 (1914): "Philosophically considered, it seems to me that legal ethics is the result of the application by thinkers, more or less profound, of the principles of the philosophy of right conduct, to the specific problems, which experience has shown, confront the lawyer, in the prosecution of his professional duties."

Grievance Committees. These chapters, with a chapter on disciplinary proceedings—powers of the courts, grounds for discipline, reinstatement, etc.—constitute Part One, "Organization of the Bar and
of Disciplinary Proceedings." In the section on "Grounds for Discipline" I have not attempted to collect all the many decided cases in
which lawyers have been disbarred, suspended, censured, or vindi-
cated, confining my discussion in the text to an analysis of the two
basic grounds for discipline, with but a few illustrative cases; [8] in
Appendix B are collected a few leading or illustrative decisions involving each of the principal grounds on which lawyers have been
disciplined.

Part Two, "The Duties and Obligations of Lawyers," comprises
five chapters. The first four cover the duties and obligations of lawyers to the public, to the courts, to clients, and to other lawyers.

The fifth chapter is entitled "Advertising and Solicitation." The
duty not to advertise or solicit professional employment is not
strictly one owing to the public, the courts, clients, or colleagues. It
is a duty to the traditions and amenities of an honorable profession
and is discussed separately at the end. It involves the consideration
primarily of ethics committee decisions. Although perhaps the least
interesting chapter to the average lawyer, it will, I believe, be the
most useful to these committees all over the country.

But before plunging into and endeavoring to define, classify, and
arrange the various duties and obligations of lawyers, I have ven-
tured to epitomize, in a section significantly entitled "Noblesse
Oblige," my idea of what a lawyer owes to his profession.

An extended discussion of the mentality and training most con-
ducive to success at the bar is outside the scope of this book.

In an article entitled "The Armament of the Lawyer" [9] James
Grafton Rogers says that he has been through the biographies of 160
lawyers and made a tabulation of the relative frequency of their
outstanding characteristics. The most frequently mentioned, he says,
and thus indicated as the sources of success, were industry, legal
learning, broad culture, strong will, oratorical power, moral courage,
and human insight or sympathy. The weaknesses most often named

[8] For an instructive summary of the Statutes and decisions in the various states relative
to discipline and disciplinary proceedings, see 52 Col. L. Rev. 1039–53 (1952).
[9] 14 A.B.A. Jour. 301 (1928).

as limitations on the lawyer's success were spasmodic effort, lack of education, unthrift, and ill health.

In a letter to the Law Alumni of the University of Illinois, dated May 13, 1935, Albert J. Harno says that he sent out letters to over 100 persons, lawyers and law teachers, to name the traits they believed an individual should possess for success in the practice of law. The following traits were the most frequently named: discrimination, character, industry, scholarship, courage, and a sense of social responsibility.

In none of these lists are mentioned imagination or wisdom and common sense, which seem to me among the most important qualities. Imagination is essential in every phase of the lawyer's experience: in litigation, to divine and supply facts which the client or the witness is loath to disclose or the importance of which he does not realize, and to anticipate the point on which the case will eventually turn; in organizing or reorganizing a business or giving business advice, to foresee the difficulties to be avoided and the advantages to be gained; imagination coupled with common sense to tell the difference between important and unimportant facts and questions, a defect which probably more than any other, accounts for the lack of success of many a learned lawyer.

I have received valuable help in the preparation of this book from a number of sources. John G. Jackson, Esq., a member of the Ethics Committee of the American Bar Association for thirteen years, read proofs of the entire book, offered many pertinent criticisms, and gave me welcome assurance as to the balance. Several of the trustees of The William Nelson Cromwell Foundation (which financed the publication), particularly S. Pearce Browning, Jr., Esq., Hon. Bruce Bromley, and Dean Ignatius M. Wilkinson, read the manuscript and made helpful suggestions. The editors of Columbia University Press have been cordially cooperative. The Foundation also contributed the valued services of Esther Brandschain, a member of the Philadelphia bar, who, for eighteen months has read, checked, and discovered authorities and helped me classify and summarize the many decisions covered. Mrs. J. Wesley Mallams, for nine years the Secretary of the Ethics Committee, has also been of much appreciated assistance, not only in preparing the manuscript, but, by reason of her familiarity with the Committee's decisions, in helping me to avoid inconsistencies in the text.

H. S. D.

Philadelphia
June 1, 1953

CONTENTS

NOBLESSE OBLIGE   3

Part One

ORGANIZATION OF THE BAR AND OF
DISCIPLINARY PROCEEDINGS

I. HISTORY OF THE BAR IN ENGLAND AND THE
    UNITED STATES   11
    The Bar in England   11
    The Bar in the United States   19

II. SANCTIONS OF PROFESSIONAL CONDUCT   22
    Nature of the Sanctions   22
    History of the Canons   23
    Force and Effect of the Canons   26
    Organization and Functions of the
        Ethics and Grievance Committees   30

III. DISCIPLINARY PROCEEDINGS   33
    Procedure for Disciplining Lawyers   33
      In England   33
      In the United States   34
      Nature of the Proceedings   35
      Distinction between Contempt and
        Disciplinary Proceedings   38
      Powers of Courts and of Legislatures
        in Disciplinary Proceedings   41
    Grounds for Discipline   42
      Moral Unfitness to Advise and Represent Clients   43

Unworthiness to Continue in the Legal Profession   44
Burden of Proof   46
Disbarment, Suspension, or Censure   46
Rights of Disciplined Lawyers   48
　　Right to Resign   48
　　Reinstatement of Lawyers Suspended or Disbarred   49
　　Rights of Lawyers Suspended or Disbarred   51

Part Two

THE DUTIES AND OBLIGATIONS
OF LAWYERS

IV. THE LAWYER'S OBLIGATIONS TO THE PUBLIC BY
　　 REASON OF THE SPECIAL PRIVILEGES ACCORDED
　　 HIM   59
　　Duty to Police the Bar   59
　　Duty to Further the Choice of Able
　　　　and Upright Judges and See to the
　　　　Removal of Those Manifestly Unworthy   60
　　Duty to Represent the Indigent   62
　　Duty Not to Stir Up Litigation   63
　　Duty Not to Aid in the Unauthorized
　　　　Practice of Law   66

V. THE LAWYER'S OBLIGATION TO THE COURTS   69
　　Duty to Observe a Respectful Attitude   69
　　Personal Relations with Judges   71
　　Understandings with the Court   73
　　Candor and Fairness to the Court   74
　　Duty to Disclose Relevant Matters Not
　　　　Brought Out by Opposing Counsel   76
　　Briefs   78
　　Alteration of Court Records   79
　　Abuse of Legal Process   79
　　"Quickie" Divorces   80
　　Duty to Be Punctual   82
　　Duty Not to Employ Dilatory Tactics   82
　　Attitude toward Jury   84

Attitude toward Witnesses 85
Appearance before Other Bodies 87

VI. THE LAWYER'S OBLIGATIONS TO HIS CLIENT 89
The Lawyer as a Fiduciary 89
Rebates and Commissions 96
Acquiring an Interest in Litigation 99
Duty to Settle Cases Where to the
Client's Advantage 101
Duty to Give Candid Advice 102
Duty Not to Represent Conflicting
Interests 103
Analysis of the Provisions 104
General Scope of the Provision 106
Committee Decisions Limiting the Application of the
Canon 107
Disclosure of Confidential Communications Not the
Sole Test 109
Cases in Which the Lawyer's Individual Interest
Conflicts with That of His Client 109
Taking Cases or Giving Advice against the Interest of
His Client or Former Client 111
Diverging Interests of Two Clients 112
Necessity for Wholehearted Service to the Second
Employment 113
Counsel for Stakeholder May Not Take Sides 113
May Not Attack the Validity or Effect of an Instrument
Which He Drew 113
Insurance Cases 114
Cases Involving Insured Minors 118
Public Prosecutors and Other Public Servants 118
Effect of Consent 120
"Collusive" Divorces 122
Manufacture of or Connivance in Procuring Ground
for Divorce 123
Deliberate Neglect to Allege or Prove a Defense 124
Agreement to Make No Defense, or to Withdraw
a Defense 125

Furnishing Otherwise Unobtainable Evidence of
    Actual Facts Constituting a Ground for Divorce   126
    Designating Lawyer for the Other Side   128
    Acceptance of Compensation from the Other Side   129
Lawyers Retired from Judicial or Public
    Positions   130
Duty Not to Disclose Confidential Communications   131
    Purpose of the Rule   132
    Scope of the Rule   133
    Application of the Rule   136
    When Disclosure Is Proper   137
Extent of Duty to Accept Professional
    Employment   139
Right to Withdraw   140
Defense of One Known to Be Guilty   142
How Far a Lawyer May Go in Supporting a
    Client's Cause   146
    Counsel's Personal Belief in His Cause   147
    Public Prosecutors   148
    Upholding the Honor of the Profession   149
    Defenses such as Usury, Infancy, Bankruptcy, Statutes
    of Frauds or of Limitations   149
Participation in Fraud or Trickery   150
Advice or Assistance in the Deliberate
    Violation of the Law   151
Countenance of Payments to Secure Specific
    Testimony   152
Employment of Coercive Tactics   153
Abuse of Legal Process   154
Employment of Underhanded Means to Get
    Evidence or Disreputable Tactics to
    Further His Case   155
Harassment of Opponent   156
Compliance with Agreements and Understandings Made
    in the Course of Conducting the Case   156
Duty on Discovery of Fraud or Imposition in His Case   156
Duty as a Prospective Witness   158
Direct Relations with Clients   159
    Intervention by Intermediary   160

Delegation of Professional Functions   160
Employment by Organization to Act for Its Employees
    or Members   161
Analysis of Problems Involved   162
History of Canon 35   163
Considerations Pro and Con   164
Canon 47 Is Decisive   165
Representation of a Group with a Common Interest
    Paying Uniform Annual Dues to Provide His
    Compensation   165
Trade Bulletins Involving Legal Questions   168
Relations with Collection Agencies   168
Compensation   169
Barristers' Fees in England   169
Lawyers' Fees in the United States   170
Right to Compensation in Certain Cases   171
Basis for Compensation   173
Right to Damages for Discharge without Cause   175
Contingent Fees   176
Expenses   178
Division of Fees   179
With a Layman or a Lay Agency   179
Employment of a Layman by a Lawyer   179
Employment of a Lawyer by a Layman   180
"Splitting of Fees" with Employers
    or Clients   181
Arrangements and Division of Fees
    between Lawyers   186
Division of Fees with Retired
    Partners or Their Estates   188

VII. THE LAWYER'S OBLIGATIONS AND RELATIONS TO OTHER
    LAWYERS   190
Encroaching on Other Lawyers   190
Courtesy and Good Faith to Other Lawyers   192
Duties of Superseding and Superseded
    Lawyers   198
Duty Not to Negotiate with One Represented
    by Counsel   201

Partnerships among Lawyers   203
    Partnership Names   206

VIII. ADVERTISING AND SOLICITATION   210
    Origin of the Proscription of Advertising
        and Solicitation by Lawyers   210
    The Legal Profession Is Not Relaxing the
        Standards   212
    History of the Canons Proscribing
        Advertising and Solicitation   215
        Canon 27   215
        Canon 43   217
        Canon 46   217
        Canon 40   218
    Scope of the Proscription of Advertising
        and Solicitation   218
    General Principles   219
    Right to Engage in an Independent Business   221
        The Rule in New York City as to an Independent
            Business   224
        Earlier Decisions by New York City Committee   225
        New York County Committee   226
        Other Decisions on Independent Business   227
    Miscellaneous Decisions as to Advertising   228
    Letterheads   228
        Letterheads of Lawyers Admitted in Different States 230
    Shingles   231
    Announcements   232
        Announcements of Special Branches   233
        New York City Committee Rulings   233
        New York County Committee Rulings   236
        Survey by the New York Bar   238
        Announcements by Lawyers Returning from
            Government Service   239
        Other Rulings Relative to Announcements   240
    Professional Cards   241
    Specialized Legal Service   242
    Telephone Books   246
    Indirect Advertising   247

Solicitation   249
   Notifying Persons Having Similar Problems   251
"Personal Relations"   252
   Information to Clients as to Changes in the Law   254
Advertisement by Bar Associations   254
   Legal Services to Low-Income Groups   257
Acquiescence in the Recommendations of
   Others   259
Legal Articles and Addresses   263
Law Lists   265
   History of the Law List Exception   265
   General Rulings   267
   Basis for Listing in a Law List   269
   Biographical and Informative Data   269
   Addresses   270
   References   271
   Clients Regularly Represented   271
   Client's Consent   272
   Legal Societies   272
   Posts of Honor   272
   Branches of the Profession Practiced   272
   Legal Authorships   273
IX. THE CANONS OF JUDICIAL ETHICS   274

APPENDICES

A. Decisions by the American Bar Association Ethics
   Committee Hitherto Unreported   283
B. Digest of Representative Court Decisions Specifying
   Grounds for Disbarment, Suspension, or Censure   304
C. Canons of Professional Ethics   309
D. Canons of Judicial Ethics   327
E. Hoffman's Fifty Resolutions in Regard to Professional
   Deportment   338
F. Code of Ethics, Alabama State Bar Association   352
G. Rules and Standards as to Law Lists   364

INDEX OF WORKS CITED   367

TABLE OF CASES   380

TABLE OF COMMITTEE DECISIONS   399

INDEX   437

LEGAL ETHICS

"True civilization is measured by the extent of Obedience to the Unenforceable."

LORD MOULTON

NOBLESSE OBLIGE

IN AMERICA, where the stability of the courts and of all departments of government rests upon the approval of the people, it is peculiarly essential that the system for establishing and dispensing justice be . . . so maintained that the public shall have absolute confidence in the integrity and impartiality of its administration. . . . It cannot be so maintained unless the conduct and motives of our profession are such as to merit the approval of all just men.

Thus begins the Preamble to the Canons.

What must be the "conduct and motives of our profession" in order that they shall "merit the approval of all just men"?

As the second paragraph of the Preamble points out, the Canons do not purport to particularize—merely to be a general guide. Since the adoption of the original thirty-two Canons in 1908 new problems and changed conditions have required and in the future will require additions, amendments, and clarification, but the basic standards of professional conduct which they embody have never been materially relaxed or the essential provisions altered; nor need they be. A lawyer who studies them thoughtfully and who wholeheartedly respects and abides by their substance and spirit will suffer no serious lapse in ethical conduct or motives.

But it is not enough for the lawyer to comply literally with the Canons and openly advocate their observance in order that his professional career shall merit the approval of all just men. The traditions of an honored profession bind him to a higher and much more difficult duty. Example is always a more potent and effective guide than mere words, which, however eloquent and stirring, can have no enduring influence unless they come from one whose life is known to follow his precepts.

The lawyer must not only be honest and upright, but must be believed to be so by clients, court, colleagues, and by his fellow citiᴌᴄᴎᴊ.[1] Nor can he prove himself thus deserving of the confidence of the community which he serves merely by observing scrupulously the letter of the law. He must be recognized as one of those exponents of true civilization who, by their lives, continually render "Obedience to the Unenforceable." "It is needful," said Justice Stone, "that we look beyond the club of the policeman as a civilizing agency to the sanctions of professional standards which condemn the doing of what the law has not forbidden." [2]

To maintain the position to which our traditions, our training, and our duties and responsibilities entitle us, we lawyers must live and act in the way which we know is right, irrespective of statutes, court decisions, canons of ethics, and disbarment proceedings.

In an address to the American Bar Association in 1910 Woodrow Wilson thus stated his idea of the status of lawyers:

> You are not a mere body of expert business advisers in the field of civil law or a mere body of expert advocates for those who get entangled in the meshes of the criminal law. You are the servants of the public, of the state itself. You are under bonds to serve the general interest, the integrity and enlightenment of law itself, in the advice you give individuals.[3]

To achieve his maximum status of usefulness, the lawyer must also be recognized as one to whom may be entrusted the most delicate confidences, with assurance that they will be handled not only with fidelity, but with understanding and sympathy. "The chief excellence of the advocate is in proportion to the facility with which he can become a party to the most momentous concerns of strangers." [4] His exceptionally broad and practical experience with the widely divergent problems of life qualifies him uniquely for such confidences.

Distinctive Characteristics of the Legal Profession

The usual reason given for different standards of conduct being applicable to the practice of law from those pertaining to business is

---

[1] "No man can ever be a truly great lawyer, who is not in every sense of the word, a good man. . . . There is no profession in which moral character is so soon fixed as in that of the law; there is none in which it is subjected to severer scrutiny by the public. It is well that it is so. The things we hold dearest on earth—our fortunes, reputations, domestic peace, the future of those dearest to us, nay, liberty and life itself, we confide to the integrity of our legal counsellors and advocates. Their character must be not only without a stain, but without suspicion. From the very commencement of a lawyer's career, let him cultivate, above all things, truth, simplicity and candor: they are the cardinal virtues of a lawyer." Sharswood, *Professional Ethics* (1854), pp. 168, 169.

[2] 48 Harv. L. Rev. 1, 13 (1934).

[3] "The Lawyer and the Community," 35 A.B.A. Reports 419, 435 (1910).

[4] Anon., "On the Principle of Advocacy," 20 Law Mag. (N.S.) 265, 283 (1854).

that the law is a "profession." This bare statement, however, does not define what constitutes a "profession" or explain the reason for the different standards.

Dean Pound, in his recently published contribution to the *Survey of the Legal Profession*, (*The Lawyer from Antiquity to Modern Times*, page 5) defines a profession as "a group of men pursuing a learned art as a common calling in the spirit of public service,—no less a public service because it may incidentally be a means of livelihood."

This tradition of public service, with the remuneration an incident, originated long ago with our legal ancestors, the barristers, in their Inns of Court. They were originally almost exclusively men of substantial origins, often younger sons of England's leading families, who for the most part were not dependent on their profession for their livelihood. As was common in that age, they looked down on "trade" and particularly on its spirit of competition and *caveat emptor*. The young men who went from Boston, New York, Philadelphia, and the South to study at the Inns of Court, and who on their return became the leaders at the bar here, brought with them these traditions, which despite the urge of "business" have been preserved and formulated by our bar associations.

Primary characteristics which distinguish the legal profession from business are:

1. A duty of public service, of which the emolument is a by-product, and in which one may attain the highest eminence without making much money.

2. A relation as an "officer of court" to the administration of justice involving thorough sincerity, integrity, and reliability.

3. A relation to clients in the highest degree fiduciary.

4. A relation to colleagues at the bar characterized by candor, fairness, and unwillingness to resort to current business methods of advertising and encroachment on their practice, or dealing directly with their clients.

While the lawyer's broad contacts with the actualities of life fit him uniquely to give wise and sympathetic advice on its many different problems, his profession has in it features which involve unique difficulties. To avoid ethical delinquencies requires not only rectitude on the lawyer's part, but also superior intelligence and imagination, more so probably than in any other calling. The reason for this is that the lawyer is constantly confronted with conflicting loyalties which he must reconcile.[5] He is answerable not only to his client whose interest it is his primary duty to serve and promote, but also to the court of which he is an officer, and further to his colleagues at the bar and to the traditions of his profession. In addition, he is not infrequently confronted with situations where his immediate personal interest apparently must run counter to that of his client. In such cases, however, if he will but believe what his better self tells him, he will find, it is confidently believed, that not only his peace of mind and self-respect, but his ultimate well-being will best be served by subordinating what seems to be his temporary personal advantage to his cardinal loyalties.

The Lawyer's Cardinal Loyalties

Neither fidelity to the court, apprehension of judicial disfavor, nor friendship and sympathy will relieve him nor should deter him from his constant obligation to see to it that no unfit person is made or continued a judge or a member of the bar, whose honor and dignity it is always his duty to uphold and maintain.

To the court he must be thoroughly candid and sincere, both in word and in action, shunning every sort of deceit or misrepresentation, preserving a self-respecting independence in the discharge of professional duty without denial or diminution of the courtesy and respect due the judicial office.

To his client he owes absolute candor, unswerving fidelity, and undivided allegiance, furthering his cause with entire devotion, warm zeal, and his utmost ability and learning, but without using means other than those addressed to reason and understanding; employing and countenancing no form of fraud, trickery, or deceit which, if brought to light, would shame his conscience or bring discredit to his profession.

To his brethren at the bar, courtesy and good faith, respecting their opinions and the relation between them and their clients, disdaining to supplant or surpass them by advertising, publicity, artifice, or by any means other than the establishment of a well-merited reputation for professional capacity, achievement, and fidelity to trust.

To himself and his profession, tireless industry, unbounded enthusiasm, delight in its problems, and joy in its struggles, and—above

[5] See Edson R. Sunderland, 21 Mich. L. Rev. 372, 383–85 (1923). Also Cheatham's Case Book, pp. 90–91, as to the lawyer's problem in reconciling his several loyalties.

all—loyalty to his own ideals and to the traditions of a noble profession.

For five hundred years it has been the fashion for uninformed people to carp at lawyers. There have, of course, always been crooked
lawyers who have pursued their crooked course without—to our
shame—being taken to task by their complaisant colleagues at the
bench and bar. There will always be such, but in no greater proportion than in other callings. The prominent positions which lawyers
have always occupied in the community have made such lapses from
rectitude the more noticeable.

In the course of my duties as chairman of the American Bar Association Ethics Committee, I have received a continual and increasing
stream of inquiries from lawyers all over the country stating delicate
and difficult problems of conduct with which they and their associates
and competitors at the bar are confronted, and asking whether the
bar association can offer guidance as to what they should do, with assurance of a sincere desire on their part to follow any suggestions
given.

The recent *Survey of the Legal Profession* shows that the bar is held
in high esteem by the great majority of responsible people in every
walk of life.[6] The confidence of the public in lawyers has been continually demonstrated by entrusting them, for five hundred years,
with a far larger proportion than any other profession or calling, of
important public posts in England and the United States.

Despite the ever-growing pressure of commercialism in all walks of
life, and of inevitable lapses by some publicity-minded members, I am
confident that the bar is today in sounder and healthier condition
than for a century; that year by year it is becoming more so, and
more than ever determined to maintain its standards. It is incumbent
on all of us who cherish our traditions and value our unique utility
for public service to see to it that there is no relaxation.

[6] See 37 Va. L. Rev. 399 (1951).

Part One

ORGANIZATION OF THE BAR AND OF DISCIPLINARY PROCEEDINGS

I

HISTORY OF THE BAR
IN ENGLAND AND
THE UNITED STATES

The Bar in England

AT THE TIME of the Norman conquest there was no class of professional advocates in England; [1] nor did William bring with him any professional lawyers or written law or jurisprudence.[2] In very early times, however, the lord defended his men [3] and the guardian represented his ward.[4] Also the champion, in trial by battle, may be considered "one of the direct ancestors of the legal profession." [5] This mode of trial was apparently brought over by the Normans, there being no allusion to it in the old Saxon laws. By royal decree Londoners were given an early franchise that no "battel" should be waged against them. Apparently hired champions were forbidden in England, but in spite of this, much hiring, direct or indirect, seems to have gone on, the same champions reappearing and fighting again and

[1] Herman Cohen, 30 Law Quart. Rev. 465 (1914).
[2] Herman Cohen, *History of the English Bar and Attornatus to 1450* (1929), pp. 38, 40.
[3] *Id.* at 10.   [4] *Id.* at 225.
[5] Edward Jenks, *Short History of English Law* (1912), p. 198.
As to trial by battle and the champion, see George Neilson, *Trial by Combat* (1890), especially chaps. 15–18, 28, and 47; see also Ashford v. Thornton, 1 B. and Ald. 405 (1818), where the procedure (which was not abolished until 1819) is discussed at length. Defendant must be ready to prove his innocence, either by defeating the plaintiff or his champion, by frightening him to default (as often happened), or by prolonging the "battel" through the day. If it lasted until the stars began to shine, defendant won the case.
For an account of such a trial where, after all formalities were arranged, one defaulted, see Lowe and Kyme v. Paramour, 3 Dyer 301a (1571). See also E. A. Kendall, *Trial by Battle* (1818), pp. 102, 104, 111–12, 142, 155 *et seq.*, 186–87, 216, 292.

again,[6] each time on behalf of a different principal, and frequently not clear of one contract until they took up another.[7]

Blackstone says that the reason that "battel" was waged by champions and not by the parties themselves in civil actions was because if the party to the suit died the suit would abate and therefore no judgment could be given for the lands in question if either of the parties was "slain in battel"; and "also that no person might claim an exemption from this trial, as was allowed in criminal cases, where the battel was waged in person." [8]

Blackstone also says that "the weapons allowed them are only batons, or staves, of an ell long, and a four-cornered leather target; so that death very seldom ensued from this civil combat." [9]

Trial by combat was greatly to the advantage of the rich litigant, who was able to hire all the good champions. Glanvill (d. 1190) welcomed trial by jury as an alternate to the duel.

Even before the conquest it was the practice of litigants to take with them their friends as advisers—*consilium*.[10] During the two hundred years succeeding the conquest this practice developed a class of legal advisers, increasingly experienced and competent in legal technicalities.[11] Although by 1150 the law was as yet hardly a con-

---

[6] Bracton (who wrote between 1250 and 1258) tells of one Elias Piggun who was found guilty by a jury of being a hired champion to whom money had been paid to undertake the warranty and who, as punishment, lost both his foot and his fist. See Neilson, *Trial by Combat,* pp. 48–49.

[7] *Id.* at 49.   [8] 3 Blackstone 339 (1765).

[9] But see Kendall, *Trial by Battle,* p. 295.

[10] Cohen, *History of the English Bar,* pp. 18, 19, 34. In 1158–63 the party "went to trial cum amicis et auxiliis meis,—the consilium"; *id.* at 66. In early days counsel were not, however, allowed to plead for the accused in the gravest cases: *id.* at 12. William S. Holdsworth, *History of English Law* (1922), II, 262. To be historically accurate, designations on a brief of counsel in addition to those actively participating should be worded: "John Jones, of Counsel *with* appellants, etc." Roscoe Pound, 19 Notre Dame Lawyer 235 (1944); Herman Cohen, 31 Law Quart. Rev. 65 (1915). Also, since there could be no partnerships between barristers who constitute the "counsel" so referred to, the designation of a law firm as "of counsel" is historically incorrect; see Thomas Leaming, *A Philadelphia Lawyer in the London Courts* (1911), pp. 78–79.

"Some there be who know not how to state their causes or to defend them in court, and some who cannot, and therefore are pleaders necessary; so that what plaintiffs and others cannot or know not how to do by themselves they may do by their serjeants, proctors, or friends." *The Mirror of Justices* (1285–90), Selden Society Publications, Vol. VII, chap. 2, sec. v, p. 47.

[11] Warvelle, in sec. 44, p. 29, of *Legal Ethics* (1902), says of the origin of barristers: "The early lawyers, in the main, seem to have been ecclesiastics, but about 1207, priests, and persons in holy orders generally, were forbidden to act as advocates in the secular courts, and from thenceforward we find the profession composed entirely of a specially trained class of laymen. It is said that when the prohibition above mentioned went into effect those of the clergy who had adopted law as a profession, and were unwilling

scious profession, we have by that time definite names of persons who were conducting cases.[12] While they could not sue for fees, a friend who was a *placitator* and who was of obvious help in the litigation expected and received a reward in the form of an honorarium.[13] These early advisers were the forerunners of the modern barristers.

In 1239 William of Drogheda of Oxford, half priest and half lawyer, who possibly practiced in the secular as well as in the ecclesiastical courts,[14] wrote a study of the trade of advocates, the aim of which was to teach his readers how to win their cases.[15] He describes procedure, gives many practical suggestions (*cautelae*), including hints for rather sharp practice, and asks his readers to spend part of the fees resulting from his advice in masses for his soul.[16] He was particularly explicit in his admonition to collect fees in advance: "Get your money while the patient is ill." [17]

There was a secular school of law in Canterbury between 1150 and 1176,[18] and a flourishing law school at Oxford in 1220.[19] London led the way to local independence and close organization.[20]

By the time of Edward I (1272–1303) "we see clearly that a legal profession is being formed." [21] This profession consisted of two branches, the pleaders (*placitatores* and *narratores,* who developed from the friend-adviser [*consilium*] and finally became the serjeants-at-law [*servientes ad legem*]) and the attorneys (*attornati*). The pleader did not represent the person of the client, but was his counsellor, supporting his cause "by his learning, ingenuity and zeal." [22] His develop-

---

to be deprived of this means of livelihood, assumed a coiffure, or close-fitting headdress, to hide the clerical tonsure, and this became the distinguishing badge of the legal profession for many years thereafter. To this circumstance is also ascribed that peculiar feature of the modern English barrister—the wig."

[12] Cohen, *History of the English Bar,* p. 169.

[13] See article by Cohen, 31 Law Quart. Rev. 62 (1915); also Cohen, *History of the English Bar,* p. 372.

[14] Cohen, *History of the English Bar,* pp. 101, 105.

[15] *Id.* at 102.   [16] *Ibid.*

[17] *Id.* at 108–09.   [18] *Id.* at 116.

[19] Cohen, *History of the English Bar,* p. 201; also article by him in 30 Law Quart. Rev. 475 (1914).

[20] Cohen, *History of the English Bar,* pp. 224, 226, 227.

[21] Holdsworth, *History of English Law,* II, 261; see also Cohen, *History of the English Bar,* pp. 142–52.

[22] Holdsworth, *History of English Law,* II, 261–62; Pound, 19 Notre Dame Lawyer 235, 236 (1944).

The *forespeca* was an intercessor who said what he was told to say; Cohen, *History of the English Bar,* pp. 3, 136. The *causidici* were pleaders. There is a reference to one in 1087; *id.* at 46–47, 118.

ment began "with a friend saying to the judges what he can for the party, then someone telling his own or the party's tale formally; then shaping his plea, and finally arguing the law." [23] The attorney, however, was more than a mere advocate, and represented the client in person. The client was privileged to disavow mistakes by his pleader, *placitator* or *narrator*,[24] it being the custom in the thirteenth century to ask a litigant whether he would abide by his pleader's statement.[25] The attorney, on the other hand, represented the person of the client,[26] and could instruct counsel and thus bind the client.[27] In the early days attorneys could be appointed only by permission of the crown,[28] and it was not until 1235 that suitors were allowed generally to be represented by attorneys.[29] One hundred and forty were appointed on the king's orders in 1292.[30]

"The attornatus was a mere man of business; the *serviens* (*ad legem*) a professional specialist." [31]

The professional lawyer and pleader was in full swing in 1300,[32] the rank of "serjeant-at-law" being officially established,[33] and there being twenty-four counsel in practice in 1310; [34] but at that time they did not examine or cross-examine witnesses, their chief work being to argue in court.[35] Probably by the time of Edward III (1327–77) they drew their own pleadings.[36]

Apparently the earliest provision of law regulating the professional conduct of lawyers was the statute, the First of Westminster, Chapter 29, in 1275, providing that "if any Serjeant, Pleader or other, do any manner of Deceit or Collusion in any King's Court or consent in deceit of the Court or beguile the Court or the Party and thereof be attainted, he shall be imprisoned for a year and a day and from thence-

23 Cohen, *History of the English Bar*, p. 181.

24 Cohen, 31 Law Quart. Rev. 65 (1915).

25 Holdsworth, *History of English Law*, II, 262–63.

26 Cohen, *History of the English Bar*, p. 136.

27 *Id*. at 296–97: "In a case in the MS cited as B (1293) the judge asked the attorney if he avowed what his serjeant had said on his behalf, and the attorney said that he did."

28 Cohen, 31 Law Quart. Rev. 63, 64 (1915).

29 Jenks, *Short History of English Law*, p. 201; Frederic W. Maitland and Francis C. Montague, *English Legal History* (1915), p. 95. Holdsworth, *History of English Law*, VI, 432: "The idea that one man can represent another is foreign to early English law." The statute of Westminster of 1275 regulated their conduct. See Cohen, 30 Law Quart. Rev. 479 (1914). Roscoe Pound, *The Lawyer from Antiquity to Modern Times* (1953), chap. IV, p. 79.

30 Cohen, *History of the English Bar*, p. 281.

31 *Id*. at 194–95. As to the derivation of *attornatus*, see Cohen, *History of the English Bar*, pp. 126–28; see also article by him in 31 Law Quart. Rev. 65–66 (1915).

32 Cohen, *History of the English Bar*, p. 203.

33 *Id*. at 218.   34 *Id*. at 216.   35 *Id*. at 111–12, 211.   36 *Id*. at 211.

forth shall not be heard to plead (conter) in [that] Court for any Man." [37]

In 1280 an ordinance [38] of the City of London recited that many "counters" had not learned their profession and were not competent. It provided that, at the request of the serjeants and counters, the mayor and aldermen should require them to be admitted and reasonably to understand their profession.[39] This ordinance defined the duties of the counter: to plead and make proffers at the bar.[40] He might not be on both sides of a case, or be a partner in the case.[41] He might not retire pending the proceedings without the consent of his client.[42]

He might receive reasonable compensation (salaire) in the form of fees,[43] in fixing the amount of which four points were to be considered: "the amount of the matter in dispute, the labour (travail) of the serjeant, his value as a pleader in respect of his learning, eloquence and repute, and the usage of the court." [44]

A lawyer appointed by the court to plead in a cause was bound to accept the assignment unless he had good cause to refuse.[45] Bullying of witnesses and parties was not permitted.[46] A lawyer might refuse to testify as to confidential communications.[47] A judge might not try a case if he had been in it while at the bar.[48]

In the middle ages both attorneys and barristers could sue for their fees, but by the early part of the seventeenth century barristers were precluded from doing so, the fee being regarded merely as an honorarium.[49] In the eighteenth century a barrister could not accept a fee from a lay client, but by the middle of the nineteenth century this was changed.[1]

When in Edward I's reign the legal profession appears as an or-

---

[37] Cohen, 30 Law Quart. Rev. 479 (1914); Cohen, History of the English Bar, pp. 189–90.

[38] See Cohen, History of the English Bar, pp. 230 et seq. There was evidently much corruption throughout the profession in these early days; id. at 164–67.

[39] See also the Statute of 1402; id. at 303.   [40] Cohen, 31 Law Quart. Rev. 69 (1915).

[41] Cohen, History of the English Bar, p. 233.   [42] Id. at 278; see A.B.A. Canon 44.

[43] Cohen, History of the English Bar, p. 235 n.; see also p. 77.

[44] Mirror of Justices (1285–90), Selden Society, VII, 48; Cohen, History of the English Bar, p. 279; see Canon 12.

[45] Cohen, History of the English Bar, p. 119; see Canon 4.

[46] Cohen, History of the English Bar, p. 119; see Canon 18.

[47] Holdsworth, History of English Law, VI, 433 (1924); see Canon 37.

[48] Cohen, 30 Law Quart. Rev. 475 (1914); see Canon 36.

[49] Holdsworth, History of English Law, VI, 440; infra, p. 169 n. 5.

[1] Holdsworth, History of English Law, VI, 444; see also Pound, 19 Notre Dame Lawyer 238 (1944).

ganized body, we find the pleaders a body distinct from the apprentices [2] and attorneys, both becoming subject to fixed rules.[3] At the
head of the profession and exercising a general control over it were
the judges and the serjeants-at-law. Beneath them, grouped together
in the four great Inns of Court—Lincoln's Inn, Gray's Inn, Inner
Temple, and Middle Temple—were the various grades of "apprentices," from the Benchers and Readers to the inner barristers or students.[4]

The serjeants, who were usually chosen from the Benchers and
Readers,[5] and had a rank equal to a knight,[6] had their own Inn, called
the Serjeant's Inn, to which the judges, who had been serjeants, also
belonged,[7] and hence addressed the serjeants as "brother." [8] No new
serjeants have been appointed since 1875, and the order is now ex-
tinct,[9] their Inn having been dissolved and its property sold.[10]

"By the end of the fourteenth century the serjeants-at-law formed
a close body or guild selected by the Crown, generally upon the nomination of the judges, from which the ranks of the bench were re-
cruited," [11] the candidates having practiced at least sixteen years.
They had until 1834 a monopoly of practice in the common pleas but
were not restricted to it.[12]

[2] The term "apprentices" is misleading. They were by no means students or underlings,
but were men of eminence in their profession (Theodore F. T. Plucknett, 48 Law Quart.
Rev. 328, 335–36 [1932]) from whose ranks the serjeants were chosen (Earl of Halsbury,
Laws of England [1931; 2d ed.], II, 475).

[3] Holdsworth, *History of English Law*, II, 405.

[4] *Id.* at 406.

"The Inns of Court first came into being after the breaking up by Henry III in the
12th and 13th centuries of the schools of law which existed in the city of London under
clerical control." The Rt. Hon. Sir David Maxwell-Fyfe, K.C., M.P., in 4 S.W. Law
Jour. 391 (1950).

[5] Holdsworth, *History of English Law*, II, 423; Pound, 19 Notre Dame Lawyer 242
(1944).

[6] Holdsworth, *History of English Law*, II, 407, and n. 4.

[7] Pound, 19 Notre Dame Lawyer 237 (1944); Leaming, *A Philadelphia Lawyer in the
London Courts*, p. 24.

[8] Jenks, *Short History of English Law*, p. 199; Pound, 19 Notre Dame Lawyer 238
(1944).

[9] Halsbury, *Laws of England* (2d ed.), II, 475.

[10] Sir D. Plunket Barton, *The Story of Our Inns of Court* (1924), pp. 10, 11; Halsbury,
Laws of England, II, 475; Leaming, *A Philadelphia Lawyer in the London Courts*, p. 23.

Thomas G. Lund Esq., Secretary of the Law Society in London, advises me that the
stained glass window from the Serjeant's Inn, containing its armorial bearings, is now
in the Hall of the Law Society in London.

[11] Holdsworth, *History of English Law*, II, 407; Pound, 19 Notre Dame Lawyer 237
(1944). From a list of seven or eight of the most able serjeants given the Chancellor by
the Chief Justice of the Common Pleas.

[12] Holdsworth, *History of English Law*, II, 412; see also Pound, 19 Notre Dame Lawyer 238 (1944).

The serjeants sat in court within the bar—a barrier of iron or wood.[13] They were addressed by one another (even the oldest by the youngest) by their surnames, without "Mr." [14] Until 1875 the judges were chosen from them. The ceremonies for their creation were lengthy and costly. They took a solemn farewell of their Inn of Court, of which they ceased to be members on becoming serjeants,[15] and were rung out of the society by the chapel bell.[16]

The Inns of Court [17] had the monopoly of calling to the bar, that is, licensing apprentices. The Benchers were their ruling body.[18]

Barristers were drawn mainly from the sons of men of independent means, or of the more prosperous and successful business men.[19]

The Readers were responsible for teaching the students, the educational system in the early days being thorough and intensely practical.[20] They then had excellent moot courts in which both Readers and Benchers participated.[21]

The main part of the education of a barrister consisted in mooting and discussion, reading and reporting, from which he learned the principles of the law, both substantive and adjective, while that of an attorney consisted in his apprenticeship to a practitioner, during which he learned the use of forms and processes.[22]

[13] Jenks, *Short History of English Law,* p. 199.

[14] Cecil Walsh, *The Advocate* (2d ed.), p. 13.

[15] Pound, 19 Notre Dame Lawyer 237 (1944); Leaming, *A Philadelphia Lawyer in the London Courts,* pp. 23–24.

[16] See the description of the ceremony in Holdsworth, *History of English Law,* II, 408–10.

[17] The four Inns of Court at their zenith in the latter half of the sixteenth century (Jenks, *Short History of English Law,* p. 199), had about 200 members each (Holdsworth, *History of English Law,* II, 415).

[18] Jenks, *Short History of English Law,* 199–200.

As to the regulation of barristers and the discipline of attorneys in England, see references by Chief Judge Cardozo in his opinion in People v. Culkin, 248 N.Y. 465 (1928).

The Readers were those who had publicly lectured at the Inn. Holdsworth, *History of English Law,* II, 423; Pound, 19 Notre Dame Lawyer 242 (1944).

[19] Holdsworth, *History of English Law,* VI, 436; Pound, 19 Notre Dame Lawyer 317 (1944).

[20] Holdsworth, *History of English Law,* II, 417, 427.

[21] *Id.* at 423 *et seq.*

"Other important forms of education in the Inns (not so much for the benefit of the students perhaps as for the more junior barristers) were bolts and moots, which in their early form are long ago obsolete. A bolt was a case propounded for argument among the inner barristers and conducted by the outer barristers. A moot (as then practiced) consisted of the putting of a doubtful case by an outer barrister in hall after supper, which was argued by one or two benchers. A mimic law suit followed in which inner and outer barristers and benchers took part." The Rt. Hon. Sir David Maxwell-Fyfe, K.C., M.P., in 4 S.W. Law Jour. 394 (1950).

[22] Holdsworth, *History of English Law,* VI, 436–37.

There is some confusion in the use of the terms utter or outer, and inner barrister. In the moot courts, held at the Inns, the Benchers, who acted as the judges, sat on the bench; the students who were the youngest members of the Inn not ready to argue in the moot or called to the bar, sat within the bar; and the outer or utter barristers, two of whom argued the moot case, sat without the bar, sitting "uttermost on the forms, which they call the Barr." [23]

The pleader stood *at the bar* or *ouster the bar,* and gained the name of *Apprenticius ad Barros* or Utter Barrister, and later of Barrister-at-Law. In court the order of precedence was Serjeants-at-Law, Benchers, and Utter Barristers, and so continued up to the 17th century. In later times the Utter Barrister was called within the Bar and became known as an Inner Barrister, and later still as a "silk," from the material of his gown, the junior barrister taking the cast-off name of Utter or Outer Barrister, or the more colloquial term of stuff gownsman. [24]

In addition to the barristers and attorneys [25] there were also the solicitors, a distinct class who, in the middle ages, were not members of the legal profession. [26] Solicitors began to appear as a professional class about 1450, but did not secure a recognized status until about fifty years later. [27] "A solicitor is one who conducts legal business on behalf of another, but is neither an attorney nor a barrister." [28] They were associated mainly with the Court of Chancery and had their own Inns of Chancery—nine or ten of them. [29] Early in the eighteenth century the solicitors substantially amalgamated with the attorneys. [30]

The term "devil" is a regular and serious name for a young barrister who, in wig and gown, serves without compensation and without fame, often for from five to seven years, supplying a junior with ammunition. [31]

[23] Pound, 19 Notre Dame Lawyer 237–43 (1944).
[24] Hugh H. L. Bellot, *The Inner and Middle Temple* (1902), p. 38.
[25] As to the training of an attorney, see Pound, 19 Notre Dame Lawyer 318–19 (1944).
[26] Holdsworth, *History of English Law,* VI, 448.
[27] *Id.* at 450.
[28] *Id.* at 449; Pound, 19 Notre Dame Lawyer 321 (1944).
[29] Leaming, *A Philadelphia Lawyer in the London Courts,* p. 22; see also Holdsworth, *History of English Law,* II, 415.
[30] Holdsworth, *History of English Law,* VI, 456–57. For a comprehensive summary of the Ethics and Etiquette of Solicitors see five very thorough and informative lectures by Thomas G. Lund, Esq., secretary of the Law Society, in 1950–51, published in two pamphlets by the Society, Chancery Lane, London W.C.2; also article by him, "The Legal Profession in England and Wales," 35 Jour. Am. Jud. Soc. 134–45 (1952). See also Wilfrid Bovey, 38 A.B.A. Reports 768–71 (1913).
[31] Leaming, *A Philadelphia Lawyer in the London Courts,* p. 30. See also An. St. (Annual Statement) (1902–03), p. 4.

An "essoiner" was an inferior rank of counsel who made excuses for non-attendance and so gained time for his client to plead.[32]

The Bar in the United States

The history of the legal profession in the United States has been so fully and clearly described in the ten chapters of Dean Pound's section of the *Survey of the Legal Profession* that it is unnecessary here to do more than give the briefest summary of his account of it.[33]

The young men who, in colonial times, went to study law at the Inns of Court, on their return became leaders in their respective communities.[34] Due to their influence and competition, high standards of education, craftsmanship, and conduct were there established and maintained in the period immediately following the Revolution.[35]

During the second third of the nineteenth century, however, there developed a growing hostility against special privileges granted by the government.[36] Professions, and particularly bar associations, were deemed undemocratic and un-American. This manifested itself everywhere in a lowering of the required qualifications of character, education, and training.[37] In a number of states [38] statutes and even constitutional provisions were passed upholding the inherent and "natural" right of every voter of good moral character to practice law. In others the right of admission was assured after a brief period of study. There was also widespread objection to the organized bar as a "secret

[32] Cohen, 31 Law Quart. Rev. 69 n. (1915).

[33] Dean Pound describes a cycle "from recognition at first that the legal profession as a whole had problems, functions and obligations transcending those of the individual lawyer and groups of lawyers, to gradual loss and finally all but giving up of the professional idea, thence to gradual regaining of that idea, and final achievement of it again in the integrated state bar of today." *The Lawyer from Antiquity to Modern Times,* p. 223, quoting George E. Brand, "Bar Organization," 34 Jour. Am. Jud. Soc. 38–39 (1950).

[34] In Virginia and South Carolina they practiced without admission by the local courts but as members of the Inn where they had studied. Dean Pound in his chapter VII of the *Survey* points out that at the time of the Revolution many of the best lawyers who had been trained in the Inns of Court were loyalists and left the country (p. 178).

[35] The oldest bar association claiming continual existence is apparently the Philadelphia Bar Association, which celebrated its 150th Anniversary in 1952. See 25 Temple Law Quart. 301 (1952).

[36] See Alfred Z. Reed, *Training for the Public Profession of the Law* (1921), pp. 85–93.

[37] In 1860 Pennsylvania was the only state which required students of law to register at the beginning of their period of study; *id.,* p. 87.

[38] Including Indiana (1850), Michigan (1850), New Hampshire (1842), Maine (1843), and Wisconsin (1849).

trade union" or a privileged class not open equally to all citizens.[39]
Even bar meetings, which had been primarily social gatherings of the
legal fraternity, or to honor a distinguished judge or lawyer, usually
recently deceased, were generally discontinued. In the period immediately after the Civil War, the bar reached its lowest ebb.

About 1875 the leaders of the bar, realizing the deplorable condition into which their profession was falling, as well as the imperative
necessity of taking a firm stand against the rising tide of commercialism and the growing influence of those who would turn the profession from a "branch of the administration of justice" into a "mere
money getting trade," began the movement for the reestablishment at
the bar of standards of character, education, and training, and also
for the organization of bar associations all over the country. This
movement has grown and prospered until now in every state it is
recognized that for the protection of the public no one may practice
law whose character has not been subjected to examination and
found worthy, and who has not passed a prescribed test as to his
education and legal training.[40] Also bar associations have been organized in all the states, in the District of Columbia, and in a great
many counties.[41] These are not merely fraternal societies, holding
annual dinners and memorial meetings, or trade associations for the
material advancement of their members, but organizations devoted to
the pursuit of a learned art in the spirit of public service.[42]

In twenty-five states the bar is "integrated," [43] whether by statute

[39] This still persists in the Abraham Lincoln argument for easy admission.

[40] The various character requirements are summarized in the section of the *Survey
of the Legal Profession* by John G. Jackson, Esq.; those as to education and legal training
in that by Orie L. Phillips and Philbrick McCoy, *Conduct of Judges and Lawyers,* chaps.
iii and iv, pp. 21–58; and that by Albert J. Harno, *Legal Education in the U.S.,* pp. 155–60.
    As to the constitutionality of legislative requirements relative to admission and dis-
barment see *infra,* p. 42.

[41] In 1952 there were 54 state bar associations: two in Virginia, two in West Virginia,
two in North Carolina—one integrated and one voluntary—and one in Hawaii, Puerto
Rico, and the District of Columbia, and more than 1000 local ones.
    The American Bar Association was organized in 1878.

[42] "It is the bar association, not the individual lawyer that can maintain high educational standards insuring a learned profession, that can maintain high standards of
character as a prerequisite of admission to practise, that can formulate and maintain
high standards of ethical conduct in relations both with clients and with courts. The
public has a deep interest in having a well organized bar, part of the machinery of
administering justice in a complex social and economic order." Roscoe Pound, *The
Lawyer from Antiquity to Modern Times,* p. 11.

[43] For the advantages of integration, see 26 Dicta 221–6 (1949). William Wicker,
"Integrated Bars," 21 Tenn. L. Rev. 708–18 (1951). W. M. Leech and M. E. Queener,

or by authorized Rule of Court, whereby every practicing lawyer must be a supporting member of the bar association and subject to its Canons and to discipline by it. In all the other states there are voluntary associations.

"Comments on the Integrated Bar," 21 Tenn. L. Rev. 719–22 (1951). George E. Brand, "Bar Organization," 34 Jour. Am. Jud. Soc. 38, 40–42 (1950), and "The Integrated Bar," 24 Ohio Bar 591–96 (1951). Howard L. Barkdull, "Methods of Strengthening Bar Associations," 35 Jour. Am. Jud. Soc. 9, 13–14 (1951).

II

SANCTIONS OF
PROFESSIONAL CONDUCT

NATURE OF THE SANCTIONS

IT IS BELIEVED IMPOSSIBLE to find or frame a satisfactory or comprehensive definition of "ethics" as applied to the legal profession. "What a lawyer may and may not do in his professional capacity" is too general to be of any practical use.

To define and classify the duties and obligations of the lawyer one must look to four different sources: (1) The statutes; (2) the common law decisions; (3) the Canons; (4) the usages, customs, and practice of the bar.

The duty to be a law-abiding citizen would not generally be classified as a principle of legal ethics, although a lawyer may be disbarred for violating the statutes relative thereto.[1] At the other end, the duty to be courteous to one's colleagues at the bar would ordinarily be considered a principle of etiquette rather than of ethics, although Canon 25 specifically condemns the ignoring of "known customs or practice of the bar."[2]

An example of a statutory and common law prohibition which, in its application to lawyers, has been included in the Canons is that against embezzlement.[3] The duty not to divulge confidential communications[4] is derived from the common law, where it is found from the early days.[5]

[1] See *infra*, p. 43. Canon 32 specifically requires the lawyer both to "observe and to advise his client to observe the statute law."

[2] See also *infra*, p. 195.   [3] See *infra*, pp. 43–44, 50, 89 *et seq.*

[4] Holdsworth, *History of English Law*, VI, 433.

[5] See *infra*, p. 131. It is interesting to note that the oft quoted admonition from the Sermon on the Mount in Matthew VI:24 against serving two masters was phrased: "No man *can* serve two masters," emphasizing not so much the fact that this is wrong, as that it will not work. It is also interesting that this admonition in Luke XVI follows immedi-

A number of the obligations defined by the Canons, such as that not to deal with one represented by a lawyer except through the lawyer, that not to advertise or solicit professional employment, and that not to steal another's clients, comprise practices which are not considered improper as applied to business generally.[6] A number of others, such as that, under Canon 34, relative to fee splitting; that, under Canon 35, requiring direct relations with the client; that, under Canon 33, relative to partnerships between lawyers; and that, under Canons 27, 43, and 46, relative to law lists and advertising, are associated peculiarly with the legal profession.

History of the Canons

The first Code of Professional Ethics in the United States was that formulated and adopted by the Alabama State Bar Association in 1887,[7] which, between 1887 and 1906, was adopted, with minor changes, in Georgia, Virginia, Michigan, Colorado, North Carolina, Wisconsin, West Virginia, Maryland, Kentucky, and Missouri. In Washington, California, and Oregon the Codes contained, as "duties" of an attorney, seven Canons taken from the oath for advocates prescribed by the laws of the Swiss Canton of Geneva.[8] The 1899 charter of the State Bar Association of Louisiana contained a Code of Ethics consisting of eight Canons substantially similar.[9] In Florida the Bar Association of Jacksonville printed in its 1906 Year Book the fifty "Resolutions in Regard to Professional Deportment" which had been formulated by David Hoffman (born 1784, died 1854) of the Baltimore bar, for adoption by his students on admission.[10]

In Idaho, Indiana, Iowa, Minnesota, Mississippi, Nebraska, Oklahoma, South Dakota, and Utah there were also, by 1908, Codes of Ethics more or less complete, as the result of codifications of statutory enactments or of the action of bar associations. During the period (1905–08) in which the American Bar Association was engaged in drafting its Canons, the bar associations of Illinois, Kansas, Massachusetts, Montana, New York, Ohio, Pennsylvania, and Vermont

---

ately after the Parable of the Unjust Steward, a flagrant violation of fiduciary fidelity and conflicting interest.

6 Note the Anti-Trust Laws.

7 See Appendix F hereto. Based largely on Sharswood's *Professional Ethics,* and Hoffman's Resolutions.

8 See 31 A.B.A. Reports 715 (1907).   9 See *Ibid.* at 714.

10 See Appendix E hereto.

had charged committees with the duty of working on Canons and of conferring with the American Bar Association Committee.

In 1905 the then President of the American Bar Association, George R. Peck, had appointed a committee of distinguished lawyers,[11] headed by Henry St. George Tucker [12] of Virginia and including Francis Lynde Stetson of New York, and subsequently [13] Judge Alton B. Parker (1906 President of the Association), Justice Brewer of the Supreme Court, and Judge Thomas Goode Jones of Alabama (author of the Alabama Code of 1887), to report on the advisability and practicability of the adoption of a Code of Ethics by the American Bar Association. This Committee having reported in 1906 that the adoption of such a Code was both advisable and practicable [14] was instructed to draft one. At the 1907 meeting the Committee submitted a report containing a compilation of the Codes of Ethics theretofore adopted in different states,[15] including reprints of the Hoffman Resolutions and of Sharswood's *Professional Ethics*. The Committee was continued and proceeded to draft a Code, the draft being printed and copies sent to all members of the Association and to the secretaries of each state bar association, with invitations for criticisms. In reply, more than a thousand letters were received, containing many valuable suggestions and excerpts from articles in professional journals, American and English, which were tabulated by the secretary of the Committee, Lucien Hugh Alexander of Pennsylvania, for use by the Committee.[16]

The report of the Committee, presented to the 1908 meeting of the Association, was debated and the thirty-two recommended Canons voted on one by one, all being approved as drafted except Canon 13 on contingent fees,[17] which was altered to its present form.

Unquestionably the primary reason for the great activity in the bar associations in framing and adopting Codes of Ethics, beginning with the Alabama Code in 1887, was the same as that which prompted

---

[11] See 31 A.B.A. Reports 680 (1907).

[12] Mr. Tucker had been President of the Association 1904–05, and it was primarily owing to his influence that the project went forward.

[13] See 33 A.B.A. Reports 573 (1908).   [14] See 31 A.B.A. Reports 681 (1907).

[15] *Id.* at 685. This summary of the different Codes is full of interesting suggestions and well worth reading.

[16] See 33 A.B.A. Reports 567–69 (1908).

[17] Canon 13, as proposed by the Committee read: "13. CONTINGENT FEES. Contingent fees may be contracted for, but they lead to many abuses and should be under the supervision of the court." See the present Canon, *infra*, p. 176, n. 7, and p. 313.

the organization of bar associations—the realization by thoughtful leaders of the bar of the growing commercialism all over the country. The consequent weakening of an effective professional public opinion clearly called for a more definite statement by the bar of the accepted rules of professional conduct. These must be made accessible, in simple form, as a guide both to law students and also to practicing lawyers, many of whom were found to have "departed from honorable and accepted standards of practice early in their careers as the result of actual ignorance of the ethical requirements of the situation." [18]

The thirty-two Canons, as adopted, received the hearty support of the bar of the entire country.[19]

In its report for 1914,[20] the Ethics Committee summarizes the actions of the different bar associations in adopting codes of professional ethics. From this report it appears that when the American Bar Association Code was adopted in 1908 there were forty-four state associations, twelve of which had adopted formal codes of professional ethics, besides two in which there were statutory attempts to define professional duties. By 1914, thirty-one had adopted the American Bar Association Code, with little or no change; Michigan, Virginia, Mississippi, Missouri, and North Carolina had adopted it in place of their own existing codes. In Pennsylvania a committee had been appointed to draft a code and had done so, but the bar association there rejected the report of its committee and substituted the American Bar Canons. In three others the codes included substantially all the provisions of the American Bar Association Code.

Since 1914 many additional states have adopted the American Bar Association Canons, substantially intact. Some have adopted them prospectively, as from time to time amended by the American Bar Association. Others have failed to include this provision with the result that, unless an American Bar Association amendment is specifically adopted by the state, it is not in force there as a state provision.

In 1928 American Bar Association Canon 28 was amended and Canons 33 to 45 adopted. Canons 11, 13, 34, 35, and 43 were amended and Canon 46 adopted in 1933. Canons 7, 11, 12, 27, 31, 33, 34, 37, 39,

[18] Report of the Committee in 1906; quoted in 21 Green Bag 271, 273 (1906); see also Charles A. Boston "Practical Activities in Legal Ethics," 62 Am. L. Reg. (now U. of Pa. L. Rev.) 103, 107–9 (1913).

[19] See statement commending it by Judge Simeon E. Baldwin of Connecticut, 8 Col. L. Rev. 541 (1908).

[20] See 39 A.B.A. Report 559–70 (1914).

and 43 were amended and Canon 47 adopted in 1937; Canon 27 was further amended in 1940, 1942, 1943, and 1951 and Canon 43 in 1942.[21]

The Canons of Judicial Ethics, Numbers 1–34, were adopted in 1924 and amended in 1933, 1937, 1950; Canons 35 and 36 were adopted in 1937 and Canon 35 amended in 1952.[22]

FORCE AND EFFECT OF THE CANONS

While it is clear that a lawyer may be disciplined for violating a Canon which forbids something not otherwise proscribed,[23] the court decisions [24] are not entirely clear as to the legal effect of a lawyer's violation of such a Canon. In an Illinois case, the court said:

The American and State Bar Associations are not legislative tribunals, and their Canons of Ethics are not of binding obligation and are not enforced as such by the courts, although they constitute a safe guide for professional

[21] These amendments are detailed in Appendix C hereto, where the text of the Canons is set out in full.

[22] See Appendix D hereto.

[23] In re Newman, 172 App. Div. 173 (1916), lawyer censured for splitting fees with a collection agency, improper only since the amendment of 1937 to Canon 34; lawyer suspended for a year for representing conflicting interests, despite his forty-four years at the bar (four-to-three decision), Lewis v. Board of Governance, 316 Pa. 193 (1934); suspended for a month for violating Canons 27, 35, and 47 in advertising the servicing, through a corporation, of a real estate transaction from its inception to its closing, including legal services, In re L. R., 7 N.J. 390 (1951); reprimanded for violating Canons 34, 35, and 47, Matter of A.B.C., 7 N.J. 388 (1951); suspended for eight months and until further order of the court for advertising for Nevada divorces, In re Schnitzer, 33 Nev. 581 (1911). See also People ex rel v. MacCabe, 18 Colo. 186 (1893); Dahl v. State Bar, 213 Cal. 160 (1931), fee splitting with adjusters; In re Information to Discipline etc., 351 Ill. 206 (1933), taking public salaries without performing any service; Carpenter v. State Bar, 210 Cal. 520 (1930), suspended for negotiating directly with other party. See also 52 Col. L. Rev. 1045, 1047 (1952).

[24] The ethics committees are not empowered to pass on questions of law (infra, p. 32). They have intimated, however, that an agreement by a lawyer to divide a fee with another lawyer who performs no service, or with the estate of a deceased partner is enforceable, App. A, 6; see also N.Y. County 161 and 352; and compare A.B.A. Op. 124. In Lilly v. Commissioner, 343 U.S. 90 (1952) the Supreme Court reversed the Tax Court, 14 T.C. 1066, and the Circuit Court of Appeals, 188 F.2d, 269, which had disallowed as "ordinary and necessary expenses" the agreed payments by an optician to oculists of one-third the price of glasses sold to the doctors' patients. The acceptance of such payments was condemned by the Canons of the American Medical Association and those in North Carolina, where they were made. The Tax Court and the court below held them thus to be in violation of public policy. The Supreme Court, while stating that if the payments had been declared unlawful by a state or Federal law this might render them non-deductible, held that the customs and actions of organized professional organizations did not of themselves constitute the "sharply defined national or state policies" the frustration of which may, as a matter of law, preclude the deduction of an expense as one ordinary and necessary in the particular business and locality.

conduct in the cases to which they apply, and an attorney may be disciplined by this court for not observing them.[25]

In the *Matter of Cohen*,[26] Chief Justice Rugg, in affirming the suspension of a lawyer for two months for advertising free legal advice, said:

Codes of legal ethics adopted by bar associations of course have no statutory force. They are illuminating as showing views entertained by organizations of members of the bar concerning tests of proper conduct for those charged with the important functions of attorneys admitted to practice within the courts. They are commonly recognized by bench and bar alike as establishing wholesome standards of professional action. . . . Advertising or soliciting business is censurable as a form of self-laudation unbecoming the traditions of a high calling. The Canon thus incorporates in the Code of Ethics an ideal standard of conduct which has been long and well recognized and upheld in theory by both bench and bar. The attorney who disregards the rule is properly subject to rebuke if not to disbarment.

In a recent Federal case, District Judge McGuire said:

Codes of ethics adopted by bar associations, of course, have no statutory force. They are indicative, however, of and reflect the attitude of the profession as a whole upon those courses of action which they frown upon and interdict, and they are commonly regarded by bench and bar alike as wholesome standards of professional ethics. The practice of law is a profession and not a trade.[27]

Cases in which a lawyer has been denied compensation because he represented conflicting interests [28] are not particularly helpful in this connection, since, irrespective of Canon 6, this has frequently been held to be violative of public policy and of the lawyer's fiduciary

---

[25] People v. McCallum, 341 Ill. 578, 590 (1930); see also Hunter v. Troup, 315 Ill. 293 (1925); but see In re Clifton, 33 Ida. 614 (1921). In A.B.A. Op. 37 (1912), Chairman Howe said: "The Canons of Professional Ethics are legislative expressions of professional opinion." In states where the Codes have been adopted by statute or by rules of the highest court, they may of course be given the full force of law.

[26] 261 Mass. 484, 487 (1928).

[27] Herman v. Acheson, 108 F. Supp. 723, 726 (1952); In re Annunziato's Est. 108 N.Y.S.2d 101, 103 (1951), Surrogate Rubinstein of King's Court, New York, said that the Canons are "entitled to the force of law."

[28] Such as Weil v. Neary, 278 U.S. 160 (1929), Anderson v. Eaton, 211 Cal. 113 (1930), Reilly v. Beekman, 24 F.2d 791 (1928). See also Gesellschaft, etc. v. Brown, 78 F.2d 410 (1935), where a lawyer formerly employed by the Alien Property Custodian was denied a quantum meruit for representing a foreign corporation in a claim against the custodian and for securing legislation from Congress; see 45 Yale L. Jour. 731 (1936). See also 52 Col. L. Rev. 1045 (1952) notes 34 and 35.

relation.[29] Similar is a Pennsylvania case [30] where a lawyer who had induced a witness to feign illness in order to have his case continued was held not entitled to recover his charges, which included an unsegregated fee for this case, even though the witness did not in fact join in the deception of the Court. Such deception required no Canon 15 or 32 to denounce its impropriety.

Cases involving solicitation are, however, instructive. In states where a statute prohibits agreements to procure cases for a lawyer, such agreements have been held unenforceable, both as in violation of the statute and "by the rule of general public policy," the court saying that even if there were no statute, the iniquity of such agreements was now so generally recognized as to render them unenforceable.[31] In solicitation cases, in states where there is no such statute, the courts have recognized a distinction between personal solicitation by the lawyer himself, and organized solicitation for him by laymen whose compensation is based on a percentage of recovery. The leading case of *Chreste* v. *Louisville Ry.*[32] was a suit by a lawyer based on the defendant's having settled direct with his client and thus deprived him of his 50 per cent contingent fee. The defense was that the case had been obtained by solicitation. The court said that,

considering the difficulty of fixing the dividing line between what is proper and improper solicitation, the uncertainty that the doctrine would introduce into all contracts between attorneys and their clients, the fact that solicitation is not condemned at common law, or denounced by our Constitution or Statutes, and the further fact that it is difficult to perceive upon what theory it can be said to be clearly injurious to the public good, we conclude that mere solicitation on the part of an attorney, unaccompanied by fraud, misrepresentation, undue influence or imposition of some kind, or other circumstance sufficient to invalidate the contract, is not of itself sufficient to render a contract between an attorney and client void on the ground that it is contrary to public policy.[33]

[29] Similarly, a lawyer has been held liable to one injured by a gross breach of his duty not to divulge confidential communications. Taylor v. Blacklow, 3 Bing. N.C. 235 (1836). See also In re Boone, 83 F. 944, 952, 957 (1897).

[30] Duffy v. Colonial Trust Co., 287 Pa. 348 (1926).

[31] Mendelson v. Gogolick, 243 App. Div. 115 (N.Y., 1934).

[32] 167 Ky. 75 (1915).

[33] See also State v. Rubin, 201 Wis. 30 (1938); Louisville Bar Association v. Hubbard, 282 Ky. 734, 739 (1940); Hightower v. Detroit Edison Co., 262 Mich. 1 (1933); in Matter of Gray, 184 App. Div. 822 (1918), the court censured respondent for the persistent personal solicitation of business men, stating that such was "repugnant to the conception of every honorable practitioner, condemned by the bench and bar alike."

In Matter of Schwarz, 231 N.Y. 642 (1921), the Court of Appeals held, affirming the Appellate Division, that a lawyer might be disbarred for distributing to former clients

The railroad, having obtained a new trial, then alleged and proved that the solicitation had been by one who was paid a monthly salary plus a fourth interest in the proceeds of all contracts brought to Chreste. On appeal the court held that this entirely changed the situation, there being "a very wide difference between the unprofessional and undignified practice of personal solicitation of business and the indefensible and vicious practice of employing agents and runners who are not lawyers to go about the country soliciting business and stirring up strife and litigation for a stipulated consideration or a contingent fee." [34] Chreste's claim was accordingly denied,[35] and he was subsequently disbarred.[36]

In a Minnesota case [37] where a lawyer was disbarred for organized solicitation of involved debtors, the court said of the contention that collection agents were permitted to solicit:

The point is in the fundamental difference between any commercial business and a profession. The vocation of a lawyer is a profession . . . his conduct is to be measured not by the indefinite, still developing and largely unwritten standards of trade and counting house, but by those of his profession, which, while they have not reached their ultimate state, have yet attained the development and degree of formulation evidenced by the Canons of Ethics.

In the Massachusetts case quoted above,[38] Chief Justice Rugg said:

It is incompatible with the maintenance of correct professional standards to employ commercial methods of attracting patronage. Advertising such as that disclosed on this record is commonly designed to stimulate public thought and challenge popular attention to the end that the business of

---

a circular letter asking them why they had not sent him any cases lately; but see the three strong dissenting opinions.

In In re Gill, 104 Wash. 160 (1918), where the three defendants each with eighteen years unblemished professional reputation, under retainer from the Merchants Protective Corporation had represented the members in actively soliciting, the court merely held the practice unprofessional, without further punishment other than the publicity of the case.

See also Gammons v. Johnson, 76 Minn. 76 (1899); Ingersoll v. Coal Co., 117 Tenn. 263 (1906).

34 Chreste v. Commonwealth, 171 Ky. 77, 97 (1916).   35 173 Ky. 486 (1917).

36 178 Ky. 311 (1917); see also In re H———— S————, 229 Mo. App. 44 (1934). See also in the Matter of Wiltse, 109 Wash. 261 (1920), disbarred for soliciting claims for draft exemption.

37 In re Disbarment of Tracy, 197 Minn. 35, 43 (1936).

38 In the Matter of Cohen, 261 Mass. 484, 488 (1928). See also People v. Berezniak, 292 Ill. 305, 315 (1920) (severe censure); In re Donovan, 43 S.D. 98 (1920), suspended six months for garbled and deceptive divorce advertisement; In re Oliensis, 26 Pa. Dist. 853 (1917) (divorce advertisement); Mayer v. State Bar of California, 86 Cal. 461, 464 (1933) (indirect divorce advertising); see also In re Roberts, 2 Cal. App.2d 70 (1934).

the advertiser may be increased. It has always been regarded as contrary to sound public policy for an attorney at law to foment litigation or to instigate law suits.

The upshot of the cases is apparently that a contract to which a lawyer is a party will not be declared void merely because its fulfillment by him will involve the breach of a Canon, or unless what the lawyer is called on to do is so flagrantly improper that the court will hold it to be void as contrary to public policy.[39] In determining what is contrary to public policy doubtless the court will take into consideration the existence of the Canons. It is conceivable also that a lawyer might be denied the assistance of the court to enforce a contract in flat violation of a Canon, although such conclusion might not apply to a layman. For example, Canon 34, as amended in 1937, forbids the division of fees for legal services, except with another lawyer, based upon a division of service or responsibility. It might well be held that a lawyer who had performed no service might be precluded from enforcing a division contract with another lawyer,[40] while a layman who had performed service might enforce such a contract against the lawyer.[41]

Organization and Functions of the Ethics and Grievance Committees

The Standing Committee on Professional Ethics of the American Bar Association came into being in 1914 pursuant to a resolution adopted at the annual meeting in 1913 to amend the constitution by providing for this Committee, and to amend the bylaws by adding the following provision:

The Committee on Professional Ethics shall communicate to the Association such information as it may collect respecting the activity of state and local bar associations in respect to the ethics of the legal profession, and it may from time to time make recommendations on the subject to the Association.[42]

In 1919 the Committee on Professional Ethics was changed to a Committee on Professional Ethics and Grievances, and its duties were fixed by the bylaws as follows:

The Committee on Professional Ethics and Grievances shall communicate to the Association such information as it may collect concerning the activ-

[39] See App. A, 6.   [40] See Reilly v. Beekman, 24 F.2d 791 (1928).
[41] See App. A, 6; see also N.Y. County 351.   [42] 39 A.B.A. Reports 559 (1914).

ities of state and local bar associations in respect to the ethics of the profession and grievances against members of the Bar, and it may from time to time make recommendations on the subject to the Association.[43]

In 1922 the bylaws of the Association were again amended to authorize the Committee on Professional Ethics and Grievances:

to express its opinion concerning proper professional conduct when consulted by members of the Association or by officers or committees of state or local bar associations. Such expression of opinion shall only be made after a consideration thereof at a meeting of the committee and approval by at least a majority of the committee.[44]

By subsequent amendment, the Committee is now authorized to express its opinions concerning proper professional or judicial conduct (but not dealing with judicial decision or discretion) when consulted by members of the bar or by any officer or committee of a state or local bar association.[45]

The American Bar Association Committee's first formal published Opinion was rendered January 15, 1924. Since then it has published 286 additional numbered Opinions, 274 of which are contained, with the Canons, in a bound volume issued by the Committee in 1947, and the balance have been published in the *American Bar Association Journal.*[46] In 1952 the Committee authorized the chairman to include, as an Appendix to the present volume, some 300 rulings by the Committee theretofore unpublished, covering points in which the Committee were all in accord and which seemed instructive.[47]

While the functions of the Committee include that of passing on violations of the Canons by members of the Association with a recommendation to the Board of Governors of censure, private or public, suspension or disbarment, it would be wholly impractical for this Committee to attempt to investigate and pass on complaints from all over the country. Hence it usually refers complaints to the local bar associations.

The Ethics Committee of the New York County Lawyers' Association was first authorized to give opinions in 1912, and through 1952 has published 418 opinions. The similar Committee of the Associa-

---

[43] 46 A.B.A. Reports 302 (1921).   [44] 48 A.B.A. Reports 172 (1923).
[45] Bylaws, Art. X, Sec. 12.
[46] 275, March, 1948; 276, April, 1948; 255 (modification), June, 1948; 277, November, 1948; 278, February, 1949; 279 and 280, October, 1949; 281, July, 1952; 282, September, 1950; 283, October, 1950; 284, October, 1951; 285, December, 1952; 286, January, 1953. Opinions 45 and 46 were withdrawn by the Committee.
[47] Appendix A hereto.

tion of the Bar of the City of New York since 1923 has issued 1,167 opinions; the Michigan Committee 150; the North Carolina Committee has in preparation a volume containing approximately 200; and the committees in Chicago, Cleveland, California, Missouri, Texas, etc., each a lesser number. Copies of these may be obtained from the several secretaries.

In many jurisdictions there are two separate committees [48] one of which hears and passes on grievances, the other devoting its attention to the construction of the Canons. In addition there is usually a committee on the unauthorized practice of the law.

The function of the American Bar Association Ethics Committee is the interpretation of the Canons; that of interpreting the rules and standards is lodged in the Law List Committee.[49]

The Ethics Committees do not pass on questions of law.[50]

Unless specific complaints are made, the American Bar Association Committee will not inquire into or enforce Canon 27 relative to the names of lawyers in publications which are not law lists; [51] nor will it advise a local bar association whether or not it should institute disciplinary proceedings.[52]

The American Bar Association Committee in an early ruling held that it would not entertain a complaint against a judge where the case was not clear and where the offense was not flagrant.[53]

Complaints against non-members should be sent to the local associations,[54] the American Bar Association's disciplinary powers being applicable only to its members.[55]

While state and local committees are not bound by the American Bar Association Opinions, it has been said that they are considered highly persuasive and to be followed unless unique local conditions are present.[56]

Where a bar association has a special committee on unauthorized practice, the ethics committee of such association is bound by its decisions as to what constitutes unauthorized practice, even though the ethics committee may not agree.[57]

[48] There are two such committees in Philadelphia, as well as in New York City and in many other associations; see also Cleveland 8.

[49] App. A, *1*. The Rules and Standards relative to the Law Lists, adopted pursuant to Canon 27, are Appendix G hereto.

[50] A.B.A. Ops. 63, 204, 209, 247; App. A, *1*.   [51] App. A, *2*.

[52] A.B.A. Op. 77; see also N.Y. City 131, 177, 320, etc.; N.Y. County 19, 20, 21, etc.

[53] App. A, *3*.   [54] Art. X, Sec. 12(*b*) of the bylaws.

[55] App. A, *4*. See *supra*, p. 31.   [56] Miss. 1.   [57] App. A, *5*.

III

DISCIPLINARY PROCEEDINGS

Procedure for Disciplining Lawyers

In England

As the admission of barristers is exclusively in the control of the Benchers of the Inns, so also is their disbarment, suspension, or other discipline for professional misconduct.[1] Proceedings for disbarment are rare, the usual practice being to suspend for a period, but even this is regarded as a blow from which no member of the profession can recover.[2] The proceedings are confidential. At the hearing of the complaint before the Benchers, who may disbench one of their own number as well as disbar a barrister, the respondent is present, but must be represented by one of the members of his Inn, he being privileged to call on any one of them to take up his case.[3] While there is an appeal to the judges as visitors,[4] apparently they always follow the decision of the Benchers,[5] who, although they need give no reason for refusing to admit, must assign a reason to disbar, which must be guilt of "conduct unbecoming his profession." [6]

A barrister desiring to become a solicitor must first be "disbarred" as a barrister, which, in such case, is on his own motion.[7]

---

[1] In a privy council case, Petition from Antigua, 1 Knapp 267, 12 E.R. 321 (1830), Lord Wynford said: "In England the courts of justice are relieved from the unpleasant duty of disbarring advocates in consequence of the power of calling to the Bar and disbarring having been in very remote times delegated to the Inns of Court. . . . The power of suspending from practise must, we think, be incident to that of admitting to practise as is the case in England with regard to attornies."

[2] Wilfrid Bovey, "The Control Exercised by the Inns of Court over Admission to the Bar in England," 38 A.B.A. Reports 767, 773-74 (1913).

[3] *Ibid.*

[4] *Ibid.* See also Manisty v. Kenealy, 24 W.R. 918 (1876).

[5] Leaming, *A Philadelphia Lawyer in the London Courts*, p. 68. Mathers, "Legal Ethics," 40 Can. L.T. 809, 819 (1920). See also as to the history of the power to disbar in England and the United States, In re Cannon, 206 Wis. 374 (1932).

[6] Alexander Pulling, *The Order of the Coif* (1897), pp. 178-79; Appeal of H. Hayward, Esq.; Pearce's, *Guide to the Inns of Court* (1855), pp. 419-20.

[7] Halsbury, *Laws of England* (2d ed.), II, 478.

In the old days a lawyer was "disbarred" by literally being cast over the bar, which was a substantial barrier of iron or wood separating the court and its official staff from litigants and others.[8] The serjeants once used the same ceremony to express their contempt for an "unhappy attorney" who presumed to assert a right to practice in the Common Pleas [9] where the serjeants held a monopoly.

In the case of solicitors, the English Solicitors Act of 1932 makes a distinction between a "removal from the Roll" by voluntary application on the part of the solicitor wishing to withdraw from practice or to become a barrister, and "striking off the Roll" in disciplinary actions because of misconduct.[10]

The solicitor may be struck off the Roll of Solicitors, for professional misconduct, by the Master of the Rolls; [11] and is also subject to disciplinary control by the Disciplinary Committee of the Law Society, appointed by the Master of the Rolls from among the present or past members of the Council of the Law Society.[12]

In the United States

The requirements, both as to character and education, for admission to the bar, have been thoroughly described in the volume of the *Survey of the Legal Profession* entitled *Bar Examinations and Requirements for Admission to the Bar* (John G. Jackson, 1952).

The practice and procedure for disciplining lawyers varies in the several states, and it would not seem worth while to attempt to detail it as of the present date, some generalizations being here sufficient.[13]

In practically all jurisdictions, a complaint of misconduct by a lawyer may be filed by anyone. In most of the states there is a grievance

[8] Pulling, *The Order of the Coif*, pp. 187, 188. Bellot, "Some Early Law Courts," 38 Law Quart. Rev. 168, 170 (1922). Byrchley's Case, Jenkyn's Rep. 262, 145 E.R. 187 (1584).

[9] Inderwick, *The Interregnum* (1891), p. 230.

[10] Jenks, *The Book of English Law* (1928), p. 88.

[11] See for a comprehensive summary of the whole subject "The Ethics and Etiquette of Solicitors," Five Lectures before the Law Society in 1950 and 1951 by Thomas G. Lund, Esq., its secretary; published by the Law Society at its Hall, Chancery Lane, London W.C.2. As to the Disciplinary Committee, see pp. 12–16 of the 1951 lectures. See also Lund, 35 Jour. Am. Jud. Soc. 134–45 (1952).

[12] Lund, p. 13 of 1951 lectures. As a practical matter the master follows the recommendation of the Committee.

[13] See as of 1946 Charles S. Potts, "Disbarment Procedure," 24 Texas Law Review 161 (February, 1946); also *Survey of the Legal Profession*, Phillips and McCoy, *Conduct of Judges and Lawyers*, chap. vi, pp. 85 to 129, and Harno, *Legal Education in the U.S.*

committee of the state bar association, and also in many of local county associations. This committee is charged with the duty of receiving and investigating such complaints, and of making preliminary findings. These are referred to a court, which may hear additional evidence from both sides, either directly or through a referee, rule on the propriety of the lawyer's conduct, and exonerate him or subject him to censure, suspension, or disbarment. In some states the court proceedings are instituted and conducted by the Attorney General or the County Attorney, or by an attorney appointed by the court. Everywhere the lawyer has the right of ultimate appeal to the highest court of the state. Everywhere he has the right to a full hearing, with ample notice.

In no states except Georgia, North Carolina, and Texas is the lawyer entitled to a jury trial.

In some jurisdictions, the bar committees have power to compel the attendance of witnesses.[14]

Nature of the Proceedings

"The power [to disbar], however, is not an arbitrary and despotic one, to be exercised at the pleasure of the court, or from passion, prejudice, or personal hostility; but it is the duty of the court to exercise and regulate it by a sound and just judicial discretion, whereby the rights and independence of the bar may be as scrupulously guarded and maintained by the court, as the rights and dignity of the court itself." [15]

To practice law, although "more than a mere indulgence, revocable at the pleasure of the court," [16] is not a property right, or a privilege protected by the Constitution,[17] but a conditional privilege.

"Membership in the bar is a privilege burdened with conditions. A fair private and professional character is one of them. Compliance with that condition is essential at the moment of admission, but it is equally essential afterwards. Whenever the condition is broken, the privilege is lost. To refuse admission to an unworthy applicant is not

14 For example, Illinois, Arkansas, New York, and the Committee of Censors of the Philadelphia Bar Association.

15 Ex parte Secombe, 19 How. 9, 13 (1856).

16 Ex parte Garland, 4 Wall. 333, 379 (1866).

17 See Bradwell v. Illinois, 16 Wall. 130 (1872); Philbrook v. Newman, 85 Fed. 139 (1898); Watson v. Maryland, 218 U.S. 173 (1910).

to punish him for past offences. The examination into character, like
the examination into learning, is merely a test of fitness. To strike the
unworthy lawyer from the roll is not to add to the pains and penalties
of crime. The examination into character is renewed; and the test of
fitness is no longer satisfied. For these reasons courts have repeatedly
said that disbarment is not punishment." [18]

A proceeding to discipline a lawyer, both in England [19] and in the
United States is neither criminal nor civil,[20] and is not founded on
legal process according to the signification of the words "per legem
terrae," as used in Magna Charta and in the Constitution and statutes.[21] A court, knowing judicially of the misconduct of an attorney,
may proceed of its own motion, without issuing any process.[22] Respondent has no constitutional right to confront witnesses [23] or, (except in Georgia, North Carolina, and Texas) to trial by jury.[24] "The
court has over attorneys a jurisdiction which is to be exercised according to a standard of conscience and not according to technical
rules," [25] including rules of evidence.[26]

In *In re Samuel Davies*,[27] the court said:

18 Cardozo, J., Matter of Rouss, 221 N.Y. 81, 84 (1917). See also, People v. Culkin, 248
N.Y. 465 (1928). In Lantz v. State Bar of California, 212 Cal. 213, 220 (1931), however,
the court said, in suspending Lantz for a year for taking undue advantage of his client
for his own benefit, that this would be "adequate punishment to be inflicted upon him,
and will be a sufficient deterrent to others who might in the future be tempted to commit
similar transgressions." Sacher v. The Association of the Bar of the City of New York
and New York County Lawyer's Association, 22 L.W. 4206 (April 5, 1954).

19 In re Hardwick, 12 Q.B.D. 148 (1883).

20 State v. Peck 88 Conn. 447 (1914), but see In re Breidt, 84 N.J.Eq. 222, 230 (1915).

21 Matter of Allin, 224 Mass. 9 (1916).

22 Randall, petitioner, 11 Allen (Mass.) 473, 479 (1865). As to the summary jurisdiction
of the court to require a lawyer to account to his client, see Costigan's Case Book, pp.
149–57.

23 People v. Stonecipher, 271 Ill. 506 (1916).

24 Ex parte Wall, 107 U.S. 265, 283, 288 (1882); see also In re Shepard, 109 Mich. 631, 636
(1896); Smith's Appeal, 179 Pa. 14, 22 (1897); also cases cited in an article by Leon Green,
"The Court's Power over Admission and Disbarment," 4 Texas L. Rev. 1 (1925) (n. 35, pp.
12–15, and n. 37, pp. 16–17). Charles S. Potts, "Trial by Jury in Disbarment Proceedings,"
11 Texas L. Rev. 28–52 (1932); Charles S. Potts, "Disbarment Procedure," 24 Texas L.
Rev. 161, 163–67 (1946).

In the Pennsylvania case above cited the court said (p. 22) "Nor is there any more
reason for calling in a jury to pass upon his misconduct, when he is put without the
bar, than for calling in one to pass upon his professional qualifications when he is
admitted within it."

See also Barach's case, 279 Pa. 89, 95 (1924). See, however, the dissenting opinions of
Justices Black and Douglas in Sacher v. United States, 343 U.S. 1, 14, 89 (1951).

25 Gould v. State, 99 Fla. 662, 671 (1930); see also Re Yablunky, 407 Ill. 111, 120 (1950).

26 See Matter of Joseph Santosuosso, 318 Mass. 489 (1945), and cases cited. In re
Durant, 80 Conn. 140, 150 (1907); In the Matter of Eldridge, 82 N.Y. 161 (1880).

27 93 Pa. 116, 121–22 (1880).

By admitting him the court presents him to the public as worthy of its confidence in all his professional duties and relations. If afterwards it comes to the knowledge of the court that he has become unworthy it is its duty to withdraw that endorsement, and thereby cease to hold him out to the public as worthy of professional employment.

. . . .

the exercise of the power is not for the purpose of enforcing civil remedies between parties, but to protect the court and the public against an attorney guilty of unworthy practices in his profession.

The court, by reason of the necessary and inherent power vested in it to control the conduct of its own affairs [all attorneys being officers of the court [28]], and to maintain its own dignity, has a summary jurisdiction to deal with the alleged misconduct of an attorney. A proceeding for disbarment is simply the exercise of jurisdiction over an officer, an inquiry into his conduct not for the purpose of granting redress to a client or other person for wrong done, but only for the maintenance of the purity and dignity of the court by removing an unfit officer.[29]

A pardon of the offense,[30] or restitution to the injured party,[31] although perhaps relevant to the severity of the discipline administered, is not a defense. Nor does the fact that respondent was acquitted of the offense charged bind the court in administering discipline.[32] *Res adjudicata* does not apply to disciplinary proceedings; [33] nor is there nor can there be any statute of limitations applicable to disciplinary proceedings.[34] However, the fact that the acts complained of occurred a long time ago, thereby increasing the difficulty of respond-

---

[28] Ex parte Garland, 4 Wall. 333, 378 (1866).

[29] Hammond, J., in Bar Association of Boston v. Casey, 211 Mass. 187, 191, 192 (1912).

[30] See In re Davies, 93 Pa. 116 (1880); Sanborn v. Kimball, 64 Me. 140 (1875); Matter of —— (an attorney), 86 N.Y. 563 (1881) State v. Snyder, 136 Fla. 875 (1939); In re Wolfe's Disbarment, 288 Pa. 331, 335–37 (1927).
"While the effect of the pardon was to relieve him of the penal consequences of his act, it could not restore his character." Clay, J., in Nelson v. Com., 128 Ky. 779, 789 (1908). Edward M. Thornton, *Attorneys at Law* (1914), sec. 863, p. 1226.

[31] In re —— (an attorney), 9 L.T. (N.S.) 299 (1863), where no one appeared on either side when the case was called, Pollock, C. B., said: "Grave charges are made against the attorney, which must be answered by him, and if not answered he ought to be punished. . . . If those whose duty it is to be here and proceed with the matter forget their duty, the court will not forget its duty, but take care that such steps are taken as will prevent a private settlement of the proceedings by smothering it and so getting rid of the matter." See also in re Harris, 88 N.J.L. 18 (1915).

[32] Re Kennedy, 18 Lanc. L. Rev. 276 (1901); Matter of Richards, 333 Mo. 907 (1933); Barach's case, 279 Pa. 89, 95 (1924); In re Wolfe's Disbarment, 288 Pa. 331, 337 (1927) (dictum); see also In re Abrams, 36 Oh. App. 384 (1930); and see Thornton, *Attorneys*, sec. 864, p. 1277.

[33] Re Bruener, 178 Wash. 165 (1934).

[34] Wilhelm's case, 269 Pa. 416, 421 (1921).

ent in making a defense, will augment the burden in his favor.[35]

Speaking for the majority of the court in *Ex parte Wall*,[36] Justice Bradley said:

"The question is," said Lord Mansfield, "whether, after the conduct of this man, it is proper that he should continue a member of a profession which should stand free from all suspicion. . . . It is not by way of punishment; but the court in such cases exercise their discretion, whether a man whom they have formerly admitted is a proper person to be continued on the roll or not."

Distinction between Contempt and Disciplinary Proceedings

In *Ex parte Terry*,[37] a case in which respondent was held in contempt for assaulting the marshal who was attempting to carry out the court's order to remove his wife from the court room, Justice Harlan said:

The power to punish for contempt is inherent in all courts; its existence is essential to the preservation of order in judicial proceedings, and to the enforcement of the judgments, orders and writs of the courts, and consequently to the due administration of justice. . . .

. . . The petitioner was not entitled, of absolute right, either to a regular trial of the question of contempt, or to notice by rule of the court's intention to proceed against him, or to opportunity to make formal answer to the charges contained in the order of commitment. . . .

. . . It was competent for the Circuit Court, immediately upon the commission, in its presence, of the contempt recited . . . to proceed upon its own knowledge of the facts, and punish the offender, without further proof, and without issue or trial in any form. . . .

Jurisdiction of the person of the petitioner attached instantly upon the contempt being committed in the presence of the court. That jurisdiction was neither surrendered nor lost by delay on the part of the Circuit Court in exercising its power to proceed, without notice and proof, and upon its own view of what occurred, to immediate punishment.

In *In re Schofield*,[38] Justice Linn said:

A contempt proceeding for misbehavior in court is designed to vindicate the authority of the court; on the other hand the object of a disciplinary proceeding is to deal with the fitness of the court's officer to continue in that office, to preserve and protect the court and the public from the official ministrations of persons unfit or unworthy to hold such office.

•   •   •   •

[35] See *infra*, p. 46.   [36] 107 U.S. 265, 273 (1882).
[37] 128 U.S. 289, 303, 307, 309, 311 (1888).   [38] 362 Pa. 201, 214, 215 (1949).

The fact that professional misconduct may also be a contempt does not bring disciplinary proceedings within the rule that one court will not punish for contempt of another tribunal. The respondent is not now charged with contempt of court but with misbehavior in his office of attorney.

In *People ex rel. v. Green,*[39] Judge Helm said:

The purpose of proceedings for contempt and those for disbarment, and the powers and duties of courts in connection therewith, must not be confused. The former may be termed a police regulation or power, for the protection of the court from present direct interference and annoyance in a trial or proceeding taking place before it; the latter is intended to protect, generally, the administration of justice, to save the legal profession from degradation by unworthy membership, and to guard the interest of litigants against injury from those intrusted with their legal business. The power to act in connection with the former is lodged in the court before or against whom the offense is committed; authority to proceed in the latter is possessed exclusively by the tribunal authorized to grant licenses admitting to the profession; the former is punished by fine or imprisonment, and in many instances the proceeding is summary and largely ex parte; the sole penalty in connection with the latter is a prohibition from practicing in courts of record, and this judgment can only be entered upon notice of the charge preferred and a full hearing in defense; ample time for preparation being given and all legitimate testimony being allowed and considered. A contempt may constitute ground for disbarment, but it by no means follows that the cause for disbarment must, in all cases, constitute a contempt.

Speaking of power of courts to punish for contempt, Judge Winslow said in *State v. Circuit Court:* [40]

It is, and must be, a power arbitrary in its nature, and summary in its execution. It is, perhaps, nearest akin to despotic power of any power existing under our form of government. Such being its nature, due regard for the liberty of the citizen imperatively requires that its limits be carefully guarded, so that they be not overstepped. It is important that it exist in full vigor; it is equally important that it be not abused. The greater the power, the greater the care required in its exercise. Being a power which arises and is based upon necessity, it must be measured and limited by the necessity which calls it into existence.

. . . .

Important as it is that courts should perform their grave public duties unimpeded and unprejudiced by illegitimate influences, there are other rights guaranteed to all citizens. . . . which are fully as important, and which must be guarded with an equally jealous care.

[39] 7 Colo. 237, 247–48 (1884).   [40] 97 Wis. 1, 8 (1897).

Accordingly the court held in that case that a newspaper article charging a judge with corrupt motives could not be considered criminal contempt, where the publication was subsequent to the conclusion of the trial.[41]

In *Cooke* v. *United States*,[42] where the contemptuous remarks relative to the judge were made in a letter to him, and not in open court, Chief Justice Taft said:

When the contempt is not in open court, however, there is no such right or reason in dispensing with the necessity of charges and the opportunity of the accused to present his defense by witnesses and argument.

. . . .

The power of contempt which a judge must have and exercise in protecting the due and orderly administration of justice and in maintaining the authority and dignity of the court is most important and indispensable. But its exercise is a delicate one and care is needed to avoid arbitrary or oppressive conclusions. This rule of caution is more mandatory where the contempt charged has in it the element of personal criticism or attack upon the judge. . . . The substitution of another judge would avoid either tendency.

Where improper statements are made during the progress of a trial, they may be contemptuous although true.[43] In this case Justice Holmes said:

When a case is finished, courts are subject to the same criticism as other people, but the propriety and necessity of preventing interference with the course of justice by premature statement, argument or intimidation hardly can be denied.

In *Sacher* v. *United States*,[44] the Supreme Court in a five-to-three decision affirmed the judgment imposing jail sentences on attorneys for Communists tried before Judge Medina. During the trial, Judge Medina had reserved the right to punish them for contempt on several occasions, but had not done so on the occurrence of each incident because he believed that this would have lessened the chances of a well-considered judgment and would have obstructed the course of the trial. The majority (per Justice Jackson) held that Judge Medina properly proceeded under Rule 42(*a*), although he postponed filing his certificate and imposing sentence until the close of the trial, since the offenses occurred in his presence and were within his personal knowledge; "summarily" said the court, does not refer to timing.

---

[41] Compare In re Pryor, 18 Kans. 72 (1877).   [42] 267 U.S. 517, 536, 539 (1925).
[43] Patterson v. Colo., 205 U.S. 454, 463 (1907). See also In re Mindes, 88 N.J.L. 117 (1915).
[44] 343 U.S. 1 (1952).

They further held that Rule 42(*b*) was for cases where the facts were not within his own knowledge and that it was only in such cases that the judge was to become a complaining witness in a proceeding before another judge.

The minority held that the postponement of sentence to the end of the trial made it clear that summary enforcement was not necessary, and that there was no reason why their guilt should not have been tried before another disinterested judge.

In *Hallinan* v. *United States*,[45] and *MacInnis* v. *United States*,[46] the two lawyers were held guilty of contempt during the trial, after a brief time for judicious consideration, but execution of sentence stayed until the conclusion of the trial. These decisions were relied on by the minority in the *Sacher* case as demonstrating the fallacy of Judge Medina's conclusion that prompt action by him would have disrupted the trial.[47]

Repeated acts of contempt may indicate lack of the sound character which is necessary for continuance at the bar.[48]

Powers of Courts and of Legislatures in Disciplinary Proceedings

While the legislature may provide that one may not practice law who has not complied with certain minimum requirements as to character [49] and preparation,[50] or that the conviction of certain specified

[45] 182 F.2d 880 (1950).   [46] 191 F.2d 157 (1951).

[47] See also as to the distinction between contempt proceedings based on disrespect to the court and disciplinary proceedings by reason thereof, In re Wallace, L.R. 1 P.C. 283 (1866); State v. Root, 5 N.D. 487, 493 (1896); Ex parte Tillinghast, 4 Pet. 108 (1830); In re Langworthy, 39 Ariz. 523 (1932); Ex parte Townley, 3 Dowl. 39, 40 (1834); 76 Cent. L. Jour. 293 (1913); State v. Circuit Court, 97 Wis. 1 (1897); State Board v. Hart, 104 Minn. 88 (1908); See also note in 53 A.L.R. 1244 (1928). See also Thatcher v. U.S., 212 Fed. 801, 807 (1914); In re Thatcher, 190 Fed. 969 (1911); In re Charles Thatcher, 80 Oh. St. 492 (1909); Bradley v. Fisher, 13 Wall. 335 (1871); Ex parte Cole, 1 McCrary 405, Fed. Cas. No. 2973 (1879); People v. News-Times Publ. Co., 35 Colo. 253, 391, 393 (1906); Patterson v. Colo., 205 U.S. 454 (1907); People ex rel Chicago Bar Association v. Standidge, 333 Ill. 361 (1928); In re Hilton, 48 Utah 172 (1916); State v. Kirby, 36 S.D. 188 (1915); 17 L.R.A. (N.S.) 572 n. (1909); 15 Ann. Cas. 205 n. (1908); and see 9 Ann. Cas. 168 n. (1908); 15 L.R.A. (N.S.) 525 n. (1910).

[48] In re Cannon, 206 Wis. 374, 409 (1932); and cf. Casper v. Kalt Co., 159 Wis. 517, 533 (1915).

A disbarred lawyer who remained silent when others, with his knowledge, frequently and publicly represented him as a licensed attorney, has been held guilty of contempt. People ex rel Colorado Bar Association v. Humbert, 86 Colo. 426 (1929).

[49] See Petition of the Board. 191 Wis. 359, 364 (1926); In re Farmer, 191 N.C. 235, 239 (1926); Spears v. California, 211 Cal. 183 (1930); Brydonjack v. State Bar, 208 Cal. 439, 443 (1929); In re Cannon, 206 Wis. 374, 397 (1932).

[50] In re Bergeron, 220 Mass. 472 (1915); Olmsted's case, 292 Pa. 96, 103 (1928); In re Bledsoe, 186 Okla. 264, 266 (1939).

offenses [1] shall preclude his admission or necessitate his disbarment, it may not constitutionally provide that certain specified qualifications shall entitle one to practice, since this is the exclusive function of the courts.[2] In a leading Maryland case,[3] the court said:

> In the last analysis the duty rests upon the courts, and the profession as a whole, to uphold the highest standards of professional conduct and to protect the public from imposition by the unfit or unscrupulous practitioner.
>
> The Court controls the situation and procedure . . . in its discretion, as the interests of justice may seem to it to require.[4]

> The right of any person to engage in the practice of the law is slight in comparison with the need of protecting the public against the incompetent.[5]

GROUNDS FOR DISCIPLINE

As indicated in the above quotations, the cases dealing with the disbarment or other discipline of lawyers involve two distinct characteristics,[6] although the distinction is often not clearly recognized:

1. Cases in which the lawyer's conduct has shown him to be one who cannot properly be trusted to advise and act for clients

2. Cases in which his conduct has been such that, to permit him to remain a member of the profession and to appear in court, would cast

---

For the requirements in the several states relative to the admission of lawyers to practice, see the section of the *Survey of the Legal Profession* summarized in 24 Pa. Bar Assn. Quart. 144 (1953); also Harno, *Legal Education in the U.S.*

[1] 7 C.J.S. (attorney and client) 737 n. 31 (1937). State v. Turner, 141 Neb. 556, 573 (1942); In re Rudd, 310 Ky. 630 (1949); In re McCoy, 239 S.W.2d 86 (1951); In re May, 239 S.W.2d 95 (1951); Matter of Donegan, 282 N.Y. 285 (1940).
In the last case cited the court said that statutes of this kind should be strictly construed.
See also Wisconsin v. O'Leary, 207 Wis. 297 (1932); Application of Levy, 23 Wash.2d 607 (1945).

[2] Re Opinion of the Justices, 279 Mass. 607, 611–13 (1932); In re Cannon, 206 Wis. 374, 397 (1932). See 80 U. of Pa. L. Rev. 1021 (1932); 8 Wis. L. Rev. 74 (1932); 16 Minn. L. Rev. 857 (1932); Blewett Lee, 13 Harv. L. Rev. 233 (1899); Andrew A. Bruce, 19 Ill. L. Rev. 1 (1924); Leon Green, 4 Tex. L. Rev. 1 (1925); W. C. Bolland, 24 Law Quart. Rev. 392 (1908); Re Platz, 42 Utah 439, 443 (1913); Hanson v. Grattan, 84 Kan. 843, 845 (1911); Petition of Splane, 123 Pa. 527, 540 (1888); Ex parte Steckler, 179 La. 410, 422 (1934); In re Lavine, 2 Cal. 2d 324, 327 (1935).

[3] Rheb v. Bar Association of Baltimore, 186 Md. 200, 205 (1946).

[4] State v. Peck, 88 Conn. 447, 452 (1914).

[5] Rugg, C. J., in In re Bergeron, 220 Mass. 472, 477 (1915).

[6] A classified summary of illustrative cases is given in Appendix B. See also Thornton, *Attorneys*, chap. xxx, pp. 1183–1278. For an excellent summary of the statutory provisions in different states, with illustrative decisions, see 52 Col. L. Rev. 1039–53 (1952).

a serious reflection on the dignity of the court and on the reputation of the profession

Moral Unfitness to Advise and Represent Clients

Many of the statutes and decisions dealing with the conviction of various crimes as ground for disbarment specify that such must be crimes involving "moral turpitude." [7] As applied to acts in a non-professional capacity, this phrase is sometimes difficult to apply. For example, was the manufacture of home brew during prohibition an act involving moral turpitude? [8] Or the fighting of a duel in another state? [9] Or participating in Florida in 1880 in a lynching? [10] Or refusing, as a bona fide conscientious objector, to further the war effort? [11]

The ultimate question in such cases on this phase of the problem is whether the lawyer has been shown to be "an unsafe person to manage the legal business of others." [12] Nor is it really important (except perhaps as the legislature's opinion of the seriousness of the offense) whether the crime of which he has been convicted is called a felony or a misdemeanor.[13]

[7] See John S. Bradway, "Moral Turpitude as the Criterion of Offenses that Justify Disbarment," 24 Cal. L. Rev. 9–27 (1935).

[8] See State v. Bieber, 121 Kan. 536 (1926); 48 A.L.R. 252 (1926). In this case, in a vigorous dissent, Judge Dawson said at page 544 that he could not bring himself "to the point of holding that by the isolated fact of having had a bottle of liquor on his kitchen shelf this man has been guilty of moral turpitude and should be deprived of his license to practice law."
Compare Rudolph v. United States, 6 F.2d 487, 488 (1925), especially Judge Robb's dissenting opinion, and Bartos v. United States District Court, 19 F.2d 722, 724 (1927); In re Minner, 133 Kan. 789 (1931).

[9] See Smith v. State, 1 Yerg. (Tenn.) 228 (1829).

[10] See Ex parte Wall, 107 U.S. 265 (1882); cf. State ex rel. McLaughlin v. Graves, 73 Ore. 331 (1914).

[11] See In re Pontarelli, 393 Ill. 310 (1946).

[12] Field, J. (dissenting), in Ex parte Wall, 107 U.S. 265, 307 (1882).
The basis for Justice Field's dissent in this case was his belief that, under the decisions, one could not be disbarred for a non-professional offense except on trial and conviction. See also In re Saddler, 35 Okla. 510, 519 (1913).

[13] See Rheb v. Bar Association of Baltimore, 186 Md. 200, 204 (1945); 52 Col. L. Rev. 1049–50 (1952).
"It is perfectly clear that the mere fact that the person has been convicted of a criminal offence does not make it imperative on the Court to strike him off the roll. There are criminal offences and criminal offences." Lopes, L.J., in In re Weare, 2 Q.B. Div. 439, 449 (1893).
The upright character necessary to entitle one to become or remain a lawyer "expresses itself, not in negatives nor in following the line of least resistance, but quite often in the will to do the unpleasant thing, if it is right, and the resolve not to do the pleasant thing, if it is wrong." Stacy, C. J., in In re Farmer, 191 N.C. 235, 238 (1926).

In cases of this class, the most obvious demonstration of a lawyer's lack of reliable character is in being proven guilty of flagrant disregard of the duties of honesty, fidelity, candor, and fairness, which, as a lawyer, he owes to clients. None would doubt that a lawyer found guilty of extortion or embezzlement from a client, or of blackmailing or deliberately deceiving him for the lawyer's advantage, should not be permitted to continue in the intimate fiduciary relation [14] with clients which the lawyer occupies. However, it has always been recognized that a dishonest business man or citizen cannot be trusted to be an honest lawyer.[15]

"It would indeed be a travesty if the court were powerless to restrain rogues from parading as its officers, simply because they were clever enough to divorce their professional lives from their private lives." [16]

"Professional honesty and honor are not to be expected as the accompaniment of dishonesty and dishonor in other relations. So it is that we, in common with other courts, hold, as did Lord Mansfield more than a century ago, that misconduct, indicative of moral unfitness for the profession, whether it be professional or nonprofessional, justifies dismissal as well as exclusion from the bar." [17]

Unworthiness to Continue in the Legal Profession

The second class of cases comprise those in which the lawyer, although apparently one who could be trusted to deal fairly with clients, has nevertheless done something so lacking in respect for the judicial office or for the good name of the community that his appearance in court would be a "scandal and contempt" to the court or an outrage to the profession, from which they should be protected.[18] Such was apparently the real basis of the decision in *Ex parte Wall*, which involved respondent's disbarment by the District Judge in Florida for taking an active part in a lynching. While Wall's reliability in serving clients was apparently not questioned,[19] it was obviously impossible

[14] See *infra*, p. 89. In Matter of Greenbaum, 161 App. Div. 558 (N.Y., 1914), respondent was disbarred for swearing to an answer which he knew to be false, in a suit against him personally.

[15] See cases *infra*, Appendix B.

[16] Matter of Fischer, 231 App. Div. 193, 202 (N.Y., 1930).

[17] State v. Peck, 88 Conn. 447, 450 (1914), and see also cases listed in n. 21, pp. 230–31 of Costigan's Case Book.

[18] See Ex parte Wall, 107 U.S. 265 (1882). See citation of Sacher case, p. 36, n. 18.

[19] That Wall's fellow citizens did not share the Supreme Court's view of the moral

for the Supreme Court to have condoned his flagrant flouting of the dignity of the District Court in staging the lynching in front of the court house during the judge's lunch hour.[20]

A similar conclusion would be called for in the case of a lawyer who assaulted a judge because of an adverse decision [21] or who repeatedly appeared in court in a state of obvious intoxication,[22] or otherwise showed clear and open disrespect for the judicial office.[23] Also, one who openly flouts the laws and encourages the overthrow of the government by force cannot be continued as a member of the bar.[24]

In certain other cases the lawyer's conduct has constituted such an outrage to his neighbors and the community that his continuance at the bar would be an obvious reflection on the whole legal profession. Such was the case of In re Hicks,[25] where a dwarf woman having the intellect of a child had become pregnant by reason of intimacy with a married lawyer with six children.[26] A questionable decision of this class is In re Welansky,[27] where respondent was the lawyer, owner,

---

iniquity of his offense was indicated by the fact that he was never disbarred by the Florida courts, but was elected and served for many years as a local judge.

According to the account of an eyewitness, the man lynched was a white man, a Scandinavian sailor, believed to be a deserter in the port of Tampa. The crime of which he was accused was breaking and entering a private residence while drunk, and insulting the female occupants, the man of the family being absent.

20 In the course of the opinion Justice Bradley said (107 U.S. at p. 274 [1882]):

"But besides the character of the act itself, as denoting a gross want of fealty to the law and repudiation of legal government, the particular circumstances of place and time invest it with additional aggravations. The United States court was in session; this enormity was perpetrated at its door; the victim was hanged on a tree, with audacious effrontery, in the virtual presence of the court! No respect for the dignity of the government as represented by its judicial department was even affected; the judge of the court, in passing in and out of the place of justice, was insulted by the sight of the dangling corpse. What sentiments ought such a spectacle to arouse in the breast of any upright judge, when informed that one of the officers of his own court was a leader in the perpetration of such an outrage?"

21 See Bradley v. Fisher, 13 Wall. 335 (1871).

22 See Wood v. State, 45 Ga. App. 783 (1937); In re Wells, 293 Ky. 201 (1943); In re Evans, 94 S.C. 414, 423 (1913); In re Macy, 109 Kan. 1 (1921); In re Osmond, 174 Okla. 561 (1935); In re Branch, 53 S.2d 317 (Fla., 1951).

23 Compare also In re Eaton, 60 N.D. 580 (1931), where respondent by libeling all connected with legal administration demonstrated an attitude wholly incompatible with that required of a member of the legal profession.

24 See Margolis's Case, 269 Pa. 206 (1921).   25 163 Okla. 29 (1933).

26 In this case the court said: "Men who are guilty of debased, wicked and immoral conduct do not have the same idea of righteous conduct that moral men possess."

Compare In re Information, etc., 351 Ill. 206 (1933), where the disciplined lawyers took public salaries without performing any service; citing Canons 12, 15, and 32.

27 319 Mass. 205 (1946).

and manager of the Cocoanut Grove night club in Boston which burned with the loss of 400 lives. After he was convicted of involuntary manslaughter he was disbarred. Although he was in the hospital at the time of the fire, he had been negligent in his instructions and provisions for safety. Apparently public opinion required his exit from the community.[28]

Burden of Proof

While the burden is on one seeking admission to the bar to show himself to be of a character "worthy of membership in an honorable profession," yet after he has been admitted and particularly where he has practiced for a considerable time without indication of any professional delinquencies, the burden is strongly in his favor and it should require clear and convincing proof to warrant his being deprived of his primary means of livelihood.[29]

"The duty of this Court," said Judge Clarke in a New York case,[30] "towards the members of the Bar, its officers, is not only to administer discipline to those found to be guilty of unprofessional conduct, but to protect the reputation of those attacked upon frivolous or malicious charges."

Disbarment, Suspension, or Censure

Ordinarily the occasion for disbarment should be the demonstration, by a continued course of conduct, of an attitude wholly inconsistent with the recognition of proper professional standards. Unless it is clear that the lawyer will never be one who should be at the bar, suspension is preferable.[31] For isolated acts, censure, private or public,

[28] See also Grievance Committee v. Broder, 112 Conn. 269 (1930), where respondent was disbarred for adultery under circumstances constituting an outrage to the community. Also In re McNeese, 346 Mo. 425 (1940) for selling opium. As to the Broder case, see, however, 79 U. of Pa. L. Rev. 506 (1931).

[29] See Re Morford, 80 A.2d 429 (Del., 1951); In re Power, 407 Ill. 525, 529 (1950).

[30] Matter of Stern, 137 App. Div. 909 (N.Y., 1910).

[31] Bradley v. Fisher, 80 U.S. (13 Wall.) 335, 355 (1871). "To deprive one of an office of this character would often be to decree poverty to himself and destitution to his family. A removal from the bar should therefore never be decreed where any punishment less severe—such as reprimand, temporary suspension, or fine—would accomplish the end desired."

See also In re Power, 407 Ill. 525 (1950); Re Diesen, 173 Minn. 297 (1927). No other charge had been brought against Diesen during his twenty years of practice. In re McDonald, 204 Minn. 62 (1938), respondent was disbarred for ambulance chasing after warning from the State Board, but with leave to apply for reinstatement after three years. Cf. Barton v. California, 209 Cal. 677 (1930); In re L. R., 7 N.J. 390 (1951).

is more appropriate.[32] Only where a single offense is of so grave a nature as to be impossible to a respectable lawyer, such as deliberate embezzlement, bribery of a juror or court official, or the like,[33] should suspension or disbarment be imposed.[34] Even here the lawyer should be given the benefit of every doubt, particularly where he has a professional record and reputation free from offenses like that charged.[35] Similarly, such extreme measures should be invoked only in case of fairly recent offenses,[36] proof in refutation of which would be reasonably available to respondent, except, of course, in cases where he was shown to have actively concealed them. Just as a lawyer who has been habitually dishonest will almost certainly revert to his low professional standards when necessity, temptation, and occasion recur, so one who has been consistently straight and upright can properly be trusted not to repeat an isolated offense unless of such a nature as of itself to demonstrate a basically depraved character.

Similarly, it not infrequently happens that certain practices, although admittedly improper and condemned by the Canons, are allowed to continue and grow without action by the bar and the courts until they become so serious as to give rise to an investigation and crusade to eliminate them. As a result, a large number of lawyers are found to have been guilty of the objectionable practices, some deliberately, others unwillingly, impelled by competition. Such a case

[32] See In re Gill, 104 Wash. 160 (1918); but see In re Bruener, 178 Wash. 165 (1934).

[33] See United States v. Costen, 38 Fed. 24 (1889), where respondent was disbarred for deliberately offering to sell privileged communications to the other side.

[34] The California Code of Ethics of 1928 provided that for the "wilful breach" of any of these rules "the offender shall be punishable by suspension from the practice of the law for a period not to exceed one year"; 204 Cal. XCI.

[35] In People v. McCallum, 341 Ill., 578, 584 (1930), Judge Heard said: "Where an attorney by his conduct has built up for himself a reputation for honesty and fair dealing, when his integrity as a lawyer is assailed such reputation is a circumstance strongly tending to prove his innocence."

In the cases of Dorsey and Carter, two lawyers disbarred by the Patent Commissioner from practicing before him for having deceived his office and the Circuit Court of Appeals twenty years before, the A.B.A. Committee refused to recommend their suspension or expulsion to the Board of Governors, each of them having offered a possible, though improbable explanation, and each having an unblemished professional record of more than fifty years. See Dorsey v. Kingsland, 173 F.2d. 405, 407–08 (1949); Kingsland v. Dorsey, 338 U.S. 318, 320 (1949).

See also Colorado Bar Association v. ———, Attorney, 88 Colo. 325 (1931); In re Diesen, 173 Minn. 297 (1928). Conversely, in Re Isserman, 9 N.J. 269 (1952), Chief Justice Vanderbilt stressed the fact that respondent had previously been suspended for two years for statutory rape. (6 N.J. Misc. 146 [1928].) As to young lawyers, see Smith v. California, 211 Cal. 249 (1930); In re Penn, 196 App. Div. 764 (N.Y., 1921); also Costigan's Case Book, pp. 200–11.

[36] But see In re Heinze, 233 Minn. 391 (1951).

was the ambulance-chasing crusade in Philadelphia in 1928, where the Philadelphia Committee of Censors, in connection with its investigation and report to the Bar Association, fixed a date in advance, advising the accident lawyers that any ambulance chasing beyond that date would be drastically dealt with, but recommending no discipline for the past offenses of which practically the entire accident bar was demonstrated to have been more or less guilty.[37]

While there has been a difference of opinion [38] as to the propriety of disciplining a lawyer for actions forbidden only by the Canons, the better opinion seems to be that this is justified.[39]

There has never apparently been any extensive attempt to remove lawyers from active practice merely because they are or have been obviously incompetent or careless in performing their professional duties.[40]

RIGHTS OF DISCIPLINED LAWYERS

Right to Resign

Whether a lawyer, charged with delinquency, should be permitted to resign either from a bar association or from the bar, is a debatable question, depending, it is believed, on whether his offense, or the circumstances under which it was committed, are such as demand publicity to prevent its repetition by others. In the American Bar Association the practice has been not to permit the resignation of members against whom charges are pending, but some exceptions have been made.[41]

[37] But see Smith v. California, 211 Cal. 249 (1930), dissent by Judge Langdon (Costigan, Case Book, p. 210; Arant, Case Book, p. 282).

[38] See, for example, State v. Rubin, 201 Wis. 30 (1930) (defendant fined $500 for manifest disrespect to the examining bar committee). Pound, J., dissenting in Matter of Schwarz, 231 N.Y. 642, 645 (1921) (Hiscock, C. J., and Cardozo, J., concurring) said: "Rules . . . which do not involve the distinction between natural right and wrong should not be too strictly applied against one whose sin has been against good taste rather than good morals." See also *supra*, pp. 43–46.

[39] There is an excellent review of the decisions in Opinion 1 of the Louisville Bar Association. See also *supra*, pp. 26 *et seq*.

[40] See Winch, "The Recall of Lawyers," 24 Green Bag 135, 136 (1912); but see Marsh v. State Bar. 210 Cal. 303 (1930); L.R.A. 1916A, 1175 n. (1916); 69 A.L.R. 705 n. (1930); L.R.A. 1915A, 663 n. (1915). See also Arant, Case Book, pp. 374–90 and 600–17; 52 Col. L. Rev. 1046–47, 1053 (1952). See, however, the following New York cases: Matter of Friedland, 238 App. Div. 215 (1933), In re Phillips, 248 App. Div. 768 (1936), In re Vandewater, 257 App. Div. 962 (1939), In re Scannell, 260 App. Div. 442 (1940), In re Virdone, 261 App. Div. 961 (1941), In re Halpern, 265 App. Div. 340 (1942), In re Holley, 271 App. Div. 225 (1946), In re Coman, 274 App. Div. 300 (1948).

[41] App. A, *8*.

Reinstatement of Lawyers Suspended or Disbarred

When a lawyer is disbarred it is because the court has concluded, after thoroughly investigating and considering the charges against him, as well as his explanation of them and his past record as a lawyer and a citizen, and after giving him the benefit of every doubt, that he is not one who should be a member of this honorable profession. If, after such investigation the court believes that his misconduct is perhaps not chronic, and that his lapse is but temporary and his point of view remediable, he should not be disbarred, but put on probation by suspension, either for a definite period, or preferably until further order of the court,[42] during which period his conduct can be under supervision. While it is, of course, always possible that a disbarred lawyer may be reinstated,[43] this, it is believed, should almost never occur except where the court concludes that the disbarment was erroneous.[44] For a lawyer who has been found guilty of an act warranting disbarment to be reinstated justly creates an impression on the public which is very bad for the reputation of the bar, the conclusion being that this is because of friendship, pity, or political influence;[45] which is not infrequently the case. In *Matter of Shepard*,[46] the court said: "When he has been once disbarred, a mistaken charity should not restore him to his position."

In *In re Kennedy*,[47] Judge Landis said:

I am, at all times, willing to receive and consider petitions emanating from such respectable sources [members of Bar]. I do not forget that, generally speaking, we should look in a Christian spirit and with leniency upon each other's shortcomings. 'For he that is without sin, let him first cast a stone.' The good wishes, therefore, of the petitioners are creditable to their hearts; but after all, they are based purely on sentiment, which has no place here. Such influences ought not to move us in the discharge of our solemn duty, the responsibility of action having been now, by these efforts, shifted upon us. The public and the bar, as well as Mr. Kennedy, deserves consideration at our hands, and it seems to me that these should be the first objects of our solicitude. Their welfare is far more important than that of any individual.

[42] See Breslin's App., 316 Pa. 392, 394 (1934). The State Bar of California does not permit a disbarred lawyer to apply for reinstatement for two years; Rules 43–45. See also Thornton, *Attorneys*, sec. 902, p. 1332.

[43] See In re Branch, 53 S.2d 317 (Fla., 1951); In re Harris, 88 N.J.L. 18 (1915).

[44] See Petition of Emmons, 330 Mich. 303 (1951). See Petition of Stalnaker, 150 Fla. 853 (1942).

[45] State v. Cannon, 199 Wis. 401 (1929); 206 Wis. 374 (1932).

[46] 35 Cal. App. 492, 501 (1917).   [47] 18 Lanc. L. Rev. 276 (1901).

The offenses committed by the petitioner were of no trifling nature. He was guilty of crimes against the Commonwealth, the penalty for which he barely escaped; he violated his oath of office, in that he did not act with due fidelity to his clients; and lastly he failed in his duty as an officer of the Court. The court can forgive the wrongs, but it does not follow that it should fully restore the offender to his prior rank. The office which he occupied, and to which he now desires to return, is too important to entrust to one who has thus proved faithless.

So long, however, as this court is as now constituted, and I speak for the whole court—where similar facts are disclosed, the rule will not be broken. Therefore, to do our share in maintaining what we believe to be the honor and integrity of the Lancaster Bar, and to aid as best we can in giving protection to this community against all such wrongdoers, we desire to say that those who, as attorneys, violate the sacred trusts conferred upon them, and for such cause are deprived of the rights and emoluments incident to our profession, will not be by us restored to their former station, but must seek in other fields the success which they by their own faults have here failed to earn.[48]

While the courts have repeatedly said that it should require much stronger proof of good character to restore a disbarred lawyer than that required on his admission,[49] nevertheless, lawyers are continually being reinstated, after disbarment, for conduct which any character committee would have unquestionably held to preclude their original admission.[50] Instances of this kind, often manifestly unjustified, are most injurious to the reputation of the bar in the eyes of the public. Courts before whom such applications come are referred with respectful insistence to Judge Landis' opinion above quoted.

On application for reinstatement of one found guilty of misappropriating the funds of clients, the mere fact that he has settled with his

[48] See also State v. Priest, 123 Neb. 241 (1932), where the court refused to reinstate one who had used his client's money, though he had made settlement, and nineteen lawyers signed his petition.

[49] See Kepler v. State Bar, 216 Cal. 52 (1932). "A court should be slow to disbar, but it should be even slower to reinstate"; Petition of Morrison, 45 S.D. 123 (1922).

[50] See also Stewart, C. J., in Matter of Palmer, 9 Ohio Circuit Court Rep. 55, 70, 71 (1894). Also 22 Ann. Cas. 813 n. (1912); Costigan, Case Book, pp. 239–40, nn. 26 and 27.

In the leading case of State v. Cannon, 199 Wis. 401 (1929); see also 206 Wis. 374 (1932); 196 Wis. 534 (1928); 17 A.B.A. Jour. 561 (1931); 80 U. of Pa. L. Rev. 1021 (1932); 8 Wis. L. Rev. 74 (1932); 16 Minn. L. Rev. 857 (1932), the court (Stevens, J.) said:

"The achievements of those who win a place for themselves by their own unaided efforts always deserve commendation. But the right of a lawyer to maintain his place at the Bar must be determined by his conduct as a minister of justice, not by his early struggles for an education. The public has a right to be protected from the unfit practitioner, without regard to whether he was required to struggle against adversity, or was reared in the lap of luxury."

See also In re Crum, 55 N.D. 876 (1927).

victims [1] or that he [2] or his friends [3] have made restitution should be of little weight. Nor should the customary petition, signed by numerous fellow members of the bar to the effect that in their opinion he "has been sufficiently punished." [4]

"The proof must be sufficient to overcome the court's former adverse judgment of the appellant's character." [5]

Similarly, the mere fact that the offense causing the disbarment has been pardoned, should not of itself be ground for reinstatement. [6]

"Where a member of the bar is charged with delinquencies, as in this case, there is but one course open to him—to come forward frankly and make such truthful explanations as he may, and with equal frankness admit his mistakes. It does not profit him before this court to rely upon technical defenses or employ sophistry in argument in an attempt to establish a superficial justification." [7]

Rights of Lawyers Suspended or Disbarred

This question is not answered merely by a statement, such as that in Section 272a of the New York Penal Law, that a disbarred lawyer may not do what one not admitted to the bar may not do. The New York County Lawyers Association Committee has held [8] that since the writing of briefs and doing legal research for attorneys constitute the practice of law, a disbarred lawyer may not do this from his own office for compensation. However, law students may properly write briefs and look up law and by the entrance requirements of many states, in order to qualify for admission they are required to serve a probationary period devoted to such activities. [9]

The Court decisions cited by the New York County Committee in

---

[1] State v. Priest, 123 Neb. 241 (1932).

[2] Petition of Morrison, 45 S.D. 123 (1922); In re Harris, 88 N.J.L. 18 (1915); Breslin's Appeal, 316 Pa. 392 (1934).

[3] Allen's case, 75 N.H. 301 (1909).

[4] See In re Enright, 69 Vt. 317 (1897). In re Pemberton, 63 P. 1043 (1901).

[5] Young, C. J., in In re Simpson, 11 N.D. 526, 528 (1903).

[6] In re Wolfe's Disbarment, 288 Pa. 331, 50 A.L.R. 380 (1927). In re Lavine, 2 Cal.2d 324, 327 (1935). See also 16 L.R.A. (N.S.) 272 n. (1908); 50 A.L.R. 384 n. (1927); 31 Col. L. Rev. 881 (1931); 3 Miss. L. Jour. 341 (1931).

[7] Per curiam, in In re Feinstein, 233 App. Div. 541 (1931). See also In re Blakesberg, 236 App. Div. 227 (N.Y., 1932).

[8] N.Y. County 400 (1951).

[9] As to what a law clerk may properly do see A.B.A. Op. 85 and Op. 97 at p. 210; N.Y. City 88, 113, 180, 320; N.Y. County 38; see also Frederick C. Hicks and Elliott R. Katz in 41 Yale L. Jour. 69, 90 (1931).

support of its ruling [10] were both cases in which the disbarred lawyer was in reality continuing to practice law under the pretense of doing non-legal work for another lawyer.

A better reason why a disbarred lawyer may not properly be employed by another lawyer, not merely to do work of a legal nature but work of any kind, was given by the same Committee in 1929, when it said:

If, as a matter of law, the disbarred attorney is forbidden to render the services described in the question, then it is clearly improper for the practicing attorney to employ him for their performance. And, as a matter of professional propriety, the employment by an attorney in good standing, of a disbarred attorney to perform any duties that lie in a doubtful zone between practising law and not practising law (including the duties specified in the question), should, in the opinion of the Committee, be disapproved because such employment tempts and conduces to the violation of the plain intendment of any decree or order of disbarment. It cannot be doubted that disbarment is always and everywhere intended to deprive the disbarred attorney of the right to practice law, and even if the disbarred attorney be employed to render such services as may not constitute "the practice of the law," yet there is in every such case the danger and likelihood that he will, under cover or cloak of such employment, perform such other services, either for his employer or for his own account, as under any construction of the law do constitute such practice.[11]

This decision was relied on by the Committee of The Association of the Bar of the City of New York in its Opinion 877 (October 8, 1943) holding that a firm of attorneys might not properly employ, either as a clerk or as an investigator, a former member of the bar who resigned after charges were brought against him, saying:

A lawyer who resigns from the bar when charges are brought against him will be looked upon with suspicion and distrust. If he prefers rather to resign than to clear his name and establish the falsity of the charges, he should be prepared thereafter to be divorced entirely from the profession.

The practice of the law requires that the highest degree of confidence and trust should exist between clients and their attorneys and between attorneys and the courts. The profession needs and is entitled to have the confidence

---

10 Matter of Treadwell, 175 App. Div. 833, 842 (1916). Matter of Sutherland, 252 App. Div. 620 (1937).

The fact that a successful litigant was represented by an unlicensed lawyer has been held ground for reversal: Bennie v. Triangle Ranch Co., 73 Colo. 586 (1923); Kaplan v. Berman, 37 Misc. 502 (N.Y., 1902). The soundness of this conclusion is believed questionable.

11 N.Y. County 186. See also App. A, 7.

of the public. The suspicion that an employee of an attorney is not trust-worthy diminishes the usefulness of that attorney and of other members of the bar. This is also true no matter what the duties of the employee are.[12]

It would seem possible that a somewhat less drastic view might be taken, under certain circumstances, of the propriety of the employ-ment, by a firm in good standing, of a lawyer who had been suspended and not permanently disbarred, the employer seeing to it that he had no contact with clients nor with court attaches or proceedings. While the suspicion that a suspended employee is not trustworthy might, of course, be related to his employer, the latter's reputation might well be sufficiently unassailable as to lead him to risk this in order to en-able him to watch over the suspended lawyer during his probationary period, which would be a distinct service to the court and to the bar.

The nature of the offense committed by the suspended or disbarred lawyer would also seem to be important. For example, where one was disbarred for grossly abusing the process of the law, for repeatedly defrauding his clients, or for embezzling trust funds, he should ob-viously not be thereafter permitted to have anything whatever to do with the practice of the law. It might be, however, that one could be suspended for an offense which would not incapacitate him from do-ing research and helping to prepare briefs in a large law office, he hav-ing no contact with clients or courts; for example, because convicted of manslaughter by reckless driving when intoxicated, or of making statements disrespectful to the court.

The Michigan Committee, in a well-considered Opinion,[13] has held that one suspended for two years "for conduct which some of the Commissioners felt merited permanent disbarment" might not dur-ing the period of his suspension complete collections in his file with-out court action, since this would leave the impression with the public and bar that he was engaging in the practice of law; nor could he

---

[12] The N.Y. City Committee also held in Opinion 923 (June 28, 1944) that a practicing firm might not properly employ, to do work of a Federal nature only, one who had resigned under charges from the New York bar although he had not resigned from the Federal courts.

The A.B.A. Committee in a hitherto unpublished (see Appendix A) ruling, 7 (1938), advised against the employment of a disbarred lawyer even to do only office work, seeing no clients, "because of the practical difficulty of confining his activities to an area which does not include practice of law, and because such employment would show dis-respect to the courts."

See also N.Y. City 571 that he might not be employed by a lawyer to do non-legal work, or N.Y. City 658, to write briefs.

[13] No. 44, October, 1939.

properly accept collections sent to him by reason of his being listed in a law list, it being his duty to notify all such lists to discontinue his listing as an attorney.

It has been held that a disbarred lawyer might properly file suit for fees earned by him while in good standing,[14] and that there was no objection to his being employed as a collector for a local concern,[15] or as a process server,[16] he being careful not to give the impression that he was acting as a lawyer; or to his accepting the nomination of Justice of the Peace, or to his acting as a real estate or life insurance agent.[17] "If," said the Michigan Committee, "he desired to regain his professional standing, he should so conduct himself at all times so there can be no criticism of his actions." [18]

The New York City Committee has also held that a lawyer properly substituted for one suspended may pay to him his disbursements [19] and also his fees earned prior to his suspension.[20]

A lawyer of whom a disbarred lawyer was a colleague prior to his disbarment, may not leave the name of the disbarred lawyer on his door, though he takes over his practice.[21]

The New York City Committee also approved the procedure by which a suspended attorney, with the full knowledge and consent of his clients, had his wife, an attorney in good standing, substituted for him to represent them, although she continued to use the same office where he and she had practiced together, he receiving no compensation for procuring or consenting to the substitution.[22]

A lawyer may represent a disbarred lawyer to recover for services prior to his disbarment and apparently not connected with his disbarment.[23] Where, however, one is represented by a disbarred lawyer, he should be advised by the lawyer on the other side to get another lawyer, and if he will not do so, his opponent's lawyer should be very careful in advising him.[24]

One to whom a disbarred lawyer turns over his cases should get authority direct from the clients, advising them of the facts, and making sure that they asked the disbarred attorney to suggest counsel.[25]

14 N.Y. City 151.
15 Mich. 44; see also N.Y. City 165. Query as to the soundness of this ruling.
16 N.Y. City 150, 165.   17 Mich. 44.
18 Ibid.   19 N.Y. City 163.
20 N.Y. City 164, 703, 753, B-83; see also App. A, 140.
21 N.Y. City 940.   22 N.Y. City 161; see also N.Y. City 162.
23 N.Y. City 753, 800; and see N.Y. County 277.
24 N.Y. City 698.   25 N.Y. City 800.

Where, however, one who was never admitted is convicted of illegally practicing, the lawyer to whom he turned over his cases may not ask the clients to pay him for what he has done, but should ask the clients to come for their papers.[26]

A lawyer who has been suspended for ten years may not, prior to the expiration of the ten years, insert a paid advertisement in papers announcing his resumption of practice.[27]

[26] N.Y. City 836.   [27] Va. 29.

Part Two

THE DUTIES AND
OBLIGATIONS
OF LAWYERS

IV

THE LAWYER'S OBLIGATIONS
TO THE PUBLIC
BY REASON OF
THE SPECIAL PRIVILEGES
ACCORDED HIM

BY HIS ADMISSION TO THE BAR, the lawyer is granted the exclusive right: (1) to hold himself out as a lawyer; (2) as such to advise clients and to represent them as an advocate; (3) to appear for them in court proceedings.

In recognition of these exclusive privileges the lawyer is charged with certain obligations to the public: (1) to see to it that those admitted to the bar are properly qualified by character, ability, and training, and that those who thereafter prove unworthy of these privileges are deprived of them; (2) to see to it that able and upright judges are chosen and that any who prove manifestly unworthy or unfit are removed; (3) to represent without charge those unable to pay; (4) not to stir up litigation; (5) not to aid in the unauthorized practice of law.

DUTY TO POLICE THE BAR

One of the principal features resulting in just public criticism of the bar is the unwillingness of lawyers to expose the abuses of which they know that certain of their brethren are guilty, as well as the reluctance of judges to disbar, suspend, or even publicly reprimand such lawyers. Much of the public suspicion of lawyers is due to the realization that most of the abuses of which lawyers are guilty could be eliminated if the bar and the courts were constantly alert and willing to do their full duty in this regard.[1]

The first sentence of Canon 29 provides:

Lawyers should expose without fear or favor before the proper tribunals corrupt or dishonest conduct in the profession,[2] and should accept without hesitation employment against a member of the Bar who has wronged his client.[3]

The third sentence provides:

The lawyer should aid in guarding the Bar against the admission to the profession of candidates unfit or unqualified because deficient in either moral character or education.

One may question whether the latter provision of the Canon is phrased as positively as it should be. It is not only the lawyer's duty to see to it that none but fit candidates are admitted,[4] but also that no lawyer is permitted to continue to practice who has proved himself untrustworthy to advise or represent clients or an unworthy member of an honorable profession.[5]

DUTY TO FURTHER THE CHOICE OF ABLE AND UPRIGHT JUDGES AND SEE TO THE REMOVAL OF THOSE MANIFESTLY UNWORTHY

Canon 2 provides:

It is the duty of the Bar to endeavor to prevent political considerations from outweighing judicial fitness in the selections of Judges. It should protest earnestly and actively against the appointment or election of those who are unsuitable for the Bench; and it should strive to have elevated thereto only those willing to forego other employments, whether of a business, political or other character, which may embarrass their free and fair consideration of questions before them for decision. The aspiration of lawyers for judicial position should be governed by an impartial estimate of their ability to add honor to the office and not by a desire for the distinction the position may bring to themselves.

In its Opinion 189 the American Bar Association Committee said:

---

[1] As to the duty of bar associations to investigate known abuses without formal complaint, see A.B.A. Ops. 2, 3, and 147; also N.Y. City 721. Most grievance committees have no power to institute such investigations of their own motion. See *supra,* pp. 30–32.

[2] It is the duty of an employee of a dishonest lawyer to leave him and report to the bar association, N.Y. County 78. His duty to the profession is higher than that to his employer.

[3] See A.B.A. Op. 144; N.Y. City 47, 91, 721, 811.

[4] As to the duty to advise the character committees regarding an applicant see N.Y. City 94.

[5] See *supra,* pp. 42–46.

Lawyers are better able than laymen to appraise accurately the qualifications of candidates for judicial office. It is proper that they should make that appraisal known to the voters in a proper and dignified manner. A lawyer may with propriety endorse a candidate for judicial office and seek like endorsement from other lawyers. But the lawyer who endorses a judicial candidate or seeks that endorsement from other lawyers should be actuated by a sincere belief in the superior qualifications of the candidate for judicial service and not by personal or selfish motives; and a lawyer should not use or attempt to use the power or prestige of the judicial office to secure such endorsement. On the other hand, the lawyer whose endorsement is sought, if he believes the candidate lacks the essential qualifications for the office or believes the opposing candidate is better qualified, should have the courage and moral stamina to refuse the request for endorsement.[6]

While lawyers may voluntarily contribute to the campaign fund of judges whose election they deem in the public interest, such contributions should in every case be reasonable and preferably be made to a campaign committee.[7]

The last two sentences of Canon 1 provide:

Whenever there is proper ground for serious complaint of a judicial officer, it is the right and duty of the lawyer to submit his grievances to the proper authorities. In such cases, but not otherwise, such charges should be encouraged and the person making them should be protected.

While the Canon does not specifically refer to the duty of the bar to see to the removal of a corrupt judge, there is no doubt as to the existence of this duty, in order to maintain the confidence of the public in the administration of justice.

In the report of the Committee of Professional Ethics of the New York State Bar Association of January 23, 1948, Chairman Wherry said: "It is as much the duty of the bar to assist in the removal of unfit members of the judicial tribunal, as to assist in securing good judicial appointments."[8]

The difficulty in inducing a member of the bar to attack a corrupt judge lies in his natural fear of reprisals in case, through influence, political or otherwise, the lawyer's efforts prove unsuccessful. As Emerson said to Justice Holmes when the Justice was a student: "If you shoot at a king, you must kill him."

---

[6] It is a lawyer's clear duty to oppose the candidacy of one whom he knows would be an unfit judge, App. A, 9.

[7] A.B.A. Op. 226; see N.Y. County 304; and Judicial Canons 30 and 32.

[8] On p. 8.

No attack or imputation of dishonesty should, of course, ever be made against a judge by a lawyer unless the judge's conduct is continued and flagrant and this is capable of demonstration by unassailable evidence. Where, however, such is the case, no fear or favor should deter the bar from proceeding.

When through age or otherwise, an able and upright judge becomes incompetent, it would seem to be the function of his colleagues on the bench, rather than the bar, to arrange that his disability does not lower the efficiency of the court.[9]

As to the relations of lawyers with judges, see Chapter V.

DUTY TO REPRESENT THE INDIGENT

From the earliest times [10] it has been the practice, when persons accused of crime are indigent, for the court to appoint counsel to defend them. Lawyers have always regarded the acceptance and performance of such service as one of the obligations incident to their professional status and privileges.[11]

Canon 4 provides: "A lawyer assigned as counsel for an indigent prisoner ought not to ask to be excused for any trivial reason, and should always exert his best efforts in his behalf."

In many jurisdictions a statutory fee is paid by the county to the lawyer so assigned. The Chicago Committee has held that a lawyer appointed by the court may, with the court's approval, accept a fee (not suggested by him) from the relatives of his client; [12] or a voluntary gift; but he may not demand a fee, directly or indirectly.[13]

Where one appointed by the court to defend a supposed indigent prisoner finds, on consulting him, that he is not in fact indigent, the lawyer may not make a private employment contract for legal services with him in lieu of the fee to be paid by the county, but must require his client to advise the court of the true facts and abide the court's redetermination as to his indigency before he can make any

9 Justice Holmes exacted from his colleagues a promise to tell him when the time came; and they did.

10 Cohen, *History of the English Bar,* p. 119. In England a serjeant was bound to accept and, "if we were to assign one of them as counsel, and he were to refuse to act we should make bold to commit him to prison." Sharswood, *Professional Ethics,* p. 92 n., quoting Chief Justice Hale.

11 See Vise v. Hamilton County, 19 Ill. 78 (1857).

12 Op. 33, p. 74; and see N.Y. County 338; Mich. 127.   13 N.Y. City 587.

agreement. Any retainer paid by the prisoner or his relatives should be returned and they be free to employ other counsel.[14]

A duty similar to that of defending indigent criminals is recognized in civil cases to worthy persons unable to pay full compensation. An enormous amount of legal advice and service is continually being given by lawyers in this way. While not perhaps as extensive as that of doctors, much of that done by the latter, especially in hospitals, is necessary to maintain their privilege to use the facilities of the hospitals for private patients, as well as to improve their technique and to keep up with medical and surgical developments. Almost all of the charitable work done by lawyers involves practically no such indirect remuneration to them.

A lawyer may properly charge a well-to-do client for services in getting his son exempted from the draft, despite regulations requiring lawyers to serve free,[15] but must advise that they can get such advice free.[16] He may make a charge to a member of the armed forces, although it is usual and proper to perform such service for nothing.[17]

He may not refuse to take a murder appeal because the client cannot pay,[18] or put off the entry of a divorce decree so long as to endanger it, because his client cannot pay his agreed fee.[19]

A lawyer may properly accept a weekly salary from a charitable organization to procure the necessary papers for indigent immigrants.[20]

As to Legal Aid Bureaus, see Chapter VIII.

DUTY NOT TO STIR UP LITIGATION [21]

At common law stirring up litigation constituted the crime (punishable by fine and imprisonment) known as maintenance, which is aggravated in case the perpetrator is a lawyer, who, by reason of his special professional privileges, is precluded from instigating, promoting, or prolonging litigation for his own benefit.

Canon 28 provides:

[14] Mich. 127.
[15] N.Y. County 149.
[16] N.Y. County 371. See also *infra*, p. 103, n. 18.
[17] App. A, *335*.
[18] N.Y. City 436.
[19] N.Y. City 494, N.Y. County 158.
[20] N.Y. City 593.

[21] This subject is of course closely related to that of advertising, and solicitation which is discussed fully *infra*, pp. 265–73. As to champerty, barratry, and maintenance, see Thornton, *Attorneys*, chap. xviii, pp. 652–87.

It is unprofessional for a lawyer to volunteer advice to bring a lawsuit, except in rare cases where ties of blood,[22] relationship or trust make it his duty to do so. Stirring up strife and litigation is not only unprofessional, but it is indictable at common law.[23]

The practice of "ambulance chasing" is so well known and so obviously improper as to require no extensive comment. It is most prevalent in large communities, and comprehensive investigations and drives to stamp it out have been held, with more or less success, usually but temporary, in many such jurisdictions.[24] It could be materially reduced by the adoption of statutes providing automatic compensation for certain classes of injuries, notably those by automobiles, on the theory that the activity giving rise to the injuries should pay for such injuries by assessment against the persons directly benefiting by the activity. The sanction of such a statute as to automobile injuries by the bar associations and its adoption by the legislatures has been continually opposed by the negligence lawyers.

A lawyer may not properly represent a runner in his suit for contingent compensation.[25]

A lawyer may not make it a practice to investigate unsatisfied judgments recovered by persons with whom he has had no previous professional or personal relations for the purpose of being employed in their collection.[26]

---

[22] For a case within the exception see N.Y. County 126.

[23] The balance of Canon 28 is as follows: "It is disreputable to hunt up defects in titles or other causes of action and inform thereof in order to be employed to bring suit or collect judgment, or to breed litigation by seeking out those with claims for personal injuries or those having any other grounds of action in order to secure them as clients, or to employ agents or runners for like purposes, or to pay or reward, directly or indirectly, those who bring or influence the bringing of such cases to his office, or to remunerate policemen, court or prison officials, physicians, hospital *attachés* or others who may succeed, under the guise of giving disinterested friendly advice, in influencing the criminal, the sick and the injured, the ignorant or others, to seek his professional services. A duty to the public and to the profession devolves upon every member of the Bar, having knowledge of such practices upon the part of any practitioner, immediately to inform thereof to the end that the offender may be disbarred."

[24] For example, in New York see In re Rothbard, 225 App. Div. 266 (1929); In re Vail, 228 App. Div. 217 (1930); In re Axtell, 229 App. Div. 323 (1930); In re Association of Bar of New York, 222 App. Div. 580–91 (1928); 52 N.Y. State Bar Assn. Reports 323 (1929); 14 A.B.A. Jour. 561, 563–64 (1928). See also 26 Ill. L. Rev. 457 (1931); 6 Cal. State Bar Jour. No. 2, p. 37, No. 3, p. 54, No. 4, p. 97, No. 6, p. 153 (1931). In Philadelphia, 1928; report of the Committee reprinted as a supplement to 14 Mass. Law Quart. No. 1 (Nov., 1928). See Ky. 1; see Hicks, Case Book, pp. 305–09. In New Jersey, In re Bar Association, 109 N.J.L. 275 (1932). Costigan, Case Book, p. 169 n. 94. In Minnesota, Weinard v. Chicago, etc. Ry., 298 Fed. 977 (1924); see also Ingersoll v. Coal Co., 117 Tenn. 263 (1906). Contracts for legal compensation obtained by the solicitation of paid agents have been held unenforceable in a number of cases. See *supra*, pp. 28 *et seq.*

[25] N.Y. City 222.   [26] N.Y. County 69, 91, 227, 291; see also 252.

He may, however, buy up claims to a refund by a bank, which will not involve litigation, using letterheads which do not mention that he is a lawyer.[27]

A lawyer may not properly initiate a meeting of the members of an automobile club, the object of which is to induce them to organize and contest legislation under his guidance; [28] nor may he volunteer information to an International Claims Commission in order to obtain the representation of such claims; [29] nor bring a strike suit.[30]

He may not purchase notes to collect at a profit; [31] or employ a runner under the guise of a bail producer; [32] or search for unknown heirs,[33] and solicit their employment of him,[34] particularly of a testator who is still alive; [35] or furnish credit reports [36] in order to obtain professional employment; or agree with a purchaser of future interests to a share of them in consideration of his services; [37] or personally or through stock ownership in a corporation buy up tax liens to enforce them.[38]

As to contingent fees, somewhat inconsistent with the principle here involved, see page 176.

The New York City Committee has stated that in its opinion a lawyer may not properly seek, in the interest of his client, to induce another lawyer to bring a suit which the latter or his client is not inclined to bring.[39] He may not, in order to obtain evidence of the commission of crime, induce the violation of law so that he may testify thereto.[40]

He may not advise a stranger [41] or the latter's lawyer of a refund which may be obtained; [42] nor, without request, investigate a husband's prior marriage with a view to getting him a new divorce.[43]

Where, in pursuing his client's interest, he discovers persons possibly responsible for a judgment debtor's debts, he may, if his client's interest requires it, look up other judgment debtors and communi-

---

[27] Mich. 91.

[28] A.B.A. Op. 8; cf. N.Y. City 134.

[29] A.B.A. Op. 9; see also A.B.A. Op. 51, Mich. 53, and N.Y. City 757, 933.

[30] N.Y. City 490.   [31] A.B.A. Op. 51; cf. N.Y. City 427, N.Y. County 324.

[32] A.B.A. Op. 147.   [33] A.B.A. Op. 173 (also App. A, 78).

[34] App. A, 78.   [35] Mich. 53.

[36] A.B.A. Op. 188; see also Mich. 51.

[37] A.B.A. Op. 176; see also Chicago 24; Ohio 2; and N.Y. City 463, 802. He may, however, represent one who has acquired condemnation awards; N.Y. City 463, 506.

[38] N.Y. County 324, see also N.Y. City 427.   [39] N.Y. City 146.

[40] N.Y. City 23.   [41] N.Y. City 640.

[42] N.Y. City 138.   [43] N.Y. County 224.

cate with their attorneys to secure their cooperation, but not employment by their clients.[44]

Although he may not acquire an interest in a corporate client which buys choses in action at a discount in order to collect them, he may represent such corporation.[45]

He may make an investment which must be protected, if necessary by litigation, where suit is an incident, but not where it is the principal idea of the purchase.[46]

A lawyer may report tax evaders provided he does not seek or accept employment to collect the tax,[47] and may litigate without compensation and with expenses reimbursed only out of the proceeds, if any, of the litigation.[48]

He may, in the interest of a client, take up a similar case to the Supreme Court, without charge to the parties who proposed not to do so,[49] and may get others to press their claims when this is obviously in the interest of his client.[50]

An agreement with the client that no part of the retainer shall be refunded in case of a reconciliation is against public policy and reprehensible.[51]

Duty Not to Aid in the Unauthorized Practice of Law

American Bar Association Canon 47, adopted in 1937, provides: "No lawyer shall permit his professional services, or his name, to be used in aid of, or to make possible, the unauthorized practice of law by any lay agency, personal or corporate."

What constitutes the "unauthorized practice of law" is a question determinable by the statutes and court decisions in the various jurisdictions and not by the ethics committees of the bar associations.[52] Where a bar association has a special committee on unauthorized prac-

---

[44] N.Y. County 228.   [45] N.Y. City 757; N.Y. County 361.
[46] Mich. 65.   [47] A.B.A. Op. 87.
[48] N.Y. City 903; and cf. infra, pp. 178 n. 27, 251.   [49] N.Y. City B-46.
[50] N.Y. County 210.   [51] Chicago, 28, p. 61.
[52] A.B.A. Ops. 198, 273; see Frederick C. Hicks and Elliott R. Katz, 41 Yale L. Jour. 69–100 (1931). Also A.B.A. Ops. 31, 35, 57, 80, 257. For definitions of what constitutes the practice of law, see Meisel v. Board of Trade, 90 Misc. Rep. 19, 21 (1915); In re Duncan, 83 S.C. 186, 189 (1909); 52 A.B.A. Reports 382 (1927). A local lawyer may, if he deems himself competent, advise on the law of another jurisdiction, A.B.A. Op. 263.

For a list of certain cases on unauthorized practice, see A.B.A. Op. 8; see also A.B.A. Op. 122. In Stark v. P. G. Garage, Inc., 7 N.J. 118 (1951), a contract by a layman to procure tax reductions on real estate, requiring a hearing before a board, was held to constitute the practice of law and to be unenforceable, it being no defense that the layman employed a lawyer to appear for him. See also Mo. 74.

tice, the ethics committee is bound by its decisions as to what constitutes unauthorized practice, even though the ethics committee may not agree.[53]

The Unauthorized Practice Committee of the American Bar Association has held that a lawyer may not accept a retainer from a corporation or association to advise or represent its stockholders, customers, or members in connection with their personal affairs, even though such service by the lawyer is to the manifest interest of the corporation or association and though in every case he has personal contact with the person advised.[54]

A lawyer may not furnish a real estate broker with abstracts and opinions for him to sell to customers; [55] nor may he cooperate with a trust company to enable it to advise its patrons in legal matters; [56] nor may he permit a lay forwarder to fix fees or to arrange conferences and contacts with clients; [57] nor may he write legal bulletins for a lay agency to enable it to get business.[58]

He may supply office space to English solicitors to enable them to meet clients and give advice on English law.[59]

A lawyer on a full-time salary may turn over to his employer fees allowed him by statute in matters in which he acted for such employer.[60]

He may not employ a patent agent, not a member of the bar, to take depositions in a patent case,[61] nor be paid an annual retainer by a patent agent to advise the latter's clients.[62]

The mere fact that a layman may perform certain services does not render them non-professional when performed by a lawyer. A.B.A. Ops. 57, 80, 257.

What is done by a law firm in the course of its law practice must be treated as a professional service. N.Y. County 420.

[53] App. A, 5.

[54] See *infra,* p. 161. There would seem to be doubt as to the soundness of this conclusion. Such service by doctors is extensively furnished without question and is furnished with increasing frequency by labor unions and other organizations. It would seem to be one of the efficient developments of modern life which it is both unwise and futile to oppose. The public, it is believed, regard such opposition as in the interest of the lawyers and not, as claimed, in the public interest. "The duty of this court is not to protect the bar from competition, but to protect the public from being advised or represented in legal matters by incompetent and unreliable persons." Hyde, J., Hulse v. Criger, 247 S.W.2d 855, 857 (1952). See also Noone in 22 A.B.A. Jour. 609, 612 (1936).

[55] Mich. 110.

[56] A.B.A. Op. 122; App. A, *290;* see also A.B.A. Ops. 31 and 41; and see N.Y. City 388.

[57] Mich. 56.

[58] Chicago 31, p. 69; see also A.B.A. Op. 273; see further as to this topic, *infra,* p. 247.

[59] N.Y. City B-61; see also N.Y. City 622.

[60] App. A, *246;* see also *infra,* pp. 97, 179, 181.

[61] N.Y. County 334.   [62] N.Y. County 336.

Provided the statute permits the organization of a corporation to help wage earners pay off their debts, a lawyer may organize and help operate it.[63]

He may direct a New Jersey lawyer as to the handling of a New Jersey estate, he representing New York heirs, and advise his clients as to their rights.[64]

[63] N.Y. City 289.   [64] N.Y. City 369; but cf. A.B.A. Op. 248, and Mo. 56.

V

THE LAWYER'S OBLIGATION
TO THE COURTS

Duty to Observe a Respectful Attitude

THE FIRST TWO sentences of Canon 1 are as follows:

It is the duty of the lawyer to maintain towards the Courts a respectful attitude, not for the sake of the temporary incumbent of the judicial office, but for the maintenance of its supreme importance. Judges, not being wholly free to defend themselves, are peculiarly entitled to receive the support of the Bar against unjust criticism and clamor.

Although it is both the right and duty of a lawyer to protest vigorously rulings on evidence or procedure or statements in the judge's charge which he deems erroneous, nevertheless, when the ruling has been finally made, the lawyer must, for the time being, accept it and invoke his remedy by appeal to the higher court. He has no right to argue to the jury that the judge's charge or rulings do not represent the law, and for him to do so constitutes both a breach of his professional obligation and a contempt of court.[1]

"The counsel in any case may or may not be an abler or more learned lawyer than the judge, and it may tax his patience and his temper to submit to rulings which he regards as incorrect, but discipline and self-restraint are as necessary to the orderly administration of justice as they are to the effectiveness of an army. The decisions of the judge must be obeyed, because he is the tribunal appointed to decide, and the bar should at all times be the foremost in rendering respectful submission." [2]

---

[1] See In re Schofield, 362 Pa. 201 (1949); also United States v. Sacher, 9 F.R.D. 394, 182 F.2d 416 (1950), 343 U.S. 1 (1952).

See also B.&O.R.R. Co. v. Boyd, 67 Md. 32, 43 (1887).

[2] Mitchell, J., in Matter of Scouten's Appeal, 186 Pa. 270, 279 (1898).

As to a charge of prejudice in a petition to remove, see Re Sherwood, 259 Pa. 254 (1918); note in L.R.A. 1918 D 450.

It is not proposed here to attempt to cite or summarize the numerous cases in which lawyers have been charged with contempt of court
based on statements or actions by them, showing disrespect for the
judicial office.[3] Such become the basis for disbarment or suspension
only when so flagrant and persistent as to indicate the lawyer's unfitness to continue as a member of the profession, in which it is funda-
mentally essential that members maintain with the courts a relation
of mutual respect and regard.

Canon 20 provides:

Newspaper publications by a lawyer as to pending or anticipated litigation
may interfere with a fair trial in the Courts and otherwise prejudice the
due administration of justice. Generally they are to be condemned. If the
extreme circumstances of a particular case justify a statement to the public,
it is unprofessional to make it anonymously. An *ex parte* reference to the
facts should not go beyond quotation from the records and papers on file
in the court; but even in extreme cases it is better to avoid any *ex parte*
statement.

The American Bar Association Committee has held that this Canon
does not preclude the issuance of statements by public officials; but an
Attorney General's statements relating to prospective or pending
criminal or civil proceedings should avoid any statement of fact likely
to create an adverse public attitude respecting the alleged actions of
the defendants in such proceedings.[4]

Where a lawyer is also editor of a newspaper, he has the right that
every editor has to criticize the decisions and motives of the court
and though he does so in language constituting a libel he may not be
held guilty of contempt, nor may he be disciplined professionally if
what he wrote did not demonstrate his unfitness to be a lawyer.[5]

While it is the duty of the bar to support the judges against unjust
criticism and public clamor, it is also their duty fearlessly to take ex-

---

"An exception may be noted to the opinion of the Bench as easily in an agreeable
and polite as in a contemptuous and insulting manner." Sharswood, *Professional Ethics*,
p. 63.

[3] As to the distinction between contempt proceedings based on disrespect to the court
and proceedings to disbar, suspend, or censure him therefor, see *supra*, pp. 38 *et seq.*

[4] A.B.A. Op. 199.

Canon 20 applies, not only to discussion in newspapers, but to any discussion in a
magazine, including legal magazines or other publications, intended or calculated to
influence the decision in a pending case in which the writer is counsel, and would also
include, by implication, similar radio and television broadcasts. App. A, 256.

[5] Ex parte Steinman and Hensel, 95 Pa. 220 (1880). For a full discussion of Canon 20,
see *Survey of the Legal Profession*, volume on *Professional and Judicial Standards and
Public Opinion* (Phillips and McCoy), pp. 154–87.

ception to judicial corruption and incompetence. In the case last cited, Chief Justice Sharswood said:

No class of the community ought to be allowed freer scope in the expression or publication of opinions as to the capacity, impartiality or integrity of judges than members of the bar. They have the best opportunities of observing and forming a correct judgment. They are in constant attendance on the courts. Hundreds of those who are called on to vote never enter a court house, or if they do, it is only at intervals as jurors, witnesses or parties. To say that an attorney can only act or speak on this subject under liability to be called to account and to be deprived of his profession and livelihood by the very judge or judges whom he may consider it his duty to attack and expose, is a position too monstrous to be entertained for a moment under our present system.[6]

When a judge is candidate for reelection, newspaper criticism of him by lawyer-editors is obviously privileged.[7]

PERSONAL RELATIONS WITH JUDGES

Canon 3 is as follows:

Marked attention and unusual hospitality on the part of a lawyer to a Judge, uncalled for by the personal relations of the parties, subject both the Judge and the lawyer to misconstructions of motive and should be avoided. A lawyer should not communicate or argue privately with the Judge as to the merits of a pending cause, and he deserves rebuke and denunciation for any device or attempt to gain from a Judge special personal consideration or favor. A self-respecting independence in the discharge of professional duty, without denial or diminution of the courtesy and respect due the Judge's station, is the only proper foundation for cordial personal and official relations between Bench and Bar.

Testimonial dinners to judges should be by one of the established bar associations, not by a self-formed committee.[8]

A loan by a lawyer to a judge is improper;[9] nor may a lawyer properly ask a judge for appointment as receiver or trustee.[10]

---

[6] 95 Pa. at 238–39.

The following is a ruling by the General Council of the English Bar in 1912: "DUTY.— According to the best traditions of the Bar of England, a barrister should, whilst acting with all due courtesy to the tribunal before which he is appearing, fearlessly uphold the interests of his client without regard to any unpleasant circumstances either to himself or to any other person . . . . any attempt to coerce or influence any Barrister in the execution of what he considers to be his duty to his client by any social pressure or disqualification is to be strongly condemned. A.S. 1912, p. 16" *The Annual Practice* (1912), p. 12.

[7] And see In re Cannon, 206 Wis. 374 (1932).   [8] N.Y. City 588, 673.

[9] A.B.A. Op. 89; App. A, 252.   [10] N.Y. County 333; see also Judicial Canon 12.

The propriety of a lawyer's practicing before a judge to whom he is related depends somewhat on the circumstances. Judicial Canon 13 provides:

He should not act in a controversy where a near relative is a party; he should not suffer his conduct to justify the impression that any person can improperly influence him or unduly enjoy his favor, or that he is affected by the kinship, rank, position or influence of any party or other person.

In its Opinion 200, the American Bar Association Committee said:

A judge should studiously avoid wherever possible every situation that might reasonably give rise to the impression on the part of litigants or of the public that his decisions were influenced by favoritism. While the Canons do not preclude a judge from sitting in a case in which a son or other relative is counsel, it is wise in such cases for the judge, where feasible, to have another judge hear the case.

It is not incumbent on a lawyer to refuse to accept employment in a case because it may be heard by his father or other relative. The responsibility is on the judge not to sit in a case unless he is both free from bias and from the appearance thereof.

The New York Committees have held that a trial judge should disqualify himself when his son, nephew, or near relation is the attorney for a party to the litigation, and that if a near relative is in the employ of such attorney, the judge should, if feasible, disqualify himself in any case in which there is a reasonable doubt as to the propriety of his presiding.[11] Where, in exceptional cases, obvious injustice would result in his not presently trying the case, he should disclose all the facts to the parties and proceed only if all counsel consent.[12]

There is no general rule relative to a judge sitting in a case tried or argued by his former partner,[13] or by the judge's former secretary.[14] Here again the responsibility is on the judge and not on the lawyer.[15] The practical problem is, of course, different in rural communities from in large cities, and in the former would be influenced by local custom.

The rule as to English barristers was thus stated in the Annual

[11] N.Y. City 607; N.Y. County 346; see also *infra*, p. 277; also Mo. 48.
[12] N.Y. City 607. See as to barristers, An. St. (1895–96), p. 6.
[13] App. A, *281;* Texas 35. See also editorial in the N.Y. Law Jour. of Aug. 23, 1938.
[14] N.Y. City 681.
[15] App. A, *281.* Any advantage that the relative, partner, or secretary might have in gaining the judge's interest and attention might be considerably offset by his ability, through familiarity with the lawyer's views, to detect flaws in his argument.

Statement by the General Council of the Bar on page 7 of its rulings for 1923:

JUDGES' SONS. There is no objection to a barrister practicing in a court where his father is one of several judges. In such case it is impossible to know beforehand which judge will in fact try a case. For example; it has never been considered improper for a barrister to appear before his father in the High Court, or in the Court of Appeals, or in the House of Lords.

The propriety of a contribution to a judge's campaign fund depends on all the attendant circumstances.[16]

A lawyer may not informally discuss a case with the judge without the other lawyer's presence, nor should the judge permit this.[17]

He may tell a judge, respectfully, either by a proper letter or by personal discussion, of a reason that it is important to his client to have an early decision, but with the other lawyer present if oral and a copy to him if written. He should ask the other lawyer to go with him to see the judge; if the other lawyer will not do so, he should tell the judge that this has been requested.[18]

UNDERSTANDINGS WITH THE COURT

A lawyer cannot be too careful scrupulously to observe every arrangement, formal or informal, or understanding with the court or made with opposing counsel in the court's presence,[19] as regards the conduct of the case. A lawyer who secures a postponement of a case by an agreement with opposing counsel and the court that "everything remains in status quo" will be severely censured for permitting and taking steps changing the status quo during the period agreed on.[20]

After getting a continuance by a statement that he did not know of his client's whereabouts, on learning of it the lawyer is bound, irrespective of his client's consent, to disclose to the court and opposing counsel that he knows this, but that it has been disclosed to him in confidence.[21]

---

[16] N.Y. County 304.   [17] App. A, *251;* Mo. 79.
[18] App. A, *255;* see also Cleveland 6. He may not properly get his clients to write to the judge criticizing his opinion; Cleveland 6.
[19] As to agreements with opposing counsel, see also *infra,* p. 156.
[20] A.B.A. Op. 25.   [21] N.Y. County 217.

Candor and Fairness to the Court

Canon 22 is as follows:

The conduct of the lawyer before the Court and with other lawyers should be characterized by candor and fairness.

It is not candid or fair for the lawyer knowingly to misquote the contents of a paper, the testimony of a witness, the language or the argument of opposing counsel, or the language of a decision or a textbook; or with knowledge of its invalidity, to cite as authority a decision that has been overruled, or a statute that has been repealed; or in argument to assert as a fact that which has not been proved, or in those jurisdictions where a side has the opening and closing arguments to mislead his opponent by concealing or withholding positions in his opening argument upon which his side then intends to rely.

It is unprofessional and dishonorable to deal other than candidly with the facts in taking the statements of witnesses, in drawing affidavits and other documents, and in the presentation of causes.

A lawyer should not offer evidence, which he knows the Court should reject, in order to get the same before the jury by argument for its admissibility, nor should he address to the Judge arguments upon any point not properly calling for determination by him. Neither should he introduce into an argument, addressed to the court, remarks or statements intended to influence the jury or bystanders.

These and all kindred practices are unprofessional and unworthy of an officer of the law charged, as is the lawyer, with the duty of aiding in the administration of justice.

The oath recommended by the American Bar Association contains a pledge that the lawyer "will never seek to mislead the judge or jury *by any artifice* or false statement of fact or law."

In an article "Relations of Bench and Bar," Justice Anglin said:

It is impossible to exaggerate the importance of being absolutely fair with the court. Candour and frankness should characterize the conduct of the barrister at every stage of his case. The court has the right to rely upon him to assist it in ascertaining the truth. *Veritas est justitiae mater.* He should be most careful to state with strict accuracy the contents of a paper, the evidence of a witness, the admissions or the argument of his opponent. Knowingly to cite an overruled case, or to refer to a repealed statute as still in force, would be unpardonable, and counsel cannot be too cautious not to make such mistakes unwittingly. A charitable construction is not always put upon such errors, and the confidence of the courts and of his professional brethren is far too important for counsel to jeopardize it lightly. The success of the advocate who enjoys this confidence is assured; while the lawyer who is not candid with the court, or who attempts to deceive or mislead it, very quickly attains an undesirable reputation. Once made such a reputation renders future success at the Bar almost an impossibility. *Falsus in uno, falsus in omnibus,* is a *maxim* not applicable exclusively to the witness.[22]

In an Illinois case [23] Judge Magruder said:

The lawyer's duty is of a double character. He owes to his client the duty of fidelity, but he also owes the duty of good faith and honorable dealing to the judicial tribunals before whom he practices his profession. He is an officer of the court—a minister in the temple of justice. His high vocation is to correctly inform the court upon the law and the facts of the case, and to aid it in doing justice and arriving at correct conclusions. He violates his oath of office when he resorts to deception, or permits his clients to do so. He is under no obligations to seek to obtain, for those whom he represents, that which is forbidden by the law. If he suffers false and perjured testimony to be presented to the presiding judge, with the possible result of inducing the latter to take jurisdiction of a cause, in which there would otherwise be no power to act, and to grant a judgment or decree which the law would prohibit if the real character of the offered testimony were known, he cannot shield himself behind his supposed obligations to his client.

A lawyer may not, in order to get decided a question of law in which he is interested, foist a fictitious controversy on the court.[24]

He may not appear for a non-existent corporation; [25] nor may he ostensibly appear for a stooge client when he really represents others.[26]

A lawyer using an accountant, employed to certify balance sheets, must disclose that he is such; [27] and one hiring a professional witness to get evidence in a divorce case cannot properly represent such witness as being a friend [28] of plaintiff.

A lawyer may not participate in a bargain with a witness as a condition of his giving evidence,[29] but this does not preclude the payment

---

22 29 Can. L. T. 1, 7–8 (1909). See also *infra*, p. 145 n. 32; also 52 Col. L. Rev. 1041 (1952).

23 People v. Beattie, 137 Ill. 553, 574 (1891).

24 In re Attorney, 10 App. Div. 491 (1896). See also N.Y. City 570, N.Y. County 171; Matter of Elsam, 5 Dowl. & Ry. 389 (1824); In re Hawes, 169 App. Div. 644 (1915); in Harbin v. Masterman, 1 Ch. 351, 371 (1896), Lord Justice Rigby said: "I wish it to be known that in my judgment, at any rate, it is not the part of a respectable solicitor to induce clients to lend their names for appeals in which they have no interest at all, in order that the solicitor himself may gain his own private ends."

See also *infra*, p. 152 n. 26, on violating a law in order to test its validity.

Where, however, a question of law should obviously be promptly decided, it is quite usual to get up a test case which the lawyers and the court realize is for the purpose of settling the law. Such a case was Mahon v. Penna. Coal Co., 260 U.S. 393 (1922); also Heisler v. Thomas Colliery Co., 260 U.S. 245 (1922).

25 N.Y. City 292.   26 N.Y. City 130.   27 A.B.A. Op. 272.

28 N.Y. City 668.   29 See *infra*, pp. 86, 152.

of actual expenses and reasonable compensation to persons who cannot afford to come and testify at the statutory fees, with no attempt to influence their testimony, the arrangement being disclosed to the court and jury.[30]

A lawyer may settle his personal civil claim if he makes no agreement not to testify in a criminal case arising out of the same matter.[31]

Counsel for a special guardian may not ask counsel for the accountants for an agreement as to his fee before filing his report with the court.[32]

Although a lawyer is not responsible for the character of bail presented by his client unless there is something suspicious to put him on inquiry,[33] a criminal lawyer was suspended for two years for telling a magistrate that bail bonds were "all right" when he knew they were not; [34] and another was disbarred for presenting to the court appeal bonds with sureties which he knew to be worthless or fictitious.[35]

As to "collusion" in divorce cases, see *infra,* pages 122–30.

DUTY TO DISCLOSE RELEVANT MATTERS NOT BROUGHT OUT BY OPPOSING COUNSEL

The extent to which it is regarded as counsel's duty to advise the court as to matters relevant to the proper decision of the case of which opposing counsel is ignorant or which he has overlooked turns on the degree to which the old idea that litigation is a game between the lawyers has been supplanted by the more modern view that the lawyer is a minister of justice.[36] Always, however, must be borne in mind the principle that the theory of our system is still that justice is best accomplished by having all the facts and arguments on each side investigated and presented with maximum vigor by opposing counsel, for decision by the court and jury.[37]

When one of the lawyers knows that a prospective juror is an em-

[30] N.Y. County 110 and cases cited therein; and see N.Y. City 86. In N.Y. City 8, it was held that with disclosure to the court, jury and counsel, a witness might be paid to waive his privilege not to testify.

[31] N.Y. County 347; N.Y. City 589.

[32] N.Y. County 247. As to the acceptance of compensation in addition to that awarded by the court for representing minors see *infra,* p. 98 nn. 29 and 30.

[33] In re Hirst, 9 Phila. 216, 217 (per Hare, P. J.) (1874).

[34] In re Sachs, 169 App. Div. 622 (N.Y., 1915).

[35] People v. Pickler, 186 Ill. 64 (1900).

[36] "Under our system of jurisprudence it is intended that a trial shall not be conducted as a game between court and counsel." Mich. 142.

[37] See *infra,* pp. 142–44.

ployee of a corporation directly interested in the outcome of the case, and such juror in answering questions concerning his impartiality fails to disclose this, it is not fair to the court for him to permit such juror to be selected.[38]

A lawyer may not close the mouth of an important witness to a murder [39] nor may he advise his client, a fugitive from justice, not to surrender, because the lawyer believes that public hysteria would prevent his getting a fair trial.[40]

The Michigan Committee has held that a lawyer who represents a defendant known by him to be a minor is bound to disclose this to the court and have a guardian appointed, since a judgment against his client would otherwise be invalid and the court's time in trying the case be wasted.[41] The New York County Committee, however, held that it was not professionally improper for defendant's counsel in a negligence case, which was dismissed for failure of proof, not to have disclosed to the court that he had in court the only eyewitness to the accident, even though plaintiff was an infant.[42]

A lawyer who has made an unwitting but material mistake in connection with proceedings in a decedent's estate is bound, on ascertaining the true facts, to disclose to the court the mistake he made, but he should not divulge privileged communications.[43]

While a lawyer should advise the court and opposing counsel of a clear mistake in computation made by his opponent,[44] he need not advise of what he believes may have been a mistake by the commissioner in applying the principles of law laid down by the Board of Tax Appeals.[45]

---

[38] N.Y. City 280.   [39] App. A, *21, 304*.   [40] *Id., 14*.

[41] Mich. 142; cf. Texas 33, holding that, where a statute made it obligatory in a divorce case to disclose whether there were any children under sixteen years of age, it was unethical for the lawyer not to disclose that the wife was pregnant. In N.Y. City 58, however, that Committee held it not improper, where counsel for the other side was out of town when a case was reached for a new trial, not to inform the court that the scope of the new trial had been limited by the order for it, he not having made affirmative representations to the court.

[42] N.Y. County 309. Query as to the soundness of this decision; also as to N.Y. City 58 in the previous note.

[43] N.Y. City 945. However, the performance of this duty to the court may, as here, result in the disclosure of an iniquity on the part of the client.

[44] N.Y. City 631; see also N.Y. County 181, 215. Canon 41 provides as follows: "When a lawyer discovers that some fraud or deception has been practiced, which has unjustly imposed upon the court or a party, he should endeavor to rectify it; at first by advising his client, and if his client refuses to forego the advantage thus unjustly gained, he should promptly inform the injured person or his counsel, so that they may take appropriate steps." Note that the Canon does not specify disclosure *to the court*.

[45] App. A, *18;* see also N.Y. City 269.

A lawyer is bound to tell the court of any decisions directly adverse to any proposition of law on which he expressly relies, of which the lawyer on the other side is apparently ignorant and which would reasonably be considered important by the judge sitting in the case.[46]

BRIEFS

A lawyer may not properly give a memorandum to the trial judge without a copy to the other side,[47] even where the court asked for it.[48] He should have a good reason for filing an additional brief after

[46] See A.B.A. Op. 280 and cases cited; also John C. Harris "Legal Ethics," 69 Albany L. Jour. 300, 303 (1907); Showell Rogers, "The Ethics of Advocacy," 15 L. Quart. Rev. 259, 275, n. (1899). Moody v. Davis, 10 Ga. 403, 410 (1851); also N.Y. City 889 and 35 A.B.A. Jour. 5 (1949).

In its Opinion 280, the American Bar Association Committee said:

"The lawyer, though an officer of the court and charged with the duty of 'candor and fairness,' is not an umpire, but an advocate. He is under no duty to refrain from making every proper argument in support of any legal point because he is not convinced of its inherent soundness. Nor is he under any obligation to suggest arguments against his position. His personal belief in the soundness of his cause or of the authorities supporting it, is irrelevant. See Canons 5 and 15.

"We would not confine the Opinion to 'controlling authorities,'—i.e., those decisive of the pending case,—but, in accordance with the tests hereafter suggested, would apply it to a decision directly adverse to any proposition of law on which the lawyer expressly relies, which would reasonably be considered important by the judge sitting on the case.

"Of course, if the court should ask if there are any adverse decisions, the lawyer should make such frank disclosure as the question seems to warrant. Close cases can obviously be suggested, particularly in the case of decisions from other states where there is no local case in point. (See *Glebe Company v. Trustees*, 37 T.L.R. 436 (1921 A.C.66) where the dicta of Lord Birkenhead are very broad. Also 15 Law Quarterly Rev. 259, 273-275; 69 Albany L.J. 300, 303; 'The Seven Lamps of Advocacy' by Edward A. Parry (1923) pp. 19-20, 'The Advocate' (Cecil Walsh) (2d Ed.) p. 100.) A case of doubt should obviously be resolved in favor of the disclosure, or by a statement disclaiming the discussion of all conflicting decisions.

"Canon 22 should be interpreted sensibly, to preclude the obvious impropriety at which the Canon is aimed. In a case involving a right angle collision or a vested or contingent remainder, there would seem to be no necessity whatever of citing even all the relevant decisions in the jurisdiction, much less those from other states or by inferior courts. Where the question is a new or novel one, such as the constitutionality or construction of a statute, on which there is a dearth of authority, the lawyer's duty may be broader. The test in every case should be: Is the decision which opposing counsel has overlooked one which the court should clearly consider in deciding the case? Would a reasonable judge properly feel that a lawyer who advanced, as the law, a proposition adverse to the undisclosed decision, was lacking in candor and fairness to him? Might the judge consider himself misled by an implied representation that the lawyer knew of no adverse authority?" See also A.B.A. Op. 146.

[47] App. A, *253*; N.Y. County 221. See also Judicial Canon 17, Appendix D.

[48] App. A, *253*; a custom to the contrary is invalid, Mich. 96. In March, 1947, the Judicial Conference adopted the following:

"The Use of Trial Memoranda in Criminal Cases.—The Conference after consideration of the report of the Committee appointed to study the subject matter, disapproved

the case has been submitted, and should send a copy to the opposing lawyer in order to enable him to reply.[49]

The New York County Committee has held it improper to make a statement in a brief to the effect that a judge, a former partner of the writer, who had rendered a decision apparently contrary to the writer's contention, approved of his present position.[50] The New York City Committee has also held that it is improper to name trial counsel "of counsel" on an appellate brief in the preparation of which he has not participated, such being contrary to the current practice.[1]

A brief which contains offensive, impertinent, or scandalous matter may be refused or stricken from the files and the writer held in contempt.[2] In a memorandum opinion the Supreme Court has said that arguments, either oral or written, must be "gracious and respectful to both the court and opposing counsel, and be in such words as may be properly addressed by one gentleman to another." [3]

ALTERATION OF COURT RECORDS

It is a most serious offense for a lawyer to make any alteration in a judgment or decree of a court; [4] or as a notary to affix his certificate to a document not actually sworn to before him [5] or to ante-date the jurat in order to further his client's interest,[6] or to swear that a legal tender was made when he knows the tender was not a legal one.[7]

ABUSE OF LEGAL PROCESS

A lawyer may not properly send to a debtor papers designed to resemble court process; [8] nor may he employ a skip-tracing plan oper-

---

the practice, prevalent in some districts, of trial judges in criminal cases receiving from the attorney on one side a brief or trial memorandum that has not been furnished to the attorney on the other side, and recommended the immediate discontinuance of such practice."

[49] N.Y. City 756.   [50] N.Y. County 34.

[1] N.Y. City B-54.   [2] Pittsburgh, etc., R. Co. v. Muncie, 166 Ind. 466 (1906).

[3] National Surety Co. v. Jarvis, 278 U.S. 610 (1928).

[4] State ex rel v. Finley, Circuit Judge, 30 Fla. 325 (1892); even as to what he considered an immaterial provision. In re P., 83 N.J.Eq. 390 (1914); see also Erskine v. Adeane, 18 Sol. J. 573 (1874); Matter of Eldridge, 82 N.Y. 161 (1880).

[5] State ex rel v. Finn, 32 Ore. 519 (1898); Griffin's Appeal, 371 Pa. 646, 651 (1952).

[6] Re Arctander, 26 Minn. 25 (1879).   [7] N.Y. City 84.

[8] A.B.A. Op. 178; App. A, 301. See also N.Y. County 392. In Illinois it is a misdemeanor to circulate papers simulating court process (Criminal Code, chap. 37, sec. 501; also in New York, Sec. 551-A of the Criminal Code; People v. Globe Jewelers, 249

ated by a lay agency to locate a debtor; [9] nor may he bring a purely vexatious suit.[10]

A lawyer may not be employed merely to serve a summons and do no more; [11] nor may he issue a subpoena returnable on a day when the case is not being called; [12] or participate in a subterfuge to avoid the homestead law.[13]

A lawyer who is a member of the legislature may not send claim letters to a debtor in an envelope marked "The Assembly, Albany," since this might mislead the debtor into thinking that political pressure would be brought to force him to pay the claim.[14]

"QUICKIE" DIVORCES

In its Opinion 84 the American Bar Association Committee held that a lawyer whose client, with no local ground for divorce, had a valid ground in another state conditioned on her obtaining a bona fide domicile therein, might not properly advise her to institute divorce proceedings there, alleging and swearing her intention to make her residence there permanently, when he knew that she intended to return as soon as the decree was signed. This decision was rendered when the law as to the binding effect of divorces in sister states was as stated by the five-to-three majority of the Supreme Court in *Andrews* v. *Andrews*.[15] This case held that the Full Faith and Credit Clause did not make binding in Massachusetts—the state of matrimonial domicile—a North Dakota divorce when the Massachusetts court found that plaintiff had gone there without a bona fide intent to change her domicile, even though defendant had appeared and consented to the decree. Domicile was essential, the court said, to jurisdiction in divorce cases, irrespective of the appearance of the parties.

In *Sherrer* v. *Sherrer*,[16] *Johnson* v. *Muelberger*,[17] and *Cook* v. *Cook*,[18] the majority of the court has since taken the position that

---

App. Div. 122 (1936). See also In re Dows, 168 Minn. 6 (1926); also 47 A.L.R. 267 n. (1927). See also Chicago 23, pp. 45–46. It is, of course, a cardinal offense deliberately to mislead the court. See 52 Col. L. Rev. 1041 (1952). See also *supra*, p. 74.

As to fraud and chicane in dealings with clients, see further *infra*, pp. 89, 102. As to how far a lawyer may properly go in furthering his client's cause, see *infra*, p. 146.

[9] N.Y. City 803, 886, 937; see also N.Y. County 254.

[10] N.Y. County 306; and cf. N.Y. County 301.

[11] N.Y. County 306.   [12] N.Y. City B-66.

[13] Texas 39.   [14] N.Y. City 682-H.

[15] 188 U.S. 14 (1903).   [16] 334 U.S. 343 (1948).

[17] 340 U.S. 581 (1951).   [18] 342 U.S. 126 (1951).

Andrews v. *Andrews* is no longer binding on this point; [19] that where defendant is represented in the divorce proceedings, the state of domicile may not disregard the decree on the basis of its finding that plaintiff's residence was merely for divorce purposes; and that local policy must give way to the Full Faith and Credit Clause as "part of the price of our Federal system." [20] Accordingly, where the defendant appears in the divorcing state, either in person or by counsel, its decree is now binding on the parties,[21] on those in privity with them,[22] and on strangers.[23]

Under these circumstances, is a lawyer justified in advising a client to go to Nevada to secure a divorce, knowing that she does not intend to acquire a bona fide domicile?

In support of the position that he may so advise and arrange for a responsible Nevada lawyer to represent her, it may be forcibly urged that her allegation of proposed "indefinite" residence will not in the least deceive the local judges [24] nor alter their "amiable inclination" toward easy divorce,[25] and that neither the court nor counsel for defendant will cross-examine her about it; that the local judges clearly understand the situation and under their practice have adopted what practically amounts to a legal fiction [26] to take the place of the statutory requirement of domicile; that if, as is most probable, the local

[19] Sherrer v. Sherrer, 334 U.S. at 353.   [20] See *id.* at 350, 354, and 355.
[21] *Id.* at 343, 350.   [22] Johnson v. Muelberger, 340 U.S. at 581, 587–89.
[23] Cook v. Cook, 342 U.S. at 126.

The principal points apparently as yet undecided are whether the court, as now constituted, will follow the majority decision in the second Williams case, 325 U.S. 226 (1945), holding the state of domicile not bound by the divorce decree of another state, in which plaintiff did not acquire a bona fide domicile, despite the appearance of the defendant; or will follow the majority in the first Williams case, 317 U.S. 287 (1942), in holding that if plaintiff does acquire such a domicile, defendant is bound by the decree though served merely by publication. See, however, Justice Jackson's dissenting opinions in the first Williams case, 317 U.S. at 316–24, in Estin v. Estin, 334 U.S. 541, 553 (1948), and in Rice v. Rice, 336 U.S. 674, 678, 680 (1949). See also L. A. Haslup, "Divisible Divorce," 3 Fla. L. Rev. 145, 171 (1950).

[24] See Justice Rutledge's dissenting opinion in the second Williams case, 325 U.S. 226, 249 (1945). Also Thomas Reed Powell, "And Repent at Leisure," 58 Harv. L. Rev. 930, 944–47 (1945).

[25] ". . . in the states which prostitute their honor in order to fatten on marital misfortune," 36 A.B.A. Jour. 107 (1950); see also Frank W. Ingram and G. A. Ballard, "The Business of Migratory Divorce in Nevada," 2 Law & Contemp. Prob. 302, 307 (1935).

[26] See L. L. Fuller, "Legal Fictions," 25 Ill. L. Rev. 363, 513, 877 (1930); Jeremiah Smith, "Surviving Fictions," 27 Yale L. Jour. 147, 317 (1917); Oliver R. Mitchell, "The Fictions of the Law," 7 Harv. L. Rev. 249 (1893); Allen M. Stearne, "Fiction," 81 U. of Pa. L. Rev. 1 (1932); Ben W. Palmer, "Legal Fictions and Red Room Wine," 38 A.B.A. Jour. 23 (1952); see also H. S. Drinker, "Ethical Problems in Matrimonial Litigation, 66 Harv. L. Rev. 443 (1953); Fowler V. Harper, "The Myth of the Void Divorce," 2 Law & Contemp. Prob. 335, 344, 345 (1935). As to a "dummy" on a bond, see N.Y. County 30.

court signs the decree after a five-minute hearing, the Nevada Supreme Court will sustain it as based on substantial evidence [27] and the Supreme Court of the United States will uphold it as against all but a local prosecution for bigamy or adultery, which will be unlikely unless, like the Williams couple, she flaunts a second marriage in the face of her indignant neighbors.

Lawyers of high standing have so advised their clients, considering that it is not their function to supervise the local Nevada or Florida courts.

Others have taken the position that under no circumstances may a lawyer advise his client to allege or swear to an untruth and that if, in view of the latest Supreme Court decisions, mere sojourn is to be made the basis of divorce jurisdiction, Nevada or Florida or the Virgin Islands must so amend their statutes.

DUTY TO BE PUNCTUAL

Canon 21 provides: "It is the duty of the lawyer not only to his client, but also the Courts and to the public to be punctual in attendance, and to be concise and direct in the trial and disposition of causes."

Repeated tardiness may amount to contempt of court.[28]

DUTY NOT TO EMPLOY DILATORY TACTICS

The American Bar Association Canons contain no provision precluding the employment of dilatory tactics except the clause in the recommended oath of admission that the candidate "will not delay any man's cause for lucre or malice"; nor should they.[29] Of this provision in the oath Sharswood says:

It refers, no doubt, primarily, to the cause intrusted to the attorney, and prohibits him from resorting to such means for the purpose of procuring more fees, or of indulging any feeling he may have against his client per-

27 Whise v. Whise, 36 Nev. 16, 23 (1913); Confer v. District Court, 49 Nev. 18, 26 (1925); Lamb v. Lamb, 57 Nev. 421, 432 (1937); Wilson v. Wilson, 66 Nev. 405 (1949).

It is not clear what the Nevada court will hold if the trial judge should ask her what she meant by "indefinitely" and she should say that she did not know whether she would go back to Philadelphia on next Thursday or Friday.

28 59 A.L.R. 1272a (1929).

29 Canon IX of the California Bar Association Code of Legal Ethics of 1910 contained a long provision specifying all sorts of dilatory proceedings as unprofessional, but in 1928 was superseded by a short provision (204 Cal. XCI) condemning appeals taken merely for delay.

sonally. . . . But it is a question, also, whether the case generally, in which he is retained, is not comprehended.[30]

The law offers innumerable opportunities and means for delay, many of which it is not only the right but the duty of the lawyer to employ for the benefit of his client; others where it is not. The point at which he should draw the line is a question which each lawyer must decide for himself under the admonition of Canon 29 to "strive at all times to uphold the honor and to maintain the dignity of the profession and to improve not only the law but the administration of justice." At one end is the clear right to take the full time allowed for an appeal, whether to determine its advisability, to perfect the papers, or what not; at the other end is the long-standing and usual requirement for counsel to certify that a motion for reargument is not for delay. Five hundred years ago the law was a game, the processes of which were continually and openly employed by means of obscure technicalities, serving no useful purpose, to defeat justice. In those days the lawyer's reputation was based in large part on his successful use of such devices. Even during recent years it was possible and regarded as entirely proper in many jurisdictions for the lawyer for a defendant by entering an unsworn general denial, to delay judgment in a defenseless case for several years.[31] Recently, with increasing insistence, the bar and the courts have taken radical steps by statutes and court rules, requiring specific averments, providing for pretrial conferences, interrogatories and specific admissions, to simplify and develop promptly and dispose of, finally and clearly, the real issues in the case.

Some lawyers are naturally imbued with the old traditions and loath to welcome the new devices which render obsolete much of that in which they have taken years to become expert, while an impatient public demands remedy of "the law's delays."

It is clearly the duty of the bar to cooperate wholeheartedly in developing all such new procedures and in making them work practically.[32]

The mere fact that a defense is on a ground that a layman would

[30] *Professional Ethics*, p. 115. For the history of the oath, see *id*. at 58–59 n., also p. 116.

[31] But see N.Y. City 85, holding that whenever any of the material allegations of fact set forth in a complaint is true, the interposing of a general denial is improper.

[32] See C. H. Tuttle, "The Ethics of Advocacy," 18 A.B.A. Jour. 849, 853 (1931).

"A law suit is something more than a game which is to be won by the player who is shrewder and more observant of the rules." Shientag, J., in Marcus v. Simotone, etc., Films, 135 Misc. 228, 229 (N.Y., 1920).

term technical is of itself no valid objection to it. "All rules are called 'technical' by those against whom they operate." [33]

As Chief Justice Sharswood said,[34] much depends on the lawyer's estimate of the case. Where a claim is manifestly unjust, but difficult to prove as such, it may be properly defended by more unsubstantial technicalities than one which is obviously just.

Dilatory proceedings are wrong when solely intended to hinder the proper presentation and development of a just cause.[35]

ATTITUDE TOWARD JURY

Canon 23 provides:

All attempts to curry favor with juries by fawning, flattery or pretended solicitude for their personal comfort are unprofessional. Suggestions of counsel, looking to the comfort or convenience of jurors and propositions to dispense with argument, should be made to the Court out of the jury's hearing. A lawyer must never converse privately with jurors about the case; and both before and during the trial he should avoid communicating with them, even as to matters foreign to the cause.

A lawyer may not, even after verdict, seek out individual jurors and interview them as to what went on in the jury room, and as to what were the salient points deemed by them of importance in reaching their verdict, even though the lawyer's purpose has no relation to the case which they decided, and is solely for the improvement of his jury technique.[36] A lawyer may not write to or communicate with jurors, either before or after trial.[37] Jurors should conduct their deliberations and reach their verdict with the assurance that, except for fraud, there will be no subsequent investigation by any one of their deliberations.[38]

It is, of course, manifestly improper for a lawyer to show any

---

[33] Sir Frederick Pollock in 18 Law Quart. Rev. 411 n. 1 (1902).

[34] *Professional Ethics*, pp. 98–99.

[35] See United States v. Frank, 53 F.2d 128 (1931). May a lawyer interpose a dilatory motion, plea, demurrer, etc., for the sole purpose of having the statute of limitations run against a defenseless claim?

[36] A.B.A. Op. 109. App. A, 257; and see Texas 26; but see N.Y. City 377, 507, B-174, holding that he may properly interview members of the jury after it has been discharged; N.Y. City B-174 not agreeing "in all respects" with A.B.A. Op. 109.

[37] App. A, 257.

[38] *Id.*, 258. A number of experienced lawyers have expressed disagreement with the broad statements in this paragraph. It has also been suggested that the fact that the Canon specifies "both before and during the trial" impliedly sanctions communications with jurors after trial.

marked attention to jurors during the trial.[39] The shadowing of jurors during a trial has been held to constitute contempt; [40] also the verbal abuse of a jury for awarding but a small amount of damages.[41]

Counsel for defendant in a personal injury case, who is also counsel for the insurance company may not misstate to the jury that the defendant was not insured, despite the fact that plaintiff's counsel, perhaps unfairly, created the impression in his examination of jurors that he was.[42]

ATTITUDE TOWARD WITNESSES [43]

Canon 39 provides:

A lawyer may properly interview any witness or prospective witness for the opposing side in any civil or criminal action without the consent of opposing counsel or party. In doing so, however, he should scrupulously avoid any suggestion calculated to induce the witness to suppress or deviate from the truth, or in any degree to affect his free and untrammeled conduct when appearing at the trial or on the witness stand.

A lawyer may properly interview witnesses for the other side without getting the consent of the other counsel [44] and even where they are under subpoena by the other side; [45] including the employee who was responsible for the accident and is joined as a defendant.[46] But under Canon 9 [47] this does not apply to the opposite party himself, though he is expected to be a witness.[48] It probably does apply, however, to the officers of a corporation having authority to bind it.[49]

[39] See In re Kelly, 243 Fed. 696 (1917). Sandstrom v. Oregon, etc., Co., 69 Ore. 194 (1914). Garvin v. Harrell, 27 Okl. 373 (1910); see also Liutz v. Denver City Tr. Co., 54 Colo. 371 (1913).

[40] Sinclair v. United States, 279 U.S. 749 (1929); see also 63 A.L.R. 1269 n. (1929); also 63 U.S. L. Rev. 345 (1929). In re Bruener, 159 Wash. 504 (1930).

[41] Tanner v. United States, 62 F.2d 601 (C.C.A., 1933); see also Ex parte Pater, 10 L.T.R. (N.S.) 376 (Q.B., 1864).

[42] N.Y. County 127. As to arguments to the jury held unduly prejudicial, see Arant's Case Book, pp. 473–77.

[43] See also *infra*, pp. 201–03.

[44] See A.B.A. Ops. 12, 14, 101, 117, 187; Mich. 41, 68, 117, 141; N.Y. City 541, B-87.

[45] A.B.A. Ops. 127, 187.   [46] N.Y. City 443.

[47] 9. NEGOTIATIONS WITH OPPOSITE PARTY. "A lawyer should not in any way communicate upon the subject of controversy with a party represented by counsel; much less should he undertake to negotiate or compromise the matter with him, but should deal only with his counsel. It is incumbent upon the lawyer most particularly to avoid everything that may tend to mislead a party not represented by counsel, and he should not undertake to advise him as to the law."

[48] A.B.A. Op. 187; Mich. 41. The mother is so far identified with her injured child that it would violate Canon 9 for her to be interviewed: App. A, 250.

[49] N.Y. City 830.

Counsel for a convicted criminal may properly visit in prison the accomplice whose testimony was largely influential in securing the conviction, in the bona fide belief that he testified falsely, and endeavor to secure a retraction.[50]

A cheap subterfuge, employed by many lawyers, particularly with an inexperienced opponent, is to ask the witness on cross-examination if he has been talked to by counsel for the side on which he has been called. It is, of course, entirely proper for counsel to go over carefully beforehand all the testimony of his witnesses, and they should be warned to be entirely frank about admitting this.

Just where is the line between developing all the facts known to the witness and indirectly coaching him by repeated statements of facts and conclusions of fact which counsel desires to establish, is, of course, a question of good faith.[1]

The Texas Committee held that in interviewing employees of the other side, full disclosure of connection with the litigation and of purpose must be made.[2]

A lawyer for the defense may not close the mouths of witnesses in a murder case,[3] or try to close those of disinterested persons who know the facts, or prevent counsel for the other side from learning such facts from them.[4]

An expert whose proposed testimony disappoints the one employing him may properly be called by the other side.[5]

It is unfair and oppressive for a lawyer to subpoena an expert chemist whom he has paid merely for an analysis and whom he has not told that he expects him to testify.[6]

A lawyer may not agree to pay a contingent fee to a witness,[7] nor advertise for a witness to testify to stated facts; although he may advertise for witnesses to a particular event or transaction.[8]

[50] A.B.A. Op. 12.

[1] Mich. 68. "His duty is to extract the facts from the witness, not to pour them into him; to learn what the witness does know, not to teach him what he ought to know." Finch, J., in Matter of Eldridge, 82 N.Y. 161, 171 (1880). See also Sharswood, *Professional Ethics*, p. 112, as to drawing affidavits which stretch the truth; also Warvelle, *Legal Ethics*, pp. 113–15.

[2] Texas 17.   [3] App. A, *21, 304;* see also *supra,* p. 77.

[4] A.B.A. Op. 131.   [5] N.Y. City 183.

[6] N.Y. City 273.

[7] N.Y. City 86; and see N.Y. City 311 (guaranty not to lose), N.Y. County 110, and cases cited; but transportation charges from without the jurisdiction may be paid without disclosure to court or counsel, N.Y. City 411. Supplemental Rule No. VIII in Arkansas specifically so provides.

[8] App. A, *305;* see also *infra,* p. 152.

He may not make "wanton, unnecessary and unreasonable" inquiry into the past of a pardoned witness.[9] He must not bully or browbeat honest witnesses; [10] where he attempts to do so the court of its own motion should promptly stop him.[11]

It is not necessary that he separate witnesses so that some shall not hear the testimony of others.[12]

The lawyer's privilege to make in judicial proceedings what would otherwise be slanderous statements relative to witnesses does not protect him from suspension or disbarment for such gross abuse of such privilege as shows him not to be a fit and proper person to remain a member of the bar.[13]

Where testimony necessary to exonerate the client may make the witness a criminal, the lawyer need not warn the witness that he is not obliged to testify, and should examine him.[14]

APPEARANCE BEFORE OTHER BODIES

Canon 26 provides:

A lawyer openly, and in his true character, may render professional services before legislative or other bodies, regarding proposed legislation and in advocacy of claims before departments of government, upon the same principles of ethics which justify his appearance before the Courts; but it is unprofessional for a lawyer so engaged to conceal his attorneyship, or to employ secret personal solicitations, or to use means other than those addressed to the reason and understanding to influence action.[15]

9 N.Y. County 43.

10 This was theoretically the rule in the earliest times; see Cohen, *History of the English Bar*, p. 119. Warvelle, *Legal Ethics,* p. 109: "He has a right to employ all the resources of his art to detect mistakes and expose falsehood but it is mean and contemptible to seek to entrap a witness into a falsehood, or to confuse and perplex him, with a design to discredit him, when counsel does not believe him to be swearing falsely." See also as to barristers, An. St. (1917), p. 7.

11 Sir John A. Boyd, "Legal Ethics," 4 Can. L. Rev. 85, 96 (1926). See also Canon 18. See W. Blake Odgers, *A Century of Law Reform* (1901), pp. 41, 42. As to the privilege of slandering a lawyer or witness in the proper furtherance of a cause, see La Porta v. Leonard, 88 N.J.L. 663 (1916); L.R.A. (1916) E. 782; Hoar v. Wood, 3 Metc. (Mass.) 193, 197 (1841); Carpenter v. Ashley, 148 Cal. 422 (1906); Rogers v. Thompson, 89 N.J.L. 639 (1916); 7 Ann. Cas. 603 n. (1907): Maulsby v. Reifsnider, 69 Md. 143, 151 (1888).

12 See App. A, 259.

13 See People v. Green, 9 Colo. 506, 533, 534 (1886); In re Adriaans, 17 App. D.C. 39 (1900).

14 N.Y. County 307.

15 "I do not believe that a lawyer has any more right, as a matter of correct public service, to hold a retainer while writing a law in the public interest and that a law which may affect his client adversely, than has a judge to hold retainers from those whose interests may be affected by the decisions which he renders or the judgment

The Illinois Bar Association adopted in 1938 an additional Canon, Number 49, defining the status and duty of a lawyer who is a member of the legislature or the occupant of a public office.

Canon 42 precluding the lawyer from agreeing with his client to pay or bear the expenses of litigation applies to the presentation and prosecution of a claim before an International Claim's Commission.[16]

A lawyer member of a committee of the legislature should make clear to his colleagues any interest of his clients which might be affected by legislation dealt with by such committee.[17]

He may not be employed to use his influence to secure a Government loan, or to have a given person appointed to office.[18]

---

which he signs. . . . Is it not as important to the public that laws be framed free of the influence, conscious or unconscious, of private interests as that they be administered free of such influence?" Wm. E. Borah, "The Lawyer and the Public," 2 A.B.A., Jour., 776, 780 (1916).

[16] A.B.A. Op. 20.   [17] App. A, 20.

[18] N.Y. City 544. As to the distinction between the status of a lawyer as an advocate in legal proceedings and as a lobbyist, see L. D. Brandeis, "The Opportunity in the Law," 39 A.L.R. (now U.S. L. Rev.) 555, 561–62 (1905), where he points out forcibly that in the latter case there is no other competent lawyer on the other side as contemplated by our system. See also Trist v. Child, 88 U.S. 441 (1874); Gesellschaft, etc., v. Brown, 78 F.2d 410 (1935).

VI

THE LAWYER'S OBLIGATIONS
TO HIS CLIENT

The Lawyer as a Fiduciary

Canon 11 [1] provides:

The lawyer should refrain from any action whereby for his personal benefit or gain he abuses or takes advantage of the confidence reposed in him by his client.

Money of the client or collected for the client or other trust property coming into the possession of the lawyer should be reported and accounted for promptly.

In *Stockton* v. *Ford*,[2] Justice Nelson said:

There are few of the business relations of life involving a higher trust and confidence than that of attorney and client, or, generally speaking, one more honorably and faithfully discharged; few more anxiously guarded by the law, or governed by sterner principles of morality and justice; and it is the duty of the court to administer them in a corresponding spirit, and to be watchful and industrious, to see that confidence thus reposed shall not be used to the detriment or prejudice of the rights of the party bestowing it.

In *Equity Jurisprudence*,[3] Story says:

The situation of an attorney or solicitor puts it in his power to avail himself not only of the necessity of his client, but of his good nature, liberality and credulity to obtain undue advantages, bargains, and gratuities. . . . By establishing the principle that while the relation of client and attorney subsists in its full vigor the latter shall derive no benefit to himself from the contracts, or bounty, or other negotiations of the former, it [the law]

---

[1] As originally enacted in 1908 the Canon read: "Money of the client or other trust property coming into the possession of the lawyer should be reported promptly, and except with the client's knowledge and consent should not be commingled with his private property or be used by him."

In 1933 this provision was amended to the form of the present second paragraph. The first paragraph was added in 1937.

[2] 52 U.S. 232, 247 (1850).   [3] (14th ed., 1918), Vol. I, sec. 433.

supersedes the necessity of any inquiry into the particular means, extent and exertion of influence in a given case; a task often difficult, and ill supported by evidence which can be drawn from any satisfactory sources. This doctrine is not necessarily limited to cases where the contract or other transaction respects the rights or property in controversy, in the particular suit in respect to which the attorney or solicitor is advising or acting for his client; but it may extend to other contracts and transactions disconnected therefrom, or at least where from the attendant circumstance there is reason to presume that the attorney and solicitor possessed some marked influence, ascendency, or other advantage over his client in respect to them.

In *Thomas* v. *Turner's Adm'r. et al.*,[4] Judge Lewis said:

. . . all dealings between attorney and client for the benefit of the former, are not only regarded with jealousy and closely scrutinized, but they are presumptively invalid, on the ground of constructive fraud; and that presumption can be overcome only by the clearest and most satisfactory evidence. The rule is founded on public policy, and operates independently of any ingredient of actual fraud, or of the age or capacity of the client, being intended as a protection to the client against the strong influence to which the confidential relation naturally gives rise.

In *Galbraith* v. *Elder*,[5] Judge Kennedy said:

The profession of a lawyer, when regulated by principles of sound morality and high mindedness, as it ever ought to be, has at all times been regarded as one of great honour and usefulness; but to render such profession either honourable or useful, it is very obvious that a most scrupulous fidelity must be for ever observed on the part of the lawyer towards his client, so that he shall never betray or take advantage, either in word or deed, of anything that has come to his knowledge by means of any communication from his client, or from papers or documents of the latter put into his hands.

In order that the interests of the client, may, in this respect, be protected and made secure, good policy would seem to require, as well as every principle of honour and fair dealing, that the counsel or attorney should not be permitted to do anything that would tend to prejudice the interest of his client, or occasion a loss to him in reference to anything upon which he was consulted.

With a view, therefore, to remove all temptation, and to prevent everything of the kind from being done, principles of expediency, as well as those of justice, require that the counsel or attorney shall derive no advantage whatever from such acts, when done by him, as may operate to the prejudice of, or occasion a loss to the client; and that all the advantage which otherwise would have arisen therefrom to the counsel, shall enure to the benefit of the client.

[4] 87 Va. 1, 12 (1890).   [5] 8 Watts (Pa.) 81, 94 (1839).

In *Young* v. *Murphy*,[6] in decreeing the cancellation of a deed which a client claimed had been given by him to his lawyer without consideration, Judge Winslow said:

Attorneys are ministers of justice as well as courts, and justice will not be contented with half-hearted service on the part of her ministers, nor will she tolerate a bargain counter within her temple. If an attorney purchase his client's property, concerning which his advice is sought, the transaction is always viewed with suspicion, and the attorney assumes the heavy burden of proving not only that there was no overreaching of the client, but that the client acted upon the fullest information and advice as to his rights. In other words, the attorney must prove *uberrima fides,* or the transaction will be set aside by the court of equity.

. . . . .

a lawyer is not permitted to traffic in his client's affairs for his own profit in disregard of the undivided loyalty commanded by his professional duties.[7]

A patent for an invention devised by a patent lawyer during his employment in connection with the apparatus covered by the patent throws on him the burden of proving his entire good faith.[8]

As regards his duty to turn over to his client inventions developed by him during his employment, the fiduciary relation of a patent lawyer is much more exacting than that of an ordinary employee. While the arrangement may possibly be such as to entitle the lawyer to retain for his own benefit ideas germinated and developed coincident with his work in the field of his employment, he should in any event give the client the first right to acquire such ideas or inventions, and in case of any doubt as to the right of the client to have them turned over to him without charge should resolve such doubt in favor of the client.[9]

Contracts between a lawyer and his client entered into after the relation of attorney and client has been established will be scrutinized with the utmost strictness, it being frequently said that they are attended by a presumption of invalidity and overreaching.[10]

In the *Matter of Howell*,[11] Judge Hogan said:

In this state it has been held that as to contracts made between the attorney and his client, subsequent to the employment which are beneficial to the attorney, it is incumbent upon the latter to show that the provisions are fair and reasonable, and were fully known and understood by the client.

[6] 120 Wis. 49, 51 (1903).   [7] In re Goldstein, 85 A.2d 361, 363–64 (Del., 1951).
[8] Goodrum v. Clement, 277 F. 586 (1922).   [9] App. A, 269.
[10] Spilker v. Hankin, 188 F.2d 35 (1951).   [11] 215 N.Y. 466, 472 (1915).

In *Bell* v. *Ramirez*,[12] Chief Justice McClendon said:

The well-established rule that the relation of attorney and client is one of *uberrima fides* rests upon the highest consideration of public policy, and agreements between them in the course of the relation are prima facie presumed to be fraudulent, the burden to show them otherwise being cast, as a matter of law, upon the attorney.

Accordingly, contracts by which lawyers have contracted for fees which the court deems exorbitant have been held invalid.[13]

The lawyer's fiduciary obligation applies to persons who although not strictly clients he has or should have reason to believe rely on him to advise them.[14] Where in the course of his investigations he discovers something which such a one should know, he should tell him of it, or at least advise him to secure separate counsel.[15] His obligation precludes his recommending an accountant to the client in consideration of the accountant's allowing him a share of his fee,[16] or otherwise using his relation in his own interest.[17]

He is bound to observe the Canons as fully when he becomes president of the company as when he was its general counsel.[18] He does not, however, owe any duty to persons with whom he has no professional relations. Accordingly, when he learns from the public record that an estate is indebted to one whom he knows, he need not tell the estate the whereabouts of the creditor, nor the latter the names and addresses of the representatives of the estate.[19]

He must not mingle the client's funds with his own.[20]

---

12 299 S.W. 655, 658 (Tex., 1927).

13 Goranson v. Solomonson, 304 Ill. App. 80 (1940). Ritz v. Carpenter, 43 S.D. 236 (1920).

14 N.Y. City 682-I; see also N.Y. City 505, N.Y. County 320; also N.Y. City 343; Mich. 150. As to when the relationship begins see Keenan v. Scott, 64 W.Va. 137 (1908). See also Mo. 29.

15 N.Y. County 90; and see N.Y. County 270, N.Y. City 682-I.

"The spirit of this rule is to be observed rather than the letter, and where counsel is aware that confidence has been reposed in him by someone not his client, but who has been assisting his client with information, he should not afterwards act against that person in any matter in which such information would be material." Annual Statement of Council of the Bar of England as to Retainer Rule XXI, *The Annual Practice* (1923), p. 2629; Annual Statement of 1896–97, p. 8.

16 N.Y. County 250. See also *infra,* pp. 96 *et seq.*　　　　　　17 N.Y. County 112, 129.

18 Matter of O'Neil, 228 App. Div. 129, 131 (1930).

19 N.Y. City 360. In this case he really wanted to have the creditor retain him to collect the debt, which the Committee said that he might not do. His asking the question of the Committee would seem to indicate the probability that he somehow would arrange to be employed.

20 N.Y. City 75. If he deposits his client's funds in his personal account, he will be liable for their loss without fault on his part, whereas if they are in a trust account he may not be (see Orrin N. Carter, *Ethics of the Legal Profession* [1915], p. 50).

When he has collected several accounts for a collection agency, he may not withhold the funds of one account to meet any obligation to him for fees on another of them,[21] nor may he make a lump settlement with a defendant against which several of his clients have claims; [22] but he may retain funds collected for the same client on another case.[23]

A lawyer may not hold up the preparation of papers to force the payment of a fee,[24] nor may he refuse to handle a debtor's bankruptcy proceedings except on condition that after the adjudication the bankrupt sign new notes to the creditors whom the lawyer represents.[25]

His fiduciary obligation is especially important where the client is not of strong mentality. While the lawyer may act for such a one whom he honestly believes to be competent,[26] he owes him a special duty not to overreach him.[27] When asked to draw a will for one whom he suspects of possibly being incompetent to execute it, he should make as exhaustive inquiry as possible under the circumstances,[28] and if his suspicion is confirmed, he should decline to do it; [29] nor should he be a subscribing witness to a will when he entertains any doubt as to the capacity of the testator.[30] If he decides to draw the will, he should retain the former will undestroyed, to have available in case of disputed capacity.[31]

He may accept employment to endeavor to persuade a relative to change his will, provided the lawyer's status be disclosed to the prospective testator.[32]

He may not properly put in the will of an old lady for whom he is collecting land contract payments and at whose death he holds for her $10,000 so collected, a provision discharging him from any sum owing by him to her at her death.[33]

He may not deliberately deceive his client, even on her doctor's advice that this is essential to her health.[34]

"It is not justifiable under any circumstances for a lawyer to double-cross a client who employs him." [35]

21 N.Y. City 152, 261; App. A, *261;* and see N.Y. City 205 and B-187.

22 Matter of Glucksman, 230 App. Div. 185 (1930); cf. Matter of Clark, 184 N.Y. 222, 233 (1906). But see Mo. 21.

23 N.Y. County 384. 24 See N.Y. City 494. 25 App. A, *271.*

26 N.Y. City 918; N.Y. City 682-A; and see Samuel Warren, *The Moral, Social and Professional Duties of Attorneys* (1870 Amer. ed.), pp. 257–59.

27 N.Y. City 918; and see N.Y. County 320, and N.Y. City 343.

28 N.Y. City 682-A. 29 *Ibid.*

30 *Ibid.;* N.Y. County 355; and cf. N.Y. County 156. 31 App. A, *16.*

32 App. A, *19.* 33 Mich. 112. 34 N.Y. County 87.

35 App. A, *12.* In N.Y. City 251 (*a*), however, it was held that a lawyer sued by a client on a loan to him might set up the defense of usury and that another lawyer might

He may not disclose provisions in a will which he has drawn for a living client.[36]

He must advise whether to pursue a tort or compensation remedy in the interest of the client.[37]

He may, with full disclosure, apply to have a clerk or stenographer appointed guardian ad litem for a client.[38]

He may not join a labor union; [39] but he may go into bankruptcy.[40]

He may buy an asset of the estate of which he is executor or attorney at a public auction conducted by a judge.[41]

A question is sometimes raised as to the propriety of a lawyer's inserting in the will a legacy to himself, or a provision appointing him executor or trustee, or one directing his executors to employ him as counsel for the estate. This, of course, depends on the surrounding circumstances. If they are such that the lawyer might reasonably be accused of using undue influence, he will be wise to have the provision inserted in a codicil drawn by another lawyer.[42] Where, however, a testator is entirely competent and the relation has been a long-standing one, and where the suggestion originates with testator,[43] there is no necessity of having another lawyer in the case of a reasonable legacy, or of a provision appointing the draftsman executor,[44] or of a direction that he be retained by the executors.[45] In the case of the latter provision it should be clearly explained to the testator that it will not be binding on the executor, who will be free to choose his own counsel,[46] since a lawyer has no vested interest in representing the estate of one whose will he has drawn.[47] The lawyer may not properly get the executors named, who are also witnesses to the will, to sign a retainer agreement with him.[48]

---

represent him in so doing. This decision, it is believed, is questionable in not giving proper effect to the lawyer's fiduciary professional status. See n. 3 p. 149.

[36] Mich. 53.   [37] Mich. 115; N.Y. City 852.

[38] N.Y. City 957.

[39] A.B.A. Op. 275; App. A, 267; N.Y. City 964; N.Y. County 376; Report of Com. of N.Y. State Bar Association for 1949, pp. 4–7.

[40] N.Y. City 368.   [41] App. A, 268.   [42] See Mich. 112; App. A, 266.

[43] It is wise to have the testator state this to a disinterested witness who can so testify if necessary.

[44] N.Y. City 14.   [45] N.Y. City 68; Mich. 120; see also Mich. 144.

[46] App. A, 263, 264, 265; N.Y. City 766. A testator may reasonably believe that it is to the distinct advantage of his estate to have the benefit of his counsel's intimate knowledge of his affairs. See Mich. 120; App. A, 266.

[47] App. A, 244.

[48] N.Y. City 766. It would seem more appropriate to have the will contain a recommendation to the executors with the testator's reasons therefor, rather than a direction.

He should not advise a client to employ an investment company in which he is interested, without informing him of this.[49]

He should tell a former client the name of a lawyer who writes to him offering to collect a judgment for 50 per cent.[50]

Although under some circumstances it is conceivable that a lawyer might borrow money from a client, the lawyer should never take advantage of the confidence reposed in him to delay payment until the statute of limitations has run, and where he did so he should not hide behind it.[1] He may loan money to a client but not as a regular practice.[2] A lawyer may not retain the funds of one client to force a settlement of the disputed claims of other clients,[3] nor may he advise his client's creditors of a collection made by him, in order that they may attach it;[4] or accept assignment to him of valid claims against a client for whom he has made a collection and deduct them in remitting.[5]

He may not apply on his claim for fees money given him by the client for another purpose,[6] or money earmarked as alimony.[7]

He may not endorse the client's name on checks collected and deposit the fund in a special account from which he pays his fees.[8] He may, however, hold postdated checks, which he has collected, so as to secure his contingent fee.[9]

Where a client introduces a woman to him for legal advice and service, the fiduciary duty to her thus arising requires him, when she tells him of her intention to marry the introducer, to tell her of various sexual offenses on the introducer's part, his introduction waiving any duty of confidence. He should then retire from further employment by her.[10]

Where a lawyer formerly employed by a public body is retained to make an application for relief to it, and in such application he includes an item which he knows it is its policy not to allow but nevertheless it does so, this being only fair, he may not call the body's atten-

49 N.Y. County 213; cf. also N.Y. City 324.   50 N.Y. City 599.

1 App. A, 262.   2 N.Y. City 533; see also B-213, B-215.   3 A.B.A. Op. 125.

4 A.B.A. Op. 163; cf. N.Y. City 279.   5 N.Y. City 364.

6 N.Y. City 786, 815; see also A.B.A. Op. 125, and see N.Y. City 217 and 296; also App. A, 261.

7 N.Y. City 482, 905; as to his right and the proper procedure to make available money collected for the client on a personal debt owed him by the client see N.Y. City 189, 203.

8 N.Y. City 205; and cf. N.Y. City 302, also 328, 331.

9 N.Y. City 272 and see N.Y. City 384.

10 N.Y. County 270. Lawyers for whose opinions I have great respect have questioned this ruling. Nevertheless, it seems to me to be sound.

tion to what he believes may have been an oversight by them. His duty is to his client and he may not give away the client's rights.[11]

While a lawyer's fiduciary position does not preclude him from pleading the statute of limitations in a claim by a client against him,[12] it may prevent the statute from running,[13] and should, of course, be pleaded only to defeat a clearly unjust claim against him.

He may, on the client's request, buy property from him, but should have him represented by independent counsel.[14] If he invests the client's money in buying mortgages from his wife, he must so advise the client.[15]

The fiduciary relation applies to the clerk of the attorney for an assignee for creditors, who may not buy an asset of the estate.[16]

When the lawyer for an administrator receives conflicting instructions from the administrator and the beneficiary, he should consult the court.[17]

REBATES AND COMMISSIONS

Canon 38, entitled "Compensation, Commissions and Rebates" provides that a lawyer "should accept no compensation, commissions, rebates or other advantages from others without the knowledge and consent of his client after full disclosure." [18]

Two different principles are involved in the application of this Canon: first, that a lawyer shall receive no secret remuneration from

[11] N.Y. City 269; see also App. A, *274;* also N.Y. City 445 as to giving away rights.

[12] App. A, *272;* N.Y. City 682-B. Compare, however, N.Y. City 251a as to the right of a lawyer to set up the defense of usury against a loan to him by a client, and the propriety of another lawyer representing him in so doing. See also Hoffman's Resolution No. XII, *infra,* p. 340.

[13] App. A, *262;* and cf. *273.*   [14] N.Y. City 685.

[15] N.Y. City 876.   [16] N.Y. County 116.

[17] N.Y. City 252.

As to the duty to have direct personal relations with clients, see *infra,* pp. 159 *et seq.*

As to the duty to protect third persons who, in the course of handling a case, he has led to rely on him for protection, see *supra,* pp. 92 n. 14 and 95 n. 10, and *infra,* p. 157 nn. 31 and 32.

As to a lawyer on retainer turning over fees earned to his retaining client, see p. 67.

As to the duty of the lawyer for the guardian of an infant, where the guardian acts arbitrarily to apply to the proper court, see N.Y. City 350.

[18] See A.B.A. Op. 196; App. A, *278;* "The vice lies in concealment from the client." N.Y. City 5, 257, 565, 881, B-207; N.Y. County 124; see also Article by E. V. Abbot in 15 Harv. L. Rev. 714 (1902), on the problem of allowances by title companies, etc., to lawyers, and other similar conflicts of interest. "If possible, do not receive any compensation in your client's business, except from your client himself; but if circumstances compel you to break the rule, tell your client what you receive." *Id.* at 724. See also Mich. 126.

Cf. Rules of Professional Conduct of the American Institute of Accountants No. (3).

the other side; second, that he must not, by accepting or bargaining for any compensation from the other side, even if fully disclosed to his client, put himself in a position which will interfere with his wholehearted duty to his client.

Full disclosure to the client solves the first difficulty unless it be that the party might not pay the commission if he thought it would go to the client, which would be solved by disclosure to the payor.[19] In this connection, however, the committees have not always analyzed clearly the effect of the lawyer's turning over, or crediting, a commission to his client, apparently regarding this as splitting a fee with a layman in violation of Canon 34. Such, however, is not the case. Where the situation is such that the lawyer might keep it without its affecting his undivided zeal to serve his client, the fact that he gets it should unquestionably affect the size of his fee.[20] Also, whatever he receives from others in the service of his client properly belongs to the client, to be payable to the client or credited against the lawyer's retainer or fee,[21] whether he is employed only for the particular service, on an annual retainer, or on a full-time salary.

There are many situations in which customary allowances, such as those by title companies, will obviously in no way interfere with the lawyer's loyalty to his client. It is cases such as these to which the concluding phrase of the Canon refers. Obviously, however, there are other cases, such as a fee from a would-be customer of a factor-client, to get him accepted as such by the factor,[22] where the client's knowledge and consent would not fully preserve the lawyer's loyalty.[23]

A lawyer may not demand or receive compensation from a mortgagor for inducing his client to grant an extension.[24]

Even with his client's consent he clearly should not accept a gift from the opposite party in appreciation of "kindness, gentleness and indulgence" after the close of the litigation,[25] this being too obviously

[19] See N.Y. County 194, N.Y. City 176; also N.Y. County 282; also *infra*, p. 98.

[20] App. A, *278*.

[21] N.Y. City 341; but see App. A, *359*; see *supra*, p. 67; also *infra*, pp. 179, 181–85.

[22] N.Y. City 602; see also App. A, *277*; N.Y. County 112; but see N.Y. City 19, the soundness of which might be questionable on this score.

[23] "Attorneys . . . should not voluntarily put themselves into positions where the conditions of their compensation may interfere with the full discharge of their duty to their clients." N.Y. County 166. Cf. N.Y. City B-217.

[24] The legal journal should not publish advertisements offering to pay finders' fees to lawyers; Cleveland B; N.Y. County 112 and cf. N.Y. City 19, N.Y. County 416.

[25] N.Y. County 317; N.Y. City 429; see also App. A, *277*; N.Y. County 101; but see N.Y. City 19.

capable of misconstruction. He may not suggest to the client an extra
fee in cases assigned to him by the court,[26] or in the absence of such
a suggestion, accept such fee except on order by the court.[27] He may,
however, with the client's knowledge of the amount of a fee allowed
by the court in a divorce action, accept a reasonable additional sum
from the client.[28]

One who has received by court order one-third of a personal injury
collection for an infant, paid into court, may, subject to disclosure
to the court, receive an additional fee from the fund for services in
getting it paid to the mother for the infant's support; [29] and, where
disclosed to the court, may accept an additional sum from the infant's
parent.[30]

An agreement, not known to the court, for a division of fees allowed counsel for the trustee in bankruptcy with counsel for the
creditors is contrary to public policy and to professional ethics and
void.[31]

A lawyer who represents a corporation buying real estate and who,
because a stockholder, charges it no fee, may properly at the corporation's request turn over to it a commission of 25 per cent of the fee
of a title company,[32] but must advise the title company if he believes
it might not, under the circumstances, be willing to make the allowance.[33] It is a breach of the good faith owed by lawyers to one another for one on a salary not to tell his forwardee that his split will
be turned over to his client.[34]

Where a lawyer was under general retainer from an association and
received from an attorney, to whom he forwarded a claim on its behalf, one-third of the fee charged by the correspondent, the New
York City Committee held that he should return this and not either
keep it or turn it over to the client.[35] The soundness of this conclusion
would appear questionable. The correspondent probably made his

---

[26] N.Y. County 338; App. A, 276.   [27] N.Y. County 338; see also N.Y. City 6.
[28] N.Y. City 27; see also Mich. 84, 123.   [29] N.Y. City 450.
[30] N.Y. City 301.

[31] Weil v. Neary, 278 U.S. 160 (1928). See also A.B.A. Op. 94 and *infra*, p. 112.

[32] N.Y. County 194. See also App. A, *278* and N.Y. County 111, 112, 124, 138, 166, 282;
see also 317. In No. 111 the committee said that even though the client consented, the
acceptance of part of an auctioneer's fees was "beneath the proper professional dignity."
See also Chicago Bar Association Resolution of 6/29/1910 quoted by Costigan, Case
Book, p. 666 n. 30.

[33] N.Y. County 194; N.Y. City 176; see also N.Y. County 282.

[34] Chicago (Costigan's Case Book, p. 631). See, however, notes 35 and 36.

[35] N.Y. City 95; N.Y. City 341 seems *contra;* see also App. A, *359;* and N.Y. City 660,
also *infra,* pp. 179, 181; and see Mo. 51.

charge sufficient to provide for the remittance.[36] The client should have the benefit of it, or, if it chooses, let its counsel keep it.

Payment of the libellant's expenses and counsel fees by the respondent, with the knowledge of all concerned, is not unusual.[37]

ACQUIRING AN INTEREST IN LITIGATION

Canon 10, entitled "Acquiring Interest in Litigation" provides: "The lawyer should not purchase any interest in the subject matter of the litigation which he is conducting." [38]

This Canon must be read in connection with Canon 28 forbidding the stirring up of litigation, as part of the age-long policy which gave rise to the statutes against champerty, maintenance, and barratry. Its purpose is to prevent lawyers from the temptation to litigate on their own account. Significantly the Canon uses the word "purchase," not "acquire." Every lawyer is intensely interested in the successful outcome of his case, not only as affecting his reputation, but also his compensation. Canon 13 specifically permits the lawyer to contract for a contingent fee which, of itself, negatives the thought that the Canons preclude the lawyer's having a stake in his litigation. As pointed out by Professor Cheatham on page 170 n. of his Case Book, there is an inescapable conflict of interest between lawyer and client in the matter of fees. Nor, despite some statements to the contrary in Committee opinions,[39] is it believed that, particularly in view of Canon 13, Canon 10 precludes in every case an arrangement to make the lawyer's fee payable only out of the results of the litigation. The distinction is between buying an interest in the litigation as a speculation, which Canon 10 condemns, and agreeing, in a case which the lawyer undertakes primarily in his professional capacity, to accept his compensation contingent on the outcome. See Hoffman's Resolution XXIV, *infra,* page 343.

Canon 10 should not apply to cases where a lawyer acquires a chose

---

[36] See App. A, 278.   [37] See *infra*, pp. 129–30.

[38] See also *supra* ("Duty Not to Stir Up Litigation"), pp. 63 *et seq.;* and see 37 Ann. Cas. 953 n. (1915). But see N.Y. City 316. See Hoffman's Resolution XXIV, *infra,* p. 343.
The London Ordinance of 1280 contained a provision forbidding a serjeant to be a partner in a case; Cohen, *History of the English Bar,* p. 234.

[39] See Mich. 72, where it was held improper, under the Michigan statute, for counsel for the libellant in a divorce case to agree to accept as part of his fee a percentage of the property settlement obtained.
See also Chicago 24, and N.Y. City 916, but query as to the soundness of these two decisions.

in action not in his professional capacity [40] but merely as an investment,[41] even though the realization on or protection of it may involve
litigation,[42] where the litigation is merely a possible incident of the
purchase and not its primary reason.[43] Nor should it apply to cases
where after the completion of litigation the lawyer accepts on account
of his fee, an interest in the assets realized by the litigation.[44] There is
a clear distinction between such cases and one in which the lawyer
speculates on the outcome of the matter in which he is employed.[45]

Although a lawyer may not acquire an interest in a client corporation which buys choses in action at a discount, he may represent such
corporation.[46]

A lawyer may not properly buy judgment notes or other choses in
action for less than their face value, with the intent of collecting
them at a profit to himself,[47] nor may he enter into an arrangement
with a layman who is in the business of buying up legacies and interests in estates under which the lawyer is to investigate and collect the
interests, receiving a share thereof as his compensation,[48] or buy an
interest in a claim which he represents.[49] A lawyer may, however, accept an interest in a patent as a fee for securing it.[1]

Where, at the request of his client, a lawyer took an assignment of
a judgment entered against his client, on payment of about 2 per cent
of the face thereof with his own funds, when later the client refused
to reimburse him or to pay him fees admittedly due him, the Chicago
Committee held that under Canon 10, the lawyer might not issue
execution and collect the judgment in order to realize the fees owing
to him.[2]

Here, again, there is a distinction between buying valid claims at
a discount and speculating on the outcome of a law suit.[3]

And see Re Est. of Sylvester, 195 Iowa 1329 (1923), and Welles v. Brown, 226 Mich.
657 (1924).

[40] Ohio 2. The Ohio Committee did not accept A.B.A. Op. 51 fully.

[41] Mich. 91.   [42] Mich. 65.   [43] *Ibid.*

[44] App. A, *280;* and see N.Y. City 714.   [45] A.B.A. Op. 279.

[46] N.Y. City 757; see also N.Y. County 324.

[47] A.B.A. Op. 51; N.Y. County 160; and see Mich. 65. The Ohio Committee does not,
however, agree with this decision where the lawyer had no professional connection with
the transactions; Ohio No. 2.

[48] A.B.A. Op. 176.

[49] See Matter of Flannery, 150 App. Div. 369, 388 (1912) (Costigan's Case Book, p.
281 n. 28).

[1] App. A, *280;* and see N.Y. City 714.

[2] Chicago 24. Query as to the soundness of this decision.

[3] N.Y. City 483; Mich. 91.

A lawyer may not buy stock in a corporation, party to a litigation, or advise others to do so; [4] nor may he contract to accept stock in the corporation to be organized, in consideration of his services in organizing a corporation to acquire a radio station and resist the application of another corporation to a license from the Federal Communications Commission.[5]

The New York City Committee has held that a New York lawyer may not properly accept from the executors of a New Jersey decedent a contingent interest in suits pending and contemplated in New York in which he is attorney, in settlement of his admitted claim for fees to the estate.[6] It has also held, however, that one might accept assignments in a similar case, where the assigned choses in action were the estate's only remaining asset and the lawyer's claim for services, which were clearly worth more than could be thus realized, constituted the only remaining claim against the estate, and where also the estate refused to present the claims for its own benefit.[7]

The American Bar Association Committee has also held that, in order to secure his fees, a lawyer may properly take title to property for which he is litigating, if this be subject to the rights of the adverse party as finally determined by the court, but may not properly convey his title to one who does not know of the condition on which he holds it.[8]

DUTY TO SETTLE CASES WHERE TO THE CLIENT'S ADVANTAGE

The last sentence of Canon 8 provides: "Whenever the controversy will admit of fair adjustment, the client should be advised to avoid or to end the litigation." [9]

For a lawyer whose mind is eagerly fixed on his compensation there very often occur situations where this tends to cloud his judgment as

---

[4] A.B.A. Op. 246.

[5] A.B.A. Op. 279. Here the lawyer was virtually made a quasi-partner in the enterprise.

[6] N.Y. City 916; but query. [7] N.Y. City 933. [8] A.B.A. Op. 29.

[9] The Good Advocate (Thomas Fuller, *The Holy State and the Profane State* [1841 ed.], Book ii, chap. 1, p. 50): "VI. He joys not to be retained in such a suit where all the right in question is but a drop, blown up with malice to be a bubble. Wherefore on such trivial matters, he pursuades his client to sound a retreat or make a composition."

"Can you not understand that though I am sure, I am not quite sure; that though the case is a bad one, it may not be quite bad enough to be thrown up? It is just the case in which a compromise is expedient. If but a quarter, or but one-eighth of the probability be with you, take your proportion of the thing at stake. But here is a compromise that gives all to each." A. Trollope, *Lady Anna* (1st ed.), Vol. I, chap. IX, p. 113.

to what is best for the client. Unless a principle is involved which it is essential that the client maintain, a settlement on a reasonable basis, on a fair estimate of the relative chances of the parties, is always better for the client than litigation, involving time, expense, and ill feeling,[10] though often considerably less fees to the lawyers. Nevertheless, the lawyer will be better off in the long run in giving sound advice and good service to his client.[11]

A clause in a retainer agreement prohibiting the client from settling without the attorney's consent is void as against public policy; [12] as is an agreement with the client that no part of the retainer shall be refunded in the event of a reconciliation between the parties.[13]

DUTY TO GIVE CANDID ADVICE

The first two sentences of Canon 8, preceding that quoted in the preceding section, are as follows:

A lawyer should endeavor to obtain full knowledge of his client's cause before advising thereon, and he is bound to give a candid opinion of the merits and probable result of pending or contemplated litigation. The miscarriages to which justice is subject, by reason of surprises and disappointments in evidence and witnesses, and through mistakes of juries and errors of Courts, even though only occasional, admonish lawyers to beware of bold and confident assurances to clients. . . .

While a lawyer must be most careful not to be oversanguine in his expressed belief as to the chance of success, he is bound to form and

---

[10] Advice by Judge Noah Davis, retired, to a young lawyer: "Young man, I have only one word of advice to give you: Settle every case that you can; but if you fight, fight like hell!" Henry Wynans Jessup, *The Professional Ideals of the Lawyer* (1925), p. 60.

In the report of Jan. 23, 1948, of the Committee on Professional Ethics of the New York State Bar Association, Chairman Wherry said (p. 9): "The function of the lawyer in our changing society is constantly developing. Today, he is called upon less often for dramatic forensic exploits than for wise counsel in every phase of life."

[11] Hoffman's practice in negotiation or compromise, as indicated by his Resolution XXXII (*infra*, p. 345), was apparently, after careful study, discussion and consideration, to determine what, under all the circumstances, was fair and feasible for his client, communicate his views frankly to counsel for the other side, and stick to it. Such a procedure, after it has had time to be recognized generally by the bar, is a great saver of time, and is believed effective, the negotiator always, of course, reserving the right to alter his views on being shown new circumstances which he had not considered. Although overshrewdness and lack of candor sometimes result in a better settlement in the individual case, a reputation for this is a great handicap in a negotiation.

[12] See In re Snyder, 190 N.Y. 66 (1907). An agreement guarantying the lawyer a stated amount in case the client does so settle is, however, apparently valid. Ward v. Orsini, 243 N.Y. 123 (1926).

[13] Chicago 28.

tell his client his real opinion as to everything the client should know,[14] and to advise him to do what he honestly believes to be in his best interest.[15]

A lawyer should not, on the advice of a physician that this is necessary to the mental health of his incompetent client, who is in an asylum, advise the incompetent that he is attempting to secure his release, when this is not so.[16] He is bound to tell the client all facts which the latter should know.[17]

He must advise a draftee who consults him that he can get free advice through the Draft Board.[18]

Duty Not to Represent Conflicting Interests

The first paragraph of Canon 6 provides:

It is the duty of a lawyer at the time of retainer to disclose to the client all the circumstances of his relations to the parties, and any interest in or connection with the controversy, which might influence the client in the selection of counsel.[19]

The injunction against being on both sides of a case goes back to the earliest times, being contained in the London Ordinance of 1280.[20]

The second and third paragraphs of Canon 6, entitled "Adverse Influences and Conflicting Interests," [21] following that just quoted, provide:

It is unprofessional to represent conflicting interests, except by express consent of all concerned given after a full disclosure of the facts. Within the meaning of this canon, a lawyer represents conflicting interests when, in behalf of one client, it is his duty to contend for that which duty to another client requires him to oppose.

The obligation to represent the client with undivided fidelity and not to divulge his secrets or confidences forbids also the subsequent acceptance

14 "And though clients sometimes have the folly to be better pleased with having their views confirmed by an erroneous opinion, than their wishes or hopes thwarted by a sound one, yet such assentation is dishonest and unprofessional." Hoffman's Resolution XXXI; *infra*, p. 345.

"There are many persons who will go from lawyer to lawyer with a case, until they find one who is willing to express an opinion which tallies with their own." Sharswood, *Professional Ethics*, p. 108.

15 A.B.A. Op. 82.   16 N.Y. County 87.   17 Canon 8, *supra*, p. 102.
18 N.Y. County 371.   19 N.Y. City 662.
20 Cohen, *History of the English Bar*, p. 233.
21 See as to conflicting interests, 23 Ann. Cas. 212 n. (1912) and 51 A.L.R., 1307 n. (1927). Professor Cheatham in his Case Book, p. 170 n., points out that there is an inescapable conflict of interest between the attorney and his client with regard to counsel fees.

of retainers or employment from others in matters adversely affecting any interest of the client with respect to which confidence has been reposed.

Next to advertising and solicitation, the application of this Canon gives rise to the most frequent requests to the Committees for guidance.

Analysis of the Provisions

Canon 6 is as it was originally enacted in 1908.

The last two paragraphs above quoted cover two distinct obligations:

First, not to represent conflicting interests except with the deliberate consent of all concerned.

Second, not to disclose or abuse professional confidence.

The second obligation, covered by the last paragraph of Canon 6, was restated more fully and more broadly by the addition of Canon 37 in 1937 [22] under the heading "Confidences of a Client." However, the reference in Canon 6 to the obligation "not to divulge" the client's "secrets or confidences" has created the impression, reflected in some of the Committee decisions hereafter discussed,[23] that the test of "conflicting interests" is whether the representation will involve the disclosure of a confidential communication. Such, however, is not the sole test. Although the disclosure of such confidences is one of the probable consequences of representing adverse interests and a potent reason for its prohibition, the first of the two paragraphs above quoted from Canon 6 covers not only cases in which confidences have been bestowed, but also those in which the lawyer assumes to represent parties having adverse interests with neither of whom he has had any previous dealings, much less confidential discussions.

In observing the admonition of Canon 6 to avoid the representation of conflicting interests, the lawyer must have in mind not only the avoidance of a relation which will obviously and presently involve the duty to contend for one client what his duty to the other presently requires him to oppose, but also the probability or possibility that such a situation will develop.[24] In such cases, as will later be pointed out,[25] even though the clients both consent to the assumption

---

[22] *Infra,* pp. 131 *et seq.*   [23] *Infra,* p. 109.

[24] The Securities and Exchange Commission has carried this idea very far in Reorganization proceedings. See W. O. Douglas "The Lawyer and Reorganizations," address quoted by Cheatham, Case Book, pp. 188–93.

[25] *Infra,* p. 120.

of the relation, the lawyer may eventually regret that he did not initially refuse to take the case. Also, even where all parties agree, the appearance of a lawyer on both sides of the same controversy,[26] particularly in cases of some notoriety, will often give an impression to the public which is most unfortunate for the reputation of the bar, and which of itself should be decisive.[27] The temptation to get into an interesting, important, or profitable case is always alluring, and the lawyer is very prone to rationalize himself into the belief that he will be able to steer safely between Scylla and Charybdis, when sober reflection or a discussion with his partners would bid him pause. Where there is any serious doubt, it should be resolved by declining the second retainer.[28] He should avoid not only situations where a conflict of interest is actually presented, but also those in which a conflict is likely to develop.[29]

"When a client employs an attorney, he has a right to presume, if the latter be silent on the point, that he has no engagements, which interfere, in any degree, with his exclusive devotion to the cause confided to him; that he has no interest, which may betray his judgment or endanger his fidelity." [30]

"The test of inconsistency is not whether the attorney has ever appeared for the party against whom he now proposes to appear, but it is whether his accepting the new retainer will require him, in forwarding the interests of his new client, to do anything which will injuriously affect his former client in any matter in which he formerly represented him, and also whether he will be called upon, in his new relation, to use against his former client any knowledge or information acquired through their former connection." [31]

The requirement of undivided fidelity by a lawyer to his client pre-

---

[26] N.Y. County 350.

[27] A lawyer should not put himself in the position where "in the public view" he will appear to be "endeavoring to take advantage of wrongs which he had previously condoned as an attorney." N.Y City 777.

[28] See N.Y. City 308, 716; N.Y. County 143.

[29] See N.Y. City 769. A lawyer who represents a mother in a negligence suit against an insured son for auto injuries should not also represent another guest where the mother is the owner of the auto and so a proper defendant as against such guest; nor should he represent the mother in a suit until all possibilities of amicable settlement are exhausted: A.B.A. Op. 99; such cases are apt to be tainted with collusion. See N.Y. City 116, 725, 809, 867; N.Y. County 279, 329. See also *infra*, pp. 114 *et seq.*

As to a lawyer acting in a case in which he will probably be an important witness, see *infra*, p. 158.

[30] Story, J., in Williams v. Reed, 3 Mason 405, 418 (1824).

[31] Morrow, J., in Re Boone 83 F. 944, 952-53 (1897).

cludes him from belonging to a labor union of his employer's employees which includes persons other than lawyers,[32] dividing his allegiance with persons other than his client.

General Scope of the Provision

"Attorneys . . . should not voluntarily put themselves into positions where the conditions of their compensation may interfere with the full discharge of their duty to their clients." [33]

"The spirit of this rule is to be observed rather than the letter, and where counsel is aware that confidence has been reposed in him by someone not his client, but who has been assisting his client with information, he should not afterwards act against that person in any matter in which such information would be material. An. St. 1896–1897 p. 8." [34]

The duty not to represent conflicting interests or to betray the confidences of a former client is not abrogated by a release signed by the former client.[35]

The injunction not to represent conflicting interests applies equally to law partners representing different clients who have interests conflicting with one another; [36] also to lawyers, not partners, having offices together; [37] and to one formerly a clerk; [38] also to a lawyer who had had an informal discussion with the lawyer for the other side during a trial, when asked to take part in an appeal.[39]

[32] A.B.A. Op. 275; App. A, *267*; N.Y. City 964; N.Y. County 376. The tradition of the unions is that the employee shall be paid according to his needs, contrary to the principle on which the lawyer's compensation should properly be based. Report of Committee on Professional Ethics for the N.Y. State Bar Association for 1949, p. 7.
The vice in these cases was the presence in the union of persons not lawyers, although they were co-employees of the same employer. A fortiori would it be improper if the union included outsiders and were under the influence of alien interests. If the organization included only lawyers it would be a sort of bar association and would not be improper unless it adopted regulations such as minimum fee schedules interfering with the individual lawyer's duty to deal directly with his client.

[33] N.Y. County 166; see also 111, 124, and 194; also A.B.A. Op. 132 and N.Y. County 419.

[34] Statement of the General Council of the Bar as to Retainer Rule XXI, *The Annual Practice* (1923), p. 2629.

[35] See In re Boone, 83 F. 944, 952, 957 (1897).

[36] A.B.A. Ops. 16, 33, 49, 50, 72, 103, 142, 185, 192, 220, 271; Mich. 122; Va. 15; N.Y. City 259. Where a junior partner, without knowing that his senior partner has been retained by the other side, begins suit against the senior's client, both should retire; N.Y. County 33.

[37] A.B.A. Op. 104; App. A, *284*; Mich. 100; see also N.Y. City 386 (the lawyer must be above suspicion). In N.Y. City 105 that Committee said: "When attorneys occupy offices together, they have a mutual relation of trust and confidence and should aid rather than rival each other." Cf. N.Y. City B-205.

[38] N.Y. City 2; N.Y. County 116.   [39] A.B.A. Op. 83; cf. N.Y. City 291.

A lawyer may not employ in a case one who is under a duty of loyalty to the other side.[40]

Canon 6 applies to the admiralty bar, despite its few members.[41]

In a case arising in New York, Judge Lacombe, when a circuit judge, held that he would not enjoin a lawyer from accepting employment which might involve a conflicting interest or the disclosure of confidential communications by a former client, it being presumed that the lawyer would act properly.[42]

One representing a creditor cannot properly accept a retainer from the debtor on condition that his client creditor be paid in full.[43]

The fact that the wife, whom he represented in a separate proceeding, has retained another lawyer does not justify a lawyer in representing the husband in a new separation proceeding [44] irrespective of the fact that no confidential communication had been made to him by her.[45]

A lawyer who was a student in a lawyer's office may not accept a retainer against his former employer involving matters of which he might have obtained knowledge while in such employment, and by reason thereof; [46] nor may one formerly employed by another lawyer accept employment to represent a client of that lawyer whom he had then served, in proceedings to require his former employer to account, particularly when his proposed employment was because of such experience.[47]

Committee Decisions Limiting the Application of the Canon

Where there is no real conflict of interest,[1] the Canon does not apply, as where the two matters are wholly unrelated to one another; [2]

---

[40] Murray v. Lizotte, 31 R.I. 509 (1910).　　　　[41] N.Y. County 20.

[42] Lalance et al. v. Haberman Co., 93 F. 197 (1899); but cf. Brown v. Miller, 286 F. 994 (C.C.A.D.C., 1923).

[43] N.Y. County 123; and cf. App. A, *10*.　　　　[44] N.Y. City 188.

[45] N.Y. City 188-A.　　　　[46] N.Y. County 11.

[47] N.Y. City 488; but cf. N.Y. City 548, apparently based on the fact that there appeared to have been no confidential communications. See *infra*, p. 109.

[1] See A.B.A. Op. 55 holding that the partner of a prosecutor in a rural community might properly defend an indigent prisoner; and see N.Y. City 119, 435, 499, 515, and 783; N.Y. County 63, 99.

A director of a corporation may be its lawyer: N.Y. City 828.

[2] See A.B.A. Ops. 72, 262; N.Y. City 79, 414, 446, 716, 732, 760, 763, 915, B-32, B-178; Mich. 7; N.Y. County 63, 240; but see N.Y. City 80, 466, 838.

See also Warvelle, *Legal Ethics* (2d ed.), p. 178 n., for a case where a lawyer who had urged the pardon of a criminal refused it after becoming governor, on further application by others. Cf. A.B.A. Op. 161. Cf. Mo. 75 (may represent juror).

ui where the lawyer is really helping his client.[3] But the fact that the
conflict is rather remote is not necessarily decisive.[4] Thus, the New
York County Committee has held that one who represented an insurance company in commercial matters might not subsequently represent a claimant against it in a negligence case; [5] while the Michigan
Committee has held that one may sue a former client, with whom all
relations had ceased, on a case involving new subject matter.[6] In such
cases it is always a question of honest judgment, in forming which the
first client's wishes should, of course, be given great weight.[7]

The New York County Committee has also held that the fact that
a lawyer represents the administrator of a decedent's estate does not
preclude him from representing one of the next of kin in a divorce
action involving attachment of respondent's interest in the estate to
pay alimony.[8] It also held, however, that a lawyer who is counsel for a
legatee under a will, and has offered the will for probate on behalf of a
child who announced her intention to contest it, may not thereafter
assist her in so doing.[9]

The fact that a lawyer has sent a case to a lawyer in another state
to represent plaintiff, which case is still pending, does not of itself
make it improper to accept from the lawyer for defendant in such case
a wholly unrelated case for another client; [10] nor is a lawyer precluded
from becoming a colleague, in other distinct matters, with one against
whom he has a case pending.[11]

A lawyer employed by a law firm may, with full disclosure to it,
properly accept employment from a lawyer for the other side in a
case conducted by him, to handle matters having no relation to the
first case; [12] and where he is assisting his lawyer-employer in a trial
he may take a position with the opposing lawyer at a higher salary
if he takes no further part in the case being tried.[13]

A lawyer may represent different interests in matters concerning
a former client where his new employment is obviously in support
of his former client's interest. Thus, one who was the lawyer for a

---

[3] Cleveland, 25 Ohio Law Reporter 569, but cf. N.Y. County 143.
[4] N.Y. City 117.   [5] N.Y. County 279; cf. N.Y. City 291.
[6] Mich. 7.
[7] N.Y. City 575; held here that one who had represented the wife in a separation
case might not, against her protest, represent her husband seeking a divorce from her
ten years later.
[8] N.Y. County 63.   [9] N.Y. County 35.   [10] N.Y. City 409.
[11] The N.Y. City Committee, however, apparently took a different view in City 662,
as to one who was merely an employee of a law firm; see, however, N.Y. City B-197.
[12] N.Y. City 662.   [13] N.Y. City 430; but see N.Y. City 662.

decedent may represent his widow in a suit against those trying to loot the estate.[14]

Disclosure of Confidential Communications Not the Sole Test

As was stated on page 104, there has been some confusion of thought in the Committee decisions as to the basis of the proscription of "conflicting interests," due possibly to the reference in the last paragraph of Canon 6 to "secrets or confidences." Thus, the New York City Committee in several decisions apparently considered it proper for a lawyer to take a case against a former client from whom the lawyer had received no information pertinent to the subsequent employment against him.[15] In another case,[16] the same Committee said that a lawyer who had negotiated an employment contract on behalf of a client with a corporation might not, after his client had got other counsel, bring a suit on behalf of the corporation to impair the value of the contract which he had drawn. The Committee held that this was so "because it might involve the use by you of information confidentially obtained during your employment by your former client." While this was, of course, a sufficient reason for the decision, a broader ground was that the lawyer might not, without consent, represent the other party to a contract which he had drawn for a former client. A more convincing analysis is that given by the New York County Committee in the passage from its Opinion 202 [17] quoted *infra,* on page 115.

Cases in Which the Lawyer's Individual Interest Conflicts with That of His Client

While there is no legal or ethical restriction to a lawyer's having a large financial interest in a corporation which he represents, there is much to be said against the wisdom of this. A lawyer should be able

14 N.Y. City B-167.

15 N.Y. City 944; and see B-32. In Opinion 944 the Committee said: "It is not professionally improper for an attorney to undertake a claim against a person or corporation who or which has formerly been his client provided that no use is made of any information confidential or otherwise which the attorney acquired in the course of his employment."

16 N.Y. City B-63.

17 See also N.Y. County 401 and cf. N.Y. County 240; however, the same confusion is found in N.Y. City 87, 383, 446, 548, 675, B-26 (where, however, consent was given), B-138, and B-172; also in N.Y. County 327, where the test of confidential communications was apparently applied; see also N.Y. City 414, 466, 515, 580; but see B-136, where, despite the fact that the other client acquiesced and there were apparently no confidences, the possibility that other matters might develop was said to be sufficient to require him to decline.

to advise and act for his client without any thought as to his individual interest, nor should he subject himself to the temptation of using for his own advantage information obtained in his professional capacity,[18] or having it said or suspected that he did. There is also a grave question as to the wisdom of representing a member of one's immediate family or an intimate friend in matters vitally affecting them. It is usually wiser to have an outside attorney and consult with him.[19]

The regular lawyer for a trust company may not accept employment by it to draw wills, without charge to the testators, in which he is expected or required to see to it that the trust company will be named as fiduciary and for whom he is assured that he will be counsel.[20] A lawyer is always in a delicate position in accepting a retainer to draw wills or trust agreements where recommended by a trust company which would like to be named trustee therein, even though supposedly on the merits only.[21] He will be too disposed to favor the trust company by naming it as trustee.[22]

The New York County Committee has held that a lawyer who is being sued personally by a husband may accept a retainer in a divorce action by his wife unless "his prejudices prevent him from giving the wife unbiased counsel," and he should not accept it if he knows that she has retained him because the lawyer is "out to ruin her husband." [23]

A group of lawyers may not agree to draw free wills making a bequest to their church. Their desire to help the church might prevent them from giving unbiased advice to the testators.[24]

The American Bar Association Committee in an early decision held that the salaried officer of a trust company might not represent it as a fiduciary and be paid counsel fees which he turns over to it.[25] The

---

[18] See Walsh, *The Advocate* (2d ed., 1926), pp. 34–36; see also N.Y. County 44, 157, and 196; and Mich. 47.

[19] See N.Y. City 769.

[20] A.B.A. Op. 122; App. A, *290;* and see as to New York, address by J. H. Cohen, 7 Ind. Law Jour. 295, 306–08 (1931); and see N.Y. City 237.

[21] See *infra*, p. 160.

[22] N.Y. City 237; see also App. A, *290;* also Hicks and Katz, 41 Yale L. Jour. 69, 83 (1931). Declaration of Principles of May 11, 1931, by City and County Associations, N.Y. Law Jour. (May 12, 1931); Year Book (1931), pp. 167–68; Cheatham, Case Book, p. 170; Hicks, Case Book, p. 531; and see 65 U.S. L. Rev. 538–55 (1931).

[23] N.Y. County 263.   [24] N.Y. City 608.

[25] A.B.A. Op. 10; approved in A.B.A. Op. 60.

The General Council of the Bar in England held in *The Annual Practice* (1933), p. 2616, that "there is no objection to a barrister who is a salaried legal adviser to a company accepting a brief on behalf of the company provided he is instructed in the usual and proper way."

soundness of the reasoning of this decision as an application of Canon 6 may be questioned. The problem is primarily one under Canons 35 and 47.[26] So long as no conflict of interest develops between the company and the beneficiaries, it would seem that the mere fact that the lawyer was a salaried officer, with administrative duties and subject to the company's master and servant direction, should not affect the problem under Canon 6; nor that under his agreement with it, his fees were turned over to it.[27]

The lawyer for county commissioners who is also a large property owner may not advise them as to their legal power to grant a reduction of assessment on the class of property in which he is interested.[28]

A lawyer may not jeopardize his client's substantial rights because the client does not pay his bill, although this may justify the lawyer in withdrawing where the client has time to protect himself.[29]

Taking Cases or Giving Advice against the Interest of His Client or Former Client

A lawyer who is an employee of a corporation should not take employee cases against it; [30] and one who ordinarily represents an insurance company in Workmen's Compensation cases should not take a case against the company brought by a general agent.[31] The lawyer for an insurance company may not advise a prospective insured.[32]

One who was formerly counsel for a corporation may not accept employment from its customers to defend suits brought by its receiver against them.[33] A lawyer may, however, try cases which are being defended by an insurance company which he formerly represented, disclosing to his new client his former relation to the insurance company.[34]

One who has represented an administratrix may not accept employment to bring an action against her in connection with her duties as such; [35] nor may the lawyer for executors represent the wife of one of them in an action for divorce; [36] but a lawyer has been held not to be precluded from representing the executor of an estate because he is

---

26 See *infra*, p. 181.
27 See App. A, *278*. The amount of the fees to be charged by a lawyer always presents an inescapable conflict of interest.
28 N.Y. County 97.
29 N.Y. City 494.
30 App. A, *289*.
31 A.B.A. Op. 112.
32 Chicago 31, p. 70.
33 N.Y. City 412.
34 N.Y. City 508.
35 A.B.A. Op. 167; and see Mich. 75.
36 N.Y. County 232; but see N.Y. City 238 (to me a questionable decision).

named one of three testamentary trustees, and thus might be in a conflicting position.[37]

One who represented a postal employee in a homicide prosecution for negligent driving may not later represent the administrator of the estate of the deceased in a claim against the Government.[38]

It is immaterial whether the lawyer ever rendered a bill to the first client or that the bill was ever paid.[39]

Although a lawyer may not represent both a bankrupt and his creditors,[40] a member of the firm to which a receiver belongs may represent co-receivers; [41] and the lawyer for a debtor may act as assignee or as the attorney for the assignee for the benefit of creditors.[42]

An agreement, not known to the court, for a division of fees allowed counsel for the trustee in bankruptcy with counsel for the creditors is contrary to public policy and to professional ethics and void.[43]

A lawyer who had represented a wife in an assault prosecution against her husband, might not, "a year or so later," represent the husband in an action against the wife for separation, based on an alleged abandonment by the wife in the interim.[44]

In the cases discussed *supra,* page 109, relative to the confusion in the Committee decisions between Canons 6 and 37 there are a number holding that one may sue a former client if his representation is ended and the matter does not involve confidential communications. Some of these it would seem difficult to reconcile.[45]

Diverging Interests of Two Clients

When the interest of clients diverge and become antagonistic, their lawyer must be absolutely impartial between them,[46] which, unless they both or all desire him to represent them both or all, usually means that he may represent none of them.[47]

---

[37] Schield's Estate, 250 S.W.2d 151 (Mo., 1952).

[38] Mich. 111.   [39] N.Y. City 392.

[40] A.B.A. Ops. 40, 103; N.Y. City 614, but see N.Y. County 22, 143, and cf. 153; see also N.Y. City 592, 653.

[41] A.B.A. Op. 271, overruling Op. 181; see also N.Y. County 272, where the divided Committee "reluctantly" approved. See also *infra,* p. 188.

[42] N.Y. City 245.   [43] Weil v. Neary, 278 U.S. 160 (1928). See also *supra,* p. 98.

[44] N.Y. City 466.

[45] For other New York City Committee decisions on conflicting interests see Nos. 493, 647, 744.

[46] N.Y. City 274, 299.

[47] See N. Y. County 151, 410; N.Y. City 122, 159, B-63.

The Alabama Code of 1887 contained in sec. 31 the following provision, which was adopted in Michigan (1897) but not concurred in by the Bar Association of any other

Necessity for Wholehearted Service to the Second Employment

Where a trust company is trustee of an estate with a life tenant and remainderman, a lawyer may not represent it as trustee and also the purchaser of real estate from the estate, in a suit to confirm the contract to purchase, favored by the life tenant and opposed and ultimately set aside by the remaindermen, through their own counsel, because of a clearly inadequate price; nor in such case may he collect fees from the estate.[48]

One representing B against C may not at the same time represent C against D;[49] nor may a lawyer, a friend of both husband and wife, who represents the wife in a divorce action, accept a retainer from the husband on certain business matters and in a negligence case; nor can he make the latter proper by withdrawing as counsel for the wife.[50]

Counsel for Stakeholder May Not Take Sides

The lawyer for a trust company, stakeholder of a fund deposited with it, may not represent a third party claiming the fund against the depositor;[1] nor may the general counsel for a corporation solicit proxies or act as proxy for one of the contesting groups of stockholders.[2]

May Not Attack the Validity or Effect of an Instrument Which He Drew

A lawyer may not accept employment to attack the validity of an instrument which he drew for a client;[3] or accept employment to take a position with regard to an instrument contrary to an opinion which he has given construing it.[4] Where two individuals for whom he drew a contract[5] or a mortgage[6] get into a dispute over it, he may not represent either.

---

state: "Where an attorney has more than one regular client, the oldest client, in the absence of some agreement, should have the preference of retaining the attorney, as against his other clients in litigation between them."

[48] A.B.A. Op. 60.   [49] N.Y. County 292.

[50] N.Y. City 769; but see N.Y. City 347; see also Mich. 70 and 102.

[1] A.B.A. Op. 218.   [2] A.B.A. Op. 86.

[3] A.B.A. Op. 64; but may attack the constitutionality of a statute passed while he was governor, A.B.A. Op. 26. The Michigan Committee, however, held in its Op. 78 that a justice of the peace who performed a marriage might not thereafter represent one of the parties in getting a divorce; see also *infra*, p. 131.

[4] N.Y. County 305; and see also N.Y. County 369.

[5] N.Y. County 151; N.Y. City B-63.   [6] N.Y. City 159.

One who represented a municipality in the preparation and validation of a bond issue may not thereafter attack its validity.[7]

One who drew a will for a decedent may not represent his widow in a suit to set it aside on the ground of insane delusions, even though he believes her case sound.[8]

A lawyer may not endeavor to enforce, for a third party, an instrument which, on behalf of another client he has led the other side to believe, to the latter's detriment, did not exist.[9]

However, the mere fact that, under a prior retainer, he has advocated views of the law and facts different from those on which his present client rests his case will not ipso facto disqualify him. He has a right to change his views.[10]

After representing clients in a patent infringement suit and helping to effect a compromise under the terms of which his clients were granted licenses under the patent, the lawyer may not later represent another client who seeks to attack its validity.[11]

Insurance Cases [12]

Difficult questions arise in cases involving insurance against negligence or title, by reason of the fact that such policies include provisions requiring the insured to give the insurance company full cooperation, to permit its lawyer to conduct the defense of claims, and to assign such claims to the insurance company as subrogee.

Also, when one who is insured injures a relative or friend he is usually quite willing to have the injured party recover from the insurance company, and to have his lawyer or one suggested by him represent such party.[13] It has been said that to permit this, even with the consent of the insured, would encourage and facilitate collusion to mulct the insurance company.[14]

Obviously, the insertion in the policy of a provision requiring the insured to permit the insurance company's lawyer to defend claims insured against, is consent in advance by the insured, obviating improper conflict of interest [15] on the part of the lawyer representing

---

[7] A.B.A. Op. 71.   [8] N.Y. County 156; see also Mich. 125.   [9] N.Y. City 337.

[10] Beck, J., in Smith v. Chicago, etc., Ry., 60 Iowa 515 (1883).

[11] A.B.A. Op. 177.

[12] See Hicks and Katz, 41 Yale L. Jour. 69, 93 (1931). In the cases summarized in this section, there are presented many of the problems discussed under the foregoing subdivisions; also problems involving consent discussed *infra,* p. 120.

[13] See N.Y. City 288, 307, 547, 725.   [14] N.Y. City 809.

[15] A.B.A. Op. 282. Similarly the lawyer designated by a bank may represent a borrower from it in connection with a loan, where the bank insists and the client is fully

the insured in a claim by a third party which gives rise to a claim on the policy, and also representing the insurer in defending such claim by the insured on the policy; [16] but after defending the insured pursuant to the clause in the policy, the same lawyer may not sue the insured for failing to cooperate as required by the policy. Irrespective of actual conflict of interest, maintenance of public confidence requires a lawyer not appear both for and against the same party in the same controversy.[17]

"The rendition of professional services by an attorney to one party to a litigation which thus establishes necessarily a relation of trust and confidence, precludes the acceptance of employment by such attorney in any subsequent phase of the same litigation from the adverse party. A client is encouraged to make full disclosure of all facts to his attorney, and he should be justified in feeling that his attorney will never be found helping the other side of the litigation. The matter is not to be determined by such facts as, that the original services were rendered on the employment of another lawyer, or that the services may have had no particular bearing upon the phase of the litigation contemplated to be conducted in behalf of the new employer, or that it is probable that no information was acquired in the first employment that might prove useful in the subsequent employment. Irrespective of any actual detriment, the first client might naturally feel that he had in some way been wronged when confronted by a final decree obtained by a lawyer employed in his behalf in an earlier part of the same litigation. To maintain public confidence in the Bar it is necessary not only to avoid actual wrong doing but an appearance of wrong doing." [18]

The lawyer for an insurance company which insured both colliding cars, who has investigated the accident and advised that both were negligent, may not take sides between the two owners by defending one against the other,[19] or against the occupants of the other car; [20] or represent the injured person in an action by another against the insured and another insurance company.[21]

---

informed: Mich. 98; query as to whether the bank's regular lawyer may; *ibid.* In N.Y. City 335, the Committee said that for a lawyer to represent both the assured and the insurer constitutes serving two masters contrary to Holy Scripture.

[16] A.B.A. Op. 282; N.Y. County 119. When they fail to cooperate he may withdraw from defending them, with proper notice to protect them. N.Y. County 318.

[17] N.Y. County 350; distinguishing N.Y. County 119; see also N.Y. County 421.

[18] N.Y. County 202; see also N.Y. County 421.

[19] Mich. 102.   [20] Mich. 70.

[21] A.B.A. Op. 247; see also in connection with an insurance company A.B.A. Op. 231.

A lawyer defending an insured (pursuant to the clause in the policy) against civil liability has no authority to represent him in a criminal proceeding growing out of the same accident, unless such authority is expressly given, and should not assume so to represent him.[22]

When a lawyer's regular client, who is insured, negligently injures the lawyer's wife, neither the lawyer nor his associate may properly represent the wife.[23]

The lawyer for the insurance company insuring the owner of a night club against liability to a patron from being injured by another patron, who investigates the shooting of one guest by another, may not thereafter represent the injured guest in a suit against the owner and a second insurance company under a statute imposing liability for injuries inflicted by intoxicated persons as the result of a sale of intoxicating liquors, the first insurance company not having consented to such suit.[24]

Counsel for an insurance company, who represented both the owner and the driver and contended that the driver was not on the owner's business, exonerating the owner and holding the driver liable, may not in subsequent garnishment proceedings to collect from the insurance company, contend that the driver was driving without the owner's consent, a criminal offense, there being no consent by the driver.[25]

However, after the insurance company which the lawyer has represented in settling with the insured car owner has paid the latter, the lawyer may, presumably with the insurance company's consent, represent such owner in an unsolicited suit against the driver who caused the accident, although the lawyer may not, prior to such settlement and complete termination of the controversy between the company and the owner, give any advice to the owner as to his right against the driver.[26]

Where the insurance company is subrogated as to the part of the claim insured against, which it has paid the insured, the latter may assign his whole claim to the insurance company so that the insurance

---

Cf. N.Y. County 279, 350; Mich. 138; as to adverse interests of persons injured in the same accident, see N.Y. City 282, 288.

[22] A.B.A. Op. 231.

[23] N.Y. City 514. There is no discussion in the opinion of consent by the regular client.

[24] A.B.A. Op. 247.   [25] A.B.A. Op. 222.

[26] Mich. 138; see also A.B.A. Op. 282.

company's lawyer may sue the negligent third party, the insured to pay his proper proportion of the counsel fee.[27]

The City Committee held that the lawyer for an insured car owner might, after the owner's and his guest's claims against a third party had been settled by the insurance company, with the owner's consent represent the guest in suing the insured owner; [28] in a case where no such consent appeared the County Committee held that the lawyer might not sue the owner (whom he represented in commercial matters) on behalf of his guest.[29]

The lawyer employed and compensated by an insurance company which carries only collision insurance may defend the insured in a "public liability and property damage" action brought by a third party against the insured, and at the same time act for the insured and the collision insurance company in a joint cross-petition against such third party.[30]

The lawyer for the insurance company may, where no conflict of interest appears, defend a criminal charge against the driver of one of the insured cars, all parties consenting.[31]

One who represented both the owner and his guest in a suit against the third party may not, without the owner's consent, represent the guest in a suit against the owner.[32]

When one who is being sued for negligence by his guest or a friend is insured, the City Committee held that his lawyer could not represent the injured party.[33] Similarly it held that a lawyer insured against injuries to third parties from defects in his property may not recommend a lawyer to one so injured, nor may the recommended lawyer accept,[34] nor may a lawyer accept a retainer when recommended by one insured (not a lawyer) to sue him for injury by such defects.[35] It does not matter, the Committee said, that the recommender is not the real party in interest. One may not recommend a lawyer to sue the recommender.

The lawyer for an insured taxicab company may not accept a retainer from one injured by a taxicab to sue the taxicab company even with the company's consent,[36] and the lawyer for the driver-owner of

[27] N.Y. County 198; A.B.A. Op. 282.   [28] N.Y. City 267.
[29] N.Y. County 279.   [30] A.B.A. Op. 282. Cf. Mich. 150.   [31] N.Y. City 783.
[32] N.Y. City 510; see also N.Y. City B-200; and N.Y. County 421.
[33] N.Y. City 288, 307, 725, 909, B-53, B-65; see also N.Y. City B-146 and B-200.
[34] N.Y. City B-40-(1); cf. N.Y. City 842.   [35] N.Y. City B-40(2).
[36] N.Y. City 288.

a car colliding with a taxicab may not represent a taxicab passenger in
a suit against the taxi driver-owner.[37]

CASES INVOLVING INSURED MINORS

Where an insured infant has been injured, the statutes of some
states provide that the settlement must be submitted to and approved
by a court. In such cases, where the parents or guardian of the infant
have come to a final agreement with the insurance company, a majority of the American Bar Association Committee held that counsel
for the insurance company might (in the interest of saving counsel
fees) prepare the papers and present the matter to the probate court
with full advice to the court as to his relationship to the company
and as to all the facts, the court making the proper inquiry and taking
any necessary steps to protect the infant's interest.[38] The New York
City Committee at first held such procedure proper though it did not
recommend it,[39] apparently following a decision of the Appellate Division.[40] Later, however, when the Wilbur case had been disapproved,[41] the New York County Committee disapproved the practice, insisting that the court have the unbiased recommendation of
a lawyer "solely representing the infant." [42] The City Committee also
followed this ruling.[43]

The proper answer would appear to turn on the amount of trouble
and responsibility which the court was willing to assume. Whatever
practice the court approves, it would seem that the lawyer, with full
disclosure, might properly follow.

Public Prosecutors and Other Public Servants

A county attorney, in charge of prosecuting crimes in his county,
should not, while in office, undertake to obtain a pardon for one convicted of crime in his county, although he had on several occasions
prior to his election appeared as counsel for him before the Pardon
Board.[44]

A public prosecutor in one state may not properly defend a person
accused of crime in another state; [45] to permit this would undermine

37 N.Y. City 282, cf. 510.
38 A.B.A. Op. 235; cf. A.B.A. Op. 102.   39 N.Y. City 170.
40 Matter of Wilbur, 228 App. Div. 197 (N.Y., 1930).
41 Matter of Paders, 250 App. Div. 418 (N.Y., 1937).
42 N.Y. County 342; see also its prior similar ruling in 183; also N.Y. County 421.
43 N.Y. City 349, 582, 617.   44 A.B.A. Op. 136; and cf. A.B.A. Op. 129; Mo. 60.
45 A.B.A. Op. 30; and see A.B.A. Ops. 39, 110, 118, 142, 242, 261; App. A, 292; Ky. 10.

confidence in him and his office.[46] A state prosecutor may, however, take cases before Federal Administrative bodies [47] and a United States attorney those on the civil side of the Federal courts,[48] or in the state courts.[49] A lawyer's induction into the service does not prevent his arguing a case against the Government,[1] and a member of Congress may try in the Federal court a civil contract case which he had prepared prior to his election to Congress.[2]

A lawyer elected judge may practice in the court to which he is elected, until his installation.[3]

A private prosecutor may not change sides.[4]

A newly elected prosecutor should withdraw his appearance on appeal by one whom he represented below on conviction for murder, though he had agreed to take the appeal.[5] An assistant prosecutor may not represent a fireman in a prosecution for reckless driving; [6] nor may a mayor and council member defend an accused where the police are the prosecutor's or complainant's witness; [7] nor may one prosecuting a defendant for assault represent him in a damage suit for independent injuries.[8] A former prosecutor may not represent, on appeal, a party prosecuted, although he is confined to the printed record; his experience with the case would enable him to piece things together.[9]

The partner of a prosecuting attorney may not defend one accused of crime in another county.[10]

A states attorney or his deputy may not appear as counsel in any divorce case where the facts involve a crime which it might be their duty to prosecute.[11]

A lawyer who is a justice of the peace may not represent one charged with an offense, civil or criminal, in connection with which he has issued a warrant.[12]

A legislator may not accept a retainer from a client interested in particular legislation other than as a member of the public.[13] It is not sufficient that he refrain from voting.[14]

[46] A.B.A. Op. 186. Cf. App. A, 292, 293; and see Cleveland 2, Mo. 59.
[47] A.B.A. Op. 262.   [48] A.B.A. Op. 278; and cf. A.B.A. Ops. 34, 77.
[49] N.Y. County 82.   [1] App. A, 286.   [2] Id. 287.
[3] N.Y. County 402; N.Y. City B-156.   [4] N.Y. City 577; cf. Mo. 33, 38.
[5] Mich. 73; see also Ky. 6. Cf. Mo. 65, 85.   [6] Mich. 109.
[7] Mich. 139; but see Mich. 132; as to a county judge in Kentucky, see Ky. 5(3).
[8] N.Y. City 303; see also Ky. 10, Utah 3.   [9] App. A, 293.
[10] A.B.A. Ops. 16, 192; Texas 23; and see Texas 37; Va. 32; also N.Y. City 259.
[11] 21 So. Dak. Bar Jour. 27 (Apr., 1952).   [12] Mich. 95; Va. 17, 35.
[13] Mich. 83; also Mich. 87; see also supra, pp. 87–88.   [14] Mich. 87.

A circuit court commissioner may advise a client, although he knows that this will prevent his performing the duties of his office in case of a subsequent dispute as to the correctness of his advice.[15]

Effect of Consent

Canon 6 forbids the representation of conflicting interests "except by express consent of all concerned given after a full disclosure of the facts."

The Chicago Association, in view of the fact that in cases involving a public interest, consent should be no justification, amended its Canon 6 to eliminate the phrase quoted. This amendment, it is submitted, was unnecessary and a mistake.[16] The Canon does not sanction representation of conflicting interests in every case where such consent is given, but merely forbids it *except* in such cases. The American Bar Association has acquiesced in the numerous decisions of its Ethics Committee construing the exception as not exclusive, and consent as unavailable where the public interest is involved.[17] There are, also, certain cases in which such representation is improper or at least unwise even with consent.[18] There are, however, not infrequently cases in which it is highly desirable and to the advantage of everyone concerned that the same lawyer should, at the desire of both parties, represent them both.[19] Where it is or becomes apparent that they should

[15] Mich. 82; where he has advised a client he is disqualified from thereafter acting on such matter in his official capacity, *ibid.*

[16] The A.B.A. Committee has repeatedly refused to approve an amendment deleting this clause, App. A, *296*.

[17] A.B.A. Ops. 16, 34, 77, etc.; N.Y. County 97; Mich. 63, 83; see also A.B.A. Op. 71.

[18] App. A, *297*; see N.Y. City 159, 288, 307, 308, 517, 685, 725, 863, 909, B-9, B-53, B-65, B-77, B-191; Mich. 109; see also App. A, *277*; but see N.Y. City 19, 347, also 547, 809, B-136, B-146; N.Y. County 143, 152, 155; and see Chicago 19, pp. 38–41; also N.Y. County 232; as to the acceptance of gifts from the other side in recognition of "kindness etc." see N.Y. County 317 and 421, N.Y. City 429. See also Ala. Code of 1887 sec. 25; 31 A.B.A. Reports 700 (1907); also A.B.A. Op. 132, and N.Y. County 419, Mo. 15.

[19] See A.B.A. Ops. 102, 224; App. A, *285, 298*; and see A.B.A. Ops. 235, 243; N.Y. County 99, 152, 155; N.Y. City 630, 650; and see Mich. 98.

See Hobart's Admr. v. Vail, 80 Vt. 152, 161 (1907); also Eisemann v. Hazard, 218 N.Y. 155, 159 (1916), where the court said that it was not always improper for a lawyer to represent conflicting interests "though the cases in which this can be done are exceptional, and never entirely free from danger of conflicting duties."

It has always been regarded as proper for the lawyer of the payee of a note authorizing any attorney to enter judgment in case of default, to do this even without consulting the maker. Warvelle, *Legal Ethics,* p. 164; A.B.A. Op. 70; and see A.B.A. Ops. 102, 165, and N.Y. County 271; cf. N.Y. County 290; the same applies to the defense of the insured

have independent counsel, the lawyer should so advise them.[20]

In order that mutual consent be effective, full disclosure must, of course, be made and the effect of the dual relationship fully explained to both parties.[21] Also, all parties concerned must consent, a majority not being enough.[22]

If, at the time the duality of representation is suggested, the lawyer has it distinctly understood with both that in the event such a conflict develops he is to represent one of them, this would seem to amount both to a consent in advance by the other under Canon 6 and to a waiver of any privilege under Canon 37.[23] Even so, the lawyer will often be wise not to allow himself to be put in the position of representing conflicting interests or of being subject to the charge of betraying professional confidence.

The New York County Committee has held that the lawyer for a creditor of an insolvent may, with this creditor's consent, represent other bona fide creditors in getting the proceedings set aside on account of fraud and collusion in which his first client was implicated.[24]

Without discussing consent, the New York City Committee held that a lawyer might not collect compensation claims for patients in

---

by the lawyer for the insurance company; N.Y. County 318; but see N.Y. City 349; and to the lawyer for a title company representing the insured as per contract; which amounts per se to a consent in advance, N.Y. County 119.

In Strong v. International B.L. & I. Union, 82 Ill. App. 426, 431 (1898), Judge Sears pointed out the distinction in cases where the lawyer virtually "acts with the consent of both adverse litigants, in the character of an umpire, for the determination of their differences," there being then no inconsistency in such employment. A lawyer who has recovered a judgment may accept a retainer from the judgment debtor to collect from a third party who owes him, and apply the amount collected on the original judgment and his fee, and when the debtor repudiates his agreement, the lawyer may have the third party enjoined from paying the debtor directly. N.Y. City 234; cf. N.Y. City 271.

[20] N.Y. County 90, 155. [21] A.B.A. Ops. 160, 224; N.Y. City 716.

[22] N.Y. City 826.

[23] N.Y. County 243(3). See N.Y. City 435 (a six-to-five decision).

In N.Y. County 389 the Committee apparently regarded it essential that consent be thus given at the time the lawyer assumed the relation which might eventually develop into a conflict. It there said: "a lawyer should not take a case against a party on whose behalf the lawyer previously acted as attorney, where such case involves or arises out of the same matter as the prior litigation, unless such possible conflict was made clear to the former client before he disclosed his case to the attorney, and the client, with full knowledge, agreed that in the event of such a subsequent litigation the attorney would be free to represent the adversary."

See also N.Y. County 397; if the two clients agree not to sue one another, the lawyer's difficulty is at least temporarily solved.

[24] N.Y. County 75.

a hospital, at its request and suggestion, and thus enable it to be paid.[25] The soundness of this decision would seem open to question.

"Collusive" Divorces [26]

From the earliest times the Common Law judges have reiterated the principle,[27] derived apparently from the ecclesiastical law,[28] that the state has an interest in the marital status of its citizens which precludes their being divorced by agreement,[29] and have thrown doubt on the validity of a divorce in the obtaining of which there has been cooperation on their part.[30]

The lawyer's duty to his client requires him to secure for the client the legal redress that the client wants, provided this can be done by proper legal means. His duty to the court requires him not to misrepresent any facts or to mislead the court. Is there an additional duty by the lawyer to the state and to the court, as its instrument, in divorce cases which may conflict with his obligation to his client? [31]

It would seem clear that a lawyer owes no duty to the state in which he practices to refrain from advising a client to go to another state in order to take advantage of laws more favorable to the redress which the client desires.[32] Thus, in its Opinion 12, a majority of the New York County Committee held it not improper for a New York lawyer to advise a client that a New York decree prohibiting marriage with

---

[25] N.Y. City 556. For clear cases involving consent, see also N.Y. City 451, 496, B-26; and see also N.Y. City 621 where consent was not apparently considered.

[26] See H. S. Drinker, "Problems of Professional Ethics in Matrimonial Litigation," 66 Harv. L. Rev. 443–64 (1953).

[27] Mich 85.   [28] Dickson v. Dickson, 9 Tenn. (1 Yerg.) 110, 112 (1826).

[29] Joel P. Bishop, *Marriage, Divorce, and Separation* (1891), Vol. II, chap. xvi, secs. 480, 481, 498; Joseph Story, *Conflict of Laws* (8th ed., 1883), chap. vii, sec. 200, p. 275.

[30] Hall v. Hall, 122 Pa. Super. Ct. 242, 246 (1936).

[31] In England the interest of the state has, since the Statute of 1860, been represented by the King's Proctor, one of whose duties it is, by leave of Court and under the direction of the Attorney General, to prevent "collusion." See Chester G. Vernier, *American Family Laws*, Vol. II (1932), sec. 80, "Proctors." Twenty-one of the states have or have had similar statutory officers who have discharged their varying duties with varying degrees of enthusiasm. *Id.*, p. 95, Table XL; see also Matter of Cahill, 66 N.J.L. 527, 530 (1901); 6 Det. L. Rev. 23, 29 (1935); 36 Col. L. Rev. 1121 (1936). Despite this, and the persistence of the idea that collusion is a bar to a divorce, probably 80 to 90 per cent of divorces are said to be the result of mutual consent. 3 Enc. Soc. Serv. 177, 182 (1937); see also P. W. Alexander, 36 A.B.A. Jour. 105, 168 (1950); Sir Henry Maine, *Ancient Law* (Pollock's ed.; 1906), pp. 28 *et seq*. That "collusion" in the broad sense is no longer recognized as a defense, see N.Y. County 37, 86.

[32] Such laws are also believed advantageous in enabling the parties to escape the humiliation of admitting in a local court the details of marital failure, an experience which many shrink from and which it seems greatly to their interest to avoid; see 2 Law & Contemp. Prob. 293, 298 (1935).

the co-respondent did not preclude her going to Connecticut and there contracting a marriage which would be recognized as valid in New York and not punishable there as a contempt of court. The Committee disapproved, however, the lawyer's having gone there with the client and "giving her away," as "likely to be misunderstood" and tending to "diminish public respect for the profession."

Similarly in its Opinion 100 a majority of the County Committee held it not improper for the lawyer for a deserted New York wife to enter into an agreement with the husband's lawyer that she make a bona fide and actual change of domicile to another state where desertion was a valid ground for divorce, he to go there and accept service and make her a substantial payment in settlement of all claims for future maintenance, with a substantial fee for her lawyer. The majority of the Committee said that it "was unable to agree with the minority that the mere fact that the statutes of New York do not provide for the relief desired in the case suggested is sufficient ground to condemn the arrangement or the participation of a New York lawyer in aid of relief elsewhere according to the law there in force."

In a later Opinion 289, the County Committee said:

Where an action for divorce has been commenced on valid grounds, facilitation of the decree by the party at fault is not in itself improper. Nor is a New York attorney to be criticized for participating in the lawful dissolution in another jurisdiction of the marriage of a New York citizen, merely because the grounds are not sufficient to obtain a divorce in New York.[33]

These decisions were based on the assumption that the Full Faith and Credit Clause would make the decree of the foreign court binding in New York. It does not follow that a lawyer may properly participate in procuring a Mexican mail-order divorce, manifestly invalid in the United States, and which can be used by his client only to misrepresent married status.[34]

MANUFACTURE OF OR CONNIVANCE IN PROCURING GROUND FOR DIVORCE

Clearly a lawyer may not originate or participate in a scheme to make it appear to the court that a ground for divorce has occurred when this is not the fact. Such is the case in the so-called "hotel di-

[33] See also its Opinions 37, 193, and 357. Opinions 214 and 791 of the New York City Committee are to the same effect.
[34] *Infra*, p. 150.

vorces," [35] prevalent in jursidictions where adultery is the only ground for divorce,[36] and based on the principle that intercourse will be presumed from apparently uninhibited opportunity.

Clearly, too, he must have no part in hiring a co-respondent to seduce the defendant in order to create ground for divorce.[37]

A very different situation is presented where defendant, without connivance or cooperation on the part of plaintiff, has actually committed adultery. Here, neither the fact that plaintiff is thoroughly delighted at what has occurred, nor the mutual desire of the parties to be divorced is really relevant to plaintiff's right to secure it, and neither lawyer is under any duty to inform the court of their respective states of mind.

DELIBERATE NEGLECT TO ALLEGE OR PROVE A DEFENSE

A more difficult question arises where the statutory ground for the divorce relied on may be dependent on the non-consent of the plaintiff. Is there a "desertion" where the defendant, although leaving with no intent to return, goes away with the expressed or silent approval and satisfaction of the plaintiff? In a divorce proceeding based on such a "desertion," is defendant or his lawyer bound to tell this to the court, or under any duty to tell of defendant's rebuffed offer to return, the latter, if known, being a bar to the divorce?

After the decision of the New York Appellate Division [38] holding that plaintiff's adultery was by way of defense only, the New York City [39] and County [40] Committees held it proper for a lawyer to accept employment to secure a divorce on the ground of adultery though knowing that his client had also committed adultery. It would seem to follow that the lawyer owes no duty to the state to disclose independent defenses to a divorce action.

[35] In Matter of Gale, 75 N.Y. 526 (1879), respondent was disbarred for such a case.

[36] In New York and until 1937 in England. On pages 1130–31 of an article in 36 Col. L. Rev. 1121 (1936), there are summarized enlightening statistics on "hotel divorces" in New York, collected by Harold R. Jackson, clerk of the Supreme Court, showing clearly that they are fictitious and "collusive." For an interesting decision by an English judge refusing to accept the customary "Mr. & Mrs. A.B.A." receipted hotel bill, with the husband's admission, as sufficient evidence of adultery, see Aylward v. Aylward, 44 T. L. Rep. 456–57 (1927–28). See also In re Cahill, 66 N.J.L. 527, 530 (1901).

[37] Irrespective of consent, the plaintiff in such case comes to court with very unclean hands. See Matter of Bayles, 156 App. Div. 663 (N.Y., 1913).

[38] Thompson v. Thompson, 127 App. Div. 296 (1908) (two of the five judges dissenting).

[39] N.Y. City 726, 951.   [40] N.Y. County 365 (overruling County 106).

AGREEMENT TO MAKE NO DEFENSE, OR TO WITHDRAW A DEFENSE

In an early opinion, Opinion 81, the New York City Committee, although sanctioning an agreement, disclosed to the court, by the parties to a divorce relative to alimony, counsel fees, and custody of children, stated flatly that a lawyer should not countenance an agreement not to defend a matrimonial action. In a later opinion, however, Opinion 314, this Committee modified the above statement, holding that a lawyer who, on behalf of a husband, had filed an answer denying adultery and alleging connivance and procurement, might properly agree with the other side, "in the absence of fraud or collusion," [41] to withdraw the defense or suffer a default in consideration of the wife's waiving all alimony and counsel fees.[42]

In its Opinion B-79 (1948) the New York City Committee held it improper for the lawyer for a wife, against whom her husband had obtained a Florida divorce without service, to agree, for a consideration, to validate the divorce and legitimize his second wife and her children, by opening the Florida proceedings, appearing therein, and permitting a decree. The Committee said that such an arrangement appeared to be "collusive" and "contrary to the public policy of this state."

The New York County Committee, in its Opinion 54, approved an agreement by counsel for the wife, sued for divorce, to bring an action for annulment and accept a fixed sum in lieu of alimony and counsel fees, the husband to discontinue the divorce action, provided the agreement be disclosed to the court in both cases. In its Opinion 192 the same Committee held that the lawyer for a wife who, for adequate cause, had sued for separation, might properly, if satisfied "of his client's good faith and of the absence of collusion," agree with the lawyer for the husband to discontinue the separation suit and sue for divorce on the ground of adultery, which the husband agreed to

[41] The injection of this phrase obviously makes the opinion difficult to evaluate; possibly "fraud or collusion" means "fraudulent collusion"; compare "unlawful collusion" in New York County 193. See n. 12 in 36 Col. L. Rev. 1121 (1936) for the differing and inconsistent definitions of "collusion" in the statutes of twenty-eight states.

[42] Compare Opinion 139 of the City Committee, where the questioning lawyer, representing the husband, stated that the proposed agreement by the husband relative to alimony, etc. reserved to him the right to defend, but that he knew of no defense and his present intention was to default, both parties desiring a divorce. Subject to full disclosure to the court, the Committee did not disapprove. See also the City Committee's No. 173.

confess and furnish adequate evidence. The Committee said, however:

Since the State has an interest in actions for divorce which should be supervised by the Court, the agreement or stipulation should be in writing and should be disclosed to the Court [43] in the divorce action, in order that the Court may be put on notice of all the circumstances and make such inquiry as those circumstances may suggest—concerning, for example, the good faith of the parties, the absence of collusion, the credibility of the witnesses and the weight that should be given to the evidence.

In a later opinion, also, Opinion 230, the same Committee approved an agreement, communicated to the court, by the wife's lawyer with the husband for an uncontested annulment, for adequate cause, the husband to pay all expenses.

Despite these decisions, the New York County Committee, in its Opinion 205, stated flatly that an agreement not to defend a divorce action was against public policy and should not be made or countenanced by a lawyer.

FURNISHING OTHERWISE UNOBTAINABLE EVIDENCE OF ACTUAL FACTS CONSTITUTING A GROUND FOR DIVORCE

A distinction may well be drawn between the prior instigation of or connivance in the acts relied on as a ground for divorce, and the facilitation of proving such acts after they have unquestionably occurred.[44] If the willingness of both parties to secure a divorce absolutely precluded each of them, under the law, from getting it, the participation of a lawyer in facilitating proof might be considered improper. However, despite statements in some opinions [45] to the contrary, it is not believed that the "collusion" doctrine is carried so far; or that this type of cooperation by a lawyer has ever been characterized as unprofessional.[46]

In its Opinion 86, a majority of the New York County Committee held it not improper for the wife's lawyer to accept the husband's

---

[43] See N.Y. County 171.

[44] As to the prior and subsequent "collusion" and the interest of the state in divorce proceedings, see decision No. 85 of the Michigan Committee (1945); advisory Opinion No. 1 to Disbarment Committee of the Supreme Court of Louisiana, 4 Tulane L. Rev. 226 (1929).

[45] See Maimone v. Maimone, 90 N.E.2d 383 (Ohio, 1949), and *infra,* p. 127 nn. 47–49.

[46] If it has, I would not agree. See also Conyers v. Conyers, 311 Ky. 468 (1949); State v. Rodgers, 129 W. Va. 174 (1946); Geis v. Gallus, 130 Ore. 619 (1929); Maroth v. Maroth, 64 N.Y. Supp.2d 260 (1946).

agreement to furnish, in consideration of a satisfactory money settlement, witnesses to flagrant acts by him, the agreement being fully disclosed to the court and the parties being told that the court might not agree.

In Opinion 132, however, the same Committee held improper an agreement by the lawyer for a white wife, by which her Negro husband, for a sum of money, agreed to furnish evidence of admitted adultery, "however desirable the dissolution of the marriage may be." In Opinion 163 also, this Committee refused to sanction an agreement by which, in return for a release of all claims, the husband agreed to furnish evidence of past adultery, not committed with the wife's connivance. A lawyer, said the Committee, should not countenance a bargain to obtain necessary testimony in a divorce suit, this being contrary to public policy.[47]

The propriety of the lawyer's conduct in cases within these last three subdivisions would appear to depend on the nature of the particular case. Where the offense relied on as ground for the divorce is clear, flagrant, and indefensible, the proposed settlement between the parties fair and reasonable, and the stipulated cooperation by the defendant merely to eliminate nuisance value, the disclosure of all the facts to the court affords adequate protection against fraudulent "collusion." [48] Where, however, the situation is such as to indicate the possibility that purchased evidence may be manufactured, the lawyer should resolve the doubt by declining to have a part in the arrangement.[49] While the decisions by the two New York Committees are on their face difficult to reconcile, it is believed that, as a practical matter, they may well have been influenced by the above considerations.

In a case where the husband gave the wife the names of witnesses to his adultery, which antedated her engaging counsel, the Disbarment Committee of the Supreme Court of Louisiana advised counsel that it was proper to use such evidence, saying:

[47] See also N.Y. City B-9 (infra, pp. 128–29); and cf. N.Y. County 165 and 205; also N.Y. City 81. In its Opinion 86, the majority of the County Committee said: "The attorney in a divorce case should regard with disfavor any offer by the adverse party to stipulate to furnish witnesses to the past offense charged, in consideration of stipulations as to alimony, release of dower, etc. (see Train v. Davidson, 20 App. Div. 577)."

[48] See N.Y. County 86 and 192. See also Hill v. Hill, 23 Cal.2d 82 (1943); Brainard v. Brainard, 82 Cal. App.2d 478 (1947); and cf. Oberstein v. Oberstein, 217 Ark. 80 (1950).

[49] See N.Y. County 132 and 163, and cf. N.Y. County 365 (overruling 106) and see N.Y. City 726, 951.

The fact that the act of the husband was committed long prior to the employment of counsel, precludes the idea of collusion on the part of either. What the law reprobates is consent divorces and any collusion between the principals or their attorneys to obtain them. This proceeds from considerations of public policy too obvious to mention. Any offer of assistance from opposing counsel in a divorce case is ordinarily to be regarded with disfavor. If the offer of assistance is conditioned on a consideration such as to limit the wife's right to alimony or to relinquish other valuable property interests, the situation is reduced to one of barter and sale and should not be countenanced. Where, however, the assistance offered has to do with giving names of witnesses to an act committed by the husband, as to which the wife neither condoned nor consented, and is not conditioned on the relinquishment of any of the wife's rights, the Committee thinks the attorneys, if satisfied with the wife's good faith, may proceed to submit the evidence; provided, the agreement so to do be in writing and be expressly made subject to the approval of the Court, and that the Court be fully informed of all the facts and circumstances at or before the trial, and the parties be advised that the Court may decline to confirm it.[50]

DESIGNATING LAWYER FOR THE OTHER SIDE

The American Bar Association, the Michigan Committee, and the two New York Committees have held that the lawyer for one spouse should not recommend a lawyer for the other,[1] or prepare the pleadings or papers or testimony for the other [2] or act for or give legal advice to the other in any respect,[3] and that disclosure to the court, even before the decree, would not make this proper.[4]

In its Opinion B-9, the New York City Committee held that the lawyer suggested by the husband might not properly represent the wife in a divorce suit based on the husband's past adultery, of which he would supply the evidence only on condition that his lawyer represent her, this being agreeable to her. The Committee said that, despite her acquiescence, the condition indicated that the husband expected some degree of allegiance from the lawyer suggested by him, which would render him "unable to represent the wife with the undivided fidelity that is required." [5]

[50] 4 Tulane L. Rev. 226, 228 (1929).
[1] A.B.A. Op. 245; N.Y. County 171, 289; see also N.Y. City 378, 530; but see N.Y. City B-128 and cf. N.Y. City 762 and 821 under the Soldiers' and Sailors' Act. Cf. also N.Y. City B-205.
[2] Mich. 85; and see A.B.A. Op. 58, Mo. 83.
[3] A.B.A. Op. 58; Chicago 19, pp. 38–41; N.Y. City B-9.
[4] N.Y. County 265; but see N.Y. County 128 (guardian), N.Y. County 357, N.Y. City 214.
[5] The Michigan Committee based its similar decision, 123, on the above ground. See also N.Y. City 378 and N.Y. County 171.

Canon 6, on which the City Committee there relied, forbids the representation of "conflicting interests except by express consent of all concerned, given after a full disclosure of the facts." Where the public interest is involved, the Committees have held that the consent of the immediate parties is insufficient.[6]

Apparently the decisions which would insulate the parties and their respective lawyers completely from one another are based on the fiction that the interests of parties to a divorce suit are necessarily and always antagonistic to one another [7] and on the further assumption that this was necessary to secure proper protection for the interest of the state in preserving their marital status. It would, however, seem very questionable as to whether such protection is needed in a bona fide case, where it is clear that the wife honestly wants the divorce and is not coerced into it by an obviously dominant husband, where the allowance proposed by him is reasonable, and where the lawyer suggested to her by the husband or by his lawyer has not theretofore represented the husband. It is manifest that such suggestion is but natural and occurs all the time in uncontested cases. To condemn it where it is openly disclosed would seem both futile and unnecessary.[8]

ACCEPTANCE OF COMPENSATION FROM THE OTHER SIDE

It is not considered unethical or apparently as indicating "collusion" for the wife's lawyer to be paid by the husband.[9] In fact many divorce statutes provide for this, as well as for alimony. There can seem to be no impropriety in a bona fide agreement to this effect, or in an agreement, disclosed to the court, with regard to property, alimony, counsel fees, and custody of children.[10]

The upshot of the foregoing would seem to be:

Collusion involving deliberate distortion of the facts constituting

---

In N.Y. City 201, however, the wife's lawyer was practically recommended by the husband, who told the lawyer the basis for a valid annulment decree. Cf. also N.Y. City 106 and see N.Y. County 128.

[6] A.B.A. Ops. 16, 34, 77. It will be noted that the Canon does not sanction the representation of conflicting interests in all cases where the immediate parties mutually consent to this but merely specifies this as a possible exception.

[7] Compare N.Y. County 99; Chicago 19, pp. 38–41.

[8] This does not, however, mean that in cases so flagrant as Staedler v. Staedler, 6 N.J. 380 (1951) (where the husband's regular lawyer managed the whole proceedings) the court should not call a halt, as it there did, suspending the lawyer for a year; and cf. Chicago 19, pp. 38–41.

[9] Mich. 84, 123; N.Y. City 27; N.Y. County 230, cf. N.Y. City 495.

[10] See N.Y. City 81, 106, 139, 173, 314, B-200; N.Y. County 54, 357.

the ground of the divorce, or connivance in inducing defendant to commit acts constituting such ground is obviously improper.

Cooperation with the other side in facilitating proof of acts theretofore committed without such connivance is not necessarily so, but where involving a money payment will be viewed with suspicion and should be fully disclosed to the court.

The mere fact that the more affluent of the parties agrees to make a payment to the other on account of counsel fees and other expenses and a lump sum or allowance is not improper where this is likewise disclosed to the Court.

As to the lawyer's duty not to advise or sanction his client's misrepresentation of her bona fide domicile in obtaining a "quickie" divorce in another state, see *supra,* page 80.

LAWYERS RETIRED FROM JUDICIAL OR PUBLIC POSITIONS

Canon 36, analogous and supplementary to Canon 6, the decisions under which also apply to cases under Canon 36,[11] provides:

A lawyer should not accept employment as an advocate in any matter upon the merits of which he has previously acted in a judicial capacity.

A lawyer, having once held public office or having been in the public employ, should not after his retirement accept employment in connection with any matter which he has investigated or passed upon while in such office or employ.

The consent or request of the public authority is not a justification.[12]

The phrase "in connection with any matter" in the second paragraph of Canon 36 was not, of course, intended to preclude the legal adviser of a government department or agent or a judge from thereafter, on his resignation, taking cases involving any questions of law in connection with which he had been engaged.[13] The purpose of the first provision is to preclude a judge from thereafter participating in litigation the merits of which he has passed on when a judge and thus taking advantage of the prestige which this would give to his present opinion and argument;[14] also that the public employee's

---

11 See A.B.A. Op. 37 (an extreme case, see dissenting opinion), 39, 49, 71, 72, 104, 128, 134, 135, 136, and 192.

The English Ordinance of 1280 forbade a judge to try a case if he had been in it while at the bar: Cohen, 30 Law Quart. Rev. 475 (1914).

12 N.Y. City 715; see also *supra,* p. 120 n. 17.

13 See Smith v. Ry Co., 60 Iowa 515 (1883); also App. A, *288.*

14 "The principle applied in those Opinions (16, 30, 34, 77, 118 & 134) is that an

action, or the judge's decision might otherwise be influenced or be thought to have been influenced, by the hope of later being employed privately to uphold or to upset what he had done or decided.[15] He should avoid even the appearance of evil.[16] In the second paragraph the words "any matter" apparently mean "any controversy" or "involving the same facts"[17] as they more clearly do in the first paragraph.[18] The duty of one while in public office to refrain from representing persons involved in matters within the scope of his duties is not specifically covered by Canon 36, but obviously comes within its spirit.[19] Such cases are covered by Canon 6 (conflicting interest) and Canon 11 (fiduciary relation).

One who has passed, as Master, on matters concerning the validity of a patent, may not thereafter accept a retainer from any party to the controversy in connection with the litigation involving it.[20]

One who, as justice of the peace, found a man guilty of assault on his wife, may not represent her in a divorce action against him.[21] Nor may he represent one in connection, civil or criminal, with an offense as to which he has issued a warrant.[22] The Michigan Committee has held that a justice of the peace who performed a marriage ceremony in connection with which it was his duty to make investigation as to the status of the parties may not appear for one of them as plaintiff pro confesso in a divorce action.[23]

The Canon does not apply to a referee where his prior connection with the matter was in a purely ministerial capacity, he making no investigation and exercising no judicial functions.[24]

Duty Not to Disclose Confidential Communications

Canon 37. Confidences of a Client.[25] It is the duty of a lawyer to preserve his client's confidences. This duty outlasts the lawyer's employment, and extends as well to his employees; and neither of them should accept em-

---

attorney holding public office should avoid all conduct which might lead the layman to conclude that the attorney is utilizing his public position to further his professional success or personal interests." A.B.A. Op. 192.

As to the use by lawyers, professionally, of their political influence, see 35 Law Notes 103 (1931).

[15] See A.B.A. Op. 37 at pp. 124 and 125.

[16] A.B.A. Op. 49; N.Y. City 759.　　　[17] See A.B.A. Op. 26, p. 106.

[18] The provision covers, however, the whole case or proceeding, and not merely some isolated part of it. Mich. 38.

[19] See Mich. 137; A.B.A. Op. 110.　　　[20] N.Y. City 759; see, however, N.Y. City 79.

[21] Mich. 81.　　　[22] Mich. 95. Cf. Mo. 38 and 66.　　　[23] Mich. 78.

[24] N.Y. County 226.

[25] The Canon, as adopted in 1928, was amended in 1937 by inserting the first sentence;

ployment which involves or may involve the disclosure or use of these confidences, either for the private advantage of the lawyer or his employees or to the disadvantage of the client, without his knowledge and consent, and even though there are other available sources of such information. A lawyer should not continue employment when he discovers that this obligation prevents the performance of his full duty to his former or to his new client.

If a lawyer is accused by his client, he is not precluded from disclosing the truth in respect to the accusation. The announced intention of a client to commit a crime is not included within the confidences which he is bound to respect. He may properly make such disclosures as may be necessary to prevent the act or protect those against whom it is threatened.

The rule of this Canon, that confidential communications by or on behalf of a client may not be disclosed without his consent, has long been a rule of the common law,[26] and is in many jurisdictions the subject of statute. As such, its application is usually a question of law rather than of ethics.[27] It is therefore deemed superfluous here to do more than refer to the decisions of the various ethics committees on the rule and the qualifications thereof.

Purpose of the Rule

The purpose of the rule was thus stated by Judge Taft:

I have recently heard an arraignment of our present judicial system in the trial of causes by a prominent, able and experienced member of the Boston Bar. . . . He feels that the procedure now in vogue authorizes and in fact requires counsel to withhold facts from the court which would help the cause of justice if they were brought out by his own statement. To remedy this he suggests that all counsel should be compelled to disclose any

---

by inserting "or may involve" on line 4, and by inserting "as may be necessary" in the last sentence.

John H. Wigmore thus states the rule (*Evidence* [3d ed.], secs. 2290–2329): "Where legal advice of any kind is sought from a professional legal adviser in his capacity as such, the communications relating to that purpose, made in confidence by the client, are at his instance permanently protected from disclosure by himself or by the legal adviser, except the protection be waived."

See also A.B.A. Op. 250, and authorities cited.

As to certain confusion of thought in the Committee decisions between Canons 6 and 37 see *supra*, pp. 104, 109, 115.

In an address before the American Law Institute in 1932, Judge Samuel Seabury, as a result of his investigation of graft in New York City, recommended that the privilege be made inapplicable to public officials or political organizations or their leaders in relation to public concessions, public contracts or favors: 18 A.B.A. Jour. 371, 372 (1932).

26 A.B.A. Op. 150; Holdsworth, *History of English Law*, VI, 433. Thornton says (*Attorneys*, sec. 94) that this rule or law was first applied in 1577 in Berd v. Lovelace, Cary, 62.

27 A.B.A. Op. 247; Chicago 27, p. 60.

facts communicated to them by their clients which would require a decision of the case against the clients. . . . To require the counsel to disclose the confidential communications of his client to the very court and jury which are to pass on the issue which he is making, would end forever the possibility of any useful relation between lawyer and client. It is essential for the proper presentation of the client's cause that he should be able to talk freely with his counsel without fear of disclosure. . . . The useful function of lawyers is not only to conduct litigation, but to avoid it, where possible, by advising settlement or withholding suit. Thus, any rule that interfered with the complete disclosure of the client's inmost thoughts on the issue he presents would seriously obstruct the peace that is gained for society by the compromises which the counsel is able to advise.[28]

Scope of the Rule

Of the Canon the American Bar Association Committee said in Opinion 250:

We think the language of the canon wherein it states specific applications of the general rule and of exceptions thereto is not intended to be all inclusive; rather that it was the purpose to state with particularity important applications and exceptions, and that it was not intended to exclude other well-recognized exceptions.

A lawyer representing a corporation may and should disclose to its directors defalcations by the manager which the lawyer learned about in connection with his representation of the corporation.[29]

"Since the privilege is for the protection of the client's interest, he may waive the privilege during his lifetime, and, after his death, his personal representative or heirs may waive the privilege." [30]

When a client becomes mentally incompetent, his lawyer may use confidential communications in having him committed; [31] and may use them to prevent the looting of his deceased client's estate.[32] Similarly, a lawyer who holds property in trust for a client, recently deceased, which will be claimed by a boy (brought up by the client but not adopted) as an illegitimate son, should advise the heirs of his

---

[28] W. H. Taft, *Ethics in Service* (1915), pp. 31–32. See also Greenough v. Gaskell, 1 Myl. & K. 98, 103 (1833).

In A.B.A. Op. 91 the Committee said: "The reason for the rule lies in the fact that it is essential to the administration of justice that there should be perfect freedom of consultation by client with attorney without any apprehension of a compelled disclosure by the attorney to the detriment of the client." See also A.B.A. Op. 23.

[29] A.B.A. Op. 202.   [30] A.B.A. Op. 91; see also N.Y. City 947.

[31] N.Y. County 88. As to testamentary matters as privileged, see 14 Ann. Cas. (1909) 601 n.; 22 Ann. Cas. 1912 A 839 n.; 41 Ann. Cas. 1916 C 1073 n.

[32] N.Y. City B-167.

knowledge of her repeated statements to him directly negativing the son's claim.[33] Here as the lawyer for the deceased he owed it to her to protect her good name, and as trustee of the fund he was obliged to see that it went to the rightful owners.

When a lawyer-client testifies in a disciplinary proceeding as to the advice given him by another lawyer, the latter is free to testify as to what advice he actually gave. By testifying the client waived the privilege.[34]

Where a client introduced a woman to his lawyer for legal advice and service, who later indicated her intention to marry such client, the lawyer is bound to advise her of various prior sexual offenses on the client's part.[35]

The duty is not owed to one who procured advice from misrepresenting his identity; [36] or where the information was obtained by the lawyer in a capacity other than legal adviser.[37]

A communication must be regarded as confidential where it possibly is so, although it is not entirely clear that the relations exist.[38] The mere fact that advice is given without charge therefor does not nullify the privilege,[39] nor does the fact that the lawyer does not take the case.[40]

"An attorney cannot destroy his client's privilege by his construction or conclusion that his client was acting as agent for another. The governing intention to determine the character in which a client speaks is a client's intent, not the attorney's construction, especially in case of conflict between them. The confidential character of com-

[33] N.Y. City 236. The Committee here said: "In the opinion of the Committee the lawyer should not attempt to deprive any person [here the rightful heirs] rightfully entitled by law; his fiduciary relations continue, and he should not attempt by any concealment to defeat the operation of law."

[34] Texas 9.

[35] N.Y. County 270. His introducing her would apparently waive the confidence. He should retire from further employment by her. See as to this case, *supra*, p. 95 n. 10.

[36] Mich. 116.

[37] App. A, *309;* N.Y. County 154 (as member of Draft Board).

[38] See Mich. 118, and cf. N.Y. City 308. As to a communication to a law student, not yet admitted but made to him as legal adviser, see cases cited by Costigan, Case Book, p. 142. The New York County Committee held it improper for a lawyer who, prior to his admission to the bar, had been a clerk for a lawyer, to defend a client against whom his employer acquired a claim for fees earned while the clerk was in the lawyer's office. N.Y. County 11. In Murray v. Lizotte, 31 R.I. 509 (1910), a lawyer was suspended for a year for engaging an investigator whom he knew had previously been employed by the other side.

[39] A.B.A. Op. 216.

[40] N.Y. City 671; see articles in n. 1, p. 506 of Arant's Case Book.

munications is not to be determined by an attorney's conclusion that the representation of one client is dominant and the matter of real importance and that of the other subordinate. The obligations of confidences may not be limited by comparisons of degrees of importance." [41]

The duty is not released by non-payment of the lawyer's fees, except insofar as the lawyer's testimony may be clearly necessary to establish his right thereto.[42]

The rule applies only where the communications by the client were made under circumstances clearly indicating that they were intended to be confidential.[43] Thus, the rule does not apply where the communication was made in the presence of the other party to the case; [44] nor where it was not made to the lawyer in the capacity of a legal adviser.[45]

Where the communication was made in the presence of a third party, if such party was present as a witness,[46] the rule does not apply,[47] but it would apply if the third party was present in such capacity as to be identified with the client; for example, where the mother [48] or a friend [49] of the client accompanied the client to the lawyer, seeking his advice.

The privilege is not nullified by the fact that the circumstances to be disclosed are part of a public record,[50] or that there are other available sources for such information,[1] or by the fact that the lawyer received the same information from other sources.[2]

Where the question involves the production of documents, it is not the document that is privileged. "It is merely the possession of the attorney that is protected." [3]

A bankrupt lawyer must advise his assignees of the nature and extent of the services rendered to each client whose account is as-

[41] N.Y. City 693.　　　　　　　　　[42] A.B.A. Op. 250, p. 501; and see N.Y. City 108.

[43] Wigmore, *Evidence*, secs. 2311–16.

[44] Doheny v. Lacy, 168 N.Y. 213, 223 (1901); Ver Bryck v. Luby, 67 Cal. App.2d 842, 844 (1945).

[45] Mich. 116.　　　　　　　　　[46] Mitchell v. Towne, 31 Cal. App.2d, 259, 265 (1939).

[47] Doheny v. Lacy, 168 N.Y. 213, 223 (1901).

[48] Bowers v. State of Ohio, 29 Ohio St. 542, 546 (1876).

[49] N.Y. City 420, "even though, because of the presence of a third person, it may not be a so-called privileged communication." But see Packer v. Rapoport, 88 N.Y.S.2d 118, 119 (1949); In re Boone, 82F. 944 (1897).

[50] Mich. 45; and see N.Y. City 839, B-138, B-147; App. A, 293.

[1] N.Y. County 401; N.Y. City B-138; and cf. N.Y. County 157.

[2] N.Y. County 157; N.Y. City 749.

[3] Shiras, J., in Liggett v. Glenn, 51 Fed. 381, 396 (1892).

signed, and cooperate in collecting them. Such information is not covered by the privilege.[4]

Application of the Rule

A lawyer may not disclose his client's funds [5] or his whereabouts [6] to the client's creditors, or to a public officer,[7] or, after the client retains another lawyer, disclose to the court the mala fides of the residence of one consulting him as to a divorce,[8] or statements by his client, a wife, as to the prior commission of a crime by her husband.[9] Nor may he disclose the name of his client, the finder of a watch, even where he is arrested for refusing to do so.[10] Nor may one who represents a corporation from time to time disclose to it the fact, communicated to him in confidence by a friend and client, employed by it, that he had embezzled its funds.[11]

A retired solicitor who has drawn a will for one who becomes of unsound mind may not, at the request of the testator's friends, turn the will over to the solicitor handling the family affairs; [12] nor may a lawyer disclose the provisions of a will which he drew for a testator not yet dead.[13]

Where a lawyer, on the instructions of his client and his injunction of secrecy, drew an alteration to his client's will appointing the lawyer's father as executor in place of a solicitor who had hitherto acted for him, he was bound not to disclose this to the other solicitor.[14]

A prosecutor may not use a phonograph record of confidential communications between the defendant in custody and his lawyer.[15]

Because a lawyer referred a client to another lawyer does not justify the first lawyer in advising the second of property of the client, in

---

[4] A.B.A. Op. 154; N.Y. City 480.

[5] A.B.A. Op. 163, or to one client the funds of another who owes the first; N.Y. City 98; see also App. A, *310.*

[6] N.Y. City 107, 108.

[7] N.Y. City 241; N.Y. County 70. See, however, *infra,* p. 137 n. 21.

[8] A.B.A. Op. 268.   [9] A.B.A. Op. 274.

[10] California Committee Q 24, 3 Cal. State Bar Jour. (April, 1929), p. 216; Costigan's Case Book, p. 147.

[11] Cleveland Committee, 25 Ohio Law Reporter 569; but see A.B.A. Op. 202.

[12] Op. of Council of the Law Society, *Law, Practice and Usage of the Legal Profession* (1923), p. 311.

[13] Mich. 53.

[14] Op. of Council of the Law Society, *Law, Practice and Usage of the Legal Profession* (1923), p. 312, 1172 (July 14, 1884) (He should have asked the testator to have someone else know about it.)

[15] A.B.A. Op. 150.

violation of Canon 37, when the client refuses to pay the lawyer's just fees.[16]

The purchase of another lawyer's practice and good will is likely to involve a violation of Canon 37.[17]

Where when representing several participants in an accident a lawyer obtains from one of them information which, by a subsequent decision, may serve to make others of those represented liable, he should retire entirely from the case.[18]

When Disclosure Is Proper

Although Canon 37 contains no specific exception covering communications where disclosure to the authorities is essential to the public safety, such is necessarily implied. Accordingly, where a lawyer has confidential information from a foreign government with which the United States is at war, he should reveal to the proper authority the fact that he has received it, and abide the latter's decision;[19] and he may tell of subversive activities by his client, the common defense transcending Canon 37.[20]

A lawyer may disclose the whereabouts of a client jumping bail.[21] The lawyer for an administrative body may reveal gross abuses by it after having advised the highest officials and refusal by them to act, the lawyer thus invoking public opinion to remedy the situation.[22]

He may advise the Industrial Commission of the nature and extent of injuries to the plaintiff in a case conducted by him, the plaintiff having falsely testified as to them.[23]

A disclosure of confidential information may be made where necessary to prevent a contemplated crime,[24] or fraud.[25]

Canon 29 is subject to Canon 37.[26] Where a fraud is possible but

---

[16] N.Y. City 682-G. [17] A.B.A. Op. 266; Chicago 32, p. 72.
[18] N.Y. City 122. Cf. Mo. 29. [19] N.Y. County 167, 168.
[20] Mich. 71; and cf. N.Y. City 484, Cleveland 6/23/45, and Mich. 88.
[21] A.B.A. Op. 155, and see 156; but see Op. 23, and N.Y. County 70; also *supra*, p. 136 n. 7.
[22] N.Y. County 339. [23] Chicago 27, pp. 59–60.
[24] A.B.A. Op. 155, 202; N.Y. County 13; "A client who consults an attorney for advice that will serve him in the commission of a fraud will have no help from the law. He must let the truth be told." Cardozo, J., in Clark v. U.S., 289 U.S. 1, 15 (1933). See Hicks, Case Book, p. 339.
[25] N.Y. County 84; see also Mich. 22 and 59; see also N.Y. City 484 (bankrupt concealing asset); but see N.Y. City 945.
The State Bar of California recommended a detailed rule to the Supreme Court, which the court did not adopt. See 16 Cal. L. Rev. 487, 494–95. (1928).
[26] N.Y. County 253, and see N.Y. County 190.

not clear, the lawyer should withdraw.[27] A lawyer should inform the surrogate of the proposed concealment by his client-executor of an existing grandchild from whom his client proposes to abstract the estate; [28] but he may not tell his client's husband of her plan to cut him out of her will as to property in her name but the result of their joint labors.[29] However, one holding a former will of a wife who had agreed to a mutual disposition of property belonging to her and her deceased husband was held bound to disclose this when she tried to avoid her obligation.[30]

A lawyer may not inform the collector of a failure by his client to disclose income,[31] or of his client's address; [32] or reveal to the authorities that his client paid for a promise of preferential treatment after induction.[33]

The exception in the second paragraph of the Canon relative to the announced intention of his client to commit a crime includes a fraud on others but not a crime or fraud which has been completed.[34] The lawyer may make such disclosures as are necessary to protect himself against false accusations,[35] or to protect his rights, including reasonable compensation,[36] but may not in order to avoid being sent to jail by the judge.[37] He may not use confidential information as to his client's funds to enable him to collect his fee,[38] but may use information not obtained from the client,[39] and in suing one client for a fee, may use non-confidential information obtained from another client.[40]

Where a lawyer's client has aided in the prosecution of charges against him, the lawyer may reveal such confidences as are material to the proceeding.[41]

The privilege is not binding where the client either conspires with

[27] N.Y. County 259.
[28] N.Y. City B-107, and see N.Y. City 70 and 945, N.Y. County 84.
[29] N.Y. County 190.   [30] N.Y. City 128.
[31] Cleveland F, and see Mich. 88.   [32] Mich. 88.
[33] N.Y. County 169.
[34] A.B.A. Op. 202; N.Y. County 253; but see Mich. 22.
[35] A.B.A. Op. 202; p. 408; N.Y. County 218.
[36] A.B.A. Op. 250; in N.Y. City 179, however, that Committee pertinently said as the basis for its decision: "It would certainly offend the sense of propriety if an attorney who was retained in a matter which from its nature was highly confidential, should, in an action for the recovery of his fees, give publicity to the very facts which he was employed to suppress."
[37] App. A, 312.   [38] N.Y. County 44.   [39] N.Y. County 196.
[40] Wash. 1.   [41] A.B.A. Op. 19.

the lawyer or deceives him,[42] or falsely accuses him,[43] but is not forfeited merely by the client's acting in bad faith to his own creditors.[44] One defamed by a former client whom he is suing for slander may, in order to protect his good name, advise other clients in the same trade of the true facts.[45]

Before making a permissible disclosure he should, if possible, notify his client of his intention to do so and give him reasonable opportunity himself to disclose the information or to show that the lawyer's information is incorrect or irrelevant.[46]

It has been held that damages may be collected by one injured by a gross breach of a lawyer's duty not to divulge confidential communications.[47]

Extent of Duty to Accept Professional Employment

Canon 31 provides: "No lawyer is obliged to act either as adviser or advocate for every person who may wish to become his client. He has the right to decline employment."

Except where assigned by the court to defend those who cannot afford to pay counsel,[48] the lawyer may choose his own cases and for any reason or without a reason may decline any employment which he does not fancy. Such is not the case, however, with regard to the barrister in England who, in the absence of special circumstances, is apparently bound to accept any brief in the courts in which he professes to practice, at a proper professional fee.[49]

A lawyer should not presume to undertake professional employment for which he is not reasonably competent but should recommend or at least associate a specialist.[50]

---

[42] Stephen, J., in Queen v. Cox, 14 Q.B.D. 153, 168 (1884).

[43] N.Y. County 218. [44] N.Y. City 108.

[45] N.Y. County 319; N.Y. City 336. [46] N.Y. City 484.

[47] Taylor v. Blacklow, 3 Bing. N.C. 235 (1836).

[48] See *supra*, p. 62. For a general statement as to the duty to one whom the lawyer believes guilty, see N.Y. City 253.

[49] Statement of the General Council (1933), p. 2610; see also E. S. Cox-Sinclair, "The Right to Retain an Advocate," 29 Law Mag. & Rev. 406 (1904).

A not wholly convincing reason suggested for the English rule by Judge Baldwin ("The New American Code of Legal Ethics," 8 Col. 1. Rev. 541, 544–45 [1908]) is that barristers are employed only by solicitors, who presumably have satisfied themselves that each case is a proper one.

[50] Warvelle, *Legal Ethics*, p. 151; A.B.A. Op. 248.

RIGHT TO WITHDRAW

Although a lawyer may refuse at his pleasure to take a case,[1] he has not the same unqualified right to withdraw once he has undertaken one, except on non-compliance with a condition imposed on the acceptance of the retainer.[2]

Canon 44 provides:

44. Withdrawal from Employment as Attorney or Counsel. The right of an attorney or counsel to withdraw from employment, once assumed, arises only from good cause. Even the desire or consent of the client is not always sufficient. The lawyer should not throw up the unfinished task to the detriment of his client except for reasons of honor or self-respect. If the client insists upon an unjust or immoral course in the conduct of his case, or if he persists over the attorney's remonstrance in presenting frivolous defenses, or if he deliberately disregards an agreement or obligation as to fees or expenses, the lawyer may be warranted in withdrawing on due notice to the client, allowing him time to employ another lawyer. So also when a lawyer discovers that his client has no case and the client is determined to continue it; or even if the lawyer finds himself incapable of conducting the case effectively. Sundry other instances may arise in which withdrawal is to be justified. Upon withdrawing from a case after a retainer has been paid, the attorney should refund such part of the retainer as has not been clearly earned.

What constitutes "good cause" depends, of course, largely on the circumstances at the time the lawyer deems it his duty to retire from the case or finds it desirable to do so. The duty to retire would be based on his being satisfied that the client is behaving or insisting that the lawyer behave in a manner contrary to ethical standards;[3] the desire to withdraw might rest merely on his not choosing any longer to represent the client, as for example where the latter refuses to pay for his services,[4] or where the client's behavior shows decided lack of

---

[1] He may not, however, refuse to represent a bankrupt except on condition that the bankrupt pay the lawyer's clients in full; App. A, *10*.

[2] N.Y. City 285; here that defendant in negligence cases be insured.

Where the lawyer of the casualty company represents an assured and the latter will not cooperate as per the clause in the policy, the lawyer may withdraw with reasonable protection to the assured. N.Y. City 335; N.Y. County 318.

[3] See N.Y. County 9, 181, 318; but see N.Y. County 110, holding it not to be good cause that the client refuses to allow him to pay a witness extra to testify.

Even though there has been impropriety on behalf of the client, the lawyer need not withdraw for the new trial if he and the client have had no part in such impropriety, A.B.A. Op. 44.

[4] N.Y. County 15; N.Y. City 786; but not where the client is perhaps unable presently to pay for them. See N.Y. City 12, N.Y. County 390. "The profession is a branch of the administration of justice and not a mere money-getting trade." Canon 12.

confidence.[5] In either case, however, he should afford the client reasonable opportunity to secure other counsel [6] with the assistance, it may be, of the court,[7] and he may not withdraw on the eve of a trial because the client refuses to pay or secure him his accrued charges.[8] Where the client is an infant, the lawyer should lay the matter before the proper court for its instructions,[9] even under circumstances where, if his client were an adult, he might properly withdraw forthwith.[10]

A lawyer learning of fraud practiced by his client on a court or administrative officer, which the client declines to disclose, must inform the injured parties,[11] and withdraw from the case,[12] despite Canon 37.[13]

The mere fact that he strongly suspects fraud by his client, while not justifying the dismissal of the client's claim, justifies the lawyer in advising the court and withdrawing.[14]

On withdrawal he must return the client's papers even though they may be used improperly; this fact the lawyer should disclose if permitted under Canon 37.[15]

A lawyer who makes it a practice to withdraw from defending a criminal on becoming convinced of his guilt should inform the client thereof before receiving a confidential communication from him; and after receiving such should not withdraw where the result would be its disclosure.[16]

One who through the indiscretion of the lawyer on the other side has received an improper and obviously confidential disclosure from him about the case should retire and hold inviolate the confidence thus obtained.[17]

On his withdrawal from a case on being satisfied after investigation that the client who had misrepresented the facts to him had really

[5] N.Y. City 950; N.Y. County 55.

[6] N.Y. County 18, 318; N.Y. City 950, B-71. In the earliest times a serjeant might not retire from pending proceedings without the consent of his client; Cohen, *History of the English Bar*, p. 234.

[7] N.Y. County 55; and see N.Y. County 158. In N.Y. County 146 the Committee said: "In the opinion of the Committee, unless the client consented to the retirement of the attorney, or to the dismissal or discontinuance of the cause, he should privately have stated to the Court his application for leave to withdraw, and the reasons therefor, and should have asked that the cause be continued to enable the client to procure other counsel."

[8] N.Y. County 18.   [9] N.Y. City 204; and see N.Y. City 350; cf. N.Y. County 318.

[10] N.Y. City 204; N. Y. County 350; see also N.Y. County 158.

[11] N.Y. County 215. Query as to his duty to advise the court. See Canon 29.

[12] N.Y. City 70; N.Y. County 9; and see N.Y. City 743.   [13] N.Y. City B-107.

[14] N.Y. County 146; see also N.Y. County 181.

[15] N.Y. City 743.   [16] A.B.A. Op. 90.   [17] A.B.A. Op. 47.

no good cause of action, the lawyer may retain from his retainer the reasonable value of his services to date.[18]

A lawyer handling a case on a contingent basis who is given proper grounds for withdrawal, in so doing is entitled to compensation on a quantum meruit basis, but not where his withdrawal is capricious.[19]

When he finds that the client has no case and the client has disappeared, he can move for leave to withdraw, advising all concerned.[20]

DEFENSE OF ONE KNOWN TO BE GUILTY

The first paragraph of Canon 5 is as follows:

It is the right of the lawyer to undertake the defense of a person accused of crime, regardless of his personal opinion as to the guilt of the accused; otherwise innocent persons, victims only of suspicious circumstances, might be denied proper defense. Having undertaken such defense, the lawyer is bound by all fair and honorable means, to present every defense that the law of the land permits, to the end that no person may be deprived of life or liberty, but by due process of law.

Although a lawyer may refuse to undertake a case which appears to him unsound or incapable of being successfully prosecuted or defended, or to defend a criminal whom he believes to be guilty,[21] he is not bound to do so.[22] Our legal system does not constitute the lawyer the judge as to the justice or soundness of the causes committed to him, but deems it in the ends of justice to have all the facts and arguments on each side of the controversy presented by expert counsel, stimulated to a maximum of industry and ingenuity by the contest, for decision by the court and jury.[23] Experience has shown that

---

[18] A.B.A. Op. 88; and see Chicago 28, pp. 61–63.

[19] N.Y. City 394.   [20] N.Y. City 477.

[21] See Canon 31 quoted *supra*, p. 139; also *infra*, p. 320.

[22] The distinction between the function and duty of the public prosecutor and the advocate is emphasized by the two paragraphs of Canon 5. See par. 2, quoted *infra*, p. 148.

[23] " 'Sir (said Dr. Johnson), a lawyer has no business with the justice or injustice of the cause which he undertakes, unless his client asks his opinion, and then he is bound to give it honestly. The justice or injustice of the cause is to be decided by the judge. Consider, sir, what is the purpose of courts of justice? It is, that every man may have his cause fairly tried, by men appointed to try causes. A lawyer is not to tell what he knows to be a lie: he is not to produce what he knows to be a false deed; but he is not to usurp the province of the jury and of the judge, and determine what shall be the effect of evidence,—what shall be the result of legal argument. As it rarely happens that a man is fit to plead his own cause, lawyers are a class of the community who, by study and experience, have acquired the art and power of arranging evidence, and of applying to the points at issue what the law has settled. A lawyer is to do for his client

in many cases a lawyer's first impression of a case has turned out on further investigation to be erroneous.[24] Judge Sharswood tells how Sir Matthew Hale at first would take no case that he believed unsound, but on later experience modified his views and altered his practice when several causes that he had condemned and rejected proved finally to be just.[25]

In the Statement of the General Council of the Bar of England for 1933, the Council says as to English barristers:

(1) Counsel has the same privilege as his client of asserting and defending the client's rights, and of protecting his liberty or life by the free and unfettered statement of every fact, and the use of every argument and obser-

---

all that his client might fairly do for himself, if he could. If, by a superiority of attention, of knowledge, of skill, and a better method of communication, he has the advantage of his adversary, it is an advantage to which he is entitled. There must always be some advantage on one side or other; and it is better that advantage should be had by talents, than by chance. If lawyers were to undertake no causes till they were sure they were just, a man might be precluded altogether from a trial of his claim, though, were it judicially examined, it might be found a very just claim.' Boswell, *The Journal of a Tour* (Temple Classics), pp. 13–14." (Costigan, Case Book, p. 298 n.)

"The lawyer who refuses his professional assistance because in his judgment the case is unjust and indefensible, usurps the functions of both judge and jury." Sharswood, *Professional Ethics*, p. 84.

"Justice is found, experimentally, to be most effectually promoted by the opposite efforts of practiced and ingenious men, presenting to the selection of an impartial judge the best arguments for the establishment and explanation of truth." Sydney Smith, *The Lawyer that Tempted Christ* (1873), p. 425.

24 " 'I have frequently been engaged in a case for the defence which, on a perusal of the brief, I have thought to be utterly hopeless, and have believed my client to be not quite so honest as he should be; but afterwards, on the facts being thoroughly sifted before a judge and jury, I have been just as firmly convinced that my first opinion was utterly erroneous.'—Serjeant Robinson, *Bench and Bar Reminiscences* (1889), p. 116."

25 Sharswood, *Professional Ethics*, p. 88. Baxter has the following note to Burnet's *Life of Hale (Hale's Works*, 1, 106): "And indeed Judge Hale would tell me that Bishop Usher was much prejudiced against lawyers because the worst causes find their advocates; but that he and Mr. Selden had convinced him of the reasons of it to his satisfaction; and that he did by acquaintance with them believe that there were as many honest men among lawyers proportionately as among any profession of men in England (not excepting bishops or divines)."

In Costigan's Case Book he quotes, on pages 453 *et seq.* (2d ed.), a number of striking instances where such proved to be the case, as well as famous cases in which distinguished lawyers have defended prisoners who had confessed their guilt.

"A client is entitled to say to his counsel, 'I want your advocacy, not your judgment; I prefer that of the Court,' " Baron Bramwell in Johnson v. Emerson, L.R. 6 Ex. 329, 367 (1871).

"The question in the American or English Court is not whether the accused be guilty. It is whether he be shown to be guilty, by legal proof, of an offense legally set forth." Geo. F. Hoar, "Oratory," 29 Scribner's Mag. 756, 758. See also Wm. Forsyth, *Hortensius* (3d ed., 1879), pp. 408, 409.

"The lawyer may present any fairly debatable law question for the Court's determination"; N.Y. County 95.

vation, that can legitimately, according to the principles and practice of
law, conduce to this end; and any attempt to restrict this privilege should
be jealously watched. (An. Stat. 1919, p. 6) [26]

Under our system, when anyone is accused of crime it is his right
to be acquitted unless proved guilty by the procedure recognized by
the law. The Sixth Amendment assures him the right to be represented by counsel, who may properly see to it that he is accorded all
his legal rights, and that "nothing be taken or be withheld from him,
save by the rules of law, legally applied." [27]

A lawyer may not, of course, put a witness on the stand whom he
knows will swear to what is not true.[28] The New York County Committee has held that a lawyer may not properly take a claim which he
is sure is void.[29] He is not, however, ultimately responsible for the
morals of his client.[30]

---

[26] *The Annual Practice* (1933), p. 2621.

[27] Canon 15, par. 3. And see IV Blackstone 356 (1765).

Judge Ellsworth, afterwards Chief Justice of the United States, advised Jeremiah
Evarts "that any cause that was fit for any court to hear was fit for any lawyer to present
on either side, and that neither judge or counsel had the right to prejudge the case
until both sides had been heard." Joseph H. Choate, *American Addresses* (1911), p. 184.

A lawyer may defend the most odious of criminals. Cleveland 15.

"The ethical question which laymen most frequently ask about the legal profession
is this: How can a lawyer take a case which he does not believe in? The profession is
regarded as necessarily somewhat immoral, because its members are supposed to be
habitually taking cases they do not believe in. As a practical matter, I think the lawyer
is not often harassed by this problem, partly because he is apt to believe at the time
in most of the cases that he actually tries, and partly because he either abandons or
settles a large number of those he does not believe in. In any event, the lawyer recognizes
that in trying a case his prime duty is to present his side to the tribunal fairly and as
well as he can, relying upon his adversary to present his case fairly and as well as he
can. As the lawyers on the two sides are usually reasonably well matched, the judge or
jury may ordinarily be trusted to make such a decision as justice demands." Louis D.
Brandeis, "The Opportunity in the Law," 39 Am. L. Rev. (now U.S. L. Rev.) 555, 561
(1905).

"Nature is very kind in allowing us to believe almost anything which it is for our
interest to advocate." C. A. Kent, "Legal Ethics," 6 Mich. L. Rev. 468, 474 (1908).

[28] A.B.A. Op. 150, p. 314. Nor should he draw affidavits which stretch the truth. Sharswood, *Professional Ethics*, p. 111–12.

[29] N.Y. County 281.

[30] See also *infra*, p. 149 and p. 196.

"The chief business of the lawyer is that of counsel as to legal rights, and the
maintenance, through the courts, of such rights. The lawyer offers himself as an expert as to the legal rights of all who ask his assistance and as to their enforcement. He
is not an expert as to moral as distinguished from legal rights. He may know less of these
than his client. There is, too, such a difference of opinion as to mere moral rights that,
generally, they do not constitute a basis for advice." Kent, "Legal Ethics," 6 Mich. L. Rev.
468, 474 (1908).

" 'No counsel,' he [Lord Langdale] said, 'supposes himself to be a mere advocate or
agent of his client to gain the victory, if he can, on a particular occasion. The zeal and

Although generally a lawyer may not interpose a pleading which he knows to be false, in New York it has been held that in a divorce action based on adultery, he may interpose a general denial where he knows that defendant is guilty but believes plaintiff will not be able to prove it.[31]

A lawyer is not bound to give his client a moral lecture. He should advise what the law requires, but should not further any of the client's unjust schemes, and should refuse to become a party to them.[32]

---

the arguments of every counsel knowing what is due to himself, and his honorable profession are qualified not only by considerations affecting his own character as a man of honor and experience and learning but also by considerations affecting the general interests of justice.' " Costigan, Case Book, p. 307.

[31] N.Y. County 206; but see U.S. v. Frank, 53 F.2d 128 (D.C.N.J., 1931).

[32] Warvelle, *Legal Ethics*, p. 156.

Quintillian: "The advocate will not undertake the defense of everyone; nor will he throw open the harbor of his eloquence as a port of refuge for pirates." Quoted by Carter, *Ethics of the Legal Profession*, p. 45. Boyd, "Legal Ethics," 4 Can. L. Rev. 85 (1905).

"It is a popular, but gross mistake, to suppose that a lawyer owes no fidelity to any one except his client; and that the latter is the keeper of his professional conscience. He is expressly bound by his official oath to behave himself in his office of attorney with all fidelity to the court as well as the client; and he violates it when he consciously presses for an unjust judgment: . . The high and honourable office of a counsel would be degraded to that of a mercenary were he compelled to do the biddings of his client against the dictates of his conscience." Gibson, C. J., in Rush v. Cavenaugh, 2 Barr (Pa.) 187, 189 (1845).

"The responsibility for advising as to questionable transactions, for bringing questionable suits, for urging questionable defenses, is the lawyer's responsibility. He cannot escape it by urging as an excuse that he is only following his client's instructions." Canon 31.

"At the trial it is his province to represent the true interests, not the aimless passions of his clients; to soften, not to exasperate hatreds." 20 Law Mag. (N.S.) 265, 282 (1854).

"The office of attorney does not permit, much less does it demand of him for any client, violation of law or any manner of fraud or chicane. He must obey his own conscience and not that of the client." Canon 15.

A pernicious advocacy of the contrary views—that the lawyer is justified even in lying in support of his client's case—has been advanced by Charles P. Curtis, Esq., of the Boston Bar, in an article in 4 Stanford Law Review 3 (1951), entitled "The Ethics of Advocacy." See Reply in 4 *Id.* 349 (1952); see also In re Napolis, 169 App. Div. 469 (N.Y., 1915).

"Although not bound to state or prove the case of an adversary, they are bound, if they anticipate it, to do so fairly; to state the entire material effect of an instrument; to produce no document with the hope of raising an impression they believe to be untrue by the ambiguity of its language; to garble nothing; to conceal nothing; to misrepresent nothing; but to present every argument and illustration which the zeal of the most earnest friendship could urge, and which are rarely urged with powerful effect unless in the conviction that they are urged for justice." 20 Law Mag. N.S. 265, 277 (1854).

How Far a Lawyer May Go in Supporting
a Client's Cause

Canon 15 [33] entitled as above provides:

Nothing operates more certainly to create or to foster popular prejudice
against lawyers as a class, and to deprive the profession of that full measure
of public esteem and confidence which belongs to the proper discharge of
its duties than does the false claim, often set up by the unscrupulous in
defense of questionable transactions, that it is the duty of the lawyer to do
whatever may enable him to succeed in winning his client's cause.

It is improper for a lawyer to assert in argument his personal belief in
his client's innocence or in the justice of his cause.

The lawyer owes "entire devotion to the interest of the client, warm
zeal in the maintenance and defense of his rights and the exertion of his
utmost learning and ability," to the end that nothing be taken or be withheld from him, save by the rules of law, legally applied. No fear of judicial
disfavor or public unpopularity should restrain him from the full discharge of his duty. In the judicial forum the client is entitled to the benefit
of any and every remedy and defense that is authorized by the law of the
land, and he may expect his lawyer to assert every such remedy or defense.
But it is steadfastly to be borne in mind that the great trust of the lawyer
is to be performed within and not without the bounds of the law. The
office of attorney does not permit, much less does it demand of him for any
client, violation of law or any manner of fraud or chicane. He must obey
his own conscience and not that of his client.

The part of the Canon in quotation marks is from Sharswood, *Professional Ethics,* pages 78–79.

As to English Barristers the General Council says: [34]

(2) It is inadvisable to lay down what a barrister defending a client on
a charge of crime may legitimately do in the course of his defence, but he
is not entitled to attribute to another person the crime with which his
client is charged wantonly or recklessly, nor unless the facts or circumstances given in evidence, or rational inferences drawn from them, raise
at the least a not unreasonable suspicion that the crime may have been
committed by the person to whom the guilt is so imputed. (An. St. 1919,
p. 6) [35]

The acceptance of a retainer to act as general counsel implies a
purpose to observe the Canons and creates no obligation to violate them in order to further the interest of the client; [36] and it is

[33] See also Canons 18, 22, 29, 30, 31, and 32.
[34] *The Annual Practice* (1933), p. 2621.
[35] See Costigan's Case Book, pp. 455–56.   [36] App. A, *11.*

not improper to represent one client only, on an annual salary.[37]

As pointed out by Judge Sharswood,[38] there is a practical difference of degree in the prosecution or defense of a claim dependent on its inherent justice. Where the other party is manifestly seeking, through the forms of law, to deny to a lawyer's client a clearly just claim or to do the client an obvious injury, the lawyer is doubly justified in availing himself of every honorable means to enable his client to succeed. In such case, however, the lawyer should make it clear to counsel on the other side that they are dealing strictly at arms length.

Counsel's Personal Belief in His Cause

The third paragraph of the Oath prescribed by the American Bar Association is as follows: "I will not counsel or maintain any suit or proceeding which shall appear to me to be unjust, nor any defense except such as I believe to be honestly debatable under the law of the land."

The first part of this provision is believed to go too far.

There are several reasons for the rule, long established,[39] that a lawyer may not properly state his personal belief either to the court or to the jury in the soundness of his case.[40] In the first place, his personal belief has no real bearing on the issue; no witness would be permitted so to testify, even under oath, and subject to cross-examination, much less the lawyer without either. Also, if expression of personal belief were permitted, it would give an improper advantage to the older and better known lawyer, whose opinion would carry more weight, and also with the jury at least, an undue advantage to an unscrupulous one. Furthermore, if such were permitted, for counsel to omit to make such a positive assertion might be taken as an admission that he did not believe in his case.[41]

He may bring a suit for divorce on a valid ground, irrespective

---

[37] N.Y. County 251.

[38] Sharswood, *Professional Ethics,* pp. 89 and 98–99.

[39] *Ibid.,* pp. 99 *et seq.*

[40] See Ala. Code of 1887, sec. 19; 31 A.B.A. Reports 697 (1907).

The last sentence of Canon 30 is as follows: "His appearance in Court should be deemed equivalent to an assertion on his honor that in his opinion his client's case is one proper for judicial determination."

[41] See Mathers, C. J., in 40 Can. L.T. 925–26 (1920); and see Wm. R. Riddell, 39 Can. L.T. 620–31 (1919); Showell Rogers, "The Ethics of Advocacy," 15 Law Quart. Rev. 259 (1899); Chas. H. Tuttle, "The Ethics of Advocacy," 18 A.B.A. Jour. 849–53, 882 (1931).

In the article last cited, the author says (p. 852): "As has well been said, we have not as yet altogether emerged from the *caveat emptor* stage of justice."

of inherent justice, and may in good faith advise against a reconcilia-tion.[42]

Public Prosecutors

The second paragraph of Canon 5, relative to the duty of public prosecutors, is:

The primary duty of a lawyer engaged in public prosecution is not to convict, but to see that justice is done. The suppression of facts or the secreting of witnesses capable of establishing the innocence of the accused is highly reprehensible.[43]

This doctrine originated in England because of the unfair advan-tage that the prosecutor originally had over the accused, in that the prisoner was at first not allowed to have counsel in cases of treason or felony; later when he was allowed them, they could not be sworn.[44]

The prosecutor should of his own motion strike from the jury one whom he knew had expressed the opinion that defendant should be convicted.[45] He may not attempt to get a plea of guilty by a threat to charge a more serious offense,[46] nor may he use newspaper publicity except where this is solely in the public interest.[47]

He should not prosecute a near relative.[48]

While a public prosecutor is not a "vindictive seeker for venge-ance," he need not call an eyewitness whose testimony he believes to be unreliable, where he so advises the defense.[49]

He may, under proper circumstances, associate a former secretary of a judge to argue a motion.[50]

Mr. Costigan has collected in his *Case Book on Legal Ethics* a num-ber of pertinent decisions and statements relative to the duty of the prosecuting attorney.[1]

[42] A.B.A. Op. 82.   [43] See N.Y. Law Jour. for Mar. 17, 1948.

[44] See James B. Thayer, *Preliminary Treatise on Evidence* (1896), pp. 157, 160, 161; 20 Law Mag. (N.S.) 265, 286 (1854).

[45] N.Y. County 145.   [46] Mich. 129.   [47] N.Y. County 103.

[48] Texas 32: "It is quite obvious that if the defendant should be acquitted, or if the District Attorney should feel after putting on his evidence that the case should be dis-missed in order to bring about substantial justice, he would never be able to explain such action to the prosecuting witness or witnesses, and they would always believe that he took such action because of his relationship to the defendant."

[49] Commonwealth v. Palermo, 368 Pa. 28, 32 (1951); see also Commonwealth v. Sacco, 259 Mass. 128, 141 (1927).   [50] N.Y. City 681.

[1] Pages 387 *et seq.;* Sir John Simon, "The Vocation of an Advocate," 25 Law Notes 228, 231 (1922). See People v. Tufts, 167 Cal. 266, 273, 274 (1914); Commonwealth v. Sacco, 259 Mass. 128, 141 (1927); Charles H. Tuttle, "The Ethics of Advocacy," 18 A.B.A. Jour. 849, 852, 853 (1931). State v. Montgomery, 56 Wash. 443 (1909); State v. Osborne,

Upholding the Honor of the Profession

The last sentence of Canon 29 requires the lawyer to "strive at all times to uphold the honor and to maintain the dignity of the profession." [2]

Defenses such as Usury, Infancy, Bankruptcy, Statutes of Frauds or of Limitations

Although Hoffman in his Resolutions XII and XIII said that he would never plead the statute of limitations when based on the mere efflux of time or that of infancy, against an honest demand, such defenses as these are deliberately offered by the law and it is the client's privilege to avail himself of them. In a case where their assertion would produce flagrant injustice, the lawyer may, of course, if he wish, refuse to take the case, or withdraw from it if this is possible without impairing the client's right, but while in the case he must advise the client of the availability of such defenses and if, despite his admonition, the client insists, assert and make them effective. [3]

---

54 Ore. 289, 296 (1909); People v. Phipps, 261 Ill. 576 (1914); Showell Rogers, "The Ethics of Advocacy," 15 Law Quart. Rev. 259 (1899). See 9 A.L.R. 197 (1920); 43 A.L.R. 109 (1926); 46 L.R.A. 641 (1927); People v. Dane, 59 Mich. 550 (1886).

See as to the other view, Warvelle, *Legal Ethics* (2d ed.), secs. 230–32, pp. 141–43.

2 Of this the New York City Committee aptly said in its Op. 834: "A lawyer should at all times conduct himself with all candor and fairness in all his dealings. Only in this way can he uphold the honor and integrity of the profession." In this opinion the Committee held that where a lawyer was approached to secure a loan and intended to arrange with his wife to make it, it would be contrary to Canons 22 and 29 for him not to tell her that he was being paid to secure the loan.

As to how far a lawyer is bound to protest the client's exaction of his pound of flesh, see *supra*, pp. 144–50, and *infra*, p. 196.

As to the impropriety of newspaper discussion of pending litigation, see Canon 20, *supra*, p. 70.

However, N.Y. City 251 (a), holds that a lawyer who had borrowed money from his client might, on suit by the client interpose the defense of usury and that another lawyer might properly represent him in so doing. The Committee said that in its opinion "as a general proposition a lawyer cannot be deprived, by reason of his professional character, from interposing a defense that is open to a layman."

While, as a matter of law, this statement may be correct in the case of a loan from one not a client, as applied to a loan by a client it is wholly at variance with the lawyer's highly fiduciary relation. Certainly the lawyer's action would not tend to uphold the honor or dignity of the profession.

3 "The defenses of infancy, statute of frauds, statute of limitations, or that a promise was gratuitous are only too often dishonorable defenses, but their abolition would probably increase rather than diminish injustice." James Barr Ames, *Lectures on Legal History* (1913), p. 448.

See also J. B. Leavitt, *Lawyer and Client in Every Day Ethics* (1910), pp. 56, 57; Forsyth, *Hortensius*, p. 402; Sharswood, *Professional Ethics* (5th ed.), pp. 98, 99.

Participation in Fraud or Trickery

The fourth paragraph of the Oath of Admission prescribed by the Association provides:

I will employ for the purpose of maintaining the causes confided to me such means only as are consistent with truth and honor, and will never seek to mislead the judge or jury by any artifice or false statement of fact or law.

A lawyer may not aid his client in perpetrating a fraud,[4] or what is virtually one,[5] or represent a client suspiciously insisting on using an assumed name.[6] When a lawyer learns that he has won his case by testimony which was deliberately false, he must disclose such falsity to those injured by its results so that they may take such steps as they are advised are necessary for the protection of their interests.[7]

He may not properly assist a client to obtain a Mexican mail-order divorce,[8] known to be wholly invalid, even though he clearly advises the client of its invalidity.[9] The client's only conceivable purpose in securing such a "divorce" is to misrepresent its validity. This is believed to be a sounder reason for the lawyer's declining to have any part in obtaining it than that given by the American Bar Association Committee [10] that "the state is a party to the matrimonial status of its citizens and insists that that status shall be dealt with only in a manner that will be recognized as according with the law of the state."

He may not employ a "skip-tracing" concern to locate debtors, which, to be successful, depends on deceit and misrepresentation; [11] nor may he obtain evidence through a misrepresenting detective; [12] and query as to the propriety of his using it.

---

[4] N.Y. County 9, 181; see also N.Y. City 535.   [5] App. A, *15*.
[6] N.Y. County 259; N.Y. City 560.   [7] N.Y. County 215; see *supra*, p. 141.
[8] A.B.A. Op. 248; N.Y. City 232, 378; but see N.Y. City 845, B-128, B-159; see also Matter of Anonymous, an Attorney, 274 App. Div. 89 (1948), and note thereon in 49 Col. L. Rev. 129 (1949).
[9] As to Mexican divorces, see "The Divorce Laws of Mexico," 2 Law & Contemp. Probl. 310 (1935); see also *supra*, p. 123. Also In re Cohen, 10 N.J. 601 (1952).
In connection with these cases a distinction may perhaps be drawn between advising a local client of his or her rights, and affirmatively participating, even to the extent of recommending a Mexican lawyer. Much can be said in favor of a lawyer's right and duty to advise an intelligent client correctly on any question of law as to which the client consults him and as to which he is competent to give advice.
[10] A.B.A. Op. 248.
[11] N.Y. City 654 (see Gumperz v. Hoffman, 245 App. Div. 622 [1935]), N.Y. City 803, 886, 937; cf. N.Y. County 254; also N.Y. City 219 (bad taste), N.Y. City 240.
[12] N.Y. City B-193.

The New York County Committee has held that a lawyer sued for negligence as the owner of an apartment which in fact he did not own might not accept a retainer from the casualty company insuring the real owner to defend and not disclose his non-ownership so that the statute of limitations might run.[13]

He may not pass off a professional witness in a divorce case as a friend of plaintiff.[14]

He may not insert in a contract a waiver which he knows is void as against public policy.[15]

He may not go back on a valid agreement with the other party in settlement of a case or institute a suit which he knows is not meritorious in order to deter such party from asserting his legal rights.[16]

He may not, when a notary, take an affidavit on the telephone, even of one whose voice he recognizes, and although it is not intended to be used in a legal or judicial proceeding.[17]

ADVICE OR ASSISTANCE IN THE DELIBERATE VIOLATION OF THE LAW

Canon 16, entitled "Restraining Clients from Improprieties," reads:

A lawyer should use his best efforts to restrain and to prevent his clients from doing those things which the lawyer himself ought not to do, particularly with reference to their conduct towards Courts, judicial officers, jurors, witnesses and suitors. If a client persists in such wrongdoing the lawyer should terminate their relation.

See also Canons 29, 41, and 44.

A lawyer may not be engaged by an organization whose members are violating the law, to defend them when they get caught;[18] but may

---

[13] N.Y. County 53; see also N.Y. City 535; as to whether he may use a forged paper on cross-examination in order to discredit a witness, see In re Metzger, 31 Hawaii 929 (1931) lawyer suspended for ten days, one judge dissenting.

Horace Binney, in his day leader of the Philadelphia bar, said of himself: "I never prosecuted a cause that I thought a dishonest one, and I have washed my hands of more than one that I discovered to be such after I had undertaken it, as well as declined many which I perceived to be so when first presented to me." C. C. Binney, *The Life of Horace Binney* (1903), p. 443.

[14] N.Y. City 668.   [15] N.Y. City B-78.

[16] N.Y. City 596; cf., however, N.Y. City 243 and 254, discussed *infra,* p. 196 n. 34.

[17] In re Napolis, 169 App. Div. 469 (1915). In New York this was a statutory misdemeanor.

[18] A.B.A. Op. 281. Bowman v. Phillips, 41 Kan. 364 (1889); Herbert W. Salus's case, 321 Pa. 81, 103, 106 (1936); Lemisch's case, 321 Pa. 110 (1936); Matter of Davis, 252 App. Div. 591 (N.Y., 1937). As to the lawyer's duty on discovery of his client's fraud or perjury, see *supra,* p. 141.

"use his influence" to get a client's son into the medical school and charge and sue for a fee for so doing.[19]

He may not advise a criminal to hide because of belief that he may not get a fair trial,[20] or to leave the jurisdiction on the ground that the law under which the criminal was subpoenaed is unconstitutional.[21] Nor may a lawyer advise an imprisoned client what to do when he escapes, or to swear to facts which the lawyer knows from the client are not true.[22]

A lawyer may not advise that it is cheaper to pay a fine than to obey a statute.[23]

Although a lawyer may advise the contest of a law's constitutionality or its construction, he may not advocate publicly nor advise the violation of a law declared valid by the highest court; [24] nor because of his personal conviction of the non-enforceability of a contract may he advise his client to flout the order of the court enforcing it; [25] nor may a lawyer violate a law in order to test its validity.[26]

Although he may not accept employment to enforce a claim which he knows to have been discharged,[27] he may sue on a business contract after the statute of limitations has run, since this, to be a defense, must be pleaded.[28]

Countenance of Payments to Secure Specific Testimony

A lawyer may not advertise for witnesses to testify to stated facts, although he may advertise as to witnesses of a particular event or transaction.[29] A lawyer may not offer a contingent fee to a witness,[30]

19 N.Y. City 327; Canon 26 provides that a lawyer may not use, to influence action, "means other than those addressed to reason and understanding."

20 Mich. 22; but see A.B.A. Op. 23.

21 N.Y. City 92; see also In re Robinson, 140 App. Div. 329 (1910). Boston v. Greenwood, 168 Mass. 169 (1897); Matter of Rouss, 169 App. Div. 629 (1915) (221 N.Y. 81 [1917] affirmed).

22 A.B.A. Op. 150; but see N.Y. County 206.

23 N.Y. County 27.　　24 N.Y. County 262.

25 Odell v. Bausch et al., 91 F.2d 359 (C.C.A., 7th) (1937).

26 N.Y. County 331; and see N.Y. County 27. As to the distinction between advice as to what the law is and advice to do specific acts, see In re Cooley, 95 N.J. Eq. 485, 490 (1924); and 28 Law Notes 203 (1925).

27 N.Y. County 281.　　28 Compare N.Y. County 61; see also supra, p. 149.

29 App. A, 305. See also supra, p. 86.

30 N.Y. City 86 (here a former employee of the other party having confidential information); and see N.Y. City 311 (guarantee not to lose); see also N.Y. County 110 and cases cited; Matter of Schapiro, 144 App. Div. 1 (1911); In re O'Keefe, 49 Mont. 369 (1914).

but may pay a witness for waiving his privilege not to testify, notice being given to court, jury, and counsel,[31] and may pay transportation expenses to an out-of-town witness without advising counsel and the court.[32]

He may not advise paying respondent to get from him evidence of his adultery.[33]

A lawyer may, however, where no likelihood of perjury appears, promise a contingent reward for desired information,[34] but not pay a former employee of the other side for confidential information,[35] or pay a bonus to one who is prohibited by law from accepting it.[36]

A lawyer should not testify for a former client when told that his overdue fee bill will not be paid unless the client wins;[37] nor may a lawyer refuse to represent a bankrupt except on condition that the bankrupt pay in full the creditors whom he represents.[38]

He need not disclose the only eyewitness, not known to the other side, though in court.[39]

EMPLOYMENT OF COERCIVE TACTICS

A lawyer may not make continuous complaints to defendant's superior in the police department[40] or in the Board of Education[41] or send to the employer a dunning letter, until after judgment is obtained; but he may do so when the claim is subject to garnishment,[42] and he may threaten a debtor to foreclose a mortgage unless the debt is paid.[43] A lawyer may not threaten a criminal action[44] or disciplinary proceedings[45] in order to effect a civil settlement, but apparently may ascertain without threat, from the debtor's employer, the amount of his salary,[46] and may, with the approval of the magistrate or prose-

[31] N.Y. City 8.
[32] N.Y. City 411; see also Matter of Schapiro, 144 App. Div. 1, 9–10 (N.Y., 1911), Matter of Robinson, 151 App. Div. 589, 600 (1912).
[33] N.Y. County 132; see *supra*, p. 127.   [34] N.Y. City 86(*b*); see also N.Y. City 325.
[35] N.Y. City 86(*c*); see also N.Y. City 311.   [36] N.Y. City B-182.
[37] N.Y. City 720.   [38] App. A, *10*.
[39] N.Y. County 309; but query as to the soundness of this ruling.
[40] N.Y. County 360; N.Y. City 677.
[41] N.Y. City 694; but as to the army, see N.Y. City B-14.
[42] N.Y. City 823, 829, 926; and see 682-B.   [43] N.Y. County 107.
[44] N.Y. City B-127; Matter of Gelman, 230 App. Div. 524 (1930); In re Joyce, 182 Minn. 156 (1930); State v. Johnson, 149 Iowa 462 (1910); but see N.Y. City 265. Cf. Mo. 32.
[45] Chicago 30, p. 67; In re Malmin, 364 Ill. 164, 177 (1936); In re Sherin, 50 S.D. 428 (1926).
[46] N.Y. City 823; as to government employee, see Chicago 8, p. 18.

cuting attorney, dismiss a criminal charge when restitution has been made.[47] Where his client has an assignment of the debtor's wages, a lawyer may ask the employer's cooperation in collecting, even after the statutory limitation period has expired.[48]

He may not demand of defendant a larger amount than he considers a proper maximum.[49]

He may not threaten more than he can reasonably do,[50] or write to a debtor that a judgment against him will injure his credit or reflect on his moral standing,[1] but may say he will sue [2] or foreclose [3] if not paid within blank days. He may bargain with a judgment creditor to reduce his claim or be thrown into bankruptcy.[4]

ABUSE OF LEGAL PROCESS

A lawyer may not send simulated court papers in demands from the debtor,[5] or permit his client to send collection letters in the lawyer's name,[6] or on his stationery,[7] or to issue a summons in his name,[8] but a lawyer may sign prepared letters of demand if personally satisfied that they state the facts fairly,[9] and may use a rubber stamp, although this is undignified.[10] A lawyer may not be employed merely to serve a summons and do no more.[11]

A lawyer mistakenly sued as the owner of a property negligently operated may not accept compensation from the casualty company to defend and not to disclose his non-ownership until the statute has run against the real owner, but should advise the plaintiff that he is not the owner.[12]

---

[47] N.Y. City 265, 276, 589; N.Y. County 347.

[48] N.Y. City 682-B; and cf. N.Y. City 684.   [49] N.Y. County 10.

[50] N.Y. City 125, and cf. N.Y. City 387, 397, 669, 684, 705, 733. Cf. Mo. 61.

[1] App. A, 303.

[2] N.Y. City 888, 926. As to procedure and form in case of a large number of claims under $10 each, see N.Y. City B-55. The letter should not suggest "embarrassment" or "prosecution."

[3] N.Y. County 107.   [4] N.Y. County 164.

[5] A.B.A. Op. 178; App. A, 301; Weiss's Appeal, 317 Pa. 415 (1935); In re Swihart, 42 S.D. 628 (1920); In re Pouker, 203 App. Div. 520 (1922); Chicago 23, p. 45, and cf. N.Y. County 392; N.Y. City 304. See also supra, pp. 79–80.

[6] A.B.A. Op. 253; Va. 14; App. A, 302.   [7] N.Y. City 939; Mich. 32.

[8] N.Y. County 102; In re Hendrick 229 App. Div. 100 (1930), respondent was suspended for a year for directing his employee to sign his client's name to a general release; and In re Batt 230 App. Div. 656 (1930), respondent was "severely censured" for repeatedly signing, without reading, papers to be filed in court.

[9] N.Y. County 300.   [10] N.Y. City 902.   [11] N.Y. County 306.

[12] N.Y. County 53. See also supra, p. 151.

A member of the legislature may not send claim letters to a debtor in an envelope marked "The Assembly, Albany," since this would mislead the debtor into thinking that political pressure would be brought to force him to pay the claim.[13]

Employment of Underhanded Means to Get Evidence or Disreputable Tactics to Further His Case

The oath recommended by the American Bar Association contains a pledge that the lawyer "will never seek to mislead the judge or jury by any artifice."

He may not install or advise a dictaphone in the house of a respondent in order to get evidence of adultery.[14]

He may not cause a defendant to be enticed out of the jurisdiction in order to enable suit to be brought on the bail bond; [15] or endeavor to close the mouths of disinterested witnesses so that the lawyer on the other side cannot find out what they know; [16] nor may he attempt to get the lawyer on the other side drunk in order to get the better of him in the case about to be tried.[17]

Where he gets the wrong license number of an offending auto, he may not serve a summons on the owners of other numbers with the hope of catching the offender, and if a lawyer does this he merits censure.[18]

A lawyer may not, on behalf of an unnamed client, agree with a corporation to disclose defalcations by employees in return for a large fee in which the lawyer will have a contingent interest.[19]

He may sue on a valid claim with garnishment for a client against another client, with the consent of both, in order to prevent another creditor from collecting a judgment until after the first is paid.[20]

Where defendant's counsel has moved without leaving an address but plaintiff's lawyer knows defendant's address, plaintiff's lawyer must advise defendant, despite his client's instructions to the contrary, of the entry of a default judgment in time to have a motion filed to open it.[21]

[13] N.Y. City 682-H; as to abuse of legal proceedings, see also 28 Mich. L. Rev. 71 (1929).
[14] N.Y. City 959, cf. N.Y. City 848.   [15] A.B.A. Op. 21.
[16] A.B.A. Op. 131; App. A, *304*.   [17] Dickens' case, 67 Pa. 169, 177 (1870).
[18] N.Y. City 266.   [19] N.Y. City 613.
[20] N.Y. County 325.   [21] N.Y. County 283.

The first sentence of Canon 30 is as follows: "The lawyer must decline to conduct a civil cause or to make a defense when convinced that it is intended merely to harass or to injure the opposite party or to work oppression or wrong."

He may not bring suit in a distant county merely in order to harass the debtor.[23]

COMPLIANCE WITH AGREEMENTS AND UNDERSTANDINGS MADE IN THE COURSE OF CONDUCTING THE CASE

Where in order to gain an advantage for his client the lawyer agrees to see to it that a creditor [24] or a witness [25] is paid out of the proceeds of a recovery, the lawyer may not, on the client's insistence, remit the full amount of the recovery to the client without making such payment.

DUTY ON DISCOVERY OF FRAUD OR IMPOSITION IN HIS CASE

Canon 41 provides as follows:

When a lawyer discovers that some fraud or deception has been practiced, which has unjustly imposed upon the court or a party, he should endeavor to rectify it; at first by advising his client, and if his client refuses to forego the advantage thus unjustly gained, he should promptly inform the injured person or his counsel, so that they may take appropriate steps.

He may not permit a client to be reimbursed, as per agreement, a counsel fee greater than was actually paid.[26]

Where a lawyer learns that in a settlement supervised by him which called for a conveyance by his client free of encumbrances, the client deliberately concealed an unpaid purchase money mortgage, the lawyer must advise the other party thereof despite the protest of his client and his new lawyer; Canon 37 does not modify Canon 41 in this regard.[27]

When he learns that his client, an executor holding a will naming others as beneficiaries, proposes to conceal the will and appropriate

---

[22] See also *supra*, p. 80 n. 10 and pp. 87, 147–48.
[23] N.Y. City 72; see also Dishaw v. Wadleigh, 15 App. Div. 205 (N.Y., 1897).
[24] N.Y. County 321; and cf. N.Y. City 54.
[25] Chicago 9, p. 19; see also N.Y. City 313.
[26] N.Y. County 303.   [27] Mich. 59, and cf. N.Y. County 215.

the property, the lawyer should advise the heirs and perhaps the prosecuting attorney.[28]

However, the mere fact that a client, plaintiff in an accident suit on a good cause of action, has falsely claimed a second accident at a later date and different place, does not necessarily require the lawyer to refuse to bring the first suit if satisfied that the fraud has been unsuccessful or abandoned, and that he can maintain the proper relations with the client and the court.[29]

When he learns that a client purchasing mortgages at a discount has been receiving from the title company, by a false representation, an allowance on account of fees in excess of those actually paid, the lawyer should endeavor to dissuade the client, and if this fails, to refuse longer to serve him.[30]

A lawyer who, in an accident case, made, with the client's approval, an agreement with the examining doctor witness, that he be paid a specified amount in the event of recovery, is professionally reprehensible in making settlement without providing for the doctor's fee.[31]

Where a lawyer employed a court reporter as a necessary part of the presentation of his client's case, the lawyer may not remit the funds collected to the client, on the latter's demand, without paying the reporter.[32]

A lawyer learning that a state administrative body which he had represented has committed and permitted grave violations of the laws may, after notice to the highest appropriate public officials and refusal by them to take any action, and resignation by the lawyer, properly make public the facts and invoke the pressure of public opinion to remedy the abuses.[33]

The lawyer for a husband and wife should, despite her objection, advise his relatives, after his death, of an agreement made by her for their benefit.[34]

As to the impropriety of advising a client to communicate directly with the other side represented by a lawyer, see *infra,* page 201.

---

[28] N.Y. County 84; see also N.Y. City 274.

In Matter of Hardenbrook, 135 App. Div. 634 (1909) (affirmed 199 N.Y. 539 [1910]) the lawyer who insisted on the truth of his client's testimony when he knew it to be false was disbarred.

[29] N.Y. County 301.   [30] N.Y. County 303.

[31] Chicago 9, p. 19; see also N.Y. City 313.

[32] N.Y. County 321; cf. N.Y. City 54.

[33] N.Y. County 339.   [34] N.Y. City B-60.

DUTY AS A PROSPECTIVE WITNESS

Canon 19 provides:

When a lawyer is a witness for his client, except as to merely formal matters, such as the attestation or custody of an instrument and the like, he
should leave the trial of the case to other counsel. Except when essential
to the ends of justice, a lawyer should avoid testifying in court in behalf
of his client.

The American Bar Association Committee has held,[35] modifying
its former opinions,[36] and following the ruling of the Philadelphia
Bar Association Committee on Professional Guidance,[37] that this
Canon does not preclude a lawyer, with full disclosure to opposing
counsel and to the court, from being a witness on behalf of a client
represented by the lawyer's partner, where his testimony relates to
matters occurring in the course of his professional duties and is in
support of the client's position, and where the lawyer's long and intimate familiarity with the details of the matter in litigation make it
important to the client to have the benefit both of the lawyer's testimony and of the professional services of his firm. The dissenting opinion by member Houghton cites a number of decisions in support
of the view that the partners in a firm may not, except as to merely
formal matters,[38] be both witness and advocate in a contested case.[39]

A lawyer may not testify as an expert for defendant corporation
which is being defended by his firm in a suit against it for a counsel
fee.[40]

He may represent a member of a secret society threatened with
expulsion in a hearing within the organization, though he may also
be a witness.[41]

A lawyer who saw an accident and handed the injured one his professional card cannot accept the case qua lawyer, both under Canon
19 and Canon 27.[42]

A lawyer who disqualifies himself in litigation because he saw the
accident and will be a witness, may not, after a successful outcome,

[35] A.B.A. Op. 220; Messrs. Houghton and Brand dissenting.
[36] A.B.A. Ops. 33, 50, 185.   [37] Feb. 10, 1941.
[38] N.Y. County 76; Mich. 103. See as to barristers, An. St. (1911), p. 11, and *id.* (1912),
p. 11.
[39] See N.Y. City 144; and see N.Y. City 727 and 763; also N.Y. City 777 where the
possibility was rather remote.
[40] N.Y. County 362.   [41] App. A, 282.
[42] N.Y. City 914; see also N.Y. City 564.

demand a share of the fee of the lawyer whom he got the client to employ; [43] but a lawyer who disqualifies himself as a witness because he drew the will making him an executor may be entitled to compensation for advice and attendance at the trial of the will case.[44]

Canon 19 does not apply to a mere formal witnessing of a will, with no conflict. If the latter develops, he must retire as soon as his client's interest permits.[45] It is not believed that there is much, if any, practical difference between an estate being represented by the partner of the witness, or by a fellow member of his bar whom the client would doubtless choose with his approval.

Canon 19 is not applicable where the lawyer is called by his adversary,[46] or to cases of surprise where there is not time for the client to get another lawyer.[47]

It is the right and duty of a lawyer to testify before the grand jury in place of his client who is ill.[48]

DIRECT RELATIONS WITH CLIENTS

Canon 35 [49] provides:

The professional services of a lawyer should not be controlled or exploited by any lay agency, personal or corporate, which intervenes between client and lawyer. A lawyer's responsibilities and qualifications are individual. He should avoid all relations which direct the performance of his duties by or in the interest of such intermediary. A lawyer's relation to his client should be personal, and the responsibility should be direct to the client. Charitable societies rendering aid to the indigent are not deemed such intermediaries.[50]

[43] A.B.A. Op. 153. He performed no legal service and assumed no legal responsibility.

[44] App. A, *283;* cf. also N.Y. City B-160, where it seemed wiser to refuse it in view of possible misconstruction.

[45] N.Y. County 28; the question of a partner's acting was not apparently considered in this case. And see N.Y. County 64. Mich. 103; and see N.Y. City B-167.

[46] Thornton, *Attorneys,* sec. 189.

[47] N.Y. County 64.   [48] N.Y. City 624.

[49] This Canon was amended in 1933 by inserting "by or" between the words "duties" and "in" on line 5, and by striking out the following concluding paragraph: "The established custom of receiving commerical collections through a lay agency is not condemned hereby."

Canon 34, forbidding a division of fees except with another lawyer, based on a division of service or responsibility, was also amended in 1937 by striking out a provision permitting a division with laymen on liquidated commercial claims.

[50] For a case within this exception, see N.Y. City 413, 593.

A labor union or a trade association would not seem to be a charitable society within the meaning of the exception. See N.Y. City 413.

Intervention by Intermediary

A lawyer may not properly draw a will on the instructions of a daughter and give it to her to have her mother sign, but should see the testatrix personally.[1] The practice of drawing wills for trust companies to have their patrons sign is wholly improper, particularly where the lawyer is expected to have the trust company named executor and trustee.[2]

A lawyer may not belong to a labor union which includes persons not lawyers. By so doing he surrenders his power of independent action.[3]

A group of lawyers may not agree to draw free wills in which a bequest is made to the church.[4]

The City Committee also held that a lawyer may not accept compensation cases to represent patients in a hospital of which he is counsel, on its recommendation, thus enabling them to pay their hospital bills.[5]

Delegation of Professional Functions

A lawyer may not delegate his professional functions.[6]

He may not make an arrangement with a broker to prepare abstracts for him to be delivered to the broker's client, the broker to arrange for and collect the lawyer's fee, the lawyer not to see the client.[7]

---

[1] Op. of Council of the Law Society (Eng.), Feb. 1, 1900; Costigan, Case Book, p. 687.

[2] App. A, *290;* and see A.B.A. Op. 41. See also *supra,* p. 110.

[3] A.B.A. Op. 275; App. A, *267;* N.Y. County 376; N.Y. City 964 (Joint Opinion). Relation to trade organizations, see N.Y. County Committee's Statement of 5/2/21; Costigan, Case Book, p. 360, N.Y. County 331.

Lawyers may organize a tax institute giving no advice or lawyers' names; N.Y. City 102.

An organization which has obtained claims by solicitation and turned them over to a lawyer may not demand them back from one whom the lawyer gets to handle them on leaving town, N.Y. City 140.

[4] N.Y. City 608. In a period of depression, however, a lawyer may properly belong to a barter group managed by an exchange, the lawyer being free to accept employment or not and to conduct the matters in which he is retained by his fellow members, N.Y. City 356.

[5] N.Y. City 556 (why not assign the claims?); and see N.Y. City 615, where he was not counsel for the hospital. Query as to this ruling.

[6] N.Y. County 102, 179, 300; Mich. 110.

"A lawyer cannot delegate to a lay employee the professional confidence reposed in him by his client, nor can he delegate to a layman the exercise of his professional discretion." A.B.A. Op. 85.

[7] Mich. 110; and cf. Mich. 136.

He may not accept employment by one in the business of looking up uncollected judgments where the investigator is really the client, although specifically authorized in each case by the client;[8] or on a contingent basis by engineers themselves employed on a contingent basis to collect damages for injuries by the construction of a subway.[9] A lawyer may, however, accept a retainer from the wife of one so badly injured that he cannot see the lawyer.[10]

A lawyer's practice and good will may not be offered for sale.[11]

A lawyer may not arrange for or permit a lawyer in another jurisdiction to appear there on behalf of his client, except with the client's prior consent.[12]

While a lawyer may properly make an accountant his messenger to carry to their mutual client the lawyer's legal opinion on an accounting question, the client realizing that the accountant is such messenger, the lawyer may not properly give legal advice to an accountant to enable the accountant to pass such advice to the client as the accountant's advice.[13]

The general counsel of a corporation may not allow the collection department in another office to use his letterhead,[14] or permit a collection agency to sign his name in making collections.[15]

He may not permit a client to send out letters stating that unless the account is paid within a stated time it will be turned over to the lawyer,[16] or in his name to issue and serve a summons,[17] but may sign demand letters prepared by the client.[18] A lawyer may, however, give an opinion to an investment association as to the taxability of income receivable from the funds invested by the association to be used by the salesmen of the association in selling its securities.[19]

Employment by Organization to Act for Its Employees or Members

Difficult questions are involved in connection with the lawyer's employment by corporations, labor unions, employer associations, automobile clubs, trade and other associations, to deal with their associate

---

[8] N.Y. County 291. He may not allow his name to be used in the promotion of his client's business. A.B.A. Op. 76.

[9] N.Y. County 296; and see Chicago 36, A.B.A. Op. 237.

[10] N.Y. City 785; and cf. N.Y. City 201. [11] N.Y. City B-142; A.B.A. Op. 266.

[12] N.Y. City 841. [13] App. A, *321;* cf. N.Y. City 682-C.

[14] N.Y. City 609, 672. [15] N.Y. City 99, Mo. 16.

[16] App. A, *302;* N.Y. City 77, 210, 462; A.B.A. Op. 68. [17] N.Y. City 129.

[18] N.Y. County 300. [19] App. A, *320.*

problems and with the problems affecting their employees, patrons or members.[20]

ANALYSIS OF PROBLEMS INVOLVED

These problems arise in several aspects:

In accordance with the first clause of the last paragraph of Canon 35, the lawyer may clearly accept employment from any such organization to render legal services in any matter in which the organization, as an entity, is itself directly interested.

The difficulty is with the last clause: "but this employment should not include the rendering of legal services to the members of such an organization in respect to their individual affairs."

This provision is obviously in furtherance of the admonitions in the first paragraph of the Canon that the lawyer's relation to his client should be personal, his responsibility to him direct, and not subject to the control or exploitation of any lay intermediary intervening between them. Consequences of such intervention, in addition to interference with the lawyer's intimate personal relation to his client, are the tendency to commercialize the profession, and promotion of the unauthorized practice of the law on the part of the organization by providing legal services and advice for its employees and members.

The Canon does not preclude counsel for a corporation or association from representing its individual employees, patrons, stockholders or members [21] or groups of them [22] provided such employment has not been the result of improper solicitation,[23] and provided such relation is personal and direct and the service paid for by the individual client or pro-rated among the group,[24] and not paid by the corporation or association.[25]

Where, however, the corporation or association employs and pays the lawyer to advise and represent its employees, patrons, or members in respect to their individual affairs, the prohibition of the Canon would seem applicable, even though the lawyer's relation is direct, although there is no conflict of interest between the client and the organization, and even though the reason and occasion for the service

---

20 See Hicks and Katz, 41 Yale L. Jour. 69, 84 (1931).

21 App. A, 316; Mich. 147 (iv).   22 Mich. 147 (v).

23 See also infra, p. 259. As to the impropriety of accepting chronic recommendations, see N.Y. County 147; N.Y. City 509, 629.

24 Mich. 147 (vii).   25 See, for example, N.Y. City 209; N.Y. County 363.

is the bona fide interest of the organization to see that it is performed. This latter consideration is particularly forcible in the case of corporations whose direct interest, as an entity, it is to see to it that their employees are kept free from legal difficulties and entanglements. Business corporations may and do to an ever increasing extent provide free medical services for their employees, as one of their conditions of employment, in order to keep them healthy, and consequently more efficient. Why not similarly free legal service and advice? Only, it would seem, because of the Canon, and of the decisions of the courts and the unauthorized practice committees that for a corporation to provide a lawyer to advise and serve its employees constitutes the unauthorized practice of the law by it. Suppose that the union contract provided, as one of the "fringe benefits," for free legal service to union employees, how would the employer comply with this requirement? Doubtless, the corporation might agree to pay the lawyers' bills of the employees, but this would be subject to obvious abuse and would not satisfactorily achieve the desired result and advantage to the employer.

Be that as it may, and despite the potent arguments advanced for the other view,[26] there would seem to be no valid basis for avoiding the direct admonition of the Canon, particularly in view of its history.

HISTORY OF CANON 35

Canon 35 was adopted in 1928. Prior thereto the American Bar Association Committee had promulgated its Opinion 8 (1925), holding that a lawyer might not accept employment as a part-time employee of the legal department of an automobile club, which as an inducement to membership offered legal services to members consisting of advice regarding laws relating to the operation of automobiles, to the violation of traffic laws, and to damage claims to persons and property. The Committee held that, although the service was for the benefit of the organization, nevertheless it involved solicitation, and also the exploitation of professional services by a lay agency, tending to commercialize the profession in that the club "pays a lawyer one amount for his services and for these services charges a different amount to the person to whom they are rendered." It was therefore held to be engaged in the unauthorized practice of the law. The Committee said:

[26] See memorandum attached to N.Y. City 413 (1934); see also N.Y. City 590 (1938).

The essential dignity of the profession forbids a lawyer to solicit business or to exploit his professional services. It follows that he cannot properly enter into any relations with another to have done for him that which he cannot properly do for himself.

It must therefore be held that the furnishing, selling or exploiting of the legal services of members of the Bar is derogatory to the dignity and self-respect of the profession, tends to lower the standards of professional character and conduct and thus lessens the usefulness of the profession to the public, and that a lawyer is guilty of misconduct, when he makes it possible, by thus allowing his services to be exploited or dealt in, for others to commercialize the profession and bring it into disrepute.

The conduct of the lawyers in question must be therefore disapproved on the ground that their relations with the club amounts to a division of professional fees with a lay agency and to an agreement with this lay agency for the exploitation of the lawyers' professional services.[27]

In 1928 Canon 35 was adopted, using considerable of the language of Opinion 8 and evidently with that Opinion in mind. Canon 35 was amended in 1933 by striking out [28] the original concluding paragraph providing that "the established custom of receiving commercial collections through a lay agency is not condemned hereby."

CONSIDERATIONS PRO AND CON

Much could be said in favor of the propriety as well as the practical wisdom of permitting a corporation to furnish, as part of its contract of employment, legal services to its employees where this is for the benefit of the corporation,[29] where the relation between the lawyer and the employee is direct and no conflict of interest exists between the employer and the employee. The Canon does not specifically cover this but is directed rather at services to members of associations. Nevertheless, in view of the apparent acceptance by the Association of Opinion 8, including the statement therein as to unauthorized practice, it would seem clear that any change in the construction of the Canon must be by an amendment.[30] Since the formation of the

[27] On page 74.

[28] Also by inserting the words "by or" between "duties" and "in" on line 5 of the first paragraph.

[29] The New York City Committee held that a lawyer may properly represent and be compensated by an employer in getting his employees exempted from the draft. N.Y. City 731, 930.

[30] Such an amendment might be by adding to Canon 35 the following: "The foregoing shall not prevent the lawyer for a corporation or other employer which, in its own interest, agrees to furnish free legal services to its employees, from accepting from it employment to render such services, provided that in every case the relations between

American Bar Association Committee on Unauthorized Practice in 1950, that Committee has ruled [31] that a corporation may not properly retain a lawyer to answer legal questions or to perform legal services for its employees (even though it be manifestly to the interest of the corporation to have its employees advised in connection with such matters), since, that Committee holds, the corporation would thus be practicing law; and that the same conclusion follows with regard to a labor union, automobile club, or association providing legal services for its members, although in each case the lawyer had direct relations with the employee member, and though the lawyer's service was restricted to matters in which there was no conflict of interest between the corporation or association and the employee or member.

CANON 47 IS DECISIVE

The American Bar Association Ethics Committee being bound by the above decisions,[32] necessarily held that such practice would violate Canon 47, condemning aid by a lawyer of the unauthorized practice of the law. The same conclusion would follow in the case of any other committee bound by decisions of its unauthorized practice committee or of the courts.[33]

Representation of a Group with a Common Interest Paying Uniform Annual Dues to Provide His Compensation

A somewhat different although related problem is presented where a group of persons having a common interest combine to employ a lawyer to protect or further such interest. If the group is small and not organized in the form of a club or association so as to constitute an entity distinct from its members, the case is evidently not covered by

the lawyer and the employee be direct and individual and involve no conflict of interest between the employee and the employer."

The adoption of such an amendment would not, of course, remedy the situation in any jurisdiction where under statute or under court rulings such practice would constitute the unauthorized practice of law.

The Principles of Medical Ethics, adopted by the American Medical Association specifically provide (Chap. III, Art. VI, Sec. 3) for agreements by a physician or group of physicians with a corporation for the treatment of its employees, called "Contract practice," which is said not to be unethical *per se.* But see Sec. 6.

[31] 36 A.B.A. Jour. 677 (1950); see also N.Y. City B-192; see also 18 Unauthorized Practice News No. 3, p. 35, where the Committee says that "the vice is that there is a divided allegiance."

[32] A.B.A. Op. 273, p. 570; App. A, *1;* see also Ky. 2.

[33] See cases cited in A.B.A. Op. 8; also Richmond Association v. Bar Association, 167 Va. 327, 339 (1937); Mo. 1, 5, 6, 7, 19.

the language of Canon 35. Thus a partnership may, it would seem, employ a lawyer on an annual retainer to handle all the legal problems not only of the firm but of the individual members, including for example individual income-tax problems, leases, or traffic violations. So, it would seem, might the immediate members of a family employ a family lawyer. It is difficult to see why the problem is basically different as the group grows larger or at what point the line should be drawn. The New York County Committee has held that it is proper for a number of property owners to combine and employ a lawyer to represent them in suits for personal injuries, each owner paying an annual fee.[34] Here there was apparently no separate entity which could be accused of the unauthorized practice of law. The same Committee, however, in an earlier ruling [35] held that where a group of business men had formed a membership corporation for the purpose of supplying them with laws and advice in connection with their business affairs, it was improper for a lawyer to accept employment from it, since this would violate Section 280 of the New York Penal Law.[36] Similarly, the New York City Committee held that a lawyer might not accept employment by an "Association of Tenants, Inc.," a membership corporation, to represent the individual members in proceedings instituted by a landlord against them, such being a violation of paragraph 2 of Canon 35.[37] In each of these cases the members paid an annual fee to defray the lawyer's charges irrespective of the extent to which they each required the lawyer's services. Wherein does this differ in practical effect from their having insurance against legal

---

[34] N.Y. County 261.   [35] N.Y. County 108, not referred to in No. 261.

[36] As construed in Matter of Co-operative Law Co., 198 N.Y. 479 (1910); Meisel v. National Jewelers, Board of Trade, 90 Misc. Rep. 19 (1915).

[37] N.Y. City B-58. Similar rulings involved a hairdressers' membership association, to defend nuisance suits by clients, B-92; a nurses' association, B-135; school teachers' association, N.Y. County 363; and an association of postal employees "all of one race," N.Y. City B-163.

See also People v. Association of Real Estate Taxpayers of Illinois, 354 Ill. 102 (1933), where defendant was a corporation organized not for profit but to protect the members against improper tax burdens. Members paid annual dues based on their real estate holdings and were represented in tax cases by the Association's attorney. The corporation was held in contempt, fined $2,500 and enjoined from further practicing law (see decision as to injunction). For an interesting commentary on this decision, see H. Weihofen, 2 U. of Chi. L. Rev. 119 (1934).

And see In re Thibodeau, 295 Mass. 374 (1936), also In re Maclub, 295 Mass. 45 (1936), and 31 Ill. L. Rev. 813–14 (1937).

In England the British Automobile Association offers its members legal services much broader than any American motor club and has been doing so for twenty-five years, with no suggestion by bench or bar that this is improper.

expenses? Could an employer not, as part of his arrangement with his employees, provide them with a policy covering their necessary legal expenses?

It is not believed that the Canon will prevent the labor unions [38] from finding lawyers to advise their members. The whole modern tendency is in favor of such arrangements, including particularly employer and cooperative health services, the principles of which, if applied to legal services would materially lower and spread the total cost to the lower income groups. The real argument against their approval by the bar is believed to be loss of income to the lawyers and concentration of service in hands of fewer lawyers. These features do not commend the profession to the public.[39]

[38] See "Labor Union Lawyers," 5 Ind. & Lab. Rel. Rev. 361 (1952).

In this connection several court decisions have involved the propriety of a lawyer's acting as regional counsel in a Legal Aid Department set up in 1930 by the Brotherhood of Railroad Trainmen throughout the country to enable their members to get the full benefit of the Federal Employers' Liability Act without being subjected to ambulance-chasing attorneys or activities of claim adjusters. The regional counsel dealt with the members personally but charged them less than the usual contingent fees, such charges providing the cost of running the department. While the members were not obliged to retain them, they were strongly and continuously urged to do so. In an Illinois case, where the railroad had settled direct with the employee after notice of his statutory lien, the court said that the railroad's defense that plaintiff's employment had been obtained by solicitation and fee splitting was "unworthy of the able lawyers who made it." (Ryan v. Penna. Ry., 268 Ill. App., 364, 373 [1932].) In two other cases (In re O'Neill, 5 F. Supp. 465, 467 [1933]; Hildebrand v. State Bar of California, 36 Cal.2d 504 [1950]) however, involving the discipline of the lawyers, they were censured by the court for participating in the plan, their employment being "channeled" by the Brotherhood "contrary to professional standards." In the California case there were strong dissents by Justices Carter and Traynor, in which it was said that the plan "in no way lowers the dignity of the profession," being "nothing more than a proper joining of forces for the accomplishment of a proper legal objective of mutual protection. . . . Thus we do not have a case where the purpose, motive and result is stirring up or exciting litigation. . . . The essential object of the instant plan is not to obtain clients for an attorney. It is to enable the organization to assist its membership in a matter of vital concern to them."

[39] The same conclusion as that in A.B.A. Op. 8 has been reached relative to service to patrons of a corporation, A.B.A. Ops. 10, 31, 41; App. A, *318;* Mich. 92; N.Y. City 1, 10, 935; N.Y. County 108; Va. 10; Mich. 147 (see end of opinion). See also N.Y. City 413 and memorandum attached thereto (semble that if the corporation is not organized for profit a different rule applies under the proviso at the end of Canon 35); the clients of a patent agent, N.Y. County 336; or real estate firm, N.Y. County 68; N.Y. City 718; a collection agency (Mich. 62; N.Y. County 47 ii(*b*), 74, 131; N.Y. City 99, 174, 513); the members of a grange (A.B.A. Op. 56) or of a bankers' (A.B.A. Op. 98), manufacturers' (A.B.A. Ops. 168, 273), nurses' (N.Y. City B-135), engineers' (App. A, *317;* N.Y. City 952; N.Y. County 296, see Costigan's Case Book, p. 655), tenants' (N.Y. City 134, B-58, B-185), school teachers' (N.Y. County 363, here held that he could accept cases brought to him by the individual member, whom he knew only through representing the association), or other association (A.B.A. Op. 162; N.Y. City 485, 718, B-92, B-99, B-170; N.Y. County 108; Mich. 92, 147); and to the members of a labor union (App.

Trade Bulletins Involving Legal Questions

Still another cognate question is as to the propriety of a manufacturers' or other trade association issuing bulletins in which it answers legal problems of general interest to the membership as a whole, although the answers are to be distributed, by means of bulletins, to the entire membership for their information but without mention of the lawyer's name, and with proper warning that the members should consult their own counsel on specific problems as to their individual affairs.[40] The danger that they may so use the information is much the same as that in connection with legal articles permitted under Canon 40.[41]

In a case dealing with legal advice to a State Bankers' Association to be included in bulletins to the members, the American Bar Association Committee said:

A lawyer is not justified in giving an opinion without an opportunity to ask the client for information as to the concrete facts in the client's case, and without an opportunity to see the instruments or documents and to ascertain the dates and other facts, which the client has not given or may not deem material. Nor can the client be safe in acting on generalizations. And, moreover, other member banks having problems similar to the question answered, may be misled into accepting the published question and answer as applicable to their own problems.[42]

Relations with Collection Agencies [43]

While a lawyer may own an interest in a collection agency which solicits business, he may not participate in its management or activities, or accept collection cases from it.[44]

With the client's knowledge and approval, a lawyer may employ

---

A, *319;* Mich. 42, 147; N.Y. City 679, B-163, B-192; he may, however, represent an injured seaman with whom, at the request of the union delegate, he enters into direct relations (N.Y. City 209); employers of labor (N.Y. City 952); or investment counsel (N.Y. 638); or health center (N.Y. City 682); or credit exchange (A.B.A. Op. 35).

[40] See A.B.A. Op. 168, 273; Mich. 147. See N.Y. County 47 i, ii, iii, iv, vii, viii, 363; and see N.Y. City 479.

[41] See *infra*, p. 263.

[42] A.B.A. Op. 98, p. 214. See also A.B.A. Op. 285 as to the propriety of a lawyer's permitting a trade association to have its counsel's name on its letterheads or bulletins; also as to barristers, An. St. (1909), p. 8.

[43] See App. A, *326–330;* Mich. 147; N.Y. County 220 and opinions cited; N.Y. County 260 and opinions cited. See also N.Y. City 99; and Hicks and Katz, 41 Yale L. Jour. 69, 86 (1931). See also *infra*, pp. 179–80.

[44] A.B.A. Op. 225; see also A.B.A. Op. 198; Chicago 23, pp. 45–46; N.Y. County 238; Mich. 134; Mo. 10.

a collection agency to collect his client's accounts,[45] and may accept employment from a collection agency whom the lawyer is actually satisfied was authorized by the client to employ him,[46] provided in each case the lawyer's fees are not fixed by the collection agency,[47] that his relations with the client are direct, and that he is always free so to deal with him, and provided that the agency does not receive a percentage,[48] or share of the lawyer's fees, the lawyer retaining all he charged.[49]

He may not withhold funds of a primary creditor to pay accounts owed him by the collection agency.[50]

Where the agency is clearly authorized by the client to receive on the client's behalf from the lawyer the amounts collected, the lawyer may so remit to him, deducting his fees.[1] The agency must in each case receive its compensation direct from the client.[2]

A lawyer may not make lower charges by reason of services performed by the employees of the collection agency. Such services should be performed by the lawyer, who should deal directly with the real client.[3]

He may accept cases in which he is recommended by a collection agency under proper circumstances, but not where he is habitually recommended without special request.[4]

COMPENSATION

Barristers' Fees in England

In England the barrister's fee has always been considered as an honorarium, which is paid him by the solicitor, his real client, and not by the party to the suit.[5]

---

[45] App. A, 326.

[46] Id., 327; and see N.Y. City 653, 682-C, 745; N.Y. County 47, vii, but see N.Y. City 261 and N.Y. County 323.

[47] N.Y. City 99(3), 634, 730.

[48] N.Y. County 47 vii, iv; but see Mich. 37, 60; cf. N.Y. City 682-C.

[49] N.Y. City 207; N.Y. County 125.   [50] N.Y. City 261.   [1] N.Y. County 51.

[2] See N.Y. County 47 ii(c); N.Y. City 745, B-69, B-93, B-139. The lawyer may adjust his compensation so as to make it possible for the client himself to pay the agency fairly; see N.Y. County 113. But see N.Y. City 730; as to which, query.

[3] N.Y. County 74; and see N.Y. County 125, and 137, N.Y. City 99, 634.

[4] N.Y. County 147; N.Y. City 509, 629. See also infra, pp. 259–60.

[5] "By the Etiquette of the Bar, in all questions of law and practice, except in cases of making a will and drawing up a marriage settlement, counsel is debarred from conferring directly with a layman . . . in bygone times, when counsel met their clients at the pillars in St. Paul's and round Doctors' Commons, the client used to deposit in the

A barrister cannot sue either the party in interest or the solicitor for a fee, even when the solicitor has collected his fee from the client, but may complain to the Statutory Committee under the Solicitors' Acts to punish the solicitor for misconduct. As between the barrister and the solicitor "in accordance with the etiquette of the profession," the solicitor is personally responsible for the barrister's professional fees whether or not the solicitor has received from his client the money to pay them.[6]

A barrister need not legally return any part of his fee if he is unable to be present at the trial or argument, unless he had made an express undertaking that he would personally attend throughout the case.[7]

Although in France a lawyer may sue to recover a fee, it is regarded by the bar as so dishonorable to do so that any lawyer bringing such a suit would be immediately stricken from the roll of attorneys.[8]

Lawyers' Fees in the United States

In the United States the lawyer has always been regarded as having a legally enforceable right to compensation for his professional services, whether by virtue of special agreement or on a quantum meruit,[9] but he cannot contract for a fee in compensation cases larger than that allowed by a statute regulating fees in such cases.[10] He may not

---

purse at the back of the advocate's gown (theoretically without the latter's knowledge) whatever honorarium he chose to mark thus delicately his sense of gratitude. Even at the present day the barrister's gown has at his back the symbol of the purse, and in front the single streamer by which originally the purse was drawn over his shoulder, so that he could, after the client had departed, acquaint himself with its contents. The principle still remains, and so between counsel and laymen who would consult them, there is a mediator in the form of a solicitor. The solicitor interviews the lay client direct and passes on the instructions thus received to the barrister. These instructions are contained in a typed sheet known as a 'brief,' and the delivery of them to the barrister is called 'briefing counsel.'

"It is considered *infra dig* for a barrister to discuss the question of fees with the solicitor so all such matters are arranged by his clerk." Marston Garcia, *A New Guide to the Bar* (6th ed., 1928), pp. 3–4.

[6] Costigan, Case Book, p. 621 n.; Annual Report of the Law Society for 1932. A solicitor may pay the barrister's fee and sue the client for it as a disbursement. McDougall v. Campbell, 41 U.C.Q.B. 332 (1877). See also An. St. (1937), p. 9.

[7] Statement of the General Council of the Bar, *The Annual Practice* (1933), p. 2617. Such is not the case in the United States; see Canon 44, last sentence; Chicago 28, p. 61.

[8] Sharswood, *Professional Ethics*, p. 152.

[9] See 127 Am. St. Rep. 841 n. (1908). History of right to sue for fees, Adams v. Stevens 26 Wend. 451 (1841).

[10] N.Y. City 941; Matter of Fisch, 188 App. Div. 525 (N.Y., 1919).

agree, in matrimonial controversies, that no part of his retainer shall be refunded in case of a reconciliation.[11]

A client is not bound to accept his lawyer's advice, but must pay for it, where he requests it, even though he does not accept or follow it.[12]

It has been held proper for a lawyer to join a "barter group" during depression times, although the association pays its expenses with a percentage of fees, furnishes the lawyer, and advertises moderately.[13]

A lawyer need not perform additional services until he is paid, except where the client would be prejudiced.[14]

He should sue for fees only when the circumstances imperatively demand it.[15] He will find it wise, it is believed, in the long run, not to accept any fee from an honest client greater than the client thinks he should pay.

He may take a conveyance to secure his fee,[16] despite Canon 10.

He may deduct a reasonable fee where none is agreed on,[17] but in case he does, he should keep the amount separate from his own funds until the client agrees;[18] and should so keep the funds received on account of another claim by the client which he holds against his fees.[19]

Right to Compensation in Certain Cases

A lawyer may properly charge a fee for securing a pardon for a convict [20] or for getting an immigrant admitted,[21] but not for using his influence to get a government loan or a person appointed to office; [22] or to get a client accepted as a customer of his factor-client.[23] Under proper conditions, he may render free services to registrants under the Selective Service Act and similar laws,[24] or may charge the widow of an enlisted man for legal services though she could get them free.[25] He may charge for services to a member of the armed

---

11 Chicago 28, p. 61.   12 App. A, *333.*

13 N.Y. City 356.   14 App. A, *334.*

15 A.B.A. Op. 250. Canon 14 provides: "Controversies with clients concerning compensation are to be avoided by the lawyer so far as shall be compatible with his self-respect and with his right to receive reasonable recompense for his services; and lawsuits with clients should be resorted to only to prevent injustice, imposition or fraud."

He may not put off the entry of a divorce decree so long as to endanger his client's rights, because she cannot pay his fee. N.Y. City 494; and cf. N.Y. County 158.

16 See Mich. 3. See *supra*, pp. 99–101.   17 A.B.A. Op. 27.

18 N.Y. County 330; see also N.Y. County 7, 66; and see N.Y. City 817, 949.

19 N.Y. County 384.   20 A.B.A. Op. 61.   21 N.Y. City 537.

22 N.Y. City 544.   23 N.Y. City 602.

24 A.B.A. Ops. 206, 211, 252, 259.   25 N.Y. County 173.

forces though it is usual and proper to do this for nothing,[26] or for advice regarding the draft, but must advise that the client may get it free.[27]

"A retaining fee is intended to remunerate counsel for being deprived, by being retained by one party, of the opportunity of rendering services to the other and of receiving pay from him, and the payment of such a fee, in the absence of an express understanding to the contrary, is neither made nor received in payment of services contemplated. . . . And it is a fee paid to counsel to make sure that he will represent and render service to his client in a given matter or matters." [28]

An agreed retaining fee is payable even though the client chooses not to avail himself of the retained lawyer's services.[29]

A lawyer assigned to defend a non-capital case may not suggest to defendant or his relatives that he receive or accept a fee from them, without a court order.[30] A lawyer representing the guardian of an infant on a contingent fee arrangement may, with full disclosure to the court, accept from its parents a guaranty of a sum to make up the lawyer's agreed fee in addition to the sum awarded by the court.[31]

In a jurisdiction where a stipulation in a note is regarded as one for liquidated damages, the recovery on this account belongs to the holder of the note, and his lawyer may accept from him less than that recovered; but where the amount recoverable is fixed and awarded by the court, it is improper for the lawyer to allow the client any part of it.[32]

In an early decision, the New York County Committee held that a

---

[26] App. A, 335.   [27] N.Y. County 371; cf. also N.Y. City 573.

[28] Conover v. West Jersey Mortgage Co., 96 N.J.Eq. 441, 451 (1924); see also Stone, C. J., in Agnew v. Walden & Son, 84 Ala. 502, 504, 505 (1887).

In Bright v. Turner, 205 Ky. 188, 191 (1924), the court said: "The retainer is for the purpose of obligating the attorney to represent the client as well as to prevent him from taking a fee on the other side."

Annual retainers from regular clients usually represent the average value of current services, which it would be difficult and burdensome to itemize.

As to general and special retainers in England, see, as to barristers, Statement of the General Council of the Bar, *The Annual Practice* (1933), p. 2626; as to solicitors, The Council of the Law Society, *Law, Practice and Usage of the Solicitor's Profession* (1923), p. 299.

[29] Union Surety, etc. Co. v. Tenny *et al.*, 200 Ill. 349 (1902).

[30] N.Y. County 338; and see as to a case where he found that the client was not actually indigent, Mich. 127; see *supra*, p. 62.

[31] N.Y. City 301.

[32] A.B.A. Op. 157. As to so-called "splitting of fees" with the client, see *infra*, p. 181. As to sharing fees with laymen, see *infra*, p. 179; with other lawyers, *infra*, p. 186.

lawyer-executor, even though he had performed legal services for the estate, could not secretly take part of the fees of counsel of record for the estate.[33] The vice was concealment of the facts from the court; in some jurisdictions lawyer-executors are allowed counsel fees subject to court approval.

A lawyer may hold a preliminary conference with a prospective client without charge but may not advertise that he does so.[34]

The New York City Committee has held that Canon 12 does not contemplate or justify a charge for a service not actually performed.[35]

A lawyer who has an annual pass on a railroad may charge fares to a client for trips on the client's business if the client knows of his pass.[36]

A lawyer on an annual retainer from a client who has not so advised his forwardee cannot claim a share of the latter's fee. If he got it, it would belong to the client.[37]

A lawyer must advise his client if he is to have a share of the charge of a colleague.[38]

A lawyer is not responsible for the payment of fees to a colleague [39] or to a lawyer whom he has superseded.[40]

His lien for services to a testator does not survive against the estate.[41]

Basis for Compensation

One of the earliest provisions of the English law regulating the conduct of lawyers was an ordinance of the City of London of 1280,[42] which provided that in fixing the amount of the compensation (salaire) of a lawyer four points were to be considered: "the amount of the matter in dispute, the labour (travail) of the serjeant, his value as a pleader (contour) in respect of his learning, eloquence (facunde) and repute (donur) and the usage of the court."[43]

Canon 12 relative to the amount of the fee, provides:

In determining the amount of the fee, it is proper to consider: (1) the time and labor required, the novelty and difficulty of the questions involved and the skill requisite properly to conduct the cause; (2) whether

---

[33] N.Y. County 26.   [34] Chicago 31, p. 70.

[35] N.Y. City B-134; but see Union Surety Co. v. Tenny, 200 Ill. 349 (1902).

[36] A.B.A. Op. 38; Mich. 64.

[37] Chicago Committee (Costigan, Case Book, p. 631).

[38] N.Y. County 184.   [39] A.B.A. Op. 63.

[40] A.B.A. Op. 130. See also infra, p. 195.

[41] Matter of Reiss, 200 Misc. 697 (N.Y., 1951).   [42] See supra, p. 15.

[43] Cohen, *History of the English Bar and Attornatus to 1450*, p. 279.

the acceptance of employment in the particular case will preclude the lawyer's appearance for others in cases likely to arise out of the transaction, and in which there is a reasonable expectation that otherwise he would be employed, or will involve the loss of other employment while employed in the particular case or antagonisms with other clients; (3) the customary charges of the Bar for similar services; (4) the amount involved in the controversy and the benefits resulting to the client from the services; (5) the contingency or the certainty of the compensation; and (6) the character of the employment, whether casual or for an established and constant client. No one of these considerations in itself is controlling. They are mere guides in ascertaining the real value of the service.

There is no ethical question involved unless fees are flagrantly excessive,[44] but in cases where they manifestly are, this is ground for suspension [45] or disbarment.[46]

While fees should ordinarily be based on a consideration of the factors stated in Canon 12, a lawyer may contract for any fee he chooses so long as it is not clearly excessive; [47] he must, however, fix his own fees and may not delegate this to a layman; [48] nor may he make a competitive bid.[49]

The Alabama Code of 1887 contained a provision to the effect that wherever possible the counsel's compensation should be agreed upon in advance. This was concurred in in the codes of nine of the other states adopting Canons prior to 1908, but not by the American Bar Association Committee. It would seem questionable as to whether such a general principle is to be recommended. Where the client wishes a general idea as to the amount of the compensation, it should, of course, be stated as nearly as may be; but with a fair client it would seem better to tell him that while it would seem that the fee would

---

[44] A.B.A. Op. 27, 190; N.Y. City 143, 794; on what is a reasonable attorney's fee, see 40 Ann. Cas. 263 n. (1916); Lauriz Vold, "Ethics and Economics in Lawyers' Fees," 8 Marquette L. Rev. 228 (1924).

[45] See Goldstone v. State Bar, 214 Cal. 490 (1931).

[46] People v. Bamborough, 255 Ill. 92 (1912); see also In the Matter of Cary, 146 Minn. 80 (1920); In the Matter of Hahn, 84 N.J.Eq. 523 (1915); 80 A.L.R. 706 n. (1932); 45 A.L.R. 1135 n. (1926).

[47] A.B.A. Op. 190. He may not allow a discount for prompt payment. A.B.A. Op. 151.

A further consideration is the eminence of the lawyer at the bar, or in the specialty in which he may be practicing. See In re Osofsky, 50 F.2d 925 (1931).

In general as to reasonableness of fees, see Irwin v. Swinney, 45 F.2d 890 (1930) (Loose Trust).

See also Woolsey, D. J., in In re Osofsky, 50 F.2d 925, 927 (1931), as to the general considerations in fixing fees and as to special reasons for liberality in bankruptcy and similar cases where it is necessary to discover assets and where the results are problematical; and the analogy in such cases to salvage in admiralty.

[48] Mich. 110.   [49] App. A, *83;* Mich. 133.

possibly run around a stated figure, the ultimate amount thereof would always be subject to his approval.

Although it is proper for the profession to combat, by a voluntary minimum fee schedule, the tendency of some members, through press of economic circumstances, to render legal services for inadequate consideration,[50] such compensation should be determined in each case and not as per such bar schedule.[1]

Right to Damages for Discharge without Cause

The decisions are in conflict as to the right of a lawyer, employed for a particular case, to compensation where he is discharged without cause or withdraws for cause. Some, on the theory that the client has a right at any time to sever their relations without cause, decline to award him damages,[2] but allow a quasi-contractual claim for services already rendered;[3] others maintain that he is entitled to the full contract amount.[4] Where, however, a lawyer was employed at $100 a week for a year, to perform all the legal services for the client which developed, it was held that this relationship was more in the nature of a master and servant one, and that where the lawyer was discharged before the end of the year, he could recover damages based on the value of the contract.[5]

---

[50] A.B.A. Ops. 28, 171, 190. Hoffman's Resolution XXVIII (*infra*, p. 344) was as follows: "As a general rule, I will carefully avoid what is called the 'taking of half fees.' And though no one can be so competent as myself to judge what may be a just compensation for my services,—yet, when the quiddam honorarium has been established by usage or law, I shall regard as eminently dishonourable all underbidding of my professional brethren. On such a subject, however, no inflexible rule can be given to myself, except to be invariably guided by a lively recollection that I belong to an honourable profession."

[1] Par. 3 of Canon 12 provides: "In determining the customary charges of the Bar for similar services, it is proper for a lawyer to consider a schedule of minimum fees adopted by a Bar Association, but no lawyer should permit himself to be controlled thereby or to follow it as his sole guide in determining the amount of his fee." See App. A, *336*. In England a solicitor may be disciplined for charging less than the scale prescribed by the committee presided over by the Lord Chancellor; 35 Jour. Am. Jud. Soc. 143–44 (1952).

[2] Matter of Dunn, 205 N.Y. 398 (1912); Martin v. Camp, 219 N.Y. 170 (1916); Lawler v. Dunn, 145 Minn. 281 (1920).

[3] See Seabury, J., in Martin v. Camp, 219 N.Y. 170, 176 (1916).

[4] Mutter v. Burgess, 87 Colo. 580 (1930); Scheinesohn v. Lemonek, 84 Ohio St. 424 (1911); 24 Ann. Cas. 1912C, 737 (1912); Bartlett v. Odd Fellows' Sav. Bank, 79 Cal. 218 (1889); French v. Cunningham, 149 Ind. 632 (1898); Moyer v. Cantieny, 41 Minn. 242 (1889); Kersey v. Garton, 77 Mo. 645 (1883); Myers v. Crockett, 14 Tex. 257 (1855); Mt. Vernon v. Patton, 94 Ill. 65 (1879). And see 15 Minn. L. Rev. 115 (1930); 14 L.R.A. (N.S.) 1095 n. (1908); 38 L.R.A. (N.S.) 389 n. (1912).

[5] Greenberg v. Remick, 230 N.Y. 70 (1920).

The tenor and spirit of Canon 14, deprecating controversies with clients regarding compensation, would seem strongly to favor the view that a lawyer should never assert a right to damages for services not actually performed. One who accepts employment by an unfair and unreasonable client assumes the risk of having his hopes frustrated. Nor does it pay, in the long run, to wrangle, much less to litigate, with such people. See Hoffman's Resolution XXVII, *infra* page 344.

Contingent Fees

Despite Canon 10 [6] precluding a lawyer from acquiring an interest in litigation which he is conducting, American Bar Association Canon 13 [7] expressly sanctions contingent fees reasonable under the circumstances, and subject as to this to court supervision, the client remaining responsible for expenses advanced by the lawyer.[8]

[6] See 20 Dickinson L. Rev. 1, 12–13 (1915); 21 Green Bag 271, 276 (1909); Greenleaf v. Minn., etc., R. Co., 30 N.D. 112, 126 (1915), Whinery v. Brown, 36 Ind. App. 276, 281 (1905). Henry W. Williams, *Legal Ethics for Young Counsel* (1906), p. 69; Edwin Countryman, "Ethics of Compensation for Professional Services 1882," 16 Amer. L. Rev. 240, 242, 249 (1882); 31 N.Y. Bar Assn. Reports 100, 101 (1908); Cohen, *The Law, Business or Profession* (1916), 205–16; 1 Ann. Cas. 299 n. (1906); 27 L.R.A. (N.S.) 634 n. (1910); 45 L.R.A. (N.S.) 750 n. (1913); 18 Ann. Cas. 1115 n. (1911), 3 A.L.R. 472 n. (1919); 40 A.L.R. 1529 n. (1926).

Canon 10 provides that a lawyer "should not purchase any interest in the subject matter of the litigation which he is conducting." While an agreement for a contingent fee might be thought contrary to the spirit of Canon 10, contingent fees are sanctioned in proper cases in order to enable clients to secure a competent lawyer, where otherwise they would not, in all probability, be able to do so. See *supra*, pp. 99–101; also *infra*, n. 8. Cf. also Rule (9) of American Institute of Accountants.

[7] Canon 13 is as follows: "A contract for a contingent fee where sanctioned by law, should be reasonable under all the circumstances of the case, including the risk and uncertainty of the compensation, but should always be subject to the supervision of a Court, as to its reasonableness." See also *supra*, p. 24, n. 17.

The Boston Bar Association, Canon XIII, contains a lengthy provision qualifying the right to agree on a contingent fee more radically than the American Bar Association form, and adding a sort of moral lecture on the subject; see N.Y. County 141. See also Hoffman Resolution XXIV, *infra*, p. 343.

[8] A.B.A. Op. 246; N.Y. County 141; Mich. 66; and see N.Y. County 175. Canon 13 of the Maine Code specifically provides: "Contingent fees are disapproved."

In an article entitled "Contingent Fees in California," 28 Cal. L. Rev. 587, 589 (1940) Professor Max Radin said: "The case for and against a contingent fee, if we disregard considerations of history and what may be called snobbery, may be briefly summarized. The contingent fee certainly increases the possibility that vexatious and unfounded suits will be brought. On the other hand, it makes possible the enforcement of legitimate claims which otherwise would be abandoned because of the poverty of the claimants. Of these two possibilities, the social advantage seems clearly on the side of the contingent fee. It may in fact be added by way of reply to the first objection that vexatious and unfounded suits have been brought by men who could and did pay substantial attorneys' fees for that purpose."

See also Buckley v. Service Transportation Corp., 277 App. Div. 224 (1950).

In a report of 1952, the Advisory Bar Committee of The Bar Association of the City of

Canon 13 applies to criminal cases. Irrespective of agreement, the lawyer should always be willing to have the court pass on the reasonableness of his charges under the various contingencies specified, and should make such charges so reasonable that if submitted to the court, it would sustain him.[9]

A lawyer may accept a percentage for collecting overdue alimony, but not a percentage of that to accrue subsequently.[10]

He may not get a percentage of a property settlement in a divorce case [11] or of alimony to be awarded [12] and where he has collected such must pay it back, as he is not in pari delicto.

The New York court has held that the provision in a contingent fee contract that the client might not make a bona fide settlement without the attorney's consent was contrary to public policy and void, but that where the client did so settle, the lawyer need not accept the agreed percentage of the settlement, but might recover on a quantum meruit.[13]

Where he is reasonably satisfied that he has a lien for fees, a lawyer may retain the papers until compensated [14] or retain a check, to the client's order, received by him,[15] but must keep the funds separate and subject to accounting.[16] He may not assign a right to a contingent fee as security for a personal loan.[17]

He may agree for a contingent fee to get legislation passed.[18]

In its Opinion 141 the New York County Committee says of the contingent fee:

It develops both in the lay and in the professional mind a conception of the practice of the law as a business, not a profession, and tends to lower the essential standards of the Bar.

The employment of a lawyer to serve for a contingent fee does not make it the client's duty to continue the lawsuit and thus increase the lawyer's profit. The lawsuit is his own. He may drop it when he will.[19]

New York recommended a contingent fee agreement of 35 per cent net to the client (exclusive of bills for medical treatment, hospital and other charges not arising in connection with the prosecuting of the claim) with a possible additional 15 per cent under exceptional circumstances, such as retrials and appeals, etc.

His share should be a percentage of the net and not of the gross. But see Mo. 20.

[9] App. A, 337. [10] N.Y. County 275.

[11] Re Est. of Sylvester, 195 Iowa 1329 (1923); Mich. 72.

[12] Welles v. Brown, 226 Mich. 657 (1924). [13] In re Snyder, 190 N.Y. 66 (1907).

[14] N.Y. City 15; see also N.Y. City 49. [15] N.Y. City 82.

[16] N.Y. County 330. [17] N.Y. County 349.

[18] N.Y. City 419; query as to this and see N.Y. County 175.

[19] Cardozo, J., in Andrewes v. Haas, 214 N.Y. 255 (1915). In re Snyder, 190 N.Y. 66 (1907); and see Ward v. Orsini, 243 N.Y. 123 (1926); Scheinesohn v. Lemonek, 84 Oh. St. 424 (1911); and cases cited. Martin v. Camp, 219 N.Y. 170 (1916).

As to a right of action by a lawyer against the other party to a suit which settles with his client and thus deprives him of his agreed contingent fee, see *supra*, pages 28–29.[20]

One handling a case on a contingent basis who is given proper grounds for withdrawal on so doing is entitled to compensation on a quantum meruit, but not when his withdrawal is capricious.[21]

Expenses

Under Canon 42,[22] the client must ultimately be responsible for the expenses of the litigation,[23] although the lawyer may advance them, subject to reimbursement.[24] A committee of lawyers to serve indigent service men may advance costs in an indigent case out of funds provided for such purpose by members of the bar.[25]

In certain cases involving claims by Indian tribes [26] where the litigation was expressly authorized by statute and necessarily involved the advance of expenses by lawyers, with a contingent fee arrangement, such advance has been approved despite the fact that the expenses would clearly not be recovered except out of the proceeds of the litigation.

If a lawyer relinquishes his fee he may advance expenses, putting the whole matter on a charity basis.[27]

Telephone calls, hotel bills, etc., are not expenses within the meaning of Canon 42; an agreement to pay costs is.[28]

A lawyer may accept and hold in escrow from a husband respondent the expenses of getting a divorce in a foreign state to the jurisdiction of which he will submit.[29]

A retainer agreement is void under which the lawyer agrees to pay the expenses in case the case is lost.[30]

---

20 Chreste v. Louisville Railroad, 167 Ky. 75 (1915). See also N.Y. City 628, and Krause v. Insurance Co., 331 Mich. 19 (1951).

21 N.Y. City 394; and see also Matter of Weitling; 266 N.Y. 184 (1935); Tillman v. Komar, 259 N.Y. 133 (1932). The value of his services in such a case is not measured by the results obtained by another lawyer.

As to proper procedure for a discharged attorney to establish his compensation, see Griffiths v. United States, 72 F.2d, 466, 468 (1934).

22 Canon 42 provides: "A lawyer may not properly agree with a client that the lawyer shall pay or bear the expenses of litigation; he may in good faith advance expenses as a matter of convenience, but subject to reimbursement."

23 A.B.A. Ops. 20, 246; Mich. 66; N.Y. City 24, 167, 374, 423, 627, 919, 955, B-213, B-215.

24 A.B.A. Op. 259; N.Y. City 207; but see N.Y. City 903.

25 A.B.A. Op. 259. See also Mo. 27.   26 App. A, *339;* N.Y. City 962.

27 N.Y. County 249; and cf. N.Y. City 24.   28 App. A, *338.*

29 N.Y. City 791.   30 Low v. Hutchinson, 37 Me. 196 (1853).

DIVISION OF FEES

With a Layman or Lay Agency

Canon 34 specifically condemns the division of fees for legal services "except with another lawyer."[31] The amendment of 1937 of this Canon struck out a clause permitting a division with laymen on the collection of liquidated commercial claims where not prohibited by statute. The Canon as originally adopted in 1928 referred to such division as by "established custom," "being a compensation for valuable services." These phrases were struck out by an amendment in 1933.[32]

This Canon precludes a division of fees with a trustee whom the lawyer represents, who is not required to perform any legal services and does not share any of the professional responsibility of the lawyer;[33] with a corporation employing the lawyer;[34] with a patent agent;[35] with an accountant,[36] though admitted to practice before the Tax Court;[37] with a lay forwarder;[38] with a collection agent;[39] with one performing "income tax service";[40] with an insurance adjuster;[41] or a justice of the peace;[42] or clerk;[43] or employment agency[44] which brings the lawyer business; with a German refugee lawyer,[45] or with lawyers of another state not admitted where the fee is earned.[46]

Employment of a Layman by a Lawyer

A layman may properly be employed by a lawyer on any agreed basis to give advice and assistance to the lawyer provided such serv-

[31] The Canon reads as follows: "No division of fees for legal services is proper, except with another lawyer, based upon a division of service or responsibility." See Mich. 24; see also *infra*, p. 188, as to a division of fees with the estate of a deceased partner.

[32] As to prior to 1933, see N.Y. County 314.

The Code of Ethics of the American Institute of Accountants also disapproves of the finder's fee by Rule 4, N.Y. County 343.

An amendment in 1933 also struck out from the concluding paragraph of Canon 35 the clause "The established custom of receiving commercial collections through a lay agency is not condemned hereby."

[33] A.B.A. Op. 18; and see N.Y. County 120.   [34] A.B.A. Op. 10; see *infra*, p. 181.

[35] A.B.A. Op. 48; N.Y. County 345.

[36] A.B.A. Op. 272; N.Y. City 147, 831; N.Y. County 344.

[37] App. A, *342;* Mich. 54.   [38] A.B.A. Op. 180.

[39] A.B.A. Op. 225; App. A, *327–30;* N.Y. County 47 ii(a), 98; Mo. 2, 31, 72.

[40] A.B.A. Op. 234.

[41] A.B.A. Op. 57, and see Op. 214; N.Y. County 286, 287; N.Y. City 258, 372, 626.

[42] N.Y. County 130.   [43] N.Y. County 80.

[44] N.Y. City 594.   [45] N.Y. City 853; and see 657.

[46] N.Y. City 925. As a practical matter, however, a lawyer from another state not infrequently participates in a litigation *pro hac vice* and receives a share of the fee.

ice does not constitute the practice of law by the layman.[47] A lawyer
may also employ a layman as a collector,[48] or to negotiate insurance
adjustments for the lawyer's approval,[49] provided the layman's service
does not constitute the practice of law and that the layman's compensation is not a proportion of the lawyer's fee.[50] Where such employment is authorized by the client, the layman's charge may be
collected by the lawyer from the client as an item of expense,[1] which
may include an agreed per diem charge for the services of laymen employed by the lawyer irrespective of the amounts paid them by the
lawyer.[2]

Employment of a Lawyer by a Layman

A lawyer may properly accept employment, on a stated salary or
any other agreed basis, from a collection agency, accountant, or other
layman to advise and assist the layman in any activity in which the
layman may lawfully engage;[3] but when a lawyer is employed by
a layman to perform legal services for the layman's client, the charge
therefor by the lawyer must be fixed by the lawyer and be paid by
the client, the layman acting as the client's agent in employing the
lawyer.[4] In such cases, even where a layman's client authorizes him
to employ a lawyer, the lawyer's charges may not be paid by the layman as a proportion of the layman's fee.[5] The lawyer may not be
employed by the layman on a salary basis to perform services for
such clients; otherwise the layman would be exploiting his legal
services and practicing law.[6] The layman may not determine the
amount of the lawyer's charges for legal services to the patron.[7]

When, with the authority or approval of a client, a lawyer employs
a layman or the layman employs a lawyer in the client's affairs, and
the client specifies what fee each shall receive, this does not constitute
a division of the lawyer's fees by the lawyer.[8]

[47] A.B.A. Op. 272; App. A, *341*. See Mo. 12, 14.   [48] App. A, *326*.
[49] N.Y. City 175, 626; N.Y. County 287.   [50] N.Y. City 175, 626.
[1] App. A, *344*; N.Y. County 343.   [2] N.Y. County 142, 343.
[3] App. A, *341*; N.Y. County 220; and see also N.Y. County 418.
[4] N.Y. County 47 ii b, 121, 220; see also N.Y. County 74; and see App. A, *343*.
[5] App. A, *343*.   [6] N.Y. County 74, 125, 220; and see Mo. 13, 22.
[7] N.Y. County 47 ii(*b*).
[8] App. A, *353*; N.Y. County 47 ii(*b*) (*c*), 113, 220; see also N.Y. City 595, 626, and cf.
N.Y. County 142.

"Splitting of Fees" with Employers or Clients

There has been some apparent confusion of thought in the Committee decisions relative to the "splitting of fees" with an employer or client. In such cases several different circumstances must be distinguished.

First, where the client is paying the lawyer out of his own pocket for legal services to him: here the net fee can be whatever they ultimately determine to be fair and proper. The "division of fees for legal services" which Canon 34 restricts to divisions "with another lawyer" is a division because of assistance by the divisee to the lawyer in serving his client. Obviously it is not intended to preclude a lawyer from making relatively low charges to any but other lawyers. A lawyer who charges a client half his usual fee for a particular service because the client is a relative or friend, or regular client or one paying an annual retainer, or even because the client himself contributes abnormal assistance in bookkeeping, negotiation, or organizing the testimony is not thereby "splitting his fee" with the client; and it makes no difference whether the lawyer charges him the lower amount, or bills him at his regular charge with a specified credit, or after billing and being paid the higher sum reconsiders and remits part of it.

A second circumstance is where by prior agreement, or by statute or court order the client's counsel fees are payable by the other party. Thus, a judgment note frequently contains a provision that in the event of suit the debtor shall pay the holder's counsel fee of 10 per cent. In such a case if on a $10,000 note the lawyer collects a $1,000 fee, keeps $500, and turns over $500 to the client, this is not the splitting of his fee with the client. The $1,000 belongs to the client, and if the lawyer is willing to accept but $500 for his legal services, he may do so without violating Canon 34. However, the receipt by the client of the $500 counsel fee which he does not pay to counsel would make him guilty of practicing law, in which the lawyer would be aiding him in violation of Canon 47. A similar conclusion would follow where a lawyer turned over to his client part of a sum payable as counsel fee by the defendant in a compensation case or by either party in a divorce case.

Third, there are cases in which the lawyer for a fiduciary earns counsel fees payable by the trust estate. In such cases, if the lawyer retains the entire fee there is obviously no question. Even if the relation between the trust company and its lawyer be regarded as one of employer and employee so that the counsel fee earned in the course of the lawyer's employment belongs to the employer, it may properly be paid to the lawyer as a necessary disbursement. Where, however, the lawyer is employed on an annual retainer or salary, whether or not a full-time employee, and under his agreement turns over to the trust company fees paid by the trust estate, the trust company which collects for its lawyer's services a different sum from what it pays him is guilty of selling his professional services, which are being thus exploited in violation of Canon 35. Here the lawyer is also aiding the trust company in practicing law. Such is the case wherever "a lay agency pays a lawyer one amount for his services and for these services charges a different amount to the person to whom they are rendered." [9] While in such cases it may be an answer to Canon 34 that the client is merely being reimbursed for the loss of time on the part of its lawyer, a layman may not thus farm out its lawyer's service. The only situations in which a lawyer may properly permit a client to receive and retain fees paid by others on account of his legal services are when such payments are to reimburse the client in whole or in part for the client's legal expenses actually incurred in the specific matter for which they are paid.

A still different question is presented where a full-time lawyer is under his contract permitted to perform on his own responsibility legal services for others but bound to turn over to his employer all fees received therefor. Such is the arrangement between a certain educational institution and members of its law faculty. Here there is no sale or exploitation of the lawyer's services since they are not performed for the employer, who has no interest in and no control or direction of them whatever. Nor would such in any sense constitute the practice of law by the university unless the total fees turned over to it exceeded the lawyer's annual salary.

The second question above discussed was squarely presented to the New York City Committee in a case where a bank had inserted in its notes a provision for a 10 per cent attorney's fee, the proceeds of which it proposed to use to defray the expense of its legal department. The Committee held that a lawyer might not accept employ-

[9] A.B.A. Op. 8. See *infra*, p. 183 n. 14.

ment to collect such notes, with the 10 per cent, unless he arranged that "under all circumstances the total of all fees so collected by the bank shall be paid over in full to the attorney." [10] Otherwise, the Committee held, the practice would result in a division of fees with the bank, a layman. The proper reason for the conclusion was, it is believed, not that this was a splitting of fees, which belonged always to the bank and not to the lawyer, who performed no legal service for the debtors requiring them to pay him a fee. If the bank retained these fees, however, it was in effect hiring a lawyer to perform legal services for which it was paid, in violation of Canon 47. Also, it would appear, the 10 per cent charge, not actually used as a reimbursement for the bank's actual legal expense in the particular case, might render the transaction usurious.[11]

The American Bar Association Committee reached a similar conclusion in a case where a corporation dealing in mortgage loans stipulated for an attorney's commission from the title companies insuring the titles on the mortgaged properties, such commission to be payable to a named attorney on the corporation's legal staff, but to be turned over by him (unknown apparently to the title company) "and used as an ordinary set-off to business expense." The Committee, without analysis of the problem, condemned the practice.[12]

In an earlier opinion [13] the American Bar Association Committee held that an automobile club which, as part of the service accorded the members in return for their annual dues, provided them with limited legal services was in effect "selling and exploiting the lawyers' professional services to its own benefit or profit. . . . Irrespective of whether they give all or only a portion of their time to the service furnished by the club, and whether they receive a salary, are paid a percentage, or are paid for each separate item of work, the result is the same so long as a lay agency pays a lawyer one amount for his services and for those services charges a different [14] amount to the person to whom they are rendered." This, the Committee held, constituted

[10] N.Y. City 478; but see N.Y. City 176.
[11] See Luzenberg v. B.&L. Assoc., 9 Tex. Civ. App. 261, 267 (1894); also Kennedy v. Richardson, 70 Ind. 524, 528 (1880).
[12] App. A, *359;* and see A.B.A. Op. 157; also White v. Lucas, 46 Iowa 319, 322 (1877); Munter v. Linn, 61 Ala. 492, 506 (1878); Hassell v. Steinmann (Tex.) 132 S.W. 948, 950 (1910); Conway v. Bank, 146 Va. 357, 364 (1926). See also *supra,* p. 97; also Mo. 43.
[13] A.B.A. Op. 8 (1925).
[14] Would it if he charged *less* than he actually paid his lawyer for the specific case? It would seem not.

the improper practice of law, referring to the comprehensive report of a New York Conference in 1920 and citing a long list of cases involving unauthorized practice. This, it is believed, was the correct analysis of the problem and not that in an opinion a year later (1926) holding that the retention of counsel fees paid to the salaried trust officer (lawyer) of a trust company for services to it as guardian constituted the sharing of fees by a lay agency.[15] "It has been argued," said the Committee,

that it would be proper for such a salaried attorney to reimburse his employer for the salary paid him for the actual portion of his time given to the trust estate. Assuming that it would be possible to actually apportion that time, how would it be possible to determine what portion was devoted to it in his capacity as a trust officer and what portion as an attorney at law? . . . Any fees charged against a trust estate for a lawyer's services should be paid to and retained by the lawyer rendering them and should not be turned over to or divided with a layman or a corporation.

Both Opinion 8 and Opinion 10 were rendered prior to the adoption of either Canon 34 or Canon 35.[16]

The New York County Committee, it is believed, analyzed the problem correctly in holding that where a lay informer had made it possible for a lawyer to collect a judgment, the lawyer might not properly divide his fee with the informer, but might make his fee to his client less in order to enable the client, himself, to compensate the informer.[17] This would not be a splitting of fees by the lawyer either with the client or with the informer.

The New York County Committee also held it proper for a lawyer, with his client's knowledge and consent, to retain commissions or rebates from printers, auctioneers, and others serving him in the client's litigation. The Committee [18] said merely that the "vice lies in concealment from the client." [19]

In a later opinion, however, the County Committee held that a lawyer representing a trade organization on an annual retainer (not apparently full time) might not properly account to it for awards to him of counsel fee and expenses in bankruptcy proceeding conducted by him in its interest, and that a retainer from the association requiring him so to account should not be accepted by him. The

---

15 A.B.A. Op. 10.   16 See, however, A.B.A. Op. 157 (last sentence).
17 N.Y. County 113.   18 N.Y. City 176 accord.
19 N.Y. County 124, citing its Op. 111, where the committee said that the acceptance from an auctioneer of half his commissions, although with the client's knowledge and consent, was "beneath the proper professional dignity."

Committee referred to and discussed only Canon 34 which it held violated by a division of compensation with his lay client.[20]

The Michigan Committee [21] held that a lawyer who received a discount from a legal publication on account of legal notices for a client might retain it with the client's knowledge and consent only if it was credited to the client's account. That Committee distinguished American Bar Association Opinion 38, holding that a lawyer who was given an annual pass by a railroad client, as part compensation for his services to it, which pass he was entitled to use on personal business, might charge another client, as expenses, railroad fares which, but for the pass, he would have had to pay. The Michigan Committee, in its decision, does not discuss the basis for the propriety of the client's receiving the discount, which, of course, is that it belongs to the client in reduction of the client's direct expense of securing the service and being in no sense a payment on account of legal services.

In another opinion the Michigan Committee held that the lawyer for a bank might not permit the bank to retain sums paid by borrowers as attorney's fees, in an amount greater than that actually paid its lawyers for the particular service, where its lawyers were so paid, or at all where the service was by the bank's full time salaried lawyer.[22] The only discussion by the Committee in this connection was of "Canon 35 forbidding the exploitation of a lawyer's services by a lay agency," which, of course, relates to Canon 47 rather than to the splitting of fees under Canon 34.

The New York County Committee has held that a lawyer may represent a layman in a suit by a layman for his agreed share of fees.[23]

A lawyer may not agree with a receiver whom he represents that they shall divide equally the aggregate fees awarded to each.[24]

A gratuity to employees based on net profits is not forbidden, but an agreement to make such distribution is inconsistent with essential dignity and tends to promote solicitation.[25]

When a lawyer makes an agreement to divide a fee with one having no right to a division, he must make up his mind whether to violate his promise or the Canon.[26] It is suggested that he should keep his

[20] N.Y. County 326; see also court decision cited therein.
[21] Mich. 64.   [22] Mich. 98.
[23] N.Y. County 351; but one may not represent a runner in a suit for his 10 per cent contingent compensation, N.Y. City 222.
[24] N.Y. County 56.   [25] N.Y. County 122.
[26] See App. A, 6; id., 352; but see N.Y. City 706.

promise, informing the Committee and expressing his regret for his not having realized his mistake.

But in a New York City case, where he agreed to divide contingently with one representing that he was a lawyer when he was not, it was held that he could use the information and not pay the agreed share.[27]

An assignment by a partner of his interest in the partnership to himself and wife by the entireties merely to save inheritance taxes, the wife being in no way involved in law practice or in any relationship with the clients, does not violate Canon 34.[28]

Arrangements and Division of Fees between Lawyers [29]

Canon 34 further provides that the division of fees for legal services between lawyers must be based exclusively on "a division of service or responsibility."

There was long at the bar a practice or custom whereby, when a lawyer, with authority from his client, forwarded a case to another lawyer for attention in the latter's jurisdiction, or merely recommended one, the forwarding lawyer was allowed one-third of the fee earned by his correspondent. This was in the nature of a "Finder's Fee," and was payable irrespective of any real service performed or responsibility assumed by the forwarding lawyer.

It was obviously the purpose of Canon 34 to condemn this, and such purpose should not be frustrated by construing the necessity of "responsibility" as being satisfied by the bare recommendation.[30] The service and responsibility must, to be effective, relate to the handling of the case.

Accordingly, it has been repeatedly held by the Committees that no right to a division arises from the mere recommendation.[31] It is

[27] N.Y. City 706.   [28] App. A, 347.

[29] See A.B.A. Op. 27; App. A, 356; N.Y. County 180.

[30] See A.B.A. Op. 204. As to the legal liability of a lawyer to his client for selecting or retaining an associate, see authorities cited in n. 2, p. 414 of that Opinion. The forwarding lawyer can, of course, absolve himself from any such responsibility by an understanding with his client.

Forwarding lawyers may reasonably expect reciprocal consideration from their forwardees. The recommender should collect his fee, if any, direct from the client; see App. A, 356. The fact that the client in most cases would not recognize any liability in such cases supports the propriety of the provision in the Canon, which was a distinct step in keeping the legal profession from becoming a mere business.

[31] A.B.A. Op. 265; N.Y. County 42, 81, 180; N.Y. City 141, 145, 686. A fortiori the recommending lawyer is not entitled to one-third or any part of the fees on future cases which the client sends direct to the recommended one. N.Y. City 790, B-154.

Rule 4 of the American Institute of Accountants also disapproves of a finder's fee: N.Y. County 343.

immaterial that neither of the lawyers knew of the Canon.[32] However, a lawyer taking over the practice of one in the service may pay him an appropriate share of the fees he receives,[33] and may use his letterhead.[34]

The phrase "another lawyer" in the Canon means one entitled to practice in the jurisdiction where the services are performed [35] and a foreign lawyer (not a partner, see *infra*, page 203) is not entitled to a division for services in the jurisdiction where he is not admitted,[36] except perhaps in connection with advice as to the law of his jurisdiction.[37]

When a claim is forwarded to another lawyer, the candor and fairness required under Canon 22 in dealings between lawyers, make it incumbent [38] on one expecting a share of the associate's fee to advise him of this at the outset,[39] the division between them or the basis thereof being agreed on in advance.[40] Where he does not do so, unless the case is one where obvious service by the forwarder is required and performed after the forwarding, the associate is warranted in assuming that the forwarder will be compensated directly by the client for whatever responsibility or service he assumes or renders.[41] Candor and fairness to the client also require the forwarder both to advise the client that he expects to share the correspondent's fee,[42] and to advise his correspondent as to any doubt he may have of the client's ability and probable inclination to pay the latter for the services requested,[43] as well as to use every effort to induce the client to pay him; [44] but in the absence of an agreement, the forwarder is not personally responsible therefor.[45]

A lawyer who forwarded a claim to another lawyer has no right whatever to share in the fee obtained by the forwardee from the client in another later independent case which the client sent direct to the forwardee.[46]

There is no "usual" basis for division,[47] nor will the Committee undertake to fix the proportions in which fees should be shared,[48] each case depending on its own peculiar facts.[49]

[32] N.Y. County 382.   [33] N.Y. City 807. See A.B.A. Op. 217.   [34] N.Y. City 808.
[35] App, A, *352*.   [36] *Ibid.;* see N.Y. City 531.
[37] N.Y. County 42.   [38] App, A, *351;* and see A.B.A. Op. 63.
[39] A.B.A. Op. 204.   [40] App, A, *354*.
[41] A.B.A. Op. 265; and see N.Y. County 184.
[42] N.Y. County 180, 184; N.Y. City 660.   [43] A.B.A. Op. 63.
[44] App, A, *355*.   [45] A.B.A. Op. 63; and see App, A, *242, 243*.
[46] App, A, *357*.   [47] *Id., 351;* A.B.A. Op. 265.
[48] A.B.A. Op. 204; and see N.Y. City B-194.   [49] A.B.A. Op. 204.

When the client specifically agrees that the forwarding lawyer shall receive one third and the forwardee two thirds contingently, Canon 34 is not involved.[50]

A receiver's partner may represent him, irrespective of the division of fees under the partnership agreement.[1]

Where joint services are rendered, the lawyer performing the major part may fix his fee and deduct it before remitting to the other.[2]

Where no basis of division with a correspondent is agreed on and there is no indication that the forwarder expected a division, and where the correspondent deals directly with the client, the correspondent may properly render a bill direct to the client for his services; but this does not preclude the forwarder from billing the client direct for his own services, from whom he should collect them.[3]

The New York City Committee has held that one on a general retainer should not retain a forwarding fee sent him by his associate, nor turn it over to his client, but should return it to the former, although with the consent of his client he may retain it.[4]

Where the client is himself a lawyer he is not entitled thereby to a share in a fee allowed his lawyer in a representative action unless he was associated and actually served *qua* lawyer;[5] and a lawyer-executor, not counsel of record, may not get part of his colleague's lawyer's fee for doing legal work, in addition to his executor's fee, the court not being advised.[6]

One engaged by a corporation as trial counsel may not properly agree to pay 25 per cent of his contingent retainer to its General Counsel, without telling the corporation.[7]

A disbarred lawyer may be paid for compensable services prior to disbarment.[8]

Division of Fees with Retired Partners or Their Estates

While it is proper for a fellow lawyer to care for the practice of a deceased colleague, this should be done primarily in the inter-

---

[50] App. A, *353*.

[1] A.B.A. Op. 271; and see Mo. 77; but see N.Y. County 272. See also *supra*, p. 112.

[2] A.B.A. Op. 27.   [3] App. A, *356*.

[4] N.Y. City 95. The soundness of this conclusion would not seem clear. Cf. A.B.A. Op. 10; see *supra*, pp. 97 and 179.

[5] N.Y. City 723.

[6] N.Y. County 26; In re Annunziato's Est. 108 N.Y.S.2d 101 (1951). New York counsel doubt the soundness of this ruling.   [7] N.Y. City 187.   [8] App. A, *361*.

est of the client until the client can make a desired substitute.[9]

A lawyer's clients are not merchandise nor is a law practice the subject of barter.[10] The purchase of a lawyer's practice and good will and the payment therefor to him [11] or to his estate [12] by a percentage of the receipts from his business is improper, since this would constitute a division of his fees with laymen, forbidden by Canon 34. It would seem, however, that a reasonable agreement to pay the estate a proportion of the receipts for a reasonable period is a proper practical settlement for the lawyer's services to his retirement or death.[13]

The library, fixtures and lease of a deceased lawyer may be advertised for sale.[14]

The widow of a deceased partner may not be employed by the survivors on a percentage basis.[15]

An advertisement of the sale of a law practice with "established clientele" is improper.[16]

An announcement "successor to the practice of" constitutes solicitation.[17]

Where an agreement was made with the widow of a deceased partner to receive a percentage of profits for his interest in the firm, this may be settled by paying her a lump sum.[18]

Where partners dissolve, one may not agree to pay the other a share of the fees from a client who objects to this, nor may the other demand it.[19]

---

[9] N.Y. City 840; see also 884.

[10] N.Y. City 355, 778, 872, 953; and see B-6(2), B-89, B-142; Wash. 3; but see N.Y. County 315.

[11] A.B.A. Op. 266; N.Y. City 110, 953(e). In its Op. 872 the New York City Committee held that while an attempt by the member of a law firm to sell his interest in the firm was inconsistent with the best concepts of legal practice, an incoming member might, on becoming a member, advance to the firm the necessary funds to pay an agreed value of the retiring partner's interest without allowance for good will or firm name.

[12] N.Y. City 894, B-44; Chicago 32, p. 72.

[13] N.Y. City B-44; N.Y. City 110. As to the right of an indigent widow of a former associate, not a partner, to share fees from his former clients, see N.Y. City 789, B-44. All paid the widow over the amount which was earned by a deceased partner will be considered a gift by the survivors to the widow. N.Y. City 789; N.Y. County 161.

[14] N.Y. City 440, B-142.   [15] N.Y. City 110; and see N.Y. City B-186.

[16] N.Y. City 778.   [17] N.Y. City B-104.   [18] N.Y. County 352.

[19] N.Y. City 610.

VII

THE LAWYER'S OBLIGATIONS
AND RELATIONS
TO OTHER LAWYERS

In addition to and distinct from the obligations imposed on members of the bar by reason of the special privileges granted to them by the public, they have voluntarily assumed, by mutual understanding and recognized custom of the bar over a long period, certain obligations to one another. The recognition and observance of these obligations is primarily what characterizes the practice of law as a profession as distinguished from a business. They constitute the most significant part of the lawyers' distinctive code of etiquette and of ethics. These obligations are:

1. Not to steal one another's clients
2. To be candid, fair, and courteous in their dealings with other lawyers
3. Not to deal directly with the clients of other lawyers
4. To avoid self-advertisement and solicitation of professional employment

The first three of these obligations are discussed in the present chapter, the fourth in Chapter VIII.

Encroaching on Other Lawyers

One of the amenities which, over many years, lawyers have recognized toward one another, is the obligation to refrain from deliberately stealing each other's clients. This, as well as the obligation not to advertise and solicit, it is impossible to define precisely. As we approach the borderline between what is generally considered proper and what is improper, the question, as in the case of many other problems of professional ethics and etiquette, becomes one of good taste.

The third paragraph of Canon 7 provides:

Efforts, direct or indirect, in any way to encroach upon the professional employment of another lawyer, are unworthy of those who should be brethren at the Bar; but, nevertheless, it is the right of any lawyer, without fear or favor, to give proper advice to those seeking relief against unfaithful or neglectful counsel, generally after communication with the lawyer of whom the complaint is made.[1]

The Canon condemns any disparagement of another lawyer in an endeavor to supplant him as sole listee in a law list.[2] A lawyer may not properly cause another's client to discontinue his services that he may replace him [3] or attempt to do so; [4] or attempt to seduce a client of his former partner by offering to serve him at reduced fees; [5] nor may one employed by another lawyer who contemplates leaving to practice independently suggest to a client of his employer that it will be to the client's advantage to substitute him.[6]

A lawyer may not properly make a competitive bid for professional service.[7]

One employed by a law firm who leaves it to engage in independent practice may send announcements to his individual clients, but not to those of the firm whom he has served; he need not, however, refuse retainers from the latter provided he did not, directly or indirectly, solicit employment by them.[8]

Where a lawyer is employed by another lawyer and the latter, on the first lawyer's going into independent practice, turns over to him a case he is handling, the first lawyer may subsequently accept, without solicitation, new cases from this client, explaining that he is no longer connected with the second lawyer.[9] "It is for the client to decide who shall represent him." [10]

---

[1] As to the respective obligations of superseding and superseded lawyers, see *infra,* p. 198.

[2] A.B.A. Op. 65. [3] A.B.A. Op. 10, p. 79.

[4] N.Y. City 837, 648; see also N.Y. City B-206.

[5] N.Y. County 189; as to accepting business from or through a former partner, see N.Y. County 403.

[6] N.Y. County 59, 109. [7] App. A, *83;* Mich. 133.

[8] App. A, *241;* and see N.Y. City 516. [9] N.Y. City 719.

[10] N.Y. City B-152; see also N.Y. City 516.

Courtesy and Good Faith to Other Lawyers

Canon 17 provides:

17. Ill-feeling and Personalities between Advocates. Clients, not law-yers, are the litigants. Whatever may be the ill-feeling existing between clients, it should not be allowed to influence counsel in their conduct and demeanor toward each other or toward suitors in the case. All personalities between counsel should be scrupulously avoided. In the trial of a cause it is indecent to allude to the personal history or the personal peculiarities and idiosyncrasies of counsel on the other side. Personal colloquies be-tween counsel which cause delay and promote unseemly wrangling should also be carefully avoided.

"Do as adversaries do in law: strive mightily but eat and drink as friends." [11]

"The highest reward that can come to a lawyer is the esteem of his professional brethren. That esteem is won in unique conditions and proceeds from an impartial judgment of professional rivals. It can-not be purchased. It cannot be artificially created. It cannot be gained by artifice or contrivance to attract public attention. It is not measured by pecuniary gains. It is an esteem which is born in sharp contests and thrives despite conflicting interests. It is an esteem commanded solely by integrity of character and by brains and skill in the honorable performance of professional duty. No subservient 'yes men' can win it. No mere manipulator or negotiator can secure it. It is essentially a tribute to a rugged independence of thought and in-tellectual honesty which shine forth amid the clouds of controversy. It is a tribute to exceptional power controlled by conscience and a sense of public duty,—to a knightly bearing and valor in the hottest of encounters. In a world of imperfect humans, the faults of human clay are always manifest. The special temptations and tests of lawyers are obvious enough. But, considering trial and error, success and de-feat, the bar slowly makes its estimate and the memory of the careers which it approves are at once its most precious heritage and an im-portant safeguard of the interests of society so largely in the keeping of the profession of the law in its manifold services." [12]

---

[11] *Taming of the Shrew,* Act I, end of Scene 2.

[12] From the address by Chief Justice Hughes at the meeting of the American Law Institute, Washington, D.C., May 7, 1936. See also Sharswood, *Professional Ethics,* pp. 75–76.

Section 26 of the Alabama Code of 1887 provided as follows:

Section 26. It is not a desirable professional reputation to live and die with—that of a rough tongue, which makes a man to be sought out and retained to gratify the malevolent feeling of a suitor, in hearing the other side well lashed and vilified.

Canon 22 contains the following:

The conduct of the lawyer before the Court and with other lawyers should be characterized by candor and fairness.

It is not candid or fair . . . in those jurisdictions where a side has the opening and closing arguments to mislead his opponent by concealing or withholding positions in his opening argument upon which his side then intends to rely.[13]

Canon 24 provides:

As to incidental matters pending the trial, not affecting the merits of the cause, or working substantial prejudice to the rights of the client, such as forcing the opposite lawyer to trial when he is under affliction or bereavement; forcing the trial on a particular day to the injury of the opposite lawyer when no harm will result from a trial at a different time; agreeing to an extension of time for signing a bill of exceptions, cross interrogatories and the like, the lawyer must be allowed to judge. In such matters no client has a right to demand that his counsel shall be illiberal, or that he do anything therein repugnant to his own sense of honor and propriety.

[13] Sharswood, *Professional Ethics,* pp. 73–74, says, immediately following the passage quoted *infra,* p. 194: "It is not only morally wrong but dangerous to mislead an opponent, or put him on a wrong scent in regard to the case . . . he who sits down deliberately to plot a surprise upon his opponent, and which he knows can succeed only by its being a surprise, deserves to fall, and in all probability will fall, into the trap which his own hands have laid. 'Whoso diggeth a pit,' says the wise man, 'shall fall therein, and he that rolleth a stone, it will return upon him.' If he should succeed, he will have gained with his success not the admiration and esteem, but the distrust and dislike of one of his associates as long as he lives. He should never unnecessarily have a personal difficulty with a professional brother. He should neither give nor provoke insult."

"However advantageous it may be in the conduct of a client's case to learn precisely what the evidence of the adversary may be, or the course of action he is planning to pursue, the lawyer should not resort to trickery to obtain the knowledge. Whatever knowledge comes to him in the natural course of events he is entitled to make use of, but for him to adopt underhanded methods to obtain it is contrary to legal ethics." Gleason L. Archer, *Ethical Obligations of the Lawyer* (1910), sec. 61, pp. 140, 141.

"A lawyer is not to eavesdrop or listen at keyholes. There are honorable ways of acquiring a knowledge, more or less accurate, of the designs and doings of the other side." John C. Reed, *Conduct of Lawsuits* (2d ed., 1885), sec. 121, p. 85.

"To avoid all harsh remark as far as possible, to reconcile opposing testimony by any theory rather than that of wilful falsehood, and never to impute it unless in the full belief that it has been committed, is the wisdom no less than the duty of the advocate." "On the Principle of Advocacy," 20 Law Mag. (N.S.) 265, 276–77 (1854).

As to customs of the bar, see also A.B.A. Op. 128, p. 274.

Canon 25 provides:

A lawyer should not ignore known customs or practice of the Bar or of a particular Court, even when the law permits, without giving timely notice to the opposing counsel. As far as possible, important agreements, affecting the rights of clients, should be reduced to writing; but it is dishonorable to avoid performance of an agreement fairly made because it is not reduced to writing, as required by rules of Court.

The Michigan Committee has said, "No client has any right to trade upon the privileges and courtesies extended to his lawyer." [14]

In its Opinion 149, the American Bar Association Committee, in discussing the obligations of a lawyer to one whom he supersedes, said:

The Committee recognizes that there are frequently personal relations between counsel in a given community which may render it embarrassing for an attorney to accept a retainer without the consent of the previous attorney, and this opinion is not to be taken as a criticism of courtesies extended by one member of the Bar to another because of such relations.

Candor and fairness require one to use every reasonable effort to induce his client to pay his foreign correspondent. [15]

Any agreement or representation which a lawyer makes for the client's benefit, he must, of course, scrupulously keep—as well as any agreement with the court or the opposing lawyer for his personal convenience, or in courtesy for the reasonable accommodation of other lawyers.

"A very great part of a man's comfort, as well as of his success at the Bar, depends upon his relations with his professional brethren. With them he is in daily necessary intercourse, and he must have their respect and confidence, if he wishes to sail along in smooth waters. He cannot be too particular in keeping faithfully and liberally every promise or engagement he may make with them. One whose perfect truthfulness is even suspected by his brethren at the Bar has always an uneasy time of it. He will be constantly mortified by observing precautions taken with him which are not used with others." [16]

A lawyer may not repudiate an oral stipulation, made in return for a favor granted, which cannot be revoked, to admit a certain fact

---

[14] Mich. 93. In this case the Committee held that where the broker of the seller of property had delivered the abstract of title to the lawyer for the buyer, the latter on repudiating the purchase might not require the lawyer to refuse to return the abstract to the broker in order to coerce the buyer to give back the deposit money.

[15] App. A, 355.

[16] Sharswood, *Professional Ethics*, p. 73.

in issue, which at the time could have been proved but now can be, if at all, only with difficulty; this despite his client's insistence and the existence of a court rule making oral stipulations unenforceable.[17]

A lawyer must also observe the customs of the bar [18] as well as the confidences of another lawyer, although indiscreetly given and improperly received,[19] and although this may entail his withdrawing from the case.[20]

Where, with his client's consent, a lawyer proposes to default and discontinue his case, proper professional courtesy would lead him to advise the other lawyer, but his failure to do so the New York County Committee did not characterize a professional misconduct.[21] In an early case the same Committee said that one employed as observer of a case on trial should advise counsel of record.[22]

A forwarding attorney who makes a separate charge should advise the forwardee of this before accepting a division of the latter's fee; [23] and it is a breach of good faith for a lawyer employed by a corporation on a salary to accept and turn over to it a forwarding fee, the forwardee not being advised of the relation.[24]

Where defendant's attorney moved without leaving an address, but plaintiff's attorney actually knows defendant's address plaintiff's counsel must notify defendant of trial despite plaintiff's instructions not to do so.[25]

"Let him shun most carefully the reputation of a sharp practitioner. Let him be liberal to the slips and oversights of his opponent wherever he can do so, and in plain cases not shelter himself behind the instructions of his client. The client has no right to require him to be illiberal—and he should throw up his brief sooner than do what revolts against his own sense of what is demanded by honor and propriety." [26]

Although a lawyer should not take technical advantage of inad-

[17] N.Y. County 31; and see Mutual Life Insurance Co. v. O'Donnell, 146 N.Y. 275, 280 (1895); New York v. Stephens, 52 N.Y. 306, 310, 311 (1873); and cf. N.Y. City 337; also N.Y. City 473.

[18] A.B.A. Op. 17, p. 91; A.B.A. Op. 128, p. 274; see also A.B.A. Op. 25.

[19] N.Y. County 245.

[20] A.B.A. Op. 47; for a somewhat similar case, see N.Y. County 245.

[21] N.Y. County 41.

[22] N.Y. County 176. New York counsel have questioned the correctness of this ruling.

[23] N.Y. County 184. See also supra, pp. 173 and 187.

[24] Chicago Committee, reported in Costigan's Case Book, p. 631.

[25] N.Y. County 283.   [26] Sharswood, Professional Ethics, pp. 74–75.

vertent oversights or defaults by his adversary which the court would properly remedy,[27] yet where a delay by the opposing lawyer is not because of illness or accident, he may not properly waive it and not inform the client. If it is proper that it be corrected, the court will do it.[28]

While he is under no obligation to correct his adversary's errors in applying the law, or those of the court,[29] it is his duty, when he finds that his adversary has made a typographical mistake or a clear error in computation to call his attention or that of the court to it, after first seeking the client's approval.[30] In case the client refuse to approve the disclosure, the lawyer should ask to be relieved.[31] Although a lawyer's position and status in having control over the incidents of litigation often give him power to sacrifice his client's substantial rights,[32] a lawyer has no right, as between him and the client to do this, and where without express authority from the client the lawyer does so, even in the honest belief that it is inequitable for the client to insist on such rights, he does the client a wrong for which he may be liable. His duty is to his client,[33] and he may not give away the client's rights or property.[34] Nor may a lawyer, in courtesy to one to whom he forwarded a claim, advise him of the location of the client's property in order that his correspondent may collect his fee.[35]

One may not attempt to get the lawyer on the other side drunk in order to take advantage of him in a case to be tried; [36] nor may he use a check sent in full settlement against a judgment entered for a larger amount just prior to receiving it.[37]

---

[27] See Canon 25; see Marcus v. Simotone, etc., 135 Misc. 228 (1929), and see N.Y. City 445.

[28] App. A, 274; see also N.Y. City 445, and Anonymous, 1 Wend. 108 (N.Y., 1828).

[29] N.Y. City 269.   [30] N.Y. City 631.   [31] Ibid.

[32] See McLyman v. Miller, 52 R.I. 374 (1932); Garrett v. Hanshue, 53 Oh. St. 482 (1895); Moulton v. Bowker, 115 Mass. 36 (1874); Wieland v. White, 109 Mass. 392 (1872) and cases cited on pp. 409–21, of Arant's Case Book.

[33] N.Y. City 269.   [34] N.Y. City 254, 269, 445, 474.

In N.Y. City 254, the Committee said: "While a lawyer may, and should, control the action of his client as to matters of practice and procedure, he may not force and compel his client to abandon legal rights affecting his property. A stipulation between attorneys is a proper method of adjusting questions of procedure, but an attorney may not stipulate away substantial rights of his client."

A lawyer is under no professional duty to coerce his client not to exact his pound of flesh: N.Y. City 243. Cf., however, N.Y. City 596.

[35] N.Y. City 682-G.

[36] Dickens' case, 67 Pa. 169, 176 (1870). See also supra, p. 155.

[37] N.Y. City 56. See also Matter of Steinberg, 233 App. Div. 301 (N.Y. 1931); Matter of Chaikin, 238 App. Div. 211 (N.Y., 1933); Matter of Ginsburg, 188 App. Div. 517 (N.Y., 1919).

He may not, despite outrageous demands by the other lawyer, advise the judge of negotiations for settlement, privileged and not in the record, involving very much lower terms.[38]

It is unethical for a lawyer to make a dictaphone record of a conference between himself and the lawyer who preceded him, even though this be admissible in evidence.[39] It is also not proper for a lawyer to discuss with another lawyer a claim by the other lawyer's client against one whom the first lawyer really represents, without telling the other lawyer this; or, having thus discussed the case in confidence, as if as a friend, later to take it to court.[40]

One lawyer should not criticize another for taking a weak case.[41]

While there is no professional impropriety in a lawyer accepting a retainer to prosecute a meritorious cause of action against another lawyer,[42] he should not use a threat of disbarment to collect money.[43]

Difficult and delicate problems not infrequently arise in connection with requests by other lawyers to testify as to the reasonableness or unreasonableness of fees in dispute, opinions of other lawyers experienced in matters of the nature involved being obviously of impressive significance in such cases.[44] While considerations of courtesy and fraternity should not deter a lawyer from so testifying as an expert,[45] it will be found that those of the highest standing and experience are usually the least apt to be dogmatic as to the precise amount which would be proper. Fortified for cross-examination with a precise prior understanding of all the circumstances surrounding the case and, if possible, with the amounts charged by him and by others in similar matters, he can say with assurance what he himself would charge in the particular case.

A statement by one lawyer to another is not necessarily protected because he says that it is "without prejudice." [46]

A lawyer learning of a tax refund possibly obtainable by other lawyers for his clients, should advise them of it, but not demand a fee;

---

[38] N.Y. City 946.

[39] N.Y. City 848 and cf. N.Y. City 290 (he may not take advantage of having overheard the other lawyer talking in the next office).

[40] N.Y. City 849.

[41] See address by C. J. Mathers in 40 Can. L.T. 925, 935–37 (1920).

[42] Canon 29; A.B.A. Op. 144; N.Y. City 47, 91, 158.

[43] N.Y. County 19; Chicago 30, p. 67, see In re Malmin, 364 Ill. 164, 177 (1936).

[44] But see Lee v. Lomax, 219 Ill. 218 (1906); Epp v. Hinton, 102 Kan. 435 (1918); Peltier v. Thibodaux, 175 La. 1026 (1932); 34 Ann. Cas. D 369 n. (1914).

[45] N.Y. County 17.　　　　　　　　[46] N.Y. City B-155.

it is, however, reprehensible for other lawyers to use the information secretly to obtain the refund without seeing to it that the informer is properly compensated, although they were not legally bound to compensate him.[47]

A lawyer is not obliged to protect the claim of another lawyer to a fee,[48] where he refers a case to the other,[49] or even where he supersedes him.[50]

He may not give memoranda to a trial judge without a copy to the other side,[1] even at the judge's request.[2]

A member of the bar is bound to disclose to other lawyers on a legislative committee an interest on his part in the subject being considered by the committee.[3]

DUTIES OF SUPERSEDING AND SUPERSEDED LAWYERS

The first two paragraphs of Canon 7 are as follows:

A client's proffer of assistance of additional counsel should not be regarded as evidence of want of confidence, but the matter should be left to the determination of the client. A lawyer should decline association as colleague if it is objectionable to the original counsel, but if the lawyer first retained is relieved, another may come into the case.

When lawyers jointly associated in a cause cannot agree as to any matter vital to the interest of the client, the conflict of opinion should be frankly stated to him for his final determination. His decision should be accepted unless the nature of the difference makes it impracticable for the lawyer whose judgment has been overruled to co-operate effectively. In this event it is his duty to ask the client to relieve him.

The client "has the right to be represented at all times by counsel of his own selection." [4]

Where a client suggests that another lawyer be associated, although it is proper for the lawyer already in charge to advise the client, with candor and in good faith, that the lawyer suggested is incompetent,

---

[47] N.Y. County 252; and see N.Y. County 227.   [48] App. A, *242*.
[49] See N.Y. City 682 G.   [50] App. A, *243*.
[1] App. A, *253;* N.Y. County 221; see also Texas 22.
In March, 1947, the Judicial Conference adopted the following resolution: "The Use of Trial Memoranda in Criminal Cases.—The Conference after consideration of the report of the Committee appointed to study the subject matter, disapproved the practice, prevalent in some districts, of trial judges in criminal cases receiving from the attorney on one side a brief or trial memorandum that has not been furnished to the attorney on the other side, and recommended the immediate discontinuance of such practice."
[2] A custom to the contrary is invalid, Mich. 96.   [3] App. A, *20, 291.*
[4] A.B.A. Op. 10; App. A, *244;* Mich. 113; cf. N.Y. City B-6, B-152; but see N.Y. County 315.

unprofessional, or personally undesirable as an associate,[5] with the facts and reasons, yet if the client persists, the association should be genuinely accepted or the first lawyer should retire.[6]

Whether or not a correspondent may deal directly with the client depends on the relationship and its history. A forwarder who remains counsel for the client and merely employs another lawyer to assist him, may insist that the forwardee deal with the client through him. On the other hand, if the first lawyer employed the second to act as attorney for the client, contemplating a direct relationship, the second lawyer may properly communicate directly with the client.[7]

In case of the superseded lawyer's retirement he must tell the client all that the latter should know about the case.[8] He may not object if the client, who is at all times entitled to be represented by such lawyers as he chooses, discusses the matter with another lawyer [9] and the latter may permit this, but it is wise for him to discuss the case with the superseded lawyer and ascertain if he has been accurately advised of the situation by the client.[10] Irrespective of Rules of Court the superseded lawyer is entitled to be notified promptly of a motion in court to remove him and substitute other lawyers [11] even though he may have been negligent in handling the matter.[12] The new lawyer may not take charge of the case until satisfied that the former lawyer has retired or been removed by the client.[13] Where, however, he proceeds with the case without knowing of the prior em-

---

[5] N.Y. County 59. As to the propriety of refusing to turn over the papers to one whom he honestly believes is imposing on an incompetent client, see N.Y. City 115.

[6] Tenney v. Berger, 93 N.Y. 524 (1883); Mich. 113.

[7] App. A, *358*.   [8] Mich. 113.

[9] *Ibid.;* but see N.Y. County 204, that the new lawyer should not advise with the client without the knowledge and consent of the first lawyer, so long as the latter is in the case; see also N.Y. County 176.

[10] App. A, *360*.   [11] A.B.A. Op. 17.

[12] *Ibid.* The Committee there said: "Even though a lawyer is found guilty of gross misconduct that fact does not relieve other lawyers from their professional obligations in their relations with him."

[13] A.B.A. Ops. 10, 130, 149, 209; App. A, *360;* and see N.Y. County 204. Here a husband against whom a large alimony award had been made was brought to the inquiring lawyer by a friend. The Committee said that the lawyer might not advise the client as to believed mistaken tactics which had resulted in the large award without the knowledge of the first lawyer and without his consent so long as he remained attorney in the case.

In A.B.A. Op. 149, the Committee said: "The Committee recognizes that there are frequently personal relations between counsel in a given community which may render it embarrassing for an attorney to accept a retainer without the consent of the previous attorney, and this opinion is not to be taken as a criticism of courtesies extended by one member of the Bar to another because of such relations."

ployment of another lawyer he may properly, on learning of it, stay
in the case, and perform his duty, and not leave defenseless the client,
who did not wish to have the other lawyer continue in the case.[14]

A superseding lawyer is not responsible for the fees due the superseded one.[15] However, the superseded lawyer is entitled to notice so
as to enable him to protect his right or lien.[16]

A lawyer has no vested right to represent his deceased client's estate,[17] even where the client so directed. It would seem doubtful if
either the client or the executors named could effectively contract
for this with the lawyer drawing the will.

A superseded lawyer may not take steps to get his client back;[18]
nor make a flagrant overcharge.[19]

One going into the armed forces may, with notice and full disclosure to his clients, turn over his practice to an associate to keep it
intact until his return, and the latter may assume charge of it, acting
for the soldier, who may remain attorney of record.[20] Under the circumstances, the soldier may be given a reasonable share even of the
fees for new business, though this perhaps be a technical violation of
Canon 34.[21]

At the request of the next of kin of a deceased attorney, another
lawyer may, subject to ratification by the executors, take over his practice, notifying his clients, with the right by them to make such substitution as they wish, continuing the deceased's name on the door
and stationery, accepting employment from such as desire it, and
properly compensating the estate for the services rendered by the
deceased.[22] But to continue the name of a deceased lawyer (whose
practice he takes over at the widow's request) in the telephone book
has been held to be misleading.[23]

Where colleagues taken in by an outside lawyer receive what they
consider a fair offer but the forwarding lawyer does not agree and
declines to submit it to the client, they are not obliged to submit it

[14] A.B.A. Op. 130.
[15] *Ibid.* See also A.B.A. Op. 63; App. A, *243*. As to the lien of the superseded lawyer,
see A.B.A. Op. 209.
[16] A.B.A. Op. 17. As to the lien of a discharged attorney, see N.Y. City 15, 628.
[17] App. A, *244;* but see N.Y. County 315, N.Y. City B-152.
[18] Mich. 99.   [19] Mich. 113.
[20] See N.Y. City 807, 808, 843, 844, 847, 862, 899 (see joint statement referred to therein
N.Y. Law Jour. Dec. 28 and 31, 1942); N.Y. City B-153; see N.Y. City 938, 926(7).
[21] N.Y. City 807, 844.   [22] N.Y. City 840.
[23] N.Y. City 884; see also, as to disbarred lawyer, N.Y. City 940.

direct, on the insistence of the lawyers for the other side, but, as per Canon 7, should advise the client that a difference of opinion has arisen between them and local counsel, and let him decide.[24]

Where on dissolution of a firm one partner assigned to the other all his interest in pending cases, and the assignee died, the New York County Committee held that the assignor might not, in good faith, even at the client's request, accept substitutions of the cases assigned, since, in view of his contract, this would constitute bad faith on his part.[25]

DUTY NOT TO NEGOTIATE WITH ONE REPRESENTED BY COUNSEL

Canon 9 provides:

A lawyer should not in any way communicate upon the subject of controversy with a party represented by counsel; much less should he undertake to negotiate or compromise the matter with him, but should deal only with his counsel. It is incumbent upon the lawyer most particularly to avoid everything that may tend to mislead a party not represented by counsel, and he should not undertake to advise him as to the law.

The lawyer's duty to refrain from advising or misleading one not represented by counsel is also discussed *supra* under his obligations as a fiduciary.[26]

Hoffman's Resolution XLIII was: "I will never enter into any conversation with my opponent's client relative to his claim or defense, except with the consent and in the presence of his counsel." See also XLIV (*infra*, page 349).

His duty not to deal directly with one represented by counsel does not apply to the interviewing of witnesses for the other party,[27] even where under the latter's subpoena,[28] including a physician [29] and also including plaintiff's assignors.[30] But Canon 9 probably precludes interviews of managing employees of a corporation having authority to bind it.[31] Canon 9 precludes the interviewing of the other party despite the fact that he will be a witness,[32] and despite his willingness to be interviewed.[33]

---

[24] N.Y. County 236; but see 235.   [25] N.Y. County 315.

[26] See *supra*, p. 92; A.B.A. Ops. 58, 101, 160; N.Y. City 343, 698; N.Y. County 90, 144, 155, 255.

[27] A.B.A. Ops. 12, 14, 101, 117, and 127.   [28] A.B.A. Op. 127.

[29] Mich. 68. But see Mo. 37.   [30] Mich. 117.   [31] See N.Y. City 830.

[32] A.B.A. Op. 187; Mich. 41.   [33] A.B.A. Op. 108. See also Mo. 84.

A mother is so far identified with her minor child that it is improper for the insurance company to be allowed to interview her where the child is represented by counsel.[34]

The Canon is not restricted to interviews to effect a compromise, but applies to all cases.[35] It also applies though the other lawyer is not counsel of record,[36] and where the lawyer merely advised or permitted his client to interview the other party.[37] It applies to interviews by the law officers of a municipality [38] and to the legal department of a corporation.[39] It precludes a lawyer who is himself defendant in an action, from settling direct with the plaintiff,[40] as well as one who is suing for a fee a client represented by a lawyer from settling direct with the client at the instance of a mutual friend who arranged the settlement without the courtesy of notice to defendant's lawyer.[41]

It forbids an American lawyer from writing to the client of a London solicitor with whom acrimonious relations have developed.[42] It does not, however, apply to a demand, with no intimation as to a settlement, direct to the other parties to return papers tentatively submitted to them.[43]

Where three persons are accused of related thefts the prosecutor may not, in proceedings against one of them, interview another who is represented by counsel, except in the latter's presence.[44]

The "wise and beneficent" aim of the Canon has been said to be to "preserve the proper functioning of the legal profession [45] as well as to shield the adverse party from improper approaches." [46] In view of the lawyer's clear duty to further compromises and end litigation,[47] it would not seem so clearly the lawyer's duty, where the parties are well known to one another—for example husband and wife—to pre-

---

[34] App. A, 250.   [35] Texas 17.

[36] N.Y. County 85; and where the lawyer doing the interviewing poses as a mutual friend and not as counsel, N.Y. City 849. The offending lawyer may not absolve himself by informing the party that she may consult her lawyer. Wash. 11.

[37] A.B.A. Op. 75; see also N.Y. City 17.   [38] A.B.A. Op. 95.

[39] N.Y. City 400; see also Chicago 6, p. 16.   [40] N.Y. City 434.

[41] N.Y. County 405; and cf. N.Y. City 849.   [42] N.Y. City 109.

[43] N.Y. County 406.   [44] App. A, 249. See also N.Y. City 111.

[45] In its Ops. 17 and 124, both involving Canon 9, the A.B.A. Committee said: "Compensation for his services is an attorney's professional right and, in matters affecting a professional right, candor and fairness require that other attorneys grant him more than the mere compliance with rules of court or with his statutory rights. They require that he be given a reasonable opportunity to assert and protect any such right which he may claim and possess, whether it be based on a lien or not."

[46] A.B.A. Op. 108.   [47] Canon 8.

vent one of them or his lawyer from discussing a settlement direct with the other whose counsel will not do so.[48]

Close questions also arise when counsel for a party to whom a proposal for settlement is made, refuses to submit it to his client. If this is because, in good faith, he believes that the settlement should not be considered, it may be that the Canon should be applied.[49] Where, however, his refusal to submit the offer is because he has an arrangement for a contingent fee,[50] or because his outstanding bill for services has not been paid,[1] it would seem that the other lawyer should be permitted at least to bring the facts before the court,[2] or even to take it up or allow his client to take it up direct with the other party, at a time and place of which the declining lawyer is advised.

Where an insured is represented by counsel for an insurance company who, because of his desire to protect the company, will not advise the insured of all his rights and risks, it may be the right and duty of counsel for the injured party so to advise the insured, after warning such counsel.[3]

A lawyer has been suspended for violating the provision precluding him from negotiating directly with the other party.[4]

PARTNERSHIPS AMONG LAWYERS

Although partnerships,[5] or sharing costs or profits[6] between barristers in England have never been permitted, they are expressly recognized by Canon 33[7] which provides: "Partnerships among lawyers

---

[48] See *contra*, N.Y. City 227, involving a breach of promise case. See *supra*, pp. 200–01.

[49] See N.Y. County 235. "The failure of one attorney to observe a Canon (Canon 8 re settlements) would not in our opinion justify a violation of another Canon by the opposing lawyer."

[50] N.Y. County 242. Compare also A.B.A. Op. 66 where, when the plaintiff's lawyer declined to comply with his agreement to furnish certain information, this was held to justify a direct demand by defendant's lawyer on the president of the plaintiff, with a copy of the letter to plaintiff's lawyer.

[1] N.Y. County 93.

[2] See N.Y. County 236; and cf. N.Y. City 350, holding that where the guardian of an infant does not agree with his counsel's recommendation for a settlement, the matter should be submitted to the court.

[3] App. A, *17*.   [4] In Carpenter v. State Bar, 210 Cal. 520 (1930).

[5] Annual statement of the General Council of the Bar, 1902–03, p. 4; see also 1937, p. 8.

[6] Consolidated Regulations of the Four Inns, No. 46 of 1947. Partnerships between solicitors are recognized.

[7] See N.Y. County 170. In an article in The Law Journal, London, reprinted in 90 N.Y. Law Jour. 2426 (Dec. 27, 1933) entitled "The Single Practitioner and Professional Misconduct," the author says: "It is a striking fact that in over 97 per cent of the cases which

for the practice of their profession are very common and are not to be condemned."

Canon 33 also provides:

. . . In the formation of partnerships for the practice of law, no person should be admitted or held out as a practitioner or member who is not a member of the legal profession duly authorized to practice, and amenable to professional discipline. . . .

Partnerships between lawyers and members of other professions or non-professional persons should not be formed or permitted where any part of the partnership's employment consists of the practice of law.

Accordingly, a lawyer may not be in partnership with an auditor [8] or layman "collector" [9] or with a patent agent, not a lawyer,[10] or with an income tax expert,[11] or certified public accountant [12] unless the practice of the firm is confined to activities permitted to the lay members [13] and the lawyer ceases to hold himself out as such; [14] nor may a layman be held out as an associate.[15]

There is no ethical objection to one being a partner in two distinct firms each practicing in a different borough,[16] but not in two firms at the same offices, which might cause confusion.[17]

Lawyers may not, in order to benefit their tax status, organize as a Massachusetts trust where but some are trustees and all are beneficiaries.[18]

They may not hold themselves out as a partnership where no real partnership in fact exists [19] or in a state where one of them is not admitted,[20] the statement "attorneys" indicating, in the absence of a specific statement to the contrary,[21] that they are all entitled to practice at the situs of the partnership.[22]

A partnership agreement may not contain a clause that the partner

---

have come before the Discipline Committee (London) since 1919 the solicitor whose conduct was complained of had no partner, and that in that period of fourteen years only five solicitors who were in partnership have been struck off the rolls."

[8] N.Y. City B-22.   [9] N.Y. County 98.

[10] A.B.A. Ops. 32, 201; N.Y. County 209, 345.   [11] A.B.A. Op. 234.

[12] A.B.A. Ops. 239, 272; and see N.Y. City 559, 831, B-137; N.Y. County 201 Miss. 1.

[13] A.B.A. Op. 257 (patent agent); and see Mich. 148.

[14] A.B.A. Op. 269 (C.P.A.) but see N.Y. City 709 (1940).   [15] A.B.A. Op. 54.

[16] N.Y. City 729.   [17] N.Y. City 579.   [18] A.B.A. Op. 283.

[19] A.B.A. Ops. 106, 115, 126, 277; Va. 33, 33-A; and cf, N.Y. City 531; App. A, *366*; N.Y. City 686, 819.

[20] A.B.A. Op. 115; N.Y. County 24 (prior to 1926, but see N.Y. County 354 adhering to this answer; also N.Y. County 197); query, however, since 1928, in view of the specific language of Canon 33.

[21] See *infra*, p. 205 n. 25.   [22] A.B.A. Op. 115.

shall not solicit or accept firm clients for two years after the term.[23]

Canon 33 clearly implies the propriety of partnerships between lawyers admitted only in different states, but provides that care be taken "to avoid any misleading name or representation which would create a false impression as to the professional position or privileges of the member not locally admitted." [24]

The partnership name may not include that of one not locally admitted, despite explanatory statements on the letterhead, shingle, etc. since the name, used where no such explanation accompanied it, would imply that all the named partners were locally admitted.[25]

While the provision in Canon 33 above referred to would seem also to justify an association of a lawyer of another state, where properly explained,[26] it would not clearly authorize a partnership or association with a foreign lawyer not entitled to practice in any jurisdiction of the United States.[27]

The New York City Committee has held that a German lawyer (non-partner) may be listed in the office directory.[28]

The American Bar Association Committee approved a Washington firm composed of members who were entitled to practice in Washington, D.C., as well as in their respective states, although in such states each member was in a separate firm.[29]

Although the New York City Committee has said that the word "associate," as applied to another lawyer, connotes a partnership,[30] I am advised by New York lawyers that under the current practice an "associate" there is regarded as one who is *not* a partner.

The American Bar Association Committee has held that one may not purport to be the "successor" of one of whom he was merely an associate not a partner.[31]

It is improper for a firm to designate as associates a foreign firm with which it has no legal relation.[32]

There may not be a dormant partner.[33]

A member of a firm entering public or private employment may continue in a partnership.[34] Where one is absent on war service, a

---

[23] N.Y. City B-6.   [24] See A.B.A. Op. 256; App. A, *365;* N.Y. City 961, B-31, B-76.
[25] N.Y. City 961; B-31, B-76, B-130, B-133, B-148, B-158; and see N.Y. County 182, 197, 354.
[26] See N.Y. City 28, 818; but see N.Y. City 925.
[27] See N.Y. County 24; also 354, and N.Y. City B-190.   [28] N.Y. City 585.
[29] App. A, *365.*   [30] N.Y. City 686.   [31] App. A, *364.*
[32] *Id.,* 366.   [33] N.Y. County 170.
[34] A.B.A. Op. 192; but see N.Y. City 448.

notice so stating may be sent to clients and fellow lawyers, his name being kept on the letterhead.[35]

Where a member is on leave to serve in Congress, the firm letterhead may state "on leave" [36] but not that he is in Congress.[37]

Partnership Names

Canon 33 provides:

In the formation of partnerships and the use of partnership names, care should be taken not to violate any law, custom, or rule of court locally applicable. Where partnerships are formed between lawyers who are not all admitted to practice in the courts of the state, care should be taken to avoid any misleading name or representation which would create a false impression as to the professional position or privileges of the member not locally admitted. . . . In the selection and use of a firm name, no false, misleading, assumed or trade name should be used. The continued use of the name of a deceased or former partner, when permissible by local custom, is not unethical, but care should be taken that no imposition or deception is practiced through this use. When a member of the firm, on becoming a judge, is precluded from practicing law, his name should not be continued in the firm name.

A partnership name may not be misleading,[38] as it would be while the firm had the name in question and one of the partners is still alive and practicing elsewhere,[39] or where there was no such partnership.[40] The use of a nom de plume,[41] assumed,[42] or trade [43] name in law practice is improper.

The individual name of one of the active partners may be adopted as the firm name.[44]

The name of one becoming a judge should be omitted [45] even if but for an interim period,[46] unless his name is the same as that of a continuing partner.[47]

The letterhead need not specify who are partners.[48]

A woman may practice under her maiden name.[49]

It is improper to retain the name of the senior partner who, though

[35] A.B.A. Op. 240.　　　[36] See *ibid.*　　　[37] App. A, *120.*
[38] A.B.A. Op. 6.　　　[39] N.Y. City 44.　　　[40] N.Y. City 819.
[41] N.Y. City 73, 235.　　　　　[42] N.Y. County 81, 348; Mich. 4, 12, 39.
[43] App. A, *375, 376;* N.Y. City B-7, B-42.
[44] N.Y. City 22; and see N.Y. City B-76.
[45] A.B.A. Op. 6; N.Y. City 40; N.Y. County 67.　　　[46] N.Y. City B-27.
[47] N.Y. County 67. If the judge was the senior, it would seem more proper to change the order of the names in such case.
[48] App. A, *129.*
[49] N.Y. City 883; An. St. (1932), p. 8; see Costigan's Case Book, p. 330.

still alive, has permanently left the jurisdiction and does not participate in the professional practice, contributing only his name and legal liability in exchange for a share of the profits. This tends to "beget the evils of increased commercialism and decreased sense of professional responsibility." [50]

One who was a mere associate is not the "successor" to the firm [1] or entitled to have such designation with the names of the former partners (one of whom is dead and the other disbarred) on the door. [2]

It is improper also to designate as "associates" a foreign firm with which there is no legal relation. [3] The firm name should not include that of a living person not admitted in the jurisdiction. [4] Where A, B, and C practiced under the name of A and C, and A and B moved to another office and practiced as A and B, they may not, by assignment to C of the right to use the name A and C, make this proper for C, in as much as the use of the name of a living person (A) would be misleading. [5]

The following firm names have been held improper: ——— & Co; [6] ——— Associates; [7] ——— and Co.; [8] Northern Law Clinic; [9] Mc-Carrus Claim Service; [10] Veterans' Legal Service. [11]

The following have been approved: S. S. Dudley & Son; [12] Firm of A. B. Smith; [13] Jones Brothers. [14]

"Blank Law Office" is proper, where the firm is composed of three Blanks and there is no other firm in the locality composed all of Blanks. [15]

The continued use of a firm name after the death of one or more of the partners designated by it is proper [16] only where sustained by

---

[50] N.Y. County 170. The name of one still alive would also seem to be a misrepresentation of his active participation. See N.Y. City 44; see also New Orleans 1/13/41; but see N.Y. City 908.

[1] App. A, *364;* and see N.Y. City 940; Wash. 3.   [2] N.Y. City 940.

[3] App. A, *366.*   [4] *Id., 368.*   [5] N.Y. City 44.

[6] N.Y. City 776. This would be an "assumed or trade name." It would also "lower the dignity of the profession," contrary to Canon 29, in adopting a designation common to business partnerships, "most of which have no generally respected or accepted Code of Ethics."

[7] A.B.A. Op. 219; App. A, *373, 374.*   [8] App. A, *377.*

[9] *Id., 376.* Full disclosure should be made to avoid the possibility of deception, A.B.A. Op. 219.

[10] App. A, *375.* But may say "formerly carried on under the name of McCarrus Claim Service, the use of which has been discontinued."

[11] N.Y. City B-7.   [12] App. A, *371.*   [13] *Id., 369.*

[14] *Id., 370.*   [15] App. A, *371.*

[16] N.Y. City 154; N.Y. County 411.

local custom [17] and not where by custom this purports to identify the active members.[18]

It is not proper to designate the name of a deceased partner in a firm of which he was not a member,[19] nor to include in the firm name that of a partner not entitled to practice in the jurisdiction.[20]

The name of the deceased partner may be carried with the dates of his birth and death,[21] although it would seem more accurately informative thus to designate the dates of his active participation in the firm. The Texas Committee held, however, that an individual lawyer might not carry on his letterhead the dates of his great-grandfather, grandfather, and father.[22]

A usual designation is to have the names of the active living partners on the left side of the letterhead, and those of deceased members, with the dates of their entry into the firm and their death, on the right.[23]

There would seem to be a question, under the wording of the Canon, as to the propriety of adding the name of a new partner and at the same time retaining that of a deceased partner who was never a partner with the new one.[24]

Continuance of the firm name is the privilege of the continuing partners and is not available to an individual member after the firm's dissolution.[25]

Lawyer employees of a firm (A and B) of non-lawyer patent agents cannot use the name A and B by grant from them to practice law when A and B retire.[26]

---

[17] A.B.A. Ops. 6 (prior to the adoption of Canon 33 in 1928), 97, 208, 267; App. A, *379;* and see New Orleans 1/13/41; N.Y. County 411. As to how "local custom" is determined, see A.B.A. Op. 11, p. 83, and Op. 24. In Nevada, Rule XVIII of Professional Conduct imposes a limit of three years. See also A.B.A. Op. 219, at pp. 434–36.

[18] A.B.A. Op. 97; cf. N.Y. County 170, in which the retention of the name of a living but dormant partner was held improper where it was apparently retained in order to give the impression that he was still active professionally.

The Chicago Bar Association added to its Canon 33 the following clause: "Firm letterheads and listings in professional directories should indicate that former partners whose names are so continued are deceased or retired."

What if he has retired and formed another firm, or practices alone?

[19] See N.Y. City B-157.

[20] N.Y. City B-31, B-130, B-133; and see N.Y. City 961, B-148, B-158.

[21] N.Y. City 818; App. A, *382, 383.*   [22] Texas 31; cf. New Orleans 1/13/41.

[23] App. A, *383.* See also App. A, *111, 112.* Retention of his name without explanation is misleading. Mo. 58.

[24] *Id. 381;* see N.Y. County 316 approving it; see also N.Y. City B-82 holding that to be proper there must in fact be continuation of the firm of which the deceased partner was a member, and that if the continuity of the firm is interrupted, the use of the firm name is no longer permissible.

[25] A.B.A. Ops. 258, 267. As to right of the widow of the deceased partner to object, see N.Y. City B-90.   [26] N.Y. City 632.

The New York City Committee has held that a lawyer son who was never associated in practice with his lawyer father but is his sole heir and administrator may, on his father's death, move into his father's office and so long as he practices alone may carry his father's name and dates on his letterhead, but may not so carry it on the letterhead of a new partnership which he proposes to form.[27] The same Committee held it ethically proper to continue the name of one who retired to become a court attendant and who did not continue to practice law.[28]

The American Bar Association Committee declined to recommend an amendment to Canon 33 to preclude the use of a deceased partner's name in the firm name.[29]

[27] N.Y. City B-62.
[28] N.Y. City 908. Query as to this ruling. As to the retention of the firm name when one of the former partners accepts public office, see A.B.A. Op. 192.
[29] App. A, 380.

VIII

ADVERTISING AND SOLICITATION

Origin of the Proscription of Advertising and Solicitation by Lawyers

The young men who, in the early days of the bar, came to the Inns of Court to study and eat the requisite dinners there in order to become barristers, were practically all the sons of well-to-do parents, who did not have to worry about earning their keep, and who traditionally looked down on all forms of trade and the competitive spirit characteristic thereof. They regarded the law in the same way they did a seat in Parliament—as primarily a form of public service in which the gaining of a livelihood was but an incident. The profession of the law hence acquired a certain traditional dignity which it has been the aim of the bar to preserve ever since.

The conditions under which the barristers practiced their profession materially contributed to this attitude. They were a select fraternity who lived together and met one another every day, both at dinner and in court, on a friendly basis.[1] Obviously this intimacy would have been impossible for men who were continually blowing their professional horns and plotting to steal away one another's clients, and hence looked down on by their colleagues.

These amenities of the profession were brought back by the many young men who, in the latter part of the eighteenth century and the first part of the nineteenth, went to the Inns of Court for their legal training and on their return became the leaders of the American bar.[2] Why is it, however, that they have persisted under the different conditions which obtain in this country, particularly in view of the competitive spirit which has characterized our industrial develop-

[1] See quotation from *Taming of the Shrew, supra,* p. 192. [2] *Supra,* p. 5.

ment and been so potent a factor in its success? If competition is indeed the life of trade; if it is not only proper and desirable for business men to advertise their wares but necessary under the Anti-Trust laws for them aggressively to compete for the patronage of their rivals' customers, why should it be improper for lawyers to do likewise?

Several considerations have led to the persistence of these rules of professional conduct and their inclusion in the Canons of Ethics.[3]

In the first place, while American lawyers are by no means as intimate a fraternity as the English barristers with whom these rules originated, still they differ radically from the milk man, the liquor dealer, or the manufacturer of cigarettes in being yesterday an antagonist and today a colleague on the same side of the counsel table. They also differ in being members of a profession.[4] This is not a fancied conceit, but a cherished tradition,[5] the preservation of which is essential to the lawyer's reverence for his calling—as well as to his regard and esteem for his fellows at the bar.[6] This latter consideration is much more potent than is commonly supposed. Although, prompted by material success, some lawyers may profess indifference to the good opinion of their fellows, actually none is thus indifferent, but each craves such recognition, the more strongly the older he grows.[7]

Furthermore, advertising, solicitation, and encroachment on the practice of others does not tend to benefit either the public or the lawyer in the same way as in the case of the sale of merchandise. While

[3] Since there is no inherent malum in se in a lawyer's advertising as the milk man does, or, like him, directly soliciting employment by one who has theretofore been represented by another lawyer, they are really rules of professional etiquette rather than of "ethics."

[4] *Supra,* pp. 4–5.

[5] "It should never be forgotten that the profession is a branch of the administration of justice and not a mere money-getting trade." Canon 12. See Barton v. State Bar of California, 209 Cal. 677, 682 (1930). In the Preamble to its elaborate Opinion 47 dealing with the lawyer's relation to collection agencies the New York County Committee said of the law:

"It is a profession, not only because of the preparation and qualifications which are required in fact and by law for its exercise, but also for the primary reason that its functions relate to the administration of justice, and to the performance of an office erected and permitted to exist for the public good, and not primarily for the private advantage of the officer. Such private advantage, therefore, can never properly be permitted to defeat the object for which the attorney's office exists as a part of the larger plan of public justice."

[6] A lawyer who advertises, solicits or steals another's clients is regarded by his brethren at the bar as one with whom it is not pleasant to associate on the terms of cordial intimacy characteristic of the relationship of lawyers to one another.

[7] See *supra,* pp. 192, 194, 195.

extensive advertising would doubtless increase litigation,[8] this has always been considered as against public policy.[9] Also, many of the most desirable clients, imbued with high respect both for their lawyer and his calling, would have no use for a lawyer who did not maintain the dignity and standards of his profession and would instinctively resent any attempt by another lawyer to encroach on their relation.[10] Also, in so much as lawyers are officers of the court, advertising and solicitation by them would lower the whole tone of the administration of justice.

Reasons frequently given for the rules proscribing advertising and soliciting are, in addition to commercializing [11] the profession, the tendency of such practices to stir up litigation, the evil effect on the ignorant of alluring assurances by the solicitors, as well as the temptation and probability that the lawyers who advertise and solicit would use improper means to make good their extravagant inducements.[12] While these considerations doubtless have contributed to the retention of the proscriptions, they do not, it is believed, account for their origin.

THE LEGAL PROFESSION IS NOT RELAXING THE STANDARDS

It is interesting to consider whether the amenities discussed in this and the preceding Chapter are being undermined and will eventually be done away with as the personal contacts of lawyers with one an-

[8] If lawyers made it a practice to advertise, doubtless the large firms, controlled by lawyers who are thoroughly opposed, could well afford to preserve at least their antebellum status, and no one except the advertising agents would be any better off.

As to permissible advertising by Bar Associations, to emphasize the advantages to the public of employing a lawyer, see *infra*, pp. 254–59.

As to permissible notices in Law Lists, see *infra*, pp. 217, 265.

[9] See the statutes condemning champerty, maintenance, and barratry. Also article by Max Radin in 24 Cal. Law Review 48 (1935), "Maintenance by Champerty."

For a thoughtful analysis of the elements of advertising and solicitation of law practice see pp. 161–162 of Professor Cheatham's Case Book, also Canon 28. It would seem doubtful that occasional personal solicitation would materially increase litigation.

[10] "The basis of the relationship between lawyer and client is one of unselfish devotion, of disinterested loyalty to the client's interest, above and beyond his own. Let the lawyer seek you for his own profit and you despise him." Julius Henry Cohen, *The Law, a Business or a Profession* (1916), p. 197.

[11] See N.Y. City B-6.

[12] ". . . the community is concerned in providing safeguards not only against deception, but against practices which would tend to demoralize the profession by forcing its members into an unseemly rivalry which would enlarge the opportunities of the least scrupulous. What is generally called the 'ethics' of the profession is but the consensus of expert opinion as to the necessity of such standards." Hughes, C. J., in Semler v. Oregon State Board of Dental Examiners, 294 U.S. 608, 612 (1935). See also Harrison Hewitt, "Advertising by Lawyers," 15 A.B.A. Jour. 116 (1925).

other become less intimate than they were when the "customs of the bar" were developed, and if and as modern business methods and practices are applied to the practice of law,[13] and how far the increasing organizations of bar associations will serve to counteract this tendency.

It is significant that, despite the recognition and adoption during recent years of business efficiency, the reluctance of lawyers improperly to advertise themselves has apparently been strengthened.[14] Judge Sharswood's *Professional Ethics,* published in 1854, contains nothing whatever about advertising. An early state Code of Ethics (*infra,* page 356) specified as proper "newspaper advertisements," tendering lawyers' services to the public, and condemned only "special solicitations of particular individuals to become clients." [15] In Warvelle's *Legal Ethics,* published in 1902, the author laments the fact that "the leaven of commercial influence is actively at work in the legal profession." [16] He approves the insertion of professional cards, announcing special branches of the profession practiced, in magazines and newspapers of high standing [17] and in village newspapers,[18] although he decries the insertion therein of a residence address, as "bad form." [19] Since 1937 all such advertisement has been condemned.[20] Of solicitation Warvelle says that the rigorous rule forbidding it "has long ceased to obtain more than a nominal observance in England, and never seems to have secured a practical recognition in the United States." [21] Boswell reports Dr. Johnson as having said, relative to the solicitation by lawyers, that he would refrain from it, "not because I should think it wrong but because I should disdain it. . . . However, I would not have a lawyer be wanting to himself in using fair means. I would have him to insert a little hint now and then, to prevent his being overlooked." [22] In England today, however, the ethics and eti-

---

13 See Fallon, V. C., in Umland v. United Pub. Serv. Co., 111 N.J. Eq. 563, 163 A, 794, 798 (1933); and articles cited in n. 1 on p. 8 of Arant's Case Book; also People v. Berezniak, 292 Ill. 305, 317 (1920); 55 A.L.R. 1313 (1928).

14 See Ky. 1. In its first published opinion the American Bar Association Committee said: "Any conduct that tends to commercialize or bring 'bargain counter' methods into the practice of the law, lowers the profession in public confidence and lessens its ability to render efficiently that high character of service to which the members of the profession are called."

15 See Report of American Bar Association (1907), p. 696.   16 On p. 59.

17 *Ibid.*   18 *Id.* at 61.   19 *Id.* at 60.

20 See A.B.A. Op. 276.

21 Warvelle, *Legal Ethics,* p. 52. The same statement is carried in the 1920 Edition, p. 50.

22 *Life of Johnson* (Everyman's Library), I, 608.

quette condemning self-advertisement and solicitation is stronger and more uncompromising than ever.[23]

While there doubtless is at present in the United States solicitation by numerous lawyers, there has not, it is believed, been any weakening of the condemnation by the bar associations of solicitation.[24] What they have done is to sanction and regulate reasonable advertising by bar associations,[25] the publication of law lists designed to enable persons who need a lawyer to choose the one best suited to their needs,[26] and to condemn, without any relaxation, all other forms of advertising and solicitation. The eagerness of the great preponderance of lawyers to comply fully with the Canons is demonstrated by their frequent requests for advice from the various ethics committees and their hearty acceptance and observance thereof.[27]

During the last half of the nineteenth century the standards of the bar undoubtedly deteriorated. However, with the organization of bar associations and the adoption and enforcement of Canons of Ethics all over the Country, these standards have steadily improved and promise so to continue. The predictions that the Bar would soon be but a money-making business have not materialized.[28]

Significant evidence of the determination of the bar not to relax its condemnation of advertising was recently furnished in connection with bold-face listing of lawyers in the alphabetical section of telephone books. The American Bar Association Committee had originally condemned this,[29] but, after reconsideration, on the ground that this section was not a law list in which anyone would look to select a lawyer, but was merely to enable him to locate one already determined upon, the Committee reversed its original ruling, although condemning bold-face listing in the classified section.[30] Bar as-

[23] See as to Barristers, Annual Statements of the General Council of the Bar for 1905–06, p. 13; for 1929, pp. 13 and 14; for 1930, p. 10; for 1932 (*The Annual Practice* [1933], pp. 2606–25); for 1936, p. 11; for 1937, pp. 4 and 8; and Order of the General Council of July 18, 1951, as to solicitors, address on Professional Conduct & Etiquette by Thomas G. Lund, Esq., secretary of The Law Society at the Society in 1950–51, pp. 10–32.

[24] In 1937 the A.B.A. Committee (p. 151 of minutes) declined to recommend the liberalization of Canon 27 in order to offset the effect of advertising by trust companies and other similar business organizations. See also N.Y. City 103 and Report of N.Y. State Committee of Jan. 28, 1948, pp. 7–8.

[25] *Infra*, p. 254.   [26] *Infra*, pp. 217, 265.

[27] See section of the *Survey of the Legal Profession* on the observance of the Canons (by Robert T. McCracken).

[28] See *Survey of the Legal Profession: Conduct of Judges and Lawyers,* Phillips and McCoy, end of chap. v, pp. 83–84.

[29] A.B.A. Op. 53, 123.   [30] A.B.A. Op. 241.

sociations and individuals from all over the country protested against this ruling and a number of the state and local ethics committees declined to follow it. Accordingly, the American Bar Association Committee in 1951, in order to secure uniformity and not to be behind any in maintaining professional standards, reverted to its former ruling.[31]

History of the Canons Proscribing Advertising and Solicitation

Canon 27

From its adoption in 1908 to September 30, 1937, Canon 27 read as follows:

The most worthy and effective advertisement possible, even for a young lawyer, and especially with his brother lawyers, is the establishment of a well-merited reputation for professional capacity and fidelity to trust. This cannot be forced, but must be the outcome of character and conduct. The publication or circulation of ordinary simple business cards, being a matter of personal taste or local custom, and sometimes of convenience, is not per se improper. But solicitation of business by circulars or advertisements, or by personal communications, or interviews, not warranted by personal relations, is unprofessional. It is equally unprofessional to procure business by indirection through touters of any kind, whether allied real estate firms or trust companies advertising to secure the drawing of deeds or wills or offering retainers in exchange for executorships or trusteeships to be influenced by the lawyer. Indirect advertisement for business by furnishing or inspiring newspaper comments concerning causes in which the lawyer has been or is engaged, or concerning the manner of their con-

---

[31] A.B.A. Op. 284. See *infra*, p. 246.

Another case in which a practice of the bar in conflict with modern business methods instead of being relaxed has recently become more exacting is in connection with the division of professional compensation with laymen. Prior to 1928 this was not condemned by the Canons, the first 32 of which were adopted in 1908. In 1928 Canon 34 was adopted, condemning this except in the case of the collection of commercial claims as between a lay forwarder and a receiving lawyer. In 1937 this Canon was amended by eliminating the exception.

Still another illustration is the elimination since the amendment of 1937 to Canon 27 of the publication of professional cards except in law lists. See A.B.A. Op. 276; also *infra*, p. 241.

An even more significant feature of Canon 34, as indicating the determination of lawyers to disassociate themselves from current competitive business practices, is seen in the provision adopted in 1928, by which divisions of fees between lawyers must be based on a division of service or responsibility, which provision eliminated the "Finder's Fee" between lawyers; *supra*, p. 186. For many years it had been the practice of lawyers, in forwarding a claim to a lawyer in another jurisdiction, to expect to receive one-third of the fee earned by the forwardee, after the manner of real estate brokers, although the forwarder performed no service whatever. See A.B.A. Ops. 204 and 265.

duct, the magnitude of the interests involved, the importance of the lawyer's positions, and all other like self-laudation, defy the traditions and
lower the tone of our high calling, and are intolerable.

The Canon was completely redrafted in 1937, principally to provide for law lists.

In 1940 the whole Canon was further amended, and again amended
in 1942 and 1943.

In 1951 the patent bar proposed and advocated an amendment to
permit admiralty and patent lawyers to state on their letterheads the
special branch practiced by them, which was approved by the House
of Delegates on September 2, 1951, and made effective, by adding to
Canon 27 the final paragraph so that the Canon now reads: [32]

27. *Advertising, Direct or Indirect.* It is unprofessional to solicit professional employment by circulars, advertisements, through touters or by
personal communications or interviews not warranted by personal relations. Indirect advertisements for professional employment such as furnishing or inspiring newspaper comments, or procuring his photograph to be
published in connection with causes in which the lawyer has been or is engaged or concerning the manner of their conduct, the magnitude of the
interest involved, the importance of the lawyer's position, and all other
like self-laudation, offend the traditions and lower the tone of our profession and are reprehensible; but the customary use of simple professional
cards is not improper.

Publication in reputable law lists in a manner consistent with the
standards of conduct imposed by these canons of brief biographical and
informative data is permissible. Such data must not be misleading and
may include only a statement of the lawyer's name and the names of his
professional associates; addresses, telephone numbers, cable addresses;
branches of the profession practiced; date and place of birth and admission to the bar; schools attended, with dates of graduation, degrees and
other educational distinctions; public or quasi-public offices; posts of
honor; legal authorships; legal teaching positions; memberships and offices in bar associations and committees thereof, in legal and scientific societies and legal fraternities; the fact of listings in other reputable law
lists; the names and addresses of references; and, with their written consent, the names of clients regularly represented. A certificate of compliance
with the Rules and Standards issued by the Special Committee on Law
Lists may be treated as evidence that such list is reputable.

It is not improper for a lawyer who is admitted to practice as a proctor
in admiralty to use that designation on his letterhead or shingle or for a
lawyer who has complied with the statutory requirements of admission
to practice before the patent office to so use the designation "patent at-

[32] For the precise language of the several changes, see Appendix C, pp. 316–18.

torney" or "patent lawyer" or "trade-mark attorney" or "trade-mark lawyer" or any combination of those terms.

Canon 43

Canon 43 as originally enacted in 1928 was entitled "Professional Card" and provided that:

The simple professional card mentioned in Canon 27 may with propriety contain only a statement of his name (and those of his lawyer associates), profession, address, telephone number, and special branch of the profession practiced.

This Canon was amended in 1933 to read as follows:

A lawyer's professional card may with propriety contain only a statement of his name (and those of his lawyer associates), profession, address, telephone number, and special branch of the profession practiced. The insertion of such card in reputable law lists is not condemned and it may there give references or name clients for whom the lawyer is counsel, with their permission.

In 1937 Canon 43 was again amended, both in its title and in its text, to read as follows:

Approved Law Lists. It shall be improper for a lawyer to permit his name to be published after January 1, 1939, in a law list that is not approved by the American Bar Association.

In 1943 the Canon was amended to its present form as follows:

43. Approved Law Lists. It shall be improper for a lawyer to permit his name to be published in a law list the conduct, management or contents of which are calculated or likely to deceive or injure the public or the profession, or to lower the dignity or standing of the profession.

The principal changes were thus the provision for law lists and the elimination of the provision permitting the designation of special branches of the profession practiced in professional cards.

Canon 46

This Canon as adopted in 1933 provided as follows:

46. Notice of Specialized Legal Service. Where a lawyer is engaged in rendering a specialized legal service directly and only to other lawyers, a brief, dignified notice of that fact, couched in language indicating that it is addressed to lawyers, inserted in legal periodicals and like publications, when it will afford convenient and beneficial information to lawyers desiring to obtain such service is not improper.

For an amendment to Canon 46 proposed by the A.B.A. Committee but not adopted by the House of Delegates, see *infra,* page 245.

Canon 40

Canon 40, adopted July 26, 1928, provides as follows:

40. Newspapers. A lawyer may with propriety write articles for publications in which he gives information upon the law; but he should not accept employment from such publications to advise inquirers in respect to their individual rights.[33]

SCOPE OF THE PROSCRIPTION OF ADVERTISING AND SOLICITATION

One of the most frequent objections to Canon 27 is that it interferes only with the little fellows, precluding them from making themselves known to prospective clients by advertising and solicitation, while the big ones not only are constantly in the public eye, but by means of their membership in clubs and their prominent participation in Community Chests and in the management of hospitals, colleges, etc., are enabled to meet and become intimate with the leaders in business as potential clients.

These criticisms ignore the distinction between giving the public the chance to see and judge of the lawyer's ability and personality, and the direct emphasis of his superiority as a lawyer.

When a lawyer has the opportunity to perform a service to the community which will place him in the public eye, he need not hesitate to seek or accept it because if successful he will appear frequently in the newspapers, and will enlarge his circle of friends and acquaintances and thus attract new clients, some possibly who have theretofore employed another lawyer. Where publicity is the normal byproduct of able and effective service, whether of a professional or non-professional character, this is a kind of "advertisement" which is entirely right and proper. Clients naturally gravitate to a lawyer who has successfully represented their friends or who has obtained the confidence of the community by effective public service. What is wrong is for the lawyer to augment by artificial stimulus the publicity normally resulting from what he does, seeing to it that his successes are broadcast and magnified. While in hypothetical cases it may often seem difficult to draw the line between what is right and what is not, actually, a lawyer soundly brought up in the law, who wholeheartedly

---

[33] See *infra,* p. 263.

accepts his professional status, will rarely have any difficulty in realizing the difference between the normal by-product of efficient service [34] and the unwholesome results of self-aggrandizement.

The distinction between a proper and an improper offer to perform professional services free of charge is well illustrated by the American Bar Association Committee's Opinions 148 and 169. In the first the Committee held it not only proper but commendable for a committee of lawyers to make a public offer to defend gratis any indigent citizens who believed their constitutional rights to be imperiled by certain legislation. Speaking for the Committee, Chairman McCracken said:

The Canon proscribing the solicitation of business is aimed at commercialization of the profession. It announces the principle that the practice of the law is a profession and not a trade, and that the effort to obtain clients by advertisement is beneath the dignity of the self-respecting lawyer. It has to do, moreover, with the effort to obtain remunerative business—the endeavor to increase the lawyer's practice with the end in view of enlarging his income. It certainly was never aimed at a situation such as this, in which a group of lawyers announce that they are willing to devote some of their time and energy to the interests of indigent citizens whose constitutional rights are believed to be infringed.

In American Bar Association Opinion 169, on the other hand, the Committee held it to be improper for a lawyer to proffer his services to various labor unions in connection with their associate problems, with the hope that these contacts would lead to his receiving employment from the members of the union.[35]

GENERAL PRINCIPLES

Advertising is not justified by local custom.[36] The fact that a court acquiesces in conduct by the lawyer in manifest violation of the Canon does not alter its impropriety.[37]

[34] "Each piece of honest professional work breeds more clients." Frank J. Loesch, "The Acquisition & Retention of a Clientage," 1 Ill. L. Rev. 455, 468 (1906). Although it takes longer to build up a practice gained by a reputation for uprightness, efficiency, and dependability and through the unsolicited recommendations of clients well served, such a practice, when established, is much more satisfactory and stable than one acquired by the go-getter devices of modern business. Many a client is traceable to a jury which has seen a lawyer perform in contrast to his colleagues, or to a defeated litigant. My revered preceptor, Samuel Dickson, once told me that a number of his best clients had come to him in the latter way.

[35] See also Archer, *Ethical Obligations of the Lawyer*, sec. 132, p. 244. A lawyer may not retain a Public Relations Counsel, N.Y. County 423.

[36] A.B.A. Ops. 4, 115; see also App. A, *156*, *157* and N.Y. City 103.

[37] A.B.A. Op. 42.

The Canon applies to the solicitation of business from other law-yers;[38] also to solicitation of employment to give lectures on legal topics.[39] Teaching law is not, however, practicing law, and the solicitation of students for law schools is not condemned.[40]

Competitive bidding on the part of lawyers for legal employment is improper.[41]

It is no excuse in advertising for what is really legal employment not to say that the advertiser is a lawyer.[42]

The Canon does not apply to the solicitation of full-time employ-ment with a corporation [43] or full [44] or part-time [45] with a law firm, or to employment by the Home Owners Loan Corporation or other Gov-ernment agency on a fee basis; [46] but does apply to part-time employ-ment by a corporation.[47] Occasional employment is not regular em-ployment within the exception.[48] A lawyer may advertise a placement bureau for lawyers.[49] In an advertisement for full-time or for non-legal work he may say he is a lawyer.[50]

Seeking election or appointment to a public office, which can be filled only by a lawyer, is not the solicitation of professional employ-ment within the Canon.[1]

[38] A.B.A. Ops. 1, 24, 36, 123, 145, 232, including patent lawyers, A.B.A. Ops. 152, 203; N.Y. City 60, 442, 468, 543, 550, 553, 562, 601, 619, 708 (quoting A.B.A. Op. 1), 735, 736, 742; N.Y. County 46, but see N.Y. City 460 (not contrary to Canons to ask them to employ him in writing briefs, though in poor taste); also N.Y. City 963 and B-42, and N.Y. County 375; *contra* to text, N.Y. City 310, where the Committee said expressly that Canon 27 "refers only to solicitation from laymen and does not prohibit proper solicita-tion inside the profession." This statement is believed to be clearly incorrect.
Query as to whether the Canon would be strictly enforced in the case of a lawyer who has become deaf and seeks employment from other lawyers whom he does not know personally. N.Y. County 280. Cf. N.Y. City 866.
Compare Rules of Professional Conduct of American Institute of Accountants Nos. (7) (10).
[39] N.Y. County 367.   [40] App. A, 52.
[41] Mich. 133; App. A, *83;* and cf. N.Y. City 545. See also 221 N.C. 606 (F., 1942). Compare Accountants Rule No. 14.
[42] A.B.A. Op. 152; App. A, *29;* Mich. 91; Cleveland 19; see also A.B.A. Op. 272, p. 565; Ohio 9; N.Y. County 332; N.Y. City 519; see also as to lawyers in law lists with laymen, A.B.A. Op. 233, 234.
[43] A.B.A. Op. 244 (overruling A.B.A. Op. 79); App. A, *26.* N.Y. City 306, 319 (but should not say "able"), 447, 734, 911; N.Y. County 373.
[44] App. A, *26.* As to the purchase or sale of a law practice, see A.B.A. Op. 266, App. A, *26.*
[45] N.Y. City B-42.
[46] A.B.A. Op. 197; such does not constitute, the Committee said, a seeking of profes-sional employment, but appointment to a position in the nature of a public office, which can be held only by a lawyer.
[47] App. A, 27.   [48] *Ibid.*   [49] *Id., 34.*
[50] N.Y. City 455.   [1] A.B.A. Op. 74.

RIGHT TO ENGAGE IN AN INDEPENDENT BUSINESS [2]

A difficult question, which has given rise to some difference of opinion in the Committees, is as to the propriety of a practicing lawyer also carrying on another business, either from his law office or elsewhere.

There is, of course, nothing in the Canons to prevent this as to an occupation entirely distinct from and unrelated to his law practice. Thus, no one would dispute the right of a lawyer to be a teacher, or a violinist or doctor or a farmer, or to sell rare postage stamps, provided he in no way used such occupation to advertise, or as a feeder to his law practice.

As the Michigan Committee aptly said in a recent case:

There is, of course, nothing to prevent a lawyer from adding to his general qualifications by becoming a certified public accountant and using his added skill in appropriate matters as they arise. It is only when the lawyer seeks to publicize the fact that he is also an accountant that the question arises.[3]

Much, of course, depends on the surrounding circumstances. In small communities where everyone knows what everyone else is doing, and where there is comparatively little remunerative law practice, it is quite the usual thing for lawyers to be engaged in collateral occupations such as licensed broker or insurance agent. If they do so using distinct letterheads and not using the other occupation as a means of solicitation or of securing employment as a lawyer, it is not considered improper.

Thus a lawyer may properly conduct an independent real estate business in another county,[4] or may offer to manage an apartment house in exchange for the use of an apartment,[5] or may publish a newspaper and write editorials, but not to exploit himself as a lawyer; [6] or may be the salaried trust officer of a bank.[7]

Where, however, the second occupation, although theoretically and professedly distinct, is one closely related to the practice of law, and one which normally involves the solution of what are essentially legal problems, it is inevitable that, in conducting it, the lawyer will be confronted with situations where, if not technically, at least in

[2] "A practicing barrister should not, as a general rule, carry on any other profession or business . . . including a financial business." *The Annual Practice* (1933), p. 2607, but a solicitor may do so. Op. of the Council of the Law Society, Nov. 10, 1905.

[3] Mich. 124.   [4] App. A, *38*.   [5] N.Y. City 344, 475; and cf. 534.

[6] App. A, *37*. Cf. Mo. 41, 80, 86.   [7] N.Y. County 267.

substance he will violate the spirit of the Canons,[8] particularly that
precluding advertising and solicitation. The likelihood of this is the
greatest when the collateral business is one which, when engaged in
by a lawyer, constitutes the practice of law,[9] and when it is conducted
from his law office.[10] Thus there is apparently no doubt as to the impropriety of conducting, from the same office, a supposedly distinct
and independent business of collection agent,[11] stock broker,[12] estate
planning,[13] insurance adjusters bureau,[14] tax consultant,[15] or mortgage
service; [16] or to organize and operate under a trade name, even though
in an adjacent office, a corporation conducting servicing business—
drafting charters and other corporate papers.[17] Clearly a lawyer may
not use his legal stationery to solicit business in the collateral line.[18]

In Opinion 57 the American Bar Association Committee, holding
that a lawyer could not properly conduct from his law office an "Insurance Adjusters' Bureau," to investigate and adjust claims for insurance companies and lawyers, said:

> It is not necessarily improper for an attorney to engage in a business;
> but impropriety arises when the business is of such a nature or is conducted
> in such a manner as to be inconsistent with the lawyer's duties as a mem-
> ber of the Bar. Such an inconsistency arises when the business is one that
> will readily lend itself as a means for procuring professional employment
> for him, is such that it can be used as a cloak for indirect solicitation on
> his behalf, or is of a nature that, if handled by a lawyer, would be regarded
> as the practice of law. To avoid such inconsistencies it is always desirable
> and usually necessary that the lawyer keep any business in which he is
> engaged entirely separate and apart from his practice of the law and he
> must, in any event, conduct it with due observance of the standards of
> conduct required of him as a lawyer.

> Some businesses in which laymen engage are so closely associated with
> the practice of law that their solicitation of business may readily become
> a means of indirect solicitation of business for any lawyer that is associated
> with them. *Opinions 31 and 35.* The adjustment of claims, the incor-
> porating of companies, and the handling of matters before governmental
> commissions and boards and in government offices fall within such classi-
> fications. It is difficult to conceive how a lawyer could conduct a claim

---

8 See N.Y. City 767 (income tax service for lawyers).

9 See A.B.A. Ops. 31, 35, 57, 194, 201, 225, 257, 272; N.Y. City 413.

10 App. A, *43.*

11 *Id., 40;* N.Y. County 260 and opinions cited; N.Y. City 211, 633; but see N.Y. City
102, 479.

12 App. A, *39.*   13 App. A, *43.*   14 A.B.A. Op. 57.

15 N.Y. County 344; and see N.Y. City B-106.

16 N.Y. City 403; and see N.Y. City 646; see also In re L. R. 7 N.J. 390 (1951).

17 N.Y. City 768; see also App. A, 77 and Mo. 3.   18 N.Y. City 636.

adjustment bureau, a company for the organization of corporations, or a bureau for securing income tax refunds, without practicing law. In performing the services which he would ordinarily render in connection with any of these activities, his professional skill and responsibility as a lawyer would be engaged. The fact that a layman can lawfully render certain service does not necessarily mean that it would not be professional service when rendered by a lawyer. On the contrary, lawyers are frequently called upon to render such service for the very reason that it can be better rendered by a lawyer.

The adjustment of insurance claims by a lawyer is professional employment. In performing such a service his professional skill and responsibility are engaged. He cannot properly render legal services to a lay intermediary for the benefit of its patrons. *Opinions 8, 31, 35, 41 and 56.* Furthermore the investigation and adjustment of insurance claims must frequently lead to some litigation, so that the solicitation of business by a bureau handling them must readily lend itself as a means of procuring professional employment for any lawyer in general practice who may be interested in or connected with it.

. . . .

If such a business and his law practice should be conducted from the same office, the public could not be expected to distinguish between his dual capacities and know when he is acting in the capacity of a lawyer and when in that of a layman.

In Opinion 272 the American Bar Association Committee, discussing the status of a lawyer who was also a C.P.A., said:

The Committee all deem it in the interest of the profession and its clients that a lawyer should be precluded from holding himself out, even passively, as employable in another independent professional capacity. We find no provision in the Canons precluding a lawyer from being a C.P.A., or from using his knowledge and experience in accounting in his law practice.

We are all confident that a lawyer could not, as a practical matter, carry on an independent accounting business from his law office without violating Canon 27.

The Committee all agree that a lawyer, who is also a C.P.A. may perform what are primarily accounting services, as an incident to his law practice, without violating our Canons. We are also agreed that he may not properly hold himself out as practicing accounting at the same office as that in which he practices law, since this would constitute an advertisement of his services as accountant which would violate Canon 27 as construed in our opinions.

The Committee further stated that a majority were of opinion that a lawyer, holding himself out as such, might not also hold himself out as a certified public accountant at *any* office without violating Canon

27, because his accounting activities would inevitably serve as a feeder to his law practice. A minority of the Committee, however, while agreeing that, as a practical matter, a lawyer could not properly carry on a considerable accounting practice and keep it independent of his law practice or avoid other violations of the Canons, nevertheless, find nothing in the Canons which precludes a lawyer from attempting to carry on both professions, wholly independent of one another, at the same time but from a different office with different stationery and where in practicing accounting the lawyer follows all the Canons pertaining to lawyers.[19]

Similarly the Ohio Committee has held [20] in effect that a lawyer may not act and be compensated both as an attorney and as a real estate broker, representing the client in a dual capacity. In this opinion, after quoting the passages from the American Bar Association Opinion 272 first above quoted, the Ohio Committee said: "When an attorney acts in two capacities in the same transaction, there is nothing independent about his professional capacities. They are wrapped together in the one transaction."

In Michigan Committee's Opinion 124, above quoted, it held it to be improper for two lawyers to announce the formation of a partnership to practice law and public accounting at the same office. The basis of this ruling was not only the probability that the accounting business would act as a feeder for the law practice, but the fact of the announcement by the lawyer, on his letterhead and shingle, that he had the added advantage of being a certified public accountant.[21]

The Rule in New York City as to an Independent Business

The two New York Committees have differed somewhat from the above. While both held it improper for a lawyer to form a partnership with a lay accountant [22] despite the fact that the latter are now governed by a Code of Ethics forbidding advertising [23] and in many other respects are similar to the Canons of the American Bar Association,[24] they both hold [25] that a lawyer who is also a certified public ac-

---

[19] See also Ky. 3, 8; Miss. 1; see also In re Tracy, 197 Minn. 35, 43 (1936), N.Y. County 418. See also Cleveland 13A.

[20] Ohio 9; and cf. Ky. 3, 8. As to the Texas Committee, see its Op. 42. See also Mo. 63.

[21] See also Mich. 39. The Michigan Committee held, however, in its Op. 28 that a lawyer's letterhead might properly specify "Doctor of Medicine" as well as "Attorney at Law"; but not "Medical Jurisprudence."

[22] New York Joint Opinion 398 (County), N.Y. City B-137.

[23] N.Y. County 399.

[24] The Michigan Committee apparently overlooked this in its Opinion 124.

[25] N.Y. City B-118, by "a bare majority"; N.Y. County 388. See also N.Y. City B-218.

countant not only may practice both professions from the same office, but may carry the designation Certified Public Accountant on his door and also, it would seem, on his letterhead,[26] and on his calling card [27] or announcement card sent to lawyers only,[28] "provided that A B and C D in the practice of their profession as certified public accountants, adhere to the professional standards applicable to attorneys at law with respect to advertising and solicitation."

"The proposed legend on the door," they said, "would merely identify the persons occupying the premises and the professions practiced by them therein, and would not constitute either advertising or solicitation by A B and C D within the meaning of Canon 27." [29]

In each case the Committee expressed disagreement with the statements from A.B.A. Opinion 272 above quoted.

The primary fallacy of these New York rulings is believed to consist in overlooking or ignoring the fact that the bare announcement on the door and letterhead that the lawyer is also a certified public accountant of itself constitutes the advertisement of a specialty by him, forbidden (except under Canon 46) to be stated anywhere except in an approved law list; this under the rulings of both New York Committees.[30]

Earlier Decisions by the New York City Committee

Prior to concurring in the Joint Opinion (New York City B-118, County 388) that a lawyer might announce "Certified Public Accountant" and also "Attorney at Law" from the same office, the New York City Committee rendered a series of opinions holding that a lawyer might properly conduct a real estate,[31] insurance,[32] brokerage business,[33] Tax Institute,[34] or loan company,[35] or business exchange bureau [36] from his law office, and might advertise and solicit in con-

[26] N.Y. City 667.   [27] N.Y. County 407.   [28] N.Y. County 96.

[29] But in No. 393 the County Committee held that a reference on the window to taxation as a specialty went beyond identification, indicating special competence. Compare its No. 391.

[30] Joint Opinion N.Y. City 963 III; see also N.Y. City 792 and 885, and N.Y. County 358, 375, 380, 391 (real estate and insurance on some other part of the window), 393; and see A.B.A. Op. 276; also N.Y. City B-211.

[31] N.Y. City 534, 717, 755, 868, 869; see also B-2, B-8 and opinions cited B-48; see also 936 where in his "independent" merchandise business he was in partnership with a disbarred lawyer.

[32] N.Y. City 25, 133, 651 (but see 652), 816, 824, but see 885.

[33] N.Y. City 787, 542.   [34] N.Y. City 102.   [35] N.Y. City 810.

[36] N.Y. City 551.

nection with such business as is customary therein.[37] These opinions
make it a condition that the business be independent and not a cloak
to feed the law practice; and some of them state generally that in carrying on such "independent" business the lawyer must not be guilty of
any practice "inconsistent with the principles which should govern
the conduct of a lawyer," [38] or language to such effect.[39] None of
these statements, however, contains the specific condition inserted
in City Opinion B-118 (and also in County 388) that in connection
with the second business they "adhere to the professional standards
applicable to attorneys at law with respect to advertising and solicitation." This qualification apparently nullifies the earlier rulings permitting the use of the methods of soliciting [40] and advertising [41] usual
in such business.

New York County Committee

The New York County Committee, in its earlier opinions, permitted an auxiliary real estate and loan brokerage,[42] investment,[43]
mortgage, and real estate information service,[44] insurance [45] or other
business [46] with the right apparently to advertise but with the qualification that the lawyer must conduct such business in accordance with
the standards of the legal profession.[47] "Where," says the County Committee, "an attorney acts qua broker as well as qua attorney, his conduct qua broker must conform to the high standards of professional
conduct imposed by the Canons of Professional Ethics." [48] This would
seem to preclude advertising or soliciting in connection with such
other business. However, in many cases the real reason for carrying
on the real estate or insurance business as a distinct activity is to be
able to solicit and advertise.[49] If a lawyer intends, in good faith, to
carry on his "independent" real estate, brokerage, or accounting busi-

---

[37] N.Y. City 534, B-2.   [38] N.Y. City 25, 133, 344, 475.
[39] N.Y. City 389, 551, 559, 868, and 869.   [40] N.Y. City 755.
[41] N.Y. City 890, B-2.
[42] N.Y. County 114, 284 (but disapproved as "tending to lower the essential dignity of
the profession"), 295; and see 380.
[43] N.Y. County 273.   [44] N.Y. County 276 (must be "distinct and apart").
[45] N.Y. County 313.   [46] N.Y. County 179; but see 368; see also 418.
[47] N.Y. County 313, 391, citing 114 and 179.
[48] N.Y. County 380. The City Committee in Ops. 787 and B-48 also made it a condition that the lawyer should not accept any legal employment flowing from the auxiliary business—perhaps an optimistic injunction.
[49] There are doubtless a few cases like that in N.Y. City 825 where the lawyer was
engaged in the collateral business prior to becoming admitted to the bar and wished
thereafter to continue.

ness without solicitation, advertising, enticing away clients or other practice forbidden by our Canons, and with no subtle expectation of obtaining clients therefor by the prospect of a more aggressively competitive attitude than is associated with lawyers, it is difficult to understand why he should deem it disadvantageous to carry on such collateral activities as an incident to his law practice, or why he should choose to dilute the prestige attached to his profession.

The correct diagnosis is believed to be that of the Michigan and American Bar Association Committees above quoted—that either he should conduct such collateral activities qua lawyer or not at all.

Other Decisions on Independent Business

A lawyer may be employed by a corporation which reports on the activities of the legislature,[50] or by one which solicits claim adjustments.[1] He may be the agent of a bonding company and write formal bonds in cases conducted by him, but he should not write large bonds in such cases where the client's adverse interest might lead him to take a chance at the expense of the insurance company which he represents.[2]

The American Bar Association Committee has held that investment[3] and marriage[4] counselling are too nearly related to the practice of law to justify a lawyer in advertising in connection with them; and reached the same conclusion relative to an income, inheritance, and government tax service.[5]

He may, however, act as notary in a case which he is conducting,[6] may properly advertise a text book written by him,[7] may endorse a law magazine,[8] and may publish a newspaper and write editorials, but not to exploit himself as a lawyer.[9]

The Texas Committee held it not improper for a law firm to advertise a dog at stud with the firm name![10]

The New York County Committee has held that for a lawyer conducting a quiz course for the bar examinations to employ solicitors

---

[50] Va. 12. [1] A.B.A. Op. 96. [2] App. A, *45*.
[3] *Id. 42, 44;* but see N.Y. County 273. [4] App. A, *41.*
[5] A.B.A. Op. 260.

[6] App. A, *46;* a fortiori may his partner or associate. In its Op. 90, however, the Michigan Committee called attention to the Michigan statute prohibiting a lawyer from taking acknowledgments as a notary in proceedings in which he was acting in a professional capacity.

[7] Mich. 6; cf. N.Y. City 89, but see App. A, *79, 89.* [8] App. A, *51, 58.*
[9] *Id., 37.* [10] Texas 28.

to obtain pupils on a commission basis was "objectionable as beneath the essential dignity of the profession." [11]

MISCELLANEOUS DECISIONS AS TO ADVERTISING [12]

A lawyer may advertise where so to do is a normal incident to his practice, as where he advertises mortgaged properties for sale.[13]

Although a lawyer, on request by a client or forwarder, may give a bond to protect his client in particular cases, he may not execute a general bond and give publicity to this, nor permit others to do so.[14] The New York County Committee said that it was derogatory of the essential dignity of the profession for a lawyer to permit a collection agency to guarantee his honesty and efficiency.[15]

A candidate for the legislature may write voters on his letterhead if not intended or calculated to advertise him as a lawyer.[16]

LETTERHEADS

"Attorney-at-law" on a letterhead implies the right to practice at the address given.[17]

A lawyer's letterhead may not carry the name of a client [18] or of a patent agent associate,[19] non-lawyer notary [20] or engineer [21] or clerk [22] or student [23] or other layman,[24] or give the names of references,[25] or state that a layman's association is associated with him in handling

[11] N.Y. County 234; but see App. A, *52*. The Council of the Bar in England held in 1912 (Ann. St., p. 13) that it was not improper for a barrister to advertise for pupils for bar examinations in the legal papers and to send circulars to the Inns of Court where neither the advertisement nor the circular disclosed his name nor the address of his chambers; cf. Va. 36 (advertisement in horse-show program). He may not, however, practice as a doctor (An. St. [1930], p. 13) or dental surgeon (An. St. [1918], p. 10). See also An. St. (1914), p. 10, *id.* (1929), p. 14, and *id.* (1935), p. 8.

[12] As to advertisements in foreign language newspapers in New York, see N.Y. City 330; also N.Y. City 83, 380, 461, 546, 563, 606, 680.

[13] A.B.A. Op. 80; and see N.Y. City B-86; N.Y. County 284 (mortgages and loans he can place, not stating he is a lawyer).

[14] A.B.A. Op. 230, App. A, *54*.   [15] N.Y. County 47 ii(*c*), and 220.

[16] App. A, *60*. Cf. Mo. 36.

[17] A.B.A. Ops. 81, 115, 256; N.Y. City 61 and see *infra*, p. 230, as to "Lawyers Admitted in Different States."

[18] Mich. 104; but see *contra* as to client's name on door, N.Y. City 611.

[19] N.Y. City 710.   [20] App. A, *123*.   [21] *Id.*, *124*.

[22] N.Y. City 667; N.Y. County 212.   [23] N.Y. City 13.

[24] N.Y. City 462, B-34; N.Y. County 358; N.Y. County 420 (a lay labor expert; such a one may not sign important letters).

[25] App. A, *121*.

collections.[26] Nor may it carry the name of another lawyer as "adjuster," such lawyer proposing to solicit adjustment work,[27] or the name of a judge or ex judge.[28]

It may not specify "Counselor at Law" and also "General Insurance," [29] or state an independent business (real estate brokerage) conducted.[30]

It may not contain a statement that the lawyer is an M.D.[31] or a C.P.A.,[32] tax consultant,[33] Doctor of Jurisprudence [34] or other degrees,[35] Mayor of ———,[36] Governor or United States Senator,[37] former District Attorney,[38] or specify other occupations in which he is engaged,[39] or that he is a member of the American Bar Association,[40] or other bar associations,[41] or that he is admitted in another state; [42] or specify as a branch practiced Medical Legal Law,[43] Medical Jurisprudence,[44] or any other branch practiced,[45] including patent law prior to the 1951 amendment,[46] or state that he is consulting counsel to other lawyers on constitutional cases.[47]

His letterhead may not carry a statement of the date when his office was opened [48] or an address where the lawyer does not actually practice.[49]

It may properly designate another lawyer, duly admitted in the jurisdiction, as "counsel." [50]

A lawyer may not permit a corporation engaged in organizing corporations for lawyers, which advertises such activity, to carry his name on their letterheads as advertising matter,[1] nor may he permit a C.P.A.[2] or a collection agency to do so.[3]

[26] A.B.A. Op. 54.   [27] A.B.A. Op. 214.
[28] App. A, *119;* see also Canon 33.   [29] N.Y. City 885.
[30] N.Y. City 542; see also *supra,* pp. 221–28.
[31] App. A, *116;* N.Y. City 792. The Michigan Committee held in its Opinion 28 that "M.D." was proper although "Medical Jurisprudence" was not.
[32] App. A, *115.* The New York rulings are to the contrary as to this. See N.Y. City 38, 667, B-15; and see N.Y. County 388.
[33] N.Y. City B-106; Cleveland 13.   [34] App. A, *116.*
[35] *Id., 121;* Mich. 28.   [36] Mich. 89.
[37] App. A, *120;* see also N.Y. County 231.   [38] App. A, *118.*
[39] *Id., 128.*   [40] *Id., 120.*   [41] *Ibid.,* N.Y. City 557, 818.
[42] App. A, *127.*   [43] A.B.A. Op. 159.
[44] A.B.A. Op. 183; Mich. 28. Cleveland C (reluctantly in the interest of uniformity). The Michigan Committee held, however, that he might properly specify both "Attorney at Law" and "Doctor of Medicine." Mich. 28.
[45] App. A, *117;* Mich. 77; N.Y. City 470, B-106; N.Y. County 231, 393.
[46] A.B.A. Op. 277. But see Mo. 69.   [47] N.Y. City 470; and see N.Y. City B-196.
[48] App. A, *113, 114.*   [49] N.Y. City 97.
[50] Mich. 77; see also N.Y. City 3, but see N.Y. City 956 and B-189.
[1] A.B.A. Op. 31.   [2] Mich. 55.   [3] Mich. 60.

One taking over the practice of a lawyer in military service may use his letterhead.[4]

As to the impropriety of a lawyer's name appearing on the letterhead of a client, see page 262. As to that of a deceased lawyer partner on the firm's letterhead, see pages 207–08.

Letterheads of Lawyers Admitted in Different States

Canon 33 clearly implies that partnerships between lawyers admitted in different States are permissible [5] provided there be no misleading name or misrepresentation of local status; and the same would seem to apply as to associates,[6] and hence justify their inclusion on the firm's letterhead, with a clear statement that the outside partners are *not* locally admitted.[7] But it is not so clear that the letterhead may properly specify one who is merely a correspondent, with no legal relation to the local lawyer.[8]

It would seem, however, that foreign lawyers not admitted in any state may not be so designated.[9]

The name of a lawyer not admitted locally may not be included in the firm name (even though he may properly be a member of the firm) despite a statement on the letterhead, shingle, and law list that he is admitted only in the foreign state, since the firm name appearing elsewhere without such explanation would imply that all the members in the name were authorized to practice locally.[10]

A lawyer not admitted locally may not be designated on a letterhead as associated in a special branch, nor if he is associated only thus may he be specified as a general associate.[11] "A lawyer's stationery should not be used to advertise his connections with lawyers in other places or to bring their names before his correspondents." [12]

A German lawyer may be given office space and may use his own letterhead as a consultant on German law.[13]

---

[4] N.Y. City 808.

[5] A.B.A. Op. 256; N.Y. City 961, B-76; see also *infra*, pp. 207–08, re partnership names.

[6] See N.Y. City 28, 818; also N.Y. County 374.

[7] N.Y. City 3; a statement that they are admitted in the other state is not a "clear" statement that they are not admitted locally. N.Y. City B-5, B-72, B-76, B-173, B-180 (as to shingle), B-181; but see *contra* N.Y. City 956; see also N.Y. City B-45 and B-189.

[8] App. A, *122*, holding such improper; but see N.Y. City 702, 818, N.Y. County 134 holding it proper.

[9] N.Y. City B-190; but see B-29; and see also N.Y. City B-196.

[10] N.Y. City 961, B-133, B-148.   [11] N.Y. City B-189; but see N.Y. City 956.

[12] N.Y. City 925; see also N.Y. City B-196.

[13] N.Y. City 585; but see also N.Y. City B-196.

SHINGLES

While some years ago the American Bar Association Committee approved certain designations on the shingle which it did not sanction on a letterhead, the rule is now the same for both.[14] The name of a managing clerk,[15] or of a student [16] or of a non-lawyer notary [17] or tax consultant,[18] not admitted, may not be on the door, nor may there be a statement that there is a certified public accountant in the office,[19] or that the lawyer displaying the shingle is a Doctor of Jurisprudence [20] or a former judge.[21] Nor may there be a statement of special branches practiced.[22]

A lawyer may not display a neon sign for a shingle.[23] The test is whether the sign is intended and calculated to enable persons looking for a lawyer, already selected, to find him, or to attract the attention of persons who might be looking for a lawyer, although not for him.[24]

The New York City Committee has held that the name of a German attorney may be placed as such on the door apart from the other lawyers,[25] as may the name of a lawyer of another state [26] provided in each case there be a statement that he is not admitted locally.

An English barrister may not have any designation on his house or chambers indicating that he is such.[27]

A lawyer may not display a sign with his name on it in a place where he does not practice, even though he has an employee there,[28] but may have it in the directory of the elevator in the hotel where his office is,[29] or a modest projecting sign where customary in the local-

14 A.B.A. Op. 214.   15 N.Y. City 65; and cf. N.Y. County 49.
16 N.Y. City 13; N.Y. County 79.   17 App. A, *123*.
18 N.Y. City 927.   19 A.B.A. Op. 272.   20 App. A, *135*.
21 *Id., 134*.
22 *Id., 136*; N.Y. City 641; Kentucky 9; N.Y. County 388, 391, 393. In its No. 391 the County Committee said that to have "Attorney, Insurance and Real Estate" on a store window was "improper in form and offensive to good taste." In N.Y. County 388, however, the Committee approved the placing on the office door of the names of lawyers who were also Certified Public Accountants, the dual designation, "merely identifying the firms occupying the premises and the professions practiced therein," and this "not constituting either advertisement or solicitation." See also *supra*, p. 225, as to letterheads.
23 Chicago 21, p. 58; Mich. 11, 14, 33; Wash. 1; N.Y. City 418; Milwaukee, June, 1952; App. A, *131; contra* Texas 38 (six to four).
24 App. A, *132*.   25 N.Y. City 585.
26 N.Y. City 600, 956, B-180; and see N.Y. County 134, 374.
27 Order of General Council of 7/18/51, Art. 5.
28 N.Y. City 97.   29 N.Y. City 835.

ity,[30] or at a client's house where he will be every evening,[31] but not just "lawyer" without his name.[32]

He should not have a shingle at his residence when he has a distinct office where he practices.[33]

As to a statement that a lawyer in another state is his correspondent, see page 230 n. 8, under "Letterheads."

As to the situation where the lawyer conducts an independent business from his law office, see pages 221–25.

Announcements

While Canon 27 contains no specific exception authorizing normal announcements by lawyers, such is obviously implied from the proscription of solicitation and advertising "not warranted by personal relations." Accordingly the various Committees have held that a lawyer opening [34] an office, or removing [35] to a new address, or admitting new members,[36] or returning from government service [37] or entering military service [38] may send a notice thereof to persons with whom he "has already established such 'personal relations' as would reasonably justify a belief that he enjoys the friendship and confidence of such person to such extent that the person receiving the announcement will consider it news of genuine interest and value." [39]

[30] N.Y. City 922; and see Mich. 34 (sign on the front of the building, where the lawyer's office is on the second floor).

[31] N.Y. City 572.   [32] Ibid.   [33] App. A, 133.

[34] See A.B.A. Ops. 194, 228, 240, 264; Mich. 19, Va. 31. The N.Y. City Committee held in No. 48 that while there was no ethical objection to a Florida lawyer announcing both in the N.Y. Law Journal and in daily papers that he was opening an office in Florida it was contrary to local custom in New York. See also N.Y. City 76 and B-12. The Michigan Committee also said in its Op. 33 that it was proper to publish in the local papers a notice of the opening or removal of a law office two or three times, when such was the local custom.

[35] Mich. 33; App. A, 142. The A.B.A. Committee has held that such notice should be by printed card mailed to regular clients, and not by newspaper advertisement, App. A, 140, 142; but may be in the legal journal, id., 141.

[36] App. A, 148. As to the dissolution of an old firm and formation of successor, in Italian paper prior to 1930, see N.Y. City 83.

[37] A.B.A. Op. 264; App. A, 143. As to this, the A.B.A. Committee thus advised an inquirer: "It is entirely proper for you to send out announcement cards that you are returning to practice at your designated offices, these to be sent to attorneys and to former clients, and to any other persons with whom your personal relations are such as to make it clear that they would be interested in knowing that you were back, but not, of course, to persons with whom you have had no professional dealings or relations and to whom this card will be merely a suggestion that they employ you." Id., 146.

[38] A.B.A. Op. 240; N.Y. City 808; see also New Orleans 1/19/44.

[39] As defined by the Michigan Committee in its Op. 28; See also N.Y. City 619, where

Such persons include those whom he may properly regard as his clients; personal friends and relatives, members of the local bar; [40] other lawyers with whom he has had professional relations, but not persons with whom he had had no such relations,[41] such as firms which he had inspected for the Department of Labor.[42]

In the case of a partner, the notice should be sent by the firm and not by the individual.[43]

Such an announcement should be "truthful, dignified, appropriate and in good taste." [44]

Announcements of Special Branches

The American Bar Association Committee has repeatedly ruled that such an announcement may not state a special branch which the lawyer intends to practice.[45] The Michigan Committee agreed with this ruling,[46] as did the Chicago Committee.[47] On the latter's recommendation, however, the Chicago Association adopted an amendment (27A) to Canon 27 permitting the statement in such announcement cards to lawyers of a "well recognized branch of the law which he is equipped to handle." [48] Rule 2, Section *b*, of the California Rules of Professional Conduct provides that a lawyer may circulate "among lawyers only, a brief dignified notice that he is rendering a specialized legal service."

The New York City and County Committees, as well as the New York State Committee, have taken positions relative to announcement cards distinctly differing from that of the American Bar Association Committee.

New York City Committee Rulings

The City Committee, in an early ruling,[49] affirmed in a later one,[50] held that a lawyer might carry on his announcement card (and also on

---

the N.Y. Committee said that the exception was "to be confined to clients and to persons nearly related to the attorney by ties of blood or by ties of intimate friendship."

[40] App. A, *146;* Mich. 28.　　　　　　　　　　[41] App. A, *146.*

[42] *Id., 145.*　　　　[43] *Id., 147.*　　　　[44] N.Y. City 963; N.Y. County 375.

[45] A.B.A. Ops. 145, 175, 183, 228, 251; App. A, *139, 144;* see also N.Y. City 792 and Mich. 28; also as to a notice to non-lawyers, N.Y. City B-188. Despite and in view of the 1951 amendment (*supra,* p. 216), the rule as to announcements applies to notices to patent and admiralty lawyers, A.B.A. Op. 277, the exception in favor of whom applies only to letterheads and shingles, A.B.A. Op. 286.　　　　[46] Mich. 124; see also Mich. 77.

[47] Chicago 11, p. 24; as to Cleveland see their C.

[48] Chicago 15, p. 34-C. See also Mo. 25, 81.

[49] N.Y. City 38.　　　　　　　　[50] N.Y. City B-15.

his letterhead) the designation "Certified Public Accountant" as well as "Attorney at Law." In a ruling prior to the 1937 amendment to Canon 27 the City Committee held that a lawyer might announce to the bar the kind of practice in which he was engaged, but that he might not solicit.[1]

Prior to the amendment of 1937 to Canon 43, which eliminated "special branch of the profession practiced" from the items which might be stated on a "professional card," the City Committee stated in several rulings that the announcement or professional card might specify such special branch [2] including "Chemical & Electro-Chemical Patent Matters," [3] "Immigration Specialist," [4] "Criminal Matters," [5] legal research,[6] personal injury cases [7] and questions involving medical knowledge.[8] Later the City Committee apparently gave no weight to the elimination by the amendment of 1937 to Canon 43 of the provision that a professional card might state a "special branch of the profession practiced," as well as the inclusion (by the amendment of 1937) in Canon 27 of the provision that among the items permissible in law lists is "branches of the profession practiced," [9] holding in a ruling of November, 1943, that it was proper under Canon 46 to *mail* to other lawyers the announcement of the specialized legal service "Trade Regulation & Patents." [10]

In a ruling of March 29, 1944, the New York City Committee held proper an announcement by notice to lawyers that the sender had resigned from a designated government position, that he intended to

---

[1] N.Y. City 60, and see N.Y. City 340, 469, 470, 586; but see N.Y. City 375 where the Committee said that the mere fact that notices were sent only to members of the bar did not justify them; also N.Y. City 497.

[2] N.Y. City 704.　　　[3] N.Y. City 135.　　　[4] N.Y. City 142.

[5] N.Y. City 711 ("expressly authorized" by Canon 46).

[6] N.Y. City 340.　　　[7] N.Y. City 486.　　　[8] N.Y. City 586.

[9] Note the singular "branch" in the provision prior to 1942 as to professional cards, the plural "branches" as to law lists, and the different phrase "specialized legal service" in Canon 46.

[10] N.Y. City 887; see also N.Y. City 469, 470. The announcement involved in 887 was apparently to be mailed only to lawyers with whom the inquirer was "socially or professionally acquainted" which would perhaps have justified it under the "personal relations" exception. The Committee did not, however, rest the decision on this ground, but said that the notice might be "sent by mail or otherwise to attorneys unknown to the sender." The statement in this Opinion 887 that American Bar Association Opinion 114 held that Canon 46 authorized the *mailing* of the announcement of a specialized legal service to other lawyers is incorrect. (See also Mich. 77; cf. N.Y. City 586 quoting Canon 46 in a case involving an announcement.) Although the headnote to A.B.A. Op. 114 (made by a subsequent secretary who prepared the bound volume for publication) referred to *mailing* to lawyers (see also Op. 194, pp. 390 and 391) the Opinion itself held merely that such a card might *not* be mailed to manufacturers and inventors.

specialize in a stated branch, not confined to one which had been held a specialized legal service.[11] This ruling was incorporated in a joint statement by the two New York Committees in December 1946.[12]

In this joint opinion the City and County Committees, after pointing out the different impression that professional announcements made on laymen from that on lawyers, said:

Consequently, the committees are now of the opinion that an attorney may properly send to lawyers only, both known and unknown to them, an announcement which includes a statement of intention to specialize in a particular branch of law, whether or not it be a recognized specialty, but that an attorney may not include such a statement in any announcement to be sent to any one who is not a lawyer unless the speciality be admiralty, patents, copyrights or trademarks. The exception is made in deference to a long standing and approved custom in the particular fields mentioned.

The City Committee later ruled that announcements of a return from government service might be published in the law journal but a limited number of times [13] and that this ruling applied only to an "event" and did not authorize a daily advertisement.[14] The City Committee also held that such a notice to lawyers might specify "International Law, Public and Private, European Civil Law and Soviet Law," [15] "Philippine War Damage Claims" [16] and "Pretrial Investigation," "Trial Preparation in Personal Injury and Negligence Actions," [17] and patents.[18] In other prior rulings it held that a professional card might not be published in programs,[19] or in trade journals; [20] that "Consultant in Matrimonial Matters only" was not a "specialized legal service" since "any competent general practitioner can handle it"; [21] that it was improper for a New York lawyer to publish a professional card in legal publications in another state, stating services available to lawyers only; [22] that "assisting lawyers in preparing pleadings" et cetera was not sufficiently specialized to authorize under Canon 46 its *mailing* to lawyers and its publication in the legal journal.[23]

[11] N.Y. City 912; see also B-164. N.Y. City 912 said, however, that "professional cards should state only the name, address and telephone number of the attorney and that he is an attorney at law." He may not include a detached statement of his qualifications, and a copy of a letter of recommendation. N.Y. City B-202.

[12] N.Y. City 963 (N.Y. County 375); but see N.Y. City B-173.

[13] N.Y. City B-25; see also B-88 and B-81.   [14] N.Y. City B-50.

[15] N.Y. City B-52; "if sent only to members of the bar."

[16] N.Y. City B-81.   [17] N.Y. City B-88.   [18] N.Y. City B-173.

[19] N.Y. City 101.   [20] N.Y. City B-11.

[21] N.Y. City 707 (improper although in law journal only).

[22] N.Y. City 736 (prior to 1942).

[23] N.Y. City 764; see also B-52.

In another opinion, however, it was said that the "limits to which one engaged in a specialized field of practice may go in indicating the same have been set (Canons 43, 46)," [24] and in still another, holding it improper to specify "M.D." in a notice to other lawyers, that the statement relative to medico-legal services was "too broad to be generally regarded as specialized and it does not appear that the services of the lawyer in question are rendered directly and only to other lawyers, which Canon 46 makes a prerequisite to the propriety of a notice of a specialized legal service (see and cf. American Bar Association Opinions 183, 36, 159, 175 & 194)." [25]

New York County Committee Rulings

The New York County Committee has also made similar rulings which it is difficult to reconcile with Canons 27 and 46 or with one another. Prior to the 1937 amendment to Canon 43, when Canon 27 expressly permitted the publication or circulation of simple business cards and Canon 43 specified that a professional card might state a "special branch of the profession practiced," it held (apparently with reluctance) that it was not unprofessional for a lawyer to publish a business card in a trade journal (this being "left to the sense of propriety of the individual practitioner") [26] as well as to address to members of the bar a printed announcement card stating that he was both an attorney at law and a certified public accountant, but without elaboration as to the services offered; [27] also, to publish in daily and trade papers a card stating "Income Tax Consultant" either with or without a statement that he was a lawyer, the County Committee regarding "such publication as a matter of personal taste." [28] It also held that "Trial Counsel Work" was a proper specialty which might be announced in the law journal [29] (though not apparently relying on Canon 46) and that "Briefing & Research" was a specialized legal service which might be announced to lawyers, known and unknown, [30]

Other rulings by the N.Y. City Committee on this general subject are Nos. 89, 93, 426, 737, 742, 822, 866, and 871.

[24] N.Y. City 767.

[25] N.Y. City 792 (Nov. 5, 1941); see also N.Y. City 426 where the Committee in disapproving the distribution by mail to attorneys of a notice announcing "specializing in the trial of negligence cases for plaintiffs," said: "Canon 27 makes no distinction between solicitation within and without the profession" and that the exception of Canon 46 "applies only to persons exclusively engaged in furnishing services to lawyers."

[26] N.Y. County 1.   [27] N.Y. County 96.

[28] N.Y. County 195; see also as to good taste, No. 348.   [29] N.Y. County 285.

[30] N.Y. County 280; by a lawyer who had become deaf.

and advertised in the legal journal,[31] that the mailing promiscuously to members of the bar of notices of "Trade Mark and Design Patents" [32] or of a special branch practiced,[33] while not "conforming to the best standards of the profession" would not be held to be "professionally improper"; also that special branches practiced might be announced on simple professional cards to lawyers in other states containing statements which "should not go beyond those permissible in approved law lists" with no statement as to any special skill,[34] but that an advertisement by a "professional card" as an "Immigration & Naturalization Consultant" in any paper other than an approved law list or legal directory was improper under Canon 27 as amended in 1937.[35]

The above rulings were all prior to the amendment of 1937 to Canon 43.

In December, 1946, the New York County Committee joined the City Committee in the latter's opinion 963, above summarized, holding that special branches might be announced to lawyers only (both known and unknown) in notices sent direct to them, or in the legal journal, and were not confined to those branches held to be a specialized legal service, but that professional cards should state only name, address, and phone number and that he is an attorney.[36] It later held that a lawyer might not refer to himself on his door, stationery, professional card, and telephone directory as specializing in "Taxation," that the only specialties which might be announced to the public were admiralty, and patents, trademarks and copyright, but that lawyers might bring their specialties to the attention of other lawyers to the extent indicated in Canon 46 as interpreted in its Opinion 375.[37] It held, however, disapproving American Bar Association Opinion 272, that a lawyer might properly carry both "attorney at law" and "certified public accountant" on the door of his office; [38] that he might, in a professional announcement, state that he was a member of the New York and Italian bars, but might not include his academic degrees or his affiliation with educational institutions.[39]

In the foregoing opinions the two New York Committees apparently expanded the exception of Canon 46 by eliminating the requirement that, in order to qualify, the lawyer must confine his practice to

---

[31] N.Y. County 348.   [32] N.Y. County 337.   [33] N.Y. County 364.
[34] N.Y. County 356.   [35] N.Y. County 366.
[36] N.Y. County 375 (N.Y. City 963).   [37] N.Y. County 393.
[38] N.Y. County 388.   [39] N.Y. County 379.

other lawyers, provided he directed his announcement to lawyers. They also expanded the exception to include any particular branch in which the lawyer intended to specialize, whether or not such branch be a recognized specialty and to permit the *mailing* of notices of a specialty direct to other lawyers.

Survey by the New York Bar

These rulings were made after the receipt of answers from the New York bar to a series of questionnaires which are summarized in the June, 1947, issue of the New York State Bar Association Bulletin.[40] By such answers, as stated by the chairman of the Ethics Committee of the State Association, "it will be seen that the Bar generally construes the Canons so as to make them practical and applicable to modern conditions."

The "modern conditions" referred to mean the increasing specialization in the legal profession making it impossible for any one lawyer and very few offices to be competent to cover every field, and both necessary and highly desirable that they shall utilize the special skills of fellow members of the bar in order to promote efficient service. The New York Committees accordingly have taken it on themselves, by judicial legislation, to treat Canon 46 as permitting the announcement to other lawyers "both known and unknown," by mailed notices, of their readiness to serve lawyers "in a particular branch of the law, whether or not it be a recognized specialty"; [41] also, that in announcements to laymen they may include a statement of specialization in admiralty and in patents, trademarks, and copyrights.

It is difficult to see where the New York Committees found in Canon 46 authority for these rulings. Apparently they consider that it will be useful and harmless for other lawyers to be informed as to the branches practiced, but deliberately ignored the conditions specified in Canon 46.

The publication of such notice, however, other than in approved law lists is confined by the New York rulings to "a limited number of times in a publication published for the use of lawyers primarily."

40 Volume 19, No. 3, at p. 152.

41 See Review of Chairman Wherry, of the State Association, in the Pamphlet on the Canons of Ethics, published 1948, pp. 60–61.

See also proposed Rule II-A recommended to the Justices of the Appellate Division, p. 9 of Report of the State Committee of Jan. 28, 1949, which, however, I am advised was not adopted by the Court.

Announcements by Lawyers Returning from Government Service

There is also a difference of opinion among the committees as to whether a lawyer returning from government service may properly specify the branch of the government with which he has served. The American Bar Association Committee holds that he may not so specify.[42] The two New York Committees, however, in a joint opinion rendered after and in recognition of the answers to the questionnaire by the members of the state bar above referred to,[43] held he might properly name the department or agency in which he had served and specify the title of the position held,[44] but without a statement of previous experience [45] and being careful to avoid an implication that he was specially qualified to handle matters with such agency; [46] and that he might not state that he intended to specialize in practice before such department or agency.[47]

The Cleveland Committee agreed with the American Bar Association Committee.[48] The Chicago Committee originally agreed with the American Bar Association Committee's Opinion 264,[49] but later expressed its approval of the joint New York opinion.[50]

It is difficult to conceive any reason for mentioning the government agency with which the lawyer has served except as the American Bar Association Committee said: "to emphasize his special familiarity with the problems of that particular government department and his acquaintance with the personnel therein, the conclusion being that

[42] A.B.A. Op. 264; also A.B.A. Op. 184. Accord New Orleans 1/29/46, 5/28/45.

[43] See *supra*, p. 238.

[44] N.Y. City 963, B-11, B-12, B-13; N.Y. County 375; but see N.Y. County 231. They hold, however, that such notice may be published in the Law Journal but a limited number of times; that it may not refer to any government position except that the resignation from which is the immediate occasion of the notice. N.Y. City B-81.

[45] N.Y. City B-11, B-13, B-173; as to continuing part time with the government see N.Y. City B-49, he may not state the position last held when he has been out for four years, N.Y. City B-81; see also N.Y. City 818.

In its Opinion 404 the County Committee expanded the scope of their construction of Canon 46 by permitting a lawyer who had resigned his government position with the Housing Rent Commissions some months before to insert an advertisement in successive issues of the New York Law Journal under the caption "Special Services for Lawyers," stating that he was formerly chief enforcement officer of the rent commission in the Brooklyn office, the committee stating that in its opinion publication in successive issues of the journal was no more objectionable than in a single issue.

[46] See A.B.A. Op. 228 and opinions cited therein.

[47] N.Y. City 963, and N.Y. County 375; subdivision II; Texas 5.

[48] Cleveland C; but recommending consideration of a change.

[49] Chicago 11, p. 24.   [50] Chicago 15, p. 33.

he is unusually well fitted to undertake professional work involving such government agency." [1]

The Committees all agree that one returning from military service may properly state the rank which he attained.[2]

Other Rulings Relative to Announcements

Announcements may not properly be published in a local newspaper.[3]

A lawyer may not announce that a foreign copyright expert is "associated," the obvious purpose of such an announcement being to solicit business, and the implication being that the associate is admitted locally.[4] He may not properly announce his connection with a firm of which he is not a partner; such an announcement should be sent out by the firm, and to lawyers and clients only.[5]

One employed by a law firm and leaving to engage in independent practice may send announcements to his individual clients but not to the firm clients whom he has served.[6]

A lawyer admitted only in New Jersey and in the Federal courts in New York may announce this in New York, and a New York firm may carry such statement on their door, specifying, however, that he is not a member of the New York bar.[7]

A foreign lawyer may properly announce to lawyers his advent to New York for consultation on the laws of his own jurisdiction,[8] but must make it clear that he has no right or intention to practice in New York.[9]

A lawyer may not advertise that he has been appointed adjuster for any insurance company.[10] As to an announcement by a suspended lawyer returning to practice, see *supra,* page 55.

[1] A.B.A. Op. 264, p. 548. Compare A.B.A. Op. 228.

[2] N.Y. City B-13; Chicago 11, p. 24.

[3] App. A, *140, 142;* the Michigan committee held (Op. 19), however, that such might be justified by local custom.

[4] N.Y. City 605.

[5] App. A, *147.* The N.Y. City committee held, however, in its Opinion 59 that one who had been a clerk with a law firm may, on starting practice, send, with the consent of such firm, announcements to clients who had known him only by his given name, stating that he was about to engage in practice and that he was formerly with such firm.

[6] App. A, *241.*

[7] N.Y. City 28, 29; and see N.Y. City 35; and cf. *supra,* p. 231.

[8] N.Y. County 354.   [9] N.Y. County 23.   [10] Va. 26.

PROFESSIONAL CARDS

Prior to the adoption of Canon 27 in 1908 "it was a long standing custom in certain smaller communities for lawyers to publish their cards in local newspapers" [11] and trade journals,[12] and it was such "local custom" to which the Canon originally referred.[13] Until the amendment of 1937, when the Canon referred to the "publications" of "ordinary simple business cards," these were held to include professional cards customarily inserted in local newspapers.[14] After that amendment, which substituted the present provision authorizing the "customary *use* of simple professional cards" as distinguished from their *"publication"* and specified the items permissible for "publication in approved law lists," the American Bar Association Committee held that the "professional card" referred to in the amended Canon now means the visiting card carried by lawyers to introduce themselves,[15] and that such cards could properly be *published* only in approved law lists.[16]

The New York County Committee said in 1932 that there was no custom in New York City for lawyers to publish their cards in New York City newspapers.[17]

Since the 1937 Amendment, also, a professional card may not state branches of the law practiced [18] or that the lawyer intends to restrict

[11] A.B.A. Ops. 24, 69; Va. 28; see also as to patent lawyers, N.Y. County 58, 337. As to cards in foreign language papers, see N.Y. City 83, 380, 461, 546, 563, 606, 680, 752; N.Y. County 223; Mo. 24, 26. But cf. N.Y. City B-132, B-176.

[12] N.Y. County 1, 195, 225.   [13] A.B.A. Op. 24; see also A.B.A. Op. 69.

[14] A.B.A. Op. 11; see A.B.A. Op. 276 where the history of Canons 27 and 43 is set out and the decisions of the Committee are fully summarized. Op. 152 was rendered in 1936, prior to the 1937 amendment.

[15] A.B.A. Op. 251, p. 504.

[16] A.B.A. Ops. 182, 203, 251, 276; see also Ops. 24, 69, 116, 175, 221. See also 4 Washington State Bar News 45 no. 12 (1950). In Ohio under Rule of Practice XXVIII, sec. 2, a professional card may be published in legal directories and newspapers. See Cleveland F; N.Y. City B-176; Mich. 5, 8, 33; Texas 25. See also N.Y. City 740, 741, 917, 924. Prior to these opinions by the A.B.A. Committee many lawyers "without thought of impropriety" authorized the publication of their cards in publications of charitable, educational and social organizations "not because the lawyers believed the advertising to possess any value, but as a contribution to the organization which solicited it," A.B.A. Op. 24 (1930). See also Mich. 135 and 151.

[17] N.Y. County 311.

[18] A.B.A. Op. 251; N.Y. City 792 (M.D.), 912; Cleveland C (reluctantly). But see N.Y. City 752 and N.Y. County 356, decided in 1941 and 1939, in which apparently the Committees overlooked the Amendment of 1937 to Canon 43 by which the inclusion of "special branches" in professional cards was no longer expressly sanctioned; see also N.Y. City 712.

his practice to a particular tribunal or to a branch of the law not constituting a recognized specialty,[19] or that he is a state senator.[20]

A foreign lawyer not admitted in any state may not have "attorney at law" or "counselor at law" on his letterheads or personal professional cards.[21]

SPECIALIZED LEGAL SERVICE

Canon 46, adopted in 1933,[22] provides:

Where a lawyer is engaged in rendering a specialized legal service directly and only to other lawyers, a brief, dignified notice of that fact, couched in language indicating that it is addressed to lawyers, inserted in legal periodicals and like publications, when it will afford convenient and beneficial information to lawyers desiring to obtain such service, is not improper.

It is not entirely clear that, in order to qualify under this provision, the lawyer must confine his practice to the specialized legal service, but in accordance with the principle of strict construction of exemptions from the general prohibition of Canon 27,[23] it would seem that he must. In any event he must confine his practice of such service to other lawyers.

As heretofore pointed out,[24] if strictly or even reasonably construed, Canon 46 is for practical purposes inoperative, since practically no lawyers render a "specialized legal service directly and only to other lawyers," or are prepared to represent (as they would do by advertising under Canon 46) that they will accept no such cases from lay clients. Also, it clearly restricts the exception to a notice "inserted in legal periodicals and like publications" obviously not including mailed notices and announcements.

As heretofore stated [25] the New York City, County, and State Committees have not apparently given weight to the requirement of Canon 46 that the specialized legal service must be rendered "only to other lawyers." [26] The American Bar Association Committee apparently overlooked the requirement as to service exclusive to other lawyers in Opinion 141, but later expressly recognized it in Opinion 194(2),

---

[19] A.B.A. Op. 175, and see A.B.A. Op. 251; Texas 15.
[20] Texas 11.   [21] N.Y. City 61.   [22] See *infra*, p. 245.
[23] See A.B.A. Ops. 145, 194; N.Y. City 707.
[24] *Supra*, pp. 233 *et seq.*   [25] *Supra*, pp. 233–38.
[26] N.Y. City 963; N.Y. County 375; but see N.Y. City Nos. 637, 641, 678, B-168, B-179.

page 391. The New York Committees have also not insisted on the condition that the notice must be confined to legal periodicals and like publications, and approved the announcement of special branches by mail to lawyers, these not being restricted to branches which constitute a "specialized legal service." [27]

The upshot of the New York rulings is that a lawyer may there announce to other lawyers a particular branch (not a recognized legal specialty) in which he intends to specialize not only in legal periodicals but in announcements mailed to lawyers [28] as if such were permitted by Canon 27 in the same way that it is authorized in "reputable law lists."

The Michigan Committee recognized the specific requirements of Canon 46 [29] as did the Chicago Committee,[30] until the Chicago Association added Canon 27A, providing that announcement cards might state "a well recognized branch of the law" in which a lawyer or firm intends to engage and which he or it is "equipped to handle." In California, Rule 2, Section *a*, of the Rules of Professional Conduct authorizes the publication in newspapers or other media cards announcing "in a dignified manner," "the line or lines specialized in" but without repetition, and the circulation "among lawyers only" of a brief, dignified notice of a specialized legal service.

The American Bar Association Committee holds that Canon 46, being an exception to the general policy of the bar against advertising, should be strictly construed, and all the requirements be enforced.[31] In Opinion 194 this Committee suggested that probably the best test as to whether a given branch was a specialized legal service under Canon 46 was whether there was generally available in his community the type of service offered by him. That Committee recognized patents, copyrights, and trademarks, and admiralty as specialized legal services despite their general availability. It was held that the following do not constitute specialized legal services: services in the preliminaries and incidents to litigation, such as filing papers, taxing costs, etc.; [32] bankruptcy and insolvency law and business reorganizations; [33]

---

[27] N.Y. City 963; N.Y. County 375.   [28] N.Y. City 963; N.Y. County 375.

[29] Mich. 28, p. 3; Mich. 128; and see Mich. 108; but see Mich. 77.

[30] Chicago 25, p. 48. The Illinois State Bar Association has had an "Experienced Lawyer Service," through which a lawyer is aided in getting in touch with experts in various fields of specialization. See R. Allan Stephens, "The Forgotten Lawyer," 21 A.B.A. Jour. 667, 670 (1935).

[31] A.B.A. Op. 145, 194, p. 391; N.Y. City 707; and see A.B.A. Op. 175.

[32] App. A., 231.   [33] *Id.*, 237.

income tax matters; [34] tax matters; [35] jury trials; [36] arguing cases in the Supreme Court; [37] consultants in Florida law; [38] the law and practice of New Jersey; [39] taxes and estates; [40] legal research and preparation of briefs for lawyers; [41] federal taxation; [42] law of a foreign country; [43] divorce practice. [44]

Canon 46 (as at present [June, 1953] worded) does not permit a mailed notice.[45]

The following have been held by the New York City and County Committees to be such specialized services: trade regulations and patents; [46] chemical and electro-chemical patent matters; [47] international and foreign matters; [48] Philippine war damages; [49] international law; [50] pretrial preparation and investigation of negligence cases; [51] trial of negligence cases; [52] consulting counsel to other lawyers in constitutional cases; [53] branches of the law which involve medical knowledge; [54] personal injury actions and "trial counsel"; [55] criminal matters; [1] brief writing; [2] trial work; [3] Louisiana law; [4] workmen's compensation claims; [5] immigration matters.[6]

The following have been held not to be specialized legal services: matrimonial matters; [7] preparation of briefs, pleadings, etc.; [8] military law; [9] Federal taxation; [10] pretrial legal bureau; [11] legal research and briefing; [12] medical jurisprudence; [13] questions of law and practice; [14] rent control matters; [15] Florida law; [16] non-resident parties; [17] canon law.[18]

The Chicago Committee defined such a specialty as a well recognized branch of the law and "one which the average lawyer in the

---

34 *Id., 238.*   35 *Ibid.*   36 *Id., 233.*
37 *Id., 234.*   38 *Id., 235.*   39 *Id., 232.*
40 *Id., 238.*   41 A.B.A. Op. 145; App. A, 236.
42 App. A, *238.*   43 A.B.A. Op. 263.   44 A.B.A. Op. 120.
45 App. A, 239; A.B.A. Op. 114 does not hold, as stated in N.Y. City 887, a mailed notice proper, despite the headnote; see *supra*, p. 234 n. 10.
46 N.Y. City 887.   47 N.Y. City 135.   48 N.Y. County 379.
49 N.Y. City B-81.   50 N.Y. City B-52.   51 N.Y. City B-88.
52 N.Y. City 469.   53 N.Y. City 470.   54 N.Y. City 586.
55 N.Y. County 299.
1 N.Y. City 711 ("expressly authorized by Canon 46").
2 N.Y. County 83.   3 N.Y. County 285; N.Y. City B-164.
4 N.Y. City 511.   5 N.Y. City 641.   6 N.Y. City 553.
7 N.Y. City 707.   8 N.Y. City 764.   9 N.Y. City B-16.
10 Mich. 124.   11 Mich. 79.
12 Mich. 94; N.Y. City 497, 764, B-10, B-120.   13 Mich. 128.
14 N.Y. City 539.   15 N.Y. City B-168.   16 N.Y. City 558.
17 N.Y. City 678.   18 N.Y. City B-188.

community is not equipped and willing to handle and is so regarded by the customs and traditions of the community." [19]

To call it a "specialized legal service" in the law journal does not make it one.[20]

The bulletin board of the bar association is not a legal journal.[21]

Separate partners may not advertise specialties.[22]

A lawyer of but three-months standing could not qualify as a specialist.[23]

One may not have a card in a legal publication in another state, saying that his services are available to lawyers only.[24]

At the meeting of the American Bar Association House of Delegates in February, 1953, the American Bar Association Ethics Committee unanimously recommended an amendment to Canon 46 to permit all lawyers to announce to other lawyers their availability in special branches, by a brief and dignified notice, either mailed to lawyers only or by insertion in a legal journal. The basis of such recommended amendment was the fact that the present Canon 46 is, for practical purposes, inoperative; that specialization in the law had in recent years developed so as to require recognition. Such announcements to lawyers only were not, it was believed, contrary to the basic spirit and purpose of Canon 27, and would serve a useful and proper purpose, both in making available to lawyers a list of specialists in different branches from whom, on investigation of their qualifications, they might choose one as an associate when needed, and also in giving young lawyers a chance to be considered in their chosen field by their colleagues at the bar. See *infra,* page 325 n. 15.

This recommendation was referred by the House back to the Committee for further consideration and report to the House at the annual meeting in August, 1953. The American Bar Association Committee, after further consideration, recommended an amendment, changed in certain features as a result of the discussion in the House in February, but permitting the announcement by lawyers to other lawyers of special branches by mailed notices and in law journals only.

Should such amendment be adopted, the discussion on pages 233–38 and 242–43 will become of historic interest only.

[19] Chicago 15, p. 34-B.
[20] N.Y. City B-105.
[21] N.Y. City 774.
[22] App. A, *218.*
[23] N.Y. City 752.
[24] N.Y. City 736; and see 741; see also Chicago 25, p. 48.

TELEPHONE BOOKS

In 1942 the American Bar Association Committee, overruling its previous Opinions 53 and 223, held that since the alphabetical sections of a telephone directory were not designed to enable readers to select a lawyer, but were used ordinarily by one to find the lawyer whom he had already chosen, the listing of a lawyer's name therein in distinctive type, being merely to facilitate this, was not improper. In 1951 the American Bar Association Committee, finding that other committees disapproved such listing [25] and receiving protests from a number of lawyers and local associations, again reversed its ruling and held such distinctive listing improper.[26]

In its Opinion 284 the American Bar Association Committee condemned a number of distinctive methods of classifying lawyers in telephone books and directories: segregating some in the classified sections in a manner differing from the general informative listing of their fellow lawyers; including not merely "display" advertising, but also bold-face type indicating "a studied purpose to single oneself for special notice over and above his fellow lawyers"; also, adding to the regular classified listing a "second line" in which the lawyer claims that he is engaged in a "specialty," obviously an attempt to make his name unduly distinctive. Obtaining varied listings demonstrates a desire to press for public attention in a similar attempt.[27] Selecting a listing different from the listing under which the rest of the lawyers appear is a clear attempt to segregate himself for special attention.[28]

A lawyer may not list his name in the telephone book followed by "legal clinic." [29] It is proper in the classified section under "attorneys" or "lawyers." [30]

A lawyer may allow his name to be in the directory of a large office building, under the classification "lawyers." [31]

An associate who at the widow's request takes over the deceased

[25] N.Y. City 357, 576, B-121; Ohio No. 5; Cal. Rule 2, sec. b (3 Cal. State Bar Jour. 56 [No. 19, 1928]); Cleveland H; New Orleans 5/22/48, 6/15/48. The Virginia Committee (Op. 30), by a majority, accepted the A.B.A. Opinion 241 and might possibly also agree with its reversal by Opinion 284. And see Mich. 46, 145; N.Y. County 298, 417.

[26] A.B.A. Op. 284; N.Y. City 357; N.Y. County 298; Va. 34.

[27] See also App. A, *149;* Mo. 26.

[28] N.Y. County 298; Cleveland C, H, I, I (sup.), 3; Mich. 46.

[29] N.Y. City 796, 892.   [30] Texas 6, 30. See also Mo. 26, 70.

[31] N.Y. City 433.

lawyer's practice may not continue the deceased lawyer's name in the telephone book.[32]

Where a lawyer's name has been omitted from a telephone directory, the proper practice is not to insert an advertisement but to send a personal letter to those whose personal relations warrant this.[33]

A lawyer may have his name in the telephone book as attorney in a different county from where his residence is, and in still another where he has a wide acquaintance,[34] and he may be listed for nearby towns in which there are no lawyers.[35]

Barristers in England may not permit their names to be inserted in the classified telephone directory.[36]

A German attorney may be listed as such.[37]

INDIRECT ADVERTISING

Under Canon 27, every indirect form of advertising, designed to secure professional employment, is improper. Typical instances of such indirect advertising, condemned by the Committees, are: the posing for pictures in connection with a divorce suit handled;[38] deliberate newspaper publicity relative to the lawyer's handling of cases;[39] the sending out of Christmas books[40] or greetings;[41] the purchase of space in a book issued in connection with a firemen's ball;[42] the sending out of match books with a lawyer's name on them,[43] or a "Lawyer's Digest,"[44] or circulars digesting local divorce laws,[45] or diaries with his name in them, even without any statement that he is a lawyer;[46] the subscription to a booklet in order to get his biography in it;[47] or the insertion of his card in a high school or college paper.[48] A lawyer, however, may answer inquiries from *Who's Who* if he did not solicit this or pay to get his name in it,[49] and may

---

[32] N.Y. City 884.   [33] App. A, *150*.   [34] N.Y. City 498.
[35] Texas 30. But see Mich. 145.
[36] Annual Statement of Council of the Bar for 1937, p. 4.
[37] N.Y. City 585.
[38] A.B.A. Ops. 42 (though the court acquiesces), 43; and cf. Mich. 58.
[39] A.B.A. Op. 140; Cleveland 17. See also as to Canon 20, *supra*, p. 70.
[40] A.B.A. Op. 59; see also Mich. 40; and cf. N.Y. City 422.
[41] A.B.A. Op. 107; Mich. 29; N.Y. City 538.
[42] Va. 16; and cf. Va. 36; and see N.Y. City 540, 695; see N.Y. City 663, 920, and B-23 stating that he may purchase space in a souvenir charitable journal "compliments of John Doe" omitting attorney-at-law and his address.   [43] App. A, *94*.
[44] N.Y. City 644; see also N.Y. City B-219, N.Y. County 415.
[45] A.B.A. Op. 73, Mich. 146.   [46] App. A, *86*.   [47] A.B.A. Op. 207.
[48] App. A, *95*; Mich. 151.   [49] App. A, *63, 64*.

gratuitously endorse a law magazine,[50] or write a complimentary letter to the publisher of a law book though he knows his letter will be used as an advertisement of the book by the publisher but not of him as a lawyer.[1] Great care should, however, be exercised by lawyers and judges in endorsing law books sold by publishers; both the lawyers and the publishers should refrain from reference to any specific causes and also from reference to the lawyer's position generally or in the particular field of work covered.[2]

He may send copies of a law article written by him to those who ask for it, but not to others where not justified by personal relations.[3]

He may not send to a law list publisher, for dissemination outside the list, information of a character not includable in the list; [4] nor send out a statement as to which lists include him.[5]

The candidate for a public office who is a lawyer may advise the public of this when the office sought is one in which his legal training adds to his qualifications to fill the office,[6] but may not use his candidacy as an excuse for advertising that he is a lawyer; [7] nor offer to serve a charity free of charge,[8] although he may actually thus serve charities without advertisement; [9] nor may he organize a corporation through which to advertise.[10]

He may not have "attorney-at-law" printed on his automobile license tags; [11] nor may he have his name with "attorney-at-law" on his pass book.[12]

He may not advertise in his name for money to be invested by his clients in chattel mortgages.[13]

The lawyer for a title company may recommend the employment of such company.[14]

As to the propriety of a lawyer's permitting a client to carry his name on the client's letterhead, etc., see page 229. As to the stamping on a legal document of the name and address of the draftsman, see page 259.[15]

50 App. A, 58; and cf. id., 57.
1 Mich. 35; he may not, however, properly join, as a lawyer, with a number of individuals and business men in full page messages congratulating the president of a labor union on his election, Wash. 10.
2 App. A, 58.   3 N.Y. City 656, 670; and see 891.
4 App. A, 90.   5 Id., 91.
6 Wash. 9; Mich. 52; Mo. 36.   7 App. A, 65; Mich. 89; Cleveland 10.
8 N.Y. City 24; N.Y. County 256; cf. A.B.A. Op. 169.
9 A.B.A. Ops. 148, 206, 211, 252, 259.   10 App. A, 66, 77.
11 Id., 87.   12 New Orleans 2/3/50. Cf. App. A, 68.
13 N.Y. City 561.   14 New Orleans 7/13/48.   15 App. A, 153; Mich. 149.

SOLICITATION [16]

There are many opinions by the various committees condemning solicitation of professional employment both directly and by various indirect approaches,[17] and in a number of cases lawyers have been refused admission,[18] suspended, or disbarred [19] for so doing.

A lawyer for a trust company may not accept employment from it to draw wills for its clients without charge to them, naming it as fiduciary, with the assurance that the lawyer will be made counsel for the estate.[20] One may not take steps to get back a client whom he has lost, although he may advise him of a claim which may be collected by him.[21] One controlling the claims of a majority of the creditors of a bankrupt for whom a receiver (represented by another lawyer) has been appointed may not properly propose to the receiver to make an agreement to vote such claims for him as trustee in consideration of his appointing such lawyer his attorney.[22] Nor may a lawyer furnish credit reports in return for future employment,[23] or offer his services free to labor organizations as to their union problems with a view to being employed by the members individually; [24] or investigate the prior marital status of one not a client with a view to employment by him in divorce proceedings,[25] or suggest settlement of his father's debts by professional services to be rendered by him to the creditors; [26] or submit, at the request of a municipality, a competitive bid for its

[16] As to ambulance chasing, see *supra,* p. 64; also Ky. 1; also in general as to solicitation, see Costigan, Case Book, pp. 351–52.
See also Principles of Medical Ethics of the American Medical Association, chap. I., sec. 4; also Rule (7) of the American Institute of Accountants.
[17] See Samuel Johnson's advice that lawyer "inject a little hint now and then" quoted *supra,* p. 213; see also Mich. 18.
[18] In re Bowers, 138 Tenn. 662 (1917); In re Application for License, 67 W.Va. 213 (1910).
[19] See *supra,* pp. 28–29; *infra,* pp. 307–08; Ky. 1.
[20] A.B.A. Op. 122; App. A, *98,* and see J. H. Cohen, 7 Ind. L. Jour. 295, 306–08 (1932), and cf. N.Y. City 566, also O. J. Seiler in 6 Cal. State Bar Jour. 153, 154 (1932), Costigan, Case Book, p. 352 n. 19.
[21] Mich. 99; cf. N.Y. City 770 holding that a lawyer learning of a legacy to one whom he does not represent should advise him of it anonymously; and see N.Y. City 910.
[22] A.B.A. Op. 78; see also N.Y. County 120; N.Y. City 618 and cases cited.
[23] A.B.A. Op. 188.
[24] A.B.A. Op. 169; App. A, *99,* and cf. A.B.A. Op. 148, *supra,* p. 162; also N.Y. County 45, 89, 222; Wash. 10. As to employment by an organization which pays him to represent the members free of additional charge, see *supra,* pp. 161–65.
[25] N.Y. County 224; and see N.Y. County 199.
[26] N.Y. County 335; see also N.Y. City 346.

proposed bond issue,[27] or maintain a branch office merely to steer clients to the main office.[28]

A patent lawyer may not properly send out letters asking for ideas as to patents, although primarily for the benefit of a corporation which he represents; [29] nor may a lawyer distribute circulars digesting the divorce laws,[30] or invite accountants and business men to use his tax library,[31] or write to various lawyers with whom he had exchanged forwarding services, ostensibly in order to secure statistics with regard to various facts,[32] or address a meeting of an automobile club called to raise funds for his employment; [33] it being apparent in such cases that the purpose was to advertise himself and offer his services as a lawyer.

A lawyer who is captain in a political precinct may not, ostensibly as such but on his legal stationery, write letters to the voters in such precinct offering to them tax service without charge.[34] For a lawyer on the faculty of a law school to employ runners or solicitors on a commission basis to solicit pupils for his bar examination quiz course is objectionable as "beneath the essential dignity of the profession." [35]

One elected to city council may not, in a letter of thanks for supporting him, sent out generally to friends and clients, say that he is not precluded by his election from practicing law; he may say this only to those who ask it.[36] A lawyer who is a candidate for mayor has been held authorized to use his letterhead in canvassing for votes.[37]

He may not procure and pay a fee to have his name written in automobile policies with direction to the insured to contact him in case of accident, etc.,[38] but may permit his name, without his solicitation, to be in a policy as the one to be notified.[39]

He may not offer a discount to members of a social club.[40]

He may not advertise free consultations,[41] or pay part of the expenses of a foreign lawyer on a trip to the United States, in order that such lawyer may get acquainted here,[42] or offer to the officers of a charity to handle their work without charge because of his interest in such charity.[43]

He may not offer his services free to real estate brokers in order, in

---

[27] Mich. 133; App. A, *83*.   [28] N.Y. City 954.   [29] App. A, *93*.
[30] A.B.A. Op. 73.   [31] Mich. 67.   [32] App. A, *92*.   [33] A.B.A. Op. 8.
[34] Chicago 18, p. 37; cf. Mich. 89. Wash. 9; Mich. 52; App. A, *65*.
[35] N.Y. County 234; but see App. A, *52*.   [36] N.Y. City B-17.
[37] Mich. 52.   [38] A.B.A. Op. 137.   [39] A.B.A. Op. 174.
[40] N.Y. County 177.   [41] N.Y. City 101; and see N.Y. County 222.
[42] N.Y. City 126.   [43] N.Y. County 256.

drafting papers, to make contacts with potential clients; [44] nor may a lawyer who is also a C.P.A. make an arrangement with a bank to make out income tax returns free for its customers in order that he may thus make their acquaintance.[45]

A lawyer may have a financial interest in a collection agency which solicits,[46] but may not participate in its management or activities or accept employment from it to collect claims.[47]

He may not, on behalf of an unnamed client, agree with a corporation to disclose defalcations by employees in consideration of a large fee, in which he will have a contingent interest.[48]

Notifying Persons Having Similar Problems

Difficult questions arise as to the propriety of notifying persons having interests similar to those of a client, of a controversy in which they should be represented and whose participation in the litigation may be of benefit to the lawyer's client, not only in dividing the expense, but also in guarding against an inconsistent or inefficient presentation of the client's contention.[49] In such cases, while it would seem clearly proper for the lawyer to see to it that these similar interests are properly represented,[50] they should be approached by the client and not by the lawyer,[1] and be made to understand that they may be represented by a lawyer of their own choosing. He may not advise them in order to get their business.[2]

The mere fact that it will be cheaper and more efficient for owners of condemned property to have one lawyer represent them all will not justify one in soliciting their cases,[3] although it is pertinent that the lawyer will not benefit.[4] Where he discovers a judgment in favor of the client of another lawyer, he may advise such lawyer of it, but not with a view to being associated in its collection.[5] A lawyer rep-

---

[44] App. A, *100*.   [45] *Id., 101*.

[46] A.B.A. Op. 225. The N.Y. County Committee "discourages" this, No. 238.

[47] A.B.A. Op. 225; see also as to relations with collection agencies, p. 168 and p. 179.

[48] N.Y. City 613.

[49] See A.B.A. Ops. 5, 111, N.Y. County 47 vi(*c*) (*d*); N.Y. County 228, and see N.Y. City 43, 155, 373; Mich. 131. "The propriety of the communication depends on the circumstances," N.Y. City 493. See also *infra*, p. 259 ("acquiescence").

[50] See N.Y. City 424, 464, 625, B-68, also N.Y. County 228.

[1] See N.Y. City 202, 425, 625, 775; N.Y. County 278; and cf. N.Y. County 47 vi(*d*); wrong where a scheme to get business, N.Y. City 381. Cf. also B-216.

[2] N.Y. City 16, 43, 103, 127, 618, 664; N.Y. County 47-V.

[3] N.Y. County 244; see also 302, 312, 331.   [4] N.Y. City 464, 625.

[5] N.Y. County 227, 228; see also N.Y. County 252; also A.B.A. Op. 9; and see N.Y. City 7, 532, 770; but see N.Y. City 177, also 642 (but query); also discussion of Chicago

resenting a creditor of a bankrupt may, solely in the interest of his client, and not in order to secure fees, solicit two other creditors in order to satisfy the provision of the bankruptcy act requiring three.[6]

Under exceptional circumstances, but only with the approval of the proper court, it may be proper for the lawyers who have created a fund to ask parties entitled to participate in it to pay their share of the expense of creating it, as a condition of such participation.[7]

A lawyer to whom one leaving the city turned over all his pending cases and who finds, after working on them, that they were obtained by a soliciting organization, need not turn them over to it on its demand, but is entitled to have each client make a demand and then to be paid proper compensation to date.[8]

One entering the army may notify his clients of the lawyer who will handle his practice.[9]

A majority only of the New York City Committee held that a firm over 100 years old might permit its description in a booklet, for which it paid no part.[10]

A lawyer may permit his name on the letterhead of a charity as legal adviser, along with that of the medical adviser.[11]

"PERSONAL RELATIONS" [12]

The phrase means primarily professional and not social relations.[13] It includes personal friends and those who have recommended the lawyer; [14] also relatives whom he discovered are entitled to a legacy.[15] When a lawyer discovers in an ancestor's will a provision inuring to the benefit of his close relatives, he may advise them of it and suggest his employment to enforce their rights.[16]

One formerly employed by a firm and starting alone may send a

---

Committee in Chicago Bulletin for 1920; quoted in Costigan, Case Book, p. 374. In N.Y. County 228 the Committee said: "The promotion of the client's interest may furnish the exception in the present case."

[6] People v. Edelson, 313 Ill. 601 (1924); People v. Ashton, 347 Ill. 570 (1932); see 25 Col. L. Rev. 492 (1925).

[7] App. A, 67.   [8] N.Y. City 140.   [9] N.Y. City 814.

[10] N.Y. City 832.   [11] N.Y. City B-95.

[12] For a definition of "personal relations" by the Michigan and New York City Committees, see *supra,* p. 232. For a general discussion, see N.Y. City 619; see also A.B.A. Op. 7.

[13] App. A, *105.*   [14] *Id., 106.*   [15] See N.Y. County 126.

[16] *Ibid.*

simple announcement to clients of the firm whom he knew well, but not solicit them.[17]

The New York County Committee held that a deaf lawyer might send to other lawyers cards stating merely willingness to serve them, without solicitation; [18] but the City Committee held that the wife of a blind lawyer had no special latitude to advertise in the law journal in his behalf.[19]

The fact that a lawyer has inspected properties as a Government agent does not justify him in subsequently sending cards to the firms inspected.[20]

One learning of a legacy to a stranger may advise him, but without solicitation, and should preferably do so anonymously.[21]

The mere fact of personal acquaintance with a lawyer does not justify solicitation of business from him.[22]

Where a judgment was temporarily uncollectible, but the debtor afterward acquired assets, the lawyer for a creditor, after collecting for his client the balance not paid by the surety, may properly advise the latter so that it can recoup, despite the fact that this may lead to his employment by the surety company. Here his relations justify this.[23]

He may not properly have his card printed on a blotter to be sent to clients and friends to be used on their desks; [24] or send announcements to the 1,800 members of his church,[25] or to 3,500 lawyers whom he has met as a Master Mason or as an assistant district attorney.[26]

He may not offer, for compensation, to give another lawyer useful information for a case being handled by the other lawyer.[27]

A lawyer representing a party to litigation in an estate, where it is to his client's interest to locate missing heirs, may broadcast the facts in order to locate them; [28] but he may not communicate with the

17 N.Y. County 109; and see N.Y. City 516.

18 N.Y. County 280. (What was the "notice" permitted in the County's opinions in this and the preceding note but a polite form of solicitation?)

19 N.Y. City 866.   20 App. A, *80.*

21 N.Y. City 770; but see N.Y. City 910, holding that one learning that his client is not entitled to a fund but that two of his step-relations are, may not tell them of it. The only question here was solicitation. See also N.Y. County 227, 228, 252; Mich. 80.

22 See N.Y. City 619, 642.   23 N.Y. County 294; but see N.Y. City 532.

24 App. A, *88.*   25 *Id., 107.*   26 N.Y. City 619.

27 N.Y. County 150; and see also N.Y. City 7, 327A, 360, 569.

28 App. A, *70;* cf. N.Y. City 812 (writing on his letterhead to possible purchasers of a plant for sale by his client).

heirs of one not yet dead with a view to advising and representing them,[29] or with the owners of unclaimed bank accounts.[30]

Information to Clients as to Changes in the Law

While a lawyer may send to his clients a summary of recent legislation, or a suggestion based on recent decisions or legislation clearly in the interest of the particular client, he may not properly send to clients generally a notice of an estate planning service which is capable of interpretation as a bid for employment.[31]

He may advise one whose will he has drawn to review it, by reason of changes in the law or of his personal affairs and beneficiaries.[32]

A lawyer may properly advise clients of new statutes [33] and send them pertinent memoranda in reference to changes in the law, in a way that does not smack of advertising,[34] but a personal letter to the client is in better taste than a circular,[35] it being improper to do this by a folder or confidential report analyzing Government regulations.[36] He may not send to a client a copy of the revenue laws or the reprint of a legal article with his name stamped on it; [37] and it is improper for a lawyer to distribute to his clients a pamphlet recommending that they submit their insurance policies to him for advice,[38] as it is for him to write to them calling attention to a new service which his office offers; [39] nor may he write generally to clients and friends [40] communicating to them the necessity and advantages of will making. It is also indelicate for him to stamp his card on the reprint of a law article written by him, even though this be sent to lawyers only.[41]

ADVERTISEMENT BY BAR ASSOCIATIONS

Lawyers naturally view with concern the encroachment on their professional employment in recent years by banks, trust companies, accountants, tax experts, and laymen proficient in the various branches of our increasingly complicated existence, most of whom

---

29 Mich. 53.

30 Mich. 51; cf. N.Y. City 138, 348.

31 App. A, 76.

32 A.B.A. Op. 210; N.Y. City 300, 722.

33 A.B.A. Op. 213.

34 App. A, 61; see also N.Y. County 248; N.Y. City 417.

35 App. A, 62.

36 N.Y. City B-3.

37 App. A, 89.

38 A.B.A. Op. 229.

39 App. A, 81.

40 N.Y. County 219; see also N.Y. County 14.

41 App. A, 82; see however, N.Y. City 891, as to sending reprints of a law article to lawyers and students, physicians and insurance men.

are free to advertise and solicit and many of whom perform what are in fact legal services despite the activities of the Unauthorized Practice Committees. The Bar Associations have accordingly modified the stringent rule forbidding all advertisement and solicitation so as to permit limited advertisement by the local associations, and by providing for approved law lists.[42]

The provision for advertisements by local bar associations was through a series of opinions by the American Bar Association Committee, written for the Committee by Judge Phillips when he was chairman.[43] These opinions, although possibly judicial legislation when rendered, have been accepted and approved by the House of Delegates, which has amended Canon 27 several times without modifying them since Opinion 179 was announced in 1938. They have been accepted by many state and local associations and not, it is believed, condemned by any. They are indicated in Opinion 121 (1934) in which the American Bar Association Committee condemned a proposed bar advertisement, purporting to be educational, but which contained pictures, was labelled "advertisement," and was so framed as to convey to the public an implication that the "principal objective was to secure professional employment for the members of the bar association rather than to perform a supposed obligation to aid and instruct the public. See Opinion 9." At the end of the opinion, however, the Committee said:

> To overcome these natural implications the articles should not contain pictures or pictorial illustrations of any character; should not be in usual advertising form and should not contain catch phrases, or other features of ordinary advertising matter; should not extol individuals. They should be in the name of the bar association and not in the name of any individual; nor should mention be made of any lawyer.
>
> The articles in purpose and effect should be for the intelligent guidance of the public and should be free from the suspicion that selfish motives are the dominant purpose.

[42] "Of course, any bar advertising will naturally have the result of giving employment to lawyers, and is so intended. The question is one of degree. A bar advertisement should not be condemned merely because it is calculated to bring business to lawyers, but should be judged as to whether the benefit to the public in learning of the advantages of employing lawyers is sufficient to justify it." App. A, *151;* and see A.B.A. Op. 172 as to proper advertising by a bar association. Cf. also Principles of Medical Ethics of the American Medical Association, Chap. I, Sec. 5.

[43] A.B.A. Ops. 179, 191, 205, 227, 259; see also 35 Journal of American Judicature Societies 11–16 (1951), and Cleveland F. As to an advertisement by a legal printer pointing out the advantage of consulting a lawyer, see N.Y. City 682-E.

The Committee, though not entirely without misgiving, sanctions the method proposed, provided always that the publications be dignified in tone and in strict conformity with the restrictions herein indicated.[44]

Opinion 179 was pursuant to a request from a local bar association for an opinion as to the propriety of its sponsoring a radio broadcast of a sketch wherein was portrayed, in rather dramatic fashion, the unfortunate consequences of the failure of a person to secure competent legal advice and assistance in the drafting and execution of his will. The Committee said:

The employment of a lawyer to protect the client's rights, advance his interests, comply with necessary legal requirements, keep within legal inhibitions, and prevent future controversy and litigation, rather than to employ a lawyer after trouble has ensued, benefits the client rather than the lawyer because the remuneration of the lawyer is generally greater from the latter than the former service. A lawyer receives much less compensation for seeing that a will is properly drafted and executed than for defending a hotly contested will case.

We recognize a distinction between teaching the lay public the importance of securing legal services preventive in character and the solicitation of professional employment by or for a particular lawyer. The former tends to promote the public interest and enhance the public estimation of the profession. The latter is calculated to injure the public and degrade the profession.

The practice of law is affected with a public interest. Society as a whole, as well as the individual client, is interested in the service rendered by the lawyer because it directly affects the maintenance of order and harmony in business and social relations and the due administration of justice. If the public interest is to be best served the profession must merit and have the confidence and respect of the public. One way to obtain that confidence and respect is to render a more useful professional service.

Advertising which is calculated to teach the layman the benefits and advantages of preventive legal services will benefit the lay public and enable the lawyer to render a more desirable and beneficial professional service. It may tend to decrease rather than increase the sum total of remuneration received by lawyers, but because of the trouble, disappointments, controversy, and litigation it will prevent, it will enhance the public esteem of the legal profession and create a better relation between the profession and the general public.

The prevention of controversy and litigation will also improve the social order. It will lessen the instances in which the lay public may feel that a

---

[44] In Mich. 61 that Committee held that the expense of circulating such articles or broadcasts might be defrayed by subscriptions to the association on the part of law firms and individuals for the whole series and not for a particular article.

person's honest intentions and desires have been frustrated by what the layman chooses to call the "technicalities" of the law. It will result in the public acquiring a higher regard for the legal profession, the judicial process, and the judicial establishments.

In carrying out a project to educate the lay public with respect to the benefits of preventive legal services, certain possible evils should be carefully guarded against.

First, it should be carried on by the organized bar in order that any semblance of personal solicitation will be avoided.

Second, that the purpose is to give the layman beneficial information, to enable lawyers as a whole to render a better professional service, to promote order in society, to prevent controversy and litigation and to enhance the public esteem of the legal profession, the judicial process and the judicial establishments, should be made plain.

Third, it must in fact be motivated by a desire to benefit the lay public and carried out in such a way as to avoid the impression that it is actuated by selfish desire to increase professional employment; and any plan, however well intended, that on trial fails to convince the lay public that the purpose is to benefit the layman and not to promote professional employment should be promptly abandoned.

Fourth, it should be carried on in a manner in keeping with the dignity and traditions of the profession. *See Opinion 121.*

The Michigan Committee said: "It is our conclusion that if the object and purposes of the broadcast are those above indicated and the limitations above stated are observed, no ethical impropriety will result." [45]

An individual lawyer may not properly distribute copies of such bar advertisements.[46]

The Washington Committee, however, has held that lawyers may hand to their clients copies of a booklet prepared by the Bar Association entitled "Have You Made a Will?" provided neither the lawyer's name or address is printed or written on it.[47]

Legal Services to Low-Income Groups

In Opinion 191 the American Bar Association Committee held that members of a Bar Association could not form a group willing to render legal services at equitable charges in accordance with ability to pay to members of low-income groups and advertise the fact that members of the group of lawyers would render such services at their respective offices between designated hours.[48]

[45] Mich. 61.   [46] Chicago 22, p. 44; see also N.Y. County 219, Mich. 10.
[47] Wash. 4.   [48] Accord N.Y. City 796, 896, B-7.

In Opinion 205 the same Committee considered a request by the bar association of a large city on a proposed plan: "to provide legal services to persons in low-income groups at charges that are reasonable and commensurate with their ability to pay." The Committee held:

We are of the opinion that the plan here presented does not fall within the inhibition of the Canon. No solicitation for a particular lawyer is involved. The dominant purpose of the plan is to provide as an obligation of the profession competent legal services to persons in low-income groups at fees within their ability to pay. The plan is to be supervised and directed by the local Bar Association. There is to be no advertisement of the names of the lawyers constituting the panel. The general method and purpose of the plan only is to be advertised. Persons seeking the legal services will be directed to members of the panel by the Bar Association. Aside from the filing of the panel with the Bar Association, there is to be no advertisement of the names of the lawyers constituting the panel. If these limitations are observed, we think there is no solicitation of business by or for particular lawyers and no violation of the inhibitions of Canon 27.

In Opinion 227 the American Bar Association Committee further considered a Lawyers' Reference Service maintained by the bar association in a large city. Relative to advertising such service, the Committee said:

Advertising of that service must be primarily to give beneficial information to the lay public and to enable lawyers generally to render a better professional service. While the fact that incidental benefits may flow to the members of the profession does not condemn such a plan, the primary object thereof, if it is to be advertised, must be benefit to the public and not to the members of the profession or any particular or selected group thereof.

The Committee advised that the proposed plan should be modified to permit registration of not only members of the particular bar association, but of all reputable members of the local bar engaged in active practice, and that the expense of maintaining it might be defrayed by a charge, imposed equally on all registrants, including nonmembers of the association. The Committee also required that registrants:

be required to agree to abide by reasonable rules and regulations promulgated by the Bar Association respecting registrants and the carrying out of the plan, and the Bar Association, with propriety, may cancel their registration for a violation of such rules or regulations.[49]

[49] Affirmed in A.B.A. Op. 260. The Association should retain the copy of the advertisement; App. A, *152*. See Mich. 10 and also Mo. 82.

In Opinion 259 the American Bar Association Committee specified certain analogous principles applicable to a committee of the American Bar Association for providing gratuitous legal service to those serving in the armed forces and their dependents.

Consistently with the foregoing, the American Bar Association Committee has held that neither a group of lawyers nor a bar association[50] may properly solicit employment for its members, nor may a county bar association publish in a local newspaper a list of its members in good standing.[1] It was held, however, that a lawyer's organization might circulate a list among themselves.[2]

While a bar association may announce in the local papers that those needing advice as to their income tax returns should consult their lawyers prior to March 1,[3] an individual lawyer may not do this, though the advertisement be headed, "To my clients." [4]

The American Bar Association Committee has held that, as a result of the sincere effort to protect the bar against improperly drawn instruments, lawyers may, at the suggestion of the bar association, stamp such instruments as having been drafted by them.[5] The Michigan Committee has also held that, with the approval of the local bar association, lawyers may stamp formal legal instruments, such as mortgages, deeds, and wills, with the name and address of the lawyer who drew them. In such case, the benefit of the information to the users of such documents, in knowing who the draftsman is, was considered to outweigh the secondary effect of advertising the lawyer.[6]

ACQUIESCENCE IN THE RECOMMENDATIONS OF OTHERS

It is clear that a lawyer may not properly suggest or bring about laudatory statements by others as to his professional attainments.[7] It is equally clear that it is not incumbent on a lawyer to offend any friend or well-wisher making such statements by disclaiming or deprecating them,[8] unless they are very blatant or unreasonably repeated,[9] or are made under circumstances which might convey the

---

[50] A.B.A. Ops. 13, 121, 172, 191, 260; N.Y. City 896.   [1] Mich. 97.

[2] App. A, 32.   [3] Mich. 86.   [4] *Ibid.*

[5] App. A, *153*. This might be considered in bad taste, as smacking of labor union technique.

[6] Mich. 149.   [7] See A.B.A. Op. 207.

[8] See N.Y. City 748, 761, B-41; N.Y. County 370; Va. 31; but see N.Y. City 615 (hospital).

[9] N.Y. County 4, 72, 147, 172; N.Y. City 509, 574.

idea that they were inspired by him,[10] or unless the lawyer does some service free in recognition of them.[11] Although the recommendation by a hospital may in some cases be proper, the practice is generally unnecessary and condemned.[12]

Just where the line should be drawn beyond which it is incumbent on the lawyer to protest it is often difficult to say. In its ultimate analysis the question, like many of those involving legal ethics, is one of good faith and good taste.

A lawyer may not permit his landlord to publish his photo in the landlord's office in order to advertise the office building.[13]

A law firm may not acquiesce in the publication by a magazine of a laudatory history of the firm.[14]

A lawyer need not object to the voluntary publication of his name, without a telephone number, once by a newspaper in a list of returned lawyer veterans available,[15] or to his being mentioned in a regular news item written by a reporter,[16] or to a chamber of commerce including him in a list of local lawyers as part of the general activity of the community,[17] or in a bar roster,[18] provided he does not pay to get it in.[19]

A lawyer may accept cases for which he is recommended by a collection agency, provided they make such recommendations only in specific cases where the lawyer's services are needed.[20]

He may permit a casualty company, required to defend all accidents against the insured, to have pasted on its policy a notice that he should be notified in the event of accident.[21]

A young lawyer may not permit his father, a business man, to send the son's professional card to a number of the business friends with whom the father has dealings.[22]

A lawyer may properly accept cases recommended to him in good faith by his brother,[23] or by an accounting firm;[24] or cases referred to him on request of the client, by the lawyer's brother, there being

---

10 See A.B.A. Op. 62; see also A.B.A. Op. 192 (5); N.Y. City 574, 781(2), 782; Mich. 101 and *supra,* p. 162.

11 N.Y. City 748; see also N.Y. County 36.   12 N.Y. City 615.

13 N.Y. County 274.   14 App. A, *79.*   15 N.Y. City B-18.

16 Mich. 15.   17 App. A, *56, 167.*   18 *Id., 168.*

19 *Id., 169;* see also N.Y. County 414.

20 N.Y. County 147; see also N.Y. City 382 (finance company which he represents, managed by a disbarred lawyer). See also as to collection agencies, *supra,* p. 168.

21 A.B.A. Op. 174; but see Va. 26.   22 N.Y. County 117.

23 N.Y. City 338.   24 N.Y. City B-110.

no suggestion of a splitting of fees,[25] or accept clients recommended bona fide to him by the secretary of a deceased lawyer, now his secretary,[26] or by a doctor friend,[27] or a union delegate.[28]

He may permit a law book publisher to use his endorsement of a law book, if not to advertise him [29] or an account in a law journal of a case with which he has been connected.[30] He may not, however, be listed as counsel for a community chest.[31]

He may not permit a clerk to refer to him on his card,[32] or an Italian firm to refer to him on their letterhead as their correspondent.[33]

He may permit a corporation which circulates laws among lawyers to send out an article by him on the Indemnification of Corporate Directors.[34]

There is a clear distinction between permitting the advertisement of a law book which he has written, and that of his law practice.[35]

He may not permit the representation that he is the lawyer for an unnamed organization and will furnish free advice to the members,[36] nor may he permit a bank to use his name to get employment in drawing wills,[37] nor accept employment by a bankers' association to answer questions by the members, to be published in its bulletin [38] nor cooperate with foreign lawyers who advertise in New York to handle business in their country.[39]

A public prosecutor may not permit the publication of a sensational story for a detective magazine with his name.[40]

It is proper for investment bankers to specify the names of the lawyers approving a bond issue, but this must not resemble a professional card; and a lawyer may permit himself to be named as counsel for a bondholders' committee in the notice to the bondholders provided this is done in good faith in order to attain public confidence and allow the bondholders to know who represents them.[41]

---

25 N.Y. County 359.   26 N.Y. City 312.   27 N.Y. City 326.
28 N.Y. City 209.   29 Mich. 35; App. A, 58; but see N.Y. City 690.
30 A.B.A. Op. 158.   31 App. A, 79; see also Mich. 49.
32 N.Y. County 49; and see N.Y. City 358.   33 N.Y. City B-190.
34 N.Y. County 370.   35 App. A, 51.
36 A.B.A. Op. 162; see also Joint Statement of Principles of the two New York Committees (N.Y. Law Jour., May 12, 1931) re Trust Companies recommending lawyers.
37 A.B.A. Op. 41.
38 A.B.A. Op. 98. As to permitting a lay organization to use him in the unauthorized practice of the law, see further *supra*, pp. 162–65.
39 N.Y. City 724.   40 Mich. 48.
41 A.B.A. Op. 100; N.Y. County 47 viii(a) (see argument); N.Y. City 287; see also N.Y. City 359.

The New York County Committee has held that a lawyer may permit a newspaper to specify him as "patent attorney" and the compiler of a list of patents issued to residents of the community.[42]

He may not permit a labor union to solicit portal to portal cases for him; [43] nor a trade association specifically to recommend him to its individual members for a litigation in which they are all engaged; [44] nor the consul of a foreign country to send home letters suggesting that the addressees communicate with him, even though it is stated that they may employ their own lawyer. He may permit them to recommend him only when they are requested to do so.[45]

His name may not appear as general counsel, he not being a full-time employee of the association, on the stationery of a building and loan association used by the officers in correspondence on its business, without the names of other officers, but may use such stationery as his own.[46] Nor may he allow a corporation,[47] or bank or trust company,[48] or a manufacturers' association,[49] or certified public accountant,[50] or tax counsel,[1] or an audit company,[2] or credit agency,[3] or collection agency,[4] or patent attorney,[5] or immigration practitioner,[6] or real estate or insurance corporation,[7] or counselor on rental problems [8] to carry his name as counsel on their letterheads, he not being a full-time employee, but may permit a non-profit group of psychologists or an educational corporation to do so.[9] He may not permit a manufacturers' association to carry his name as general counsel on bulletins sent to their members.[10] The test as between Opinion 100 and Opinion 285 is whether the information as to who is counsel for the organization is clearly and primarily in its interest and has not the effect of unduly advertising him.[11]

[42] N.Y. County 174.   [43] Mich. 101.
[44] Mich. 147.   [45] Mich. 105.
[46] Chicago 20, p. 42; but see N.Y. County 47 viii(b); see also A.B.A. Op. 285 and cf. New Orleans 3/7/47.
[47] A.B.A. Ops. 31, 285; Mo. 17, 18, 28; but see N.Y. City 816.   [48] A.B.A. Op. 41.
[49] A.B.A. Op. 285; see N.Y. County 47 viii(b), (c), (d); and see N.Y. County 136.
[50] N.Y. City B-109; Mich. 55.
[1] N.Y. City B-110, N.Y. City B-114 (overruling N.Y. City 66); but see N.Y. City 284.
[2] N.Y. City 66, B-114.   [3] N.Y. City 160, B-69 (full statement), 456.
[4] N.Y. County 136, overruling 47 viii(d); Mich. 60; N.Y. City 581; but see N.Y. City 90.
[5] N.Y. City 795; see also N.Y. County 214.
[6] 4 Cal. State Bar Jour. 32, Q. 31 (Part 1, 1929).
[7] N.Y. City 816.   [8] Mich. 114.
[9] N.Y. City B-171; and see N.Y. City 604, 612 (amateur baseball club), but see N.Y. City 615.
[10] A.B.A. Op. 285.
[11] See N.Y. City 604, N.Y. County 47 viii(a). But see 4 Cal. State Bar Jour. 33, Q. 35 (Part 1, 1929) (auto club pamphlets).

As to the propriety of representing an association of business men to perform legal services for it and also such of the members as it refers to them in collection and bankruptcy proceedings, prompted by the interest of the organization, in good faith to protect the interest of its members see pages 162 *et seq.*[12]

LEGAL ARTICLES AND ADDRESSES

Canon 40, adopted in 1928, provides:

A lawyer may with propriety write articles for publications in which he gives information upon the law; but he should not accept employment from such publications to advise inquirers in respect to their individual rights.

Prior to the adoption of Canon 40,[13] it was held to be improper under Canon 27 for a lawyer to conduct a daily column in a newspaper answering questions propounded by readers, diminishing the lawyer's sense of personal responsibility and his direct contact with the client.

The application of Canon 40 to borderline cases always involves the question of good faith on the part of the lawyer and of the publisher or sponsor of the article or address.

The transgression of ethical principles primarily to be guarded against are:

(1) The improper advertisement of the lawyer (Canon 27)

(2) The giving by him of legal advice to persons with whom he has not the personal contact and background required between lawyer and client to make his advice reliable [14] (Canon 35)

(3) Enabling the lay publisher, sponsor, or broadcaster to give legal advice, constituting the unauthorized practice of law (Canon 47)

The American Bar Association Committee has rendered a number of formal opinions construing Canon 40 and pointing out the dangers and difficulties inherent in its application.[15]

---

12 See N.Y. County 47 iii(*a*) (*d*) (*e*); 47 iv(*a*); 47 vi; 47 viii(*c*) (*d*); but see N.Y. County 136, where is modified its Opinion 47 viii(*d*) in deference to its Unlawful Practice Committee.

13 N.Y. County 203; N.Y. City 62.

14 "A lawyer is not justified in giving an opinion without an opportunity to ask the client for information as to the concrete facts in the client's case, and without an opportunity to see the instruments or documents and to ascertain the dates and other facts, which the client has not given or may not deem material. Nor can the client be safe in acting on generalizations." A.B.A. Op. 98, p. 214.

15 A.B.A. Ops. 92, 98, 121, 141 (containing questionable dicta as to Canon 46), 162,

The Michigan Committee has also discussed these problems in several opinions,[16] as have the New York City,[17] the New York County,[18] and the Chicago Committees.[19]

Whether or not the lawyer is paid for articles is not decisive.[20]

Such articles or addresses should in no event contain or be accompanied by any statements tending or intended to advertise him.[21]

It is believed that Canon 40 was designed primarily to sanction articles in law magazines or occasional articles in other publications and that it would be difficult if not impossible to conceive of a daily, weekly, or monthly column in a newspaper or magazine devoted to the discussion of legal matters which would not, sooner or later, violate Canon 40 and also Canons 27, 35, and 47. What the readers of such columns want is not a general discussion such as they can find in a law book or in an article in a law magazine, but something practical which they can apply to their own personal experience. Laymen usually are unable to formulate questions clearly to such a column and a lawyer answering such is apt to follow what he thinks his readers want to hear about and to answer the personal problem which he sees behind their questions. This is what the publishers will ultimately see that they get.

While theoretically radio broadcasts might come within the principles under which legal articles are permitted under Canon 40, as a practical matter it is difficult to believe that such would not also violate Canons 27, 35, and 47; [22] a fortiori would this be so as to a televised address.

In a radio address only the speaker's name and the fact that he is a lawyer should be stated, not his firm or address.[23]

While articles in law magazines or articles in a newspaper sponsored

---

270, 273; see also 42, 166, 168. See also the opinions of this Committee relative to advertising by bar associations discussed *supra*, pp. 254–57.

[16] Mich. 2, 6, 9, 13, 57, 61, 106, 119.

[17] N.Y. City 224, 270, 353, 354, 399, 410, 428, 452 (radio), 476, 518, 578, 584, 656, 661, 670, 691, 700, 873, 891, 931, 935. B-24, B-67, B-131.

[18] N.Y. County 203, 264, 340, 370, 396.

[19] Chicago 26, pp. 50–57, 64–66. The Chicago Association after its Committee had disapproved legal columns in publications, passed an amendment to its Canon 40 specifically condemning this. See also Mo. 76.

[20] N.Y. City 224, 353, 661.

[21] Va. 37. As to the impropriety of the distribution by a lawyer generally of articles written by him, see *supra*, pp. 247–48.

[22] See App. A, *228;* also Mich. 61, 119; N.Y. City 691, 873; but see N.Y. City 578, also as to a radio broadcast by a judge, A.B.A. Op. 166.

[23] N.Y. City 584; see also N.Y. City 224, 428, 452.

by a local or junior bar association may be signed by the lawyer author,[24] or a single article on a legal subject in a fraternity magazine written at the request of the editor,[25] as a general rule the signing of such articles in a manufacturer's bulletin has been condemned.[26] Where the opinions of a lawyer to a manufacturers' association are published in its bulletins, his name should not be stated and the bulletin should state that the readers should consult their own lawyer for advice on the matters involved.[27]

Articles in lay publications should not contain references to decided cases.[28]

LAW LISTS

History of the Law List Exception

The first mention in the Canons of law lists was in the 1933 amendment of Canon 43, which altered it to read:

43. Professional Card. A lawyer's professional card may with propriety contain only a statement of his name (and those of his lawyer associates), profession, address, telephone number, and special branch of the profession practiced. The insertion of such card in reputable law lists is not condemned and it may there give references or name clients for whom the lawyer is counsel, with their permission.

Prior to this amendment, Canon 43, as adopted in 1928, read:

43. Professional Card. The simple professional card mentioned in Canon 27 may with propriety contain only a statement of his name (and those of his lawyer associates), profession, address, telephone number and special branch of the profession practiced.

In 1943 Canon 43 was further amended, with title changed to its present form:

43. Approved Law Lists. It is improper for a lawyer to permit his name to be published in a law list the conduct, management or contents of which are calculated or likely to deceive or injure the public or the profession, or to lower the dignity or standing of the profession.

[24] App. A, 226.

[25] A.B.A. Op. 141; here the lawyer also sent his picture. See also A.B.A. Op. 162, the dicta in which perhaps go farther than the Committee's later Opinions 270 and 273 would warrant.

[26] A.B.A. Op. 273. But see N.Y. City B-24. In Mich. 106 where a single newspaper article is approved under the lawyer's name, it is recommended that the lawyer specifically warn the paper against a laudatory comment. See also Mich. 119.

[27] A.B.A. Ops. 273, 285.   [28] App. A, 227.

See also the provision relative to law lists in Canon 27, page 216.

The Special Committee on Law Lists was authorized and appointed in 1937 on the recommendation of a Special Committee which for two years had been studying the subject. This Committee was authorized to formulate Rules and Standards governing law lists on the compliance with which the Committee issues a "Certificate of Compliance," which makes the list a "reputable" or "approved" law list in which, under Canon 27, a member of the American Bar Association may properly be listed. A copy of these Rules and Standards in effect as of 1953, is Appendix G hereto.

The Law Lists had their origin some time prior to the adoption of the original Canons in 1908.[29] Several prominent and highly respectable lawyers had compiled for their own use and that of their friends at the bar a list of competent and reliable lawyers in different cities to whom they might refer matters requiring legal services in such localities, which lists were later taken over, in some cases by their descendants, in others by persons purchasing the right to publish the list. The publishers of these lists instituted the practice of making a charge to the listees for the privilege of being listed either exclusively, or with a limited number of other lawyers in their locality, the amount charged being related to the amount of business normally available in the locality and to the number of other listees therein. The lists selected the lawyers listed as those whom they undertook to recommend as competent and reliable for the service in which the list specialized. Some of the lists bonded their listees and required them to report all items coming to them over the list, being thus able to revise their listing fees from time to time as the business received by the various listees increased.[30]

---

[29] In 1867 a selective list of lawyers "The Reference Register and Law List" was established in England and between 1870 and 1872 three selective lists, Hubbell's Legal Directory, The Wilbur Attorneys' Directory, and the Rand-McNally Bank Recommended Attorneys were published in the United States. Many other selective lists followed. One of the first of the modern law lists was created in 1890 by Mr. Walter S. Carter of the prominent law firm of Carter, Hughes & Dwight, which included Mr. Carter's son-in-law, Charles Evans Hughes. It consisted of one representative in each large city, chosen by Mr. Carter. He published and circulated his list among lawyers until his death ten years later. Thereafter, a number of other lists were compiled in much the same manner, including the Russell Law List (successor of the Carter List), the B.A. Law List, the American Lawyers Quarterly, the U.S. Fidelity & Guaranty List and others. When the Canons, including Canon 27, were adopted in 1908, a number of these lists were well known and extensively used. As to Law Lists before 1937, see N.Y. City No. 395.

[30] See A.B.A. Op. 255 for a summary of the practical operation of the lists.

The recognition of Law Lists in the Canons, by which a lawyer is permitted to pay a considerable sum for the express purpose of having himself advertised as available and recommended as a lawyer, constituted an obvious exception to the rule of the profession condemning advertising and solicitation.[31] The amendment was adopted by the Association after lengthy discussion and debate, on the insistence of a substantial part of the membership (principally those specializing in the collection of commercial claims) that they be given some relief against the advertising by the collection agencies, as well as the conviction by the Association that the maintenance of law lists was so much in the public interest that the legal profession should approve listings of lawyers in lists properly supervised by the Association. Canon 27 as amended specifically provides that publication in *reputable* lists *in a manner consistent with the standards of conduct imposed by these Canons,* is permissible. Section 3 of the Rules and Standards provides for refusal or revocation of the certificate of compliance for any list whose publication or distribution encourages "any act or thing which directly or indirectly violates the Canons of Ethics of the Association." [32]

English solicitors may not pay to have their names in a list of recommended solicitors.[33]

General Rulings

The American Bar Association Ethics Committee has held that it will not pass directly on what is or is not a "reputable" list,[34] this being the function of the Special Committee on Law Lists, the Ethics Committee confining its advice to specific questions involving the con-

[31] As to the rule approving the insertion of cards in lists of lawyers and collection agencies and in local papers, prior to 1928, see N.Y. County 47 ix; also No. 239, where a majority of the County Committee said: "Then, as to the propriety of a lawyer paying for the insertion of his name in such a list. This Committee recognizes the fact [that] lists of reputable capable lawyers are of much use to merchants and lawyers as well. Although strictly speaking, such a payment is for an advertisement, yet where the amount paid is insignificant, the Committee is of the opinion that the same answer should be given as it gave to Question No. 1, that it is a matter of personal taste."

The New York City Committee (majority) concurred in the above in its Opinion 31, although recognizing the "indefinite implication" of the word "insignificant."

As a matter of fact, the payments are by no means "insignificant." See also 3 Cal. State Bar Jour. 54 (No. 3, Pt. I, 1928); Costigan's Case Book, p. 340.

[32] A law list should have a reasonable time to comply with the requirements for becoming a reputable list, App. A, *162.*

[33] 51 Law Notes 353 (Eng., 1932).   [34] App. A, *164.*

struction of the Canons, as, for example, whether the publication of a list has departed, in specified particulars, from the "standards of conduct imposed by these Canons." [35]

As heretofore stated,[36] since the amendment of 1937 a lawyer may not insert a professional card in any publication other than an approved law list or legal directory.[37]

Law schools, fraternities, service clubs, and bar associations may publish rosters, registers, catalogs, or lists of their members, with their names, addresses, and occupations, which are not law lists, where no charge is made for listing and there is no suggestion that the names of lawyers are listed as probably available for professional employment, or to promote, solicit, or secure professional employment.[38]

A lawyers' organization may circulate a list of its members among themselves.[39]

A lawyer may properly apply to be listed in an approved list [40] and may employ an organization to advise him as to the merits of the different lists.[41] He may give to the list data to enable it to rate him.[42] He may not, however, send out statements as to which lists include him,[43] or send to a law list publisher, for dissemination outside the list, information of a character not properly includable in the list.[44]

A list may not distinguish listees by bold-face type,[45] or state that the lawyer's honesty and efficiency are bonded or guaranteed.[46] Nor is it proper in the arrangement for listing to include a clause under which the lawyer waives claims for fees in cases where money collected is not remitted or the forwarder notified of collection within five days.[47]

Lawyers may not properly be listed with laymen; [48] an exception to this rule has been made, however, in the case of the American and Chicago Patent Associations, which, although they now include some patent agents not members of the bar, do not admit any additional

---

[35] See for example A.B.A. Ops. 123, 233, 234.   [36] *Supra*, p. 241.

[37] A.B.A. Ops. 182, 260, 276; see also New Orleans 7/2/51; Mo. 73; see also A.B.A. Op. 133, N.Y. City B-214.

[38] App. A, *31;* see also N.Y. County 414; and N.Y. City B-195; see also Va. 38 as to roster of specialties.   [39] App. A, *32.*

[40] A.B.A. Op. 65; but not in order that he may supplant an existing listee.

[41] App. A, *161.*   [42] *Id., 55, 165.*   [43] *Id., 91.*

[44] *Id., 90.*   [45] A.B.A. Op. 123.

[46] N.Y. County 47 ix(d), 239; N.Y. City 31; 47 A.B.A. Reports 285 (1923), and see A.B.A. Op. 230.

[47] App. A, *163.*   [48] A.B.A. Ops. 233, 234; App. A, *166.*

laymen.[49] A lawyer may not be the sole listee in any locality in a list which he controls.[50]

A list must not hold any lawyer out as undertaking to do anything that he is not legally qualified and entitled to do, and where his right to do anything is qualified, the qualification must be stated.[1]

A lawyer need not object to having his name in a list of lawyers of the community published by the local chamber of commerce, or in a Bar roster, but must not pay to get it in.[2]

Basis for Listing in a Law List

Proper considerations for listing are legal ability, character, financial worth, and promptness in discharging obligations.[3] The ownership of real estate is not a proper basis,[4] or that the lawyer is bonded,[5] or that he is a member of a particular bar association.[6] While a higher charge may properly be made for representation in a large and productive community, such charge may not properly be graded on the amount received over the list, since this would constitute a splitting of fees condemned by Canon 35.[7]

Biographical and Informative Data

No data may appear in the listing except such as is expressly authorized by Canon 27.[8] The test is not as to what is useful to the bar.[9] Biographical data may not be given by reference to some other publication.[10] It may state that he advises on the law of a foreign country, but not that he has an associate admitted there.[11]

One may not be listed as successor to a lawyer whose practice he purchases, but with whom he never was a partner.[12]

There is no rule requiring that all the personnel of the listee's office be listed.[13] "Associates" may include past associates,[14] but if such are no longer with the office, the relationship and dates must be specified.[15] Lawyers admitted in different states may be listed, if the exact status of each is made clear.[16]

---

[49] App. A, 203. [50] A.B.A. Op. 255. [1] App. A, 159.
[2] Id., 167, 168, 169; N.Y. City 740. [3] App. A, 171.
[4] Id., 172. [5] Id., 172, 177, N.Y. County 47 ix(d), 185, 239.
[6] App. A, 173. [7] Id., 174; N.Y. County 47 ix(c); N.Y. City 502.
[8] App. A, 156; see also A.B.A. Op. 123, rendered prior to the amendment of 1937.
[9] App. A, 157. [10] Id., 176. [11] A.B.A. Op. 263.
[12] App. A, 179. [13] Id., 160. [14] Id., 178.
[15] Ibid. [16] A.B.A. Op. 256; N.Y. City 728, 857. See also supra, p. 230.

A list may not state that the firm employs a foreign lawyer not admitted in the jurisdiction.[17]

United States lawyers not admitted in a foreign country and not maintaining an office there, but qualified as advisers on the laws of such country, may be listed in the foreign section of a law list, with a statement that the lawyers are merely advisers on the laws of such country and a clear statement as to where their offices are located.[18]

A United States lawyer not admitted in a foreign country may not be listed for such country, but if a lawyer or firm maintains an office in a foreign country in charge of a resident lawyer or partner, admitted to practice there, the listing for the foreign country is permissible provided it makes clear that the foreign office is in charge of a local lawyer duly admitted to practice there, and that other members of the firm are not admitted to practice there.[19]

A firm maintaining an office in another state having a member admitted there must state clearly that he is the only member there admitted.[20]

The listing in a special section of foreign lawyers resident locally is permitted, but their address should not be given in care of the local firm.[21]

The date of the founding of an office may be stated in a law list as part of the "informative" date authorized by Canon 27.[22]

Addresses

The address of a lawyer's office specified in a law list should be one where he actually practices, and must not be misleading. If a residence address is given, it should be identified as such in case the city or other place of residence is not the same as that in which the law office is located.[23]

"What constitutes a bona fide office will depend upon particular facts and circumstances. Whether the lawyer has a lease of the office, a telephone there, his name on the building directory or office door, and whether there is some one in the office to transact his business, are elements which may be helpful in the determination of such a question—but cannot be regarded as the sole or absolute tests." [24]

It is proper to list a branch office in another state in charge of local

17 App. A, *180*.　　　　　　18 *Id., 181*.　　　　　　　　19 *Id., 182*.
20 *Id., 183;* see also N.Y. City 925.　　21 App. A, *184;* and *supra*, p. 230.
22 *App. A, 185*.　　　　　　23 A.B.A. Op. 249.
24 A.B.A. Op. 249. See also App. A, *187, 188, 189*.

counsel to investigate and adjust claims;[25] but not to have a "branch office" in a store managed by another and useful only to feed business to the lawyer.[26]

References

Prior to the amendment of 1943, it was improper to publish references other than "clients regularly represented," with their consent.[27] Lawyers as well as lay clients may be given as references.[28] Prior to the redrafting of Canon 43 by the amendment of 1942, it provided that a professional card might "give references or name clients for whom the lawyer is counsel, with their permission." Under this provision the formal consent of the client was necessary to list him as a reference.[29] The revision of Canon 43 and the amendment of 1937 to Canon 27 require the client's consent only if he is to be listed as a client. The reference may not state that more names will be furnished on request, since this would imply that there are many more.[30]

Clients Regularly Represented

A lawyer may not list as a client a person whom he knows has made arrangements with other lawyers regularly to represent him, although with the client's consent the lawyer may list him as a reference;[31] but where a former client is named as a reference, it must not state that he is a former client.[32]

Occasional employment by a company which has a general counsel is not "regular" employment permitting the naming of the client in a law list.[33]

Instead of naming the clients, the list may state that they will be given on request.[34]

The statement "representing over 50 insurance companies," or "counsel for several companies" or "A. B. Co. and affiliates" is improper.[35] The designation of "bank clients" or "insurance clients" is proper.[36]

25 App. A, *190*. 26 Mich. No. 26; see also N.Y. City No. 362, and Mo. 8.
27 A.B.A. Op. 236; App. A, *192*. 28 A.B.A. Op. 119.
29 A.B.A. Op. 123. 30 App. A, *193*. 31 *Id., 199*.
32 *Id., 194*. 33 *Id., 198*. 34 *Id., 200*.
35 *Id., 197*. 36 *Ibid.*

Client's Consent

The publisher of the list may rely on the lawyer's statement that such consent has been given, in the absence of advice or appearance to the contrary.[37]

Legal Societies

The American Bar Association Committee has given the following definition:

Within the meaning of Canon 27 a Legal Society is a membership organization composed predominantly of members of the Bar, the object of which is to cultivate the science of jurisprudence, promote reforms of the law and facilitate the administration of justice, and which does not itself engage in commercial or business transactions or render professional or commercial services or serve as a means of inducing or consummating commercial or business transactions with, or the rendition of professional or commercial services by, its members.[38]

An association which includes laymen is not a "legal society," [39] but exceptions have been recognized of associations which now only admit lawyers although some laymen are still members.[40]

The Maritime Law Association is a legal society, but the Commercial Law League is not.[41]

Posts of Honor

After numerous rulings and advice to the Law List Committee as to what were or were not "posts of honor" the American Bar Association Committee finally adopted the rule that a "post of honor" was whatever the listee considers such, but must be inserted under the specific heading "Posts of Honor." [42] As a practical result, the items that a lawyer so chooses to list give a fair indication of his distinction.

Branches of the Profession Practiced

A good deal of the confusion which has existed relative to the publication of cards and announcements by lawyers, has resulted from a failure to distinguish between "branches of the profession" which under Canon 27 may be published in reputable law lists and only thus, and "a specialized legal service" a brief and dignified notice of which, under Canon 46, might be given only when "rendered directly and

---

37 *Id., 196.*   38 *Id., 201.*   39 *Id., 202.*
40 *Id., 203.*   41 *Id., 204.*   42 *Id., 206, 207.*

only to other lawyers," "indicating that it is addressed to lawyers, inserted in legal periodicals and like publications, when it will afford convenient and beneficial information to lawyers desiring to obtain such service. . . ."

"Branches of the profession practiced" is thus of much broader scope than "specialized legal service," as provided in Canon 46 [43] and includes any distinct body of law, nor is it necessary that the lawyer listing it make a specialty of it in his practice, as he must to qualify under Canon 46.

There is no provision in the Canons authorizing the statement of either a special branch of the law practiced by a lawyer on his letterhead,[44] or a specialized legal service anywhere but in legal periodicals and like publications and then only on the conditions specified in Canon 46.[45]

A "branch" is a field of law and not a tribunal [46] and does not refer to work before a special tribunal.[47] The proper way to state a branch is "Law of Negligence," "Anti-trust law," "law of decedent's estates" etc., and not "insurance matters" etc.[48]

The special branches practiced by individual members of the firm may not be specified.[49] "Consultant" or "specializing in corporation law" are improper since they imply exceptional proficiency.[50] "Organization management and control" and "policy and contract claims" are too vague.[51] It is proper to state a branch in a law list as "exclusively" or "only" practiced.[52]

As an exception to the general rule of Canon 27 the law list provision is to be strictly construed.[53]

Legal Authorships

They should include the title of the matter written.[54]

[43] See A.B.A. Op. 194, p. 390.
[44] See *supra*, p. 229; and see A.B.A. Ops. 182, 260, 276; App. A, *117*, but see Mich. No. 77.
[45] See *supra*, pp. 233, 242.   [46] App. A, *211*.   [47] *Id., 212*.
[48] *Id., 211*.   [49] *Id., 218*.   [50] *Id., 213, 214*.
[51] *Id., 215*.   [52] *Id., 216*.
[53] A.B.A. Ops. 145, 194; see also N.Y. City No. 707.   [54] App. A, *220*.

IX

THE CANONS OF
JUDICIAL ETHICS

THE FIRST THIRTY-FOUR Canons of Judicial Ethics were adopted by
the American Bar Association in 1924. They had been prepared by
a committee appointed in 1922, of which Chief Justice Taft was chairman, the other members being Leslie C. Cornish, Chief Justice of
Maine; Robert von Moschzisker, Chief Justice of the Supreme Court
of Pennsylvania; Charles A. Boston (a former President of the Association), of New York; and Garret W. McEnerney,[1] of California.

Canons 28 and 30 were amended in 1933, and Canons 35 and 36
were adopted in 1937. Canon 28 was further amended in 1950 and
Canon 35 in 1952.

While to some it may seem presumptuous for lawyers to formulate
Canons for judicial behavior, the Preamble to the Judicial Canons,
emphasizing that "the character and conduct of a judge should never
be objects of indifference," offers them "as a proper guide and reminder for judges, and as indicating what the people have a right to
expect of them."

In 1945 the American Bar Association Ethics Committee, recognizing the primary function of the judges to pass on their own conduct, recommended to the Board of Governors to authorize the appointment of an Advisory Committee of five judges, to whom the
Committee might turn for advice in cases involving the questioned
propriety of judicial conduct. The original members of this Committee were Circuit Judge Biggs, of Wilmington, Delaware; District
Judge Laws, of Washington, D. C.; Circuit Judge Swan, of New
Haven, Connecticut; District Judge Wilkin, of Cleveland, Ohio; and

---

[1] Mr. McEnerney succeeded George Sutherland, of Wisconsin, originally a member,
who retired, and was in turn succeeded in 1923 by Frank M. Angellotti, of California.

Judge Shientag, of New York City. Chief Justice Hyde, of Missouri, succeeded Judge Shientag after the latter's death in 1952.

While the occasions for calling on them for advice have been infrequent, when consulted they have been most helpful in giving authority to the Committee's rulings.

The Judicial Canons speak for themselves and require no extended comment or interpretation.

Canon 1 points out that the assumption of the office of judge imposes on him duties to the state, to litigants before him, to lawyers, witnesses, jurors and attendants, as well as to the law itself.

Canon 2 reminds the judge that "courts exist to provide justice and thus to serve the public interest" and warns him to "avoid unconsciously falling into the attitude of mind that the litigants are made for the courts instead of the courts for the litigants."

Canon 3 refers to the reciprocal duty of State and Federal judges to support the dual system.

Canon 4, entitled "Avoidance of Impropriety," states that not only the judge's official conduct but also his personal behavior in every day life must be beyond reproach, "free from impropriety and from the appearance of impropriety."

A judge may not properly accept from a lawyer an inadequately secured loan; [2] or participate in a radio program sponsored by a commercial concern, at which legal advice is given; [3] nor may he conduct a newspaper column of comment on current news items and matters of general interest.[4] It would, however, seem entirely proper for a judge to take part in a mock trial, managed by a local bar association, and in a court room, in the evening, for the purpose of acquainting the public with the essential incidents of judicial proceedings.

A lawyer may not properly give presents to or bestow favors on judges before whom he might appear as counsel or litigant, nor may a judge accept such from lawyers, litigants or their friends.[5]

There has been some question as to the propriety of a judge's voluntarily appearing as a character witness for one accused of crime. In an early ruling the American Bar Association Committee held that "in some situations" he might do so in a court where he did not sit.[6] Where a judge has had peculiarly intimate experience and contact

[2] A.B.A. Op. 89.   [3] A.B.A. Op. 166.   [4] A.B.A. Op. 52.
[5] Cleveland 13.   [6] A.B.A. Op. 15 (1929); see also Mich. 50.

with the defendant, rendering him acquainted with relevant characteristics with which others are not equally familiar, doubtless such a situation might be presented. In the ordinary case, however, defendant's lawyer calls on a judge as a character witness primarily to secure the advantage of the prestige attached to his judicial position, an advantage to which a jury will usually give undue weight, and to which the defendant is not entitled. In all but very exceptional cases it is believed that the judge should ask to be excused.[7]

Canons 5 and 6 summarize the "Essential Conduct of a Judge."

Canon 7 is entitled "Promptness." In an article in the *Atlantic Monthly*[8] Lord Moulton gave expression to a profound thought which should never be forgotten by lawyers and judges who cherish the honor and noble traditions of their profession: "The real greatness of the nation, its true civilization, is measured by the extent of Obedience to the Unenforceable."

The judges who habitually keep litigants, lawyers, witnesses and attendants waiting on their convenience, relying on the fact that they are not subject to discipline therefor, are probably the last to recognize themselves as essentially uncivilized.

Canon 8 emphasizes the necessity of efficient court organization and cooperation for the promotion of the effective administration of justice.

Canons 9 and 10 stress consideration for jurors, witnesses, and attendants, both on the part of the court and of court officers and attendants subject to the court's direction and example, particularly courtesy by the court to counsel. An uncivil and discourteous judge cannot realize how the regard and the respect for him by the bar are thus destroyed.

Canon 11 points out the duty of the judge to criticize and correct unprofessional conduct on the part of lawyers. Too often, it is feared, judges learn of such misconduct, yet either from friendship or from a hesitation to make trouble, do nothing about it. One of the principal reasons for the public's suspicion of lawyers is the justified belief that lawyers and judges are loath to proceed against lawyers known or strongly suspected of wrongdoing.

Canon 12 is directed at the abuses in connection with the appoint-

---

[7] See report of special committee of the American Bar Association on this problem. 36 A.B.A. Jour. 630 (1950).

[8] 134 Atlantic Monthly 1, 13 (1924).

ment of trustees, masters, referees, guardians, etc., for reasons other than the necessity therefor, and their selection on a basis other than character and fitness. Such selection is sometimes at the suggestion of outsiders; also the allowance of excessive compensation, which, as the Canon points out, is not justified by the failure of counsel to object.[9]

Canon 13 deals with the problem presented when a relative is a party to a controversy before the judge. This, together with Canon 14, entitled "Independence," Canon 24 entitled "Inconsistent Obligations," Canon 26 entitled "Personal Investments and Relations," Canon 29 entitled "Self Interest," Canon 32 entitled "Gifts and Favors," and Canon 33 entitled "Social Relations" cover the same general ground with regard to the judge as Canon 6 of Professional Ethics [10]—the duty to avoid every situation where personal interest may contaminate judicial impartiality.

It is obvious that a judge should not sit in a case in which a near relative is a party. Some judges offer not to sit if they hold stock in a corporate party. It is not so clear that he may not try one in which his son is counsel.[11] In the latter case he should, it is believed, avoid, if possible, sitting without colleagues. There would, however, appear to be no impropriety in a judge's being a member of an appellate court before which his former partner argues an appeal.[12] In close cases the judge must be influenced not merely by the possibility of bias on his part, but by the fact that to the public it may so appear. In such cases it is an individual problem for the judge.

Canon 15 is directed at the tendency of some judges unduly to interfere in the examination of witnesses and by the interruption of an argument by counsel. A wise, experienced, and patient judge can properly draw the line between courteous and tactful intervention in the interest of expedition and clarity,[13] and one prompted by impatience or a tendency to be dictatorial.

By Canon 16 the judge is warned of the dangers inherent in *ex parte* applications, and urged to be sparing in their allowance and careful in safeguarding them.

[9] See N.Y. County 422 (1953).

[10] Canon 6, "Adverse Influences and Conflicting Interests." In A.B.A. Op. 22 that Committee held it improper for a judge to be a member of the National Guard or of the Reserve Officers Corps, but reversed this ruling in Op. 215.

[11] See A.B.A. Op. 200; see also *supra*, p. 72; also as to barristers, An. St. (1895–96), p. 6.

[12] But see A.B.A. Op. 142.

[13] One of the judge's duties is to "render it disagreeable for counsel to talk nonsense." Sharswood, *Professional Ethics*, p. 63.

Similarly Canon 17 frowns on all private interviews in the absence of opposing counsel, as well as the receipt of briefs and written communications without copies to the other side.[14]

Canon 18 is directed against an abuse of discretion in granting continuances without proper ground therefor, resulting in unreasonable delay and in injustice to the party and counsel whose case has been carefully prepared.

Canons 19 and 20 discuss the principles to be observed in the preparation of decisions and written opinions. Counsel are entitled, it is pointed out, to a reasoned discussion of points seriously argued; questions which will arise in a new trial should be settled; decisions should be as succinct as the case demands, and should be directed to the constructive development of the law rather than to the enhancement of the judge's individual reputation.

Canon 21 decries the indulgence of the judge's idiosyncracies.

Canon 22 emphasizes the duty to secure to defeated counsel a full review on a fair record.

Canon 23 points out the judge's exceptional opportunity and duty to promote constructive legislation, especially that relating to procedure.

Canon 24 condemns the acceptance of inconsistent obligations.

Canon 25 is directed at and condemns the practice of some judges in using the prestige of their office to further business ventures and particularly charitable enterprises. It is manifestly improper for a judge thus mildly to coerce members of the bar to contribute to his favorite charity,[15] nor should he be director of a bank.[16] He may not allow his name to be used in the solicitation of a fund to defend one accused of crime.[17]

Canon 26 suggests that a judge's personal investments be confined to those in enterprises which are not apt to involve any litigation in his court, and to those of a non-speculative nature.

Canon 27, while recognizing the propriety of a judge's acting as a fiduciary in proper cases, confines this to those cases where this will in no way interfere with the proper performance of his judicial duties.

---

[14] See also *supra*, pp. 78, 198.   [15] A.B.A. Op. 238.

[16] A.B.A. Op. 254. He may, however, it is believed, serve as director of a private family corporation. He should not sell bonds or allow his name to be used in connection with such sale. N.Y. County 133. See also N.Y. City B-203.

[17] Mich. 143; see also Mich. 30, 43.

Canon 28, entitled "Partisan Politics," as amended in 1933, condemned all participating in political campaigns and discussions, including speeches, endorsement of candidates, and contributions.[18] In 1950 it was amended by adding the following provision:

Where, however, it is necessary for judges to be nominated and elected as candidates of a political party, nothing herein contained shall prevent the judge from attending or speaking at political gatherings, or from making contributions to the campaign funds of the party that has nominated him and seeks his election or reelection.

Canon 29, entitled "Self-interest," is the judicial equivalent of Professional Canon 6. It points out, however, that if a case involving the judge personally gets into his court, he need not resign as judge, but must, of course, refrain from any participation in the case.[19]

Canon 30 entitled "Candidacy for Office," as amended in 1933, embodies the judge's duty when a candidate for office, whether judicial [20] or non-judicial.[21] In a number of cases judges have deliberately ignored the admonition that before running for a non-judicial office, they should resign their judicial position, in some cases relying on the fact that their predecessors in such violation of the Canon have not been disciplined therefor. In its Opinion 193, the American Bar Association Committee sought (unsuccessfully) to preclude this by a full statement of its construction of Judicial Canon 30.

Canon 31 is entitled "Private Law Practice." In jurisdictions where judicial compensation is not sufficient to provide an adequate living and where, in consequence, judges are permitted to engage in private practice, they are nevertheless precluded by the Canons enjoining the representation of conflicting interests, from acting in any matters where such is the case. See also Professional Canons 6 and 41. A lawyer may in no event practice in the court in which he sits as judge.[22] He may, however, properly act as arbitrator, or write or lecture on legal subjects where this does not interfere or conflict with his judicial duties.[23]

18 A.B.A. Op. 113; Mo. 57.   19 See A.B.A. Op. 170.

20 A candidate for judge should not radio-cast opinions on legal problems: A.B.A. Op. 93; or solicit the aid of lawyers by letter or otherwise: A.B.A. Ops. 105, 139, 189; see also Op. 226; but may state in his campaign literature that he is a lawyer, Mich. 36. See also Mich. 74.

21 See A.B.A. Ops. 193 and 195; cf. also Op. 164; also Mich. 121, 154, and Cleveland 11.

22 A.B.A. Ops. 142, 143. See Mo. 30, 67.

23 As to the conflicting obligations of prosecutors and of judges of inferior courts in representing defendants in criminal cases, see A.B.A. Ops. 30, 39, 55, 110, 135, 138, 142, 161, 242. See also Cleveland 12 and N.Y. City B-203.

Canon 32 cautions the judge against receiving gifts and favors from litigants or lawyers.

Canon 33 entitled "Social Relations" seeks to draw a proper line between social ostracism and seclusion, and the appearance of suspicious intimacy.

Canon 34, with which the Canons originally adopted in 1924 concluded, summarizes the judicial obligation as follows:

In every particular his conduct should be above reproach. He should be conscientious, studious, thorough, courteous, patient, punctual, just, impartial, fearless of public clamor, regardless of public praise, and indifferent to private political or partisan influences; he should administer justice according to law, and deal with his appointments as a public trust; he should not allow other affairs or his private interests to interfere with the prompt and proper performance of his judicial duties, nor should he administer the office for the purpose of advancing his personal ambitions or increasing his popularity.

Canons 35 and 36, as adopted in 1937, were very strict in precluding unnecessary publicity of court proceedings, as unbefitting the dignity and decorum of the administration of justice.[24]

In 1952, in response to a strong desire by the bar associations to acquaint the public with the nature and seriousness of naturalization proceedings, the House of Delegates, on the recommendation of the American Bar Association Ethics Committee, amended Canon 35, as below indicated, to read as follows:

Proceedings in court should be conducted with fitting dignity and decorum. The taking of photographs in the court room, during sessions of the court or recesses between sessions, and the broadcasting *or televising* of court proceedings are calculated to detract from the essential dignity of the proceedings, *distract the witness in giving his testimony,* degrade the court, and create misconceptions with respect thereto in the mind of the public and should not be permitted.

Provided that this restriction shall not apply to the broadcasting or televising, under the supervision of the court, of such portions of naturalization proceedings (other than the interrogation of applicants,) as are designed and carried out exclusively as a ceremony for the purpose of publicly demonstrating in an impressive manner the essential dignity and the serious nature of naturalization.

Canon 36 remains as adopted in 1937, as follows:

Proceedings in court should be so conducted as to reflect the importance and seriousness of the inquiry to ascertain the truth.

24 A.B.A. Ops. 67, 212. See also Cleveland 18; Mich. 1.

The oath should be administered to witnesses in a manner calculated to impress them with the importance and solemnity of their promise to adhere to the truth. Each witness should be sworn separately and impressively at the bar of the court, and the clerk should be required to make a formal record of the administration of the oath, including the name of the witness.

APPENDIX A

DECISIONS BY THE
AMERICAN BAR ASSOCIATION
ETHICS COMMITTEE
HITHERTO UNREPORTED

Functions of Committees

1. The function of the Ethics Committee is the interpretation of the Canons; that of interpreting the rules and standards is the Law List Committee. The Ethics Committee does not pass on questions of law, and will take no action while legal proceedings are pending.
2. The Ethics Committee will not inquire into or enforce Canon 27 relative to the names of lawyers in publications which are not law lists unless specific complaints are made.
3. The Committee in an early ruling (1922) held that it would not entertain a complaint against a judge where the case was not clear and where the offense was not flagrant.
4. Complaints against non-members and occasionally complaints against members are sent to the local associations. The American Bar Association's disciplinary powers are applicable to its members only.
5. Where a bar association has a Committee on Unauthorized Practice, the Ethics Committee of that association is bound by its decisions as to what constitutes unauthorized practice, even though such Ethics Committee may not agree.

Legal Effect of the Canons

6. No decisions have been found holding that a contract is void or unenforceable merely because a lawyer is party to a transaction in violation of a Canon, where the practice is not one which is held unlawful apart from the Canon. Accordingly, where a lawyer has agreed to divide his fee with a trust officer of a bank, who is also a lawyer, but who has performed no service, if he agrees in violation of the Canons

to pay the trust officer, he does so at his peril; and similarly in the case of an agreement to pay 40 per cent to the estate of a deceased partner.

DISBARMENT

7. The Committee advised against the employment of a disbarred lawyer, even to do only office work and seeing no clients, "because of the practical difficulty of confining his activities to an area which does not include practice of law, and because such employment would show disrespect to the courts."

8. The practice in the American Bar Association has been not to accept the resignation of a member against whom charges are pending.

DUTY OF THE LAWYER TO THE PUBLIC

9. It is the duty of a lawyer to oppose an unfit candidate for a judge.

GENERAL DUTY OF UPRIGHT BEHAVIOR [1]

10. He may not refuse to represent a bankrupt except on condition that the bankrupt pay the lawyer's clients in full.

11. The acceptance of a retainer to act as general counsel implies a purpose to observe the Canons and creates no obligation to violate them in order to further the interest of his client.

12. A lawyer employed by a convicted felon who has hidden jewelry may not make an agreement to accept part of the jewelry for his fee provided its whereabouts be disclosed to him, his purpose being not to keep the jewelry but to tell its whereabouts to the authorities. "It is not justifiable under any circumstances for a lawyer to double-cross a client who employs him."

14. A lawyer of a fugitive from justice may not properly advise him not to surrender because he believes that public hysteria would prevent his getting a fair trial.

15. The seller of a valuable machine, not paid for, endeavored to recover. It was attached to the real estate and under local law the mortgagee of the real estate had a right superior to that of the vendor. The mortgagee was not interested in the machine but connived with the vendee-mortgagor to squeeze out the vendor by asserting his superior right, the machine to be turned over to the vendee on payment by the latter of all the mortgagee's expenses, including counsel fees. The Committee advised the inquiring chairman of a local grievance committee that it was improper for the lawyers of the mortgagee and vendee to represent them in carrying out this scheme.

16. Where a lawyer who had drawn a will for a client when of undoubted mental capacity is asked to draw a new will for him when there is

[1] See also "Duty to Client, Fiduciary."

some slight doubt as to his capacity, he may do so, but should retain the old will; and he should turn over to the client's new and responsible lawyer a copy of a will he drew for such a one.

17. Where the insurance policy requires that the insured shall allow the insurer to defend, this is a consent under Canon 6.

18. Where a judgment was entered in connection with a tax deficiency passed upon by the Board of Tax Appeals, and by reason of a possibly erroneous application of the principles laid down, the commissioner had computed the deficiency too favorably to the lawyer's client, the lawyer is not censurable for failing to disclose his belief that a mistake of law had been made by the commissioner.

19. A lawyer may accept employment to endeavor to persuade a relative to change his will provided the lawyer's status be disclosed to the proposed testator.

20. A member of the bar is bound to disclose to other lawyers on a legislative committee an interest on his part in the subject being considered by the committee.

21. He may not close the mouth of an important witness to a murder. (See also 304.)

DUTY NOT TO ADVERTISE OR SOLICIT

Full v. Part-Time Positions

26. A lawyer may advertise his desire to acquire an interest in a firm or a full-time position on a salary basis with a business corporation.

27. A lawyer may not solicit a bank for the position of general counsel where this position is not a full-time one; but he may apply for a full-time position in the patent department of a corporation.

Immaterial That There Is No Statement That He Is a Lawyer

29. The fact that an advertisement for what is legal work does not state that the advertiser is a lawyer is no justification of it.

Bar Rosters, etc.

31. Law schools, fraternities, service clubs, and bar associations may publish rosters, registers, catalogs, or lists of their members, with their names, addresses, and occupations, which are not law lists, where no charge is made for listing and there is no suggestion that the names of lawyers are listed as probably available for professional employment, or to promote, solicit, or secure professional employment.

32. A lawyers' organization may circulate a list of its members among themselves.

34. A lawyer may advertise a placement bureau for lawyers.

Right to Conduct an Independent Business

37. He may publish a newspaper and write editorials but not to exploit himself as a lawyer.
38. While he may conduct a real estate business in another county,
39. he can hardly conduct a stock business,
40. or operate a collection agency,
41. or a marriage counselling bureau,
42. or an investment counsel service,
43. or estate planning or any other business, from his law office without violating Canon 27.
44. As to investment counsel, an inquirer was advised by the chairman, with the approval of the Committee, as follows:

".. . If you conduct your investment advisory business from a distinct office, under distinct letterheads, with no thought or purpose of using this business as a feeder for the law practice; if you give the business a distinct non-legal name, such as 'expert advice on investments' and if in actual practice the carrying on of such a business does not develop into what is apparently a feeder for the law business, the advertisement of such distinct branch would not, under the rulings of the Committee, violate the canon.

"You must bear in mind, nevertheless, that any activity carried on by a lawyer which measurably uses his legal knowledge and training (such as making out income tax returns) is considered by the Committee the practice of law, even though it may properly be done by one not a member of the bar. Also, in a community where one is generally known by all business men as a lawyer, it might well be impossible to divorce two occupations so nearly related as investment counsel and legal advice.

"While, as I stated, theoretically you might advertise as an expert on investments and steer clear of the inhibition of Canon 27, I should think that as a practical matter you were so likely sooner or later, particularly in a small community, to run afoul of Canon 27, that you would be wiser not to advertise, but to permit your proficiency as investment adviser to become known through the cumulative satisfaction of your clients." (See also 76.)

45. He may be the agent of a bonding company and write formal bonds in cases he is in, but should not write large bonds where the client's adverse interest might lead him to take a chance at the expense of the insurance company.
46. A lawyer or his partner or associate may act as notary in a case which he is conducting provided no local statute forbids this.

Law Books and Teaching v. Law Practice

51. There is a clear distinction between permitting the advertisement of law books and of a law practice.

52. Teaching law is not practicing law, and the solicitation of students in law schools is not forbidden by Canon 27.

Certain Activities Which Are Proper for a Lawyer

54. A lawyer may bond himself, but may not give publicity to this.
55. He may properly answer questions by a list publisher as to the proper rating of other lawyers,
56. and may permit a chamber of commerce to include him in a list of lawyers as part of the general activity of the community,
57. and may, in the preface of a law book, acknowledge the assistance of other lawyers in writing it.
58. Great care should be exercised by lawyers and judges in endorsing law works sold by publishers; both the lawyers and the publishers should refrain from reference to any specific causes and also from reference to the lawyers' position generally or in the particular field of work covered.
60. A candidate for the legislature may write to voters on his letterhead if not intended as an advertisement.
61. He may advise clients of administrative orders or changes in the law in a manner that does not smack of advertising,
62. a personal letter to the client being in better taste than a circular.
63. It is not improper for a lawyer in good faith to fill out answers to applications from *Who's Who*,
64. although this may be done in such a way as to amount to advertising, in violation of Canon 27,
65. as may the publicity in connection with his candidacy for a political office,
66. or the use of a corporation organized by him.
67. Under exceptional circumstances but only with the approval of the proper court, it may be proper for the lawyers who have created a fund to ask parties entitled to participate in it to pay their share of the expenses of creating it, as a condition of such participation.
68. He may have "attorney at law" printed on his checks.
70. Where he represents a party in litigation whose interest it is to locate missing heirs, he may publicize the facts for this purpose.
76. While a lawyer may send to his clients a summary of recent legislation changing the law, or a suggestion based on recent decisions or legislation clearly in the interest of the particular client, he may not properly send to clients generally a notice of an estate planning service which is capable of interpretation as a bid for employment.
77. A lawyer may not, through a corporation organized by him, solicit employment in organizing corporations;
78. nor may he search for unknown heirs and solicit their employment of him.

79. A law firm may not acquiesce in the publication by a magazine of a laudatory history of the firm, or allow itself to be listed as counsel for a community chest.
80. The fact that a lawyer has inspected properties as a Government agent does not justify him in subsequently sending cards to the firms inspected.
81. He may not properly write to advise clients of a new service which his office offers,
82. or stamp his professional card on the reprint of a law article by him.
83. He may not properly submit a competitive bid for his services to the Government or other bodies and persons requiring legal services.

Examples of Indirect Solicitation

86. A lawyer may not properly distribute generally diaries with his name on them even though he does not state that he is a lawyer,
87. or have an insignia on his automobile license plates indicating, directly or indirectly, that he is a lawyer;
88. nor may he properly have his card printed on a blotter to be sent to clients and friends to be used on their desks;
89. nor may he send to a client a copy of the revenue laws or a reprint of a legal article with his name stamped on it;
90. nor send to a law list publisher for dissemination outside the list, information of a character not properly includable in the list;
91. nor send out a statement as to which lists include him.
92. It was considered by the Committee to be indirect solicitation for a lawyer to secure statistics from various practicing lawyers with whom he had exchanged business, relative to various facts;
93. or for a patent lawyer himself to send out letters asking for ideas to patent, although primarily for the benefit of a corporation which he represented.
94. He may not send out match boxes with his name and address printed on them,
95. or insert his card in the high school or college paper.

Indirect Purchase of Practice

98. A lawyer may not offer to draw a will for nothing provided the client will recommend him to the executor as counsel to be employed in the settlement of the estate;
99. nor may he offer his services free to labor unions with the hope of obtaining employment by the members;
100. nor to real estate brokers in order, in drafting papers, to make contacts with potential clients;
101. nor may a lawyer, who is also a C.P.A. make an arrangement with a bank to make out tax returns free for its customers in order that he thus may make their acquaintance.

Personal Relations

105. This means primarily professional relations and not social relations.
106. " 'Personal relations,' means either intimate friendship (which would prompt the addressee to be interested in the fact of Mr. S.'s becoming a lawyer, apart from any possibility of sending him business) or some prior indication by the addressee that when Mr. S. was admitted he wished to know about it."
107. It would not justify the sending of an announcement to the 1,800 members of his church.

LETTERHEADS

111. A letterhead may name the living members of the firm on one side and the deceased ones with the dates of membership on the other side;
112. or may place "(deceased)" after the names of the latter.
113. It is not proper for a letterhead to state the date when an office was established.
114. It is improper to date each letter: "Feb. 4—of the X Law Office the 97th year—1939."
115. A lawyer's letterhead should not state that he is a C.P.A.;
116. or M.D. or Doctor of Jurisprudence;
117. or specify any branch practiced by him other than specified in the 1951 amendment;
118. or state that he has been States Attorney,
119. or judge,
120. or that he is a member of a stated bar association, or a Senator or Governor, or a member of Congress,
121. or list his degrees or give references;
122. or give the names as associates of persons having no legal relations to the firm,
123. or the name of a non-lawyer notary,
124. or of an engineer;
127. or state that he is admitted in another state;
128. or specify other occupations in which he is engaged.
129. It need not specify who are the partners.

SHINGLES

131. A neon sign is improper as a shingle.
132. The test is whether the sign is intended and calculated to enable persons looking for a lawyer, already selected, to find him, or to attract the attention of persons who might be looking for a lawyer although not for him.
133. He should not have a shingle at his residence when he has an office where he practices.
134. It is improper to state on his door that he was formerly a judge,

135. or that he is a doctor of jurisprudence;
136. or to state a special branch practiced, other than specified in the 1951 amendment.

ANNOUNCEMENTS

139. An announcement of one returning from service should not specify special branches practiced,
140. and should not be published in a newspaper,
141. but may be in the legal journal.
142. Notice of the removal of an office to another building should be by printed card mailed to regular clients and not be by newspaper advertisement.
143. On returning from military service a lawyer may send a dignified notice to former clients and members of the bar so stating,
144. but may not state his specialty.
145. He may not send an announcement card to firms which he had inspected from the Department of Labor.
146. As to the card on returning to practice the Committee said:
    "It is entirely proper for you to send out announcement cards that you are returning to practice at your designated offices, these to be sent to attorneys and to former clients, and to any other persons with whom your personal relations are such as to make it clear that they would be interested in knowing that you were back, but not, of course, to persons with whom you have had no professional dealings or relations and to whom this card will be merely a suggestion that they employ you."
147. If a partner or associate, the notice should be sent by the firm and not by the individual.
148. An announcement of the admission of new members to a firm may be sent to persons who might be regarded as interested to know of it.

TELEPHONE DIRECTORIES

149. It is improper to classify lawyers in a telephone directory under several titles in addition to that of lawyers, such as Contract Lawyers, Copyright Lawyers, Patent Lawyers, Trade Mark Lawyers. (See Opinion 284.)
150. Where by mistake a lawyer was omitted from the telephone book, the proper practice is not to insert an advertisement but to send a letter to those whose personal relations warrant this.

BAR ASSOCIATION ADVERTISING

151. "Any bar advertising will naturally have the result of giving employment to lawyers, and is so intended. The question is one of degree. A bar advertisement should not be condemned merely because it is cal-

culated to bring business to lawyers, but should be judged as to whether the benefit to the public in learning of the advantages of employing lawyers is sufficient to justify it."

152. The bar association doing the advertising should retain title to the copy.

153. As a result of the sincere effort of the bar to protect the public against improperly drawn instruments, lawyers may (at the suggestion of the bar association) stamp such instruments as having been drafted by them.

Law Lists

GENERAL PRINCIPLES

156. Canon 27 (with Canon 46) states all the exceptions to the general rule prohibiting direct or indirect advertising by lawyers. What is not specified is not permissible.

157. The test is not what is useful but what is expressly permitted.

159. ". . . The gist of the matter seems to be that the listing shall tell the truth, the whole truth, and nothing but the truth. It must not hold any lawyer out as undertaking to do anything that he is not legally qualified and entitled to do, and where his right to do anything is qualified, the qualification must be stated."

160. A list need not specify the entire personnel of a law firm.

161. A lawyer may pay an agency to advise him as to the lists in which it is advisable for him to be included.

162. The law list committee should wait a reasonable time to permit the law list publisher to have it approved.

163. A listing contract may not provide that legal fees will be waived where a collection is not remitted within five days.

164. The A.B.A. Committee will not pass directly on what constitutes a "reputable" list, this being the function of the Special Committee on Law Lists.

165. A lawyer may give to a list data to enable it to rate him.

166. He may not properly be listed with laymen.

167. A lawyer need not object to having his name in a list of lawyers in the community published by the local chamber of commerce,

168. or in a bar roster,

169. but may not pay to get it in.

BASIS FOR LISTING

171. Proper considerations for listing by the publisher of a law list are legal ability, character, financial worth, promptness in discharging obligations.

172. A lawyer may not be listed on the basis of being the owner of real estate, this to be indicated by a symbol, or on the basis that he is bonded,

173. or that he is a member of a particular bar association.

174. Although a higher list charge may be exacted for listing in larger communities where the responsibility of the list for efficient service is greater, nevertheless fees for listing should not be based on fees received or likely to be. To permit this would in effect be paying the lay agency for the business it might direct to the lawyer.

BIOGRAPHICAL SKETCH

176. A biographical sketch may not show that the lawyer is the compiler of a digest of the laws of a foreign country. It may show that he was or is counsel for or member of a committee for revising statutes or codes, but biographical data may not be given by reference to some other publication.

177. It may not state that he is bonded.

178. "Associates" may include past as well as present associates, but in the case of past associates the nature of the relationship and the dates should be indicated.

179. One may not be listed as successor to a lawyer whose practice he purchases but with whom he never was a partner.

180. A list may not state that the firm employs a foreign lawyer not admitted in the jurisdiction.

181. United States lawyers not admitted in a foreign country and not maintaining an office there, but qualified as advisers on the laws of such country, may be listed in the foreign section of a law list, with a statement that the lawyers are merely advisers on the laws of such country and a clear statement as to where their offices are located.

182. A United States lawyer not admitted in a foreign country may not be listed for such country, but if a lawyer or firm maintains an office in a foreign country in charge of a resident lawyer or partner, admitted to practice there, the listing for the foreign country is permissible provided it makes clear that the foreign office is in charge of a local lawyer duly admitted to practice there, and that other members of the firm are not admitted to practice there.

183. A firm maintaining an office in another state having a member admitted there must state clearly that he is the only member there admitted.

184. Foreign lawyers, resident in New York, not admitted to practice there, may be listed under "foreign lawyers resident in New York (not admitted to practice in New York)" but not in care of a New York firm, even though the address be the same as that of a New York firm.

185. The date of founding an office may be stated in a law list as part of the authorized informative data.

OFFICE

187. "There is no canon or ruling of the Committee that a practicing lawyer must confine himself to one office in the county where he is admitted to practice. We have ruled that he may maintain an office

at his home in addition to his regular office, provided he makes it clear that the home office is at his home. It is also not necessary that a lawyer be at a specific office for any particular number of hours in a day. If circumstances warrant it, a lawyer or firm may properly maintain a branch office for the convenience of clients, provided there is someone in the office to make appointments with clients, which he could keep there. Wherever this Committee has sanctioned the maintenance of branch offices, they have been the bona fide branch offices of the lawyer, and not merely a fiction office for him, which is really the office of some other lawyer with whom he has no real connection.

"The question arises most frequently in connection with listings in law lists. The Law List Committee has instructed the publishers to ascertain from listees of branch offices the following information:

"1. Do you have a lease from the building for space occupied or a sublease from a tenant of said building?

"2. Do you have a telephone for your office?

"3. Do you have your name on the directory of the building and on the door of your office?

"4. Is there someone qualified to transact business for you and in your behalf, if you do not spend all your time there?"

188. A lawyer may maintain an office in conjunction with his home where such office is completely established and maintained as a full-time law office.

"The mere fact that it is physically located under the same roof as the lawyer's home should not compel its listing as a residence if the lawyer objects to doing so. But in every instance where a lawyer maintains in conjunction with his residence an office which is anything less than a fully equipped maintained office it must be designated as a residence address."

189. An office which is a mere front is not bona fide.

190. A firm was held justified in maintaining offices in other states, in charge of a local lawyer, duly admitted there, to investigate insurance claims, and so stating in a law list.

REFERENCES

192. References were not permissible prior to 1943.

193. The reference may not state that more names will be furnished on request, since this implies that there are many more.

194. Where a former client is named as a reference, it must not state that he is a former client.

CLIENTS REGULARLY REPRESENTED

196. A law list publisher may rely on a lawyer's statement that the client's consent has been given except where the facts are reasonably suspicious.

197. Clients may be classified, but a general statement, such as "repre-

senting over 50 insurance companies," or "counsel for several companies," is improper, or "A. B. Co. and affiliates & associated companies."

198. Occasional employment by a company which has a general counsel
is not "regular" employment permitting the naming of the client in
a law list.

199. One may not list as a client a person whom he knows has made arrangements with other lawyers regularly to represent them, although,
with his consent, he may list him as a reference.

200. Instead of naming clients, the list may state that their names will be
given on request.

LEGAL SOCIETIES

201. "Within the meaning of Canon 27 a Legal Society is a membership
organization composed predominantly of members of the Bar, the
object of which is to cultivate the science of jurisprudence, promote
reforms of the law and facilitate the administration of justice, and
which does not itself engage in commercial or business transactions
or render professional or commercial services or serve as a means of
inducing or consummating commercial or business transactions with,
or the rendition of professional or commercial services by, its members."

202. An association which includes laymen is not a legal society;

203. but the American Patent Association and the Chicago Patent Association may be listed, as they now admit only lawyers.

204. The Maritime Law Association is a legal society, but the Commercial
Law League is not.

POSTS OF HONOR

206. The 1942 amendment broadened this exception beyond public posts.

207. After giving detailed answers to the Law List Committee for some
years the Ethics Committee finally defined posts of honor as follows:
"Any office or position to which a listee is elected or appointed by
another person or persons, and which he deems a 'post of honor' and
designates as such in his biographical data shall be regarded as coming within that phrase."

BRANCHES

211. A branch should be stated as "corporation law," "law of insurance,"
etc.,

212. and not as a tribunal, as "practice before the I.C.C.,"

213. or as "specializing in corporation law," since this implies exceptional
proficiency,

214. as does "consultant in law."

215. "Organization, management and control" and "policy and contract
claims" are too indefinite.

216. The list may specify a branch as practiced "exclusively,"
218. The specialities for individual partners may not be specified.

LEGAL AUTHORSHIPS

220. Legal authorships should include the title of the matter written.

LEGAL ARTICLES, SPEECHES, RADIO, TV

CANON 40

226. Articles on legal subjects in a newspaper sponsored by the local or junior bar association may be signed by the authors and are proper if bona fide.
227. Articles in lay publications should not contain references to decided cases, nor should such an article say that reference to decided cases will be furnished on request.
228. A lawyer may not answer on a radio program specific questions with reference to the law; for a lawyer thus to answer general questions is fairly certain to involve him, sooner or later, in the violation of Canon 40 and Canon 27.

SPECIALIZED LEGAL SERVICES

CANON 46

231. Services to lawyers in the preliminaries and incidents to litigation, such as filing papers, taxing costs, etc., are not a specialized legal service under Canon 46.
232. nor is the "law and practice of New Jersey,"
233. nor jury trials,
234. nor arguing cases in the Supreme Court,
235. nor consultant on Florida law,
236. nor conducting a legal research bureau for lawyers,
237. nor bankruptcy and insolvent law and reorganizations,
238. nor tax matters, income tax matters, federal taxation, or taxes and estates.
239. Canon 46 applies only when the service is solely to other lawyers, and does not permit a mailed notice.

FAIRNESS TO OTHER LAWYERS

241. A lawyer has been employed by a firm on its staff for ten years at a salary and in addition has been allowed to handle cases for his own clients, keeping the fees. One of the clients offers to give him a retainer to become that client's general counsel. The Committee held that where this was not solicited directly or indirectly he might accept it. Where he leaves the firm to establish his own private practice he

may send an announcement to his individual clients but not to the clients of the firm whom he had served.

242. A lawyer is under no duty to protect the fee owing to another lawyer,
243. even where he supersedes him.
244. A lawyer has no vested interest to represent the estate of one whose will he has drawn. The executors have the right to choose their own lawyer.

Duty Not to Approach the Other Party

CANON 9

249. Where three persons are accused of related thefts, the prosecutor may not, in the proceedings against one of them, interview another of them represented by counsel, except with the latter's lawyer.
250. The mother of an injured minor child is so far identified with it that it is improper for the insurance company to interview her where the child is represented by counsel.

Duty and Relations to the Court

251. A lawyer may not informally discuss a case with the judge without the other lawyer's presence, nor should the judge permit this.
252. A lawyer may not directly or indirectly make a loan to a judge.
253. It is improper to hand any brief or memorandum to the judge without giving a copy to the other side, even with the judge's permission.
255. A lawyer may tell a judge respectfully of a reason that it is important to the client to have an early decision, either by proper letter or by personal discussion, but with the other lawyer present if oral and a copy to him if written. He should ask the other lawyer to go with him to see the judge. If the other lawyer will not do so, he should tell the judge that this has been requested.
256. Canon 20, precluding newspaper discussion of pending litigations, applies not only to discussion in newspapers, but to any discussion in a magazine, including legal magazines or other publications, intended or calculated to influence the decision in a pending case in which the writer is counsel, and would also include, by implication, similar radio and television broadcasts.

Duty toward Jurors

257. A lawyer may not write to or communicate with jurors either before or after trial.
258. Jurors should conduct their deliberations and reach their verdict with the assurance that, except for fraud, there will be no subsequent investigation by any one of their deliberations.
259. The separation of witnesses is not required.

DUTY TO THE CLIENT

261. A lawyer may not deduct fees owed by one client from the account collected for another one through a collecting agent.

262. Although under some circumstances it is conceivable that a lawyer might borrow money from a client, he should never take advantage of the confidence reposed in him to delay payment until the statute of limitations has run and where he does so he should not hide behind it.

263. Because of the knowledge and experience of the testator's lawyer with his affairs and property, it is often to the advantage of the estate that he represent the executor in its administration, and where the testator himself desires this it is not improper for the lawyer to insert an appropriate provision in the will or in a supplementary instruction to the executor so suggesting,

264. the testator being advised by him, however, that such a provision in his will is not mandatory on the executor, no matter what its terms,

265. and the executor being always free to choose his own counsel.

266. In such cases, as well as in cases where the testator desires to name the lawyer as executor or trustee or to leave him a legacy, the lawyer should consider having the testator submit the will to another lawyer prior to its execution.

267. A lawyer may not join a union of the employer's employees.

268. An executor lawyer may buy an asset at an auction conducted by a judge.

269. As regards his duty to turn over to his client inventions developed by him during his employment, the fiduciary relation of a patent lawyer is much more exacting than that of an ordinary employee. While the arrangement may possibly be such as to entitle the lawyer to retain for his own benefit ideas germinated and developed coincident with his work in the field of his employment, he should in any event give the client the first right to acquire such ideas or inventions, and in case of any doubt as to the right of the client to have them turned over to him without charge should resolve such doubt in favor of the client.

271. A lawyer may not refuse to handle a debtor's bankruptcy proceedings except on condition that after the adjudication the bankrupt sign new notes to the creditors whom the lawyer represents.

272. It is not unethical to bring a suit barred by the statute of limitations, which may be waived;

273. conversely a lawyer may set up the statute of limitations in a suit against him personally, unless he has done something to lull the other side.

274. Where a delay by counsel on the other side is not because of illness or accident, the lawyer may not waive such delay and not inform his client. If it is proper that it should be corrected, the court can do this.

Rebates, etc.

CANON 38

276. Where a court fixes a fee as reasonable, it is improper to make an additional charge.

277. A lawyer should not, even with the approval of his client, accept a commission from an insurance company which issued the policies as to which the lawyer gave an advisory opinion.

278. ". . . A lawyer may not properly accept a gratuity . . . from anyone without his client's knowledge and consent, and if he does so the gratuity really belongs to the client, who, of course, may make the attorney's fee more generous by reason of it, but is not bound to do so."

Financial Interest in Litigation

280. A lawyer may acquire interest in a patent for his fee.

Conflict of Interest

281. The former partner of a judge may appear before him. There is no general two-year rule, as in some states.

282. A lawyer may represent the member of a secret society threatened with expulsion, in a hearing within the society, though he may also be a witness.

283. A lawyer, who disqualified himself as a witness because he drew the will making him executor, was held entitled to receive compensation for advice and attendance at the trial of the will case.

284. Two lawyers who share offices, though not partners, bear such a close relation to one another as to bring Canon 6 into play.

285. A salaried patent lawyer for one corporation may accept a position as patent lawyer in another, though the latter is engaged in litigation with the first, provided the first consents and the lawyer did not participate in any matter involving knowledge of facts gained while he was in the employ of the first.

286. A lawyer's induction into the military service does not prevent his arguing a case against the Government,

287. nor his election to Congress from going on with a case in the Federal court.

288. One employed by an agency of the United States may write and publish a treatise involving legal problems in such agency and express his opinions contrary to those held in such department, he not then being employed in such department, although employed in another Government department.

289. A lawyer who is an employee should not take employee cases against the company.

290. He may not be paid by a trust company to draw wills naming it as trustee.
291. A lawyer must disclose to the other members of the bar association committee any interest he has which would unduly influence him in work or recommendations for the committee.
292. Since a prosecuting attorney cannot take a private case involving the same facts after his term of office is over, a fortiori he cannot take it while he is still serving.
293. A former prosecutor may not, on an appeal, represent a party prosecuted, though he is confined to the printed record. His experience would enable him to piece things together.

Consent of the Client

296. The Committee has several times refused to recommend the omission from Canon 6 of the phrase "except by express consent etc."
297. It may well be the case that information acquired by a lawyer who is representing both parties is so important and personal as to make it unwise and in bad taste for him subsequently to represent one of them against the other, even with the latter's consent.
298. With the consent of both the vendors and vendees, the lawyer for the vendor may draw the conditional sales contract to be used.

How Far a Lawyer May Go in Protecting His Client's Interest

301. A lawyer may not simulate legal papers,
302. or provide his clients with blanks to send to debtors stating that unless payment is made within seven days the account will be turned over to the named lawyer for collection,
303. or write to a debtor that a judgment against him will injure his credit or reflect on his moral standing.
304. A lawyer may not close the mouths of witnesses in a murder case. (See also 21.)
305. It is improper to advertise for witnesses to testify to certain described facts, but is proper to advertise as to witnesses for a particular event or transaction.

Privileged Communications

309. A communication is not within the privilege where the facts were learned in a capacity other than attorney.
310. Where Canon 37 precludes the disclosure of an asset which the creditors should get, the lawyer must withdraw without compensation if the client refuses to allow him to disclose it.
311. Query as to whether the amount of a fee paid by a client is privileged under Canon 37.
312. He should refuse to disclose a privileged communication though the court send him to jail.

Intermediaries

CANON 35

316. A lawyer may represent an association and also in good faith represent certain individual members of it,
317. but one employed and paid by an association of engineers may not advise the members.
318. It is improper for a corporation to furnish advice to its employees through its lawyers.
319. A lawyer may not be employed by a union to advise its members.
320. A lawyer may give an opinion to an investment association as to the taxability of income receivable from the funds invested in the association, to be used by the salesmen of the association in selling its securities,
321. but may not advise an accountant so as to enable him to pass on the advice to his clients as his own.

Collection Agents

326. A lawyer may hire a layman on a specified commission basis to make collections, provided this does not involve the lawyer's splitting his fees with him.
327. There is no reason why a collection agency may not be properly designated by a creditor as his agent to employ an attorney on prescribed terms. The essential point of ethics is that the attorney shall represent the creditor and not the credit bureau, and that the credit bureau under no circumstances whatever shall receive a proportion of the lawyer's fee. Where authorized, it is proper for the collection agent to suggest a lawyer's name, unsolicited by the lawyer.
328. Where a credit bureau is authorized to retain a lawyer and does so, the lawyer has a duty to get in direct touch with the creditor, unless the creditor specifically authorizes the credit bureau to conduct the correspondence and the arrangement with the lawyer as the creditor's agent. When a lawyer so designated collects an account, he may properly deduct the agreed fee and remit the balance direct to the creditor unless the creditor specifically authorizes the credit bureau to require as the creditor's agent the remittance in the net amount collected to be sent to the credit bureau from which the credit bureau could deduct its agreed compensation.
329. The lawyer designated should not recognize the credit bureau as his client where he knows that the claim is not owned by the credit bureau, and should recognize the credit bureau as the creditor's agent only to the extent that the creditor has specifically authorized.
330. "With the client's knowledge and approval the lawyer may properly employ collection agents and accept employment from them where

they are clearly authorized by the client to choose him, provided always that the agency does not share the lawyer's fees."

Compensation

333. A client is not bound to accept the lawyer's advice, but must pay for it even though he does not accept it.

334. A lawyer need not perform additional services until he is paid, except where the client would be prejudiced.

335. A lawyer may charge a fee to a member of the armed forces, though it is usual and proper to do such service for nothing.

336. It is improper for members to pledge their local bar association to observe its minimum schedule.

337. Canon 13 applies to criminal cases. Irrespective of agreement, the lawyer should always be willing to have the court pass on the reasonableness of his charges under the various contingencies specified, and should make such charges so reasonable that if submitted to the court, it would sustain him.

Expenses

338. Telephone calls, hotel bills, etc., are not "expenses" within the meaning of Canon 42. An agreement to pay costs is.

339. Where litigation was under the supervision of a Government agency which made it a condition of employment that the expenses were collectible solely out of the recovery, the Committee advised several lawyers that although in violation of the letter of Canon 13, the Committee would take no action.

DIVISION OF FEES WITH LAYMEN

341. A lawyer may properly employ a layman, at a stated salary, to advise and assist him in his law practice. A lawyer also may be employed at a stated salary by a layman to advise and assist him in any activity in which the layman may lawfully engage, but in the latter case the lawyer may not hold himself out to the public as engaged in the practice of the law or give legal advice, nor may the employment involve a division of fees or profits by the lawyer to layman.

342. The mere fact that an accountant is admitted to practice before the Tax Court does not make it proper for a lawyer to permit a division of fees between him and such accountant.

343. Where a client authorizes an accountant to employ a lawyer, the lawyer's fee should not be paid by the accountant as a proportion of the accountant's fee, or vice versa.

344. A lawyer may, with a client's approval, employ an accountant and pay him an agreed sum and collect it from the client as an item of expense.

347. An assignment by a partner of his interest in the partnership to him-

self and wife by the entireties merely to save inheritance taxes, the wife being in no way involved in law practice or in any relationship with the clients, does not violate Canon 34.

DIVISION OF FEES BETWEEN LAWYERS

351. The arrangement with a correspondent should be clearly set out at the beginning. There is no "usual" basis for division.
352. "Another lawyer" in Canon 34 means one practicing in the jurisdiction where this service is performed. If he is not, he may be paid fair compensation but not a percentage.
353. When the client specifically agrees that the forwarding lawyer shall receive one third and the forwardee two thirds contingently, Canon 34 is not involved.

RELATIONS BETWEEN LAWYERS

354. A lawyer retaining a correspondent on a contingent fee should disclose to him his contingent fee arrangement with the client; not to do so is neither fair nor candid.
355. Candor and fairness require one to use every reasonable effort to induce his client to pay his foreign correspondent.
356. Where no basis of division with a correspondent is agreed on and there is no indication that the forwarder expected a division, and where the correspondent deals directly with the client, the correspondent may properly render a bill direct to the client for his services; but this does not preclude the forwarder from billing the client direct for his own services, from whom he should collect them.
357. A lawyer who forwarded a claim to another lawyer has no right whatever to share in the fee obtained by the forwardee from the client in another later independent case which the client sent direct to the forwardee.
358. Whether or not a correspondent may deal directly with the client depends on the relationship and its history. A forwarder who remains counsel for a client may insist that the forwardee deal with the client through him. On the other hand, if the first lawyer employed the second as attorney for the client, contemplating a direct relationship between them, the second may properly communicate directly with the client.
359. A lawyer devoting his entire time to one client for an agreed salary may not ethically turn over to the client, to be applied by it as a setoff to the expense of maintaining its legal department, the premiums paid to him by a title company insuring real estate on which, under the lawyer's supervision, his client acquired mortgages.
360. When retained in a matter previously handled by another, a lawyer should make sure that his client has discharged the other lawyer and

has so advised him. While it is not necessary for him to communicate with the other lawyer, it is courteous for him to do so. It is often wise to give the other an opportunity to state any facts which the client has refrained from telling him and which might influence him not to proceed with the case.

361. A disbarred lawyer may be paid for compensable services prior to disbarment.

Partnerships between Lawyers

364. A lawyer may not purport to be the successor of one of whom he was merely an associate, not a partner.

365. A Washington, D.C., firm was approved where composed of members each entitled to practice there as well as in their respective states, although in such states each was in a separate firm.

366. It is improper for a firm to designate as associates a foreign firm with which it has no legal relation.

Firm Names

368. The firm name should not include that of a living person not admitted in the jurisdiction.

369. "The Firm of A. B. Smith" was considered proper if in accord with local custom,

370. as was Jones Brothers,

371. and C. S. Dudley & Son, or "Blank Law office," composed of three Blanks with no other such local firm.

373. Doe & Doe Associates, has been held improper,

374. as has Householder Associates,

375. McCarrus Claim Service, and

376. Northern law clinic;

377. nor may the name end with "and Co."

379. Under Canon 33 the names of deceased partners may be retained where in accordance with local custom.

380. The Committee has refused to recommend an amendment precluding this.

381. It would seem questionable under the wording of Canon 33 whether the firm name could properly include both that of a deceased partner and that of one who had never been a partner with him.

382. A firm may retain the name of a deceased partner if his name is listed below with a statement that he is deceased,

383. but an approved practice is to have the living members listed on the left of the letterhead with the deceased on the right with the dates of admission and retirement.

APPENDIX B

DIGEST OF
REPRESENTATIVE COURT DECISIONS
SPECIFYING GROUNDS FOR
DISBARMENT, SUSPENSION,
OR CENSURE

I

Conduct indicating that the lawyer is not one who can properly be trusted to advise and act for clients

ACTS DONE IN A PROFESSIONAL CAPACITY

Conversion

In the Matter of Stern, 120 App. Div. 375 (1907)—Disbarred
In re Radford, 168 Mich. 474 (1912)—Disbarred
In re Graffius, 241 Pa. 222 (1913)—Disbarred
In re Yablunky, 407 Ill. 111 (1950)—Disbarred

Solicitation, Then Conversion

In re Thorn, 164 App. Div. 151 (1914)—Disbarred
In re Cruickshank, 47 Cal. App. 496 (1920)—Disbarred
Alexander's Case, 321 Pa. 125 (1936)—Disbarred

Betrayal of Client's Interest

United States v. Costen, 38 Fed. 24 (1889)—Disbarred
In re Boone, 83 Fed. 944 (1897)—Disbarred
Matter of Allin, 224 Mass. 9 (1916)—Disbarred

Gross Neglect

Matter of Boehm, 150 App. Div. 443 (1912)—Censured
Marsh v. State Bar of California, 210 Cal. 303 (1930)—Suspended one year
Matter of Friedland, 238 App. Div. 215 (1933)—Suspended 6 months

Fraudulent Schemes

People v. Macauley, 230 Ill. 208 (1907)—Disbarred
The People v. Gilmore, 345 Ill. 28 (1931)—Disbarred
People v. Heald, 123 Colo. 390 (1951)—Suspended 6 months

Commingling

In re Cusack, 231 App. Div. 186 (1930)—Suspended 2 years
Peck v. State Bar of California, 217 Cal. 47 (1932)—Suspended one year
Matter of Coit, 251 App. Div. 154 (1937)—Severely censured
In re Melin, 410 Ill. 332 (1951)—Suspended 3 months

ACTS DONE IN A NON-PROFESSIONAL CAPACITY

Embezzlement as Public Official

Jerome's Case, 1 Cro. Cr. 74 (1627)—Disbarred
Delano's Case, 58 N.H. 5 (1876)—Disbarred
Matter of Fridigen, 196 App. Div. 413 (1921)—Disbarred
In re Lynch, 238 S.W.2d 118 (1951)—Disbarred

Other Embezzlements

In re Wilson, 79 Kans. 674 (1909)—Disbarred
Chicago Bar v. Meyerovitz, 278 Ill. 356 (1917)—Disbarred
In re Turner, 104 Wash. 276 (1918)—Suspended one year

Theft

Ex parte Brounsall, 2 Cowp. 829 (1778)—Disbarred
In re Henry, 15 Ida. 755 (1909)—Disbarred

Extortion

Matter of Coffey, 123 Cal. 522 (1899)—Disbarred

Other frauds

In re Wilson, 79 Kans. 450 (1909)—Disbarred
In re Isaacs, 172 App. Div. 181 (1916)—Disbarred
Matter of Greenwald, 278 App. Div. 76 (1951)—Disbarred

II

Conduct such that to allow him to remain as a member of the profession and appear in court would cast serious reflection on the dignity of the court and the reputation of an honorable profession

MARKED DISRESPECT

To the Court

People v. Green, 7 Colo. 237 (1883)—Disbarred

United States v. Green, 85 F. 857 (1898)—Disbarred
State v. McClaugherty, 33 W.Va. 250 (1888)—Disbarred
Matter of Rockmore, 127 App. Div. 499 (1908)—Suspended 6 months
Re Thatcher, 80 Ohio St. 492 (1909)—Disbarred
Matter of Humphrey, 174 Cal. 290 (1917)—Suspended 2 years
In re Graves, 64 Cal. App. 176 (1923)—Suspended

To Fellow Members of the Bar

Dickens' case, 67 Pa. 169 (1870)—Suspended 6 years
In re Adriaans, 17 App. Cases D.C. 39 (1900)—Disbarred

To the Law

"TAKING LAW INTO OWN HANDS"

Dormenon's Case, 1 La. 129 (1810)—Disbarred
Ex parte Wall, 107 U.S. 265 (1883)—Disbarred
State v. Graves, 73 Ore. 331 (1914)—Suspended 3 months

HELPING OTHERS FLOUT LAWS DURING WAR

In re Hofstede, 31 Ida. 448 (1918)—Disbarred
In re Arctander, 110 Wash. 296 (1920)—Disbarred
In re Wiltse, 109 Wash. 261 (1920)—Disbarred
In re O'Connell, 184 Cal. 584 (1920)—Disbarred
Margolis' case, 269 Pa. 206 (1921)—Disbarred
In re Smith, 133 Wash. 145 (1925)—Disbarred

EVASIONS OF PROHIBITION LAWS

State v. Johnson, 174 N.C. 345 (1917)—Disbarred
In re Callicotte, 57 Mont. 297 (1920)—Disbarred
In re Finch, 156 Wash. 609 (1930)—Disbarred

EVASIONS OF OTHER LAWS

In re Peters, 73 Mont. 284 (1925)—Disbarred
In re Diesen, 173 Minn. 297 (1927)—Suspended 3 years
In're Hatch, 10 Cal.2d 147 (1937)—Suspended 10 years

TIE UP WITH RACKETEERS

Wolfe's Disbarment, 288 Pa. 334 (1927)—Disbarred
In re Moses, 186 Minn. 357 (1932)—Disbarred
Matter of Richards, 333 Mo. 907 (1933)—Disbarred
In re Disbarment Proceedings, 321 Pa. 81 (1936)—Disbarred

ABUSE OF LEGAL PROCESS

By Varied Schemes and Sharp Practice

In re Shepard, 109 Mich. 631 (1896)—Disbarred
In re Durant, 80 Conn. 140 (1907)—Disbarred

Wernimont v. State Bar, 101 Ark. 210 (1911)—Disbarred
Matter of Bayles, 156 App. Div. 663 (N.Y., 1913)—Disbarred
Matter of Hansen, 182 App. Div. 568 (N.Y., 1918)—Disbarred
Matter of Chaikin, 238 App. Div. 211 (N.Y., 1933)—Suspended one year
In re Schachne, 5 F. Supp. 680 (1934)—Suspended 5 years
In re Weiss, 20 D. & C. 666 (1934)—Disbarred; affirmed in 317 Pa. 415
    (1935)

By Bribery and Extortion

Matter of Schapiro, 144 App. Div. 1 (N.Y., 1911)—Disbarred
Matter of Robinson, 151 App. Div. 589 (N.Y., 1912)—Disbarred
Matter of Rouss, 221 N.Y. 81 (1917)—Disbarred
Re Crum, 55 N.D. 876 (1927)—Suspended 6 months
Chernoff's Case, 344 Pa. 527 (1942)—Disbarred
In re Wein, 73 Ariz. 225 (1952)—Disbarred

PERSONAL BEHAVIOR

Sex Offenses

In re Wallace, 323 Mo. 203 (1929)—Disbarred
In re Hicks, 163 Okla. 29 (1933)—Disbarred
Grievance Comm. v. Broder, 112 Conn. 269 (1930)—Disbarred
In re Heinze, 233 Minn. 391 (1951)—Disbarred

Disreputable Business Connection

In re Marsh, 42 Utah 186 (1914)—Disbarred
Matter of Fischer, 231 App. Div. 193 (N.Y., 1930)—Suspended one year
In re McNeese, 346 Mo. 425 (1940)—Disbarred

Miscellaneous Conduct

Matter of Mills, 1 Mich. 392 (1850)—Back for retrial
In re Wells, 293 Ky. 201 (1943)—Suspended 6 months

VIOLATION OF THE CANONS

Advertising and Solicitation

SELF-ADVERTISEMENT

The People v. MacCabe, 18 Colo. 186 (1893)—Suspended 6 months
Matter of Schnitzer, 33 Nev. 581 (1911)—Suspended 8 months
The People v. Berezniak, 292 Ill. 305 (1920)—Censured
In re Donovan, 43 S.D. 98 (1920)—Suspended 6 months
Barton v. State Bar of California, 209 Cal. 677 (1930)—Reprimanded
Libarian v. State Bar, 25 Cal.2d 314 (1944)—Suspended 1 year

SOLICITATION—USE OF RUNNERS, FEE SPLITTING

Chreste v. Commonwealth, 171 Ky. 77 (1916)—Disbarred

Matter of Rothbard, 225 App. Div. 266 (N.Y., 1929)—Disbarred
In re Greathouse, 189 Minn. 51 (1933)—Severely censured
In re Disbarment Proceedings, 321 Pa. 81 (1936)—Disbarred
In re Wright, 232 P.2d 398 (Nev., 1951)—Suspended 6 months

SOLICITATION AND EXPLOITATION

In re Tracy, 197 Minn. 35 (1936)—Disbarred

Excessive Fees

Matter of Fisch, 188 App. Div. 525 (N.Y., 1919)—Warning
Goldstone v. State Bar of California, 214 Cal. 490 (1931)—Suspended 3
    months

Dealing Directly with Opposing Party Who Has Representation

Carpenter v. State Bar, 210 Cal. 520 (1930)—Suspended 3 months

Practicing with Disbarred Lawyer

In re Quitman, 152 App. Div. 865 (N.Y., 1912)—Disbarred
Matter of Mainiere, 274 App. Div. 17 (N.Y., 1948)—Suspended 6 months

APPENDIX C

CANONS OF
PROFESSIONAL ETHICS[1]

PREAMBLE

IN AMERICA, where the stability of Courts and of all departments of government rests upon the approval of the people, it is peculiarly essential that the system for establishing and dispensing Justice be developed to a high point of efficiency and so maintained that the public shall have absolute confidence in the integrity and impartiality of its administration. The future of the Republic, to a great extent, depends upon our maintenance of Justice pure and unsullied. It cannot be so maintained unless the conduct and the motives of the members of our profession are such as to merit the approval of all just men.

No code or set of rules can be framed, which will particularize all the duties of the lawyer in the varying phases of litigation or in all the relations of professional life. The following canons of ethics are adopted by the American Bar Association as a general guide, yet the enumeration of particular duties should not be construed as a denial of the existence of others equally imperative, though not specifically mentioned.

1. THE DUTY OF THE LAWYER TO THE COURTS

It is the duty of the lawyer to maintain towards the Courts a respectful attitude, not for the sake of the temporary incumbent of the judicial office, but for the maintenance of its supreme importance. Judges, not being wholly free to defend themselves, are peculiarly entitled to receive the support of the Bar against unjust criticism and clamor. Whenever there is proper ground for serious complaint of a judicial officer, it is the right and duty of the lawyer to submit his grievances to the proper authorities.

[1] These canons, to and including Canon 32 and the recommended oath, were adopted by the American Bar Association at its Thirty-first Annual Meeting at Seattle, Washington, on August 27, 1908. The supplemental canons, 33–45, were adopted at the Fifty-first Annual Meeting at Seattle, Washington, on July 26, 1928. Canons 11, 13, 34, 35 and 43 were amended, and Canon 46 was adopted, in 1933. Canons 7, 11, 12, 27, 31, 33, 34, 37, 39 and 43 were amended, and Canon 47 was adopted, in 1937. Canon 27 was further amended in 1942, 1943 and 1951, and Canon 43 was further amended in 1942.

In such cases, but not otherwise, such charges should be encouraged and the person making them should be protected.

2. The Selection of Judges

It is the duty of the Bar to endeavor to prevent political considerations from outweighing judicial fitness in the selections of Judges. It should protest earnestly and actively against the appointment or election of those who are unsuitable for the Bench; and it should strive to have elevated thereto only those willing to forego other employments, whether of a business, political or other character, which may embarrass their free and fair consideration of questions before them for decision. The aspiration of lawyers for judicial position should be governed by an impartial estimate of their ability to add honor to the office and not by a desire for the distinction the position may bring to themselves.

3. Attempts to Exert Personal Influence on the Court

Marked attention and unusual hospitality on the part of a lawyer to a Judge, uncalled for by the personal relations of the parties, subject both the Judge and the lawyer to misconstructions of motive and should be avoided. A lawyer should not communicate or argue privately with the Judge as to the merits of a pending cause, and he deserves rebuke and denunciation for any device or attempt to gain from a Judge special personal consideration or favor. A self-respecting independence in the discharge of professional duty, without denial or diminution of the courtesy and respect due the Judge's station, is the only proper foundation for cordial personal and official relations between Bench and Bar.

4. When Counsel for an Indigent Prisoner

A lawyer assigned as counsel for an indigent prisoner ought not to ask to be excused for any trivial reason, and should always exert his best efforts in his behalf.

5. The Defense or Prosecution of Those Accused of Crime

It is the right of the lawyer to undertake the defense of a person accused of crime, regardless of his personal opinion as to the guilt of the accused; otherwise innocent persons, victims only of suspicious circumstances, might be denied proper defense. Having undertaken such defense, the lawyer is bound, by all fair and honorable means, to present every defense that the law of the land permits, to the end that no person may be deprived of life or liberty, but by due process of law.

The primary duty of a lawyer engaged in public prosecution is not to convict, but to see that justice is done. The suppression of facts or the secreting of witnesses capable of establishing the innocence of the accused is highly reprehensible.

6. Adverse Influences and Conflicting Interests

It is the duty of a lawyer at the time of retainer to disclose to the client all the circumstances of his relations to the parties, and any interest in or connection with the controversy, which might influence the client in the selection of counsel.

It is unprofessional to represent conflicting interests, except by express consent of all concerned given after a full disclosure of the facts. Within the meaning of this canon, a lawyer represents conflicting interests when, in behalf of one client, it is his duty to contend for that which duty to another client requires him to oppose.

The obligation to represent the client with undivided fidelity and not to divulge his secrets or confidences forbids also the subsequent acceptance of retainers or employment from others in matters adversely affecting any interest of the client with respect to which confidence has been reposed.

7. Professional Colleagues and Conflicts of Opinion [2]

A client's proffer of assistance of additional counsel should not be regarded as evidence of want of confidence, but the matter should be left to the determination of the client. A lawyer should decline association as colleague if it is objectionable to the original counsel, but if the lawyer first retained is relieved, another may come into the case.

When lawyers jointly associated in a cause cannot agree as to any matter vital to the interest of the client, the conflict of opinion should be frankly stated to him for his final determination. His decision should be accepted unless the nature of the difference makes it impracticable for the lawyer whose judgment has been overruled to co-operate effectively. In this event it is his duty to ask the client to relieve him.

Efforts, direct or indirect, in any way to encroach upon the professional employment of another lawyer, are unworthy of those who should be brethren at the Bar; but, nevertheless, it is the right of any lawyer, without fear or favor, to give proper advice to those seeking relief against unfaithful or neglectful counsel, generally after communication with the lawyer of whom the complaint is made.

8. Advising upon the Merits of a Client's Cause

A lawyer should endeavor to obtain full knowledge of his client's cause before advising thereon, and he is bound to give a candid opinion of the merits and probable result of pending or contemplated litigation. The miscarriages to which justice is subject, by reason of surprises and disappointments in evidence and witnesses, and through mistakes of juries and errors of Courts, even though only occasional, admonish lawyers to beware of bold and confident assurances to clients, especially where the

[2] Canon 7 was amended in 1937 by substituting "professional employment," for "business" in the last paragraph.

employment may depend upon such assurance. Whenever the controversy will admit of fair judgment, the client should be advised to avoid or to end the litigation.

9. NEGOTIATIONS WITH OPPOSITE PARTY

A lawyer should not in any way communicate upon the subject of controversy with a party represented by counsel; much less should he undertake to negotiate or compromise the matter with him, but should deal only with his counsel. It is incumbent upon the lawyer most particularly to avoid everything that may tend to mislead a party not represented by counsel, and he should not undertake to advise him as to the law.

10. ACQUIRING INTEREST IN LITIGATION

The lawyer should not purchase any interest in the subject matter of the litigation which he is conducting.

11. DEALING WITH TRUST PROPERTY [3]

The lawyer should refrain from any action whereby for his personal benefit or gain he abuses or takes advantage of the confidence reposed in him by his client.

Money of the client or collected for the client or other trust property coming into the possession of the lawyer should be reported and accounted for promptly, and should not under any circumstances be commingled with his own or be used by him.

12. FIXING THE AMOUNT OF THE FEE [4]

In fixing fees, lawyers should avoid charges which overestimate their advice and services, as well as those which undervalue them. A client's ability to pay cannot justify a charge in excess of the value of the service, though his poverty may require a less charge, or even none at all. The reasonable requests of brother lawyers, and of their widows and orphans without ample means, should receive special and kindly consideration.

In determining the amount of the fee, it is proper to consider: (1) the time and labor required, the novelty and difficulty of the questions involved and the skill requisite properly to conduct the cause; (2) whether the acceptance of employment in the particular case will preclude the lawyer's

---

[3] Canon 11 was amended in 1933. The original Canon was worded as follows:
"Money of the client or other trust property coming into the possession of the lawyer should be reported promptly, and except with the client's knowledge and consent should not be commingled with his private property or be used by him."

It was further amended in 1937, by inserting the first paragraph above.

[4] Canon 12 was amended in 1937 by substituting "employment" for "business" in the second paragraph, and by inserting the next to last paragraph, beginning "In determining the customary charges, etc."

appearance for others in cases likely to arise out of the transaction, and in which there is a reasonable expectation that otherwise he would be employed, or will involve the loss of other employment while employed in the particular case or antagonisms with other clients; (3) the customary charges of the Bar for similar services; (4) the amount involved in the controversy and the benefits resulting to the client from the services; (5) the contingency or the certainty of the compensation; and (6) the character of the employment, whether casual or for an established and constant client. No one of these considerations in itself is controlling. They are mere guides in ascertaining the real value of the service.

In determining the customary charges of the Bar for similar services, it is proper for a lawyer to consider a schedule of minimum fees adopted by a Bar Association, but no lawyer should permit himself to be controlled thereby or to follow it as his sole guide in determining the amount of his fee.

In fixing fees it should never be forgotten that the profession is a branch of the administration of justice and not a mere money-getting trade.

13. CONTINGENT FEES [5]

A contract for a contingent fee, where sanctioned by law, should be reasonable under all the circumstances of the case, including the risk and uncertainty of the compensation, but should always be subject to the supervision of a court, as to its reasonableness.

14. SUING A CLIENT FOR A FEE

Controversies with clients concerning compensation are to be avoided by the lawyer so far as shall be compatible with his self-respect and with his right to receive reasonable recompense for his services; and lawsuits with clients should be resorted to only to prevent injustice, imposition or fraud.

15. HOW FAR A LAWYER MAY GO IN SUPPORTING A CLIENT'S CAUSE

Nothing operates more certainly to create or to foster popular prejudice against lawyers as a class, and to deprive the profession of that full measure of public esteem and confidence which belongs to the proper discharge of its duties than does the false claim, often set up by the unscrupulous in defense of questionable transactions, that it is the duty of the lawyer to do whatever may enable him to succeed in winning his client's cause.

It is improper for a lawyer to assert in argument his personal belief in his client's innocence or in the justice of his cause.

The lawyer owes "entire devotion to the interest of the client, warm

[5] Canon 13 was amended in 1933. The original Canon was worded as follows:
"Contingent fees, where sanctioned by law, should be under the supervision of the Court, in order that clients may be protected from unjust charges."

zeal in the maintenance and defense of his rights and the exertion of his utmost learning and ability," to the end that nothing be taken or be withheld from him, save by the rules of law, legally applied. No fear of judicial disfavor or public unpopularity should restrain him from the full discharge of his duty. In the judicial forum the client is entitled to the benefit of any and every remedy and defense that is authorized by the law of the land, and he may expect his lawyer to assert every such remedy or defense. But it is steadfastly to be borne in mind that the great trust of the lawyer is to be performed within and not without the bounds of the law. The office of attorney does not permit, much less does it demand of him for any client, violation of law or any manner of fraud or chicane. He must obey his own conscience and not that of his client.

16. Restraining Clients from Improprieties

A lawyer should use his best efforts to restrain and to prevent his clients from doing those things which the lawyer himself ought not to do, particularly with reference to their conduct towards Courts, judicial officers, jurors, witnesses and suitors. If a client persists in such wrong-doing the lawyer should terminate their relation.

17. Ill-feeling and Personalities between Advocates

Clients, not lawyers, are the litigants. Whatever may be the ill-feeling existing between clients, it should not be allowed to influence counsel in their conduct and demeanor toward each other or toward suitors in the case. All personalities between counsel should be scrupulously avoided. In the trial of a cause it is indecent to allude to the personal history or the personal peculiarities and idiosyncrasies of counsel on the other side. Personal colloquies between counsel which cause delay and promote unseemly wrangling should also be carefully avoided.

18. Treatment of Witnesses and Litigants

A lawyer should always treat adverse witnesses and suitors with fairness and due consideration, and he should never minister to the malevolence or prejudices of a client in the trial or conduct of a cause. The client cannot be made the keeper of the lawyer's conscience in professional matters. He has no right to demand that his counsel shall abuse the opposite party or indulge in offensive personalities. Improper speech is not excusable on the ground that it is what the client would say if speaking in his own behalf.

19. Appearance of Lawyer as Witness for His Client

When a lawyer is a witness for his client, except as to merely formal matters, such as the attestation or custody of an instrument and the like, he should leave the trial of the case to other counsel. Except when essential to the ends of justice, a lawyer should avoid testifying in court in behalf of his client.

20. Newspaper Discussion of Pending Litigation

Newspaper publications by a lawyer as to pending or anticipated litigation may interfere with a fair trial in the Courts and otherwise prejudice the due administration of justice. Generally they are to be condemned. If the extreme circumstances of a particular case justify a statement to the public, it is unprofessional to make it anonymously. An *ex parte* reference to the facts should not go beyond quotation from the records and papers on file in the court; but even in extreme cases it is better to avoid any *ex parte* statement.

21. Punctuality and Expedition

It is the duty of the lawyer not only to his client, but also to the Courts and to the public to be punctual in attendance, and to be concise and direct in the trial and disposition of causes.

22. Candor and Fairness

The conduct of the lawyer before the Court and with other lawyers should be characterized by candor and fairness.

It is not candid or fair for the lawyer knowingly to misquote the contents of a paper, the testimony of a witness, the language or the argument of opposing counsel, or the language of a decision or a textbook; or with knowledge of its invalidity, to cite as authority a decision that has been overruled, or a statute that has been repealed; or in argument to assert as a fact that which has not been proved, or in those jurisdictions where a side has the opening and closing arguments to mislead his opponent by concealing or withholding positions in his opening argument upon which his side then intends to rely.

It is unprofessional and dishonorable to deal other than candidly with the facts in taking the statements of witnesses, in drawing affidavits and other documents, and in the presentation of causes.

A lawyer should not offer evidence which he knows the Court should reject, in order to get the same before the jury by argument for its admissibility, nor should he address to the Judge arguments upon any point not properly calling for determination by him. Neither should he introduce into an argument, addressed to the court, remarks or statements intended to influence the jury or bystanders.

These and all kindred practices are unprofessional and unworthy of an officer of the law charged, as is the lawyer, with the duty of aiding in the administration of justice.

23. Attitude toward Jury

All attempts to curry favor with juries by fawning, flattery or pretended solicitude for their personal comfort are unprofessional. Suggestions of counsel, looking to the comfort or convenience of jurors, and propositions to dispense with argument, should be made to the Court out of the jury's hearing. A lawyer must never converse privately with jurors about the case; and both before and during the trial he should avoid communicating with them, even as to matters foreign to the cause.

24. Right of Lawyer to Control the Incidents of the Trial

As to incidental matters pending the trial, not affecting the merits of the cause, or working substantial prejudice to the rights of the client, such as forcing the opposite lawyer to trial when he is under affliction or bereavement; forcing the trial on a particular day to the injury of the opposite lawyer when no harm will result from a trial at a different time; agreeing to an extension of time for signing a bill of exceptions, cross interrogatories and the like, the lawyer must be allowed to judge. In such matters no client has a right to demand that his counsel shall be illiberal, or that he do anything therein repugnant to his own sense of honor and propriety.

25. Taking Technical Advantage of Opposite Counsel; Agreements with Him

A lawyer should not ignore known customs or practice of the Bar or of a particular Court, even when the law permits, without giving timely notice to the opposing counsel. As far as possible, important agreements, affecting the rights of clients, should be reduced to writing; but it is dishonorable to avoid performance of an agreement fairly made because it is not reduced to writing, as required by rules of Court.

26. Professional Advocacy Other than before Courts

A lawyer openly, and in his true character may render professional services before legislative or other bodies, regarding proposed legislation and in advocacy of claims before departments of government, upon the same principles of ethics which justify his appearance before the Courts; but it is unprofessional for a lawyer so engaged to conceal his attorneyship, or to employ secret personal solicitations, or to use means other than those addressed to the reason and understanding, to influence action.

27. Advertising, Direct or Indirect [6]

It is unprofessional to solicit professional employment by circulars, advertisements, through touters or by personal communications or interviews

---

[6] From its adoption in 1908 to September 30, 1937, Canon 27 read as follows:
"The most worthy and effective advertisement possible, even for a young lawyer, and

not warranted by personal relations. Indirect advertisements for professional employment such as furnishing or inspiring newspaper comments, or procuring his photograph to be published in connection with causes in which the lawyer has been or is engaged or concerning the manner of their conduct, the magnitude of the interest involved, the importance of the

---

especially with his brother lawyers, is the establishment of a well-merited reputation for professional capacity and fidelity to trust. This cannot be forced, but must be the outcome of character and conduct. The publication or circulation of ordinary simple business cards, being a matter of personal taste or local custom, and sometimes of convenience, is not per se improper. But solicitation of business by circulars or advertisements, or by personal communications, or interviews, not warranted by personal relations, is unprofessional. It is equally unprofessional to procure business by indirection through touters of any kind, whether allied real estate firms or trust companies advertising to secure the drawing of deeds or wills or offering retainers in exchange for executorships or trusteeships to be influenced by the lawyer. Indirect advertisement for business by furnishing or inspiring newspaper comments concerning causes in which the lawyer has been or is engaged, or concerning the manner of their conduct, the magnitude of the interests involved, the importance of the lawyer's positions, and all other like self-laudation, defy the traditions and lower the tone of our high calling, and are intolerable."

The Canon was completely redrafted in 1937, to read as follows:

"The customary use of simple professional cards is permissible. Publication in approved law lists and legal directories, in a manner consistent with the standard of conduct imposed by these Canons, of brief biographical data is permissible. This may include only a statement of the lawyer's name and the names of his professional associates, addresses, telephone numbers, cable addresses, special branches of the profession practiced, date and place of birth and admission to the Bar, schools attended with dates of graduation and degrees received, public offices and posts of honor held, bar and other association memberships and, with their consent, the names of clients regularly represented. This does not permit solicitation of professional employment by circulars, or advertisements, or by personal communications or interviews not warranted by personal relations. It is unprofessional to endeavor to procure professional employment through touters of any kind. Indirect advertisements for professional employment, such as furnishing or inspiring newspaper comments, or procuring his photograph to be published in connection with causes in which the lawyer has been or is engaged or concerning the manner of their conduct, the magnitude of the interest involved, the importance of the lawyer's position, and all other like self-laudation, offend the traditions and lower the tone of our profession and are reprehensible."

In 1940 the whole Canon was further amended to read as follows:

"It is unprofessional to solicit professional employment by circulars, advertisements, through touters or by personal communications or interviews not warranted by personal relations. Indirect advertisements for professional employment, such as furnishing or inspiring newspaper comments, or procuring his photograph to be published in connection with causes in which the lawyer has been or is engaged or concerning the manner of their conduct, the magnitude of the interest involved, the importance of the lawyer's position, and all other like self-laudation, offend the traditions and lower the tone of our profession and are reprehensible; but the customary use of simple professional cards is not improper.

"Publication in approved law lists in a manner consistent with the standards of conduct imposed by these canons of brief biographical and informative data is permissible. Such data must not be misleading and may include only a statement of the lawyer's names and the names of his professional associates; addresses, telephone numbers, cable addresses; branches of the profession practiced; date and place of birth and admission to the bar; schools attended, with dates of graduation, degrees and other educa-

lawyer's position, and all other like self-laudation, offend the traditions and lower the tone of our profession and are reprehensible; but the customary use of simple professional cards is not improper.

Publication in reputable law lists in a manner consistent with the standards of conduct imposed by these canons of brief biographical and informative data is permissible. Such data must not be misleading and may include only a statement of the lawyer's name and the names of his professional associates; addresses, telephone numbers, cable addresses; branches of the profession practiced; date and place of birth and admission to the bar; schools attended, with dates of graduation, degrees and other educational distinctions; public or quasi-public offices; posts of honor; legal authorships; legal teaching positions; memberships and offices in bar associations and committees thereof, in legal and scientific societies and legal fraternities; the fact of listings in other reputable law lists; the names and addresses of references; and, with their written consent, the names of clients regularly represented. A certificate of compliance with the Rules and Standards issued by the Standing Committee on Law Lists may be treated as evidence that such list is reputable.

It is not improper for a lawyer who is admitted to practice as a proctor in admiralty to use that designation on his letterhead or shingle or for a lawyer who has complied with the statutory requirements of admission to practice before the patent office to so use the designation "patent attorney" or "patent lawyer" or "trade-mark attorney" or "trade-mark lawyer" or any combination of those terms.

---

tional distinctions; public or quasi-public offices; posts of honor; legal authorships; legal teaching positions; memberships and offices in bar associations and committees thereof, in legal and scientific societies and legal fraternities; the fact of listings in other approved law lists; such other information as the Rules and Standards as to Law Lists expressly permit; and, with their written consent, the names of clients regularly represented."

In 1942 it was again amended by changing the second paragraph to read as follows:

"Publication in reputable law lists in a manner consistent with the standards of conduct imposed by these canons of brief biographical and informative data is permissible. Such data must not be misleading and may include only a statement of the lawyer's name and the names of his professional associates; addresses, telephone numbers, cable addresses; branches of the profession practiced; date and place of birth and admission to the bar; schools attended, with dates of graduation, degrees and other educational distinctions; public or quasi-public offices; posts of honor; legal authorships; legal teaching positions; memberships and offices in bar associations and committees thereof, in legal and scientific societies and legal fraternities; the fact of listings in other reputable law lists; and, with their written consent, the names of clients regularly represented. A certificate of compliance with the Rules and Standards issued by the Special Committee on Law Lists may be treated as evidence that such list is reputable."

In 1943 this second paragraph was again amended to its present form by inserting "the names and addresses of references" near the end of the items permitted to be stated in law lists.

In 1951, at the instance of the Patent Bar, the Canon was further amended by adding the final paragraph quoted in the text above.

28. Stirring Up Litigation, Directly or through Agents [7]

It is unprofessional for a lawyer to volunteer advice to bring a lawsuit, except in rare cases where ties of blood, relationship or trust make it his duty to do so. Stirring up strife and litigation is not only unprofessional, but it is indictable at common law. It is disreputable to hunt up defects in titles or other causes of action and inform thereof in order to be employed to bring suit or collect judgment, or to breed litigation by seeking out those with claims for personal injuries or those having any other grounds of action in order to secure them as clients, or to employ agents or runners for like purposes, or to pay or reward, directly or indirectly, those who bring or influence the bringing of such cases to his office, or to remunerate policemen, court or prison officials, physicians, hospital *attachés* or others who may succeed, under the guise of giving disinterested friendly advice, in influencing the criminal, the sick and the injured, the ignorant or others, to seek his professional services. A duty to the public and to the profession devolves upon every member of the Bar having knowledge of such practices upon the part of any practitioner immediately to inform thereof, to the end that the offender may be disbarred.

29. Upholding the Honor of the Profession

Lawyers should expose without fear or favor before the proper tribunals corrupt or dishonest conduct in the profession, and should accept without hesitation employment against a member of the Bar who has wronged his client. The counsel upon the trial of a cause in which perjury has been committed owe it to the profession and to the public to bring the matter to the knowledge of the prosecuting authorities. The lawyer should aid in guarding the Bar against the admission to the profession of candidates unfit or unqualified because deficient in either moral character or education. He should strive at all times to uphold the honor and to maintain the dignity of the profession and to improve not only the law but the administration of justice.

30. Justifiable and Unjustifiable Litigations

The lawyer must decline to conduct a civil cause or to make a defense when convinced that it is intended merely to harass or to injure the opposite party or to work oppression or wrong. But otherwise it is his right, and, having accepted retainer, it becomes his duty to insist upon the judgment of the Court as to the legal merits of his client's claim. His appearance in Court should be deemed equivalent to an assertion on his honor that in his opinion his client's case is one proper for judicial determination.

[7] Canon 28 was amended in 1928 by inserting the words "or collect judgment."

31. Responsibility for Litigation [8]

No lawyer is obliged to act either as adviser or advocate for every person who may wish to become his client. He has the right to decline employment. Every lawyer upon his own responsibility must decide what employment he will accept as counsel, what causes he will bring into Court for plaintiffs, what cases he will contest in Court for defendants. The responsibility for advising as to questionable transactions, for bringing questionable suits, for urging questionable defenses, is the lawyer's responsibility. He cannot escape it by urging as an excuse that he is only following his client's instructions.

32. The Lawyer's Duty in Its Last Analysis

No client, corporate or individual, however powerful, nor any cause, civil or political, however important, is entitled to receive nor should any lawyer render any service or advice involving disloyalty to the law whose ministers we are, or disrespect of the judicial office, which we are bound to uphold, or corruption of any person or persons exercising a public office or private trust, or deception or betrayal of the public. When rendering any such improper service or advice, the lawyer invites and merits stern and just condemnation. Correspondingly, he advances the honor of his profession and the best interests of his client when he renders service or gives advice tending to impress upon the client and his undertaking exact compliance with the strictest principles of moral law. He must also observe and advise his client to observe the statute law, though until a statute shall have been construed and interpreted by competent adjudication, he is free and is entitled to advise as to its validity and as to what he conscientiously believes to be its just meaning and extent. But above all a lawyer will find his highest honor in a deserved reputation for fidelity to private trust and to public duty, as an honest man and as a patriotic and loyal citizen.

33. Partnerships—Names [9]

Partnerships among lawyers for the practice of their profession are very common and are not to be condemned. In the formation of partnerships

[8] Canon 31 was amended in 1937 by substituting "employment" for "business" in the third sentence.

[9] Prior to this amendment in 1937 Canon 33 read as follows:

"Partnerships among lawyers for the practice of their profession are very common and are not to be condemned. Certain courts require that lawyers practicing before them shall appear individually and not as members of partnerships. In the formation of partnerships care should be taken not to violate any law locally applicable; and where partnerships are formed and permitted between lawyers who are not all admitted to practice in the local courts, care should also be taken to avoid any misleading name or representation which would create a false impression as to the professional position or

and the use of partnership names care should be taken not to violate any law, custom, or rule of court locally applicable. Where partnerships are formed between lawyers who are not all admitted to practice in the courts of the state, care should be taken to avoid any misleading name or representation which would create a false impression as to the professional position or privileges of the member not locally admitted. In the formation of partnerships for the practice of law, no person should be admitted or held out as a practitioner or member who is not a member of the legal profession duly authorized to practice, and amenable to professional discipline. In the selection and use of a firm name, no false, misleading, assumed or trade name should be used. The continued use of the name of a deceased or former partner, when permissible by local custom, is not unethical, but care should be taken that no imposition or deception is practiced through this use. When a member of the firm, on becoming a judge, is precluded from practising law, his name should not be continued in the firm name.

Partnerships between lawyers and members of other professions or non-professional persons should not be formed or permitted where any part of the partnership's employment consists of the practice of law.

34. Division of Fees [10]

No division of fees for legal services is proper, except with another lawyer, based upon a division of service or responsibility.

---

privileges of the member not locally admitted. In the formation of partnerships for the practice of law, no person should be admitted who is not a member of the legal profession, duly authorized to practice, and amenable to professional discipline. No person should be held out as a practitioner or member who is not so admitted. In the selection and use of a firm name, one not admitted to practice in the local courts should not be named, lest such use of his name should mislead as to his professional position or privileges. And no false or assumed or trade name should be used to disguise the practitioner or his partnership. The continued use of the name of a deceased or former partner is or may be permissible by local custom, but care should be taken that no imposition or deception is practiced through this use. If a member of the firm becomes a judge, his name should not be continued in the firm name, as it naturally creates the impression that an improper relation or influence is continued or possessed by the firm.

"Partnerships between lawyers and members of other professions or non-professional persons should not be formed or permitted where a part of the partnership business consists of the pactice of law."

[10] Canon 34 was amended September 30, 1937, by striking out the last sentence, which read as follows: "But sharing commissions between forwarder and receiver, at a commonly accepted rate, upon collection of liquidated commercial claims, though one be a lawyer and the other not, is not condemned hereby, where it is not prohibited by statute."

Prior to the amendment of this Canon on August 31, 1933, this last sentence read as follows: "But the established custom of sharing commissions at a commonly accepted rate, upon collections of commercial claims between forwarder and receiver, though one be a lawyer and the other not (being a compensation for valuable services rendered by each), is not condemned hereby, where it is not prohibited by statute."

35. INTERMEDIARIES [11]

The professional services of a lawyer should not be controlled or exploited by any lay agency, personal or corporate, which intervenes between client and lawyer. A lawyer's responsibilities and qualifications are individual. He should avoid all relations which direct the performance of his duties by or in the interest of such intermediary. A lawyer's relation to his client should be personal, and the responsibility should be direct to the client. Charitable societies rendering aid to the indigents are not deemed such intermediaries.

A lawyer may accept employment from any organization, such as an association, club or trade organization, to render legal services in any matter in which the organization, as an entity, is interested, but this employment should not include the rendering of legal services to the members of such an organization in respect to their individual affairs.

36. RETIREMENT FROM JUDICIAL POSITION OR PUBLIC EMPLOYMENT

A lawyer should not accept employment as an advocate in any matter upon the merits of which he has previously acted in a judicial capacity.

A lawyer, having once held public office or having been in the public employ, should not after his retirement accept employment in connection with any matter which he has investigated or passed upon while in such office or employ.

37. CONFIDENCES OF A CLIENT [12]

It is the duty of a lawyer to preserve his client's confidences. This duty outlasts the lawyer's employment, and extends as well to his employees; and neither of them should accept employment which involves or may involve the disclosure or use of these confidences, either for the private ad-

11 Canon 35 was amended August 31, 1933, by inserting the words "by or" between the words "duties" and "in" on line 5 and by striking out the following concluding paragraph:

"The established custom of receiving commercial collections through a lay agency is not condemned hereby."

12 Prior to its amendment in 1937, Canon 37 read as follows:

"The duty to preserve his client's confidences outlasts the lawyer's employment, and extends as well to his employees; and neither of them should accept employment which involves the disclosure or use of these confidences, either for the private advantage of the lawyer or his employees or to the disadvantage of the client, without his knowledge and consent, and even though there are other available sources of such information. A lawyer should not continue employment when he discovers that this obligation prevents the performance of his duty to his former or to his new client.

"If a lawyer is falsely accused by his client, he is not precluded from disclosing the truth in respect to the false accusation. The announced intention of a client to commit a crime is not included within the confidences which he is bound to respect. He may properly make such disclosures as to prevent the act or protect those against whom it is threatened."

vantage of the lawyer or his employees or to the disadvantage of the client, without his knowledge and consent, and even though there are other available sources of such information. A lawyer should not continue employment when he discovers that this obligation prevents the performance of his full duty to his former or to his new client.

If a lawyer is accused by his client, he is not precluded from disclosing the truth in respect to the accusation. The announced intention of a client to commit a crime is not included within the confidences which he is bound to respect. He may properly make such disclosures as may be necessary to prevent the act or protect those against whom it is threatened.

38. COMPENSATION, COMMISSIONS AND REBATES

A lawyer should accept no compensation, commissions, rebates or other advantages from others without the knowledge and consent of his client after full disclosure.

39. WITNESSES [13]

A lawyer may properly interview any witness or prospective witness for the opposing side in any civil or criminal action without the consent of opposing counsel or party. In doing so, however, he should scrupulously avoid any suggestion calculated to induce the witness to suppress or deviate from the truth, or in any degree to affect his free and untrammeled conduct when appearing at the trial or on the witness stand.

40. NEWSPAPERS

A lawyer may with propriety write articles for publications in which he gives information upon the law; but he should not accept employment from such publications to advise inquirers in respect to their individual rights.

41. DISCOVERY OF IMPOSITION AND DECEPTION

When a lawyer discovers that some fraud or deception has been practiced, which has unjustly imposed upon the court or a party, he should endeavor to rectify it; at first by advising his client, and if his client refuses to forego the advantage thus unjustly gained, he should promptly inform the injured person or his counsel, so that they may take appropriate steps.

[13] Canon 39 was amended to the above form in 1937, prior to when it read as follows:
"Compensation demanded or received by any witness in excess of statutory allowances should be disclosed to the court and adverse counsel.

"If the ascertainment of truth requires that a lawyer should seek information from one connected with or reputed to be biased in favor of an adverse party, he is not thereby deterred from seeking to ascertain the truth from such person in the interest of his client."

42. Expenses

A lawyer may not properly agree with a client that the lawyer shall pay or bear the expenses of litigation; he may in good faith advance expenses as a matter of convenience, but subject to reimbursement.

43. Approved Law Lists [14]

It is improper for a lawyer to permit his name to be published in a law list the conduct, management or contents of which are calculated or likely to deceive or injure the public or the profession, or to lower the dignity or standing of the profession.

44. Withdrawal from Employment as Attorney or Counsel

The right of an attorney or counsel to withdraw from employment, once assumed, arises only from good cause. Even the desire or consent of the client is not always sufficient. The lawyer should not throw up the unfinished task to the detriment of his client except for reasons of honor or self-respect. If the client insists upon an unjust or immoral course in the conduct of his case, or if he persists over the attorney's remonstrance in presenting frivolous defenses, or if he deliberately disregards an agreement or obligation as to fees or expenses, the lawyer may be warranted in withdrawing on due notice to the client, allowing him time to employ another lawyer. So also when a lawyer discovers that his client has no case and the client is determined to continue it; or even if the lawyer finds himself incapable of conducting the case effectively. Sundry other instances may arise in which withdrawal is to be justified. Upon withdrawing from a case after a retainer has been paid, the attorney should refund such part of the retainer as has not been clearly earned.

[14] As amended August 27, 1942.

Canon 43, as originally enacted in 1928, was entitled "Professional Card" and provided:

"The simple professional card mentioned in Canon 27 may with propriety contain only a statement of his name (and those of his lawyer associates), profession, address, telephone number and special branch of the profession practiced."

The Canon was amended in 1933 to read as follows:

"A lawyer's professional card may with propriety contain only a statement of his name (and those of his lawyer associates), profession, address, telephone number, and special branch of the profession practiced. The insertion of such card in reputable law lists is not condemned and it may there give references or name clients for whom the lawyer is counsel, with their permission."

In 1937 it was again amended, both in its title and in its text, to read as follows:

"*Approved Law Lists.* It shall be improper for a lawyer to permit his name to be published after January 1, 1939, in a law list that is not approved by the American Bar Association."

In 1942 it was amended to its present form, as above quoted.

45. Specialists

The canons of the American Bar Association apply to all branches of the legal profession; specialists in particular branches are not to be considered as exempt from the application of these principles.

46. Notice of Specialized Legal Service [15]

Where a lawyer is engaged in rendering a specialized legal service directly and only to other lawyers, a brief, dignified notice of that fact, couched in language indicating that it is addressed to lawyers, inserted in legal periodicals and like publications, when it will afford convenient and beneficial information to lawyers desiring to obtain such service, is not improper.

47. Aiding the Unauthorized Practice of Law [16]

No lawyer shall permit his professional services, or his name, to be used in aid of, or to make possible, the unauthorized practice of law by any lay agency, personal or corporate.

[15] Adopted August 31, 1933.

In February, 1953, the Ethics Committee recommended to the House of Delegates the adoption of an amendment to Canon 46, to read as follows:

"A lawyer, approved by his state or local bar association as a specialist in a particular branch of the law, may send to lawyers only, and publish in a legal journal, a brief and dignified announcement of his availability to serve other lawyers in connection therewith."

The House referred this back to the Committee for further study and report.

[16] Adopted September 30, 1937.

OATH OF ADMISSION

THE GENERAL PRINCIPLES which should ever control the lawyer in the practice of his profession are clearly set forth in the following Oath of Admission to the Bar, formulated upon that in use in the State of Washington, and which conforms in its main outlines to the "duties" of lawyers as defined by statutory enactments in that and many other States of the Union —duties which they are sworn on admission to obey and for the wilful violation of which disbarment is provided:

I DO SOLEMNLY SWEAR:

I will support the Constitution of the United States and the Constitution of the State of ....

I will maintain the respect due to Courts of Justice and judicial officers;

I will not counsel or maintain any suit or proceeding which shall appear to me to be unjust, nor any defense except such as I believe to be honestly debatable under the law of the land;

I will employ for the purpose of maintaining the causes confided to me such means only as are consistent with truth and honor, and will never seek to mislead the Judge or jury by any artifice or false statement of fact or law;

I will maintain the confidence and preserve inviolate the secrets of my client, and will accept no compensation in connection with his business except from him or with his knowledge and approval;

I will abstain from all offensive personality, and advance no fact prejudicial to the honor or reputation of a party or witness, unless required by the justice of the cause with which I am charged;

I will never reject, from any consideration personal to myself, the cause of the defenseless or oppressed, or delay any man's cause for lucre or malice. SO HELP ME GOD.

We recommend this form of oath for adoption by the proper authorities in all the States and Territories.

APPENDIX D

CANONS OF JUDICIAL ETHICS [1]

ANCIENT PRECEDENTS

"AND I CHARGED your judges at that time, saying Hear the causes between your brethren, and judge righteously between every man and his brother, and the stranger that is with him.

"Ye shall not respect persons in judgment; but ye shall hear the small as well as the great; ye shall not be afraid of the face of man; for the judgment is God's; and the cause that is too hard for you, bring it unto me, and I will hear it."—*Deuteronomy,* I, 16–17.

"Thou shalt not wrest judgment; thou shalt not respect persons, neither take a gift; for a gift doth blind the eyes of the wise, and pervert the words of the righteous."—*Deuteronomy,* XVI, 19.

"We will not make any justiciaries, constables, sheriffs or bailiffs, but from those who understand the law of the realm and are well disposed to observe it."—*Magna Charta,* XLV.

"Judges ought to remember that their office is *jus dicere* not *jus dare;* to interpret law, and not to make law, or give law. . . ."

"Judges ought to be more learned than witty; more reverend than plausible; and more advised than confident. Above all things, integrity is their portion and proper virtue. . . ."

"Patience and gravity of hearing is an essential part of justice; and an over speaking judge is no well-tuned cymbal. It is no grace to a judge first to find that which he might have heard in due time from the Bar, or to show quickness of conceit in cutting off evidence or counsel too short; or to prevent information by questions though pertinent."

"The place of justice is a hallowed place; and therefore not only the Bench, but the foot pace and precincts and purprise thereof ought to be preserved without scandal and corruption. . . ."—*Bacon's Essay "of Judicature."*

[1] These Canons, to and including Canon 34, were adopted by the American Bar Association in 1924.

Canons 28 and 30 were amended in 1933. Canons 35 and 36 were adopted in 1937. Minor grammatical changes were also made in a number of the Canons in 1937.

Preamble

In addition to the Canons for Professional Conduct of Lawyers which it has formulated and adopted, the American Bar Association, mindful that the character and conduct of a judge should never be objects of indifference, and that declared ethical standards tend to become habits of life, deems it desirable to set forth its views respecting those principles which should govern the personal practice of members of the judiciary in the administration of their office. The Association accordingly adopts the following Canons, the spirit of which it suggests as a proper guide and reminder for judges, and as indicating what the people have a right to expect from them.

1. Relations of the Judiciary

The assumption of the office of judge casts upon the incumbent duties in respect to his personal conduct which concern his relation to the state and its inhabitants, the litigants before him, the principles of law, the practitioners of law in his court, and the witnesses, jurors and attendants who aid him in the administration of its functions.

2. The Public Interest

Courts exist to promote justice, and thus to serve the public interest. Their administration should be speedy and careful. Every judge should at all times be alert in his rulings and in the conduct of the business of the court, so far as he can, to make it useful to litigants and to the community. He should avoid unconsciously falling into the attitude of mind that the litigants are made for the courts instead of the courts for the litigants.

3. Constitutional Obligations

It is the duty of all judges in the United States to support the federal Constitution and that of the state whose laws they administer; in so doing, they should fearlessly observe and apply fundamental limitations and guarantees.

4. Avoidance of Impropriety

A judge's official conduct should be free from impropriety and the appearance of impropriety; he should avoid infractions of law; and his personal behavior, not only upon the Bench and in the performance of judicial duties, but also in his everyday life, should be beyond reproach.

5. Essential Conduct

A judge should be temperate, attentive, patient, impartial, and, since he is to administer the law and apply it to the facts, he should be studious of the principles of the law and diligent in endeavoring to ascertain the facts.

6. Industry

A judge should exhibit an industry and application commensurate with the duties imposed upon him.

7. Promptness

A judge should be prompt in the performance of his judicial duties, recognizing that the time of litigants, jurors and attorneys is of value and that habitual lack of punctuality on his part justifies dissatisfaction with the administration of the business of the court.

8. Court Organization

A judge should organize the court with a view to the prompt and convenient dispatch of its business and he should not tolerate abuses and neglect by clerks, and other assistants who are sometimes prone to presume too much upon his good-natured acquiescence by reason of friendly association with him.

It is desirable too, where the judicial system permits, that he should cooperate with other judges of the same court, and in other courts, as members of a single judicial system, to promote the more satisfactory administration of justice.

9. Consideration for Jurors and Others

A judge should be considerate of jurors, witnesses and others in attendance upon the court.

10. Courtesy and Civility

A judge should be courteous to counsel, especially to those who are young and inexperienced, and also to all others appearing or concerned in the administration of justice in the court.

He should also require, and, so far as his power extends, enforce on the part of clerks, court officers and counsel civility and courtesy to the court and to jurors, witnesses, litigants and others having business in the court.

11. Unprofessional Conduct of Attorneys and Counsel

A judge should utilize his opportunities to criticize and correct unprofessional conduct of attorneys and counsellors, brought to his attention;

and, if adverse comment is not a sufficient corrective, should send the matter at once to the proper investigating and disciplinary authorities.

12. Appointees of the Judiciary and Their Compensation

Trustees, receivers, masters, referees, guardians and other persons appointed by a judge to aid in the administration of justice should have the strictest probity and impartiality and should be selected with a view solely to their character and fitness. The power of making such appointments should not be exercised by him for personal or partisan advantage. He should not permit his appointments to be controlled by others than himself. He should also avoid nepotism and undue favoritism in his appointments.

While not hesitating to fix or approve just amounts, he should be most scrupulous in granting or approving compensation for the services or charges of such appointees to avoid excessive allowances, whether or not excepted to or complained of. He cannot rid himself of this responsibility by the consent of counsel.

13. Kinship of Influence

A judge should not act in a controversy where a near relative is a party; he should not suffer his conduct to justify the impression that any person can improperly influence him or unduly enjoy his favor, or that he is affected by the kinship, rank, position or influence of any party or other person.

14. Independence

A judge should not be swayed by partisan demands, public clamor or considerations of personal popularity or notoriety, nor be apprehensive of unjust criticism.

15. Interference in Conduct of Trial

A judge may properly intervene in a trial of a case to promote expedition, and prevent unnecessary waste of time, or to clear up some obscurity, but he should bear in mind that his undue interference, impatience, or participation in the examination of witnesses, or a severe attitude on his part toward witnesses, especially those who are excited or terrified by the unusual circumstances of a trial, may tend to prevent the proper presentation of the cause, or the ascertainment of the truth in respect thereto.

Conversation between the judge and counsel in court is often necessary, but the judge should be studious to avoid controversies which are apt to obscure the merits of the dispute between litigants and lead to its unjust disposition. In addressing counsel, litigants, or witnesses, he should avoid a controversial manner or tone.

He should avoid interruptions of counsel in their arguments except to clarify his mind as to their positions, and he should not be tempted to the unnecessary display of learning or a premature judgment.

16. Ex parte Applications

A judge should discourage *ex parte* hearings of applications for injunctions and receiverships where the order may work detriment to absent parties; he should act upon such *ex parte* applications only where the necessity for quick action is clearly shown; if this be demonstrated, then he should endeavor to counteract the effect of the absence of opposing counsel by a scrupulous cross-examination and investigation as to the facts and the principles of law on which the application is based, granting relief only when fully satisfied that the law permits it and the emergency demands it. He should remember that an injunction is a limitation upon the freedom of action of defendants and should not be granted lightly or inadvisedly. One applying for such relief must sustain the burden of showing clearly its necessity and this burden is increased in the absence of the party whose freedom of action is sought to be restrained even though only temporarily.

17. Ex parte Communications

A judge should not permit private interviews, arguments or communications designed to influence his judicial action, where interests to be affected thereby are not represented before him, except in cases where provision is made by law for *ex parte* application.

While the conditions under which briefs of argument are to be received are largely matters of local rule or practice, he should not permit the contents of such brief presented to him to be concealed from opposing counsel. Ordinarily all communications of counsel to the judge intended or calculated to influence action should be made known to opposing counsel.

18. Continuances

Delay in the administration of justice is a common cause of complaint; counsel are frequently responsible for this delay. A judge, without being arbitrary or forcing cases unreasonably or unjustly to trial when unprepared, to the detriment of parties, may well endeavor to hold counsel to a proper appreciation of their duties to the public interest, to their own clients, and to the adverse party and his counsel, so as to enforce due diligence in the dispatch of business before the court.

19. Judicial Opinions

In disposing of controverted cases, a judge should indicate the reasons for his action in an opinion showing that he has not disregarded or overlooked serious arguments of counsel. He thus shows his full understanding of the case, avoids the suspicion of arbitrary conclusion, promotes confidence in his intellectual integrity and may contribute useful precedent to the growth of the law.

It is desirable that Courts of Appeals in reversing cases and granting new trials should so indicate their views on questions of law argued before them and necessarily arising in the controversy that upon the new trial counsel may be aided to avoid the repetition of erroneous positions of law and shall not be left in doubt by the failure of the court to decide such questions.

But the volume of reported decisions is such and is so rapidly increasing that in writing opinions which are to be published judges may well take this fact into consideration, and curtail them accordingly, without substantially departing from the principles stated above.

It is of high importance that judges constituting a court of last resort should use effort and self-restraint to promote solidarity of conclusion and the consequent influence of judicial decision. A judge should not yield to pride of opinion or value more highly his individual reputation than that of the court to which he should be loyal. Except in case of conscientious difference of opinion on fundamental principle, dissenting opinions should be discouraged in courts of last resort.

20. Influence of Decisions upon the Development of the Law

A judge should be mindful that his duty is the application of general law to particular instances, that ours is a government of law and not of men, and that he violates his duty as a minister of justice under such a system if he seeks to do what he may personally consider substantial justice in a particular case and disregards the general law as he knows it to be binding on him. Such action may become a precedent unsettling accepted principles and may have detrimental consequences beyond the immediate controversy. He should administer his office with a due regard to the integrity of the system of the law itself, remembering that he is not a depositary of arbitrary power, but a judge under the sanction of law.

21. Idiosyncrasies and Inconsistencies

Justice should not be moulded by the individual idiosyncrasies of those who administer it. A judge should adopt the usual and expected method of doing justice, and not seek to be extreme or peculiar in his judgments, or spectacular or sensational in the conduct of the court. Though vested with discretion in the imposition of mild or severe sentences he should not compel persons brought before him to submit to some humiliating act or discipline of his own devising, without authority of law, because he thinks it will have a beneficial corrective influence.

In imposing sentence he should endeavor to conform to a reasonable standard of punishment and should not seek popularity or publicity either by exceptional severity or undue leniency.

22. Review

In order that a litigant may secure the full benefit of the right of review accorded to him by law, a trial judge should scrupulously grant to the defeated party opportunity to present the questions arising upon the trial exactly as they arose, were presented, and decided, by full and fair bill of exceptions or otherwise; any failure in this regard on the part of the judge is peculiarly worthy of condemnation because the wrong done may be irremediable.

23. Legislation

A judge has exceptional opportunity to observe the operation of statutes, especially those relating to practice, and to ascertain whether they tend to impede the just disposition of controversies; and he may well contribute to the public interest by advising those having authority to remedy defects of procedure, of the result of his observation and experience.

24. Inconsistent Obligations

A judge should not accept inconsistent duties; nor incur obligations, pecuniary or otherwise, which will in any way interfere or appear to interfere with his devotion to the expeditious and proper administration of his official functions.

25. Business Promotions and Solicitations for Charity

A judge should avoid giving ground for any reasonable suspicion that he is utilizing the power or prestige of his office to persuade or coerce others to patronize or contribute, either to the success of private business ventures, or to charitable enterprises. He should, therefore, not enter into such private business, or pursue such a course of conduct, as would justify such suspicion, nor use the power of his office or the influence of his name to promote the business interests of others; he should not solicit for charities, nor should he enter into any business relation which, in the normal course of events reasonably to be expected, might bring his personal interest into conflict with the impartial performance of his official duties.

26. Personal Investments and Relations

A judge should abstain from making personal investments in enterprises which are apt to be involved in litigation in the court; and, after his accession to the Bench, he should not retain such investments previously made, longer than a period sufficient to enable him to dispose of them without serious loss. It is desirable that he should, so far as reasonably possible, refrain from all relations which would normally tend to arouse the suspicion that such relations warp or bias his judgment, or prevent his impartial attitude of mind in the administration of his judicial duties.

He should not utilize information coming to him in a judicial capacity for purposes of speculation; and it detracts from the public confidence in his integrity and the soundness of his judicial judgment for him at any time to become a speculative investor upon the hazard of a margin.

27. EXECUTORSHIPS AND TRUSTEESHIPS

While a judge is not disqualified from holding executorships or trusteeships, he should not accept or continue to hold any fiduciary or other position if the holding of it would interfere or seem to interfere with the proper performance of his judicial duties, or if the business interests of those represented require investments in enterprises that are apt to come before him judicially, or to be involved in questions of law to be determined by him.

28. PARTISAN POLITICS [2]

While entitled to entertain his personal views of political questions, and while not required to surrender his rights or opinions as a citizen, it is inevitable that suspicion of being warped by political bias will attach to a judge who becomes the active promoter of the interests of one political party as against another. He should avoid making political speeches, making or soliciting payment of assessments or contributions to party funds, the public endorsement of candidates for political office and participation in party conventions.

He should neither accept nor retain a place on any party committee nor act as party leader, nor engage generally in partisan activities. Where, however, it is necessary for judges to be nominated and elected as candidates of a political party, nothing herein contained shall prevent the judge from attending or speaking at political gatherings, or from making contributions to the campaign funds of the party that has nominated him and seeks his election or re-election.

29. SELF-INTEREST

A judge should abstain from performing or taking part in any judicial act in which his personal interests are involved. If he has personal litigation in the court of which he is judge, he need not resign his judgeship on that account, but he should, of course, refrain from any judicial act in such a controversy.

[2] Canon 28 was amended in 1933. The original Canon was worded as follows:
"While entitled to entertain his personal views of political questions, and while not required to surrender his rights or opinions as a citizen, it is inevitable that suspicion of being warped by political bias will attach to a judge who becomes the active promoter of the interests of one political party as against another. He should avoid making political speeches, making or soliciting payment of assessments or contributions to party funds, the public endorsement of candidates for political office and participation in party conventions."

The Canon was further amended in 1951 by adding the last sentence of the second paragraph.

30. CANDIDACY FOR OFFICE [3]

A candidate for judicial position should not make or suffer others to make for him, promises of conduct in office which appeal to the cupidity or prejudices of the appointing or electing power; he should not announce in advance his conclusions of law on disputed issues to secure class support, and he should do nothing while a candidate to create the impression that if chosen, he will administer his office with bias, partiality or improper discrimination.

While holding a judicial position he should not become an active candidate either at a party primary or at a general election for any office other than a judicial office. If a judge should decide to become a candidate for any office not judicial, he should resign in order that it cannot be said that he is using the power or prestige of his judicial position to promote his own candidacy or the success of his party.

If a judge becomes a candidate for any judicial office, he should refrain from all conduct which might tend to arouse reasonable suspicion that he is using the power or prestige of his judicial position to promote his candidacy or the success of his party.

He should not permit others to do anything in behalf of his candidacy which would reasonably lead to such suspicion.

31. PRIVATE LAW PRACTICE

In many states the practice of law by one holding judicial position is forbidden. In superior courts of general jurisdiction, it should never be permitted. In inferior courts in some states, it is permitted because the county or municipality is not able to pay adequate living compensation for a competent judge. In such cases one who practises law is in a position of great delicacy and must be scrupulously careful to avoid conduct in his practice whereby he utilizes or seems to utilize his judicial position to further his professional success.

He should not practise in the court in which he is a judge, even when

[3] Canon 30 was amended in 1933. The original Canon was worded as follows:

"A candidate for judicial position should not make or suffer others to make for him, promises of conduct in office which appeal to the cupidity or prejudices of the appointing or electing power; he should not announce in advance his conclusions of law on disputed issues to secure class support, and he should do nothing while a candidate to create the impression that if chosen, he will administer his office with bias, partiality or improper discrimination.

"While holding judicial office he should decline nomination to any other place which might reasonably tend to create a suspicion or criticism that the proper performance of his judicial duties is prejudiced or prevented thereby.

"If a judge becomes a candidate for any office, he should refrain from all conduct which might tend to arouse reasonable suspicion that he is using the power or prestige of his judicial position to promote his candidacy or the success of his party.

"He should not permit others to do anything in behalf of his candidacy which would reasonably lead to such suspicion."

presided over by another judge, or appear therein for himself in any controversy.

If forbidden to practise law, he should refrain from accepting any professional employment while in office.

He may properly act as arbitrator or lecture upon or instruct in law, or write upon the subject, and accept compensation therefor, if such course does not interfere with the due performance of his judicial duties, and is not forbidden by some positive provision of law.

32. Gifts and Favors

A judge should not accept any presents or favors from litigants, or from lawyers practising before him or from others whose interests are likely to be submitted to him for judgment.

33. Social Relations

It is not necessary to the proper performance of judicial duty that a judge should live in retirement or seclusion; it is desirable that, so far as reasonable attention to the completion of his work will permit, he continue to mingle in social intercourse, and that he should not discontinue his interest in or appearance at meetings of members of the Bar. He should, however, in pending or prospective litigation before him be particularly careful to avoid such action as may reasonably tend to awaken the suspicion that his social or business relations or friendships constitute an element in influencing his judicial conduct.

34. A Summary of Judicial Obligation

In every particular his conduct should be above reproach. He should be conscientious, studious, thorough, courteous, patient, punctual, just, impartial, fearless of public clamor, regardless of public praise, and indifferent to private political or partisan influences; he should administer justice according to law, and deal with his appointments as a public trust; he should not allow other affairs or his private interests to interfere with the prompt and proper performance of his judicial duties, nor should he administer the office for the purpose of advancing his personal ambitions or increasing his popularity.

35. Improper Publicizing of Court Proceedings [4]

Proceedings in court should be conducted with fitting dignity and decorum. The taking of photographs in the court room, during sessions of the court or recesses between sessions, and the broadcasting or televising of court proceedings are calculated to detract from the essential dignity of the

[4] Canon 35 was amended in 1952 by adding "or televising" and "distract the witness in giving his testimony" in the first paragraph and by adding the second paragraph.

proceedings, distract the witness in giving his testimony, degrade the court, and create misconceptions with respect thereto in the mind of the public and should not be permitted.

Provided that this restriction shall not apply to the broadcasting or televising, under the supervision of the court, of such portions of naturalization proceedings (other than the interrogation of applicants) as are designed and carried out exclusively as a ceremony for the purpose of publicly demonstrating in an impressive manner the essential dignity and the serious nature of naturalization.

36. Conduct of Court Proceedings [5]

Proceedings in court should be so conducted as to reflect the importance and seriousness of the inquiry to ascertain the truth.

The oath should be administered to witnesses in a manner calculated to impress them with the importance and solemnity of their promise to adhere to the truth. Each witness should be sworn separately and impressively at the bar of the court, and the clerk should be required to make a formal record of the administration of the oath, including the name of the witness.

[5] Adopted September 30, 1937.

APPENDIX E

HOFFMAN'S FIFTY RESOLUTIONS
IN REGARD TO
PROFESSIONAL DEPORTMENT [1]

I

I WILL NEVER permit professional zeal to carry me beyond the limits of sobriety and decorum, but bear in mind, with Sir Edward Coke, that "if a river swell beyond its banks, it loseth its own channel."

II

I will espouse no man's cause out of envy, hatred or malice toward his antagonist.

III

To all judges, when in court, I will ever be respectful; they are the law's viceregents; and whatever may be their character and deportment the individual should be lost in the majesty of the office.

IV

Should judges, while on the bench, forget that, as an officer of their court, I have rights, and treat me even with disrespect, I shall value myself too highly to deal with them in like manner. A firm and temperate remonstrance is all that I will ever allow myself.

V

In all intercourse with my professional brethren, I will always be courteous. No man's passions shall intimidate me from asserting fully my

[1] These resolutions were written by David Hoffman, of the Baltimore Bar, for the assistance of the young practitioner. Hoffman said: "We therefore submit to him the following resolutions, to be adopted by him as guides, never to be departed from, and to which he will ever be faithful. We have preferred to frame them in the manner of resolutions, rather than of didactic rules, hoping they may thereby prove more impressive, and be the more likely to be remembered."—David Hoffman, *A Course of Legal Study* (2d ed., 1836), II, 751. The resolutions are found there on pages 752–75.

own or my client's rights; and no man's ignorance or folly shall induce me to take any advantage of him; I shall deal with them all as honorable men, ministering at our common altar. But an act of unequivocal meanness or dishonesty, though it shall wholly sever any personal relation that may subsist between us, shall produce no change in my deportment when brought in professional connection with them; my client's rights, and not my own feelings, are then alone to be consulted.

VI

To the various officers of the court I will be studiously respectful, and specially regardful of their rights and privileges.

VII

As a general rule, I will not allow myself to be engaged in a cause to the exclusion of, or even in participation with, the counsel previously engaged, unless at his own special instance, in union with his client's wishes; and it must, indeed, be a strong case of gross neglect or of fatal inability in the counsel, that shall induce me to take the cause to myself.

VIII

If I have ever had any connection with a cause, I will never permit myself (when that connection is from any reason severed) to be engaged on the side of my former antagonist. Nor shall any change in the formal aspect of the cause induce me to regard it as a ground of exception. It is a poor apology for being found on the opposite side, that the present is but the ghost of the former cause.

IX

Any promise or pledge made by me to the adverse counsel shall be strictly adhered to by me; nor shall the subsequent instructions of my client induce me to depart from it, unless I am well satisfied it was made in error; or that the rights of my client would be materially impaired by its performance.

X

Should my client be disposed to insist on captious requisitions, or frivolous and vexatious defenses, they shall be neither enforced nor countenanced by me. And if still adhered to by him from a hope of pressing the other party into an unjust compromise, or with any other motive, he shall have the option to select other counsel.

XI

If, after duly examining a case, I am persuaded that my client's claim or defense (as the case may be), cannot, or rather ought not to be sustained,

I will promptly advise him to abandon it. To press it further in such a case, with the hope of gleaning some advantage by an extorted compromise, would be lending myself to a dishonorable use of legal means in order to gain a portion of that, the whole of which I have reason to believe would be denied to him both by law and justice.

XII

I will never plead the Statute of Limitations when based on the mere efflux of time; for if my client is conscious he owes the debt, and has no other defense than the legal bar, he shall never make me a partner in his knavery.

XIII

I will never plead or otherwise avail of the bar of Infancy against an honest demand. If my client possesses the ability to pay, and has no other legal or moral defense than that it was contracted by him when under the age of twenty-one years, he must seek for other counsel to sustain him in such a defense. And although in this, as well as in that of limitation, the law has given the defense, and contemplates, in the one case, to induce claimants to a timely prosecution of their rights, and in the other designs to protect a class of persons, who by reason of tender age are peculiarly liable to be imposed on,—yet, in both cases, I shall claim to be the sole judge (the pleas not being compulsory) of the occasions proper for their use.

XIV

My client's conscience and my own are distinct entities: and though my vocation may sometimes justify my maintaining as facts or principles, in doubtful cases, what may be neither one nor the other, I shall ever claim the privileges of solely judging to what extent to go. In civil cases, if I am satisfied from the evidence that the fact is against my client, he must excuse me if I do not see as he does, and do not press it; and should the principle also be wholly at variance with sound law, it would be dishonorable folly in me to endeavor to incorporate it into the jurisprudence of the country, when, if successful, it would be a gangrene that might bring death to my cause of the succeeding day.

XV

When employed to defend those charged with crimes of the deepest dye, and the evidence against them, whether legal or moral, be such as to leave no just doubt of their guilt, I shall not hold myself privileged, much less obliged, to use my endeavors to arrest or to impede the course of justice, by special resorts to ingenuity—to the artifices of eloquence—to appeals to the morbid and fleeting sympathies of weak juries, or of temporizing courts

—to my own personal weight of character—nor finally, to any of the over-weening influences I may possess from popular manners, eminent talents, exalted learning, etc. Persons of atrocious character, who have violated the laws of God and man, are entitled to no such special exertions from any member of our pure and honorable profession; and, indeed, to no inter-vention beyond securing to them a fair and dispassionate investigation of the facts of their cause, and the due application of the law; all that goes beyond this, either in manner or substance, is unprofessional, and proceeds, either from a mistaken view of the relation of client and counsel, or from some unworthy and selfish motive which sets a higher value on professional display and success than on truth and justice, and the substantial interests of the community. Such an inordinate ambition I shall ever regard as a most dangerous perversion of talents, and a shameful abuse of an exalted station. The parricide, the gratuitous murderer, or other perpetrator of like revolting crimes, has surely no such claim on the commanding talents of a profession whose object and pride should be the suppression of all vice by the vindication and enforcement of the laws. Those, therefore, who wrest their proud knowledge from its legitimate purposes to pollute the streams of justice and to screen such foul offenders from merited penal-ties, should be regarded by all (and certainly shall by me) as ministers at a holy altar full of high pretention and apparent sanctity, but inwardly base, unworthy, and hypocritical—dangerous in the precise ratio of their commanding talents and exalted learning.

XVI

Whatever personal influence I may be so fortunate as to possess shall be used by me only as the most valuable of my possessions, and not be cheap-ened or rendered questionable by a too frequent appeal to its influence. There is nothing more fatal to weight of character than its common use; and especially that unworthy one, often indulged in by eminent counsel, of solemn assurances to eke out a sickly and doubtful cause. If the case be a good one, it needs no such appliance; and if bad, the artifice ought to be too shallow to mislead any one. Whether one or the other, such personal pledges should be very sparingly used and only on occasions which ob-viously demand them; for if more liberally resorted to, they beget doubts where none may have existed, or strengthen those which before were only feebly felt.

XVII

Should I attain that eminent standing at the bar which gives authority to my opinions, I shall endeavor, in my intercourse, with my junior brethren, to avoid the least display of it to their prejudice. I will strive never to forget the days of my youth, when I too was feeble in the law, and without standing. I well remember my then ambitious aspirations (though timid and modest) nearly blighted by the inconsiderate or rude and arrogant deportment of some of my seniors; and I will further remember that the vital spark of my early ambition might have been wholly extinguished, and my hopes forever ruined, had not my own resolutions, and a few generous acts of some others of my seniors, raised me from my depression. To my juniors, therefore, I shall ever be kind and encouraging; and never too proud to recognize distinctly that, on many occasions, it is quite probable their knowledge may be more accurate than my own, and that they, with their limited reading and experience, have seen the matter more soundly than I, with my much reading and long experience.

XVIII

To my clients I will be faithful; and in their causes zealous and industrious. Those who can afford to compensate me, must do so; but I shall never close my ear or heart because my client's means are low. Those who have none, and who have just causes, are, of all others, the best entitled to sue, or be defended; and they shall receive a due portion of my services, cheerfully given.

XIX

Should my client be disposed to compromise, or to settle his claim, or defense; and especially if he be content with a verdict or judgment, that has been rendered; or having no opinion of his own, relies with confidence on mine, I will in all such cases greatly respect his wishes and real interests. The further prosecution, therefore, of the claim or defense (as the case may be), will be recommended by me only when, after mature deliberation, I am satisfied that the chances are decidedly in his favor; and I will never forget that the pride of professional opinion on my part, or the spirit of submission, or of controversy (as the case may be) on that of my client, may easily mislead the judgment of both, and cannot justify me in sanctioning, and certainly not in recommending, the further prosecution of what ought to be regarded as a hopeless cause. To keep up the ball (as the phrase goes) at my client's expense, and to my own profit, must be dishonorable; and however willing my client may be to pursue a phantom, and to rely implicitly on my opinion, I will terminate the controversy as conscientiously for him as I would were the cause my own.

XX

Should I not understand my client's cause, after due means to comprehend it, I will retain it no longer, but honestly confess it, and advise him to consult others, whose knowledge of the particular case may probably be better than my own.

XXI

The wealthy and the powerful shall have no privilege against my client that does not equally appertain to others. None shall be so great as to rise, even for a moment, above the just requisitions of the law.

XXII

When my client's reputation is involved in the controversy, it shall be, if possible, judicially passed on. Such cases do not admit of compromise; and no man's elevated standing shall induce me to consent to such a mode of settling the matter: the amende from the great and wealthy to the ignoble and poor should be free, full and open.

XXIII

In all small cases in which I may be engaged I will as conscientiously discharge my duty as in those of magnitude; always recollecting that "small" and "large" are to clients relative terms, the former being to a poor man what the latter is to a rich one; and, as a young practitioner, not forgetting that large ones, which we have not, will never come, if the small ones, which we have, are neglected.

XXIV

I will never be tempted by any pecuniary advantage however great, nor be persuaded by any appeal to my feelings however strong, to purchase, in whole or in part my client's cause. Should his wants be pressing, it will be an act of humanity to relieve them myself, if I am able, and if I am not, then to induce others to do so. But in no case will I permit either my benevolence or avarice, his wants or his ignorance, to seduce me into any participation of his pending claim or defense. Cases may arise in which it would be mutually advantageous thus to bargain, but the experiment is too dangerous, and my rule too sacred to admit of any exception, persuaded as I am that the relation of client and counsel, to be preserved in absolute purity, must admit of no such privilege, however guarded it may be by circumstances; and should the special case alluded to arise, better would it be that my client should suffer, and I lose a great and honest advantage, than that any discretion should exist in a matter so extremely liable to abuse, and so dangerous in precedent.

And though I have thus strongly worded my resolution, I do not thereby mean to repudiate, as wholly inadmissible the taking of contingent fees— on the contrary, they are sometimes perfectly proper and are called for by public policy, no less than by humanity. The distinction is very clear. A claim or defense may be perfectly good in law, and in justice, and yet the expenses of litigation would be much beyond the means of the claimant or defendant—and equally so as to counsel, who, if not thus contingently compensated in the ratio of the risk, might not be compensated at all. A contingent fee looks to professional compensation only on the final result of the matter in favor of the client. None other is offered or is attainable. The claim or defense never can be made without such an arrangement; it is voluntarily tendered, and necessarily accepted or rejected, before the institution of any proceedings.

It flows not from the influence of counsel over client, both parties have the option to be off; no expenses have been incurred; no moneys have been paid by the counsel to the client; the relation of borrower and lender, of vendor and vendee, does not subsist between them,—but it is an independent contract for the services of counsel to be rendered for the contingent avails of the matter to be litigated. Were this denied to the poor man, he could neither prosecute nor be defended. All of this differs essentially from the object of my resolution, which is against purchasing, in whole or in part, my client's rights, after the relation of client and counsel, in respect to it, had been fully established—after the strength of his case has become known to me—after his total pecuniary inability is equally known—after expenses have been incurred which he is unable to meet—after he stands to me in the relation of a debtor and after he desires money from me in exchange for his pending rights. With this explanation I renew my resolution never so to purchase my client's cause, in whole or in part; but still reserve to myself, on proper occasions, and with proper guards, the professional privilege (denied by no law among us) of agreeing to receive a contingent compensation freely offered for services wholly to be rendered, and when it is the only means by which the matter can either be prosecuted or defended. Under all other circumstances, I shall regard contingent fees as obnoxious to the present resolution.

XXV

I will retain no client's funds beyond the period in which I can, with safety and ease, put him in possession of them.

XXVI

I will on no occasion blend with my own my client's money. If kept distinctly as his it will be less liable to be considered as my own.

XXVII

I will charge for my services what my judgment and conscience inform me is my due, and nothing more. If that be withheld it will be no fit matter for arbitration, for no one but myself can adequately judge of such services, and after they are successfully rendered, they are apt to be ungratefully forgotten. I will then receive what the client offers, or the laws of the country may award,—but in either case he must never hope to be again my client.

XXVIII

As a general rule I will carefully avoid what is called the "taking of half fees." And though no one can be so competent as myself to judge what may be a just compensation for my services, yet when the quiddam honorarium has been established by usage or law, I shall regard as eminently dishonorable all underbidding of my professional brethren. On such a subject, however, no inflexible rule can be given to myself, except to be invariably guided by a lively recollection that I belong to an honorable profession.

XXIX

Having received a retainer for contemplated services, which circumstances have prevented me from rendering, I shall hold myself bound to refund the same, as having been paid to me on a consideration which has failed; and, as such, subject to restitution on every principle of law, and of good morals,—and this shall be repaid not merely at the instance of my client, but ex mero motu.

XXX

After a cause is finally disposed of, and all relation of client and counsel seems to be forever closed, I will not forget that it once existed; and will not be inattentive to his just request that all of his papers may be carefully arranged by me, and handed over to him. The execution of such demands, though sometimes troublesome, and inopportunely or too urgently made, still remains a part of my professional duty, for which I shall consider myself already compensated.

XXXI

All opinions for clients, verbal or written, shall be my opinions, deliberately and sincerely given, and never venal and flattering offerings to their wishes or their vanity. And though clients sometimes have the folly to be better pleased with having their views confirmed by an erroneous opinion than their wishes or hopes thwarted by a sound one, yet such assentation is dishonest and unprofessional. Counsel, in giving opinions, whether they perceive this weakness in their clients or not, should act as judges, responsible to God and man, as also especially to their employers, to advise them soberly, discreetly, and honestly, to the best of their ability, though the certain consequence be the loss of large prospective gains.

XXXII

If my client consents to endeavors for a compromise of his claim or defense, and for that purpose I am to commune with the opposing counsel or others, I will never permit myself to enter upon a system of tactics, to ascertain who shall overreach the other by the most nicely balanced artifices of disingenuousness, by mystery, silence, obscurity, suspicion, vigilance to the letter, and all of the other machinery used by this class of tacticians to the vulgar surprise of clients, and the admiration of a few ill-judging lawyers. On the contrary, my resolution in such a case is to examine with great care, previously to the interview, the matter of compromise; to form a judgment as to what I will offer or accept; and promptly, frankly, and firmly to communicate my views to the adverse counsel. In so doing no lights shall be withheld that may terminate the matter as speedily and as nearly in accordance with the rights of my client as possible; although a more dilatory, exacting, and wary policy might finally extract something more than my own or even my client's hopes. Reputation gained for this species of skill is sure to be followed by more than an equivalent loss of character; shrewdness is too often allied to unfairness, caution to severity, silence to disingenuousness, wariness to exaction to make me covet a reputation based on such qualities.

XXXIII

What is wrong is not the less so from being common. And though few dare to be singular, even in a right cause, I am resolved to make my own, and not the conscience of others, my sole guide. What is morally wrong cannot be professionally right, however it may be sanctioned by time or custom. It is better to be right with a few, or even none, than wrong, though with a multitude. If, therefore, there be among my brethren any traditional moral errors of practice, they shall be studiously avoided by me, though in so doing I unhappily come in collision with what is (erroneously, I think) too often denominated the policy of the profession. Such cases, fortunately, occur but seldom, but when they do, I shall trust to that moral firmness of purpose which shrinks from no consequences, and which can be intimidated by no authority, however ancient or respectable.

XXXIV

Law is a deep science; its boundaries, like space, seem to recede as we advance; and though there be as much of certainty in it as in any other science, it is fit we should be modest in our opinions, and ever willing to be further instructed. Its acquisition is more than the labor of a life, and after all can be with none the subject of an unshaken confidence. In the language, then, of a late beautiful writer, I am resolved to "consider my own acquired knowledge but as a torch flung into an abyss, making the darkness visible, and showing me the extent of my own ignorance." (Jameson.)

XXXV

I will never be voluntarily called as a witness in any cause in which I am counsel. Should my testimony, however, be so material that without it my client's cause may be greatly prejudiced, he must at once use his option to cancel the tie between us in the cause, and dispense with my further services or with my evidence. Such a dilemma would be anxiously avoided by every delicate mind, the union of counsel and witness being usually resorted to only as a forlorn hope in the agonies of a cause, and becomes particularly offensive when its object be to prove an admission made to such counsel by the opposite litigant. Nor will I ever recognize any distinction in this respect between my knowledge of facts acquired before and since the institution of the suit, for in no case will I consent to sustain by my testimony any of the matters which my interest and professional duty render me anxious to support. This resolution, however, has no application whatever to facts contemporaneous with and relating merely to the prosecution or defense of the cause itself; such as evidence relating to the contents of a paper unfortunately lost by myself or others—and such like matters, which do not respect the original merits of the controversy, and which, in truth, add nothing to the once existing testimony; but relate merely to matters respecting the conduct of the suit, or to the recovery of lost evidence; nor does it apply to the case of gratuitous counsel,—that is, to those who have expressly given their services voluntarily.

XXXVI

Every letter or note that is addressed to me shall receive a suitable response, and in proper time. Nor shall it matter from whom it comes, what it seeks, or what may be the terms in which it is penned. Silence can be justified in no case; and though the information sought cannot or ought not to be given, still decorum would require from me a courteous recognition of the request, though accompanied with a firm withholding of what has been asked. There can be no sure indication of vulgar education than neglect of letters and notes; it manifests a total want of that tact and amenity which intercourse with good society never fails to confer. But that dogged silence (worse than a rude reply) in which some of our profession indulge on receiving letters offensive to their dignity, or when dictated by ignorant importunity, I am resolved never to imitate—but will answer every letter and note with as much civility as may be due, and in as good time as may be practicable.

XXXVII

Should a professional brother, by his industry, learning and zeal, or even by some happy chance, become eminently successful in causes which give him large pecuniary emoluments, I will neither envy him the fruits of his toils or good fortune, nor endeavor by any indirection to lessen them, but rather strive to emulate his worth, than enviously to brood over his meritorious success, and my own more tardy career.

XXXVIII

Should it be my happy lot to rank with, or take precedence of my seniors, who formerly endeavored to impede my onward course, I am firmly resolved to give them no cause to suppose that I remember the one, or am conscious of the other. When age and infirmities have overtaken them, my kindness will teach them the loveliness of forgiveness. Those again, who aided me when young in the profession shall find my gratitude increase in proportion as I become the better able to sustain myself.

XXXIX

A forensic contest is often no very sure test of the comparative strength of the combatants, nor should defeat be regarded as a just cause of boast in the victor, or of mortification in the vanquished. When the controversy has been judicially settled against me, in all courts, I will not "fight the battle o'er again," coram non judice; nor endeavor to persuade others, as is too often done, that the courts were prejudiced—or the jury desperately ignorant—or the witnesses perjured—or that the victorious counsel were unprofessional and disingenuous. In such cases, Credat Judaeus Appella!

XL

Ardor in debate is often the soul of eloquence, and the greatest charm of oratory. When spontaneous and suited to the occasion, it becomes powerful. A sure test of this is when it so alarms a cold, calculating and disingenuous opponent, as to induce him to resort to numerous vexatious means of neutralizing its force—when ridicule and sarcasm take the place of argument—when the poor device is resorted to of endeavoring to cast the speaker from his well-guarded pivot, by repeated interruptions, or by impressing on the court and jury that his just and well-tempered zeal is but passion, and his earnestness but the exacerbation of constitutional infirmity—when the opponent assumes a patronizing air, and imparts lessons of wisdom and of instruction! Such opponents I am resolved to disappoint, and on no account will I ever imitate their example. The warm current of my feelings shall be permitted to flow on; the influences of my nature shall receive no check; the ardor and fullness of my words shall not be abated—for this would be to gratify the unjust wishes of my adversary, and would lessen my usefulness to my client's cause.

XLI

In reading to the court or to the jury, authorities, records, documents or other papers, I shall always consider myself as executing a trust, and as such, bound to execute it faithfully and honorably. I am resolved, therefore, carefully to abstain from all false or deceptious readings, and from all uncandid omissions of any qualifications of the doctrines maintained by me, which may be contained in the text or in the notes; and I shall ever hold that the obligation extends not only to words, syllables, and letters, but also to the modus legendi. All intentional false emphasis and even intonations in any degree calculated to mislead, are petty impositions on the confidence reposed, and whilst avoided by myself, shall ever be regarded by me in others as feeble devices of an impoverished mind, or as pregnant evidences of a disregard for truth, which justly subjects them to be closely watched in more important matters.

XLII

In the examination of witnesses, I shall not forget that perhaps circumstances and not choice have placed them somewhat in my power. Whether so or not, I shall never esteem it my privilege to disregard their feelings, or to extort from their evidence what, in moments free from embarrassment, they would not testify. Nor will I conclude that they have no regard for truth and even the sanctity of an oath, because they use the privilege accorded to others, of changing their language and of explaining their previous declarations. Such captious dealing with the words and syllables of a witness ought to produce in the mind of an intelligent jury only a reverse effect from that designed by those who practice such poor devices.

XLIII

I will never enter into any conversation with my opponent's client, relative to his claim or defense, except with the consent and in the presence of his counsel.

XLIV

Should the party just mentioned have no counsel, and my client's interest demand that I should still commune with him, it shall be done in writing only, and no verbal response will be received. And if such person be unable to commune in writing, I will either delay the matter until he employs counsel, or take down in writing his reply in the presence of others; so that if occasion should make it essential to avail myself of his answer, it may be done through the testimony of others, and not by mine. Even such cases should be regarded as the result of unavoidable necessity, and are to be resorted to only to guard against great risk, the artifices of fraud, or with the hope of obviating litigation.

XLV

Success in any profession will be much promoted by good address. Even the most cautious and discriminating minds are not exempt from its influence; the wisest judges, the most dispassionate juries, and the most wary opponents being made thereby, at least, more willing auditors—and this, of itself, is a valuable end. But whilst address is deservedly prized, and merits the highest cultivation, I fully concur in sentiment with a high authority, that we should be "respectful without meanness, easy without too much familiarity, genteel without affectation, and insinuating without any art or design."

XLVI

Nothing is more unfriendly to the art of pleasing than morbid timidity (bashfulness—mauvaise honte).

All life teems with examples of its prejudicial influence, showing that the art of rising in life has no greater enemy than this nervous and senseless defect of education. Self-possession, calmness—steady assurance—intrepidity—are all perfectly consistent with the most amiable modesty, and none but vulgar and illiterate minds are prone to attribute to presumptuous assurance the apparently cool and unconcerned exertions of young men at the bar. A great connoisseur in such matters says, that "what is done under concern and embarrassment is sure to be ill done"; and the judge (I have known some) who can scowl on the early endeavors of the youthful advocate who has fortified himself with resolution, must be a man poor in the knowledge of human character, and perhaps, still more so in good feelings. Whilst, therefore, I shall ever cherish these opinions, I hold myself bound to distinguish the arrogant, noisy, shallow, and dictatorial impudence of some, from the gentle, though firm and manly, confidence of others—they who bear the white banner of modesty, fringed with resolution.

XLVII

All reasoning should be regarded as a philosophical process—its object being conviction by certain known and legitimate means. No one ought to be expected to be convinced by loud words—dogmatic assertions—assumption of superior knowledge—sarcasm—invective; but by gentleness, sound ideas, cautiously expressed by sincerity—my ardor without extravasation. The minds and hearts of those we address are apt to be closed when the lungs are appealed to instead of logic; when assertion is relied on more than proof; and when sarcasm and invective supply the place of deliberate reasoning. My resolution, therefore, is to respect courts, juries, and counsel as assailable only through the medium of logical and just reasoning; and by such appeals to the sympathies of our common nature as are worthy, legitimate, well-timed, and in good taste.

XLVIII

The ill success of many at the bar is owing to the fact that their business is not their pleasure. Nothing can be more unfortunate than this state of mind. The world is too full of penetration not to perceive it, and much of our discourteous manner to clients, to courts, to juries, and counsel, has its source in this defect. I am, therefore, resolved to cultivate a passion for my profession; or, after a reasonable exertion therein, without success, to abandon it. But I will previously bear in mind, that he who abandons any profession will scarcely find another to suit him; the defect is in himself; he has not performed his duty, and has failed in resolutions, perhaps often made, to retrieve lost time, the want of firmness can give no promise of success in any vocation.

XLIX

Avarice is one of the most dangerous and disgusting of vices. Fortunately its presence is oftener found in age than in youth; for if it be seen as an early feature in our character it is sure, in the course of a long life, to work a great mass of oppression, and to end in both intellectual and moral desolation. Avarice gradually originates every species of indirection. Its offspring is meanness; and it contaminates every pure and honorable principle. It cannot consist with honesty scarce a moment without gaining the victory. Should the young practitioner, therefore, on the receipt of the first fruits of his exertions, perceive the slightest manifestations of this vice, let him view it as his most insidious and deadly enemy. Unless he can then heartily and thoroughly eradicate it, he will find himself, perhaps slowly, but surely, capable of unprofessional—mean—and, finally, dishonest acts, which as they cannot be long concealed, will render him conscious of the loss of character; make him callous to all the nicer feelings; and ultimately so degrade him, that he consents to live upon arts, from which his talents, acquirements, and original integrity would certainly have rescued him, had he, at the very commencement, fortified himself with the resolution to reject all gains save those acquired by the most strictly honorable and professional means. I am, therefore, firmly resolved never to receive from any one a compensation not justly and honorably my due; and, if fairly received, to place on it no undue value; to entertain no affection for money, further than as a means of obtaining the goods of life, —the art of using money being quite as important for the avoidance of avarice, and the preservation of a pure character, as that of acquiring it.

With the aid of the foregoing resolutions, and the faithful adherence to the following and last one, I hope to attain eminence in my profession, and to leave this world with the merited reputation of having lived an honest lawyer.

L

LAST RESOLUTION: I will read the foregoing forty-nine resolutions twice every year during my professional life.

APPENDIX F

CODE OF ETHICS [1]

ALABAMA STATE BAR ASSOCIATION

DECEMBER 14, 1887
FEBRUARY 7, 1899

See 118 Ala. XXIII–XXXIV

PREAMBLE

THE PURITY AND EFFICIENCY of judicial administration, which, under our system, is largely government itself, depend as much upon the character, conduct, and demeanor of attorneys in this great trust, as upon the fidelity and learning of courts or the honesty and intelligence of juries.

HIGH MORAL PRINCIPLE ONLY SAFE GUIDE

"There is, perhaps, no profession after that of the sacred ministry, in which a high-toned morality is more imperatively necessary than that of the law. There is certainly, without any exception, no profession in which so many temptations beset the path to swerve from the lines of strict integrity; in which so many delicate and difficult questions of duty are constantly arising. There are pitfalls and man-traps at every step, and the mere youth, at the very outset of his career needs often the prudence and self-denial, as well as the moral courage, which belongs commonly to riper years. High moral principle is his only safe guide; the only torch to light his way amidst darkness and obstruction."—Sharswood.

A SUMMARY OF THE DUTIES OF ATTORNEYS

A comprehensive summary of the duties specifically enjoined by law upon attorneys, which they are sworn "not to violate," is found in section 791 of the Code of Alabama.

These duties are:

[1] The Alabama Code of Ethics was written by Thomas Goode Jones (1844–1914), Montgomery, who served his state as Speaker of the House, Governor of Alabama, Member of Constitutional Convention 1901, and United States District Judge, Middle and Northern Districts of Alabama, 1901–14.

"1st. To support the constitution and laws of this State and the United States.

"2nd. To maintain the respect due to courts of justice and judicial officers.

"3rd. To employ, for the purpose of maintaining the causes confided to them, such means only as are consistent with truth, and never seek to mislead the judges by any artifice or false statement of the law.

"4th. To maintain inviolate the confidence, and, at every peril to themselves, to preserve the secrets of their clients.

"5th. To abstain from all offensive personalities, and to advance no fact prejudicial to the honor or reputation of a party or witness, unless required by the justice of the cause with which they are charged.

"6th. To encourage neither the commencement nor continuance of an action or proceeding from any motive of passion or interest.

"7th. Never to reject, for any consideration personal to themselves, the cause of the defenseless and oppressed."

No Set Rule for Every Case

No rule will determine an attorney's duty in the varying phases of every case. What is right and proper must, in the absence of statutory rules and an authoritative code, be ascertained in view of the peculiar facts, in the light of conscience, and the conduct of honorable and distinguished attorneys in similar cases, and by an analogy to the duties enjoined by statute, and the rules of good neighborhood.

The following general rules are adopted by the Alabama State Bar Association for the guidance of its members:

Duty of Attorneys to Courts and Judicial Officers

1. The respect enjoined by law for courts and judicial officers is exacted for the sake of the office, and not for the individual who administers it. Bad opinion of the incumbent, however well founded, can not excuse the withholding of the respect due the office, while administering its functions.

Criticism of Judicial Conduct

2. The proprieties of the judicial station, in a great measure, disable the judge from defending himself against strictures upon his official conduct. For this reason, and because such criticisms tend to impair public confidence in the administration of justice, attorneys should, as a rule, refrain from published criticism of judicial conduct, especially in reference to causes in which they have been of counsel, otherwise than in courts of review, or when the conduct of a judge is necessarily involved in determining his removal from or continuance in office.

Avoid Unusual Hospitality to Judges

3. Marked attention and unusual hospitality to a judge, when the relations of the parties are such that they would not otherwise be extended, subject both judge and attorneys to misconstruction, and should be sedulously avoided. A self-respecting independence in the discharge of the attorney's duties, which at the same time does not withhold the courtesy and respect due the judge's station, is the only just foundation for cordial personal and official relations between bench and bar. All attempts by means beyond these to gain special personal consideration and favor of a judge are disreputable.

Support Courts and Judges in All Proper Ways

4. Courts and judicial officers, in their rightful exercise of their functions, should always receive the support and countenance of attorneys against unjust criticism and popular clamor; and it is an attorney's duty to give them his moral support in all proper ways, and particularly by setting a good example in his own person of obedience to law.

Candor and Fairness Should Characterize Attorney

5. The utmost candor and fairness should characterize the dealings of attorneys with the courts and with each other. Knowingly citing as authority an overruled case, or treating a repealed statute as in existence; knowingly misquoting the language of a decision or text book; knowingly misquoting the contents of a paper, the testimony of a witness, or the language or argument of opposite counsel; offering evidence which is known the court must reject as illegal, to get it before the jury, under guise of arguing its admissibility, and all kindred practices, are deceits and evasions unworthy of attorneys.

Purposely concealing or withholding in the opening argument, positions intended finally to be relied on, in order that opposite counsel may not discuss them, is unprofessional. Courts and juries look with disfavor on such practices, and are quick to suspect the weakness of the cause which has need to resort to them.

In the argument of demurrers, admission of evidence, and other questions of law, counsel should carefully refrain from "side-bar" remarks and sparring discourse, to influence the jury or bystanders. Personal colloquies between counsel tend to delay, and promote unseemly wrangling, and ought to be discouraged.

Attorneys Should Be Punctual

6. Attorneys owe it to the courts and the public whose business the courts transact, as well as their own clients, to be punctual in attendance on their causes; and whenever an attorney is late he should apologize or explain his absence.

Display of Temper Should Be Avoided

7. One side must always lose the cause; and it is not wise, or respectful to the court, for attorneys to display temper because of an adverse ruling.

DUTY OF ATTORNEYS TO EACH OTHER, TO CLIENTS AND THE PUBLIC

Uphold Honor of Profession

8. An attorney should strive, at all times, to uphold the honor, maintain the dignity, and promote the usefulness of the profession; for it is so interwoven with the administration of justice, that whatever redounds to the good of one advances the other; and the attorney thus discharges, not merely an obligation to his brothers, but a high duty to the State and his fellow man.

Prejudice Should Not Be Stirred Up

9. An attorney should not speak slightingly or disparagingly of his profession, or pander in any way to unjust popular prejudices against it; and he should scrupulously refrain at all times, and in all relations of life, from availing himself of any prejudice or popular misconception against lawyers, in order to carry a point against a brother attorney.

Duties to Be Performed within Limits of Law

10. Nothing has been more potential in creating and pandering to popular prejudice against lawyers as a class, and in withholding from the profession the full measure of public esteem and confidence which belong to the proper discharge of its duties, than the false claim, often set up by the unscrupulous in defense of questionable transactions, that it is an attorney's duty to do everything to succeed in his client's cause.

An attorney "owes entire devotion to the interest of his client, warm zeal in the maintenance and defense of his cause, and the exertion of the utmost skill and ability," to the end, that nothing may be taken or withheld from him, save by the rules of law, legally applied. No sacrifice or peril, even to loss of life itself, can absolve from the fearless discharge of this duty. Nevertheless, it is steadfastly to be borne in mind that the great trust is to be performed within and not without the bounds of the law which creates it. The attorney's office does not destroy the man's accountability to the Creator, or loosen the duty of obedience to law, and the obligation to his neighbor; and it does not permit, much less demand, violation of law, or any manner of fraud or chicanery, for the client's sake.

Fearlessly Expose Unprofessional Conduct

11. Attorneys should fearlessly expose before the proper tribunals corrupt or dishonest conduct in the profession; and there should never be

any hesitancy in accepting employment against an attorney who has wronged his client.

Defense and Prosecution of Criminal Cases

12. An attorney appearing or continuing as private counsel in the prosecution for a crime of which he believes the accused innocent, forswears himself. The State's attorney is criminal, if he presses for a conviction, when upon the evidence he believes the prisoner innocent. If the evidence is not plain enough to justify a nolle pros., a public prosecutor should submit the case, with such comments as are pertinent, accompanied by a candid statement of his own doubts.

Present Such Defenses as Law of Land Permits

13. An attorney cannot reject the defense of a person accused of a criminal offense, because he knows or believes him guilty. It is his duty by all fair and honorable means to present such defenses as the law of the land permits; to the end that no one may be deprived of life or liberty, but by due process of law.

Must Not Be a Party to Oppression

14. An attorney must decline in a civil cause to conduct a prosecution, when satisfied that the purpose is merely to harass or injure the opposite party, or to work oppression and wrong.

No Private Argument to Judge

15. It is bad practice for an attorney to communicate or argue privately with the judge as to the merits of his cause.

Newspaper Advertising

16. Newspaper advertisements, circulars and business cards, tending professional services to the general public, are proper; but special solicitation of particular individuals to become clients ought to be avoided. Indirect advertisement for business, by furnishing or inspiring editorials or press notices, regarding causes in which the attorney takes part, the manner in which they were conducted, the importance of his positions, the magnitude of the interests involved, and all other like self-laudation, is of evil tendency and wholly unprofessional.

Avoid Newspaper Discussion of Legal Matters

17. Newspaper publications by an attorney as to the merits of pending or anticipated litigation, call forth discussion and reply from the opposite party, tend to prevent a fair trial in the courts, and otherwise prejudice the due administration of justice. It requires a strong case to justify such publications; and when proper, it is unprofessional to make them anonymously.

Better for Attorney Not to Be a Witness

18. When an attorney is a witness for his client except as to formal matters, such as the attestation or custody of an instrument and the like, he should leave the trial of the case to other counsel. Except when essential to the ends of justice, an attorney should scrupulously avoid testifying in court in behalf of his client, as to any matter.

Avoid Assertion of Belief as to Justice of Client's Case

19. The same reasons which make it improper in general for an attorney to testify for his client, apply with greater force to assertions, sometimes made by counsel in argument, of personal belief of the client's innocence or the justice of his cause. If such assertions are habitually made they lose all force and subject the attorney to falsehoods; while the failure to make them in particular cases will often be esteemed a tacit admission of belief of the client's guilt, or the weakness of his cause.

Disreputable to Stir Up Litigation

20. It is indecent to hunt up defects in titles and the like and inform thereof, in order to be employed to bring suit; or to seek out a person supposed to have a cause of action, and endeavor to get a fee to litigate about it. Except where ties of blood, relationship or trust, make it an attorney's duty, it is unprofessional to volunteer advice to bring a law suit. Stirring up strife and litigation is forbidden by law, and disreputable in morals.

Confidences between Client and Attorney

21. Communications and confidence between client and attorney are the property and secrets of the client, and can not be divulged, except at his instance; even the death of the client does not absolve the attorney from his obligation of secrecy.

Secrets of Client Not to Be Divulged

22. The duty not to divulge the secrets of clients extends further than mere silence by the attorney, and forbids accepting retainers or employment afterwards from others involving the client's interests, in the matters about which the confidence was reposed. When the secrets or confidence of a former client may be availed of or be material, in a subsequent suit, as the basis of any judgment which may injuriously affect his rights, the attorney can not appear in such case without the consent of his former client.

Attorney Not to Attack Instruments Drawn by Himself

23. An attorney can never attack an instrument or paper drawn by him for any infirmity apparent on its face; nor for any other cause where confidence has been reposed as to the facts concerning it. Where the attorney

acted as a mere conveyancer, and was not consulted as to the facts, and unknown to him, the transaction amounted to a violation of the criminal laws, he may assail it on that ground, in suits between third persons, or between parties to the instrument and strangers.

Personal Services before Bodies Other than Courts

24. An attorney openly, and in his true character, may render purely professional services before committees, regarding proposed legislation, and in advocacy of claims before departments of the government, upon the same principles of ethics which justify his appearance before the courts; but it is immoral and illegal for an attorney so engaged to conceal his attorneyship, or to employ secret personal solicitations, or to use means other than those addressed to the reason and understanding, to influence action.

Attorney Not to Represent Conflicting Interests

25. An attorney can never represent conflicting interests in the same suit or transaction, except by express consent of all so concerned, with full knowledge of the facts. Even then, such a position is embarrassing, and ought to be avoided. An attorney represents conflicting interests, within the meaning of this rule, when it is his duty, in behalf of one of his clients, to contend for that which duty to other clients in the transaction requires him to oppose.

Reputation of a "Rough Tongue" Not Desirable

26. "It is not a desirable professional reputation to live and die with— that of a rough tongue, which makes a man to be sought out and retained to gratify the malevolent feeling of a suitor, in hearing the other side well lashed and vilified."

Client Is Not the Keeper of the Attorney's Conscience

27. An attorney is under no obligation to minister to the malevolence or prejudices of a client in the trial or conduct of a cause. The client can not be made the keeper of the attorney's conscience in professional matters. He can not demand as of right that his attorney shall abuse the opposite.

Ill-feeling of Clients Not to Be Entertained by Lawyers

28. Clients, and not their attorneys, are the litigants; and whatever may be the ill-feeling existing between clients, it is unprofessional for attorneys to partake of it in their conduct and demeanor to each other, or to suitors in the case.

Personalities in Argument Should Be Avoided

29. In the conduct of litigation and the trial of causes the attorneys should try the merits of the cause, and not try each other. It is not proper

to allude to, or comment upon, the personal history, or mental or physical peculiarities or idiosyncrasies of opposite counsel. Personalities should always be avoided, and the utmost courtesy always extended to an honorable opponent.

Attorney Controls Incidents of Trial

30. As to the incidental matters pending the trial, not affecting the merits of the cause, or working substantial prejudice to the rights of the client, such as forcing the opposite attorney to trial when he is under affliction or bereavement; forcing the trial on a particular day to the serious injury of the opposite attorney, when no harm will result from a trial at a different time; the time allowed for signing a bill of exceptions, crossing interrogatories, and the like; the attorney must be allowed to judge. No client has a right to demand that his attorney shall be illiberal in such matters, or that he would do anything therein repugnant to his own sense of honor and propriety; and if such a course is insisted on the attorney should retire from the cause.

Giving Preference as to Retainer

31. Where an attorney has more than one regular client, the oldest client, in the absence of some agreement, should have the preference of retaining the attorney, as against his other clients in litigation between them.

Assurances of Success to Client Not to Be Made

32. The miscarriages to which justice is subject, and the uncertainty of predicting results, admonish attorneys to beware of bold and confident assurances to clients, especially where the employment depends upon the assurance, and the case is not plain.

Promptness and Punctuality

33. Prompt preparation for trial, punctuality in answering letters and keeping engagements, are due from an attorney to his client, and do much to strengthen their confidence and friendship.

Things Attorney Should Disclose to Client

34. An attorney is in honor bound to disclose to the client at the time of retainer, all the circumstances of his controversy, which might justly influence the client in the selection of his attorney. He must decline to appear in any cause where his obligation or relations to the opposite parties will hinder or seriously embarrass the full and fearless discharge of all his duties.

Client Should Have Attorney's Candid Opinion

35. An attorney should endeavor to obtain full knowledge of his client's cause before advising him, and is bound to give him a candid opinion

of the merits and probable result of his cause. When the controversy will admit of it he ought to seek to adjust it without litigation, if practicable.

Evidence as to Agreements with Client

36. Where an attorney, during the existence of the relation, has lawfully made an agreement which binds his client, he cannot honorably refuse to give the opposite party evidence of the agreement, because of his subsequent discharge or instructions to that effect by his former client.

Client's Money a Sacred Fund

37. Money or other trust property coming into the possession of the attorney, should be promptly reported, and never commingled with his private property or used by him, except with the client's knowledge and consent.

Attorney Not to Borrow from Client

38. Attorneys should, as far as possible, avoid becoming either borrowers or creditors of their client; and they ought scrupulously to refrain from bargaining about the subject matter of the litigation, so long as the relation of attorney and client continue.

Offer of Client to Furnish Additional Counsel

39. Natural solicitude of clients often prompts them to offer assistance of additional counsel. This should not be met, as it sometimes is, as evidence of want of confidence; but after advising frankly with the client, it should be left to his determination.

Better to Reduce Important Agreements to Writing

40. Important agreements affecting the rights of clients should, as far as possible, be reduced to writing; but it is dishonorable to avoid performance of an agreement fairly made, because not reduced to writing as required by rules of court.

Known Customs of Bar to Be Followed

41. An attorney should not ignore known customs or practice of the bar of a particular court, even when the law permits, without giving opposing counsel timely notice.

Notify Client of Proposed Compromises

42. An attorney should not attempt to compromise with the opposite party, without notifying his client, if practicable.

Rule When Counsel Differ as to Vital Matters

43. Where attorneys jointly associate in a cause cannot agree as to any matter vital to the interest of their client, the course to be pursued should

be left to his determination. The client's decision should be cheerfully acquiesced in, unless the nature of the difference makes it impracticable for the attorney to co-operate heartily and effectively; in which event, it is his duty to be asked to be discharged.

Duty of Attorney Coming into a Case

44. An attorney coming into a cause in which others are employed, should give notice as soon as practicable and ask for conference, and if the association is objectionable to the attorney already in the cause, the other attorney should decline to take part, unless the first attorney is relieved.

No Discussion of Merits of Cause with Opposite Party

45. An attorney ought not to engage in discussion or arguments about the merits of the case with the opposite party, without notice to his attorney.

Better to Agree on Fee in Advance

46. Satisfactory relations between attorney and client are best preserved by a frank and explicit understanding at the outset, as to the amount of the attorney's compensation; and, where it is possible, this should always be agreed on in advance.

Suing a Client for a Fee

47. In general, it is better to yield something to a client's dissatisfaction at the amount of the fee, though the sum be reasonable, than to engage in a law suit to justify it, which ought always to be avoided, except as a last resort to prevent imposition or fraud.

Value of Attorney's Services Not to Be Overestimated

48. Men, as a rule, overestimate rather than undervalue the worth of their services, and attorneys in fixing their fees should avoid charges which unduly magnify the value of their advice and services, as well as those which practically belittle them. A client's ability to pay can never justify a charge for more than the service is worth; though his poverty may require a less charge in many instances, and sometimes none at all.

A Regular Client May Be Charged Less

49. An attorney may charge a regular client, who entrusts him with all his business, less for a particular service than he would charge a casual client for like services. The element of uncertainty of compensation where a contingent fee is agreed on, justifies higher charges than where compensation is assured.

Matters to Be Considered in Fixing Fees

50. In fixing fees the following elements should be considered: 1st. The time and labor required, the novelty and difficulty of the questions involved, and the skill requisite to properly conduct the cause. 2d. Whether the particular case will debar the attorney's appearance for others in cases likely to arise out of the transaction, and in which there is a reasonable expectation that the attorney would otherwise be employed; and herein of the loss of other business while employed in the particular case, and the antagonism with other clients growing out of the employment. 3d. The customary charges of the Bar for similar services. 4th. The real amount involved and the benefit resulting from the services. 5th. Whether the compensation was contingent or assured. 6th. Is the client a regular one, retaining the attorney in all his business? No one of these considerations is in itself controlling. They are mere guides in ascertaining what the service was really worth; and in fixing the amount it should never be forgotten that the profession is a branch of the administration of justice and not a mere money-getting trade.

Contingent Fees

51. Contingent fees may be contracted for; but they lead to many abuses, and certain compensation is to be preferred.

Services to Family of a Deceased Lawyer

52. Casual and slight services should be rendered without charge by one attorney to another in his personal cause; but when the service goes beyond this an attorney may be charged as other clients. Ordinary advice and services to the family of a deceased attorney should be rendered without charge in most instances; and where the circumstances make it proper to charge, the fees should generally be less than in case of other clients.

Treat Witnesses and Parties Fairly

53. Witnesses and suitors should be treated with fairness and kindness. When essential to the ends of justice to arraign their conduct or testimony, it should be done without vilification or unnecessary harshness. Fierceness of manner and uncivil behavior can add nothing to the truthful dissection of a false witness's testimony, and often rob deserved strictures of proper weight.

Duty of Court to Attend to Comfort of Jurors

54. It is the duty of the court and its officers to provide for the comfort of jurors. Displaying special concern for their comfort, and volunteering to ask favors for them, while they are present—such as frequent motions to adjourn trials, or take recess, solely on the ground of the jury's fatigue, or hunger, and uncomfortableness of their seats, or the court-room, and

the like—should be avoided. Such intervention of attorneys, when proper, ought to be had privately with the court; whereby there will be no appearance of fawning upon the jury, nor grounds for ill-feeling of the jury towards the court or opposite counsel, if such requests are denied. For like reasons, one attorney should never ask another in the presence of the jury, to consent to its discharge or dispersion; and when such a request is made by the court, the attorneys, without indicating their preference, should ask to be heard after the jury withdraws.

No Private Conversations with Jurors

55. An attorney ought never to converse privately with jurors about the case; and must avoid all unnecessary communication, even as to matters foreign to the cause, both before and during the trial. Any other course, no matter how blameless the attorney's motives, gives color to the imputing evil designs, and often leads to scandal in the administration of justice.

Duty When Appointed by Court to Defend Prisoner

56. An attorney assigned as counsel for an indigent prisoner ought not to ask to be excused for any light cause, and should always be a friend to the defenseless and oppressed.

APPENDIX G

RULES AND STANDARDS
AS TO LAW LISTS

Adopted by the House of Delegates
September 30, 1937 [1]

Special Committee on Law Lists:

That the Special Committee on Law Lists be authorized and directed to

(*a*) procure information regarding Law Lists and from time to time advise members of the Association thereof;

(*b*) recommend to the Association for adoption from time to time such standards or rules, and amendments thereof, for Law Lists as may seem in the interest of the public;

(*c*) adopt, and from time to time amend, such reasonable rules and regulations for the conduct of its authorized activities as it may find desirable;

(*d*) endeavor to protect the public and members of the profession from dishonest, fraudulent or unworthy conduct of persons who represent, or claim to represent, Law Lists;

(*e*) cooperate with law enforcement officers and others interested in the censure or punishment of such dishonest, fraudulent or unworthy conduct;

(*f*) investigate annually at the expense of publishers of Law Lists which shall request the committee to do so, whether such publishers respectively are complying with the provisions of the Rules and Standards as to Law Lists;

(*g*) issue an annual certificate of compliance to the publisher of any Law List which the Committee, upon such investigation, finds has complied with the Rules and Standards as to Law Lists of the Association and the regulations of the committee; and revoke, conditionally or otherwise, the certificate issued to the publisher of any such Law List if the committee finds that the publisher thereof, after receiving such certificate has violated any of such rules, standards or regulations;

[1] With amendments made October, 1941, August, 1942 and February, 1944.

(*h*) take such action as it may deem advisable to cause the issuance or revocation of a certificate to be made known to the members of the Association;

(*i*) advise each bar association having disciplinary jurisdiction, of information which may indicate dishonorable, fraudulent, or unworthy conduct of a lawyer whose name is presented in a law list.

Rules and Standards as to Law Lists:

That the following Rules and Standards, and each of them, be adopted as and for Law Lists which request a certificate of compliance:

1. Every list of attorneys at law, legal directory or other instrumentality maintained or published primarily for the purpose of circulating or presenting the name or names of any attorney or attorneys at law as probably available for professional employment, shall be deemed a Law List.

2. The purchase or use of a Law List the publisher of which has a certificate of compliance may be recommended to attorneys at law, or laymen, by its issuer, only on the basis of the circulation, physical makeup and accuracy thereof, and the extent to which lawyers listed therein have been investigated. Efforts by the issuer of a Law List to otherwise secure employment for any attorney listed therein, or presented thereby, shall be deemed ground for not issuing a certificate of compliance, or for the revocation of the certificate if it has already been issued.

3. No certificate of compliance shall be issued to the publisher of any Law List or continue unrevoked

(*a*) if, in connection with the preparation, publication, distribution or presentation thereof, the issuer does, causes, permits to be done, encourages or participates in the doing of, any act or thing which, directly or indirectly, violates the Canons of Ethics of this Association, or which constitutes the unlawful practice of the law;

(*b*) which shall be conducted upon a basis which does not tend to promote the public interest, or which employs a practice not in accord with a high standard of business conduct;

(*c*) or if the price for representation, or listing therein, or for a copy of the list, is not uniform within reasonably prescribed areas;

(*d*) or if any obligation is assumed by either user or attorney, to employ, exclusively or preferentially, in the forwarding, receiving or exchange of legal business, the attorneys listed therein;

(*e*) or if in the physical makeup thereof, preferential prominence shall be given to the name of any attorney or attorneys listed therein, by different size or character of type, underscoring or other methods employed by printers for emphasis or to attract attention; but the foregoing shall not prohibit the publication in the geographical section of a Law List of such professional card as the Canons permit or of a reference there to such card in another section of the book;

(*f*) or if the issuer thereof shall endeavor to direct, or control, the professional activities of any attorney listed therein or presented thereby;

(g) or if such Law List shall be published or issued as a part of any professional, commercial, trade or business publication or journal;

(h) or if the issuer thereof shall neglect or refuse to promptly and fully (a) notify the Association through the committee, in writing, of any payment or payments made by such issuer, or by an indemnitor, upon claims against a listed attorney, or (b) cooperate, at the request of the Association, through the committee, in the investigation, ascertainment and proof of the facts of such claims.

4. The publisher of a Law List which has received a certificate of compliance from the committee may rate its listees in a manner not disapproved of by the committee.

5. The committee shall make and promulgate such regulations as may be necessary to administer these Rules and Standards.

INDEX OF WORKS CITED

	Page	Note
Abbot, E. V. 15 Harv. L. Rev. 714	96	18
Alexander, P. W. "The Follies of Divorce," 36 A.B.A. Jour. 105.	81	25
Ibid.	122	31
Ames, James Barr. Lectures on Legal History	149	3
Anglin, Francis Alexander. "Relations of Bench and Bar," 29 Can. L.T. 1.	75	22
Anonymous. "On the Principles of Advocacy," 20 Law Mag. (N.S.) 265.	2	4
Ibid.	4	4
Ibid.	145	32
Ibid.	148	44
Ibid.	193	13
Arant, Herschel Whitfield. Cases and Other Materials on the American Bar and Its Ethics.	ix	1
Ibid.	xi	5
Ibid.	48	37
Ibid.	48	40
Ibid.	85	42
Ibid.	134	40
Ibid.	193	13
Ibid.	196	32
Ibid.	213	13
Archer, Gleason L. Ethical Obligations of the Lawyer.	193	13
Ibid.	219	35
Baldwin, Simeon E. "The New American Code of Legal Ethics," 8 Col. L. Rev. 541.	25	19
Ibid.	139	49
Ballard, G. A., and Frank W. Ingram. "The Business of Migratory Divorce in Nevada," 2 Law & Contemp. Prob. 302.	81	25
Barkdull, Howard L. "Methods of Strengthening Bar Associations," 35 Jour. Am. Jud. Soc. 9.	21	43
Ibid.	255	43
Barton, D. Plunket. The Story of Our Inns of Court.	16	10
Bellot, Hugh H. L. The Inner and Middle Temple.	18	24
—— Some Early Law Courts. 38 Law Quart. Rev. 168.	34	8
Binney, C. C. The Life of Horace Binney.	151	13
Bishop, Joel P. Marriage, Divorce and Separation.	122	29

	Page	Note
Blackstone, Sir William. Commentaries.	12	8
Ibid.	144	27
Bolland, W. C. 24 Law Quart. Rev. 392.	42	2
Borah, Wm. E. "The Lawyer and the Public," 2 A.B.A. Jour. 776.	88	15
Boston, Charles A. "Practical Activities in Legal Ethics," 62 Am. L. Reg. (now U. of Pa. L. Rev.), 103.	25	18
—— "The Source and Formulation of Ethical Precepts," 78 Cent. L. Jour. 400.	xi	7
Boswell, James. The Journal of a Tour.	143	23
—— The Life of Samuel Johnson.	213	22
Bovey, Wilfrid. "The Control Exercised by the Inns of Court over Admission to the Bar in England," 38 A.B.A. Rep. 768.	18	30
Ibid.	33	2
Ibid.	33	3
Ibid.	33	4
Boyd, Sir John A. "Legal Ethics," 4 Can. L. Rev. 85.	87	11
Ibid.	145	32
Bracton.	12	6
Bradway, John S. "Moral Turpitude as the Criterion of Offenses that Justify Disbarment," 24 Calif. L. Rev. 9.	43	7
Brand, George E. "Bar Organization," 34 Jour. Am. Jud. Soc. 38–45.	19	33
Ibid.	21	43
—— "The Integrated Bar," 24 Ohio Bar 591.	21	43
Brandeis, L. D. "The Opportunity in the Law," 39 Am. L. Rev. (now U.S.L. Rev.) 555.	88	18
Ibid.	143	27
Bruce, Andrew A. 19 Ill. L. Rev. 1.	42	2
Burnet, Gilbert. Life of Hale.	143	25
Carter, Orrin N. Ethics of the Legal Profession.	92	20
Ibid.	145	32
Cheatham, Elliott E. Cases and Materials on the Legal Profession	ix	1
Ibid.	xi	5
Ibid.	6	5
Ibid.	103	21
Ibid.	104	24
Ibid.	110	22
Ibid.	212	9
Choate, Joseph H. American Addresses.	144	27
Cohen, Felix S. Ethical Systems and Legal Ideals.	xi	7
Cohen, Herman. History of the English Bar and Attornatus to 1450.	11	2
Ibid.	11	3
Ibid.	11	4
Ibid.	12	10
Ibid.	13	12
Ibid.	13	13
Ibid.	13	14
Ibid.	13	15
Ibid.	13	16
Ibid.	13	17

	Page	Note
Ibid.	13	18
Ibid.	13	19
Ibid.	13	20
Ibid.	13	21
Ibid.	13	22
Ibid.	14	23
Ibid.	14	26
Ibid.	14	27
Ibid.	14	30
Ibid.	14	32
Ibid.	14	33
Ibid.	14	34
Ibid.	14	35
Ibid.	14	36
Ibid.	15	37
Ibid.	15	38
Ibid.	15	39
Ibid.	15	41
Ibid.	15	42
Ibid.	15	43
Ibid.	15	44
Ibid.	15	45
Ibid.	15	46
Ibid.	62	10
Ibid.	87	10
Ibid.	99	39
Ibid.	103	20
Ibid.	141	6
Ibid.	173	43
—— 30 Law Quart. Rev. 465.	11	1
Ibid.	13	19
Ibid.	14	29
Ibid.	15	37
Ibid.	15	48
Ibid.	130	11
—— 31 Law Quart. Rev. 62.	12	10
Ibid.	13	13
Ibid.	14	24
Ibid.	14	28
Ibid.	14	31
Ibid.	15	40
Ibid.	19	32
Cohen, J. H. Address, 7 Ind. Law Jour. 295.	110	20
Ibid.	249	20
—— The Law, Business or Profession.	176	6
Ibid.	212	10
Costigan, George P. Cases on the Legal Profession and Its Ethics	ix	1
Ibid.	36	22
Ibid.	44	17
Ibid.	47	35

	Page	*Note*
Costigan, George P. Cases on the Legal Profession and Its Ethics.	48	37
Ibid.	50	50
Ibid.	64	24
Ibid.	98	32
Ibid.	98	34
Ibid.	100	49
Ibid.	134	38
Ibid.	136	10
Ibid.	143	23
Ibid.	143	25
Ibid.	145	30
Ibid.	146	35
Ibid.	148	1
Ibid.	160	1
Ibid.	160	3
Ibid.	167	39
Ibid.	170	6
Ibid.	173	37
Ibid.	195	24
Ibid.	206	49
Ibid.	249	16
Ibid.	249	20
Ibid.	252	5
Ibid.	267	31
Countryman, Edwin. "Ethics of Compensation for Professional Services," 16 Am. L. Rev. 240.	176	6
Cox-Sinclair, E. S. "The Right to Retain an Advocate," 29 Law Mag. & Rev. 406.	139	49
Curtis, Charles P. "The Ethics of Advocacy," 4 Stanford L. Rev. 3.	145	32
Douglas, W. O. The Lawyer and Reorganizations.	104	24
Drinker, H. S. "Ethical Problems in Matrimonial Litigation," 66 Harv. L. Rev. 443.	81	26
Ibid.	122	26
—— Answer to Charles P. Curtis, 4 Stanford L. Rev. 349.	145	32
Forsyth, William. Hortensius.	143	25
Ibid.	150	3
Fuller, L. L. 25 Ill. L. Rev. 363.	81	26
Fuller, Thomas. The Holy State and the Profane State.	101	9
Garcia, Marston. A New Guide to the Bar.	170	5
Green, Leon. "The Courts' Power over Admission and Disbarment," 4 Tex. L. Rev. 1.	36	24
Ibid.	42	2
Halsbury, Earl of. Laws of England.	16	2
Ibid.	16	9
Ibid.	16	10
Ibid.	33	7
Harno, Albert J. Legal Education in the United States.	20	40
Ibid.	34	13
Ibid.	42	50

	Page	Note
Harper, Fowler V. "The Myth of the Void Divorce," 2 Law & Contemp. Prob. 335.	81	26
Harris, John C. "Legal Ethics," 69 Albany L. Jour. 300.	78	46
Haslup, L. A. "Divisible Divorce," 3 Fla. L. Rev. 145.	81	23
Hewitt, Harrison. "Advertising by Lawyers," 15 A.B.A. Jour. 116.	212	12
Hicks, Frederick C. Organization and Ethics of the Bench and Bar.	ix	1
Ibid.	64	24
Ibid.	110	22
Ibid.	137	24
Hicks, Frederick C., and Elliott R. Katz. "The Practice of Law by Laymen and Lay Agencies," 41 Yale L. Jour. 69.	51	9
Ibid.	66	52
Ibid.	110	22
Ibid.	114	12
Ibid.	162	20
Ibid.	168	43
Hoar, George F. "Oratory," 29 Scribner's Mag. 756.	143	25
Holdsworth, William S. History of English Law.	12	10
Ibid.	13	21
Ibid.	13	22
Ibid.	14	25
Ibid.	14	29
Ibid.	15	47
Ibid.	15	49
Ibid.	15	1
Ibid.	16	3
Ibid.	16	4
Ibid.	16	5
Ibid.	16	6
Ibid.	16	11
Ibid.	16	12
Ibid.	17	16
Ibid.	17	17
Ibid.	17	18
Ibid.	17	19
Ibid.	17	20
Ibid.	17	21
Ibid.	17	22
Ibid.	18	26
Ibid.	18	27
Ibid.	18	28
Ibid.	18	29
Ibid.	18	30
Ibid.	22	4
Ibid.	132	26
Hughes, Charles E. Address.	192	12
Inderwick, Frederick Andrew. The Interregnum.	34	9
Ingram, Frank W., and G. A. Ballard. "The Business of Migratory Divorce in Nevada," 2 Law & Contemp. Prob. 302.	81	25
Jackson, John G. Survey of the Legal Profession.	20	40

	Page	Note
Jackson, John G. Survey of the Legal Profession.	34	
Jenks, Edward, Short History of English Law.	11	5
Ibid.	14	29
Ibid.	16	8
Ibid.	17	13
Ibid.	17	17
Ibid.	17	18
—— The Book of English Law.	34	10
Jessup, Henry Wynans. The Professional Ideals of the Lawyer.	102	10
Katz, Elliott R., and Frederick C. Hicks. "The Practice of Law by Laymen and Lay Agencies," 41 Yale L. Jour. 69.	51	9
Ibid.	66	52
Ibid.	110	22
Ibid.	114	12
Ibid.	162	20
Ibid.	168	43
Kendall, E. A. Trial by Battle.	11	5
Ibid.	12	9
Kent, C. A. "Legal Ethics," 6 Mich. L. Rev. 468.	144	27
Ibid.	144	30
Leaming, Thomas. A Philadelphia Lawyer in the London Courts.	12	10
Ibid.	16	7
Ibid.	16	10
Ibid.	17	15
Ibid.	18	29
Ibid.	18	31
Ibid.	33	5
Leavitt, J. B. Lawyer and Client in Every Day Ethics.	149	3
Lee, Blewett. 13 Harv. L. Rev. 233.	42	2
Leech, W. M., and M. E. Queener. "Comments on the Integrated Bar," 21 Tenn. L. Rev. 719.	20	43
Loesch, Frank J. "The Acquisition and Retention of a Clientage," 1 Ill. L. Rev. 455.	219	34
Lund, Thomas G. "The Legal Profession in England and Wales," 35 Jour. Am. Jud. Soc. 134–45.	18	30
Ibid.	34	11
Ibid.	175	1
—— 5 Lectures before the Law Society, re solicitors.	18	30
Ibid.	34	11
Ibid.	34	12
Ibid.	214	23
Maine, Sir Henry. Ancient Law.	122	31
Maitland, Frederic W., and Francis C. Montague. English Legal History.	14	29
Mathers, Thomas Graham. "Legal Ethics," 40 Can. L.T. 809	33	5
Ibid.	147	41
Ibid.	197	41
Maxwell-Fyfe, Rt. Hon. Sir David 4 S.W. L. Jour. 391.	16	4
Ibid.	17	21

	Page	Note
McCoy, Philbrick, and Orie L. Phillips. Conduct of Judges and Lawyers, in Survey of the Legal Profession.	20	40
Ibid.	34	13
Ibid.	70	5
Ibid.	214	28
McCracken, Robert T. Observance of Canons, in Survey of the Legal Profession.	214	27
Mirror of Justices, The Selden Society Publications.	12	10
Ibid.	15	44
Mitchell, Oliver R. "The Fictions of the Law," 7 Harv. L. Rev. 249.	81	26
Montague, Francis C., and Frederic W. Maitland. English Legal History.	14	29
Moulton, Lord. "Law and Manners," 134 Atl. Monthly 1.	2	
Ibid.	276	8
Neilson, George. Trial by Combat.	11	5
Ibid.	12	6
Ibid.	12	7
Noone, Charles A. 22 A.B.A. Jour. 609.	67	54
Odgers, W. Blake. A Century of Law Reform.	87	11
Palmer, Ben W. "Legal Fictions and Red Room Wine," 38 A.B.A. Jour. 23.	81	26
Parry, Edward A. The Seven Lamps of Advocacy.	78	46
Pearce, Robert A. Guide to the Inns of Court.	33	6
Phillips, Orie L., and Philbrick McCoy. Conduct of Judges and Lawyers, in Survey of the Legal Profession.	20	40
Ibid.	34	13
Ibid.	70	5
Ibid.	214	28
Plucknett, Theodore F. T. 48 Law Quart. Rev. 328.	16	2
Pollock, Sir Frederick. 18 Law Quart. Rev. 411.	84	33
Potts, Charles S. "Disbarment Procedure," 24 Tex. L. Rev. 161.	34	13
Ibid.	36	24
—— "Trial by Jury in Disbarment Proceedings," 11 Tex. L. Rev. 28.	36	24
Pound, Roscoe. The Lawyer from Antiquity to Modern Times, in Survey of the Legal Profession.	5	
Ibid.	14	29
Ibid.	19	33
Ibid.	19	34
Ibid.	20	42
—— "Legal Profession in the Middle Ages," 19 Notre Dame Lawyer 229–44.	12	10
Ibid.	13	22
Ibid.	15	1
Ibid.	16	5
Ibid.	16	7
Ibid.	16	8
Ibid.	16	11
Ibid.	16	12
Ibid.	17	15
Ibid.	17	18

	Page	Note
—— 19 Notre Dame Lawyer 229–44.	17	19
Ibid.	18	23
Ibid.	18	25
Ibid.	18	28
Powell, Thomas Reed. "And Repent at Leisure," 58 Harv. L. Rev. 930.	81	24
Pulling, Alexander. The Order of the Coif.	33	6
Ibid.	34	8
Queener, M. E., and W. M. Leech. "Comments on the Integrated Bar," 21 Tenn. L. Rev. 719.	20	43
Quintillian. Institutes of Oratory.	145	32
Radin, Max. "Contingent Fees in California," 28 Calif. L. Rev. 587.	176	8
—— "Maintenance by Champerty," 24 Calif. L. Rev. 48.	212	9
Reed, Alfred Z. Training for the Public Profession of the Law.	19	36
Ibid.	19	37
Reed, John C. Conduct of Lawsuits.	193	13
Riddell, William R. 39 Can. L. T. 620.	147	41
Robinson, Sergeant. Bench and Bar Reminiscences.	143	24
Rogers, James Grafton. 14 A.B.A. Jour. 301.	xii	
Rogers, Showell. "The Ethics of Advocacy," 15 L. Quart. Rev. 259.	78	46
Ibid.	147	41
Ibid.	148	1
Rules of Professional Conduct of the American Institute of Accountants.	96	18
Ibid.	176	6
Ibid.	179	32
Ibid.	186	31
Ibid.	220	38
Ibid.	220	41
Ibid.	249	16
Seabury, Samuel. 18 A.B.A. Jour. 371.	132	25
Seiler, O. J. 6 Calif. St. Bar Jour. 153.	249	20
Shakespeare, William. Taming of the Shrew.	192	11
Ibid.	211	1
Sharswood, George. Professional Ethics.	4	1
Ibid.	23	7
Ibid.	62	10
Ibid.	70	2
Ibid.	83	30
Ibid.	84	33
Ibid.	86	1
Ibid.	103	14
Ibid.	143	23
Ibid.	143	25
Ibid.	143	28
Ibid.	147	38
Ibid.	147	39
Ibid.	150	3
Ibid.	170	8
Ibid.	192	12

	Page	Note
Ibid.	193	13
Ibid.	194	16
Ibid.	195	26
Ibid.	277	13
Simon, Sir John. "The Vocation of an Advocate," 25 Law Notes 228.	148	1
Smith, Jeremiah. "Surviving Fictions," 27 Yale L. Jour. 147.	81	26
Smith, Sydney. The Lawyer that Tempted Christ.	143	23
Stearne, Allen M. "Fiction," 81 U. of Pa. L. Rev. 1.	81	26
Stephens, R. Allan. "The Forgotten Lawyer," 21 A.B.A. Jour. 667.	243	30
Stone, Harlan F. "The Public Influence of the Bar," 48 Harv. L. Rev. 1, 13.	4	2
Story, Joseph. Equity Jurisprudence.	89	3
—— Conflict of Laws.	122	29
Sunderland, Edson R. 21 Mich. L. Rev. 372.	6	5
Taft, W. H. Ethics in Service.	133	28
Thornton, Edward M. Attorneys at Law.	37	30
Ibid.	37	32
Ibid.	42	6
Ibid.	49	42
Ibid.	63	21
Ibid.	132	26
Ibid.	159	46
Trollope, Anthony. Lady Anna.	101	9
Thayer, James B. Preliminary Treatise on Evidence.	148	44
Tuttle, C. H. "The Ethics of Advocacy," 18 A.B.A. Jour. 849.	83	32
Ibid.	147	41
Ibid.	148	1
Vernier, Chester G. American Family Laws.	122	31
Vold, Lauriz. "Ethics and Economics in Lawyers' Fees." 8 Marquette L. Rev. 228.	174	44
Walsh, Cecil. The Advocate.	17	14
Ibid.	78	46
Ibid.	110	18
Warren, Samuel. The Moral, Social and Professional Duties of Attorneys.	93	26
Warvelle, George W. Legal Ethics.	12	11
Ibid.	86	1
Ibid.	87	10
Ibid.	107	2
Ibid.	121	19
Ibid.	139	50
Ibid.	145	32
Ibid.	149	1
Ibid.	213	21
Weeks, Edward T. Attorneys.	ix	1
Weihofen, H. 2 U. of Chi. L. Rev. 119.	166	37
Wicker, William. "Integrated Bars," 21 Tenn. L. Rev. 708.	20	43
Wigmore, John H. Evidence.	132	25
Ibid.	135	43

	Page	*Note*
Williams, Henry W. Legal Ethics for Young Counsel.	176	6
Wilson, Woodrow. "The Lawyer and the Community," 35 A.B.A.		
Reports 419.	4	3
Winch, Louis H. "The Recall of Lawyers," 24 Green Bag 135.	48	40

MISCELLANEOUS REFERENCES

69 Albany L. J. 300	78	46
American Bar Association Journal		
14 A.B.A. Jour. 301	xii	9
Ibid. 561	64	24
17 *ibid.* 561	50	50
35 *ibid.* 5	78	46
36 *ibid.* 107	81	25
Ibid. 630	276	7
Ibid. 677	165	31
American Bar Association Reports		
31 A.B.A. Rep. 680	24	11
Ibid. 681	24	14
Ibid. 685	24	15
Ibid. 687	48	40
Ibid. 696	213	15
Ibid.	213	16
Ibid.	213	17
Ibid.	213	18
Ibid.	213	19
Ibid. 697	147	40
Ibid. 700	120	18
Ibid. 714	23	9
Ibid. 715	23	8
33 *ibid.* 567	24	16
Ibid. 573	24	13
39 *ibid.* 559	25	20
Ibid. 559	30	42
46 *ibid.* 302	31	43
47 *ibid.* 285	268	46
48 *ibid.* 172	31	44
52 *ibid.* 382	66	52
American Law Reports		
3 A.L.R. 472	176	6
9 *ibid.* 197	149	1
40 *ibid.* 1529	176	6
43 *ibid.* 109	149	1
45 *ibid.* 1135	174	46
47 *ibid.* 267	80	8
48 *ibid.* 252	43	8
50 *ibid.* 380	51	6
Ibid. 384	51	6
51 *ibid.* 1307	103	21
53 *ibid.* 1244	41	47

	Page	Note
55 *ibid.* 1313	213	13
59 *ibid.* 1272	82	28
63 *ibid.* 1269	85	40
69 *ibid.* 705	48	40
80 *ibid.* 706	174	46
127 American State Reports 841	170	9
Annotated Cases		
1 Ann. Cases 299	176	6
7 *ibid.* 603	87	11
9 *ibid.* 168	41	47
14 *ibid.* 601	133	31
15 *ibid.* 205	41	47
18 *ibid.* 1115	176	6
22 *ibid.* 813	50	50
Ibid. 839	133	31
23 *ibid.* 212	103	21
24 *ibid.* 737	175	4
34 *ibid.* 369	197	44
37 *ibid.* 953	99	38
40 *ibid.* 263	174	44
41 *ibid.* 1073	133	31
Annual Practice (England)		
Ibid. 1912	71	6
Ibid. 1923	92	15
Ibid.	106	34
Ibid. 1933	110	25
Ibid.	144	26
Ibid.	146	34
Ibid.	170	7
Ibid.	172	28
Ibid.	214	23
Ibid.	221	2
Annual Report of Law Society (England) 1932	170	6
Annual Statement of the General Council (England), 1895–96, p. 6	72	12
Ibid.	93	10
Ibid.	277	11
Ibid., 1896–97, p. 8	92	15
Ibid., 1902–03, p. 4	18	31
Ibid.	203	5
Ibid., 1905–06, p. 13	214	23
Ibid., 1911, p. 11	158	38
Ibid., 1912, p. 11	158	38
Ibid., p. 13	228	11
Ibid., 1914, p. 10	228	11
Ibid., 1917, p. 7	87	10
Ibid., 1918, p. 10	228	11
Ibid. 1929, pp. 13–14	214	23
Ibid., p. 14	228	11
Ibid., 1930, p. 10	214	23
Ibid., p. 13	228	11
Ibid., 1932, p. 8	206	49

	Page	Note
Annual Statement of the General Council (England), 1935, p. 8	228	11
Ibid., 1936, p. 11	214	23
Ibid., 1937, p. 4	214	23
Ibid.	247	36
Ibid., p. 8	214	23
Ibid.	203	5
Ibid., p. 9	170	6
Ibid., 1939, p. 8	168	42
California Code of Ethics	47	34
Ibid.	82	29
16 California L. Rev. 487	137	25
6 California State Bar Jour. Nos. 2, 3, 4	64	24
76 Cent. L. Jour. 293	41	47
25 Columbia L. Rev. 492	252	6
31 *ibid.* 881	51	6
36 *ibid.* 1121	122	31
Ibid.	124	36
Ibid.	125	41
49 *ibid.* 129	150	8
52 *ibid.* 1039–53	xi	6
Ibid.	xii	8
Ibid.	26	23
Ibid.	27	28
Ibid.	42	6
Ibid.	43	13
Ibid.	48	40
Ibid.	75	22
Ibid.	80	8
7 C.J.S. 737	42	1
Council of Law Soc. 1900 (England)	160	1
Ibid. 1905	71	6
—— Law, Practice and Usage of the Legal Profession 1923	136	12
Ibid.	136	14
Ibid.	172	28
6 Det. L. Rev. 23	122	31
20 Dick. L. Rev. 1	176	6
26 Dicta 221	20	43
3 Enc. Soc. Serv. 177	122	31
General Council of the Bar (England)	139	49
21 Green Bag 271	25	18
Ibid.	176	6
26 Ill. L. Rep. 457	64	24
31 Ill. L. Rev. 813	166	37
"Labor Union Lawyers," 5 Ind. and Labor Rel. Rev. 361	167	38
2 Law & Contemp. Problems 293	122	32
Ibid. 310	150	9
28 Law Notes 203	152	26
35 *ibid.* 103	131	14
51 *ibid.* 353	267	33
15 Law Quart. Rev. 250	78	46

	Page	Note
L.R.A. 1915 A. 663	48	40
Ibid., 1916 A. 1175	48	40
Ibid., 1916 E. 782	87	11
Ibid., 1918 D. 450	69	2
14 L.R.A. (N.S.) 1095	175	4
15 *ibid.* 525	41	47
16 *ibid.* 272	51	6
17 *ibid.* 572	41	47
27 *ibid.* 634	176	6
38 *ibid.* 389	175	4
45 *ibid.* 750	176	6
46 *ibid.* 641	149	1
14 Mass. Law Quart. 1	64	24
28 Mich. L. Rev. 71	155	13
15 Minn. L. Rev. 115	175	4
16 *ibid.* 857	42	2
Ibid.	50	50
3 Miss. L. Jour. 341	51	6
N.Y. Law Jour., May 1931	110	22
Ibid.	261	36
Ibid., Dec. 1933 ("The Single Practitioner and Prof. Misconduct")	203	7
Ibid., Aug. 1938	72	13
Ibid., Dec. 1942	200	20
Ibid., Mar. 1948	148	43
31 N.Y. Bar Assn. Rep. 100	176	6
52 N.Y. State Bar Assn. Rep. 323	64	24
19 N.Y. State Bar Bull. 152	238	40
N.Y. State Bar Ethics Com. Rep. 1948, p. 8	61	8
Ibid., p. 9	102	10
Ibid., pp. 7–8	214	24
Ibid., 1949, pp. 4–7	94	39
Ibid., p. 7	106	32
Order of the General Council 7/18/51 (England)	231	27
24 Pa. Bar Assn. Quart. 144	42	50
Principles of Medical Ethics	165	30
Ibid.	249	16
Ibid.	255	42
21 So. Dak. Jour. 27	119	11
25 Temple Law Quart. 301	19	35
4 Tulane L. Rev. 226	126	44
Ibid.	128	50
37 Va. L. Rev. 399	7	6
63 U.S.L. Rev. 345	85	40
65 *ibid.* 538	110	22
79 U. of Pa. L. Rev. 506	46	28
80 *ibid.* 1021	42	2
Ibid.	50	50
8 Wis. L. Rev. 74	42	2
Ibid.	50	50
45 Yale L. Jour. 731	27	28

TABLE OF CASES

	Page	Note
A.B.C., Matter of, 7 N.J. 388	26	23
Abrams, In re, 36 Ohio App. 384	37	32
Adams v. Stevens, 26 Wend. (N.Y.) 451	170	9
Adriaans, In re, 17 App. cases D.C. 39	87	13
	306	
Agnew v. Walden & Son, 84 Ala. 502	172	28
Alexander's Case, 321 Pa. 125	304	
Allen's Case, 75 N.H. 301	51	3
Allin, Matter of, 224 Mass. 9	36	21
	304	
Anderson v. Eaton, 211 Cal. 113	27	28
Andrewes v. Haas, 214 N.Y. 255	177	19
Andrews v. Andrews, 188 U.S. 14	80	15
Annunziato's Est., In re, 108 N.Y.S.2d 101	27	27
	188	6
Anonymous, 1 Wend. (N.Y.) 108	196	28
Anonymous, an Attorney; Matter of, 274 App. Div. (N.Y.) 89	150	8
Application of Levy, 23 Wash.2d 607	42	1
Arctander, In re, 110 Wash. 296	306	
Arctander, Re, 26 Minn. 25	79	6
Ashford v. Thornton, 1 B. and Ald. 405	11	5
Attorney, In re, 10 App. Div. (N.Y.) 491	75	24
Attorney, In re ———, an, 9 L.T. (N.S.) 299	37	31
Attorney, Matter of ———, an, 86 N.Y. 563	37	30
Axtell, In re, 229 App. Div. (N.Y.) 323	64	24
Aylward v. Aylward, 44 T.L. Rep. 456	124	36
B. & O. R.R. Co. v. Boyd, 67 Md. 32	69	1
Bar Association of Boston v. Casey, 211 Mass. 187	37	29
Barach's Case, 279 Pa. 89	36	24
	37	32
Bartlett v. Odd Fellows' Savings Bank, 79 Cal. 218	175	4
Barton v. State Bar of California, 209 Cal. 677	46	31
	211	5
	307	
Bartos v. United States District Court, 19 F.2d 722	43	8
Batt, In re, 230 App. Div. (N.Y.) 656	154	8
Bayles, Matter of, 156 App. Div. (N.Y.) 663	124	37
	307	

	Page	Note
Beattie, People v., 137 Ill. 553	75	23
Bell v. Ramirez, 299 S.W. (Tex.) 655	92	12
Bennie v. Triangle Ranch Co., 73 Colo. 586	52	10
Berd v. Lovelace, Cary 62	132	26
Berezniak, People v., 292 Ill. 305	29	38
	213	13
	307	
Bergeron, In re, 220 Mass. 472	41	50
	42	5
Blakesberg, In re, 236 App. Div. (N.Y.) 227	51	7
Bledsoe, In re, 186 Okla. 264	41	50
Boehm, Matter of, 150 App. Div. (N.Y.) 443	304	
Boone, In re, 83 F. 944	28	29
	105	31
	106	35
	135	49
	304	
Boston v. Greenwood, 168 Mass. 169	152	21
Bowers, In re, 138 Tenn. 662	249	18
Bowers v. State of Ohio, 29 Ohio St. 542	135	48
Bowman v. Phillips, 41 Kan. 364	151	18
Bradley v. Fisher, 13 Wall. (U.S.) 335	41	47
	45	21
	46	31
Bradwell v. Illinois, 16 Wall. (U.S.) 130	35	17
Brainard v. Brainard, 82 Cal. App.2d 478	127	48
Branch, In re, 53 S.2d (Fla.) 317	45	22
	49	43
Breidt, In re, 84 N.J. Eq. 222	36	20
Breslin's Appeal, 316 Pa. 392	49	42
	51	2
Bright v. Turner, 205 Ky. 188	172	28
Broder, Grievance Comm. v., 112 Conn. 269	46	28
	307	
Brounsall, Ex parte, 2 Cowp. 829	305	
Brown v. Miller, 286 F. 994	107	42
Bruener, In re, 159 Wash. 504	85	40
Bruener, In re, 178 Wash. 165	37	33
	47	32
Brydonjack v. State Bar, 208 Cal. 439	41	49
Buckley v. Service Transp. Co., 277 App. Div. (N.Y.) 224	176	8
Byrchley's Case, Jenkyn's Rep. 262	33	8
Cahill, In re, 66 N.J.L. 527	122	31
	124	36
Callicotte, In re, 57 Mont. 297	306	
Cannon, In re, 206 Wis. 374	33	5
	41	48
	41	49
	42	2
	49	45

	Page	Note
Cannon, In re, 206 Wis. 374	50	50
	71	7
Cannon, State v., 196 Wis. 534	50	50
Cannon, State v., 199 Wis. 401	49	45
	50	50
Carpenter v. Ashley, 148 Cal. 422	87	11
Carpenter v. State Bar, 210 Cal. 520	26	23
	203	4
	308	
Cary, Matter of, 146 Minn. 80	174	46
Casper v. Kalt Co., 159 Wis. 517	41	48
Chaikin, Matter of, 238 App. Div. (N.Y.) 211	196	37
	307	
Chernoff's Case, 344 Pa. 527	307	
Chicago Bar v. Meyerovitz, 278 Ill. 356	305	
Chreste v. Commonwealth, 171 Ky. 77	29	34
	307	
Chreste v. Commonwealth, 178 Ky. 311	29	36
Chreste v. Louisville Ry., 167 Ky. 75	28	32
	178	20
Chreste v. Louisville Ry., 173 Ky. 486	29	35
Clark v. United States, 289 U.S. 1	137	24
Clark, Matter of, 184 N.Y. 222	93	22
Clifton, In re, 33 Ida. 614	27	25
Coffey, Matter of, 123 Cal. 522	305	
Cohen, In re, 10 N.J. 601	150	9
Cohen, Matter of, 261 Mass. 484	27	26
	29	38
Coit, Matter of, 251 App. Div. (N.Y.) 154	305	
Cole, Ex parte, 1 McCrary 405	41	47
Colorado Bar Asso. v. ———, Attorney, 88 Colo. 325	47	35
Coman, In re, 274 App. Div. (N.Y.) 300	48	40
Commonwealth v. Palermo, 368 Pa. 28	148	49
Commonwealth v. Sacco, 259 Mass. 128	148	49
	148	1
Confer v. District Court, 49 Nev. 18	82	27
Conover v. West Jersey Mortgage Co., 96 N.J. Eq. 441	172	28
Conway v. Bank, 146 Va. 357	183	12
Conyers v. Conyers, 311 Ky. 468	126	46
Cook v. Cook, 342 U.S. 126	80	18
	81	23
Cooke v. United States, 267 U.S. 517	40	42
Cooley, In re, 95 N.J. Eq. 485	152	26
Co-operative Law Co., Matter of, 198 N.Y. 479	166	36
Cruickshank, In re, 47 Cal. App. 496	304	
Crum, In re, 55 N.D. 876	50	50
	307	
Culkin, People v., 248 N.Y. 465	17	18
	36	18
Cusack, In re, 231 App. Div. (N.Y.) 186	305	

	Page	Note
Dahl v. State Bar, 213 Cal. 160	26	23
Davies, In re, 93 Pa. 116	36	27
	37	30
Davis, Matter of, 252 App. Div. (N.Y.) 591	151	18
Delano's Case, 58 N.H. 5	305	
Dickens' Case, 67 Pa. 169	155	17
	196	36
	306	
Dickson v. Dickson, 9 Tenn. (1 Yerg.) 110	122	28
Diesen, In re, 173 Minn. 297	46	31
	47	35
	306	
Dishaw v. Wadleigh, 15 App. Div. (N.Y.) 205	156	23
Doheny v. Lacy, 168 N.Y. 213	135	44
	135	47
Donegan, Matter of, 282 N.Y. 285	42	1
Donovan, In re, 43 S.D. 98	29	38
	307	
Dormenon's Case, 1 La. 129	306	
Dorsey v. Kingsland, 173 F.2d 405, 338 U.S. 318	47	35
Dows, In re, 168 Minn. 6	80	8
Duffy v. Colonial Trust Co., 287 Pa. 348	28	30
Duncan, In re, 83 S.C. 186	66	52
Dunn, Matter of, 205 N.Y. 398	175	2
Durant, In re, 80 Conn. 140	36	26
	306	
Eaton, In re, 60 N.D. 580	45	13
Eisemann v. Hazard, 218 N.Y. 155	120	19
Eldridge, Matter of, 82 N.Y. 161	36	26
	79	4
	86	1
Elsam, Matter of, 5 Dowl. & Ry. 389	75	24
Emmons, Petition of, 330 Mich. 303	49	44
Enright, In re, 69 Vt. 317	51	4
Epp v. Hinton, 102 Kan. 435	197	44
Erskine v. Adeane, 18 Sol. J. 573	79	4
Estate of Sylvester, 195 Iowa 1329	100	39
	177	11
Estin v. Estin, 334 U.S. 541	81	23
Evans, In re, 94 S.C. 414	45	22
Ex parte Brounsall, 2 Cowp. 829	305	
Ex parte Cole, 1 McCrary 405	41	47
Ex parte Garland, 4 Wall. (U.S.) 333	35	16
	37	28
Ex parte Pater, 10 L.T.R. (N.S.) 376	85	41
Ex parte Secombe, 19 How. (U.S.) 9	35	15
Ex parte Steckler, 179 La. 410	42	2
Ex parte Steinman and Hensel, 95 Pa. 220	70	5
	71	6
Ex parte Terry, 128 U.S. 289	38	37

	Page	Note
Ex parte Tillinghast, 4 Pet. 108	41	47
Ex parte Townley, 3 Dowl. 39	41	47
Ex parte Wall, 107 U.S. 265	36	24
	38	36
	43	10
	43	12
	44	18
	45	20
	306	
Farmer, In re, 191 N.C. 235	41	49
	43	13
Feinstein, In re, 233 App. Div. (N.Y.) 541	51	7
Finch, In re, 156 Wash. 609	306	
Fisch, Matter of, 188 App. Div. (N.Y.) 525	170	10
	308	
Fischer, Matter of, 231 App. Div. (N.Y.) 193	44	16
	307	
Flannery, Matter of, 150 App. Div. (N.Y.) 369	100	49
Frank, United States v., 53 F.2d 128	84	35
	145	31
French v. Cunningham, 149 Ind. 632	175	4
Friedland, Matter of, 238 App. Div. (N.Y.) 215	304	
	48	40
Gale, Matter of, 75 N.Y. 526	124	35
Gammons v. Johnson, 76 Minn. 76	29	33
Galbraith v. Elder, 8 Watts (Pa.) 81	90	5
Garland, Ex parte, 4 Wall. 333	35	16
	37	28
Garrett v. Hanshue, 53 Ohio St. 482	196	32
Garvin v. Harrell, 27 Okla. 373	85	39
Geis v. Gallus, 130 Ore. 619	126	46
Gelman, Matter of, 230 App. Div. (N.Y.) 524	153	44
Gesellschaft, etc., v. Brown 78 F.2d 410	27	28
	88	18
Gill, In re, 104 Wash. 160	29	33
	47	32
Ginsburg, Matter of, 188 App. Div. (N.Y.) 517	196	37
Goldstein, In re, 85 A.2d (Del.) 361	91	7
Goldstone v. State Bar, 214 Cal. 490	174	45
	308	
Goodrum v. Clement, 277 F. 586	91	8
Goranson v. Solomonson, 304 Ill. App. 80	92	13
Gould v. State, 99 Fla. 662	36	25
Glucksman, Matter of, 230 App. Div. (N.Y.) 185	93	22
Graffius, In re, 241 Pa. 222	304	
Graves, In re, 64 Cal. App. 176	306	
Gray, Matter of, 184 App. Div. (N.Y.) 822	28	33
Greathouse, In re, 189 Minn. 51	308	
Greenbaum, Matter of, 161 App. Div. (N.Y.) 558	44	14
Greenberg v. Remick, 230 N.Y. 70	175	5

	Page	Note
Greenleaf v. Minn. etc. R. Co., 30 N.D. 112	176	6
Greenough v. Gaskell, 1 Myl. & K. 98	133	28
Grievance Committee v. Broder, 112 Conn. 269	46	28
	307	
Griffin's Appeal, 371 Pa. 646	79	5
Griffiths v. United States, 72 F.2d 466	178	21
Gumperz v. Hoffman, 245 App. Div. (N.Y.) 622	150	11
H——— S———, In re, 229 Mo. App. 44	29	36
Hahn, In re, 84 N.J. Eq. 523	174	46
Hall v. Hall, 122 Pa. Sup. Ct. 242	122	30
Hallinan v. United States, 182 F.2d 880	41	45
Halpern, In re, 265 App. Div. (N.Y.) 340	48	40
Hansen, Matter of, 182 App. Div. (N.Y.) 568	307	
Hanson v. Grattan, 84 Kan. 843	42	2
Harbin v. Masterman, 1 Ch. 351	75	24
Hardenbrook, Matter of, 135 App. Div. 634; Aff. 199 N.Y. 539	157	28
Hardwick, In re, 12 Q.B.D. 148	36	19
Harris, In re, 88 N.J.L. 18	37	31
	49	43
	51	2
Hassell v. Steinmann 132 S.W. (Tex.) 948	183	12
Hatch, In re, 10 Cal.2d 147	306	
Hawes, In re, 169 App. Div. (N.Y.) 644	75	24
Heinze, In re, 233 Minn. 391	47	36
	307	
Heisler v. Thomas Colliery Co., 260 U.S. 245	75	24
Hendrick, In re, 229 App. Div. (N.Y.) 100	154	8
Henry, In re, 15 Ida. 755	305	
Herbert W. Salus's Case, 321 Pa. 106	151	18
Herman v. Acheson, 108 F. Supp. 723	27	27
Hicks, In re, 163 Okla. 29	45	25
	307	
Hightower v. Detroit Edison Co., 262 Mich. 1	28	33
Hildebrand v. State Bar of California, 36 Cal.2d 504	167	38
Hill v. Hill, 23 Cal.2d 82	127	48
Hilton, In re, 48 Utah 172	41	47
Hirst, In re, 9 Phila. 216	76	33
Hoar v. Wood, 3 Metc. 193	87	11
Hobart's Adm'r. v. Vail, 80 Vt. 152	120	19
Hofstede, In re, 31 Ida. 448	306	
Holley, In re, 271 App. Div. (N.Y.) 225	48	40
Howell, Matter of, 215 N.Y. 466	91	11
Hulse v. Criger, 247 S.W.2d 855	67	54
Humphrey, Matter of, 174 Cal. 290	306	
Hunter v. Troup, 315 Ill. 293	27	25
Ingersoll v. Coal Co., 117 Tenn. 263	29	33
	64	24
In re Abrams, 36 Ohio App. 384	37	32
In re Adriaans, 17 App. Cases D.C. 39	87	13
	306	

	Page	Note
In re ———, an Attorney, 9 L.T. (N.S.) 299	37	31
In re Annunziato's Estate, 108 N.Y.S.2d 101	27	27
	188	6
In re Application for license, 67 W. Va. 213	249	18
In re Arctander, 110 Wash. 296	306	
In re Association of Bar of New York, 222 App. Div. (N.Y.) 580	64	24
In re Attorney, 10 App. Div. (N.Y.) 491	75	24
In re Axtell, 229 App. Div. (N.Y.) 323	64	24
In re Bar Association of New Jersey, 109 N.J.L. 275	64	24
In re Batt, 230 App. Div. (N.Y.) 656	154	8
In re Bergeron, 220 Mass. 472	41	50
	42	5
In re Blakesberg, 236 App. Div. (N.Y.) 227	51	7
In re Bledsoe, 186 Okla. 264	41	50
In re Boone, 83 F. 944	28	29
	105	31
	106	35
	135	49
	304	
In re Bowers, 138 Tenn. 662	249	18
In re Branch, 53 S.2d (Fla.) 317	45	22
	49	43
In re Breidt, 84 N.J. Eq. 222	36	20
In re Bruener, 159 Wash. 504	85	40
In re Bruener, 178 Wash. 165	37	33
	47	32
In re Cahill, 66 N.J.L. 527	122	31
	124	36
In re Callicotte, 57 Mont. 297	306	
In re Cannon, 206 Wis. 374	33	5
	41	48
	41	49
	42	2
	49	45
	50	50
	71	7
In re Clifton, 33 Ida. 614	27	25
In re Cohen, 10 N.J. 601	150	9
In re Coman, 274 App. Div. (N.Y.) 300	48	40
In re Cooley, 95 N.J. Eq. 485	152	26
In re Cruickshank, 47 Cal. App. 496	304	
In re Crum, 55 N.D. 876	50	50
	307	
In re Cusack, 231 App. Div. (N.Y.) 186	305	
In re Davies, 93 Pa. 116	36	27
	37	30
In re Diesen, 173 Minn. 297	46	31
	47	35
	306	

	Page	Note
In re Disbarment Proceedings, 321 Pa. 81	306	
	308	
In re Donovan, 43 S.D. 98	29	38
	307	
In re Dows, 168 Minn. 6	80	8
In re Duncan, 83 S.C. 186	66	52
In re Durant, 80 Conn. 140	36	26
	306	
In re Eaton, 60 N.D. 580	45	13
In re Enright, 69 Vt. 317	51	4
In re Evans, 94 S.C. 414	45	22
In re Farmer, 191 N.C. 235	41	49
	43	13
In re Feinstein, 233 App. Div. (N.Y.) 541	51	7
In re Finch, 156 Wash. 609	306	
In re Gill, 104 Wash. 160	29	33
	47	32
In re Goldstein, 85 A.2d (Del.) 361	91	7
In re Graffius, 241 Pa. 222	304	
In re Graves, 64 Cal. App. 176	306	
In re Greathouse, 189 Minn. 51	308	
In re H——— S———, 229 Mo. App. 44	29	36
In re Hahn, 84 N.J. Eq. 523	174	46
In re Halpern, 265 App. Div. (N.Y.) 340	48	40
In re Hardwick, 12 Q.B.D. 148	36	19
In re Harris, 88 N.J.L. 18	37	31
	49	43
	51	2
In re Hatch, 10 Cal.2d 147	306	
In re Hawes, 169 App. Div. (N.Y.) 644	75	24
In re Heinze, 233 Minn. 391	47	36
In re Hendrick, 229 App. Div. (N.Y.) 100	154	8
In re Henry, 15 Ida. 755	305	
In re Hicks, 163 Okla. 29	45	25
	307	
In re Hilton, 48 Utah 172	41	47
In re Hirst, 9 Phila. 216	76	33
In re Hofstede, 31 Ida. 448	306	
In re Holley, 271 App. Div. (N.Y.) 225	48	40
In re Information to Discipline, etc., 351 Ill. 206	26	23
	45	26
In re Isaacs, 172 App. Div. (N.Y.) 181	305	
In re Isserman, 6 N.J. Misc. 146, 9 N.J. 269	47	35
In re Joyce, 182 Minn. 156	153	44
In re Kelly, 243 F. 696	85	39
In re Kennedy, 18 Lanc. L. Rev. 276	37	32
	49	47
In re L.R. 7 N.J. 390	26	23
	46	31

	Page	Note
In re Langworthy, 39 Ariz. 523	41	47
In re Lavine, 2 Cal.2d 324	42	2
	51	6
In re Lynch, 238 S.W.2d (Ky.) 118	305	
In re Maclub, 295 Mass. 45	166	37
In re Macy, 109 Kan. 1	45	22
In re Malmin, 364 Ill. 164	153	45
	197	43
In re Marsh, 42 Utah 186	307	
In re May, 239 S.W.2d (Ky.) 95	42	1
In re McCoy, 239 S.W.2d (Ky.) 86	42	1
In re McDonald, 204 Minn. 62	46	31
In re McNeese, 346 Mo. 425	46	28
	307	
In re Melin, 410 Ill. 332	305	
In re Metzger, 31 Hawaii 929	151	13
In re Mindes, 88 N.J.L. 117	40	43
In re Minner, 133 Kan. 789	43	8
In re Morford, 80 A.2d (Del.) 429	46	29
In re Moses, 186 Minn. 357	306	
In re Napolis, 169 App. Div. (N.Y.) 469	145	32
	151	17
In re Newman, 172 App. Div. (N.Y.) 173	26	23
In re O'Connell, 184 Cal. 584	306	
In re Oliensis, 26 Pa. Dist. 853	29	38
In re O'Neill, 5 F. Supp. 465	167	38
In re Osmond, 174 Okla. 561	45	22
In re Osofsky, 50 F.2d 925	174	47
In re P., 83 N.J. Eq. 390	79	4
In re Pemberton, 63 P. 1043	51	4
In re Penn, 196 App. Div. (N.Y.) 764	47	35
In re Peters, 73 Mont. 284	306	
In re Phillips, 248 App. Div. (N.Y.) 768	48	40
In re Pontarelli, 393 Ill. 310	43	11
In re Power, 407 Ill. 525	46	29
	46	31
In re Pryor, 18 Kans. 72	40	41
In re Quitman, 152 App. Div. (N.Y.) 865	308	
In re Radford, 168 Mich. 474	304	
In re Roberts, 2 Cal. App.2d 70	29	38
In re Robinson, 140 App. Div. (N.Y.) 329	152	21
In re Rothbard, 225 App. Div. (N.Y.) 266	64	24
	308	
In re Rudd, 310 Ky. 630	42	1
In re Sachs, 169 App. Div. (N.Y.) 622	76	34
In re Saddler, 35 Okla. 510	43	12
In re Scannell, 260 App. Div. (N.Y.) 442	48	40
In re Schachne, 5 F. Supp. 680	307	
In re Schnitzer, 33 Nev. 581	26	23
	307	

	Page	Note
In re Schofield, 362 Pa. 201	38	38
	69	1
In re Shepard, 109 Mich. 631	36	24
	306	
In re Sherin, 50 S.D. 428	153	45
In re Simpson, 11 N.D. 526	51	5
In re Smith, 133 Wash. 145	306	
In re Snyder, 190 N.Y. 66	102	12
	177	13
	177	19
In re Swihart, 42 S.D. 628	154	5
In re Thatcher, 190 F. 969, 80 Ohio St. 493	41	47
	306	
In re Thibodeau, 295 Mass. 374	166	37
In re Thorn, 164 App. Div. (N.Y.) 151	304	
In re Tracy, 197 Minn. 35	29	37
	224	19
	308	
In re Turner, 104 Wash. 276	305	
In re Vail, 228 App. Div. (N.Y.) 217	64	24
In re Vandewater, 257 App. Div. (N.Y.) 962	48	40
In re Virdone, 261 App. Div. (N.Y.) 961	48	40
In re Wallace, 323 Mo. 203	307	
In re Wallace, L. R. 1 P.C. 283	41	47
In re Weare, 2 Q.B. Div. 439	43	13
In re Wein, 73 Ariz. 225	307	
In re Welansky, 319 Mass. 205	45	27
In re Wells, 293 Ky. 201	45	22
	307	
In re Wilson, 79 Kans. 450	305	
In re Wilson, 79 Kans. 674	306	
In re Wright, 232 P.2d (Nev.) 398	308	
In re Yablunky, 407 Ill. 111	36	25
	304	
Irwin v. Swinney, 45 F.2d 890	174	47
Isaacs, In re, 172 App. Div. (N.Y.) 181	305	
Isserman, In re, 6 N.J. Misc. 146, 9 N.J. 269	47	35
Jerome's Case, 1 Cro. Cr. 74	305	
Johnson v. Emerson, L.R. 6 Ex. 329	143	25
Johnson v. Muelberger, 340 U.S. 581	80	17
	81	22
Joyce, In re, 182 Minn. 156	153	44
Kaplan v. Berman, 37 Misc. 502	52	10
Keenan v. Scott, 64 W. Va. 137	92	14
Kelly, In re, 243 F. 696	85	39
Kennedy, In re, 18 Lanc. L. Rev. 276	37	32
	49	47
Kennedy v. Richardson, 70 Ind. 524	183	11
Kepler v. State Bar, 216 Cal. 52	50	49
Kersey v. Garton, 77 Mo. 645	175	4

	Page	Note
Kingsland v. Dorsey, 338 U.S. 318	47	35
Krause v. Insurance Co., 331 Mich. 19	178	20
Lalance et al v. Haberman Co., 93 F. 197	107	42
Langworthy, In re, 39 Ariz. 523	41	47
Lamb v. Lamb, 57 Nev. 421	82	27
Lantz v. State Bar of California, 212 Cal. 213	36	18
La Porta v. Leonard, 88 N.J.L. 663	87	11
Lavine, In re, 2 Cal.2d 324	42	2
	51	6
Lawler v. Dunn, 145 Minn. 281	175	2
Lee v. Lomax, 219 Ill. 218	197	44
Lemisch's Case, 321 Pa. 110	151	18
Levy, Application of, 23 Wash.2d 607	42	1
Lewis v. Board of Governance, 316 Pa. 193	26	23
Librarian v. State Bar, 25 Cal.2d 314	307	
Liggett v. Glenn, 51 F. 381	135	3
Lilly v. Commissioner, 343 U.S. 90	26	24
Liutz v. Denver City Trucking Company, 54 Colo. 371	85	39
Louisville Bar Association v. Hubbard, 282 Ky. 734	28	33
Low v. Hutchinson, 37 Me. 196	178	30
Lowe and Kyme v. Paramour, 3 Dyer 301a	11	5
L.R., In re, 7 N.J. 390	26	23
	46	31
Luzenberg v. B. & L. Association, 9 Tex. Civ. App. 261	183	11
Lynch, In re, 238 S.W.2d 118	305	
McCoy, In re, 239 S.W.2d 86	42	1
McDonald, In re, 204 Minn. 62	46	31
McDougall v. Campbell, 41 U.C.Q.B. 332	170	6
McLyman v. Miller, 52 R.I. 374	196	32
McNeese, In re, 346 Mo. 425	46	28
	307	
MacInnis v. United States, 191 F.2d 157	41	46
Maclub, In re, 295 Mass. 45	166	37
Macy, In re, 109 Kan. 1	45	22
Mahon v. Penna. Coal Co., 260 U.S. 393	75	24
Maimone v. Maimone, 90 N.E.2d (Ohio) 383	126	45
Mainiere, Matter of, 274 App. Div. (N.Y.) 17	308	
Malmin, In re, 364 Ill. 164	153	45
	197	43
Manisty v. Kenealy, 24 W.R. 918	33	4
Marcus v. Simotone, 135 Misc. 228	83	32
	196	27
Margolis's Case, 269 Pa. 206	45	24
	306	
Maroth v. Maroth, 64 N.Y.S.2d 260	126	46
Marsh, In re, 42 Utah 186	307	
Marsh v. State Bar, 210 Cal. 303	48	40
	304	
Martin v. Camp, 219 N.Y. 170	175	2
	175	3

	Page	Note
	177	19
Matter of A.B.C., 7 N.J. 388	26	23
Matter of Allin, 224 Mass. 9	36	21
	304	
Matter of Anonymous, an Attorney, 274 App. Div. (N.Y.) 89	150	8
Matter of ———, an Attorney, 86 N.Y. 563	37	30
Matter of Bayles, 156 App. Div. (N.Y.) 663	124	37
	307	
Matter of Boehm, 150 App. Div. (N.Y.) 443	304	
Matter of Cary, 146 Minn. 80	174	46
Matter of Chaikin, 238 App. Div. (N.Y.) 211	196	37
	307	
Matter of Clark, 184 N.Y. 222	93	22
Matter of Coffey, 123 Cal. 522	305	
Matter of Cohen, 261 Mass. 484	27	26
	29	38
Matter of Coit, 251 App. Div. (N.Y.) 154	305	
Matter of Cooperative Law Co., 198 N.Y. 479	166	36
Matter of Davis, 252 App. Div. (N.Y.) 591	151	18
Matter of Donegan, 282 N.Y. 285	42	1
Matter of Dunn, 205 N.Y. 398	175	2
Matter of Eldridge, 82 N.Y. 161	36	26
	79	4
	86	1
Matter of Elsam, 5 Dowl. & Ry. 389	75	24
Matter of Fisch, 188 App. Div. (N.Y.) 525	170	10
	308	
Matter of Fischer, 231 App. Div. (N.Y.) 193	44	16
	307	
Matter of Flannery, 150 App. Div. (N.Y.) 369	100	49
Matter of Fridigen, 196 App. Div. (N.Y.) 413	305	
Matter of Friedland, 238 App. Div. (N.Y.) 215	304	
	48	40
Matter of Gale, 75 N.Y. 526	124	35
Matter of Gelman, 230 App. Div. (N.Y.) 524	153	44
Matter of Ginsburg, 188 App. Div. (N.Y.) 517	196	37
Matter of Glucksman, 230 App. Div. (N.Y.) 185	93	22
Matter of Gray, 184 App. Div. (N.Y.) 822	28	33
Matter of Greenbaum, 161 App. Div. (N.Y.) 558	44	14
Matter of Greenwald, 278 App. Div. (N.Y.) 76	305	
Matter of Hansen, 182 App. Div. (N.Y.) 568	307	
Matter of Hardenbrook, 135 App. Div. 634; Aff. 199 N.Y. 539	157	28
Matter of Howell, 215 N.Y. 466	91	11
Matter of Humphrey, 174 Cal. 290	306	
Matter of Mainiere, 274 App. Div. (N.Y.) 17	308	
Matter of Mills, 1 Mich. 392	307	
Matter of O'Neil, 228 App. Div. (N.Y.) 129	92	18
Matter of Paders, 250 App. Div. (N.Y.) 418	118	41
Matter of Palmer, 9 Ohio Cir. Ct. Rep. 55	50	50
Matter of Reiss, 200 Misc. 697	173	41

	Page	Note
Matter of Richards, 333 Mo. 907	37	32
	306	
Matter of Robinson, 151 App. Div. (N.Y.) 589	153	32
	307	
Matter of Rockmore, 127 App. Div. (N.Y.) 499	306	
Matter of Rouss, 169 App. Div. 629; (Aff.) 221 N.Y. 81	36	18
	152	21
	307	
Matter of Santosuosso, 318 Mass. 489	36	26
Matter of Schapiro, 144 App. Div. (N.Y.) 1	152	30
	153	32
	307	
Matter of Schwarz, 231 N.Y. 642	28	33
	48	38
Matter of Scouten's Appeal, 186 Pa. 270	69	2
Matter of Shepard, 35 Cal. App. 492	49	46
Matter of Steinberg, 233 App. Div. (N.Y.) 301	196	37
Matter of Stern, 120 App. Div. (N.Y.) 375	304	
Matter of Stern, 137 App. Div. (N.Y.) 909	46	30
Matter of Sutherland, 252 App. Div. (N.Y.) 620	52	10
Matter of Treadwell, 175 App. Div. (N.Y.) 833	52	10
Matter of Weitling, 266 N.Y. 184	178	21
Matter of Wilbur, 228 App. Div. (N.Y.) 197	118	40
Matter of Wiltse, 109 Wash. 261	29	36
	306	
Maulsby v. Reifsnider, 69 Md. 143	87	11
May, In re, 239 S.W.2d (Ky.) 95	42	1
Mayer v. State Bar of California, 86 Cal. 461	29	38
Meisel v. National Jewelers Board of Trade, 90 Misc. 19	66	52
	166	36
Melin, In re, 410 Ill. 332	305	
Mendelson v. Gogolick, 243 App. Div. (N.Y.) 115	28	31
Metzger, In re, 31 Hawaii 929	151	13
Mills, Matter of, 1 Mich. 392	307	
Mindes, In re, 88 N.J.L. 117	40	43
Minner, In re, 133 Kan. 789	43	8
Mitchell v. Towne, 31 Cal. App.2d 259	135	46
Moody v. Davis, 10 Ga. 403	78	46
Morford, In re, 80 A.2d (Del.) 429	46	29
Morrison, Petition of, 45 S.D. 123	50	49
	51	2
Moses, In re, 186 Minn. 357	306	
Moulton v. Bowker, 115 Mass. 36	196	32
Moyer v. Cantieny, 41 Minn. 242	175	4
Mt. Vernon v. Patton, 94 Ill. 65	175	4
Munter v. Linn, 61 Ala. 492	183	12
Murray v. Lizotte, 31 R.I. 509	107	40
	134	38
Mutter v. Burgess, 87 Colo. 580	175	4
Mutual Life Ins. Co. v. O'Donnell, 146 N.Y. 275	195	17

	Page	Note
Myers v. Crockett, 14 Tex. 257	175	4
Napolis, In re, 169 App. Div. (N.Y.) 469	145	32
	151	17
National Surety Co. v. Jarvis, 278 U.S. 610	79	3
Nelson v. Commonwealth, 128 Ky. 779	37	30
Newman, In re, 172 App. Div. (N.Y.) 173	26	23
New York v. Stephens, 52 N.Y. 306	195	17
Oberstein v. Oberstein, 217 Ark. 80	127	48
O'Connell, In re, 184 Cal. 584	306	
Odell v. Bausch et al, 91 F.2d 359	152	25
O'Keefe, Re, 49 Mont. 369	152	30
Oliensis, In re, 26 Pa. Dist. 853	29	38
Olmsted's Case, 292 Pa. 96	41	50
O'Neil, Matter of, 228 App. Div. (N.Y.) 129	92	18
O'Neill, In re, 5 F. Supp. 465	167	38
Opinion of the Justices, 279 Mass. 607	42	2
Osmond, In re, 174 Okla. 561	45	22
Osofsky, In re, 50 F.2d 925	174	47
P., In re, 83 N.J. Eq. 390	79	4
Packer v. Rapoport, 88 N.Y.S.2d 118	135	49
Paders, Matter of, 250 App. Div. (N.Y.) 418	118	41
Palmer, Matter of, 9 Ohio Cir. Ct. Rep. 55	50	50
Pater, Ex parte, 10 L.T.R. (N.S.) 376	85	41
Patterson v. Colorado, 205 U.S. 454	40	43
	41	47
Peck v. State Bar of California, 217 Cal. 47	305	
Peltier v. Thibodaux, 175 La. 1026	197	44
Pemberton, In re, 63 P. 1043	51	4
Penn, In re, 196 App. Div. (N.Y.) 764	47	35
People v. Ashton, 347 Ill. 570	252	6
People v. Bamborough, 255 Ill. 92	174	46
People v. Beattie, 137 Ill. 553	75	23
People v. Berezniak, 292 Ill. 305	29	38
	213	13
	307	
People v. Culkin, 248 N.Y. 465	17	18
	36	18
People v. Dane, 59 Mich. 550	149	1
People v. Edelson, 313 Ill. 601	252	6
People v. Gilmore, 345 Ill. 28	305	
People v. Globe Jewelers, 249 App. Div. (N.Y.) 122	79	8
People v. Green, 7 Colo. 237	39	39
	305	
People v. Green, 9 Colo. 506	87	13
People v. Heald, 123 Colo. 390	305	
People ex rel Colorado Bar v. Humbert, 86 Colo. 426	41	48
People v. Macauley, 230 Ill. 208	305	
People ex rel v. MacCabe, 18 Colo. 186	26	23
	307	
People v. McCallum, 341 Ill. 578	27	25

	Page	Note
	47	35
People v. News-Times Publ. Co., 35 Colo. 253	41	47
People v. Phipps, 261 Ill. 576	148	1
People v. Pickler, 186 Ill. 64	76	35
People v. Real Estate Taxpayers of Ill., 354 Ill. 102	166	37
People ex rel Chicago Bar v. Standidge, 333 Ill. 361	41	47
People v. Stonecipher, 271 Ill. 506	36	23
People v. Tufts, 167 Cal. 266	148	1
Peters, In re, 73 Mont. 284	306	
Petition of Emmons, 330 Mich. 303	49	44
Petition of Morrison, 45 S.D. 123	50	49
	51	2
Petition of Splane, 123 Pa. 527	42	2
Petition of Stalnaker, 150 Fla. 853	49	44
Petition of the Board, 191 Wis. 359	41	49
Petition from Antigua, 1 Knapp 267	33	1
Philbrook v. Newman, 85 F. 139	35	17
Phillips, In re, 248 App. Div. (N.Y.) 768	48	40
Pittsburgh etc. R. Co. v. Muncie, 166 Ind. 466	79	2
Platz, Re, 42 Utah 439	42	2
Pontarelli, In re, 393 Ill. 310	43	11
Pouker, Re, 203 App. Div. (N.Y.) 520	154	5
Power, In re, 407 Ill. 525	46	29
	46	31
Pryor, In re, 18 Kans. 72	40	41
Queen v. Cox, 14 Q.B.D. 153	139	42
Quitman, In re, 152 App. Div. (N.Y.) 865	308	
Radford, In re, 168 Mich. 474	304	
Randall, petitioner, 11 Allen (Mass.) 473	36	22
Re Allin, 224 Mass. 9	36	21
Re Arctander, 26 Minn. 25	79	6
Re O'Keefe, 49 Mont. 369	152	30
Re Platz, 42 Utah 439	42	2
Re Pouker, 203 App. Div. (N.Y.) 520	154	5
Re Sherwood, 259 Pa. 254	69	2
Reilly v. Beekman, 24 F.2d 791	27	28
	30	40
Reiss, Matter of, 200 Misc. 697	173	41
Rheb v. Bar Association of Baltimore, 186 Md. 200	42	3
	43	13
Rice v. Rice, 336 U.S. 674	81	23
Richards, Matter of, 333 Mo. 907	37	32
	306	
Richmond Association v. Bar Association, 167 Va. 327	165	33
Ritz v. Carpenter, 43 S.D. 236	92	13
Roberts, In re, 2 Cal. App.2d 70	29	38
Robinson, In re, 140 App. Div. (N.Y.) 329	152	21
Robinson, Matter of, 151 App. Div. (N.Y.) 589	153	32
	307	
Rockmore, Matter of, 127 App. Div. (N.Y.) 499	306	

	Page	Note
Rogers v. Thompson, 89 N.J.L. 639	87	11
Rothbard, In re, 225 App. Div. (N.Y.) 266	64	24
	308	
Rouss, Matter of, 169 App. Div. 629; Aff. 221 N.Y. 81	36	18
	152	21
	307	
Rubin, State v., 201 Wis. 30	28	33
	48	38
Rudd, In re, 310 Ky. 630	42	1
Rudolph v. United States, 6 F.2d 487	43	8
Rules and Regulations of the North Carolina Bar, 221 N.C. (F.) 606	220	41
Rush v. Cavenaugh, 2 Barr (Pa.) 187	145	32
Ryan v. Penna. Ry. 268 Ill. App. 364	167	38
Sacco, Commonwealth v., 259 Mass. 128	148	49
	148	1
Sacher, United States v., 9 F.R.D. 394; 182 F.2d 416	69	1
Sacher v. United States, 343 U.S. 1	36	24
	40	44
	69	1
Sachs, In re, 169 App. Div. (N.Y.) 622	76	34
Saddler, In re, 35 Okla. 510	43	12
Salus's Case, Herbert W., 321 Pa. 106	151	18
Sanborn v. Kimball, 64 Me. 140	37	30
Sandstrom v. Oregon etc. Co., 69 Ore. 194	85	39
Santosuosso, Matter of, 318 Mass. 489	36	26
Scannell, In re, 260 App. Div. (N.Y.) 442	48	40
Schachne, In re, 5 F. Supp. 680	307	
Schapiro, Matter of, 144 App. Div. (N.Y.) 1	152	30
	153	32
	307	
Scheinesohn v. Lemonek, 84 Ohio St. 424	175	4
	177	19
Schield's Estate, 250 S.W.2d (Mo.) 151	112	37
Schnitzer, In re, 33 Nev. 581	26	23
	307	
Schofield, In re, 362 Pa. 201	38	38
	69	1
Schwarz, Matter of, 231 N.Y. 642	28	33
	48	38
Scouten's Appeal, Matter of, 186 Pa. 270	69	2
Secombe, Ex parte, 19 How. 9	35	15
Semler v. Oregon State Board of Dental Examiners, 294 U.S. 608	212	12
Shepard, In re, 109 Mich. 631	36	24
	306	
Shepard, Matter of, 35 Cal. App. 492	49	46
Sherin, In re, 50 S.D. 428	153	45
Sherrer v. Sherrer, 334 U.S. 343	80	16
	81	19
	81	20
	81	21

	Page	Note
Sherwood, Re, 259 Pa. 254	69	2
Simpson, In re, 11 N.D. 526	51	5
Sinclair v. United States, 279 U.S. 749	85	40
Smith v. California, 211 Cal. 249	47	35
	54	37
Smith v. Chicago, etc. Ry., 60 Iowa 515	114	10
	130	13
Smith, In re, 133 Wash. 145	306	
Smith v. State, 1 Yerg. (Tenn.) 228	43	9
Smith's Appeal, 179 Pa. 14	36	24
Snyder, In re, 190 N.Y. 66	102	12
	177	13
	177	19
Spears v. California, 211 Cal. 183	41	49
Spilker v. Hankin, 188 F.2d 35	91	10
Splane, Petition of, 123 Pa. 527	42	2
Staedler v. Staedler, 6 N.J. 380	129	8
Stalnaker, Petition of, 150 Fla. 853	49	44
Stark v. P. G. Garage, Inc., 7 N.J. 118	66	52
State v. Bieber, 121 Kan. 536	43	8
State v. Cannon, 196 Wis. 534	50	50
State v. Cannon, 199 Wis. 401	49	45
	50	50
State v. Circuit Court, 97 Wis. 1	39	40
	41	47
State v. Finley, 30 Fla. 325	79	4
State v. Finn, 32 Ore. 519	79	5
State (ex rel. McLaughlin) v. Graves, 73 Ore. 331	43	10
	306	
State v. Johnson, 174 N.C. 345	306	
State v. Johnson, 149 Iowa 462	153	44
State v. Kirby, 36 S.D. 188	41	47
State v. McClaugherty, 33 W.Va. 250	306	
State v. Montgomery, 56 Wash. 443	148	1
State v. Osborne, 54 Ore. 289	148	1
State v. Peck, 88 Conn. 447	36	20
	42	4
	44	17
State v. Priest, 123 Neb. 241	50	48
	51	1
State v. Rodgers, 129 W.Va. 174	126	46
State v. Root, 5 N.D. 487	41	47
State v. Rubin, 201 Wis. 30	28	33
	48	38
State v. Snyder, 136 Fla. 875	37	30
State v. Turner, 141 Neb. 556	42	1
Steckler, Ex parte, 179 La. 410	42	2
Steinberg, Matter of, 233 App. Div. (N.Y.) 301	196	37
Steinman and Hensel, Ex parte, 95 Pa. 220	70	5
	71	6

	Page	Note
Stern, Matter of, 120 App. Div. (N.Y.) 375	304	
Stern, Matter of, 137 App. Div. (N.Y.) 909	46	30
Stockton v. Ford, 52 U.S. 232	89	2
Strong v. International B.L. & I. Union, 82 Ill. App. 426	121	19
Sutherland, Matter of, 252 App. Div. (N.Y.) 620	52	10
Swihart, In re, 42 S.D. 628	154	5
Sylvester, Estate of, 195 Iowa 1329	100	39
	177	11
Tanner v. United States, 62 F.2d 601	85	41
Taylor v. Blacklow, 3 Bing. N.C. 235	28	29
	139	47
Tenney v. Berger, 93 N.Y. 524	199	6
Terry, Ex parte, 128 U.S. 289	38	37
Thatcher, In re, 190 F. 969, 80 Ohio St. 492	41	47
	306	
Thatcher v. United States, 212 F. 801	41	47
Thibodeau, In re, 295 Mass. 374	166	37
Thomas v. Turner's Adm'r., 87 Va. 1	90	4
Thompson v. Thompson, 127 App. Div. (N.Y.) 296	124	38
Thorn, In re, 164 App. Div. (N.Y.) 151	304	
Tillinghast, Ex parte, 4 Pet. 108	41	47
Tillman v. Komar, 259 N.Y. 133	178	21
Townley, Ex parte, 3 Dowl. 39	41	47
Tracy, In re, 197 Minn. 35	29	37
	224	19
	308	
Train v. Davidson, 20 App. Div. (N.Y.) 577	127	47
Treadwell, Matter of, 175 App. Div. (N.Y.) 833	52	10
Umland v. United Pub. Serv. Co., 111 N.J. Eq. 536	213	13
Union Surety, etc. Co. v. Tenny et al, 200 Ill. 349	172	29
	173	35
United States v. Costen, 38 F. 24	47	33
	304	
United States v. Frank, 53 F.2d 128	84	35
	145	31
United States v. Green, 85 F. 857	306	
United States v. Sacher, 9 F.R.D. 394, 182 F.2d 416	69	1
United States, Sacher v. 343 U.S. 1	36	24
	40	44
	69	1
Vail, In re, 228 App. Div. (N.Y.) 217	64	24
Vandewater, In re, 257 App. Div. (N.Y.) 962	48	40
Ver Bryck v. Luby, 67 Cal. App.2d 842	135	44
Virdone, In re, 261 App. Div. (N.Y.) 961	48	40
Vise v. Hamilton County, 19 Ill. 78	62	11
Wall, Ex parte, 107 U.S. 265	36	24
	38	36
	43	10
	43	12
	44	18

	Page	*Note*
Wall, Ex parte, 107 U.S. 265	45	20
	306	
Wallace, In re, 323 Mo. 203	307	
Wallace, In re, L.R. 1 P.C. 283	41	47
Ward v. Orsini, 243 N.Y. 123	102	12
	177	19
Watson v. Maryland, 218 U.S. 173	35	17
Weare, In re, 2 Q.B. Div. 439	43	13
Weil v. Neary, 278 U.S. 160	27	28
	98	31
	112	43
Wein, In re, 73 Ariz. 225	307	
Weinard v. Chicago Ry., 298 F. 977	64	24
Weiss's Appeal, 317 Pa. 415, 20 D & C 666	154	5
	307	
Weitling, Matter of, 266 N.Y. 184	178	21
Welansky, In re, 319 Mass. 205	45	27
Welles v. Brown, 226 Mich. 657	100	39
	177	12
Wells, In re, 293 Ky. 201	45	22
	307	
Wernimont v. State Bar, 101 Ark. 210	307	
Whinery v. Brown, 36 Ind. App. 276	176	6
Whise v. Whise, 36 Nev. 16	82	27
White v. Lucas, 46 Iowa 319	183	12
Wieland v. White, 109 Mass. 392	196	32
Wilbur, Matter of, 228 App. Div. 197	118	40
Wilhelm's Case, 269 Pa. 416	37	34
Williams v. North Carolina, 317 U.S. 287	81	23
Williams v. North Carolina, 325 U.S. 226	81	23
	81	24
Williams v. Reed, 3 Mason 405	105	30
Wilson v. Wilson, 66 Nev. 405	82	27
Wilson, In re, 79 Kans. 450	305	
Wilson, In re, 79 Kans. 674	305	
Wiltse, Matter of, 109 Wash. 261	29	36
	306	
Wisconsin v. O'Leary, 207 Wis. 297	42	1
Wolfe's Disbarment, 288 Pa. 331	37	30
	37	32
	51	6
	306	
Wood v. State, 45 Ga. App. 783	45	22
Wright, In re, 232 P.2d (Nev.) 398	308	
Yablunky, In re, 407 Ill. 111	36	25
	304	
Young v. Murphy, 120 Wis. 49	91	6

TABLE OF COMMITTEE DECISIONS

AMERICAN BAR ASSOCIATION

Opinion	Page	Note	Opinion	Page	Note
1	220	38	13	259	50
2	60	1	14	85	44
3	60	1		201	27
4	219	36	15	275	5
5	251	49	16	106	36
6	206	38		119	10
	206	45		120	17
	208	17		129	6
7	252	12		130	14
8	65	28	17	195	18
	66	52		199	11
	163			199	12
	164	27		200	16
	165	33		202	45
	167	39	18	179	33
	182	9	19	138	41
	183	13	20	88	16
	184			178	23
	250	33	21	155	15
9	65	29	22	277	10
	251	5	23	133	28
	255			137	21
10	110	25		152	20
	167	39	24	208	17
	179	34		220	38
	184			241	11
	184	15		241	13
	188	4		241	16
	191	3	25	73	20
	198	4		195	18
	199	13	26	113	3
11	208	17		131	17
	241	14	27	171	17
12	85	44		174	44
	86	50		186	29
	201	27		188	2

Opinion	Page	Note	Opinion	Page	Note
28	175	50	50	106	36
29	101	8		158	36
30	118	45	51	65	29
	130	14		65	31
	279	23		100	40
31	66	52		100	47
	67	56	52	275	4
	167	39	53	214	29
	222	9		246	
	229	1	54	204	15
	262	47		229	26
32	204	10	55	107	1
33	106	36		279	23
	158	36	56	167	39
34	119	48	57	66	52
	120	17		67	52
	129	6		179	41
	130	14		222	9
35	66	52		222	14
	168	39		222	
	222	9	58	128	2
36	220	38		128	3
37	27	25		201	26
	130	11	59	247	40
	131	15	60	110	25
38	173	36		113	48
	185		61	171	20
39	118	45	62	260	10
	130	11	63	32	50
	279	23		173	39
40	112	40		187	38
41	67	56		187	43
	160	2		187	45
	167	39		200	15
	261	37	64	113	3
	261	41	65	191	2
	262	48		268	40
42	219	37	66	203	50
	247	38	67	280	24
	264	15	68	161	16
43	247	38	69	241	11
44	140	3		241	13
45	31	46		241	16
46	31	46	70	121	19
47	141	17	71	114	7
	195	20		120	17
48	179	35		130	11
49	106	36	72	106	36
	130	11		107	2
	131	16		130	11

Opinion	Page	Note	Opinion	Page	Note
73	247	45	103	106	36
	250	30		112	40
74	220	1	104	106	37
75	202	37		130	11
76	161	8	105	279	20
77	32	52	106	204	19
	119	48	107	247	41
	120	17	108	201	33
	129	6		202	46
	130	14	109	84	36
78	249	22	110	118	45
79	220	43		279	23
80	66	52	111	251	49
	67	52	112	111	31
	228	13	113	279	18
81	228	17	114	234	10
82	103	15		244	45
	148	42	115	204	19
83	106	39		204	20
84	31	46		204	22
85	51	9		219	36
	160	6		228	17
86	113	2	116	241	16
87	66	47	117	85	44
88	142	18		201	27
89	71	9	118	118	45
	275	2		130	14
90	141	16	119	271	28
91	133	28	120	244	44
	133	30	121	255	
92	263	15		257	
93	279	20		259	50
94	98	31		263	15
95	202	38	122	66	52
96	227	1		67	56
97	51	9		110	20
	208	17		249	20
	208	18	123	214	29
98	167	39		220	38
	168	42		268	35
	261	38		268	45
	263	14		269	8
	263	15		271	29
99	105	29	124	26	24
100	261	41		202	45
101	85	44	125	95	3
	201	26		95	6
	201	27	126	204	19
102	118	38	127	85	45
	120	19		201	27

Opinion	Page	Note	Opinion	Page	Note
	201	28		152	22
128	130	11	151	174	47
	193	13	152	220	38
	195	18		220	42
129	118	44		241	14
130	173	40	153	159	43
	199	13	154	136	4
	200	14	155	137	21
	200	15		137	24
131	86	4	156	137	21
	155	16	157	172	32
132	106	33		183	12
	120	18		184	16
133	268	37	158	261	30
134	130	11	159	229	43
	130	14	160	121	21
135	130	11		201	26
	279	23	161	107	2
136	118	44		279	23
	130	11	162	167	39
137	250	38		261	36
138	279	23		263	15
139	279	20		265	25
140	247	39	163	95	4
141	263	15		136	5
	265	25	164	279	21
142	106	36	165	120	19
	118	45	166	264	15
	277	12		264	22
	279	22		275	3
	279	23	167	111	35
143	279	22	168	167	39
144	60	3		168	40
	197	42		264	15
145	220	38	169	248	8
	233	45		249	24
	242	23	170	279	19
	243	31	171	175	50
	244	41	172	255	42
	273	53		259	50
146	78	46	173	65	33
147	60	1	174	250	39
	65	32		260	21
148	248	9	175	233	45
	249	24		241	16
149	194			242	19
	199	13		243	31
150	132	26	176	65	37
	136	15		100	48
	144	28	177	114	11

Opinion	Page	Note	Opinion	Page	Note
178	79	8	200	277	11
	154	·5	201	204	10
179	255			222	9
	255	43	202	133	29
	256			136	11
180	179	38		137	24
181	112	41		138	34
182	241	16		138	35
	268	37	203	220	38
	273	44		241	16
183	229	44	204	32	50
	233	45		186	30
184	239	42		187	39
185	106	36		187	48
	158	36		187	49
186	119	46		215	31
187	85	44	205	255	43
	85	45		258	
	85	48	206	171	24
	201	32		248	9
188	65	36	207	247	47
	249	23		259	7
189	279	20	208	208	17
190	174	44	209	32	50
	174	47		199	13
	175	50		200	15
191	255	43	210	254	32
	257		211	171	24
	259	50		248	9
192	106	36	212	280	24
	119	10	213	254	33
	130	11	214	179	41
	130	14		229	27
	205	34		231	14
	209	28	215	277	10
192(5)	260	10	216	134	39
193	279	21	217	187	33
194	222	9	218	113	1
	232	34	219	207	7
	242	24		207	9
	243			208	17
	243	31	220	106	36
	273	43		158	35
	273	44	221	241	16
195	279	21	222	116	25
196	96	18	223	246	
197	220	46	224	120	19
198	66	52		121	21
	168	44	225	168	44
199	70	4		179	39

Opinion	Page	Note	Opinion	Page	Note
	222	9		139	50
	251	46		150	8
	251	47		150	10
226	61	7	249	270	23
	279	20		270	24
227	255	43	250	132	25
	258			133	
228	232	34		135	42
	233	45		138	36
	239	46		171	15
	240	1	251	233	45
229	254	38		241	15
230	228	14		241	16
	268	46		241	18
231	115	21		242	19
	116	22	252	171	24
232	220	38		248	9
233	220	42	253	154	6
	268	35	254	278	16
	268	48		31	46
234	179	40	255	266	30
	204	11		269	50
	220	42	256	205	24
	268	35		228	17
	268	48		230	5
235	118	38		269	16
	120	19	257	66	52
236	271	27		67	52
237	161	9		204	13
238	278	15		222	9
239	204	12	258	208	25
240	206	35	259	171	24
	206	36		178	24
	232	34		178	25
	232	38		248	9
241	214	30		255	43
	246	25		259	
242	118	45	260	227	5
	279	23		258	49
243	120	19		259	50
244	220	43		268	37
245	128	1		273	44
246	101	4	261	118	45
	176	8	262	107	2
	178	23		119	47
247	32	50	263	66	52
	115	21		244	43
	116	24		269	11
	132	27	264	232	34
248	68	64		232	37

Opinion	Page	Note	Opinion	Page	Note
	239		276	31	46
	239	42		213	20
	240	1		215	31
265	186	31		225	30
	187	41		241	14
	187	47		241	16
	215	31		268	37
266	137	17		273	44
	161	11	277	31	46
	189	11		204	19
	220	44		228	46
267	208	17		233	45
	208	25	278	31	46
268	136	8		119	47
269	204	14	279	31	46
270	264	15		100	45
	265	25		101	5
271	106	36	280	31	46
	112	41		78	46
	188	1	281	31	46
272	75	27		151	18
	179	36	282	31	46
	180	47		114	15
	204	12		115	16
	220	42		116	26
	222	9		117	27
	223			117	30
	224		283	31	46
	225			204	18
	231	19	284	31	46
273	66	52		215	31
	67	58		246	
	165	32		246	25
	167	39		246	26
	168	40	285	31	46
	264	15		168	42
	265	25		262	46
	265	26		262	47
	265	27		262	49
274	136	9		262	10
275	31	46		265	27
	94	39	286	31	46
	106	32		233	45
	160	3	287	31	46

AMERICAN BAR ASSOCIATION
HITHERTO UNPUBLISHED DECISIONS [1]

Decision	Page	Note	Decision	Page	Note
1	32	49	40	222	11
	32	50	41	227	4
	165	32	42	227	3
2	32	51	43	222	10
3	32	53		222	13
4	32	55	44	227	3
5	32	57	45	227	2
	67	53	46	227	6
6	26	24	51	227	8
	30	39		261	35
	30	41	52	220	40
	185	26		228	11
7	52	11		250	35
	53	12	54	228	14
8	48	41	55	268	42
9	61	6	56	260	17
10	107	43	57	248	50
	140	1	58	227	8
	153	38		247	38
11	146	36		248	50
12	93	35		248	2
14	77	40		261	29
15	150	5	60	228	16
16	93	31	61	254	34
17	203	3	62	254	35
18	77	45	63	247	49
19	93	32	64	247	49
20	88	17	65	248	7
	198	3		248	10
21	77	39	66	250	34
	86	3	67	252	7
26	220	43	68	248	12
	220	44	70	253	28
27	220	47	76	254	31
	220	48	77	222	47
29	220	42		248	10
31	268	38	78	65	33
32	259	2		65	34
	268	39	79	227	7
34	221	4		260	14
37	221	6		261	31
	227	9	80	253	20
38	221	4	81	254	39
39	222	12	82	254	41

[1] The text of these decisions is given in Appendix A, *supra*, pp. 283–303.

Decision	Page	Note	Decision	Page	Note
83	191	7	134	231	21
	220	41		231	22
	249	27	135	231	20
86	247	46		231	21
87	248	11	136	231	22
88	253	24	139	233	45
89	227	7	140	54	20
	254	37		232	35
90	248	4		240	3
	268	44	141	232	35
91	248	5	142	232	35
	268	43		240	3
92	250	32	143	232	37
93	250	29	144	233	45
94	247	43	145	233	42
95	247	48	146	232	37
98	249	20		233	40
99	249	24		233	41
100	251	44	147	233	43
101	251	45		240	5
105	252	13	148	232	36
106	252	14	149	246	27
107	253	25	150	247	33
111	208	23	151	255	42
112	208	23	152	258	49
113	229	48	153	248	15
114	229	48		259	5
115	229	32	156	219	36
116	229	31		269	8
	229	34	157	219	36
117	229	45		269	9
	273	44	159	269	1
118	229	38	160	269	13
	229	39	161	268	41
119	229	28	162	267	32
120	206	37	163	268	47
	229	37	164	267	34
	229	40	165	268	42
	229	41	166	268	48
121	228	25	167	260	17
	229	35		269	2
122	230	8	168	260	18
123	228	20		269	2
	231	17	169	260	19
124	228	21		269	2
127	229	42	171	269	3
128	229	39	172	269	4
129	206	48		269	5
131	231	23	173	269	6
132	231	24	174	269	7
133	232	33	176	269	10

Decision	Page	Note	Decision	Page	Note
177	269	5	238	244	34
178	269	14		244	35
	269	15		244	40
179	269	12		244	42
180	270	17	239	244	45
181	270	18	241	191	8
182	270	19		240	6
183	270	20	242	187	45
184	270	21		198	48
185	270	22	243	187	45
187	270	24		198	50
188	270	24		200	15
189	270	24	244	94	47
190	271	25		198	4
192	271	27		200	17
193	271	30	246	67	60
194	271	32	249	202	44
196	272	37	250	85	48
197	271	35		202	34
	271	36	251	73	17
198	271	33	252	71	9
199	271	31	253	78	47
200	271	34		78	48
201	272	38		198	1
202	272	39	255	73	18
203	269	49	256	70	4
	272	40	257	84	36
204	272	41		84	37
206	272	42	258	84	38
207	272	42	259	87	12
211	273	46	261	93	21
	273	48		95	6
212	273	47	262	95	1
213	273	50		96	13
214	273	50	263	94	46
215	273	51	264	94	46
216	273	52	265	94	46
218	245	22	266	94	42
	273	49		94	46
220	273	54	267	94	39
226	265	24		106	32
227	265	28		160	3
228	264	22	268	94	41
231	243	32	269	91	9
232	244	39	271	93	25
233	244	36	272	96	12
234	244	37	273	96	13
235	244	38	274	96	11
236	244	41		196	28
237	243	33	276	98	26

Decision	Page	Note	Decision	Page	Note
277	97	22	320	161	19
	97	25	321	161	13
	120	18	326	168	43
278	96	18		169	45
	97	20		169	46
	98	32		180	48
	99	36	327	168	43
	111	27		169	46
280	100	40		179	39
	100	1	328	168	43
281	72	13		179	39
	72	15	329	168	43
282	158	41		179	39
283	159	44	330	168	43
284	106	37		179	39
285	120	19	333	171	12
286	119	1	334	171	13
287	119	2	335	63	17
288	130	13		172	26
289	111	30	336	175	1
290	67	56	337	177	9
	110	20	338	178	28
	110	22	339	178	26
	160	2	341	180	47
291	198	3		180	3
292	118	45	342	179	37
	119	46	343	179	4
293	119	47		179	5
	119	9	344	180	1
	135	50	347	186	28
296	120	16	351	187	38
297	120	18		187	47
298	120	19	352	185	26
301	79	8		187	35
	154	5		187	36
302	154	6	353	180	8
	161	16		188	50
303	154	1	354	187	40
304	77	39	355	187	44
	86	3		194	15
	155	16	356	186	29
305	86	8		186	30
	152	29		188	3
309	133	37	357	187	46
310	136	5		187	47
312	138	37	358	199	7
316	162	21	359	97	21
317	167	39		98	35
318	167	39		183	12
319	168	39	360	199	10

Decision	Page	Note	Decision	Page	Note
	199	13		207	15
361	188	8	373	207	7
364	205	31	374	207	7
	207	1	375	206	43
365	205	24		207	10
	205	29	376	206	43
366	204	19		207	9
	205	32	377	207	8
	207	3		207	9
	207	4	379	208	17
368	207	4	380	209	29
369	207	13	381	208	24
	207	14	382	208	21
370	207	14	383	208	21
371	207	12		208	23

CALIFORNIA

		Page	Note
3	3 Cal. St. Bar Jour. 54	267	31
19	3 Cal. St. Bar Jour. 56	246	25
24	3 Cal. St. Bar Jour. 216	136	10
31	4 Cal. St. Bar Jour., No. 2, 32	262	6
35	4 Cal. St. Bar Jour., No. 2, 33	262	11

CHICAGO

Opinion	Page	Note	Opinion	Page	Note
6	202	39		99	39
8	153	46		100	2
9	156	25	25	243	30
	157	31		245	24
11	233	47	26	264	19
	239	49	27	132	27
	240	2		137	23
15	233	48	28	66	51
	239	50		102	13
	245	19		142	18
18	250	34		170	7
19	120	18		171	11
	128	3	30	153	45
	129	7		197	43
	129	8	31	67	58
20	262	46		111	32
21	231	23		173	34
22	257	46	32	137	17
23	80	8		189	12
	154	5	33	62	12
	168	44	36	161	9
24	65	37			

CLEVELAND

	Page	Note		Page	Note
25 Ohio Law			I supp.	246	28
Reporter 569	108	3	2	119	46
	136	11	3	246	28
6/23/45	137	20	6	73	18
B	97	24	8	32	48
C	229	44	10	248	7
	233	47	11	279	21
	239	48	12	279	23
	241	18	13	229	33
	246	28		275	5
F	138	31	13a	224	19
	239	16	15	144	27
	255	43	17	247	39
H	246	25	18	280	24
	246	28	19	220	42
I	246	28			

KENTUCKY

Opinion	Page	Note	Opinion	Page	Note
1	64	24	6	119	5
	213	14	7		
	249	16	8		
	249	19		224	19
2	165	32		224	20
3	224	19	9	231	22
	224	20	10	118	45
5(3)	119	7		119	8

LOUISIANA

Opinion	Page	Note
1	126	44

LOUISVILLE BAR ASSOCIATION

Opinion	Page	Note
1	48	39

MICHIGAN

Opinion	Page	Note	Opinion	Page	Note
1	280	23	5	241	16
2	264	16	6	227	7
3	171	16		264	16
4	206	42	7	107	2

Opinion	Page	Note	Opinion	Page	Note
	108	6		54	18
8	241	16	45	135	50
9	264	16	46	246	25
10	257	46		246	28
	258	49	47	110	18
11	231	23	48	261	40
12	206	42	49	261	31
13	264	16	50	275	5
14	231	23	51	65	36
15	260	16		254	30
18	249	17	52	248	6
19	232	34		250	34
	240	3		250	37
22	137	25	53	65	29
	138	34		65	35
	152	20		94	36
24	179	31		136	13
26	271	26		254	29
28	224	21	54	179	37
	229	31	55	229	2
	229	35		262	50
	229	44	56	67	57
	232	39	57	264	16
	233	40	58	247	38
	233	45	59	137	25
	243	29		156	27
29	247	41	60	169	48
30	278	16		229	3
32	154	7		262	4
33	231	23	61	256	44
	232	34		257	45
	232	35		264	16
	241	16		264	22
34	232	30	62	167	39
35	248	1	63	120	17
	261	29	64	173	36
36	279	20		185	21
37	169	48	65	66	46
38	131	18		100	42
39	206	42		100	43
	224	21		100	47
40	247	40	66	176	8
41	85	44		178	23
	85	48	67	250	31
	201	32	68	85	44
42	168	39		86	1
43	278	16		201	28
44	53	13	70	113	50
	54	15		115	20
	54	17	71	137	20

Opinion	Page	Note	Opinion	Page	Note
72	99	39	99	200	18
	177	11		249	21
73	119	5	100	106	37
74	279	18	101	260	10
75	111	35		262	43
76			102	113	50
77	228	45		115	19
	228	50	103	158	38
	233	46		159	45
	234	10	104	228	18
	243	29	105	262	45
	273	44	106	264	16
78	113	3		265	26
	131	23	108	243	29
79	244	11	109	119	6
80	253	21		120	18
81	131	21	110	67	55
82	120	15		160	6
83	119	13		160	7
	120	17		174	48
84	98	28	111	112	38
	129	9	112	93	33
85	122	27		94	42
	126	44	113	198	4
	128	2		199	6
86	259	3		199	8
	259	4		199	9
87	119	13		200	19
88	137	20	114	262	8
	138	31	115	94	37
	138	32	116	134	36
89	229	36		135	45
	248	7	117	85	44
	250	34		201	30
90	227	6	118	134	38
91	65	27	119	264	16
	100	41		264	22
	100	3		265	26
	220	42	120	94	45
92	167	39		94	46
93	194	14	121	279	21
94	244	12	122	106	36
95	119	12	123	98	28
	131	22		128	5
96	78	47		129	9
	198	2	124	221	3
97	259	1		224	
98	115	15		224	24
	120	19		232	46
	185	22		244	10

Opinion	Page	Note	Opinion	Page	Note
125	114	8	139	119	7
126	96	18	141	85	44
127	62	12	142	76	36
	63	14		77	41
	172	30	143	278	17
128	243	29	144	94	45
	244	13	147	167	39
129	148	46		168	40
130				168	43
131	251	49		262	44
132	119	7	147(iv)	162	21
	174	49	147(v)	162	22
133	191	7	147(vii)	162	24
	220	41	148	204	13
	249	27	149	248	15
134	168	44		259	6
135	241	16	150	92	14
136	160	7		117	30
137	131	19	151	241	16
138	116	21		247	48
	116	26	154	279	19

MISSISSIPPI

Opinion	Page	Note	Opinion	Page	Note
1	32	56		224	19
	204	12			

MILWAUKEE

Opinion	Page	Note
June, 1952	231	23

MISSOURI

Opinion	Page	Note	Opinion	Page	Note
1	165	33	17	262	47
2	179	39	18	262	47
3	222	17	19	165	33
5	165	33	20	177	8
6	165	33	21	93	22
7	165	33	22	180	6
8	271	26	24	241	11
10	168	44	25	233	48
12	180	47	26	241	11
13	180	6		246	27
14	180	47		246	30
15	120	18	27	178	25
16	161	15	28	262	47

Opinion	Page	Note	Opinion	Page	Note
29	92	14	63	224	20
	137	18	65	119	5
30	279	21	66	131	22
31	179	39	67	279	21
32	153	44	69	229	46
33	119	4	70	246	30
36	228	16	72	179	39
	248	6	73	268	37
37	201	29	74	66	52
38	119	4	75	107	2
	131	22	76	264	19
41	221	6	77	188	1
43	183	12	79	73	17
48	72	11	80	221	6
56	68	64	81	233	48
57	279	17	82	258	49
58	208	23	83	128	2
59	119	46	84	201	33
60	118	44	85	119	5
61	154	50	86	221	6

NEW ORLEANS

Opinion	Page	Note	Opinion	Page	Note
1/13/41	207	50	3/7/47	262	46
	208	17	5/22/48	246	25
	208	22	6/15/48	246	25
1/19/44	232	38	7/13/48	248	14
5/28/45	239	42	2/3/50	248	12
1/29/46	239	42	7/2/51	268	37

NEW YORK CITY

Opinion	Page	Note	Opinion	Page	Note
1	167	39	14	94	44
2	106	38	15	177	14
3	229	50		200	16
	230	7	16	251	2
5	96	18	17	202	37
6	98	27	19	97	22
7	251	5		97	24
	253	27		97	25
8	76	30		120	18
	153	32	22	206	44
10	167	39	23	65	40
12	140	4	24	178	23
13	228	23		178	27
	231	16		248	8

Opinion	Page	Note	Opinion	Page	Note
25	225	32		129	10
	226	38	82	177	15
27	98	28	83	228	12
	129	9		232	36
28	205	26		241	11
	230	6	84	79	7
	240	7	85	83	31
29	240	7	86	76	30
31	267	31		86	7
	268	46		152	30
35	240	7	86(b)	153	34
38	229	32	86(c)	153	35
	233	49	87	109	17
40	206	45	88	51	9
43	251	49	89	227	7
	251	2		236	23
44	206	39	90	262	4
	207	50	91	60	3
	207	5		197	42
47	60	3	92	152	21
	197	42	93	236	23
48	232	34	94	60	4
49	177	14	95	98	35
54	156	24		188	4
	157	32	96		
56	196	37	97	229	49
58	77	41		231	28
	77	42	98	136	5
59	240	5	99	161	15
60	220	38		167	39
	234	1		168	43
61	228	17		169	3
	242	61	99(3)	169	47
62	263	13	101	250	41
65	231	15	102	160	3
66	262	1		222	11
	262	2		225	34
68	94	45	103	214	24
70	138	28		219	36
	141	12		251	2
72	156	23	105	106	37
73	206	41	106	129	5
75	92	20		129	10
76	232	34	107	136	6
77	161	16	108	135	42
79	107	2		136	6
	131	20		139	44
80	107	2	109	202	42
81	125		110	189	11
	127	47		189	13

Opinion	Page	Note	Opinion	Page	Note
	189	15	164	54	20
111	202	44	165	54	15
113	51	9		54	16
114			167	178	23
115	199	5	170	118	39
116	105	29	173	125	42
117	108	4		129	10
119	107	1	174	167	39
122	112	47	175	180	49
	137	18		180	50
125	154	50	176	97	19
126	250	42		98	33
127	251	2		183	10
128	138	30		184	18
129	161	17	177	32	52
130	75	26		251	5
131	32	52	179	138	36
132			180	51	9
133	225	32	183	86	5
	225	38	187	188	7
134	65	28	188	107	44
	167	39	188(a)	107	45
135	234	3	189	95	7
	244	47	201	129	5
138	65	42		161	10
	254	30	202	251	1
139	125	42	203	95	7
	129	10	204	141	9
140	160	3		141	10
	252	8	205	93	21
141	186	31		95	8
142	234	4	207	169	49
143	174	44		178	24
144	158	39	209	162	25
145	186	31		168	39
146	65	39		261	28
147	179	36	210	161	16
150	54	16	211	222	11
151	54	14	214	123	33
152	93	21		128	4
154	207	16	217	95	6
155	251	49	219	150	11
158	197	42	222	64	25
159	112	47		185	23
	113	6	223		
	120	18	224	264	17
160	262	3		264	20
161	54	22		264	23
162	54	22	227	203	48
163	54	19	232	150	8

Opinion	Page	Note	Opinion	Page	Note
234	120	19	288	114	13
235	206	41		116	21
236	134	33		117	33
237	110	20		117	36
	110	22		120	18
238	111	36	289	68	63
240	150	11	290	197	39
241	136	7	291	106	39
243	151	16		108	5
	196	34	292	75	25
245	112	42	296	95	6
251(a)	93	35	299	112	46
	96	12	300	254	32
	149	2	301	98	30
252	96	17		172	31
253	139	48	302	95	8
254	151	16	303	119	8
	196	34	304	154	5
257	96	18	306	220	43
258	179	41	307	114	13
259	106	36		117	33
	119	10		120	18
261	93	21	308	105	28
	169	46		120	18
	169	50		134	38
265	153	44	309		
	154	47	310	220	38
266	155	18	311	86	7
267	117	28		152	30
269	77	45		153	35
	96	11	312	261	26
	196	29	313	156	25
	196	33		157	31
	196	34	314	125	
270	264	17		129	10
271	120	19	316	99	38
272	95	9	319	220	43
273	86	6	320	32	52
274	112	46		51	9
	157	28	324	95	49
276	154	47	325	153	34
279	95	4	326	261	27
280	77	38	327	152	19
282	116	21	327(a)	253	27
	118	37	328	95	8
283			329		
284	262	1	330	228	12
285	140	2	331	95	8
286			335	115	15
287	261	41		140	2

Opinion	Page	Note	Opinion	Page	Note
336	139	45	382	260	20
337	114	9	383	109	17
	195	17	384	95	9
338	260	23	386	106	37
340	234	1	387	154	50
	234	6	388	67	56
341	97	21	389	226	39
	98	35	392	112	39
343	92	14	394	142	19
	93	27		178	21
	201	26	395	266	29
344	221	5	397	154	50
	226	38	398		
346	249	26	399	264	17
347	113	50	400	202	39
	120	18	403	222	16
348	254	30	409	108	10
349	118	43	410	264	17
	120	19	411	86	7
350	96	17		153	32
	141	9	412	111	33
	141	10	413	159	50
	203	2		163	26
353	264	17		167	39
	264	20		222	9
354	264	17	414	107	2
355	189	10		109	17
356	160	4	417	254	34
	171	13	418	231	23
357	246	25	419	177	18
	246	26	420	135	49
358	261	32	422	247	40
359	261	41	423	178	23
360	92	19	424	251	50
	253	27	425	251	1
362	271	26	426	236	23
364	95	5		236	25
368	94	40	427	65	31
369	68	64		65	38
372	179	41	428	264	17
373	251	49		264	23
374	178	23	429	97	25
375	234	1		120	18
377	84	36	430	108	13
378	128	1	433	246	31
	128	5	434	202	40
	150	8	435	107	1
380	228	12		121	23
	241	11	436	63	18
381	251	1	440	189	14

Opinion	Page	Note	Opinion	Page	Note
441			484	137	20
442	220	38		137	25
443	85	46		139	46
445	96	11	485	167	39
	196	27	486	234	7
	196	28	488	107	47
	196	34	490	65	30
446	107	2	493	112	45
	109	17		251	49
447	220	43	494	63	19
448	120	15		93	24
	205	34		111	29
450	98	29		171	15
451	122	25	495	129	9
452	264	17	496	122	25
	264	23	497	234	1
455	220	50		244	12
456	262	3	498	247	34
460	220	38	499	107	1
461	228	12	502	269	7
	241	11	505	92	14
462	161	16	506	65	37
	228	24	507	84	36
463	65	37	508	111	34
464	251	50	509	162	23
	251	4		169	4
466	107	2		259	9
	109	17	510	117	32
	112	44		118	37
468	220	38	511	244	4
469	234	1	513	167	39
	234	10	514	116	23
	244	52	515	107	1
470	229	45		109	17
	229	47	516	191	8
	234	1		191	10
	234	10		253	17
	244	53	517	120	18
473	195	17	518	264	17
474	196	34	519	220	42
475	221	5	530	128	1
	226	38	531	187	36
476	264	17		204	19
477	142	20	532	251	5
478	183	10		253	23
479	168	40	533	95	2
	222	11	534	221	5
480	136	4		225	31
482	95	7		226	37
483	100	3	535	150	4

Opinion	Page	Note	Opinion	Page	Note
	151	13	579	204	17
537	171	21	580	109	17
538	247	41	581	262	4
539	244	14	582	118	43
540	247	42	583		
541	85	44	584	264	17
542	225	33		264	23
	229	30	585	205	28
543	220	38		230	13
544	88	18		231	25
	171	22		247	37
545	220	41	586	234	1
546	228	12		234	8
	241	11		234	10
547	114	13		244	54
	120	18	587	62	13
548	107	47	588	71	8
	109	17	589	76	31
550	220	38		154	47
551	225	36	590	163	26
	226	39	592	112	40
553	220	38	593	63	20
	244	6		159	50
556	122	25	594	179	44
	160	5	595	180	8
557	229	41	596	151	16
558	244	16		196	34
559	204	12	599	95	50
	226	39	600	231	26
560	150	6	601	220	38
561	248	13	602	97	22
562	220	38		171	23
563	228	12	604	262	9
	241	11		262	11
564	158	42	605	240	4
565	96	18	606	228	12
566	249	20		241	11
569	253	27	607	72	11
570	75	24		72	12
571	53	12	608	110	24
572	232	31		160	4
	232	32	609	161	14
573	172	27	610	189	19
574	259	9	611	228	18
	260	10	612	262	9
575	108	7	613	155	19
576	246	25		251	48
577	119	4	614	112	40
578	264	17	615	160	5
	264	22		259	8

Opinion	Page	Note	Opinion	Page	Note
	260	12	652	225	32
	262	9	653	112	40
617	118	43		169	46
618	249	22	654	150	11
	251	2	656	248	3
619	220	38		264	17
	232	39	657	179	45
	252	12	658	53	12
	253	22	660	98	35
	253	26		187	42
621	122	25	661	264	17
622	69	59		264	20
624	159	48	662	103	19
625	251	50		108	11
	251	1		108	12
	251	4		108	13
626	179	41	663	247	42
	180	49	664	251	2
	180	50	667	225	26
	180	8		228	22
627	178	23		229	32
628	178	20	668	75	28
	200	16		151	14
629	162	23	669	154	50
	169	4	670	248	3
630	120	19		264	17
631	77	44	671	134	40
	196	30	672	161	14
	196	31	673	71	8
632	208	26	675	109	17
633	222	11	677	153	40
634	169	47	678	242	26
	169	3		244	17
635			679	168	39
636	222	18	680	228	12
637	242	26		241	11
638	168	39	681	72	14
640	65	41		148	50
641	231	22	682	168	39
	242	26	682(a)	93	26
	244	5		93	28
642	251	5		93	29
	253	22		93	30
643			682(b)	96	12
644	247	44		153	42
646	222	16		154	48
647	112	45	682(c)	161	13
648	191	4		169	46
650	120	19		169	48
651	225	32	682(e)	255	43

Opinion	Page	Note		Opinion	Page	Note
682(g)	137	16			60	3
	196	35		722	254	32
	198	49		723	188	5
682(h)	80	14		724	261	39
	155	13		725	105	29
682(i)	92	14			114	13
	92	15			117	33
684	154	48			120	18
	154	50		726	124	39
685	96	14			127	49
	120	18		727	158	39
686	186	31		728	269	16
	204	19		729	204	16
	205	30		730	169	47
690	261	29			169	2
691	264	17		731	164	29
	264	22		732	107	2
693	135	41		733	154	50
694	153	41		734	220	43
695	247	42		735	220	38
698	54	24		736	220	38
700	264	17			245	24
702	230	8		737	236	23
703	54	20		740	241	16
704	234	2			269	2
705	154	50		741	241	16
706	185	26			245	24
	186	27		742	220	38
707	235	21			235	22
	242	23			236	23
	243	31		743	141	12
	244	7			141	15
	273	53		744	112	45
708	220	38		745	169	46
709	204	14			169	2
710	228	19		748	259	8
711	234	5			260	11
	244	1		749	135	2
712	241	18		752	241	11
714	100	44			241	18
	100	1			245	23
715	130	12		753	54	20
716	105	28			54	23
	107	2		754		
	121	21		755	225	31
717	225	31			226	40
718	167	39		756	79	49
719	191	9		757	65	29
720	153	37			66	45
721	60	1			100	46

Opinion	Page	Note	Opinion	Page	Note
759	131	16	796	246	29
	131	20		257	48
760	107	2	800	54	23
761	259	8		54	25
762	128	1	802	65	37
763	107	2	803	80	9
	158	39		150	11
764	235	23	807	187	33
	244	12		200	20
	244	8		200	21
766	94	46		230	4
	94	48	808	187	34
767	222	8		200	20
	236	24		232	38
768	222	47	809	105	29
	225	31		114	14
769	105	29		120	18
	110	19	810	225	35
	113	50	811	60	3
	225	31	812	253	28
770	249	21	814	252	9
	251	5	815	95	6
	253	21	816	225	32
774	245	21		262	47
775	251	1		262	7
776	207	6	817	171	18
777	105	27	818	205	26
	158	39		208	21
778	189	10		229	41
	189	16		230	6
781(2)	260	10		230	8
782	260	10		239	45
783	107	1	819	204	19
	117	31		206	40
785	161	10	821	128	1
786	95	6	822	236	23
	140	4	823	153	42
787	225	33		153	46
	226	48	824	225	32
789	189	13	825	226	49
790	186	31	826	121	22
791	123	33	828	107	1
	178	29	829	153	42
792	225	30	830	85	49
	229	31		201	31
	233	45	831	179	36
	236	25		204	12
	241	18	832	252	10
794	174	44	834	149	2
795	262	5	835	231	29

Opinion	Page	Note	Opinion	Page	Note
836	55	26	888	154	2
837	191	4	889	78	46
838	107	2	890	226	41
839	135	50	891	248	3
840	189	9		254	41
	200	22		264	17
841	161	12	892	246	29
842	117	34	894	189	12
843	200	20	896	257	48
844	200	20		259	50
	200	21	899	200	20
845	150	8	902	154	10
846			903	66	48
847	200	20		178	24
848	155	14	905	95	7
	197	39	908	207	50
849	197	40		209	28
	202	36	909	117	33
	202	41		120	18
852	94	37	910	249	21
853	179	45		253	21
857	269	16	911	220	43
862	200	20	912	235	11
863	120	18		241	18
866	236	23	914	158	42
	253	19	915	107	2
867	105	29	916	99	39
868	226	39		101	6
869	226	39	917	241	16
870			918	93	26
871	236	23		93	27
872	189	10	919	178	23
	189	11	920	247	42
873	264	17	922	232	30
	264	22	923	53	12
876	96	15	924	241	16
877	52		925	179	46
881	96	18		205	26
883	206	49		230	12
884	189	9		270	20
	200	23	926	153	42
	247	32		154	2
885	225	30	926(7)	200	20
	225	32	927	231	18
	229	29	930	164	29
886	80	9	931	264	17
	150	11	933	65	29
887	234	10		101	7
	244	45	935	167	39
	244	46		264	17

Opinion	Page	Note		Opinion	Page	Note
936	225	31			160	3
937	80	9		B-2	225	31
	150	11			226	37
938	200	20			226	41
939	154	7		B-3	254	36
940	54	21		B-5	230	7
	200	23		B-6(2)	189	10
	207	1		B-6	198	4
	207	2			205	23
941	170	10			212	11
944	109	15		B-7	206	43
945	77	43			207	11
	137	25			230	7
	138	28			257	48
946	197	38		B-8	225	31
947	133	30		B-9	120	18
949	171	18			127	47
950	141	5			128	3
	141	6			128	
951	124	39		B-10	244	12
	127	49		B-11	235	20
952	167	39			239	44
953	189	10			239	45
953(e)	189	11		B-12	232	34
954	250	28			239	44
955	178	23		B-13	239	44
956	229	50			239	45
	230	7			240	2
	230	11		B-14	153	41
	231	26		B-15	229	32
957	94	38			233	50
959	155	14		B-16	244	9
961	204	24		B-17	250	36
	205	25		B-18	260	15
	208	20		B-22	204	8
	230	5		B-23	247	42
	230	10		B-24	264	17
962	178	26			265	26
963	220	38		B-25	235	13
	233	44		B-26	109	17
	235	12			122	25
	237	36		B-27	206	46
	239	44		B-29	230	9
	239	47		B-31	204	24
	242	26			205	25
	243	27			208	20
	243	28		B-32	107	2
963 III	225	30			109	15
964	94	39		B-34	228	24
	106	32		B-40(1)	117	34

Opinion	Page	Note	Opinion	Page	Note
B-40(2)	117	35	B-82	208	24
B-41	259	8	B-83	54	20
B-42	206	43	B-86	228	13
	220	38	B-87	85	44
	220	45	B-88	235	13
B-44	189	12		235	17
	189	13		244	51
B-45	230	7	B-89	189	10
B-46	66	49	B-90	208	25
B-48	225	31	B-92	166	37
	225	48		167	39
B-49	239	45	B-93	169	2
B-50	235	14	B-95	252	11
B-52	235	15	B-99	167	39
	235	23	B-101	235	19
	244	50	B-104	189	17
B-53	117	33	B-105	245	20
	120	18	B-106	222	15
B-54	79	1		229	33
B-55	154	2		229	45
B-58	166	37	B-107	138	28
	167	39		141	13
B-60	157	34	B-109	262	50
B-61	67	59	B-110	260	24
B-62	209	27		262	1
B-63	109	16	B-114	262	1
	112	47		262	2
	113	5	B-118	224	25
B-65	117	33		225	
	120	18	B-120	244	12
B-66	80	12	B-121	246	25
B-67	264	17	B-127	153	44
B-68	251	50	B-128	128	1
B-69	169	2		150	8
	262	3	B-130	205	25
B-71	141	6		208	20
B-72	230	7	B-131	264	17
B-76	204	24	B-132	241	11
	205	25	B-133	205	25
	206	44		208	20
	230	5		230	10
	230	7	B-134	173	35
B-77	120	18	B-135	166	37
B-78	151	15		167	39
B-79	125		B-136	109	17
B-81	235	13		120	18
	235	16	B-137	204	12
	239	44		224	22
	239	45	B-138	109	17
	244	49		135	50

Opinion	Page	Note	Opinion	Page	Note
B-138	135	1		231	26
B-139	169	2	B-181	230	7
B-142	161	11	B-182	153	36
	189	10	B-185	167	39
	189	14	B-186	189	15
B-146	117	33	B-187	93	21
	120	18	B-188	233	45
B-148	205	25		244	18
	208	20	B-189	229	50
	230	10		230	7
B-152	191	10		230	11
	198	4	B-190	205	27
	200	17		230	9
B-153	200	20		261	33
B-154	186	31	B-191	120	18
B-155	197	46	B-192	165	31
B-156	119	3		168	39
B-157	208	19	B-193	150	12
B-158	205	25	B-194	187	48
	208	21	B-195	268	38
B-159	150	8	B-196	229	47
B-160	159	44		230	9
B-163	166	37		230	12
	168	39		230	13
B-164	235	11	B-197	108	11
	244	3	B-200	117	32
B-167	109	14		117	33
	133	32		129	10
	159	45	B-202	235	11
B-168	242	26	B-203	278	16
	244	15		279	23
B-170	167	39	B-205	106	37
B-171	262	9		128	1
B-172	109	17	B-206	191	4
B-173	230	7	B-207	96	18
	235	12	B-211	225	30
	235	18	B-212	69	50
	239	45	B-213	95	2
B-174	84	36	B-214	268	37
B-176	241	11	B-215	95	2
	241	16	B-216	251	1
B-178	107	2	B-217	97	23
B-179	242	26	B-219	247	44
B-180	230	7			

NEW YORK COUNTY

Opinion	Page	Note	Opinion	Page	Note
1	236	26	4	259	9
	241	12	7	171	18

Opinion	Page	Note		Opinion	Page	Note
9	140	3		47	180	4
	141	12			180	7
	150	4			180	8
10	154	49		ii(c)	169	2
11	107	46			180	8
	134	38			228	15
12	122			iii	168	40
13	137	24		iii(a)	263	12
14	254	40		iii(d)	263	12
15	140	4		iii(e)	263	12
17	197	45		iv	168	40
18	141	6		iv	169	48
	141	8		iv(a)	263	12
19	32	52		v	251	2
	197	43		vi	263	12
20	32	52		vi(c)	251	49
	107	41		vi(d)	251	49
21	32	52			251	1
22	112	40			263	12
23	240	9		vii	168	40
24	204	20			169	46
	205	27			169	48
	285	3		viii	168	40
26	173	33		viii(a)	261	41
	188	6			262	11
27	152	23		viii(b)	262	46
	152	26			262	49
28	159	45		viii(c)	262	49
30	81	26			263	12
31	195	17		viii(d)	262	49
33	106	36			263	12
34	79	50			262	4
35	108	9		ix	267	31
36	260	11		ix(c)	269	7
37	122	31		ix(d)	268	46
	123	33			269	5
38	51	9		49	231	15
41	195	21			261	32
42	186	31		51	169	1
	187	37		53	151	13
43	87	9			154	12
44	110	18		54	125	
	138	38			129	10
45	249	24		55	141	5
46	220	38			141	7
47	211	5		56	185	24
47 i	168	40		57		
ii	168	40		58	241	11
ii(a)	179	39		59	191	6
ii(b)	167	39				

Opinion	Page	Note	Opinion	Page	Note
	199	5	98	179	39
61	152	28		204	9
63	107	1	99	107	1
	107	2		120	19
	108	8		129	7
64	159	45	100	123	
	159	47	101	97	25
66	171	18	102	154	8
67	206	45		160	6
	206	47	103	148	47
68	167	39	106	124	40
69	64	26		127	49
70	136	7	107	153	43
	137	21		154	3
72	259	9	108	166	35
74	167	39		167	39
	169	3	109	191	6
	180	4		253	17
	180	6	110	76	30
75	121	24		86	7
76	158	38		140	3
78	60	2		152	30
79	231	16	111	98	32
80	179	43		106	33
81	186	31		184	19
	206	42	112	92	17
82	119	49		97	22
83	244	2		97	24
84	137	25		98	32
	138	28	113	169	2
	157	28		180	8
85	202	36		184	17
86	122	31	114	226	42
	126			226	47
	127	47	116	96	16
	127	48		106	38
87	93	34	117	260	22
	103	16	119	115	16
88	133	31		115	17
89	249	24		121	19
90	92	15	120	179	33
	121	20		249	22
	201	26	121	180	4
91	64	26	122	185	25
93	203	1	123	107	43
95	143	25	124	96	18
96	225	28		98	32
	236	27		106	33
97	111	28		184	19
	120	17	125	169	49

Opinion	Page	Note	Opinion	Page	Note
	169	3		201	26
	180	6	156	93	30
126	64	22		114	8
	252	15	157	110	18
	252	16		135	1
127	85	42		135	2
128	128	4	158	63	19
	129	5		141	7
129	92	17		141	10
130	179	42		171	15
131	167	39	160	100	47
132	127		161	26	24
	127	49		189	13
	153	33	163	127	
133	278	16		127	49
134	230	8	164	154	4
	231	26	165	127	47
136	262	49	166	97	23
	262	4		98	32
	263	12		106	33
137	169	3	167	137	19
138	98	32	168	137	19
141	176	7	169	138	33
	176	8	170	203	7
	177			205	33
142	180	2		207	50
	180	8		207	18
143	105	28	171	75	24
	108	3		126	43
	112	40		128	1
	120	18		128	5
144	201	26	172	259	9
145	148	45	173	171	25
146	141	7	174	262	42
	141	14	175	176	8
147	162	23		177	18
	169	4	176	195	22
	259	9		199	9
	260	20	177	250	40
149	63	15	179	160	6
150	253	27		226	46
151	112	47		226	47
	113	5	180	186	29
152	120	18		186	31
	120	19		187	42
153	112	40	181	77	44
154	134	37		140	3
155	120	18		141	14
	120	19		150	4
	121	20	182	205	25

Opinion	Page	Note	Opinion	Page	Note
183	118	42	219	254	40
184	173	38		257	46
	187	41	220	168	43
	187	42		180	3
	195	23		180	4
185	269	5		180	6
186	52	11		180	8
189	191	5		228	15
190	137	26	221	78	47
	138	29		198	1
192	125		222	249	24
	127	48		250	41
193	123	33	223	241	11
	125	41	224	65	43
194	97	19		249	25
	98	32	225	241	12
	98	33	226	131	24
	106	33	227	64	26
195	236	28		198	47
	241	12		251	5
196	110	18		253	21
	138	39	228	66	44
197	204	20		251	49
	205	25		251	50
198	117	27		251	5
199	249	25		253	21
201	204	12	230	126	
202	109			129	9
	115	18	231	229	37
203	263	13		229	45
	264	18		239	44
204	199	9	232	111	36
	199	13		120	18
205	126		233		
	127	47	234	228	11
206	145	31		250	35
	152	22	235	201	24
209	204	10		203	49
210	66	50	236	201	24
211				203	2
212	228	22	238	168	44
213	95	49		251	46
214	262	5	239	267	31
215	77	44		268	46
	141	11		269	5
	150	7	240	107	2
	156	27		109	17
217	73	21	241	176	8
218	138	35	242	203	50
	139	43	243(3)	121	23

Opinion	Page	Note	Opinion	Page	Note
244	251	3	281	144	29
245	195	19		152	27
	195	20	282	97	19
247	76	32		98	32
248	254	34		98	33
249	178	27	283	155	21
250	92	16		195	25
251	147	37	284	226	42
252	64	26		228	13
	198	47	285	236	29
	251	5		244	3
	253	21	286	179	41
253	137	26	287	179	41
	138	34		180	49
254	80	9	289	123	
	150	11		128	1
255	201	26	290	120	19
256	248	8	291	64	26
	250	43		161	8
259	138	27	292	113	49
	150	6	293		
260	168	43	294	253	23
	222	11	295	226	42
261	166	34	296	161	9
	166	35		167	39
262	152	24	297		
263	110	23	298		
264	264	18		246	25
265	128	4		246	26
267	221	7		246	28
270	92	15	299	244	55
	95	10	300	154	9
	134	35		160	6
271	120	19		161	18
272	112	41	301	80	10
	188	1		157	29
273	226	43	302	251	3
	227	3	303	156	26
274	260	13		157	30
275	177	10	304	61	7
276	226	44		73	16
277	54	23	305	113	4
278	251	1	306	80	10
279	105	29		80	11
	108	5		154	11
	116	21	307	87	14
	117	29	309	77	42
280	220	38		153	39
	236	30	311	241	17
	253	18	312	251	3
			313	226	45

Opinion	Page	Note	Opinion	Page	Note
	226	47	343	179	32
314	179	32		180	1
315	189	10		180	2
	196	4		186	31
	200	17	344	179	36
	201	25		222	15
316	208	24	345	179	35
317	97	25		204	10
	98	32	346	72	11
	120	18		249	26
318	115	16	347	76	31
	120	19		154	47
	140	2	348	206	42
	140	3		236	28
	141	6		237	31
	141	9	349	177	17
319	139	45	350	105	26
320	92	14		115	17
	93	27		116	21
321	156	24		141	10
	157	32	351	30	41
323	169	46		185	23
324	65	31	352	26	24
	65	38		189	18
	100	46	353		
325	155	20	354	204	20
326	185	20		205	25
327	109	17		205	27
329	105	29		240	8
330	171	18	355	93	30
	177	16	356	237	34
331	152	26		241	18
	160	3	357	123	33
	251	3		128	4
332	220	42		129	10
333	71	10	358	225	30
334	67	61		228	24
335	249	26	359	261	25
336	67	62	360	153	40
	167	39	361	66	45
337	237	32	362	158	40
	241	11	363	162	25
338	62	12		166	37
	98	26		167	39
	98	27		168	40
	172	30	364	237	33
339	137	22	365	124	40
	157	33		127	49
340	264	18	366	237	35
342	118	42	367	220	39

Opinion	Page	Note	Opinion	Page	Note
368	226	46	392	79	8
369	113	4		154	5
370	259	8	393	225	29
	261	34		225	30
	264	18		229	45
371	63	16		231	22
	103	18		237	37
	172	27	396	264	18
372			397	121	23
373	220	43	398	224	22
374	230	6	399	224	23
	231	26	400	51	8
375	220	38	401	109	17
	225	30		135	1
	233	44	402	119	3
	235	12	403	191	5
	237	36	404	239	45
	239	44	405	202	41
	239	47	406	203	43
	243	27	407	225	27
	243	28	410	112	47
376	94	39	411	207	16
	106	32		207	17
	160	3	414	260	19
379	237	39		268	38
	244	48	415	247	44
380	225	30	416	97	24
	226	42	417	246	25
	226	48	418	180	3
382	187	32		224	19
384	93	23		226	46
	171	19	419	106	33
388	224	25		120	18
	225		420	67	52
	229	32		228	24
	231	22	421	115	17
	237	38		115	18
389	121	23		117	32
390	140	4		118	42
391	225	29		120	18
	225	30	422	277	9
	226	47	423	219	35
	231	22			

OHIO

Opinion	Page	Note	Opinion	Page	Note
2	65	37	5	246	25
	100	40	9	220	42
	100	47		224	2

TEXAS

Opinion	Page	Note		Opinion	Page	Note
5	239	47		27		
6	246	30		28	227	10
9	134	34		30	246	30
10					247	35
11	242	20		31	208	22
15	242	19		32	148	48
17	86	2		33	77	41
	202	35		35	72	13
22	198	1		37	119	10
23	119	10		38	231	23
24				39	80	13
25	241	16		42	224	20
26	84	36				

UTAH

Opinion	Page	Note
3	119	8

VIRGINIA

Opinion	Page	Note		Opinion	Page	Note
10	167	39		31	232	34
12	227	50			259	8
14	154	6		32	119	10
15	106	36		33	204	19
16	247	42		33a	204	19
17	119	12		34	246	26
26	240	10		35	119	12
	260	21		36	228	11
28	241	11			247	42
29	55	27		37	264	21
30	246	25		38	268	38

WASHINGTON

Opinion	Page	Note		Opinion	Page	Note
4 Wash. State Bar News, No. 12, 45	241	16		4	257	47
				9	248	6
					250	34
1	138	40		10	248	1
	231	23			249	24
3	189	10		11	202	36
	207	1				

INDEX

Abuse of legal process, 79, 154

Acceptance of professional employment, duty as to, 139

Acquiescence
in recommendations of others as solicitation, 259
duty to accept court rulings, subject to right of appeal, 69

Acquiring interest
in litigation, 65, 99
conveyance to secure fee, 101

Address, lawyer's in law lists, 270

Addresses, radio and television broadcasts, 263

Admission to the bar
requirements, 20, 34-35
constitutionality of legislative requirements, 42

Adverse decisions, duty to disclose to court, 78

Advertising and solicitation (Canons 27, 40, 43, 46; *see also* full analysis in Table of Contents, Chapter VIII)
law lists, 265-73
origin of rule proscribing, 210
reasons given for, 212
no relaxation in modern times, 212
scope of proscription, 218
history of Canons proscribing advertising, 215
no excuse not to say he is a lawyer, 220
proscription extends to soliciting other lawyers, 220
proper and improper publicity, 219
proper where a normal incident of practice, 228
proper where for full-time position, 220
proper in seeking election to public office, 220
not authorized by local custom, 219
or by court acquiescence, 219
independent business, right to engage in, 221-28

announcements, 232
special branches, 233
rulings by the New York Committees, 233
survey by the New York bar, 238
lawyers returning from government service, 239
in foreign language papers, 228 n. 12
professional cards, 241
telephone books, 246
specialized legal service, 242
indirect advertising, 247
solicitation, 249
notification of persons having similar problems, 251
personal relations, justifying, 252
information as to change of laws, 254
reminders as to wills, 254
by bar associations, 254
of service to low-income groups, 257
legal articles and broadcasts, 263
acquiescence in encomiums of others, 259
see also Ambulance chasing, Branches of the profession, Bulletins, Letterheads, Shingles

Advice, duty to give candid advice to clients, 102

Advising on foreign law, proper for local lawyer, 66 n. 52

Agreement of testator that his lawyer represent his estate not binding on executors, 94

Agreements
with the court, 73
between lawyer and client, necessity of utmost good faith, 89
with other lawyers, duty as to compliance with, 156
see also Candor and fairness

Alabama Code of 1887, quoted, 352-63

Allowances, *see* Rebates

Alteration of court records, 79

Ambulance chasing, 64

American Bar Association
  organized 1878, 20 n. 41
  Canons of Ethics adopted, 24-26
  Ethics Committee, establishment of, 30
    functions and jurisdiction of, 32
    opinions of, weight given to, 32 n. 56
    opinions hitherto unreported, 283-303
  Canons of Professional Ethics, quoted,
    309-26
  Canons of Judicial Ethics, quoted, 327-
    37
Announcements
  special branches, 233
  decisions by the New York Committees,
    233
  survey by the New York bar, 238
  lawyers returning from government
    service, 239
  other rulings, 240
Appointment as trustee, etc., by court,
  276-77
Apprentice, 16 n. 2
Approved law lists, see Law Lists
Armed forces, see Military forces
Articles, legal (Canon 40), 263-65
Assignment of law practice, 189
Association, employing lawyer to advise
  members, 161-65
Associations, bar, see Bar associations
Attornati, 13-14
Attorneys, early history of, 13-14
Authorships in law lists, 273

Bankruptcy
  defense of, 149
  lawyer may go into, 94 n. 40
Bar
  English, brief history, 11
  American, brief history, 19
  admission to, requirements for, 20, 34-35,
    42
  integrated, 20
  see also Duties of lawyers
Bar associations
  history, 20
  duty of, to expose and remedy improper
    practices, 60
  fee schedules of, not binding, 175
  advertisements by, 254-57
  see also Advertising, by bar associations;
    Bar; Ethics Committees
Barratry, 63, 99
Barristers, 13-18
  fees in England, 169
Battle, trial by, 11-12
Benchers, 16, 33

Biographical material, in law lists, 269
Bold-face listing, in telephone books and
  directories, 214, 246
Bolt, in the Inns of Court, 17 n. 20
Bond, lawyer may give, but not advertise
  giving, 228, 268, 269
Borrowing from client, 95
Branches of profession
  what they are, 272-73
  may not be stated on letterhead, 229
  — on shingle, 231
  — in announcements, 233-38
  — on professional cards, 241
  may be in law lists, 272
  see also Advertising and solicitation
Briefs
  definition of, 170 n. 5
  duty of lawyer regarding, 78, 198, 278
Bulletins, trade, lawyer's name in, 168, 261
  see also Advertising
Bullying witnesses
  in early days, 15
  in modern times, 87
Burden of proof, in disciplinary proceedings, 46
Business, independent
  right of lawyers to engage in, 221-23
  New York Committee decisions, 224-27
  decisions by other committees, 227-28

Candid advice, duty to give to clients, 102
Candor and fairness, duty of
  with court, 74
  with clients, 102
  with other lawyers, 192
Canons of Judicial Ethics
  discussed, 274-81
  quoted, 327-37
  see also Judges, Courts
Canons of Professional Ethics
  history of, 23
  force and effect of, 26
  no recent relaxation in enforcement, 212
  construction, exceptions strictly con-
    strued, 242, 243, 273
    statement of specific applications and
      exceptions, not exclusive, 133
  Canon 1, respect due the court, 69
  Canon 2, selection of good judges, 60
  Canon 3, personal relations with judges,
    71
  Canon 4, counsel for indigent, 62
  Canon 5, defense of those accused, 139,
    142
  Canon 6, conflict of interest, 103-29
  Canon 7, professional colleagues, 190

Canon 8, duty to give candid advice, 102
Canon 9, negotiations with opposing party, 54 n. 24, 201
Canon 10, acquiring interest in litigation, 99
Canon 11, dealing with trust property, fiduciary relation, 89
Canon 12, fixing amount of fees, 173
Canon 13, contingent fees, 176
Canon 14, suing client for fee, 171
Canon 15, how far he may go in supporting client's cause, 146
Canon 16, restraining client for improprieties, 151-52
Canon 17, ill feeling and personalities between advocates, 192
Canon 18, treatment of witnesses and litigants, 85, 146
Canon 19, lawyer as witness, 158
Canon 20, newspaper discussion of cases, 70
Canon 21, expedition and punctuality, 82
Canon 22, candor and fairness, to court, 74
— to other lawyers, 192
— to client, 102
Canon 23, attitude to jury, 84
Canon 24, right to control incidents of trial, 193
Canon 25, taking technical advantage of opponent, 194-96
Canon 26, advocacy before other bodies, 87
Canon 27, advertising, direct or indirect, 210-73
  history of, 215
Canon 28, stirring up litigation, 63
Canon 29, upholding the honor of the profession, 149
Canon 30, justifiable and unjustifiable litigation, 139, 149
Canon 31, responsibility for litigation, 139
Canon 32, lawyer's ultimate duty, 320
Canon 33, partnerships, 203
  partnership names, 206
Canon 34, division of fees, with laymen, 179
— with retired lawyers or their estates, 188
— with other lawyers, 186
— "splitting" fees with clients, 97, 179, 181-85
Canon 35, intermediaries, 160
Canon 36, retirement from public employment, 130

Canon 37, confidences of a client, 132-37
  the exceptions stated do not exclude others, 133
Canon 38, rebates and commissions, 96
Canon 39, witnesses, 85
Canon 40, legal articles, newspapers, radio and television broadcasts, 263
Canon 41, divulgence of fraud and deception, 156
Canon 42, expenses, 178
Canon 43, law lists, 265
Canon 44, withdrawal, 140
Canon 45, specialists, 233, 242, 272
Canon 46, specialized legal service, 242
  special branches, 272
Canon 47, unauthorized practice, 66, 165
Canons quoted, 309-25
Canterbury, law school there in 1160, 13
Cards, professional, 241
Censure, when preferable to disbarment or suspension, 46-48
  see also Disciplinary proceedings
Certified public accountant, conducting business of from law office, 223-27
Champerty, 63, 99
Champions in trial by battle, 11-12
Character requirements for admission, 20, 34-35
Character witness, judge as, 275-76
Characteristics of lawyers, xii-xiii
Chicanery, see Fraud
Clients (see also analysis in Table of Contents, Chapter VI)
  always entitled to lawyer of their own choosing, 94, 198, 199
  consent necessary to inclusion of names in law lists, 272
  duty of lawyer to, as a fiduciary, 89, 96
— not to accept rebates or commissions, 96
— not to acquire an interest in litigated matters, 99-101
— to settle cases where to client's advantage, 101
— to give candid advice, 102
— not to represent conflicting interests (see also Conflicting interests), 103-30
— to give wholehearted service, 113
— not to attack an instrument drawn by him, 113
— in insurance cases, 114
— to insured minors, 118
— as public prosecutors, 118
  consent, where effective and where not, 120

Clients (Continued)
    collusive divorces (see also Divorces), 122
    on retirement from public position, 130
    confidential communications (see also
        Confidential communications), 131-
        39
    acceptance of employment, 139
    right to withdraw, 140
    defense of one known to be guilty, 142
    personal belief in justice of client's cause,
        147
    newspaper discussion of pending causes,
        70
    permissible and improper practices in
        supporting client's cause, 146
    defense of usury, etc., 149
    improper practices in client's service:
        participation in fraud, 150
        Mexican divorces, 150
        assisting in violating the law, 151
        payments to secure testimony, 152
        employment of coercive tactics, 153
        abuse of legal process, 154
        employment of underhanded methods,
            155
        harassment of the other side, 156
    duty to comply with agreements, 156
    — on discovery of client's fraud, 156
    — as a prospective witness, 158
    — of direct relation with clients, 159
        intervention of intermediary, 160
        delegation of professional functions,
            160
        employment by an organization, 161-
            65 (analysis of problem, 162; history
            of Canon 35, 163; considerations
            pro and con, 164; Canon 47, 165)
        representation of group with common
            interest, 165
    permitting inclusion of name in trade
        bulletins, 168
    relations with collection agencies, 168
    compensation, see Compensation, Divi-
        sion of fees
    division of fees with client, 181
    see also Conflicting interests, Confiden-
        tial communications, Divorces,
        Fraud, Noblesse oblige
Codes of ethics, force and effect of, 26
Coercive tactics, 153
Coif, origin of, 12 n. 11
Colleagues at the bar, duties to (see also
    analysis in Table of Contents, Chap-
    ter VII)
    not to encroach on practice, 190
    courtesy and good faith, 192

differences of opinion between, duty in
    case of, 198, 200-01
duties of superseding and superseded
    lawyers, 198
in connection with proffered association
    of, 198
not to negotiate with clients of op-
    ponent, 201
see also Partnerships
Collection agencies, relations of lawyers
    with, 168, 179-80, 222 n. 11
Collusion, in divorce cases, 80, 122
Commercialization, spread of has not un-
    dermined lawyers' standards, 7, 212
Commissions and rebates, 96
Committee on Ethics, see American Bar
    Association, Ethics Committee
Common interest, right to solicit those
    having, 251
Compensation
    of early lawyers, 15
    right to in England, 169
    — in U.S., 170
    basis of, 173
    contingent fees, 176
    damages for discharge, 175
    expenses, 178
    division of fees, 179
        Committee will not fix, 187 n. 48
        with laymen, 179
        between lawyers, 186
        with one in military service, 200
        with retired lawyers and their estates,
            188
        splitting with clients, 97, 179, 181-85
    acceptance of compensation from the
        other side in divorce cases, 129
    duty as to indigent, 62
    — as to persons of moderate means, 257
    testimony as to reasonableness, 197
    acceptance of interest in litigation as a
        fee, 99-101
    see also Canon 12; Canon 13; Canon 14;
        Canon 34; Canon 35; Executor,
        where lawyer and; Forwarding
        lawyer
Competitive bidding for legal employment
    improper, 174, 191, 220, 249-50
Compromise, duty to promote, 101
Confidences of opposing lawyer, 195
Confidential communications, 131-39
    conflict of interest distinguished, 104,
        109, 115
    exceptions enumerated, do not exclude
        others, 133
    recognized in early days, 15, 132

purpose of the rule, 132
scope of the rule, 133
application of the rule, 136
when disclosure proper, 137
duty on discovery of fraud or perjury by his client, 141, 151
Conflicting loyalties, lawyer must reconcile, 5-6, 101-02
in divorce cases, 80-82, 122 *et seq.*
see also Confidential communications
Conflict of Interest, duty not to represent when there is (*see also* full analysis in Table of Contents, Chapter VI)
serving two masters, 22 n. 5, 115 n. 15
Canon 6 on, 103
analysis of problem, 104
distinction between this and confidential communications, 104, 109, 115
test of inconsistency, 105
scope of the provision, 106
applies to former employee, 106
applies to partners, 106
and to admiralty bar, 107
attacking an instrument which he drew, 113
client's interest and individual interest of lawyer, 109
collusive divorces, 122-29
neglect to prove defense, 124
consent, effect of, 120
cases where ineffective and unwise, 120
consent in advance, 121
consent ineffective where public officer, 120, 129, 130
injunction to prevent representation, 107 n. 42
insurance cases, 114
insured minors, 118
public prosecutors and other public servants, 118
that of former client, 111
receiver's partner may represent him, 112, 188
Conflict of opinion, between colleagues (Canon 7), 198, 200-01
Connivance in divorce cases, 123
Consent to conflict of interest, 120, 121, 129
Consilium, early advocate, 12
Conter, 15
Contempt, distinguished from disciplinary proceedings, 38, 41 n. 47
Contingent fees, 176
Continuance, abuse of discretion in granting, 278
Construction of Canons

function of Ethics Committee, 31
exceptions not exclusive, 133
strict construction of exceptions, 242
re law lists, 273 n. 53
Contracts
between lawyer and client, 91
with client to represent his estate, 94, 198, 199, 200 n. 17
Control over incidents of litigation, 193
Corporation
employing lawyer to advise employees, 161 *et seq.*
lawyer officer of, 98, 110-11
Counter, 15
Counsel, implication of the term, 12 n. 10
see also Lawyers
Court, *see also* Judges
Court reporter, obligation to see paid, 157 n. 32
Courtesy and good faith
to the court, 69
to clients, 89-96, 102
to other lawyers, 192
may sue another lawyer in a meritorious case, 197
Court proceedings, publicity to, 280
Court records, alteration of, 79
Courts
power of to discipline lawyers, 38
duties of lawyers to, 69-87
to see to the appointment of able, upright judges, 60
respectful attitude toward, 69
personal relations with, 71, 275
discussion of pending cases with, 71, 73, 275
agreements and understandings with, 73
of candor and fairness to, 74
dilatory tactics, 82
disclosure of relevant matters to, 76
briefs, 78
respect of lawyers for legal process, 79, 154
punctuality, 82
behavior to judges, 69
behavior of lawyers to witnesses, 85
contribution to judge's campaign fund, 73 n. 16
Customs of the bar, duty to observe, xi, 22, 195

Damages, rights of lawyer to, on improper discharge, 175

Deceit
    may not deceive client, 93, 102-03
    no participation in, 150
Decisions, duty to disclose to court de-
    cisions overlooked by adversary, 78
Definitions of ethics, xi
Delay, lawyer's duty not improperly to de-
    lay the proceedings, 82
Delays, lawyer's duty to remedy ineffective
    procedure, 83
Delegation of professional functions, 160
    et seq.
Devil, young barrister, 18
Dilatory tactics, extent of the duty not to
    employ, 82
Directories, see Telephone books
Direct relations, necessity of with client,
    159 et seq.
Disbarred lawyers, rights of, 51
Disbarment, see Discipline
Disciplinary proceedings
    nature of, 35-38
    res judicata does not apply to, 37
    contempt distinguished from, 38
    powers of court and legislature, 41
    burden of proof in, 46
    disbarment, suspension, or censure, 46
    isolated acts not ordinarily grounds for
        disbarment, 46-47
    relevance of record and reputation of
        accused, 47
    restitution no defense, 37
    reinstatement, 49
    resignation, 48
    sympathy should not mitigate discipline,
        49-50, 59
Discipline, grounds for
    moral unfitness to advise or represent
        clients, 43
    unworthiness to continue a member of
        an honorable profession, 44
    incompetence as ground for, 48 n. 40
    procedure in England, 33
    — in U.S., 34
    for violating canons, 34-35
Disclosure, duty of to court, of relevant
    matters, 76
    see also Confidential communications
Discount for prompt payment, lawyer may
    not allow, 174 n. 47
Divergence of interests represented, duty
    where, 112
Division of fees, see Compensation, divi-
    sion of fees
Divorce cases, recent supreme court de-
    cisions, 80-82

Divorces
    "quickie," 80
    collusive, 122-30
    interest of state, 122-30
    connivance in procuring, 123
    manufacture of cause of action (hotel
        divorces), 123
    agreement not to defend, 125
    agreement to furnish necessary evidence,
        126
    designation of lawyer for other side, 128
    compensation from other side, 129
    securing Mexican divorces, 123, 150
Doctor witness, obligation to see paid, 157
    n. 31
Domicile
    in divorce cases, 80-82
        misstatement of in divorce cases, 80
Double-cross client, lawyer may never, 93
Drogheda, William of, 13
Duties of lawyers to the public
    to police the bar, 59
    to further the choice and continuance of
        proper judges, 60
    to represent the indigent, 62
    not to stir up litigation, 63
    not to aid unauthorized practice, 66
    to the court, 69-88
    to clients, 89
    to other lawyers, 190 et seq.
    not to advertise and solicit, 210 et seq.
    advice to one not represented, 54 n. 24,
        92, 201
    see also Noblesse Oblige; Clients, duties
        of lawyer to; Colleagues, duties of
        lawyer to; Public, duties of lawyer
        to

Educational requirements of lawyer, 20,
    34, 41-42
Employment, professional, extent of duty
    to accept, 139
Encroaching on other lawyer's practice,
    190
Essoiner, 19
Estate of client not bound by his direc-
    tion that his lawyer represent it,
    94, 198, 199
Ethics
    definitions of, xi, 22
    sanctions, 22
    see also Advertising and solicitation;
        Alabama State Bar Association Code
        of Ethics; American Bar Associa-
        tion, Committee on Ethics; Canons
        of Professional Ethics; Cards, pro-

fessional; Clients, duties of lawyer to; Colleagues, duties of lawyer to; Compensation; Conflicting interests; Courts, duties of lawyers to; Discipline; Hoffman's Fifty Resolutions; Law; Law lists; Letterheads; "Noblesse Oblige"; Oath of Admission; Public, duties of lawyer to; Special branches

Ethics Committee of the American Bar Association
organization of, function and jurisdiction, 30
does not pass on questions of law, 26 n. 24, 32

Ethics committees
history, organization, and functions of, 30
opinions, numbers of, x n. 2, 31-32

Etiquette of the bar, xi, 27, 211 n. 3

Exclusive privileges accorded lawyers, 59

Executor
lawyer who is, is he entitled to a colleague lawyer's share of fee for legal work, in addition to executor's fee? 188 n. 6
right to have counsel of his choice despite agreement by testator, 94, 198

Ex parte applications, 277

Expenses
lawyer may not pay, 178
definition of, 178

Fairness, see Candor and fairness

Feeder, independent business as, 221 et seq.
branch office as, 271 n. 26

Fees, see Compensation

Fictitious controversy, may not foist on court, 75 n. 24

Fiduciary
lawyer as, 89, 160
who is a lawyer may be represented by his partner, 188

Finder's fee, 186-87

Force and effect of the Canons of Professional Ethics, 26

Foreign language papers, advertising in, 228 n. 12

Foreign law, advising on by local lawyer proper, 66 n. 52

Forespeca, 13 n. 22

Forwarding fee, none ipso facto under Canon 34, 186-87
see also Compensation

Forwarding lawyer, duty to advise forwardee that he makes separate charge, 195
see also Compensation, division of fees

Fraternity rosters, 268

Fraud
constructive, in dealings by a lawyer with his client for his own benefit, 90
participation in, 150
duty on discovery of client's, 141, 156

Frauds, statute of, defense of, 149

Full-time position, lawyer may advertise for, 220

Funds, mingling client's with his own, 92 n. 20

Game, law suit not a mere game, 83 n. 32

Gifts from opponents, 96-97

Good taste, many ethical problems involve, 190-91, 260, 277

Good will, lawyer's may not be offered for sale, 161, 189

Government service
lawyer entering may turn over practice to another, 188-89
taking over practice of one entering, 200
letterhead of lawyer entering, 230
announcements by lawyer returning from, 239

Grievance committees, and ethics committees, history, organization, and functions, 23, 30

Guilt, knowledge by lawyer of, effect of, 142-43

Guilty person, lawyer's right to defend one known to be guilty, 142

Harassment of other side, 87, 156

History of bar
in England, 11
in the United States, 19

Hoffman's Fifty Resolutions, quoted, 338-51

Honorarium, of early lawyers, 15, 169 n. 5

Hotel divorces, 123-24

How far a lawyer may go in supporting client's cause, 146

Imagination, importance of in lawyer's make-up, xiii

Improprieties, restraining clients from, 151-52

Improvement of the law, duty as to, 83, 278

Incompetence
  as ground for disbarment, 48 n. 40
  of judges, duty of court to take action, 62
Independent business, *see* Business, in-
    dependent
Indigent, duty to represent, 62
Indirect advertising, 247
  see also Advertising and solicitation
Infancy, defense of, 149
Informative data, in law lists, 269
Inns of Court, 16
Insurance cases, conflicting interest in, 114
Integrated bar, 20
Interest in litigation
  duty not to acquire, 63-66, 99
  conveyance to secure fee, 99-101
  contingent fee as, 99-101
Interests, conflicting, *see* Conflict of in-
    terest, 103-30
Intermediary, intervention by, 160
Inventions, duty to turn over to client, 91
Investment advisory service, may not con-
    duct from law office, 227

Judges
  duties of lawyers to, *see* Courts, duties of
    lawyers to
  essential conduct of, *see* Judicial Canons
    5, 6, and 34
  respect due, 69
  personal relations of lawyers with, 71,
    275
  partner appearing before, 72, 277
  relative appearing before, 72, 277
  request for early decision from, how
    properly made by lawyer, 73
  understandings with lawyers, 73
  as character witnesses, 275-76
  personal investments, 278
  private practice, engaging in, 279
  engaging in partisan politics, 279
  candidacy for office, 279
    where non-judicial, duty to resign, 279
  danger of ex parte applications, 277
  decisions and opinions of, principles
    relative to, 278
  personal interest in litigation, 279
  social relations, 280
  publicizing court proceedings, 280-81
  ⟨ radio and television, 280
  duty of judges
  — acting as fiduciary, 278-79
  — to be free from the appearance of
      impropriety, 275
  — not to accept favors from lawyers or
      litigants, 275, 280

— to be courteous, 276
— to be prompt, 276
— in making appointments, 276-77
— to have efficient court organization,
    276
— to criticize and correct improper con-
    duct of lawyers, 276
— not to interfere unduly, 277
— not to indulge his idiosyncracies, 278
— to secure for defeated counsel full re-
    view on fair record, 278
— not to use prestige of office to pro-
    mote pet enthusiasms, 278
— to promote constructive legislation,
    278
Judicial Canons, 274-81
Jurors, attitude and behavior of lawyers
    to, 84
Jury trial, no right to in disbarment pro-
    ceedings, 35, 36 n. 24

Knowledge of guilt, effect of by lawyer, 142

Labor union
  lawyer may not join one which includes
    non-lawyers, 94 n. 39, 160
  employing lawyer to advise members,
    161-65
Law
  practice of, what constitutes unauthor-
    ized, 36, 165
  violation of, assistance in, 151
Law lists
  history of the exception,
    exception to be strictly construed, 242,
    243, 273
  general rulings, 267
  basis for listing, 269
  biographical matter, 269
  addresses, 270
  references, 271
  client's consent, 272
  clients regularly represented, 271
  legal societies, 272
  posts of honor, 272
  branches of the profession, 272
  authorships, 273
  rules and standards of, quoted, 364-66
Law schools
  early in England, 13
  rosters, 268
Lawyer, suit against another, 197
Lawyers
  inherent powers of, not covered in this
    book, xi

characteristic traits, xii-xiii
cardinal loyalties, 6
exclusive privileges accorded lawyers, 59
solicitation of, proscribed, 220
see also Advertising and solicitation; Canons of Professional Ethics; Clients, duty of lawyer to; Colleagues, duty of lawyer to; Courts, duty of lawyer to; Public, duty of lawyer to
Lay intermediaries, intervention by, 160
Layman
  employment by lawyer, 179
  employment of lawyer by, 180
  partnership with, proscribed, 204
  listing with layman, 268
Legal articles (Canon 40), 263-65
Legal process, abuse of, 79, 154
Legal profession, characteristics of, 5
Legal societies, in law lists, 272
Legislative bodies
  appearance of lawyer before, 87
  duty of lawyer as member of, 88
Legislature, powers re discipline, 41
Letterheads
  what they may and may not contain, 228
  lawyer entering government service, 230
  lawyers admitted in different states, 230
  of clients may not carry lawyer's name, 229, 262
Liens, lawyers', this book does not cover, xi
Limitation of actions
  taking advantage of, 149
  against client, 95, 96, 151 n. 13
Litigation
  acquiring interest in, 64, 99
  stirring up, 63-66
Loan, to client, 95
Lobbyist, lawyer as, 87-88
Local custom
  retention of deceased or retired partners' name, 207-08
  does not justify advertising, 219
London, Ordinance of 1280, 15
Low-income groups, services to, 257
Loyalties
  cardinal loyalties of lawyers, 6
  lawyer must reconcile conflicting, 5-6, 80-82, 101-02
  in divorce cases, 122
Lump settlements, 93

Maintenance, 63, 99
Marriage, *see* Matrimonial litigation

Marriage counselling, announcing from law office, 227
Massachusetts trust, lawyers may not form to practice law, 204
Master and servant v. lawyer and client, 182
Matrimonial litigation, ethical problems in connection with, 80, 122
Mexican divorces, securing, 123, 150
Military service, *see* Government service
Mingling clients' funds with his own, 92 n. 20
Minors, insured, conflicting interests, 118
Misrepresentation, lawyer must have no participation in, 150-51, 155, 156
Moot courts, 17
Moral lecture, counsel not bound to give to client, 144-45, 149
Moral turpitude, as ground for disbarment, 43
Mother, as identified with infant party, 98 n. 29, 105 n. 29, 135 n. 48

Names, partnership, *see* Partnership names
Narratores, 13-14
Negotiation with client of another lawyer, 201
Neon sign, improper as shingle, 231
Newspaper
  discussion of pending laws, 70
  criticisms of decisions, 70
  see also Advertising and solicitation
"Noblesse Oblige," 3
Notary
  lawyer may act as in case which he conducts, 227
  may not take phone affidavit, 151
Notice, to persons with similar problems, 251
  see also Announcements

Oath of Admission, quoted, 326
Obedience, to rulings of court subject to right of appeal, 69
"Obedience to the Unenforceable," 2, 4, 276
Office, lawyer's branch, 270-71
Office, public, *see* Public position
"One package service" in divorce cases (Staedler), 129 n. 8
Opinions of the American Bar Association Ethics Committee, x, 30-31
Opposing lawyer
  mistakes by, duty to correct, 76
  duties to, 190-206
  confidences of, 195
Outer or utter barristers, 18
Oxford, law school in 1220, 13

Pardon
  no defense to discipline, 37
  or basis for reinstatement, 51
Partner
  lawyer may represent fiduciary partner,
      112, 188
  judge sitting in case when counsel is
      former partner, 72, 277
  lawyer may not do what partner may
      not, 106
Partnership names
  inclusion of one accepting public posi-
      tion, 206
  where one deceased, 207-08
Partnerships
  among lawyers, 203
  lawyers admitted in different states, 204
Patent lawyers, Canons apply to, 220 n.
      38
Patents, duty to turn over to client, 91
Perjury, duty on discovery of by client, 141,
      151
Personal belief, in justice of case, 147
Personal relations
  with judges, 71
  justifying solicitation, 252
Placitator, 14
Police the bar, duty of lawyers to, 59
Position, full-time, lawyer may advertise
      for, 220
Posts of honor, in law lists, 272
Powers of lawyers, inherent, this book does
      not cover, xi
Practice of law
  nature of right to, 35
  what constitutes, 66 n. 52
  may not be offered for sale, 161, 189
Preamble to Canons quoted, 3, 309
Prejudice, statement by a lawyer "without
      prejudice" not necessarily a protec-
      tion, 197
Privileged communications, see Confiden-
      tial communications
Privileges of lawyers, 59
Professional cards, 241
Professional employment
  what is, 66 n. 52
  extent of duty to accept, 139
Profession, legal
  characteristics of, 5, 7, 29
  educational and character requirements
      for admission, 20, 34-35
  duty of lawyer to, not encroach on an-
      other's practice, 190
  — not to advertise or solicit, 210
  — not to deal with another's client, 201

Proof, burden of in disciplinary proceed-
      ings, 46
Prosecutors, public, may not change sides,
      118, 148
Public relations counsel, lawyer may not
      retain, 219 n. 35
Public position
  retirement from, duty on, 130
  name of one accepting in partnership,
      206
Public, duties of lawyer to
  to police the bar, 59
  to further the choice and continuance
      of proper judges, 60
  to represent the indigent, 62
  not to stir up litigation, 63
  not to aid the unauthorized practice of
      law, 66
  see also "Noblesse Oblige"
Public prosecutors, duties of, may not
      change sides, 118, 148
Public service, tradition of lawyers in, 5
Punctuality
  duty of lawyers as to, 82
  duty of judges as to, 276
Punishment, discipline not designed as,
      35-36

"Quickie" divorces, 80
Quiz course, conduct of by lawyers, 227-28

Radio broadcasts
  by lawyers, 263, 264
  of court proceedings, 280
Readers, in English bar, 17
Rebates and commissions, duty of lawyer
      not to receive secret, 96
Receiver, his partner may represent him,
      112, 188
Recommendations, acquiescence in, 259-63
Recommending lawyer for other side, 117,
      128
Record of accused lawyer, relevance in
      disciplinary proceedings, 44, 46-47
References, in law lists, 271
Reinstatement of disbarred lawyers, 49
Relative, judge sitting in case when rela-
      tive or former partner is counsel,
      72, 277
Reputation of accused lawyer, relevancy
      in disciplinary proceedings, 44, 47
Residence, in law lists, 270
Resignation, right of lawyer to withdraw
      from bar, 48
Res judicata, does not apply to disciplinary
      proceedings, 37

Respect due the court, 69

Restitution, no defense to disciplinary proceeding, or ground for reinstatement, 37, 50-51

Restraining clients from improprieties, 151-52

Retaining fee, definition of, 172

Retirement, from judicial position, 130

Retirement from public position, conflicting employment, 130

Rosters, 268

Rules and standards as to law lists, quoted, 365-66

Runners, 29, 64
  right to represent, 64

Sale of law practice not proper, 161, 189

Sanctions relative to professional conduct, statutes, court decisions, Canons and customs, 22

Sergeant at law, in English law, 14-18

Servientes ad legem in English law, 13

Service, tradition of public duty to give wholehearted, 5, 113
  see also Clients, duty to; Public, duty to

Serving two masters, quotation of phrase, 22 n. 5, 115 n. 15
  see also Conflict of interest

Settlement, duty to promote, 101

Shingles
  principles relative to, 231
  neon sign improper, 231

Signs, see Shingles

Skip-tracing, lawyer may not employ, 79-80, 150

Slander, of witness or party, when proper, 87

Solicitation, see Advertising and solicitation

Solicitors, 18, 34

Special branches
  on letterheads, 229
  on shingles, 231
  in announcements, 233-38
  in professional cards, 241-42
  proposed amendment of Canon 46, 245
  in law lists, 272-73

Specialized legal service (Canon 46), 242, 325

Splitting of fees
  with client or employee, 67, 97, 179, 181
  with layman, 179
  with other lawyers, 186
  with retired partner, 188-89
  with estate of deceased partner, 188-89

Stamping instruments with draftsman's name, 259

Stakeholder, duty of lawyer as, 113

State, interest in matrimonial status of citizens, 122, 150

Statute of frauds, defense of, 149

Statute of limitations
  against client, 95, 96, 151 n. 13
  defense of, 149

Stirring up litigation, duty not to, 63

Stooge client, should not appear for, 75

Suing fellow lawyer, permissible, 197

Suit for fees
  permissible in the U.S., 170
  to be avoided if possible, 171

Superseding and superseded lawyers, duties to and of, 194, 198

Support of client's cause, how far a lawyer may go in, 146

Survey of legal profession, 5, 7, 34

Survey of the New York bar, relative to announcements, 238

Suspended lawyers, rights of, 51-55

Suspension, when preferable to disbarment, 46-48
  see also Disciplinary proceedings

Sympathy, should not mitigate discipline of lawyers, 49, 59

Sympathy and understanding
  necessity of to lawyer, 4
  his experiences develop, 5

Technical defenses
  in disbarment proceedings, 51
  duty as to, 83-84

Telephone books, name in, 246

Testimony
  in divorce cases, 126
  payments to secure, 152
  as to fees of others, 197

Trade bulletins, mentioning counsel, 168

Trial by "battel," 11

Trustee, lawyer as, 89 et seq.

Unauthorized practice, duty not to further, 66, 165

Underhanded methods, duty not to use, 155

Understandings
  with court, 73
  with clients, 91
  with opposing lawyer, duty to observe, 156, 194

Unenforceable, see "Obedience to the Unenforceable"

Union, lawyer may not join one that in-
　　cludes non-lawyers, 94 n. 39, 160
Unjust steward, parable of, 22 n. 5
Usury, defense of, when available, 93 n.
　　35, 96 n. 12, 149
Utter barristers, different meanings of
　　term, 18

Vested interest, lawyer has none in right to
　　represent client's estate, 94
Violation of law, assistance in, 151

Wholehearted service, duty to give, 113
Wig, origin of, 12 n. 11
William of Drogheda, 13
Wills
　　appointing himself fiduciary, 94
　　drawing for incompetent, 93
　　— for trust company, 110, 160, 249
　　inserting legacy to himself, 94

direction in, to employ draftsman, 94
Withdrawal
　　right of, 140
　　right on, 141
Without prejudice, statement to other
　　lawyer to this effect not necessarily
　　a protection, 197
Witness
　　bullying of, not permitted in early days,
　　　15
　　— or at present, 87
　　duty as to interviewing witnesses of op-
　　　ponent, 201-02
　　lawyer as prospective witness, 158
　　judge as character witness, 275
　　lawyer may not bargain with witness to
　　　secure testimony, 75, 86
　　lawyer may not advertise for witnesses
　　　to testify to stated facts or particular
　　　event, 152